HIGHWAY HEATH

THE STORY IN FACT AND FICTION OF HOUNSLOW HEATH IN MIDDLESEX

By

GORDON S. MAXWELL

with a Foreword by

SIR MONTAGU SHARPE, K.C., V.Lt.

With a Frontispiece by
Donald Maxwell, Old Prints,
Drawing and Photographs.

HERITAGE PUBLICATIONS
Hounslow Leisure Services

Reprinted 1994
Heritage Publications
■ Hounslow Leisure Services

ISBN 1899144005

Printed in Great Britain by
Antony Rowe Ltd, Chippenham, Wiltshire

ON HOUNSLOW HEATH, 1735.

From the painting by Donald Maxwell.

HIGHWAYMAN'S HEATH

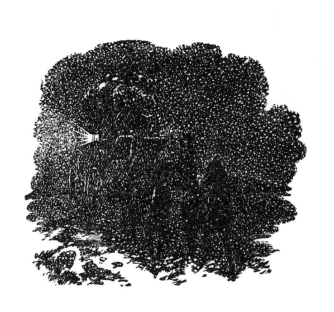

FOREWORD

By SIR MONTAGU SHARPE, K.C., V.Lt.,
President London and Middlesex Archaeological Society.

MIDDLESEX having never possessed a County town in the ordinary meaning of the term, and at all times overshadowed by the proximity of the Metropolis—for even in Saxon times it is mentioned as " owing obedience to London "—has, in consequence, been erroneously supposed to possess little or no local history of general interest.

If this idea still persists it should now be laid to rest by Mr. Gordon S. Maxwell's excellent book entitled *Highwayman's Heath*. It is an admirable and a comprehensive work, enlarging our knowledge of past times in the South-Western parts of Middlesex lying between the rivers Brent and Colne.

From the title it might be supposed that the text is confined to the misdeeds of notorious highwaymen upon the historic and dreaded Heath. This is by no means so, for Mr. Maxwell, in pursuit of his quest, which he has so deeply at heart, has from extensive reading and infinite research, together with personal visits into the parishes surrounding the Heath, succeeded in accumulating a valuable store of information. With this is a map of the locality and many illustrations.

I commend this book to every reader interested in the past and varied life in rural Middlesex, now fast disappearing as it becomes absorbed in a uniform assemblage of urban habitations.

To

CAPTAIN S. J. HOLLOWAY, M.C.

In remembrance of our life-long
friendship and our mutual love of
literature.

ACKNOWLEDGEMENTS.

In other parts of this book I have acknowledged many courtesies and kindnesses I have received " on the road," but there are one or two names I still must mention.

Sir Montagu Sharpe has given me several suggestions with regard to the early history of Middlesex. The value of this friendly co-operation from so great a scholar and authority on the county is incalculable.

I have to thank Mr. Harold Groom, Heston and Isleworth Borough Librarian, for his keen interest and practical help. My brother, Donald Maxwell, has lent me several of his drawings for reproduction, and my son, Colin Maxwell, has helped me with the map, drawings and photographs

I certainly cannot let this go to press without recording my grateful thanks to Mr. Frank Jennings for his generous and valuable help while it was running as a serial and its production in book form.

THE GREAT WEST ROADS NEAR LONDON.

A ballad of two Middlesex highways
—The Staines and Bath Roads—over
Hounslow Heath ; and all those lands
that do adjacent lie.

1. Early Days. Prehistoric to B.C. 55.

Here mighty brontosaurus dwelt
Long eons before the forest felt
Stone axes hew for early Celt
  A trackway through these regions.
Where roamed the rude primordial
  man,
" Before our history books began,"
And later Caesar led the van
  Of Rome's invading legions.

2. Early Days. B.C. 55 to A.D. 1016.

Here Trinobantes once held sway,
Till beaten in the bloody fray
When Caesar crossed the Thames this
  way,
  By Brent's confluent tide.
Rome's eagles gone, the Danish horde
Across this swampy forest sward
Were driven by the Saxon sword
  Of Edmund Ironside.

3. A Royal Chase. Disafforested in 1227.

In mediaeval days this ground
A Royal Chase, where ran the hound
Till stag or savage boar were found
  To die by kingly arrow.
But now these fields where vision
  brings
A glimpse of falcon's swooping wings,
See far more Cabbages than Kings,
  Which spring beneath the harrow.

4. Hounslow Hamlet awakens to life. 1227 to 1650.

Where woodman's huts and cattle
  byres
Clustered by charcoal-burner's fires,
Close to the home of ancient Friars
  That stood twixt forest ways.
For centuries in deep repose
Of ancient peace, before it rose
To play an active part in those
  Post-chaise and stage-coach days.

5. A Sleepy Queen. 1579.

Elizabeth (of course) slept here,
For Gresham's Osterley was near,

Where walls would rise (or disappear !),
  Tradition here was born.
She seemed to rest her sleepy head
In ev'ry house that had a bed.
Though wide awake to make her bread
  From Heston's growing corn.

6. Shakespeare and Bacon at Twickenham Park.

" Who is this Mr. Bacon, pray,
Who says he wrote my latest play ? "
The Bard, to settle this, they say,
  To Thames from Avon travelled.
P'raps here they hatched a little plot,
As who should write and who should
  not,
Which tied the critics in that knot
  Some claim is still unravelled.

7. A Royal Chaser. 1670.

Though Rumour states a Royal chase
Of quite another kind took place ;
The Merry Monarch's gloomy face
  In Feltham lanes was seen.
Blaize Farm stood here where this
  occurred.
When Charles the Second (so I've
  heard)
Pursued a different sort of bird,
  When Nell Gwynne was his Quean.

8. The Great Heath Camp. 1688·

'Twas James the Second's idle hope
To gain allegiance to the Pope,
But people thought " Come rack—
  Come rope "
  A dangerous salvation.
Then James tried military force,
But twenty thousand foot and horse
Could not awe London, though
  of course.
It caused his abdication.

9. " Coaching Days and Coaching Ways," and " Tales of a Wayside Inn." 1650 to 1840.

At Hounslow Town fresh horses wait,
When, swinging through the turnpike
  gate,
We " spring our cattle " down the
  " straight "
  That's called The King's Highway.

The coach-guard on his yard o' tin
Wakes echoes from each wayside inn
(What yarns those hostelries could
    spin,
What tales of yesterday !).

10. Highwaymen : 1650 to 1800.

What memories those roads bequeath,
That traverse Hounslow's dreaded
    Heath,
Where ev'ry tree might hold beneath
A masked and pistolled rider.
Dick Turpin rode his gallant mare
Along the moonlit roads, near where
Gavotte was danced by ladye faire,
With Claude Duval beside her.

11. The Bow Street Runners chase Galloping Dick and Jerry Abershawe. 1780 to 1790.

The Runners here had many a chase,
Across the Heath at break-neck pace,
But did not always win the race
    (Or legends so relate),
For Ferguson and Abershawe
Escaped the Robin Redbreasts' maw
On swifter steeds, by leaping o'er
    The Colnbrook turnpike-gate.

12. Relics and Visions. Various dates.

Here Hatton's Hiding Hole is seen,
And Bedfont's Peacocks skirt the
    green,
With Cranford's Cage, which oft has
    been
    The captured footpad's prison.
From Perry Oaks the Last Wolf's ghost
Through Heath Row leads a lupine
    host,
To howl by Whitton's Bloody Post,
    With other spectres risen.

13. A Great Mansion 1. 1415.

Of Syon House and its demesne
I scarce can write, too oft the scene
Of vivid story has it been,
    Which English History yields.
Since Henry, fresh from Agincourt,
This chantry built on Thames fair
    shore
Has tasted peace—then stress—then
    war,
    In its riparian fields.

14. A Great Mansion 2. Lady Jane Gray and Catherine Howard. 1553 and 1542.

Poor Lady Jane—the Nine Day's
Queen—

The most pathetic figure seen
On Syon's sometimes bloodstained
    screen,
    The Crown was offered here.
A second queen from here was rowed,
To die for Henry's " moral " code,
But Thames bore back another load—
    The Royal murderer's bier.

15. A Great Mansion 3. Guy Fawkes' midnight visit. Nov. 5, 1605. "The Naval battle of Syon," 1642.

Here plotters at the dead of night
Assured Guy Fawkes " Twill be all
    right,
Just fire the train—you'll soon see
    light ;
    If you don't lose your head ! "
Here Cavaliers and Roundheads fought
The only " naval " action sought
By Cromwell's " fleet," which made
    its port
    Deep in the river bed !

16. The Arterial Road 1. Gunnersbury to the Old Bath Road. In modern times.

Where apple orchards used to bloom
The shapes of ugly factories loom,
And smoke-clouds temper mid-day
    gloom
    To twilight murkiness.
Here speeding through the livelong
    day
The Juggernauts of Petrol slay
Unwary folk who cross this way
    Of Blood and Ugliness !

17. The Arterial Road 2. Bath Road to Staines. In modern times.

A scar that sears the county's face,
This new road yet knows not the place
Where lurks some half-forgotten trace
    Of peaceful old-world village.
That belt of trees which skirts the way,
May hide old farms or churches grey,
Where waving wheat or unmown hay
    still Speak of rural tillage.

18. The Future.

What ghosts must wander up and down
These western roads to London town,
Where in its turn each gave renown
    To passing generation.
Dull folk whose mental eyes are blind
These heathland spectres will not find,
Though it requires no psychic mind,
    —But just imagination.

AUTHOR'S PREFACE.

" Shall ancient Hounslow then be lost to fame,
And dull oblivion desecrate the name ?
No—from the Nine we this advice receive,
That in their records Hounslow's name shall live."

            Rev. Wetenhall Wilkes, 1747.

ONE night I had a dream—a vision, if you will. I was on a vast heath stretching desolate and wild for miles. I was alone yet in the midst of a great company—of ghosts that moved as shadows around me. Not malevolent spectres, you understand, but vastly interesting, for in their dim outlines I recognised many famous in history, song and story.

Soon I was conscious of several maidens approaching; they wore white robes and each carried a casket. The leading one spoke: " We are the Nine Muses, and I am Clio, the Muse of History. From our caskets we have scattred jewelled beads over the Heath. Take this cord and thread as many of these as you can—and you will have a string of beads that will surprise many by its brilliance.

I glanced at the cord in my hand and when I looked up I was alone again. Gone were the Nine; vanished were the ghosts of yesteryear; but around me lay some of the jewels of which Clio had spoken. Some were easy to find, but others were half hidden in the grass and bushes.

So I began to search and to string these beads on to the magic cord. Then I woke.

This vision on the old-time Heath of Hounslow gives the clue to the writing of this book. Beads of history and story lie around in plenty; some have already been picked up, but others were harder to find, though they proved well worth the searching.

The following verses, that tell of a few of these beads, must be the introduction to this book. The verses were written on a summer's morn as I sat on Hounslow Heath, creating mental pictures of its wonderful yesterday.

LIST OF ILLUSTRATIONS.

LIST OF ILLUSTRATIONS—*continued.*

CONTENTS.

CONTENTS—*continued.*

HIGHWAYMAN'S HEATH
BOOK ONE.

CHAPTER I.

A Topographical Mystery.

I T is an extraordinary thing in these days, when so much "research-light" has been turned upon almost every town, village or district in Great Britain, that the once famous Hounslow Heath in Middlesex can boast of no historian. Paradoxically enough, however, there can be very few places in our shires that have been referred to more often in all sorts and conditions of books; in history, in literature, in topographical works, and most of all, in fiction. But all these mentions are more or less scrappy, in passing, or as a setting for a story, and the strange fact still remains that there does not exist any one volume whose sole topic is Hounslow Heath—that is until the appearance of the book which you are now reading.

What is the reason for this neglect? At first thought it is, perhaps, a little hard to find one definite reason; the answer is rather made up of several forces of circumstance.

First of all, there is not one square foot of Hounslow Heath, as such, existing to-day. This may surprise some, but it is correct. It is true that a few hundred acres still remain as a drilling and cavalry exercising ground near the Barracks, but that is "enclosed" and only unofficially accessible to the public.

The fact that this is often overlooked was emphasised by a magazine story I read recently, in which the author told of a motor-cyclist riding at night over Hounslow Heath, and went on to describe the Heath as he imagined it to be; what he described was the Heath of the eighteenth century, and he had obviously laid the scene of a modern story in a place he had never visited.

Although no actual Heath now remains, there are still plenty of heath-like scenes there; especially in the twilight, when the growing dark-ness turns the fruit-bushes and flat cabbage fields into the scrubby waste of former days, and it is possible to see, at that time of day, the Heath very much as it was once, a visualisation helped by the fact that many of the fields are hedgeless. Perhaps, the best impression of this sort can be obtained on that stretch of flat road that lies between the Bath Road, just past Cranford Bridge and the village of Hatton. I have often stood on that road in the early night and imagined I could see the Hounslow Heath of old, and thought what it must have looked like to the traveller in those days—except that I had the advantage of knowing that nothing more alarming than a rabbit or a bat was likely to cross my path, whereas the fears of my confrere of bygone days would have been very real ones that were more likely than not to be fulfilled before he reached his journey's end.

Another reason of the neglect of Hounslow Heath is that it is so near London; people will write books on the Lakes, on Dartmoor, on the Broads or any other place that is more difficult to reach; places which, perhaps, may be able to score scenically over Hounslow Heath, but are " left at the post " as regards romantic memories.

An Englishman has been described as one " who travels in every country but his own," and a Londoner is this condensed. The latter will take infinite pains to explore places much farther afield and completely ignore those near at hand. He will strain his eyes to see what is on the horizon and not notice what is just beyond his own doorstep.

A third reason is that Hounslow Heath lies in Middlesex. Here again we enter the realms of paradox, for Middlesex is, at once, the most neglected and the most persecuted of all the English counties. Middlesex has suffered, and always will suffer, from having London within its borders; for in spite of the municipal boundary made when the L.C.C. formed the new county of London, from a topographical point of view, London is still in Middlesex—or if it is not (apart from the L.C.C. boundary) where London ends and Middlesex begins, I will not venture to say; the " line " changes almost every day.

When I say Middlesex is neglected, I mean from the historian's point of view, more especially the writers of books on Modern England. For instance, H. V. Morton, in two books which I admire immensely, has emphasised this; when he heard the *Call of England* it was not loud enough to echo " Middlesex," or when he went *In Search of England* he did not look closely enough to find this " unknown " county by the Thames; yet I will venture to say, and I am ready to prove my words against all comers, that Middlesex, the smallest county but one, has (and not merely in proportion to its size) more of historical and topographical interest within its borders than any other in the British Isles.

This point of neglect is again brought home in a publication of quite a different nature, entitled *Britain Beautiful,* of which I am also an admirer as a fine piece of work. Here, too, Middlesex is sadly neglected; there are certainly twenty-five most interesting photographs, but some 280 lines only of letterpress, nearly 100 of which are devoted to one " show " place of the county, Hampton Court. But then, I suppose, in a publication of this sort, about a hundred people look at the pictures to one who reads the text and as I say, the photographs are good; though it is to be regretted that the writer of the wording beneath one of them badly mixes up Hayes in Middlesex with Hayes in Kent. He is not alone in this, newspapers often do it and even worse things; why, I recently saw a photo in a paper of the " Old Berkeley Coach on the way to Oxford " passing through West Wickham, which is in Kent, when it was really going through West Wycombe, which is in Bucks.

So much for the neglect of Middlesex; I could quote numerous similar examples. Now for the persecution. Middlesex is fighting for her life; like many a mortal beauty, all men's hands seem against her. Perhaps her worst foe is the builder, before whose hand of devastation the farms and fields of rural Middlesex are fast disappearing—though luckily they have not quite all gone yet.

The builder is not, however, the only foe, though often coming in the wake of a greater. Were it not for the saner counsels that have happily prevailed the great estates of Middlesex would have fared even worse than they have done. Often I wonder if we are mad as a nation—at least the municipal part of us. Otherwise, how can we account for the state of mind that would have destroyed Chiswick House and its grounds to erect an electric power station, or the suggestion, recently put forward, of turning the grounds of Syon House into a sewage works!

If the despoilers of Middlesex could have their horrid way, all the fine old houses and estates on this side of London would soon be swept away in the name of "improvements." I mentioned the saner counsels; thank Heaven they have saved Chiswick House with the spirited help of Mr. John Burns, and also rescued Gunnersbury Park and Cranford Park from the builders.

The list could be extended, but it is a melancholy story, with a few bright spots. To tabulate only a few from memory whose fates were recently decided or are still in the balance, we can note the following historic estates that have come into the unpleasant limelight after centuries of delightful obscurity in the depths of rural Middlesex.

Ken Wood was saved only by agitation from having blocks of flats erected on its grounds. Chiswick House, that fine old 18th century mansion whose grounds are an "earthly paradise" and hardly altered at all since the 18th century, was only saved from becoming a power station after much protest. Syon Park, the fine Thames-side estate at Isleworth, was threatened by the sewage spectre. Gunnersbury Park and its two mansions have luckily been saved. Swakeleys at Ickenham, one of the finest Jacobean mansions in England, is saved as a club, but its grounds are completely spoilt and its general effect quite ruined by bungalows almost up to its doors. Boston Manor, Brentford, is saved after a "fight." Hanworth Park is now a Flying School. Headstone Manor, that fine old moated grange, has only been snatched from the builder at the last moment.

The historic estate of Canons at Edgware is now being built over, though the mansion is still standing. Harefield Place is being cut up into lots; a fate that has also befallen Arno's Grove at Southgate. Bentley Priory, now held by the R.A.F., with its beautiful grounds and literary memories, may yet be saved for the people. Cranford Park is empty but, luckily, no longer "on the danger list." Osterley Park, with its beautiful meadows where we can wander, is still with us, but for how long? Garrick Villa at Hampton is now flats. Orleans House, Twickenham, has recently been demolished, though I'm glad to say York House and its fine gardens have been saved, and also White Webbs, Enfield.

Dawley Farm, Harlington, what is left of Lord Bolingbroke's famous mansion, which has points in its story that would rival any mansion in England, is in danger of demolition to make way for a gramophone factory. This old house that can tell stories—*quietly*—more fascinating than any record ever could be, is in danger of being swept away to add to the world's noise. O tempora. O mores. Then—even though we must finish on a melancholy note—the Tube—that evil burrower whose breath is even more devastating than the Great Worm of Lambton, has invaded that beautiful and still rural corner of Middlesex where lies the hamlet of Cockfosters and the beautiful estate of Trent Park. Sic transit gloria Middlesexi. Not content with ruining Edgware in the same county and Morden in Surrey, this worm is now burrowing its destructive way to feed on the vitals of another victim. But then, think of the dividends, my tear vriends.

I could go on but, in spite of the brighter notes here and there, it is all too depressing.

Oh, yes; I know all about the "commercial reasons"; but don't we spend millions on "palatial" super-picturehouses; and yet destroy living pictures of old England, near London, that untold millions can never restore to us after it is too late ?

That, I think, is another sign of our madness as a nation. People come from the ends of the earth to see the pleasures of our countryside, and yet we seem to be doing all we can to destroy the very things that attract visitors to our shores. Looking at it from the very lowest standpoint—the commercial—where is the sense of that ?

If the much-talked-of Green Belt round London had been begun even as late as just after the Great War it would not have been too late. These estates could have been linked up and this, now only a dream of what might have been, would be an accomplished fact. No sane person imagines this "belt" to be two complete circles, say a mile apart; it could have been an irregular and more charming belt than that in which the connecting link between two existing commons and estates might be only an avenue of trees in parts; but it would have been enough. Let them build outside or inside this irregular circle, but let the "belt" itself be inviolate from the hand of the vandal, so that the citizens of the world's greatest city might still have a touch of real country breeze to fan their cheeks when they crossed London's "doorstep."

In future, in this book, I shall refer to the old and the present country that was once Hounslow Heath under that name; the context, and the intelligence of the reader, will easily differentiate between the two.

The Hounslow Heath district (apart from the present Heath) is notable in many ways, as I trust these pages will show, but there is one thing about it (hardly understood generally I am afraid, but it is only one of the many things concerning it that seem ignored by the average person) and that is the fact that here—only about a dozen miles from the world's largest city — there is a tract of open country *twenty-five miles square still untouched by a single inch of railway line.* If anything this is an under-estimate of area; look on a map and you will see that this statement, almost unbelievable at first, is strictly true. Is there any other district within the same distance of London that can claim this? I think not.

         *   *   *   *   *   *

The way of the digressor is hard. I have been led away from Hounslow Heath on many side tracks into other parts of historic Middlesex —albeit a fascinating thing either on wheels or afoot—but we must resist it. Anyhow, for the present, and get back to our Heath—get back, in fact, from mention of some of the county's beauty spots to what some think one of its ugly spots; for it is sometimes argued of the countryside that what was once Hounslow Heath is flat and uninteresting. I agree to the former—half of it, certainly, is flat—but it is very far from being uninteresting to those with a spark of imagination; and it is little use going rambling anywhere without a grain or two. Most people invariably misjudge this part of Middlesex; they dash by it, along the Great West Road—of which more anon—in a car, see the said flat cabbage fields and nothing beyond that; either with physical or mental eyes. They do not know and cannot imagine what lies beyond the trees that flank these cabbages; their imaginations being on the level of that humble but useful vegetable, they are quite incapable of rising higher.

They do not realise that behind those trees lie still unspoiled villages village greens, meadowlands, streams and even ruins, as well as many relics of bygone days, quaint little country inns, where one may still drink a pint of beer with a yokel to whom London, even to-day, is but a faint echo, though under a dozen miles away. Add to these charms many a legend and tale of old England in song and story that had its genesis in this quiet countryside.

Evidence of the lack of an understanding mind is often being thrust upon me. Two men have made pretty much the same remark to me. One, a barrister, who ought to have known better, spoke sneeringly when he said " What a terrible part it is, just beyond Hounslow; the most dull and uninteresting bit round London." I questioned him, and it was as I thought; all he had done was to pass three times along the main road in a car, without stopping, and he had not the faintest idea of what lay beyond his cabbage-fringed vision. I did not tell him; his tone was so " superior " that I left him to wallow in his crass ignorance.

The other man spoke in quite a different style, more in despair. " What *can* you see to interest you round Hounslow ? " he asked me. He was a very different type from the first man, and I led him by the hand and showed him something of what interested me. He was sportsman enough to own he spoke without knowledge, and now he is keen on further exploration.

The story of Hounslow Heath is a long one, stretching back into the dawn of our history, when the early Britons and the Romans, possibly, fought for its possession. It has its niche in military annals; it has played its part in science, history and topography, while its records in agriculture are varied. Yet, in spite of all these things, it has one memory that crowds out all others. Mention the two words, Hounslow Heath, and what thought flies instantly to the mind of any English-speaking person, whether he be in Tooting or Timbuctoo? Highwaymen. . . . .

The Highwaymen of Hounslow Heath. There's romance in those five words that appeals to the imagination more than mention of any other famous robbers in the world's history.

There may be thrills in other names—in the mention of the Bush-rangers of Australia; the Road Agents of the Wild West, or the Bad Men of Arizona, the Pirates of the Spanish Main, the Coasts of Barbary, or the China Seas, the Brigands of Old Spain, the Head Hunters of Borneo, the Robbers of the Rhine, or even Robin Hood and his merry men in Sherwood Forest. I would not rob any of these of their fame, evil—and popular—as it may be; but I still think that none of them has quite the romantic spark which fires the imagination as much as the mention of the Highwaymen of Hounslow Heath.

Before we get on with the story of these picturesque Night Riders—picturesque that is to us as we see them through the glamour of years, whatever may have been the opinions of the travellers on the Western Road when they caught sight of the same gentry lurking in the dark o' the moon, by the wayside—we must devote some attention to the history, past and present, of the spot where they once played the High Toby.

To those who are anxious to get on to the highwaymen episodes as quickly as possible—and are too conscientious merely to skip—this may be the pill in the jam; but, believe me, it is a pill of a very pleasant taste and there will be still plenty of jam left when you have swallowed it. . .

CHAPTER II.

The Riddle of a name, and the former extent of the Great Heath.

THE derivation of the name Hounslow is still undecided. Ingenious theories have been put up by some students of nomenclature to be knocked down by others, who, in turn, offer suggestions. Where those more learned disagree I will not venture on any new theory, but own to being an honest agnostic and confess I do not know. It may be worth while, however, to note the various ideas on this somewhat elusive theme.

J. E. B. Gover, who probably knows more than most on this subject, in *The Place Names of Middlesex* gives these spellings—all differing little in comparison with some places: " 1086 Honeslaw (Domesday), 1216-1307 Hundeslawe, 1327-1446 Houndeslowe, 1535 Hounslowe. The mound or tumulus of Hund, Anglo-Saxon ' hloew '; Middle English ' lawe-lowe '= mound or tumulus; also rising ground, only in Hounslow (as regards Middlesex). The literal meaning of Hund is dog, but here used as a personal name as the genitive ' s ' shows, cf., ' on hundes hloew ' in ancient deeds."

Gover makes no mention of Lyson's far-fetched derivation. I have every respect for Lyson, as author of the topographers' "Bible," as regards London's environs; but it is hard to agree with his fanciful conclusion when he says: "The old name of Hounslow-heath was Hundeslawe. Qu. Hound's lawe? To *lawe* a hound was an obsolete word for laming him, by cutting out one of the balls of his foot, which was done by the foresters to all dogs kept on the King's forests that could not be drawn through a stirrup provided for that purpose, and kept in the house where the swan-mote was held. Hounslow-heath was within the forest of Staines."

Thorne politely differs from this, though he offers no alternative, merely stating that Lyson's theory "may be taken for what it is worth." Walford was another agnostic and, as he did not know, wisely says nothing; but D. Loinaz in the *Home Counties Magazine* says: "The Domesday Honeslaw gave its name to one of the six original Hundreds of Middlesex, but is now within the Hundred of Isleworth, comprising the parishes of Isleworth, Heston and Twickenham in addition to Hounslow, which is well to remember, though it throws no light on the present controversy." Aungier, in his book *Syon Monastery*, suggests that the name might be derived from the Saxon *Hundes* and might mean the " place where the dogs are kept." Such a derivation, suggestive of the forest or the chase, accords very well with the character of the locality in those far-off times, when the whole stretch of country from Staines to Brentford, and from Harmondsworth to Hampton, was one vast forest, dotted here and there with enclosures granted from time to time by royal favour.

"From Stanes to Brayneford," writes Camden in 1586, " all that which lies between the high roade along Hundeslawe and The Thamis was called the forest or Warren of Stanes, but Henry III. deforested and dewarrened it in 1227." The glimpse then that is afforded us of Hounslow in those ancient times, if we accept Aungier's derivation, is that of a few foresters' huts placed at some convenient spot in the great forest, and hard by, the

6

more important outbuildings in which the King's hounds were housed. The chosen spot would probably be not too remote from the old Roman highway which, as Camden says, "passes through Brayneford and so over Hundeslaw Heath." But the Domesday form of the name (Honeslaw) would seem fatal to Aungier's derivation.

On this W. Paley Baildon comments: "This suggested derivation of Hounslow seems more than usually crude and unconvincing. The fact that in 1086 Hounslow gave its name to the Hundred, provides a clue for the true explanation. *Hund,* genitive *hundes,* is the Saxon word for the hundred; hlaw is the Saxon for a small hill, still in use in the alternative forms of *law* (e.g., Berwick Law) and *low* (e.g., Arbour Low). Hundes-law simply means the hill at which the Hundred Court met. These courts in early times met in the open air, at some natural or artificial feature of the country, a hill, a tree, a stone, a bridge, a cross, or the like. Assuming, as seems reasonably probable, that the Domesday Hundred of Honeslaw was co-extensive with the modern Hundred of Isleworth, a glance at the map will show that Hounslow is the most convenient place possible for the three centres of population, the parishes of Isleworth, Heston and Twickenham.

The "hill" of Hounslow is not very lofty, though the road certainly rises from Isleworth; anyhow it is but a little extra piece of the "nominal mystery" of Hounslow. Here are the theories, real or imaginary, and the reader must form his own conclusions; for it is unlikely that fresh evidence will now come to light.

If I should venture on an opinion, probably I should incline rather to the folk-moot idea than to the hounds—but one cannot be dogmatic on so visionary a point.

The fact that Hounslow is within two parishes only adds to the confusion, for some old writers say Heston and some Isleworth when they both really mean Hounslow, according to which part of it they refer—though the meaning can generally be gathered from the context.

* * * * *

The exact extent of Hounslow Heath in olden days was probably never known quite accurately; and to tell its confines to an acre was almost impossible in a place straggling over fourteen parishes.

In Luke Pope's *History of Middlesex* we read "Hounslow Heath extended into the several parishes and hamlets of Isleworth, Braynford, Twickenham, Heston, Feltham, Harlington, Craynford, Harmondsworth, Stanwell, Hanworth, Bedfont, Hampton, Hounslow and Teddington."

Even more vague is another old account which says "Hounslow Heath once extended to the pales of Bushey Park, and into the parishes of Brentford, Twickenham, Teddington, Harmondsworth, et cetera." The et cetera may apparently be taken how we like.

In most of these places it is fairly clear how they came to be included in the heath country, though in others now quite separate from Hounslow it is more or less conjecture. For instance, Twickenham probably meant the Common (now the Green); Hampton must also have been its common (now no more), while Teddington would almost certainly be the upper part, probably Fulwell Golf Links and part of Bushy Park.

Even the official accounts of the extent of the Heath vary. The earliest survey of any importance was in 1546, when 4,293 acres was given; in Rocques map of Middlesex in 1754 the extent is stated to be 6,658 acres, an appreciable increase; while in a survey of 1810 the figures dropped again to 5,000 acres; though unofficial enclosures—or land grabbing—probably account for the last discrepancy.

Another old account says, more vaguely still, that the Heath "extended for five miles beyond the Town with a lateral measurement of much the same distance." This would make it twenty-five square miles; an approximation probably fairly accurate, though the lateral measurement seems rather under-estimated. Anyhow it is these twenty-five square miles we are exploring in this book.

In Sir Montagu Sharpe's valuable monograph, *The Forests of Middlesex*, we read: "The Royal Forest of Staines extended into 14 parishes and covered some 23,000 acres of land, and included Sunbury Heath and a large portion of the Great Heath of Hounslow. . . . As Staines Forest was not disafforested under the General Statute of Forests, it would seem that the order turning this district into a Royal Preserve was made by one of the earlier Norman kings at some period anterior to the reign of Henry II. (1154). The effect of this arbitrary decree upon a cultivated district is well pictured by John of Salisbury, writing in the 12th century: 'Husbandmen with their harmless herds and flocks are driven from their well-cultivated fields and pastures that wild beasts may range in them without interruption.' "

The Charter of Henry III. in 1227 which disafforested this part will be found in full in this book. It is rather quaintly worded, and enacts "in protection of the people of all the county of Middlesex that lived in this region should not be molested by the King's men—no warrener or forester or Justice of the Forest shall or may anything meddle with their lands or woods." Exactly how or to whom this ex-forest was apportioned is a little vague, for it was mainly wild waste land for centuries after this. In the Parliamentary Survey of Hampton Court (1653) it is termed "The Great Heath, commonly called Hounslow Heath."

It is a curious anomaly that this Heath, with boundaries so visionary, should have been chosen for the commencement of an undertaking looked upon as the last word in accuracy—the Ordnance Survey—but so it was. Walter Jerrold has a concise account of these famous beginnings in the measurement of our land, part of which reads: "In 1784 Hounslow Heath was the scene of the beginning of General William Roy's trigonometrical survey. It was on the Heath that the General measured his Base Line. The work occupied nearly three months. When in 1792 the General Ordnance Survey of the British Isles was begun, operations were commenced by re-measuring of Roy's Hounslow base line, and the result was within two and three-quarter inches of his measurement."

It is interesting to note that Henry Cavendish, the brilliant but eccentric scientist, was present on this occasion, for we read in General Roy's book *An Account of the Measurement of the Base Line upon Hounslow Heath*: "On the 16th day of April, 1784, Mr. Cavendish and Mr. Blagdon accompanying the President of The Royal Society (Sir J. Banks) we began our observations at a place called King's Arbour, at the north-west extremity of the Heath, between Cranford Bridge and Longford; and having proceeded from thence through the narrow gorge formed by Hanworth Park and Hanworth Farm, we finished at Hampton, near the east side of Bushy Park, at the south-east extremity; the total distance. from the Survey of Middlesex, being upwards of five miles." The map in this

A Reconstruction by Colin Maxwell and A. H. Palmer.

"THE OLDEST INHABITANT."

The Brontosaurus roamed the Heath some 100,000,000 years ago.

CAESAR'S CAMP - KING'S ARBOUR.

book is most interesting and worth consulting for details not shown on general maps of the district. In that fascinating book, *The Map of England,* Sir Charles Close writes: " Let us accompany Roy in the first of his labours in this great operation, that is, the measurement of a base. He chose Hounslow Heath for this purpose. It was decided to employ soldiers on the duty of clearing the ground and for furnishing ' the necessary centinels for guarding the apparatus,' and accordingly a party of the 12th Regiment of Foot was ordered to march from Windsor to Hounslow Heath, where they encamped. The base was measured by long glass tubes. . . . His Majesty (George III.) deigned to honour the operation by his presence, entering minutely into the work of conducting it, which met with his gracious approbation (and he probably understood it as much as one of the sheep grazing near!).

" The respectable and worthy President of the Royal Society," this interesting, but fulsome, account continues, for it is quoted from a contemporary source, " ever zealous in the cause of science, repeatedly visited the Heath, and in the final stages ordered his tents to be continually pitched near at hand, where his immediate guests, and the numerous visitors whom curiosity drew to the spot, met with the most hospitable supply of every necessary, and even elegant refreshment." I wonder if the love for science or the " elegant refreshment " drew the more!

In a catalogue of French books I recently found the following: *Description des Moyens employés pour mésurer le Base de Hounslow-Heath dans la Province de Middlesex, 1784.* It was like meeting an old friend in fancy dress.

The disappearance of the Heath was gradual. During the reign of Henry VIII. a Bill was framed for enclosing it and assigning the allotments to the inhabitants of the several parishes concerned, but it was not carried into effect. Meanwhile, " land-grabbing " went on pretty considerably; and not by the " common people " but by noblemen who wished to increase the acreage of their estates—as in the case of the Duke of Argyle at Whitton.

It was at the end of the 18th and the beginning of the 19th centuries that the Enclosures Act fell like an axe on Hounslow Heath, or as one writer puts its: " In 1795 the people of Isleworth made an attempt to get it enclosed into small farms, but it was not till 1813 that, by Act of Parliament, the great enclosure took place, when almost every acre then capable of profitable cultivation was enclosed and the aspect of the country for miles round thereby materially altered; the soil was poor, but it tempted the land-hungry."

In Peter Foot's *Agriculture of Middlesex* this Bill of Henry VIII.'s is quoted; but too long to give in full. The spelling is quaint and it speaks of the " wast grounde and soyle commonly called Hounsloo-Hethe in the King's County of Middlesex," and goes on to complain of the " barreness and infertylitie thereof by waunte of dylygence and industryes of men in cultivating all manner of grayne, grasse, woodes and other necessarie thynges."

There is another account written about the time of Foot's book, which says much the same in modern language, for in Middleton's *Agriculture of Middlesex* we read of " such parts of Hounslow Heath as lie within the parishes of Twickenham, Teddington and Hanworth, in case they were enclosed would let for very high rents. The rest of Hounslow Heath is land

of such good quality that it is disgraceful to the county that it should
remain in its present unproductive state, when most or all of it might be
subjected to the fructifying influence of irrigation and in consequence be
brought to yield a produce of upwards of 10l. an acre per annum," which
was the beginning of the rich farmlands we see on the old-time Heath
to-day.

CHAPTER III.

When Hounslow Heath formed part of the Forest of Middlesex.

CHANCE, which plays so great a part in all phases of life, despite the
teachings of the sternly practical, enabled me to begin the history
of Hounslow Heath eons earlier than I had hoped to do. I
cannot give the exact date, but it recalls the days when mammoths
roamed and British-born lions made their homes in that wild waste; where,
at an even earlier age, the brontosaurus and the ichthyosaurus went about
their awful occasions in the swamps, and the pterodactyl circled its
leathern-winged flight above them.

My authority is the famous geologist, Sir Roderick Murchison,
as I came across in his writings, quite unexpectedly, this
arresting paragraph: "In the low tracts of England, where tranquil
lacustine (lake-like) deposits have occurred, their bones—even those of the
lion—have been found so perfectly unbroken and unworn in the fine gravel
in which they are heaped up, that few persons would be disposed to deny
that such feline, and other animals, including the mammoth, once roamed
over the British Isles.

"When the great estuary of the Thames spread far inland, and the
plains of Hyde Park, Chelsea, Hounslow and Uxbridge were under water,
the slightly elevated parts around these swamps would be feeding grounds
for the great quadrupeds whose bones are found in the gravel of the
adjacent rivers and estuaries."

There is evidence for all this, but more startling is a statement related
in *Speculum Britanniae*, 1593, "made by the Travaill and view of John
Norden," who is certainly a "diehard" for the county's antiquity, for he
says that Berosus, the son of Japhet (grandson of Noah), was an inhabitant
of Middlesex, where he settled 252 years after the Flood! Unfortunately
no authority is given for this illuminating information.

The history of the Heath in early days has to be gathered from various
writers, some of whom include it (though not always by name) when
speaking of the Great Forest of Middlesex, of which it once formed a
part, usually referred to in this district of the county as the Forest, or
Warren, of Staines. I do not pretend that the sources quoted are at all
complete, but they will, at least, give us some idea of this wild desolate
region in bygone times.

Edward Clodd's *Primitive Man* will be found a most useful little book
for those who would read more of these very early days; in fact, the author

touches on this actual district when he speaks, in passing, of "the early history of man and the conditions of the Thames Valley when he and a strange group of animals lived there in a dim and dateless past."

In *Origines Celticae* Edwin Guest writes: "I believe the district of Middlesex in the early Roman period was merely a march (roughly a boundary) of the Catuvellauni, a common through which ran a wide trackway, but in which was neither town, village or inhabited house. We have Caesar's authority for saying that the imperfectly civilised races of the period prided themselves in having a belt of desolate country round their settlements, and I have little doubt that between Brockley Hill and the Thames all was wilderness, from the Lea to the Brent and beyond." This would, of course, include all that tract of country later known as Hounslow Heath.

The Archaeology of Middlesex and London is a most interesting book as far as it goes, but I cannot help thinking that the Heath district, rich as it is in story, is somewhat neglected by C. E. Vulliamy, the author. "In early Saxon days," he writes, "the woods of Middlesex were infested by robbers, and honest men passed through them with loud shouting and the blowing of horns." Personally I should imagine this method was as likely to attract as scare robbers.

We certainly have a little of Hounslow later on in this book, when we read "One of the most interesting of our local hoards of the Bronze Age is the one found at Hounslow. It is especially remarkable as containing examples of the flat axe, the palstave and the socketed celt—types which, as we have seen, represent successive stages of invention. There were also gouges and spear-heads, part of a knife, fragments of swords, and a singular curved implement made apparently by hammering down the edge of a broken sword or dagger. They are now in the British Museum." When I tried to see these the attendant could not find them. The particular gallery was under repair at the time, which may have had something to do with it.

The same writer also speaks of a later discovery here: "There was a curious find made in 1864 by men digging in a field at Hounslow. They came upon a small collection of animal figures in bronze, together with a small bronze wheel. The date of these animals must be regarded as Celtic, but not probably much superior to the Roman dominion. These models were probably amulets or badges for ornamental purposes."

Something of the beginnings of Middlesex will be found in *Wanderings In Anglo-Saxon Britain,* by Arthur Weigall, and we also read of the great forest from a writer called T. Cromwell, the author of a *Life of Oliver Cromwell,* and possibly a relation. In the Introduction to his *History of Clerkenwell,* in which he touches upon other parts of early Middlesex, he says: "The term forest had a wider import at that period than now. It included desert not less than wooded land, which, though neither marked by more than the ordinary abundance of trees, nor by sterility, was yet unappropriated upon any terms of tenure or service.

"Forming an original portion of that extensive tract, even long afterwards known as the Forest of Middlesex, it probably still afforded many traces of the old empire of the woods. . . . . Thus the monk Fitz-Stephen, who wrote his curious description of London not much more than a century afterwards, informs us of the delight of the citizens in hawks and hounds, and of their *right* to hunt in this forest.

"That valuable record, the Conqueror's Survey, indeed makes no reference of any ecclesiastical structure in all Middlesex; and though unexceptional instances might be adduced of the existence of churches at that period, upon which the Domesday Book is silent, yet the proofs afforded by the same venerable document, that a very large portion of the county was then forest-land, added to our knowledge that the temporalities of the clergy in the reign of William were comparatively small, add weight to its negative evidence in this case."

The statement anent the Middlesex churches in *Domesday* is misleading; there is certainly mention of several priests resident in the various districts, which in the ordinary way would surely imply some sort of a church, if only a rude Saxon wattle-and-daub structure.

"It is as well to point out," writes Eyre, "that the term ' disafforesting ' would not necessarily mean that the forest lands were cleared by the removal of trees, although that was probably the ultimate result. When a district was disafforested it simply ceased to be kept as a royal preserve and was thrown open to the people. The result of this would probably be the cutting down of quantities of timber and the clearing of large tracts for meadow and arable land. Thus the order for disafforestation usually marked the beginning of the work of clearing the district, which may actually have remained uncleared for centuries." As was probably the case in this part of Middlesex.

It is hard (for which we should be thankful) to get away from quoting old Stow, the Elizabethan topographer, and he reminds us that "in the second year of Henry IV. the forest of Staines was disafforested." This would make it in 1400; but we know from many other sources that this took place in 1227, and according to modern authorities (*Victoria County History* and other books) Stow was in error on this point, which mistake apparently arose from the misreading of the charter granted by the King in the latter year. Well, in a monumental work such as Stow's a mistake or two may well creep in.

It is amusing to note in conclusion to this chapter Stow's plaintive remark concerning the disafforestation in question: "Since which time the suburbs about London hath been also mightily increased with buildings." This was written in 1598. I wonder what he would say now !

Writing of the early days in *Hallowed Spots of Ancient London* Eliza Meteyard draws a vivid picture of the future Hounslow Heath: "On the Middlesex shore of the Thames was undulating meadow-land, varied by breadths of primeval trees; and these lent their shadow and dipped their branches often into the stream itself. Lesser streams emerged from the gloom of the woods and flowed down by turfy banks into the river; whilst at the rear stretched a dense woodland, forming a portion of what was afterwards known as the forest of Middlesex.

"This woodland extended on either side, and at one period or another was covered with trees of gigantic growth, which, swept down in some great convulsion of nature as a whirlwind or an earthquake, are found— even occasionally at this day—root upwards in the soil. To the north of this forest round London rose a heathy upland of which Hampstead Heath formed a small portion to the north as Hounslow Heath did to the west. These heaths were probably never more than partially wooded.

"Such was the primitive aspect of the surroundings of ancient London —a wilderness varied by stream and upland, precisely as may be seen at the present day in New Zealand, or the more remote states of North America."

It was not until the days of the Ancient Britons that the history of Hounslow Heath began to emerge out of the mists of the past, when it became traceable from authentic sources rather than from conjecture.

The Catuvellauni and the Trinobantes were the first known inhabitants of Middlesex, though we seem to meet more of the latter in the Heath country. Their name literally means " dwellers between three rivers," and it is sometimes written Trinovantes. " It is the Latinised form of the British word Trinobantys," says one authority, " or ' dwellers over the water,' with reference to the estuary of the Thames, which then severed Essex and Middlesex from Kent and Surrey." (Why *then?* Doesn't it still?)

The sway of this tribe extended, of course, far beyond Hounslow Heath, for the Trinobantes occupied all Middlesex, Herts and Essex. They are recorded to have been " the bravest people in the island "; there seems to have been a traitor in their camp, however, for it is said that it was by Mandubratius, a chieftain of this tribe, that Julius Caesar was invited to invade this island.

The Trinobantes, however, under Cassivelaunus, rose against the Imperial Eagles and after fighting bravely, but vainly, against a stronger foe " retired into the marshes and there protracted a desperate resistance." These marshes probably included Hounslow Heath.

According to an ancient M.S. description of Middlesex this part was once called " The Valley of the Trinobantes," and described as " all lowland, marshy, boggy and woody," until the time of the Saxons, when husbandry began here. There is evidence that Caesar himself was here, for his army crossed the Thames at Brentford (about three miles away, and in those days almost part of the heath) in pursuit of Cassivelaunus. Caesar probably stayed with his army at the camp on the Heath.

Many writers speak of this camp in passing, such as Cooke's *Topography of Middlesex,* when we are told that " Upon Hounslow Heath are the remains of several ancient camps," which is interesting but hardly informative, though it gives us an impetus to seek further. Camden in his *Britanniae* (1586) is a little more explicit when he says " on the north end of the Heath towards King's Arbour is a Roman camp; a simple work and not large."

It was Dr. Stukeley, the 18th century antiquarian, in his *Itinerarium Curiosium* who really first drew serious attention to this camp on what he calls " the via Trinobantica," of which he has a plan in the book " Caesar's Camp on Hounslow Heath." He writes: " It is very perfect, 60 paces square. It is to be seen on the way to Longford: I showed it to Lord Hertford and to Lord Winchelsea, who measured it and expressed the greatest pleasure at the sight." This camp, however, seems rather small for the several thousand men Caesar is known to have with him. Possibly it was one of several.

Brewer, in his *History of Middlesex* (1816), comments on this: " It is observed by Stukeley that a portion of a Roman road, one quarter of a mile long, is still perfect to the east of the brook where the powder mills are on Hounslow Heath, at which place the common road goes southward to pass it. By this is meant a part of the presumed Roman road leading from Regnum to London, which is believed to have run in the same direction as the present road from Staines to Turnham Green."

C. E. Vulliamy in his *Archaeology of Middlesex* rather sneers at Stukeley, especially his account of the Roman camp at King's Arbour, though he owns it has since been ploughed flat, and it is also now partly covered by trees. The author forgets that *Itinerarium Curiosium* in which Stukeley records his discoveries, was written in 1723 and many changes can take place in two hundred years. I could tell him of more drastic changes in six months. It is easy enough to sneer at Stukeley as "ingenious and imaginative"; the old antiquarian nevertheless did a good deal of sound work, which has been of great use to those who have followed.

Vulliamy's book is a most fascinating one and has afforded me many hours of interest; it is a work of very deep research, but like all works of this nature, it has strange gaps and one of these is the rather scanty information he has concerning Hounslow Heath, though what he does say is intensely interesting and enough to make us want more.

Lyson has very little to say of this camp, dismissing it in one paragraph: " A little to the east of Heathrow, on Hounslow Heath, within Harmondsworth Parish, are very perfect remains of an ancient camp, single trenched, about 300ft. square."

I have explored this part, committing the sin of trespass, but found no trace whatever now of this camp and supposed it to be destroyed, a supposition confirmed by a reference to the *Victoria County History,* which tells us: " Three-quarters of a mile north-east of Heath Row, immediately south of the Bath Road, a small square camp about 380 feet square was extant until the autumn of 1906. It is now ploughed perfectly flat, leaving no trace." (There is a plan of the camp in this volume).

The immediate (if temporary) inhabitants of the site knew nothing whatever of Romans, though they were at least willing to lend themselves as subjects for a pictorial *jeu d'esprit—* the Romans and the Romanies—but when I went a week later to show them the photo I found the wandering gypsies gone; their camp fires were cold and the spot where their caravans had rested was once more left to the ghosts of Caesar's legions.

The Heath Row camp, though the most important, was not the only one hereabouts; in fact, there were several, although some of them may be the remains of trenches dug by the armies encamped here during the Civil War. Speaking of camps, however, the *Victoria History* has mention of two smaller ones: " To the east of Osterley Park was a small circular earthwork 200 feet in diameter inclusive, with an entrance on the eastern side," and again: " There is an earthwork situated on Hounslow Heath towards Twickenham against the boundary of the cemetery; it has now all but perished; the slightest depression in the ground is only just discernible." These camps were probably not Roman.

Frankly, anyone would be ill-advised to waste much time searching for these Roman camps; there is so little left of them now, even the actual sites are more or less conjecture, except that at Heath Row. The evidence on paper is stronger than on the face of the land and small references continually crop up, such as a note in Burlington's *British Traveller:* " In the road from Staines to Uxbridge is a small village called King's Arbour, near which are the remains of two Roman camps." The traveller who went from Staines to Uxbridge via King's Arbour would be rather out of his way, though it is quite possible that the road by the more direct route over Staines Moor in those days might sometimes have been impassable.

Only one of these other camps is mentioned by name, of which we get a clue from Cooke's book already mentioned: " On Hounslow Heath, near Cranford, are two royal camps marked on the map " (he refers to an old map at Syon House), " by name of Shakesbury Hills, mentioned by no writer I know of." I cannot find this marked on any general map of the county, though I have found a reference to it in a book, for Lambert in his *London and its Environs* says " on Hounslow Heath are the vestiges of several ancient camps, two of which are called Caesar's Camp and Shakesbury Camp."

Cooke's topography goes a litle adrift here (in company with his grammar), for Sir Montagu Sharpe informs me that Shakesbury Hill was a Roman camp—the term " hill " probably refers to an artificial mound, as in other places. " The Ordnance describes Shakesbury as a camp," he says, " but it is only a little east of King's Arbour. Why two camps so close?" He supplies the probable explanation to this when he adds: " Theodosius (c. 368) divided his army around London and defeated the Picts and Scots. I think he threw up the little camps in Middlesex."

To revert to the departure of the Romans from our shores and the coming of the Saxons. There was, so Besant tells us, " Stubborn fighting still for many years in the country about and beyond the great Middlesex forest." That the Saxons conquered is told from the name they gave to this part—the dwelling of the Middle Saxons—shortened to Middlesex.

It was a dim and mysterious period—sometimes called " The Two Lost Centuries of British History "—when practically nothing (beyond conjecture) is known even of the history of London, so it is hardly surprising that there is no history traceable to so desolate a region as Hounslow Heath. I would advise everyone to read that wonderful chapter (in Besant's London) called *After the Romans*. It is a fine piece of imaginative writing and contains the clearest reconstruction I know—anyhow in mentally " pre-digested " form for the busy man—of this period of London history, so fascinating because so inscrutable.

" We have seen the evidence of history," writes Besant, " let us consider next the evidence of topography," and goes on to speak of " the dreary uncultivated plains, covered with fens and swamps, stretching from the walls of London to the lower slopes of the northern hills and away to the westward to the foot of an immense forest, as yet wholly untouched, afterwards called the Middlesex forest "; and later on he mentions these parts being composed of " swampy moorlands followed by an impenetrable forest."

Although not mentioned by name—for this was a period long before it had one—we know that one of these marshy regions—half swamp and half forest—must have been that part of the country afterwards known as Hounslow Heath.

In Sharon Turner's *History of the Anglo-Saxons* there is a list of the numbers and conditions of the Saxon races of Middlesex at the time of the Domesday Survey, and from which has been drawn up an interesting table, though it does not throw much light on our particular district, for it does not specify the localities occupied by the various classes of population.

A gazetteer informs us that " numerous Celtic or early British, Roman and Saxon coins have been found on the Heath," but it gives no information as to the exact spots of this treasure trove, traces of which may still remain under the earth.

There are few traces of the Danes in this district, though they exist in other parts of the county, the nearest to Hounslow being, I think, Staines and Brentford. In the *Domesday Tables* there is mention of the payment of "Danegeld" for Middlesex.

Writing on this subject Sir Montagu Sharpe has a note: "A.D. 880. The Valley of the Thames which included Middlesex passed to Guthrum and Dane Law." Though this would include Hounslow Heath in a general way, the fact that no particular mention of this district under the Danes can be found is easily explained. It was far too desolate a region to attract marauders. There would be no loot for these Viking pirates on this bare swampy heathland.

Of the "Norman Conquest" of Hounslow Heath we have strong evidence in the first topographical book ever written—the *Domesday Book*—where the accounts of the early Heath villages make interesting reading. It shows, too, how many villages and hamlets existed in this region even in those early days. Here is the record concerning Hounslow: "Honeslaw.—Assessed for 70 hides. The land is 55 carucates. In the demesne there are 6½ hides and 6 ploughs. Among the free-men and the villeins there are 20 ploughs and 11 more could be made. A priest has 3 virgates there, and 51 villeins each with 1 virgate and 24 villeins each with ½ a virgate, and 6 cottagers. A foreigner and a certain Englishman have 4 hides and they are proved knights. The rank or station of these persons is uncertain. Under them reside 21 villeins and bordars and there are 6 of the lord's villeins who hold 2 hides and ½ a virgate. There are 2 mills of 10 shillings value. Meadow for 20 ploughs. Pasture for cattle of the village. One weir and a half of 12 shillings and eightpence value. Wood for 500 pigs. For the herbage 12 pence, with all its profits, and is worth 72 pounds; the same when received; in the time of King Edward 80 pounds. Earl Algar held this manor."

In Camden's *Britannia* we read "From Staines to Brentford all that which lies between the high road along Hounslow and the Thames was called the Forest or Warren of Staines," and that the original warren of Staines extended to 23,000 acres—a huge area, as we have already noticed.

For many hundred years the Heath probably remained in much the same state. "To some extent," says one writer, commenting on Elizabethan days, "no doubt Hounslow and the neighbouring districts shared in London's development. The prosperous 'merchant adventurer' of the city could now build himself a country residence within easy reach of town. Such residences sprang up all round London, not a few in and about Isleworth, and some, though not so many, in Hounslow.

"But the greater benefit accrued to Hounslow, though it may have taken years before the full force of it began to be felt, from the fact that the disafforestment not only gave an impetus to the development of the suburb and brought cultivators upon land hitherto wild, but also it involved a development of travel and traffic: situated on the common highway, the prosperity of the place could not but be enhanced by the growth of such road usage."

Another writer who touches on the great forest in this part of England is A. M. Eyre, who says: "After the Roman occupation of Britain ceased the roads were quickly overgrown and lost sight of, becoming as densely wooded as of yore and the forest of Middlesex became the refuge of outlaws, robbers and wild beasts. . . . . . *Domesday Book* provides ample evidence that Middlesex was still in Norman times an unusually

WHERE HEATH AND RIVER MEET.
Old England—Brentford.

Etching by Seymour Haden.

THE ROMANS AND THE ROMANIES.
Gypsies on the site of the Roman
Camp.

Photo by F. Ash.

densely wooded country. There is no record in actual measure of the amount of woodland, but food was provided for 20,000 swine." Fitzstephen, a monk of Canterbury, writing (circa 1170), refers to the lands on the "other" side of London (i.e. from Canterbury), which in its western portion must have included our Heath. "Here are fields for pasture," it is stated, "and a delightful plain of meadow-land, interspersed with flowing streams, on which stand mills whose clack is very pleasing to the ear. Close by lies an immense forest, in which are densely wooded thickets, the coverts of game, red and fallow deer, boars and wild bulls." This is a little less grim than many of the accounts of the early days of these parts.

The term "No Man's Land" is usually considered to have been invented during the Great War, but it appears in the Middlesex section of *Domesday,* where it is stated of a certain Hundred in this county: "The King holds 12 acres of the land of No-Mans-land. It is worth five shillings."

Probably the best, and certainly the most imaginative account, we have of the county hereabout in these early days is found in Sir Montagu Sharpe's *Middlesex in British, Roman and Saxon Times,* where the author visualises a Roman camp near Brentford and mentions "the cattle and ponies which graze on the heathland a mile higher up the trackway, or among the forest glades"—this was, of course, Hounslow Heath. Of this camp, near the Butts at Brentford, this writer says: "In form it was circular with entrances from the north to south. On the west the ditch and earthwork extend to within 70 yards of the Brent, while on the east the trackway, now the Boston Road, took its present semi-circular course to avoid the camp. The defence works consisted of a ditch and a bank, on the top of which stood a dense hedge of boughs and thorn bushes. Within the fort are rudely constructed huts of the tribesmen who guard the ford and portal to their county. Close to hand are some pits covered over with bushes and reeds, containing corn grown on the little clearings in the adjoining woodland. Further on stand the byres for the cattle and rough ponies, which graze on the heathland a mile higher up the trackway, or amongst the forest glades. By the entrances is a row of brightly painted war chariots, in which are placed weapons ready for use, while some gaunt and savage dogs lie beneath them."

There is a fine imaginative touch about this description; a quality very noticeable about this writer's work. He goes on: "The writer was once on Hounslow Heath looking at a cannon buried muzzle downward, which, with another, had marked the base for a trigonometrical survey, when a cottager informed him that it had been used in a battle on the Heath against Julius Caesar." This old cannon is still to be seen at King's Arbour.

"The Hundred of Spelthorne derived its name from a venerable and once well-known tree—viz., Spelthorne, the Tree of Speech"; appropriately so named when discussions were thorny. Its site is unknown, but it may provisionally be placed by Thamesis Street (Staines Road) at Hounslow. (Other authorities place this tree at Stanwell, Sunbury and Ashford Commons variously).

"There have been dug up on the Heath relics of ancient Britons, palstaves, celts (stone implements), swords and three small figures of boars."

"In Saxon times the Hundred Court held its sittings in the open air. The Hundred of Honeslow derived its name from a small artificial hill known as 'Hones-Klaw,' or 'hound's mound,' which formerly stood by the Bath Road on Smallbury Green (Isleworth). It was one of the

botonini, or landmarks of the long forgotten Roman survey of Middlesex.
" After the fall of London, about 600 A.D., the stream of East Saxon
invaders coming in from Herts to occupy their newly acquired territory
came down by the old mid-Middlesex forest trackway, and by the waterways of the Lea and the Thames. Uniting at Brentford they would soon
spread over the adjoining rich districts of Isleworth, Hounslow, and Twickenham; then came settlements appearing like little islands of cultivation
in the midst of forest waste and common. The villages were groups of
wooden homesteads with barns and cattle sheds, surrounded by rough
stockades and destitute of roads."

It is a temptation to quote more of these fascinating passages, but these
will at least give, in clear and vivid glimpses, mental pictures of the past
that are unforgetable.

I once saw an old rhyme (originally written of Tottenham wood, I
believe) thus adapted:
> " When Hounslow Heath is all afire,
>   Then Hounslow roads are nought but mire,"
a couplet certainly applicable to these parts, for I have seen the after-glow
of a stormy sunset when the Heath roads seemed enveloped in fiery vapour,
with the wet, steaming surfaces touched with ruddy reflections from the
skies. The old roads across the Heath counrty, leading directly towards
the westering sun, are wonderful spots for observing the beauties of sunset.

CHAPTER VI

The Parable of the Mustard Pot.

IT frequently happens when looking for the mustard pot that your eyes
roam the dinner table in search of it, only to discover it just in front
of your plate—the most simple simile proving the truth of the saying
" What is nearest the eye is hardest to see."

This is the position of Middlesex among the English counties; so near
London, it is often almost unknown even to Londoners (perhaps more than
any). They rush through it to get to other places, but leave it unexplored.
Yet, paradoxically enough, most people think they know Middlesex or, as
a pathetic alternative, think there is nothing to know about it.

Before the story of any special part of a county be read some knowledge of it as a whole is desirable, if only from a comparative value,
especially as we are studying it in a bygone age, when legend and truth are
intermixed.

This section will consist of the views of others, adverse and favourable, of this small shire as a whole, but it should be remembered that the
subsequent chapters deal only with the south-west corner of the county.

I shall write in this chapter more of opinions than of general history,
interesting as the latter is, to which some guide can be gathered from
various books mentioned.

There are, of course, many modern things in Middlesex that need no
explaining; things we could do without; such as an ugly bit of " strip "
building on an old coach road, too blatant to call for anything but a passing
curse; but we shall wander freely in these pages in that delightful half-and-
half land, where many things that are true enough are so linkec with the
past as to make them a joy to the discoverer.

The prejudice against Middlesex which exists to-day is no new thing, and the most stupid remark about the county is found in Cobbett's *Rural Rides* (a fascinating book nevertheless): " All Middlesex is *ugly,* notwithstanding the millions it is continually sucking from the rest of the Kingdom, and though the Thames and its meadows are seen from the road, the country is not less ugly from Richmond to Chertsey Bridge, through Twickenham, Hampton, Sunbury and Shepperton, than it is elsewhere. The soil is a gravel at bottom with a black loam at top near the Thames; further back it is a sort of spewy gravel, and the buildings consist generally of tax-eaters, showy, tea-garden-like boxes, and of shabby dwellings of labouring people, who, in this part of the country, look dirty and have every appearance of drinking gin."

Cobbett, who is all the funnier because he was not intentionally humorous, is equally vitriolic about the Heath, when he says " Hounslow Heath, which is only a little worse than the general run, is a sample of all that is bad in soil and villainous in look, yet this is now enclosed and what they call cultivated. Here is fresh robbery of villages, hamlets, and farm and labourers' buildings and abodes. But there is one of those *' vast improvements, ma'am,'* called *Barracks.* What an ' improvement ! ' "

The heavy satire of Cobbett continues in this strain on other pages, but it must be remembered that he was a politician and agriculturist, and cared not a fig for pictorial effects or romantic story.

It might even be possible to divide some of the opinions from various books about Middlesex into " for " and " against," for it is curious to note that the writers seldom adopt a neutral position; there is the one side that run it down, usually due to ignorance or more often indifference, and the others who have that rare gift called understanding, who write strongly in its favour. To follow Cobbett's violent abuse there is another unconsciously humorous account in *In and out of London,* a book of entirely different stamp. It is really an excellent little volume, but from the point of view of the exploration of this county it is comic.

The author, W. J. Loftie, an antiquarian of some note, writes: " The natural features of Middlesex are covered by an impenetrable veil. Rivers and ravines are masked, hills are levelled, marshes are hidden, a flood of brick fills up the hollows; the brooks run far underground. The flats are elevated, and the heights depressed The tide of buildings surges on, swallowing up in its course fields and gardens, parks and woods, uprooting trees, blasting flowers, shutting out even the air and winds of Heaven. There is something appalling in the resistless growth of London. Middlesex is nearly eaten up. The old form of the country, as it lay face to the sky, is wholly lost. It is overwhelmed and obliterated."

And now comes the amazing part—for the writer confesses that his researches into Middlesex led him no further north than Kilburn and no further west than Notting Hill ! Beyond these spots he apparently did not penetrate—it was too far in the wilds to be safe!

Yet this book was not written of the days of the brontosaurus, or even the highwayman, but in the comparatively modern days of 1875; though early enough for the parts of the county with which we deal to be undiscovered country.

In another, a much earlier and different type of book, something of the same kind is found; for in Fynes Moryson's *Itinerary* he writes—in 1605 —" Middlesex County was of old inhabited by the Trinobantes. In this county is the King's stately palace, Hampton Court, having many court-yards compassed with sumptuous buildings."

In spite of a further 1,950 pages—in which he wanders all over Europe, this is all he can find to say about Middlesex. I'm afraid it was the old story of neglecting good things near at hand to rush off, and sometimes fare worse, to see things far off.

It is in a way, however, an extraordinary book of travel, and he tells us of the labour he had in writing it, for he wrote it first in Latin (for some unexplained reason!) and then translated it into English. "To save expenses," he tells us, "I wrote the greatest part with my owne hand, and almost all the rest with the slow pen of my servant," and there follows a remark which I can heartily endorse ! "I found the bulke thereof to swel. Then I chose rather to suppresse it, than to make my Gate bigger than my Citie." Evidently this old rambler found a great deal of matter in his wanderings, which grew to more than he thought—I found the same, with this difference—he found his all over a continent, but I found mine in one corner of England's second smallest county—all that part that was once the Heath of Hounslow!

I bought a little book recently called *An Appendix to English Ecclesiology.* It has no title page, so I do not know the author or date, but the former simply does not know what he is talking about. This is how he dismisses the interesting churches of Middlesex: " This county is very poor in an ecclesiological point of view. Its churches are never on the grand scale and are little worth of notice." I wonder if he has ever seen any of them, or is it a case of the general sneer against Middlesex, by the stupidly ignorant, extending to its churches ? A far better book is J. H. Sperling's *Church Walks in Middlesex;* though it is strange to find, while almost every church in the county is described, there is no mention of that of Hounslow.

An amazing statement, hard to understand, is made by John B. Firth in his *Middlesex* in the " The Little Guides," which volume, despite some sins of both omission and commission, is really useful. " Middlesex," he writes, " has practically no history save in reference to the capital city of London." To begin with London, though certainly *in* Middlesex, is *not* the capital of the county (which is Brentford), and the rest of the statement is just silly; for in this case it cannot be due to the usual ignorance.

One does not expect to find much topographical information beyond the conventional in Gazetteers, but that in *The New Gresham Encyclopaedia* seems more than usually stupid: " Middlesex is almost entirely covered with urban districts and towns, all suburbs of London." Comment is needless.

An even more stupid statement about this county is that of a modern writer, E. W. Swanton, in the *Evening Standard,* who says: " Middlesex is just London and its northerly tentacles and can lay little claims on natural loyalty." Again comment on such ignorance would be waste of time.

To close the " against " section we will notice these writers who touch on the Hounslow Heath district, and begin with Thorne in his *Environs of London,* written in 1876. " The immediate neighbourhood of Hounslow," he says, " is flat, monotonous and uninteresting," a remark which Thorne, whose book is so wonderful a piece of research, should never have made, for he refutes his own words completely.

Then follows Walford, two years later, in *Round About London* : "The country round Hounslow is flat and uninteresting to the last degree and offers few attractions to the pedestrian." Now Walford, an F.S.A., should certainly have known better, and again he contradicts himself in his *Greater London.*

In *An Old-Fashioned Journey,* J. J. Hissey, that delightful explorer who spent his time driving about England in pre-motor days, writes in 1884, "The country round Hounslow is flat and uninteresting to a degree. In the old coaching days the Heath—long since all enclosed—bore a well-earned, though ill, reputation, and was a spot travellers were generally only too pleased to pass safely without misadventure or an acquaintance with the 'knights of the road.' Traversing such spots in the olden days must have been exciting enough to the nervous and lonely wayfarer and not altogether an excitement of an agreeable nature; then the Heath must have presented a very different appearance to the peaceful, not to say dull, prosaic look it now bears."

Then there is Hughson's opinion in his well-known *Circuit of London* in 1809, which is a good one to quote between the "against" and "fors," as it is a sort of "no-man's land" in views: "Hounslow Heath consists of a lean and hungry gravel, equally unsightly to the eyes, and unprofitable to the cultivator. The County of Middlesex has certainly its share of beauty and fertility; but the quantity of waste land does not entitle it to the high praise for richness of soil which some writers have lavished upon it. The cows for milking are the largest and finest in the Kingdom."

In the Middlesex section of J. Nightingale's *English Topography,* written in 1816, we read: "The surface of this county, though gently waving, can make no pretensions to what is called the picturesque. No rugged woody mountains, nor craggy ivy-bound rocks here present themselves to intercept the traveller on his way, or to captivate the fancy of the painter, but the more chaste and ornamented scenes may be found in many parts of the county."

I should like to have quoted more of this quaint description, for the writer goes on to describe the "great houses" in the same flamboyant style. He even tells us there were "2,811 houses a-building" at that period, in spite of their being 4,326 *un*-inhabited houses, but adds, hopefully, that "the return of peace will lessen this number considerably." The building history of Middlesex in the days following the Napoleonic wars has certainly repeated itself—only more so—after the Great War a hundred years later.

Now for a few "fors." As a counterblast to Cobbett's vitriolic remark is that of a far greater writer, who certainly knew what he was saying when he wrote: "An acre in Middlesex is better than a principality in Utopia." This was Lord Macaulay's opinion.

Then there is Camden's quaint description (1586): "The air (of Middlesex) is exceedingly beautiful, and the soil fertile; the houses and villages everywhere neat and stately, and there is no part of it but affords a great many remarkables."

We shall have occasion to quote Camden elsewhere, for his is one of the best accounts of the old Middlesex tribe, the Trinobantes; and perhaps a slight digression will be forgiven to notice some of the quaint botanical information imparted by this old historian concerning Hounslow Heath. He tells us that "a wanderer on the Heath may meet a Lycopediuminndatum." This sounds a first cousin to the brontosaurus, but it was only a flower.

There is an interesting appendix to one eighteenth century edition of Camden which mentions a good deal on this topic. It seems that in these times an energetic gentleman called Mr. Doody was busy in searching for such plants and we read (among many like entries): "Mr. Doody nettled cowsilk in some ditches on Hounslow Heath." Mr. Doody seems to have had a special "nose" for finding curiously named plants hereabouts, among which were "Cocks-foot grass," "Biting Fleabane," "Impatient lady's smock," "Hairy impatient cuckow-flower," "Stinking gladvin," "Mouse-tail," "Hound's tongue," and "Horse-tail."

Mr. Doody was not a "comic" character in a paper (as his name might suggest) but a scientist of some note and at one time Curator of the Chelsea Physic Garden; and of whom more will be found in that interesting book *The Apothecary's Garden*, by F. W. Drewitt.

Nothing, in a book of such peripatetic information as we roam in imagination over the Heath country, is more easy than to get led away from the historical main theme, to which we must now return.

Norden a few years later in his *History of Middlesex* also says curiously: "Myddlesex is above all other shyres grac'd; it is plentifully stored and as it seemeth beautiful with many faire and comely buildings, beautified with rare inventions, with gardens of delectable walks, arbres, allies, and a great varietie of pleasing dainties and orchards of sundrie delicate fruits . . . . the face of Myddlesex is most beautiful, the fields fresh and greene, the valleys delightful to behold, the townes, villages and stately buildings, enterlaced with the pleasant woodes, are glorious to be seen."

Dr. Peter Heylin, a seventeenth century writer, says: "Middlesex is not so large as other counties, but far more remarkable for sumptuous houses, well-built villages, a fertyle soyle and temperate air, a county happy above others . . . . . Across the wild hethelandes of Hounslow the Saxons advanced into the desert of Middlesex."

Leigh Hunt, who was born in the county in 1784 but writing in 1828, says: "Middlesex in general is a scene of trees and meadows, of greenery, and nestling cottages; it is a place mostly lying out of the way of innovation, therefore it has the pure sweet air of antiquity about it."

Coming down to more modern writers, who, from the point of view of their opinions of Middlesex are really more valuable, there were published in 1868 in *All the Year Round* an anonymous series of articles entitled *As the Crow Flies* (subsequently re-issued in book-form under the title of *A Tour Through England* by Walter Thornbury). They begin *Due West : Hounslow Heath :* "Swift in a phantom mail coach, the ghosts of four 'spankers' whirl us along the great west road. The phantom guard blows a blast as we sweep on with whizzing wheels between the broad nursery gardens.

"Were we magicians we should at once call together the dispersed atoms of the highwaymen who rattled in chains above the Hounslow furze bushes. From the roots of the fir trees, and the earth beneath the brambles, from the flints of the roadside and the water of the rivulets, we would collect the fragments of the wicked bodies, until once more the 'Captain' who swore 'by the bones of Jerry Abershaw' should appear in his black mask, gold-laced cocked hat, and scarlet roquelaure, with his silver 'hops,' bestriding his chestnut mare, the bold and reckless rascal of the pleasant days when thirteen gibbets stood at one time near Bason Bridge on the road to Heston.

"If any highwaymen who galloped to the gallows could see Hounslow Heath now he would wonder where the four thousand acres that covered fourteen parishes had shrunk to. He would find only a few dozen acres of grass field enclosed for cavalry drill on one side of the road, and a few dozen acres of rough furze and bramble on the other.

"Hounslow was dependent on the coaches; every third house was still an inn. Ruined stables and faded inn signs still testify to the old prosperity of the place. The spankers strike out and away they go. . . . .

"High and swift up in the soft blue air the crow passes over Middlesex, and bright pasture, where the Thames winds like a tangled silver thread. Down from the clouds he will drift to any village in his way that has a legend, any town that has a tradition, any old house that has been consecrated by genius, or associated with any passage of human nature. His scent will be keen for old legend and odd biographical incident." This extract is, by suggestion as it were, a wonderful opinion of what the writer thought of the county.

A few years later the author of *The Homes of London* says : "Almost every square mile in the county of Middlesex has been the scene of historical events, or has acquired its name from some characteristic of its own "; while that imaginative writer, Edwin Lester Arnold, says: "We need not go a hundred miles from London to obtain country as fair and uncontaminated as may be found this side of Scotland. Once the hum of the busy town is dropped behind it is no mean discovery that the county of Middlesex opens up fresh, sparkling and restful; bird and beast and flower flourish, men are as simple and children as chubby as though we had wandered into some Devonshire wilderness." It must be remembered, though, that in 1895, when this was written, there were no motors .

Two years before this H. S. Vaughan in his *Way About Middlesex,* speaking of the riverside parts of the county—" whose loveliness of scenery is proverbial,"—says: "Middlesex may be said to be uncommonly well timbered, this feature being a direct survival of that period in its history when most of its surface was covered by dense forests. Wooded parks, private and public, abound; copses and plantations give the land in many parts, as seen from any height, an aspect of being still a forest; and in almost every district hedge elms and oaks line the fields, convert the manor lanes into shady avenues, and, except where swept away by the spreading building operations, continue to fringe the main turnpikes, which are the direct successors, in many cases, of the old Roman and Celtic roads through the jungle. For the rest, the land is almost entirely under pasture, or market garden; and the constant succession of flat and gently undulating green meadows—tenanted as a rule by scanty herds, would soon prove monotonous were it not relieved by the varied form and colour of spinney and woodland, and the flash of many a willow-bowered stream.

Yet within the memory of living man the surface of Middlesex was not so entirely green; there are still old inhabitants of villages who can recall the harvest times of their youth, when the fields were yellow with the wheat crop for miles; but foreign competition has accomplished what bad seasons could never do, and the Middlesex farm that used to employ twenty hands now requires barely six. If anyone finds the scenery of the county at times a trifle monotonous, let him be gently remonstrated with by Richard Jeffries. "How few, how very few seem to appreciate the quiet beauty of this lovely country. Somehow, they do not seem to see it—to look over it; there is no excitement in it, for one thing. They can see a great deal in Paris, but nothing in an English meadow."

A. R. Hope Moncrieff in his book *Middlesex (1907)*, has a delightful word-picture of the county: " Around such flats as Staines Moor and Harmondsworth (both formerly parts of Hounslow Heath) in a county so recklessly labelled 'all ugly' one can find much pleasant and not a little charming scenery of a truly English type. If a jury of my fellow-country-men and gentle readers be not now ready to give a verdict of Slander against Cobbett, let them go forth to examine with their own eyes the evidence on which I have been able to discharge my duty as advocate for Middlesex."

Again the same author reminds us " Its (Middlesex) very misfortune of being so near a rich city contributes one feature of ornament in, notably, frequent parks, pleasure grounds and gardens. Its hills, vales and woods can boast a special interest in having, perhaps, inspired more of our great poets than has any larger English county . . . . its charms are often neglected by those who hurry over its dusty or muddy roads to reach neighbouring bounds that have not always a better right to give themselves airs of rurality."

Although these words were penned a few years ago they are still luckily true to-day, even if the scope of rural Middlesex is somewhat contracted; and they were written by one who had the rare gift of understanding.

Some of the most sympathetic touches of any writer on this county are found in *Middlesex to Wit* by Clive R. Fenn. This is really an account of the Middlesex War Hospitals, when many of the " great houses " were thus used, but there are delightful touches on the district.

" Superficial writers," he writes, " say that Hounslow is awful. It is nothing of the kind, only a hard-working, commonsense town which sees as straight as the old Roman road through it to Staines, or its newer brother to Bath past the quite fascinating Cranford region. Right and left of these roads is countryside which charms."

Here again is a wonderful sentence of a war-time Middlesex: " In those villages of dreamland—for you find them in out of the way corners of this old county along with many an old romance—there was much to stir the heart. It is no use blinking the sadness of those days. There was the empty chair in the little cottage down the winding lane where the banks were flecked with scarlet poppies and the pale pink dog-rose floated against the blue of the sky as well as in the big house. The old barge horse was doing his bit along the canal which lies, like a silver thread, amidst the woods and meadows." Or again: " Western Middlesex is often accounted dull and uninteresting by motorists as they sweep on, turning homely scenery into something grotesque, regardless of anything but speed. But it is always worth while to stop and look. In the glimmer, half mystic, of the green lanes there is something which is matchless in its import. You need to linger in Middlesex. Then you will love it, its homely touches, the odd little pastoral fragments of villages down by the gleaming water-side, the dumpy churches, the safeness of the view, all pleasant and homely and habitual; something which thrills because it seems to say ' Here is peace.'—So the frantic motorist, that cormorant for speed, who races through Middlesex may be pitied, for he does not see many things worthy of inspection. . . . . .

Photo by F. Ash.

THE TOWER OF MYSTERY.
Old Shot Tower at Hanworth Powder
Mills.

Photo by N. Mayger.

**SAXON COINS DUG UP ON
HOUNSLOW HEATH.**

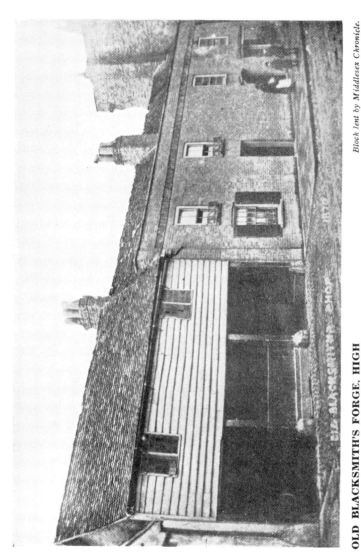

Block lent by Middlesex Chronicle.

**OLD BLACKSMITH'S FORGE. HIGH
STREET, HOUNSLOW.**
Where the coach horses were shod.

"There are those who look upon Middlesex as something of a jumble. The county is regarded as less of a county than a few cheap remnants left over after the metropolis has taken its pick. This is a mistake. Middlesex has its fragmentary features, but it has managed none the less to retain its proper character. It is sadly divided, but not, thank goodness, against itself. Middlesex has suffered from overmuch regard for London."

Rev. P. H. Ditchfield, whom as a boy it was my good fortune to know, who has written so charmingly on old England, brings to my mind most vividly some of the villages of old Middlesex when he writes (in his *English Villages*): "It is no small thing to live in such a 'City of Memories' as every village is, when at every turn we meet something that reminds us of the past and recalls the pleasing associations of old village life. To those used to the din, turmoil and hurry of a large town the delicious calm and quietude of an old English village is most grateful.

"To live in memory of the lives and customs of our forefathers, of the strange events that have happened on the very ground on which we are standing, will make us delight in our villages. In the large towns old features are fast disappearing, historical houses are pulled down and everything is being modernised; but in the country it is not so difficult to let one's thoughts wander into the past and picture the old village life of bygone times."

* * * * *

In a chapter like this I make no attempt to preserve a strict chronology, so make no excuses for here introducing more opinions some years apart. The first is from that interesting—but rather incomplete—little book *Middlesex* wherein G. F. Bosworth writes : "Fortunately there are parts of Middlesex which retain some of their old characteristics. A recent writer on the county says that 'though the great cornland of Middlesex has largely become pasture or market gardens, and old-fashioned farmsteads are few and far between, there are still some "rustic" bits to be seen away from the highways.' The same writer also remarks that 'If in Middlesex we have a district lacking any of the more striking beauties even of some of its newest neighbours, we have one that can vie with the best of them in the variety and multiplicity of its associations with men and events.' " There is scarcely a parish in the county without its memories of someone who made himself famous.

The second one is Defoe's *Tour Through Britain* when he writes: "There is an incredible number of fine houses in Middlesex built within these last few years. That England never had such a glorious show to make in the world before . . . . I find 2,000 houses which in other places would pass for palaces in the little towns and villages of the county of Middlesex."

Defoe goes on to say that if he described all he found it would take "2 or 3 volumes equal to this to describe those in the county of Middlesex only." It would seem that since Defoe's day some of these 2,000 "palaces" have disappeared but, fine as some of the old houses of the county are, 2,000 seems a generous estimate.

It would be easy to go on quoting references to Middlesex from different writers, with varying degrees of mention of Hounslow and its vicinity, but with a final "assorted bunch" from among my notes this chapter must be closed.

Of the county and its inhabitants in Saxon days, especially of the fighting between Caesar and the Trinobantes, a good description will be found in *The Chronicles of England,* by Joseph Strutt; while in *Bygone Middlesex* William Andrews relates other antiquities of Middlesex history. *The Description of the County of Middlesex*   (1775) is a fair example of its type, which rather "skim the surface."

The Visitation of Middlesex : 1663, edited by Joseph Foster, is chiefly concerned with the old county families, and most useful as a reference book ; while the *Middlesex County Records,* edited by H. J. and W. le Hardy, will be found informative, especially from the accounts of old-time criminal cases.

One writer who shows a rare insight into his subject—more unusual in the case of Middlesex than of most places—is Stanley R. Baron, for in his article (in *The News-Chronicle*) entitled *Look Behind the Hedges,* dealing with the "unknown" aspect of this county, he has a very real under-standing of a thing most writers either ignore or miss entirely through a lack of this gift.

In Regency days I find notes of two more books.   *London and its Environs,* by the Rev. Henry Hunter, has a sentence, written in 1811, that might equally well apply to-day : "Some of the remote parts of Middlesex out of the course of the main roads appear to be little affected by the influence of the town and are as merely rural as the most distant part of the provinces"; while in *A Family Tour through the British Empire* (1812), by Priscilla Wakefield, one of those books written to improve the minds of the young, we find this bit of good advice: "Mr. Franklin urged that the tour of his pupils was incomplete without examining the numerous elegant towns, villages and seats that are so thickly strewed throughout the county of Middlesex." He did not take his young charges there, it is true, but he at least pointed the way.

For a "general utility" book on this county there is probably no better one than *Highways and Byways in Middlesex,* by Walter Jerrold, whose fairly recent death we all deplore. It is a book in which I take a special interest, quite apart from its subject, for I was in a sense present at its con-ception, it being my good fortune as a youngster to accompany the author on several rambles in different parts of the county when he was gathering material for the volume—days of delightful exploration, and for me of learning, which will always remain a cherished memory.

Rev. P. H. Ditchfield, in his *Counties of England* has a good general description of Middlesex, not very full, but, as far as it goes, excellent; while the author of a more recent book, *Rambles in the Home Counties,* W. A. Hirst, speaks truly when he says: "Few counties are more neglected than Middlesex; for Londoners, ignorant of London, are still more ignorant of their county, while people who come to see London do not find time to visit the adjoining districts. Fuller remarks: 'Middlesex is in effect but the suburbs at large of London, replenished with the retiring houses of the gentry and citizens thereof, besides many palaces of noblemen and three Royal mansions.' There are still pretty country walks to be found in Middlesex, nor is it in historical and archaeological interest below the average."

This last sentence is a very mild estimate, as I hope these pages will show, and even Fuller's remark could do with some qualification; written in the seventeenth century the word "suburb" meant "sub urbe" (reading "sub" as "outside") with a rather wider meaning than is now generally given to the word. Fuller lived at Cranford, which even to-day cannot be called suburban; it is still an old-world country village—despite would-be despoilers who are building ugly new roads on its fringes. We can imagine what a delightful place it must have been in the days of Fuller's incumbency.

In the R.A.C. Road Gazette the section of Middlesex is a strange mixture. The average motorist does not care much about this county (thank goodness) except to rush through it at "a rate o' knots," and the compiler of this section of the gazetteer has tried to steer a middle course; in the main he has succeeded, for his information is really quite full for such a book—in spite of some glaring errors both historical and topographical.

There is quite a good foreword, by R. A. Moss, in which he writes: "It is true that to many city goers Middlesex is *primarily* a land of dreams—places mainly to sleep in. Yet this familiar wheel-trodden shire is also a touring ground crowded with interest, and parts of it remain still scented with the gracious fragrance of green untainted country. Middlesex would invite the tourist's close attention if it possessed only Hampton Court, whereas its attractions include Bushy Park, Twickenham—and all that the name implies to literary students—Chiswick, Wembley, Harrow, Staines, Sunbury, Teddington, and a score of other interesting, pretty and more or less celebrated places."

Middlesex is "a land of dreams"—yes, and in spite of those who seem, in parts, to be trying to turn these into nightmares, we can still find in this delectable county "such stuff as dreams are made on."

In Ralph Nevill's entertaining book we find some *Echoes : Old and New* notes, well worth reading, on old Middlesex; but the last advocate I shall produce (though many more on both sides could be quoted) is a writer who has a very sympathetic touch He is J. Penderel-Brodhurst, and though some years have passed since these words were penned, it is good to find that much of what he has written is still to be seen to-day.

"The hills in Middlesex are few," begins the article. "Its flat acres are cultivated to every hedge. But if Middlesex is less profusely picturesque, in human and historic interest it is unapproachable by any other county. Its historic houses are legion, for the circumstance that its rural portions have for two centuries been mere suburbs of the seat of Empire has made it the abiding place of a crowd of personages whose shades still loom large. Nearly all our great men in history, in letters, and in art, have lived in Middlesex.

"It is a rich, productive bit of country, crowded with market gardens, and though it cannot be said that a perspective of bean fields and cabbage plantations is superlatively pictorial, yet there are seasons of the year, and hours of the day, when such a prospect is clothed with mystic charm. In spring the belts of blossoming orchards, which define the long vistas of white and powdery roads, atone for the superabounding presence of the cabbage. In autumn the perfumed blossom has changed to clusters of faintly odorous fruit, which, in ripened hues of gold and purple, spangle the background of brilliant green.

"The fall of dusk over these stretches of flat fields with a darkling distance of woodland, and a square grey church tower for diversity, is always fascinating. The dull transitional grey seems slowly to descend to earth. Just above the treetops it intermingles with the white chilly vapour which rises from the land; for in these western parts of Middlesex there is abundance of water in canals and little rivers, while the Thames is never far away. The mist winds in and out among the trees, slowly surrounding trunk and branches with tender mystery as of semi-diaphanous veil of gauze. This is the most silent hour of the autumn day. The caw of the rooks high in the elms ceased an hour ago; the small birds sleep; all the sounds of country life are stilled; and the tramp of a tarrying labourer, or the rarer flash of a carriage dashing homeward, alone break the eerie stillness."

The author has certainly caught the old-world atmosphere of the county, and a little further on he writes of another phase of the same theme—that of some of the old houses—in an equally fascinating way. Of those in the scope of this book he says: "Between Hounslow and West Drayton is one of the most historically attractive portions of Middlesex. Within an easy walk there is Hayes, with its Archiepiscopal Rectory House; Harlington with the scanty remains of Dawley and abounding memories of Bolingbroke; Cranford with its haunted Manor House and its flavour of Berkleian romance; Uxbridge with its proud pretension of the county town to the prejudice of Brentford.

"It is a land of long-descended legends, of ghostly visitants in panelled chambers, of confused traditions of feudal splendour and ecclesiastical consequence. The last waning of romance linger around these ancient Middlesex mansions and tales of old time still are told in the sequestered villages, whose people have changed in little, often not even in religion, since the last moat was dug in England."

Whether the author of these wonderful lines is still alive I cannot say —it is nearly fifty years since they were written and the style is of a mature rather than a youthful mind.

If he is alive he is probably rather an old gentleman by now, but I should love to take him—in a bath chair if necessary—to revisit some of these spots in old Middlesex that he loved so well. I could show him most of them unaltered in some corner or other; true I might have to search a little further down the lane or to dodge some new block of houses, but I could find them. As for the old mansions, all those he mentions are still standing to-day and the same ghosts of the past stalk through their empty corridors, where I trust they will hold sway for many a long year—for even if we may not believe in them we are loth to lose our traditional family spectres.

It is evident that the spell of old Middlesex was upon the writer of that article, as it has been, I confess, upon me. It is a spell that can be felt, but never properly explained as one wanders about in what may seem an aimless way, but really mentally alert, a little perhaps in the spirit of Wordsworth's line (in his *Ode to Immortality*): "Moving about in Worlds not realised"—a world half real and half imaginary; that is to say in actual places peopled with folk of imaginative memory; losing touch with the present as one rubs shoulders (if this be possible!) with shadows that once walked this wonderful "stage" —where we can see the shade of Bolingbroke in his splendid obscurity at Dawley Farm with the rather pathetic little deformed figure of his famous visitor—"the Wasp of Twickenham" as Pope was known— whose brilliant brain was housed in so poor a dwelling. We meet, too, the ghost of the Countess of Berkeley at Cranford, who, for all her humble birth, was an aristocratic and stately old lady; we see the man who caught Guy Fawkes, Lord Knyvett, in his peaceful retirement at Stanwell Place; the Duke of Argyll in his beautiful wooded retreat at Whitton; the great

Sir Thomas Gresham at Osterley Park, and many another whose name is written in the history of England, but whom we view, more or less, in private life.

Kings and Queens, too, stride over our stage. Queen Elizabeth hunting at Hanworth and sleeping (of course!) at Osterley and several other places; we catch glimpses of Henry VIII. at Hanworth, and of James II. mournfully viewing the failure of his idea to overawe London with his camp at Hounslow Heath that became a fair ground; and we also see the gloomy countenance of the "Merry" Monarch as he rode over the Heath to visit Sweet Nell of Old Drury at the little farm at Feltham. Then there are many glimpses of road life—stage coaches, chaises, barouches, and such like vehicles—and, of course, highwaymen.

The list is incomplete, there are others, but these will be enough to show that it is sometimes very much worth while to become a dreamer in old Middlesex. People have often laughed at me for this—with a sneer mixed up with the laugh sometimes—and yet these dull-wits will crowd into a cinema and "swallow" the screeching screeds of Hollywood, which the poor "muts" (to use Hollywoodian "English") imagine to be "slices of life"—they sneer at me as a dreamer—but I'll wager the "pictures" I see in these old Middlesex villages and mansions are a thousand times more vivid than their machine-made absurdities.

And why shouldn't we dream? After all it's about the only thing that is not taxed nowadays—to put the thing on a sound financial basis! It's true, perhaps, that in these days our dreams can be nightmares at times, but there are others, such as I have mentioned, that bring a little solace to a harrassed mind—so leave us poor dreamers in peace, you superior folk. But this "isolation" has its compensations—we are not overjostled by Philistines as we roam in this dreamland of romance and history.

And so I ask you, as you follow me through these pages, to "wake up and dream." I think you will not be disappointed when we reach our Journey's End.

CHAPTER IV.
Of Heathen Agriculture.

IN referring to the dwellers in and around Hounslow as heathens I mean no disrespect to them, merely using the word in its real sense, apart from its modern corrupted meaning. I could also call them pagans and yet not insult them in the least, for this word had originally exactly the same meaning. The Italian Pagini (from which comes pagans) literally means a dweller in the country, as our word heathen means a dweller on the heath

Taking English words alone, it is curious how many have got entirely altered in meaning from their original sense. There is no need to give a list, but the worst change is the word "star." In pre-war days this meant something beautiful that brought us, visually at least, nearer Heaven. Now what is a "star"? A grinning ape who acts for the films, who is far more likely to remind us of Hell than the celestial regions. I was once introduced to a "film star." She might have been good-looking if her face could have been seen behind the powder, rouge and the "posed" expressions; but for vacuity of mind and the murder of the King's English

—well, she was a star that had strayed far from the 'eavenly 'eights. . . .
    We are straying ourselves, though, and must get back to the Heath.
In spite of highwaymen and military camps, agriculture has always
flourished more or less prosperously on the farms in the neighbourhood of Hounslow, Cobbett's vitriolic criticisms notwithstanding.
Even before the enclosures began, during the latter decades of the
eighteenth and the earlier ones of the nineteenth centuries, there were
many farms scattered about the Heath, and these of course increased rapidly
after the passing of the Acts. To-day Hounslow Heath is almost entirely
agricultural, though its wheat lands and hay crops have mostly given
place to cabbage fields, fruit farms and market gardens.
    Cobbett was always unfair to Middlesex, a spot that was to him as a
red rag to a bull. Here is one of his comments, from his *Rural Rides,* on
this country in general and Hounslow Heath in particular, written in the
year 1822: " A more ugly country than that between Egham and Kensington
would be, with great difficulty, found in England. Flat as a pancake, and
until you come to Hammersmith the soil is a nasty stony dirt upon a bed
of gravel. Hounslow Heath, which is only a little worse than the general
run, is a sample of all that is bad in soil and villainous in look. Yet this
is now enclosed, and what they call ' cultivated.' Here is a fresh robbery
of villages, hamlets, and farm and labourers' buildings and abodes. . . ."
Yet, in spite of Cobbett, the Heath soil is very fertile, as it was in his
time.
    It is more pleasant to read old Norden's earlier account (1593) of the
same district, when he says quaintly: " The soil of Middlesex is excellent,
fat and fertile, and full of profite; it yieldeth corn and graine, not only
in abundance, but most excellent good wheat, especially about Heston-
Hounslow, which place may be called Granarium tritici regalis, from the
singularitie of the corne. The rainge of this especiall corne seemeth to
extend from Heston-Hounslow to Harrow-on-the-Hill, between which, as
in the midway, is Perivale. Yet doth not this so fruitful soyle yield comfort to the wayfaring man in winter time, by reason of the claiesh nature
of the soyle, which after it hath tasted of the autumne showers, waxeth
both dyrtie and deep, but unto the countrie swaine it is a sweet and
pleasant garden in regard to his hope of future profite, for
                ' The deep and dirtie loathsome soyle
                Yields golden gaine to payneful toyle,'
and the industrious and paineful husbandmen will refuse a pallace to
droyle in these golden puddles."
    In another part of his book the same writer has more praise for
Heston, which he calls " A most fertile place of wheate, yet not so much
to be commended for the quantitie, as for qualitie; for the wheate is most
pure, accompted the purest in many shires; and therefore Queen Elizabeth
hath the most part of her provision from that place for manchet for her
Highness' own diet as is reported."
    Humour lurks in unexpected places and often pops up when least
expected; one would not look for it in an old agricultural journal, yet it
was certainly there, though unconsciously, which added to its flavour. I
was recently looking through some copies of the *Farmer's Magazine* for the
years 1800-1810, for any odd information I could glean about Middlesex
agriculture of those days, and the humour was more in the titles of the
articles than in the matter. For instance, the gentleman who wrote *An
Essay on Turnips* was in deadly earnest; he must have been, for he goes on

for *twenty pages* on this illuminating topic. I confess that I have not read it all, but the man who can write that number of pages on turnips compels my admiration; I doubt if I could write twenty lines about them.

The author of this article, however, has a serious rival in another farmer, who contributed sixteen pages on manure, and, in a noble effort to tone down an unsavoury topic by a little artistry in his title, calls his effort *Reflections upon Ordure*. This noble essay in its turn was not without its rival, for a few weeks later followed another article on the same subject— a modest ten pages only—which, as far as I read, seemed pretty much the same as the first one, with one notable difference The second essayist was a real John Blunt, if he didn't call a spade a spade he probably termed it a sanguinary shovel. No titular frills for him, no disguising his topic with flowery words, for with monosyllabic directness he calls his article *Muck*.

When we have recovered from the shock of so much outspokeness of our straight-from-the-shoulder friend, we are soothed down a few pages further on by a return to a little nearer the Muse (not mews), for we find an article entitled *The Propagation and Improvement of Vegetables by the Concurrence of Art and Nature*. Even if we do not read the article, its title is gratifying.

We are not left in peace for long, however, for a little later we come across an article entitled *Sheep Pox*, in which the details are almost sickening in their outspokenness. In this I suspect the hand of John Blunt again, and perhaps he was right. *The Farmer's Magazine* was hardly likely, in those days, to have been found in the boudoirs of young ladies, and from a farmer's point of view it was probably more help to speak plainly than to describe the symptoms of the unfortunate animal as if it were suffering from a slight headache.

Soon we are destined for another shock, though of quite a different nature, for we come across a twelve page review of a book of *Literary and Political Essays*, which, as it contains not a mention of anything appertaining to farming and in a day when many farmers were unable even to read themselves, seems rather unusual. The next article gets down to " brass tacks " again, for it deals with a very real problem of agricultural life in those days, though the author chooses to wrap up his subject in long phrases, even calling it *On the Augmentation of Stipends in Victual*.

And so the amazing magazine goes on, giving us all sorts of out-of-the-way information from a *Recipe for Hay Tea*, whatever that may be, to (Apt Alliterations Artful Aid) *Slaying Slugs by Sprinkling Sulphur*. The chief object of the conductor (as he is always termed, and never Editor) seems to be to appeal to the " mental noses " of his readers, and the varied odours wafted through these pages is extraordinary; we pass from apple blossom to onions, from hops to sweet peas, from " apple potatoes " to " potato oats " (sic), and from farm refuse to roses, in a most inconsequential way. I do not know what the circulation of this magazine was, but the conductor did his utmost to make it a best smeller.

Quite apart from these humorous bits there is a great deal of interest in this old book, and when I bought three leather-bound copies from the penny-box of an old bookshop I had as much entertainment for threepence (without tax) as if I had paid five times that amount at the local " pictures " for an " alleged " comedy that would have probably depressed me. Certainly it would not have given me the vivid mental pictures of old England that these volumes conjured up.

There is a fair amount of information about bygone Middlesex in these pages, when the county was deep in the country, and some entertaining pieces refer to the agriculture around Hounslow Heath. For instance, we are told how the osiers, which always flourished at Sunbury, a few miles away, were introduced into the more marshy waste lands of the Heath as a "new industry" after the enclosures; the author ending a really interesting article with the old saw, imported from the Fens, that a "willow will buy a horse before an oak will buy a saddle."

"Imported" industries seem to have been tried a good deal at Hounslow about this time and quite a little sensation was caused by the appearance of two Sussex ploughing oxen upon the Heath, and a spirited correspondence is found upon the pros and cons of oxen as compared with horses for the plough.

In 1805 we read of another "imported" industry in the introduction of hops to Hounslow Heath. This experiment to rival "The Garden of England" was not successful, however; apparently the soil was not suitable, though the writer of the article is more apt to blame the insects, which, he tells us, "maliciously followed the hops from Kent to attack them with great vehemence in their new habitation." This "trek" of malicious and determined insects on their way from Kent to Middlesex must have been an interesting sight, especially their crossing of the Thames.

In Middleton's *Agriculture of Middlesex,* written towards the close of the eighteenth century, we read something of the oxen in this county, and some notes comparing their work with that of horses. One of the chapters in this book is entitled "Middlesex Farmhouses"; this led me to expect something from it, but it is highly technical; the writer did not worry about any picturesque features. On curious fact in this book is a suggestion that an arterial road be built north of Brentford to avoid the smell of the filth in the High Street of that town. Now such a road *has* been built, some hundred and thirty odd years later, I often choose to go along Brentford High Street to avoid the smell of the motors on the arterial road!

Hounslow to-day does not witness anything so exciting in agriculture as oxen and hops, it being mainly given over to market gardens. A writer on Middlesex about twenty years ago says: "At the present day very little wheat is grown in the county, and there are whole parishes, such as Heston, once famous for the quality of its grain, where not one bushel is now raised. Agricultural Middlesex, indeed, is almost wholly given over to market gardening, the produce comprising 'top' fruit, 'soft' fruit, root crops and vegetables, which are conveyed by road to London.

"West Middlesex, especially that part where once the great heath of Hounslow stretched far and wide of the town, is now mostly farms of from 50 to 100 acres in size, and employ far more labour than they would if they were devoted to ordinary agriculture. There are also large nursery garden, dairy farms and stud farms."

This is pretty much as it is to-day, though I think the market gardens have swamped the dairy and stud farms, anyhow as regards the parts round the Heath. One of the best descriptions of the Hounslow countryside under modern conditions is in a book called *The Eyes of the Thames,* by Arthur T. Pask. Although written some forty years ago practically no alterations as regards the main essentials will be found to-day.

The chapter is entitled *A London Orchard* and begins: "The sun is somewhat low in the cool turquoise sky, and over the rich fields of Heston and Hounslow light fleecy clouds are floating. On the banks of the little

FARM CARTS HOLD THEIR OWN
At the Middlesex Agricultural Show at
Harlington.

" WHO SAID TRACTORS ? "
A study in conscious pride at the Harlington show.

river Crane water-wagtails are hopping to and fro, and the sleepy-eyed Alderney is chewing the cud on the damp grass beneath the heavy topped pollards. Light gusts of wind and rain have chilled the air, and the Worton Road is decked here and there with pools that glisten in the now mellowing light of the sun.

"Yet, as the wind has gone down and the rain has drifted off to the Harrow hills, it is pleasant walking between the trim hedges, over which now and again a weary cart horse out at grass, thrusts his head, blinking his eyes and twitching his ears at the cloud of tiny gnats rising from the low ditch. Past the meadows the air is filled with a curious wavering odour, sometimes aromatic, sometimes sharp and pungent, sometimes sweet and faint; still it is an odour which, if rather offensive, is far from unpleasant. It is that which is even to be found close by a large orchard when the ground is wholly given up to fruit growing.

"As the clock strikes five you find yourself in front of a low green paling, which shuts off a trim garden and a good sized cottage from the road. Beside the cottage stand an old yew and a big acacia. Walking through the garden and past these, and skirting the cottage, you come to a good old English garden, set in the midst of a mighty orchard. The garden is a simple stretch of grass, decked with a patriarchal apple tree, and bordered by plain beds, filled with the famous old rosebushes—a garden such as might have formed the pleasaunce of a manor house centuries ago. Passing beneath an arch of white clematis and Jacob's ladder, and following a narrow path there is to be seen an apiary numbering some thirty hives; for the market-gardener here is a great believer in the good work of the bees in carrying the precious pollen.

"Away from the sleeping bees, you enter a roadway, which stretches far away between the heavy laden fruit trees. To the right and left are long avenues of apple standards, while beneath the trees the ground is covered with gooseberries, currants and raspberries. Close here are a number of women mounted on short ladders and plucking the fruit from some low trees; as to the younger women, many of them are comely enough, a few North-country lassies who have stayed beyond the soft fruit season, but the majority are natives of the district, who, however, will soon be leaving this orchard in the Thames Valley for the hop grounds on the banks of the Medway."

Then the author breaks into a personal touch and complains of the bad language used by these orchard workers, and on this point he waxes eloquently sad when he says: "In their short print dresses and with red cotton handkerchiefs tied over their heads the girls look well enough to form a study for a picture; but despite rosy cheeks, blue eyes and agile forms, the romance is soon broken when they open their mouths. If ever a rival could be found for Billingsgate it would be in some London market orchard, for these girls are as foul tongued as a lighterman on the Pool. But if the girls are somewhat rough, the orchard men are worse, they are quarrelsome, foul-mouthed and drunken."

There is a good deal more in this strain and all I can say is that things must have altered in the forty years since these words were written; for one thing, other forms of work now attract the local girls and as to the men, I have talked often to these farm workers round Hounslow and always found them civil enough. Far from being quarrelsome I have always found them perfectly friendly; I cannot honestly say I have ever spoken to a drunken one and if their language were a little free at times it was certainly nothing to shock an old sailor like myself.

The author soon gets back to pleasanter topics, however, and ends his chapter with another pleasing word picture of scenes that can still be seen to-day, hardly altered at all except that motor lorries have taken the place of the old market waggons which, the drivers fast asleep, the clever old cart horses pulled on through the night, unguided, to Covent Garden.

"Morland, the painter," proceeds this account, "was partial to subjects taken from the Thames orchards, and many of his best works have stayed in the neighbourhood of Hounslow, Isleworth and Twickenham, since they were first painted. I know a friend living in the high road, not a mile off, who has a very characteristic Morland of the old tilted market boats which were used sometimes to carry produce to London.

"The yellow light of the sun glistens on the fruit of the thousands of trees, and you cannot help but feel that it is this thrice blessed district that the great Thames Valley poet termed a 'calm of plenty.' The monks of the neighbouring Hounslow Monastery were wise in their generation when they laid hands on the rich lands by the Crane and the Thames.

"Among other beauties of this grand old orchard are the yew hedges, a century old. The grandfather of the present owner, even in his day, knew how a good hedge breaks up the draught of wind, instead of, like a brick wall, only turning it in another direction.

"The men in the yard are busy packing great wains with sieves of apples, while the contented fowls are sleepily clucking about the yard, and as we pass out of the orchard into the bye-road leading to Hounslow the sun is sinking beneath the horizon, leaving behind it a long line of burnished copper and a fading blush on the twilight sky.

"From the leaves of the fruit trees, the water drops are falling and plashing on the moist road. The restless tom-tit is still stirring in the hedges, and from afar-off come the shrill voices of the village children, the barking of a dog, and the whistle of a steam-tug forging its way against the stream of the Thames.

"From the small hill by Worton Manor rises a melodious harmony. A group of garden girls are singing a good old country ballad; two of them carry large bundles on their heads, which they poise by no means ungracefully. In the background of warm twilight is the cool crescent of a new moon. It is like a picture by Fred Walker, yet it is a reality and not a half-Classic idyll; and it seems to say that some spirit of poetry still dwells even amid the turmoil of a Middlesex orchard."

A pleasant picture this of the Hounslow Heath countryside forty years ago, and although the author does not actually specify to which farm he alludes I have a pretty shrewd suspicion in my own mind that I know the one he means. It is still there and it would be almost possible to-day to see a picture very much the same as he did then. The "girls" might now be older women and the ballad a modern jazz, if they sing at all, but in the main essentials it is a picture that this district still can show—but for how long ?   *   *   *   *   *

I recently came across an interesting letter from a farmer in these parts, written in 1804, for in those days "settlers" in the wilds of Middlesex wrote home as from an unknown land, much in the same way a settler in the wilds of Africa would do to-day; in fact, the latter, with the wireless and telegraph is sometimes much "nearer" London, as regards news anyhow, than the Middlesex farmer of bygone days.

"When I first took up my residence in the Hounslow district of Middlesex," writes this one, "I was astonished to see how different its agriculture was conducted from what was practised in Essex and other counties." It seems that the natives of Middlesex strongly resented this "foreign" invasion of their soil, for the writer goes on to say: "The prejudice is, however, strong against me and this has not been lessened by my bringing servants from Essex."

Then follow technical details regarding ploughs and soils, after which we notice the influence of the then recent Enclosure Acts, for the writer continues: "In Middlesex I find we have farmers of every description, and the *cast* is more diversified. The land here is nearly all in the hands of bankers, East and West India merchants, cockneys, bakers, brewers, officers, and in short, almost every character except the real farmer.

"The wheats around Hounslow, though partially blighted, are not so materially injured as in Essex." Then again follow more technical details of agriculture and he continues with a reiterated moan: "Labour of all kinds is exceedingly dear, as much as 12s. a week is commonly given. These terribly high rates of pay are the ruin of farming in these parts." I wonder what the present Trades Unions would say to such "excessive" wages.

These high wages, however, were not the only grievance of this old time Hounslow farmer, for he ends his epistle on a tragic note that, I am sure, must touch every honest English heart. "Taxes, wages of labour and every species of out-payment have increased and are increasing and ought to be diminished," he complains bitterly. "But even worse is at hand and that is the heavy and impolitic imposts upon malt; these have created a cursed and unwholesome beverage of a sort of indifferent beer, more properly hogs-wash, made of anything but malt and hops; by which the hard-working farmers and good people of England in general are in danger of being *poisoned*." There is quite a modern flavour in this pathetic wail; it might almost apply to some of our post-war beer. . . . .

Nowadays Hounslow—or the county of Middlesex generally—is not noted for its sheep; you may see a small isolated flock on some farms still, it is true, but sheep are more the exception round Hounslow than the rule.

Yet at one time the Heath was almost as famous for its sheep as the South Downs are to-day, as exemplified by Pope, for in his *Imitations of Horace* (1733) occur the lines

"To Hounslow Heath I point, and Banstead Down,
Thence comes your mutton and these chicks my own."

It seems that many experiments in sheep breeding were carried on upon the Heath, and G. A. Cooke, in his *Description of Middlesex,* written in the early years of the last century, has a note on this old time industry in this part; which is interesting, though a little contradictory, for he begins by telling us that Middlesex was not famous for its own breed of sheep and then goes on to mention famous breeders of the county.

"Hounslow Heath and its adjoining pastures," he writes, "are the chief places where sheep are kept and this seems more for the sake of folding than for the hope of sending a superior kind of mutton to market; in fact, sheep folding is very extensively practised on the Heath where many thousands of sheep are fed, particularly in the part towards Harmondsworth.

"The method of breeding house lambs in this county is as follows. The ewes are always, without exception, of Dorsetshire breed, and the rams always of the county of Middlesex. The choice given by the breeders to the Middlesex rams in preference to those of any other county in the Kingdom is extraordinary."

Sir Joseph Banks, the scientist, who lived near the Heath at Spring Grove, Smallbury Green, then a hamlet between Isleworth and Hounslow, was a keen breeder. There is a note from a woollen merchant of the day in answer to a request from Sir Joseph, as to the success of his experiments, in which he says: "Upon the whole, the cloth you send me, which is made from your Spanish sheep reared upon Hounslow Heath, may be ranked with the best superfine cloth manufactured in England."

The old books that mention Hounslow Heath, and in those early days most writers touched on the agriculture for which it became so famous, seem numberless. I am almost afraid to continue my searches among the byways of Bookland for fear of finding matter that *should* be included in these pages, but for which there is really no space. A few more, however, will have to suffice here before we pass on.

In *Middlesex in Domesday Survey,* written by Edward Griffith in 1859, we read: "Its most productive portion next to Stebenhithe (Stepney) was between the Thames and the Coln, and the northern woodlands, though we can recollect much of the waste land of Hounslow Heath before it was reduced to tillage as at present." Then Peter Haylyn, a writer on Middlesex in the seventeenth century, published a book with one of those curious titles with which our ancestors sometimes loved to label their works: *Mikrokosnios: A Little Description of the Great World.* In *England Displayed,* a book of some hundred years later, the writer goes to the other extreme, for under "*Husbandry of Middlesex*" all he tells us is how much beer a day was allowed to farm labourers. No doubt, however, a vital question.

In *The Modern Universal British Traveller* for 1774 all the writer can find to say under "*Natural History for Middlesex*" is a long article on manure, while another writer, a few years later, tells us that the reason Hounslow Heath is so productive is the habit of the inhabitants to take the mud from the ponds and spread it over the whole heath ! Let's hope labour was cheap in those days !

We can take as a final example here of these old agricultural writers one who tells us, in 1805, "Some parts of Hounslow Heath, recently enclosed from the waste, are laid out in fields for the grazing of cattle, particularly horses and cows, and others are cultivated as gardens for vegetables; the art of gardening being here brought to much greater perfection than in any other part, not only of Great Britain, but, perhaps of the known world. The more distant parts of the heath abound with fertile meadows and produce great quantities of the most excellent grain."

*   *   *   *   *   *

One of the pleasantest functions at which I have played the role of humble, but intensely appreciative, spectator is the Middlesex Agricultural Show where the Bath Road crosses the Heath at Harlington. It is a scene of amazing contrasts that in these days after the Great War there is a distinct touch of the unreal, almost magic, about it.

To begin with, it is a strange feeling to get out of a District electric train and after a short journey on a motor-bus to walk into a field where everything speaks of real rural England. Yet that is what I did—for the motors that rushed up and down the Bath Road adjoining the field were of less account than the flies that buzzed about our ears. The Ploughing Match interested me most—real old-fashioned horse instruments, too; none of your modern motor-ploughs for these sturdy Middlesex yeomen. The marvellously straight furrows carved out of the brown earth by these septuagenarian husbandmen, for most seemed to be old, was an invigorating sight that made mere onlookers from " Lunnon " feel strangely ignorant.

I had a long talk with one white-headed old man, and entertaining company I found him. He was a delightful personality, who seemed to blend in his nature, quite unconsciously, a respectful deference and a sturdy independence in his own views. He paid me the compliment of assuming that I knew as much of ploughing as he did, nor was this a pose; it was more the inherent modesty of a true scholar and though he would never have applied such a term to himself, it was true enough in his own way. Hiding my ignorance as well as I could I listened to his talk, in which was the real old country " burr."

I was far beyond my depths in technical details—he even went into the comparative merits of the " wheel " and the " swivel " plough, at which I nodded sagely, but did not confess that this was the first intimation that there *were* two sorts. What pleased me most was his perfectly natural use of the old Saxon word " lea " for field or meadow. Surely this delightful old man was a descendant of the original Middle-Saxons, who once inhabited and gave the name to this county. I am glad that my old friend won first prize for ploughing that day.

I was loth to part with him and invited him to share my modest midday meal of bread and cheese and beer at the Old Magpies, that quaint thatched inn not far away across the road.

" Thankee, sir," he replied, " don't mind a glass o' beer but I brought my dinner wi' me," and he went over to a small bundle, tied in a white cloth, by the hedge (I was sorry not to see traditional red handkerchief). In keeping with his personality and his talk I expected him to produce a hunk of bread and a piece of fat pork, after the true country style. I had, however, rather a shock; he certainly produced the hunk of bread and the pork—but the latter was a tin of pork and beans. It was the only modern touch about him. Perhaps he noticed my surprise, for he said " Yes, I'm a bit partial to this 'ere. My son, who was in the army, brought some home and I finds a tin very tasty.'

We ate our meal on a bench outside the inn just the same, and he entertained me with stories of ploughing matches of fifty years ago in the same fields. He even described with great details the ploughing suppers they used to have afterwards in those days. Altogether my talk with this old farm labourer—for he aspired to no other title—was a real tonic and I sincerely hope it is not the last time we shall smoke a friendly pipe together.

Yet when the vapid and callow youths, who rush up and down the Great West Road in their " sports models " at excessive speed to others discomfort, pass this old man trudging along the roadside on his way home from his work, they would merely look upon him contemptuously, if they noticed him at all, as a " mere labourer," who should get out of their lordly way. He may be that—for " Ambition did not mock his useful toil; his homely joys and destiny obscure " (to paraphrase *the* Elegy)—but of one

thing I am certain and that is that this old man had far more character
than those said youths.

There were other things to see at the show besides the ploughing;
vegetables of all sorts—potatoes, beets, turnips and many others—were on
view, as well as fruit, poultry and butter; in fact, all the usual attributes
of a real country show that owed nothing to London, so near and yet so
very far away. It was a scene which Thomas Hardy would have delighted
to describe. The ploughing it was that gave the show its distinctive touch,
which in my case was accentuated by my talk with that old ploughman,
born and bred, as he proudly told me, on Hounslow Heath.

*   *   *   *   *   *

When I got home that evening I turned up my copies of the old
Farmer's Magazine to see if I could find anything of the old-time ploughing
matches in Middlesex. There were certainly a few notes on ploughing in
this county, though no mention of the matches, but there was an article
of some fourteen pages on Ploughing Matches in general, which though
written in 1801, might well have applied to what I had witnessed that day.

An even more powerful simile was an article in a journal for 1850
which I came across, describing an actual ploughing match in Middlesex
(the place was not mentioned) : " A pretty sight truly. A faint haze of
mist curtained the scene from infinity; the sun shining with more bright-
ness than warmth; a gay crowd in rural finery; these make the accessories
of the picture. But the horses ! Away with your foppish exquisites of the
chase, and your airy nothings of the turf; for examples of dignity, joined
to force, you must look at these giant-limbed mighty-boned brutes moving
slow in pairs. Do you mean to tell me there is no conscious pride in that
sweeping arch of the neck? The shaggy fetlock is laid down as lightly
as the foot of a fay, not to bruise the mould. Art, too, has been called in;
tail and mane are streaming with ribbons and a rosette adorns the forehead, while the harness is studded with sparkling bits of polished brass."

These words were written of this old Middlesex ploughing match some
eighty years ago. On this last September morning the scene was enacted
again with little difference, if one could forget the motor-tractors—poor,
ugly, unromantic things that even the fine shire horses pulling the ploughs
seemed to despise.

BOOK TWO.

CHAPTER VI.

How the Monks of olden time heard a strange story from a wandering mendicant.

MANY people, I find, have never heard of a monastery at Hounslow, so completely has all trace of it disappeared; yet a little research into various books has yielded a fair crop of information concerning this forgotten medieval religious house.

Although some authorities give the date of its foundation as 1296 there is evidence that it was really founded in 1211. Probably the best account of all is in Aungier's *Syon Monastery*, though it is too long to quote. One of the best shorter accounts is in *A History of Heston and Isleworth*, by G. E. Bate, an excellent little book, to which I have been much indebted elsewhere also.

Another good description is that of D. Loinaz (in *The Home Counties Magazine*), who quotes some of the lesser known authorities. " Early in the 13th century, about 1211, a Priory of Friars of the Order of the Holy Trinity was founded at Hounslow," he writes, " in all probability the first house of its kind in England." The order was first instituted in France in 1198 by SS. Jean de Martha and Felix de Valois. King John, about 1214, granted Letters of Protection to the brethren of "The Hospitall of Hundeslawe," and in 1296 Edward I. granted to the Priory the right to hold a weekly market.

The Issue Roll of *The Pell Records* has a note under the date 1371: " Edward III. To the Minister and Brethren of Hundeslowe. The money delivered to them in discharge of the 10 marks which the Lord King commanded to be paid to them of his alms, for the salvation of the soul of Philippa (of Hainault), late Queen of England, his Consort, £6 13s. 4d."

Leland's *Itinerary* (1542) has the following reference to this Priory: " From Brentford to Hundeslawe is two miles. There was in the west ende of the town an house of the Freres of the Ordre of the Title of the Trinitie"; and Norden, in his *Speculum Britanniae* (1593), writes: " Hunslow belongeth unto two parishes, the north side of the street (i.e. the High Street) to Heston and the south to Isleworth. There is a chapell of ease which belonged unto the fryerie there disolved, which fryerie after the dissolution was by exchange given to Lord Windsore by King Henry VIII. Afterwards it came to Auditor Roan by purchase, who hath bestowed the same chappelle and 40s. per annum upon the inhabitants, to the ende and upon condition that they shall maintain a minister there. There is a faire house erected where the friery was, belonging to the heires of Auditor Roan. In the chappelle was buried Sir George Windsor, Knight. In that place lie many of the Windsors."

There were in all about twelve of these Trinitarians or Maturine Friaries in England. The former name they derived from their dedicating their churches to the Holy Trinity, the latter from their having had their first house near St. Maturine's Chapel in Paris.

Fosbrooke's *British Monarchism* gives the following particulars of this Order: " Government by a Minister; vow of chastity and poverty; third part of incomings to be devoted to redemption of Christian captives from infidels (referring to the Crusades); all Churches to be of plain work, and dedicated to the Trinity; sleep in their cloaths; no featherbeds nor counterpanes, only pillows allowed. No accusation without proof, or the accuser to undergo the punishment the accused had been liable to." All the revenues were divided into three parts—one for their own maintenance, one for the relief of the poor, and one for the ransom of Christians taken captive by infidels.

The Hounslow Trinitarians held land in Bedfont, Heston, Hatton, Harlington and Uxbridge, in addition to their lands in Hounslow, but they were not a wealthy community. At the time of their suppression by Henry VIII. the gross annual valuation of their holdings was not more than £85 15s., or £64 8s. net.

The Manor of Hounslow, including the site of the Trinitarian Hospital, was annexed by Henry VIII. to the Honour of Hampton Court, and leased in 1539 for a period of twenty-one years to Richard Awnsham, and in 1553 by Edward VI. to the Marquis of Northampton for a similar term, upon the expiration of the former lease. The reversion of these properties, consisting of the hospital. 117 acres of land, with appurtenances, together with the fair, market, court-leet, etc., was sold in 1557 to Lord Windsor for £905; and in 1571 a later Lord Windsor sold them to Anthony Roan, the Queen's Auditor, who lived at Hounslow, for £300 (reserving to himself the manor, with the right to holding courts in the great hall of the manor house).

They were, however, repurchased by the fifth Lord Windsor in 1594, and transferred by him with the manor to Thomas Crompton. In 1625 the estate was conveyed by Crompton's daughter, Lady Lyttleton, to Justinian Povey. It was sold by the Povey family in 1671 to James Smith and Henry Meuse, from whom it passed the following year to Henry Sayer, in whose family it remained until 1705, when it was purchased by Whitelock Bulstrode, of Cliffords Inn. It was again sold in 1818 to Thomas Cane. Lysons, writing in 1795, says: " The manor house stands at the western extremity of the town and adjoins the Heath; it is an ancient brick structure." The grounds of Holy Trinity Church were the site of the old manor house. In 1795, therefore, the Heath extended eastwards to Holy Trinity, and this part of the town was then the western extremity; and here the town ended and the Heath began. To-day what we know as the Heath lies a mile or more to the westward.

The monks of Hounslow, often known as Redemptionists because of their vow to redeem captives, wore a distinctive dress of white robes with a red and blue cross on the left breast. In G. E. Bate's book there is an interesting item I have not seen in any other source. It is usual to associate Henry VIII. with the dissolving of monasteries, as he did this one, and it is rather refreshing to look at the other side of the picture, and to find him actually *admitted* as member of a monastic house. Yet this happened here. " It seems strange to find that Henry VIII. was a Brother of the House of the Holy Trinity at Hounslow," writes Mr. Bate, " for in

THE MONKS' CHAPEL, HOUNSLOW.
Demolished 1828.   *Block lent by Middlesex Chronicle*

" HOLLAND IN MIDDLESEX."   *Drawn by R. Gammon of the News-Chronicle*

"OURS IS THE HEATH COUNTRY."

A scene near Harlington Corner. *Photo by F. Ash.*

RECLAIMED HEATHLAND. *Photo by F. Ash.*

Near Stanwell.

the British Museum a document is preserved which records his admission to the Confraternity of the Order in 1508, when he was Prince of Wales. It is drawn up by Father Ralph Bekwith, 'Minister domus de Houndeslowe,' and the Convent of the same. The occasion was one of importance, for the deed is richly illuminated in colours. Henry's Coat of Arms is worked into the initial letter, and the decorative border contains the badge of the Trinitarians, bearing three ostrich feathers and red Tudor roses. At the end is a form of absolution." Dissolution, however, seems to have been more in the King's mind a few years later. Did he remember, it is to be wondered, that he was breaking up his *own* monastery when he issued orders for the spoliation of this house. Perhaps, however, he merely considered he was taking his own property.

A sidelight on this dissolution appears in the same book: "The King's Escheator for the county of Middlesex who should have dealt with the matter was Robert Cheeseman, of Southall, Falconer to Henry VIII. In 1538 we find him making a lease for 80 years with William Hyde, the minister or prior, and the brethren. Cheeseman was to receive the barns, stables and orchards, 'in or about the said monastery of the Trynyte of Hounslow,' except the church chambers where the minister 'and convent do lye, the kechyn, brewhouse and bakehouse.' In return Cheeseman was to pay £10 to the Minister and £16 to the brethren every year. The King's Commissioner, Richard Layton, heard of this arrangement and reported the matter to Thomas Cromwell, the Vicar-General and enemy of the friars. He upset the agreement, confiscated the friar's property and turned them adrift."

There are several other accounts at which we can glance in passing; they may overlap in parts, but all are interesting. It will be best, perhaps, to deal with them chronologically.

In *The Modern Universal British Traveller,* an eighteenth century journal, we read: "At Hounslow was antiently a convent of British friars; but no remains of the building are now to be seen. This place being situated on the high western road has many good inns. Here is a chapel of ease and a charity school."

Lysons, a few years later, says: "The priory at Hounslow was founded in the 13th century, but by whom or at what time is uncertain; though it has been thought that it was founded by some of the Windsor family, but there appears no other grounds for the supposition than that they were an ancient and opulent family situated in the neighbourhood (at Stanwell), and that they chose (though not till the beginning of the 16th century) the chapels belonging to the priory as their place of burial."

It is surprising to find so great a topographer as Lysons so shaky about the early history of the Priory, as it is not at all difficult to find this out. "The only remaining part of the priory," he continues, "is the chapel, which exhibits evident traces of the architecture of the 13th century, particularly in the stone-stalls, three of which are to be seen in the chancel, and a double piscina, with the narrow pointed arches divided by a column. The chapel consists of a chancel, nave and aisle.

"Hounslow Priory bore for its arms Gules, a Lion rampant guardant, per fesse Or and Argent, between three plates, each charged with a cross of the first." Lysons says a good deal more, but it has all been covered by the other quotations, the authors of which probably purloined it from Lysons to begin with.

In *The Beauties of England* it is stated that the Manor and the site
of Hounslow Priory was in 1705 purchased by Whitelocke Bulstrode, the
author of the *Treatise on Transmigration, Compendium of Crown Laws,*
and other works, who enlarged the manor house, an ancient brick
structure facing the Heath at the western extremity of Hounslow, and also
repaired the chapel which contains his monument.   Care should be taken
not to confuse him with Bulstrode Whitelocke, which is often done, for the
latter, though I believe a relation, had no connection with Hounslow.   I
would like to quote what the D.N.B. and Aungier have to say of Whitelocke
Bulstrode, but space forbids, so must merely refer the reader to those
books.   In the chapel was a mutilated escutcheon, with the arms and
quarterings of the Windsor family, who have been supposed, but
erroneously, to have founded the priory.

In Cooke's *Topography of Middlesex,* an early nineteenth century book,
it is stated that " the only remaining part of the conventual buildings is the
chapel.   In the south wall of the chancel are three ancient stone stalls, and
a double piscina, with narrow pointed arches, divided by a column.   In the
nave is a small monument, with the effigies of a man in armour and his
wife, kneeling; on the floor is a brass plate to the memory of Thomas
Lupton, who died in 1512, and his wife Alice.   In the windows of the south
aisle there is some painted glass, representing the figure of St. Katherine,
and other subjects."

Cobbett, in his *History of the Reformation,* speaks of it as a " friary ";
while Thorne tells us: " A priory of the Brethren of the Holy Trinity
existed at Hounslow in 1296.   The priory continued down to the Dissolution and is often referred to.   It had at least one distinguished member,
Robert de Hounslow, a native of the town, died 1430, Grand Provincial of
the Order for England, Ireland and Scotland, and eminent in his day as a
writer.   The chapel of the priory continued to be used as the chapel-of-ease
for Hounslow until the present church was built.   The old chapel was a
small building of the Decorated period, but had been often repaired and
was in a bad state.   The present Church is a plain white brick building,
Gothic, of the year 1835."

Walford tells us, " This ancient chapel has now entirely disappeared,
and in its place—although perhaps not quite on the same site—has arisen
another Church, dedicated to the Holy Trinity.   It is constructed of white
brick, and is a plain edifice in the Italian style, with a bell-turret and
surmounted by twelve cupolas.   The building was enlarged by the addition
of a chancel in 1856, and was reseated in 1880, when three stained glass
windows were added."

The two best known Priors of Hounslow were Clement Maydestone and
Robert Hounslow.   The former, whose dates seem rather uncertain, for all
the *D.N.B.* gives is " fl. 1410," was ordained deacon at Hounslow in that
year, and priest two years later.   He was a prolific writer on religious
matters, and his best known works are *The Life of Richard Scrope* (Archbishop of York) and *Directorium Sacerdotum*; the latter book being printed
some years later (1487) by Caxton.   The former work, however, has more
interest for us here, for it contains one of the strangest minor stories of
English history, which had its beginning at Hounslow in the time of
Maydestone.

It is related how one evening, shortly after the death of Henry IV.,
the monks were at supper in the refectory of this heathside Priory, when
there came a loud knocking at the outer door.   The monkish custodian

reported to the prior, who sat at the head of the table, that a stranger was without and sought refreshment and shelter. The Prior bade the door-keeper admit him, and a wild-eyed figure entered, dishevelled and stained with travel. Food and drink were placed before him, and, his appetite satisfied, he told his hosts a weird and fantastic tale. He was, he asserted, one of three men who threw the corpse of the late King into the River Thames, between Barking and Gravesend, whilst it was being conveyed from Westminster to Canterbury for interment, but that the chest, covered with cloth of gold, in which the body had lain, was still carried with great pomp and honour into the Cathedral and buried with full state.

This extraordinary story naturally caused a great sensation among the monks, and in time it spread far beyond the confines of this monastery, probably with embellishments. There was nothing unusual about the fact that it became a nine-days' wonder—the strange part was that it became a four-hundred-and-nineteen-*years'* wonder; for it was after the lapse of all that time, that is in 1832, so firmly had the story taken a hold on public imagination, that the tomb of Henry IV. at Canterbury was actually opened, in the presence of the Bishop of Oxford, the Dean of Canterbury, and other distinguished persons, and the body of the King was found to have been inside the coffin, thus finally disproving the unlikely story told by a wandering mendicant at Hounslow Priory so long before. The surprising thing is that so wild a tale, entirely unsupported by any evidence and coming from so unreliable a source, should have been believed at all, even by the most credulous and simple-minded of monks.

Those who wish for further details of this extraordinary affair will find it in *The Testimony of Clement Maydstone*, translated from a Latin MS. of 1440; and also in Strickland's *Queens of England,* which has details of the exhumation, though not very pleasant reading.

* * * * * *

Curiously enough Robert de Hounslow is not mentioned in the *D.N.B.*, but here is Fuller's quaint account of him in *The Worthies*: "Robert de Hounslow was born in this county of Middlesex at Hounslow. He was a Fryer of the Order of the Holy Trinity. To give this Order their due much good did redound from their endeavours, for this Robert being their provinciale rich people by him were exhorted, and their almes collected. He wrote many *Synodall Sermons* and *Epistles of Consequence* to severall persones of qualitie, to stir up their liberalitie. He flourished Anno Domini 1430, a most remarkable year by our foresaid author, assigned either for the flourishing, or for the Funeralls of eleven famous writers; yet so our Robert leads all the rest by his book *De Illustribus Angliae Scriptoribus.*"

The site of the old monk's market and fair was probably near the Polytechnic in Hanworth Road, and there is still a street called Fair Street. This was certainly the site in later years when a market toll stood here.

"A fair was of greater importance in the Middle Ages than now," writes Mr. Bate. "Not only did jugglers, minstrels and dancers attend to amuse the people, but much trade was transacted. Peddlers, who were the retailers of those days, brought their wares, and the inhabitants for miles around brought in their produce. Huts, tents and stalls were erected, and the friars went round collecting toll from all who sold. The friars were also responsible for just dealing; they tested the measures used and could hold a court to try offenders.

"Hounslow fair lasted longer than the friars, for after the Dissolution we find the right to hold the fair and market being sold along with the friars' property. One of the customs, that of taking a toll called ' show penny ' from every house that sold liquor, and every shop and stall during the fair, was continued by the Lords of the Manor until the beginning of the ninetenth century."

The monastery chapel also existed long after the Dissolution, though all the other buildings disappeared. The former was used, as we have seen, as the parish church till about 1828, when it was demolished, and the present church begun more or less on the same site. It is possible that some remains still exist underground, for I have in my cuttings-book a newspaper paragraph of September, 1928, that reads: " When the workmen were digging out foundations at Hounslow they found a heap of building materials, believed to have been part of the 13th century Chapel of the Trinitarian Brothers of Redemption, who had their chief monastery there." Mr. Thomas Woods' auction rooms in Bell Road are the remains of an old mansion known as The Priory, a typical 18th century building, as the interior still shows, and nothing like old enough once to have been part of the actual Priory, though probably built on land once owned by the monks.

In Mr. G. E. Bate's book on the history of this church we find an unusual paragraph: " The new church was opened in December, 1829, but owing to a technical error was not consecrated until 1836." I have never before heard of a church that was forgotten to be consecrated in time for the opening.

The spirit of the Hounslow Trinitarians remained, in a measure, active long after this time, for there was an old charity in operation some centuries later, by which twelve boys were taught and clothed here, chiefly out of the offertory at the Sacrament, and which also enacted that " a two-penny loaf of good bread shall also be given to every child that comes to church on Sundays, morning and afternoon."

Another link with this old monastery is a sepulchral inscription in the Church of the Grey Friars (Christ Church), Newgate Street, London, which reads:—

> " Fr.Willmus Appthomas de ordre sci
> trinitie de Hounslow. Ob. 13. June 1478."

Little enough by which to recall the story of this once famous monastery—this inscription some miles away, and a heap of building rubbish thrown up by a workman's spade. These things tangible—but a wealth of memories.

CHAPTER VII.

Of Hounslow Town that has no History.

IT is curious at first thought, if understandable later, that Hounslow itself, which gave its name to a district so crowded with vivid memories, should, as a town, be practically without history.

Yet such is the case, for though it is certainly mentioned in the *Domesday Book* there is nothing to record of this place—with the single exception of its vanished monastery—until the middle of the seventeenth century and through the eighteenth, and even then its story is wrapped up in the history of coaching, for Hounslow in the days of what "glory" it ever had owed it entirely to its position on the Great West Road out of London.

History, in the generally accepted but elastic term, it had none, and the first real notice ever taken of the place was its mention in the *Parliamentary Survey* of 1650, which states: "The town of Hounslow containes 120 houses, most of them inns and alehouses depending upon travellers." The few houses not inns were mostly inhabited by horsekeepers and others who gained their livelihood from the road.

"Now at about this time the use of coaches was rapidly coming into vogue in England," says one chronicle. "It was no longer considered, as it had been, effeminate for men to travel by coach rather than on horseback; the old prejudices were dying under the obvious advantages of the new mode of travel. The coach did for travel in those early days what the railway did at a later period and the aeroplane later still; it lessened distances, at least, figuratively. With the growth of travel the prosperity of Hounslow increased; it was a natural halting place for traffic to and from London on the western road. It became essentially a posting station, about 500 vehicles passing through it daily. By the end of the eighteenth century it had probably attained its zenith in this respect.

"What animated scenes must have been witnessed here in bygone days, especially on market day, or during the eight days of the annual fair, when the surrounding villages and hamlets would each send its quota to swell the variegated crowds, bent on fun and bargains. Above the din of the merchants and merrymakers would sound continually the horns of the incoming and outgoing coaches, and at every inn all would be bustle and hurry. At these fairs the lord of the manor levied toll on all sellers; for every horse 4d., on every score of sheep 4d., for each cow or calf 2d., for each pig 1d., a penny from every house selling liquor and the same from all shops and stalls, as well as 'show pennies'—probably amusement booths.

"There was a dark side to this bright scene, in sharp contrast to this merry picture; for there was one spot, scarcely a stone's throw from the fair grounds, where the festive gave place to the gruesome. This was at the junction of the Bath and Staines roads. There criminals, brought from London and elsewhere, were gibbetted, for the improvement presumably of the morals of residents and passers-by."

The quotation about the 120 inns is usually all most writers say of Hounslow, and honestly I don't know that I can say very much more,

45

though I will do my best to trace what little claim to historical fame it
possesses.

Its mention in the *Domesday Book* (quoted elsewhere) is purely a
nominal one as the then name of the Hundred, and not as a
" Vill.' It gives us no mental picture of what the village was like in
those early days; we can only imagine it as a collection of wayside huts.
The way was a Roman one but had been neglected into little more than a
pack-horse track. The huts were the homes of the Forest Keepers, for then
the Warren (or Forest) of Staines was a Royal preserve, and perhaps a
few colliers (charcoal burners) carried on their sombre trade within its
precincts.

The Calendar of State Papers and *The Patent Rolls* are mines of
information from the reigns of Edward I. to Henry VIII., and contain many
references to Hounslow Heath. Even later we find occasional items in
these pages, though not so numerous as the earlier dates; such as: " 1656.
Petitions granted to John Cook, Gentleman, for the encouragement of his
manufacture of sword and rapier blades at Hounslow."

All what may be called " standard references " to Hounslow bear a
strong family likeness, for the old topographers had a knack of cribbing
from each other quite shamelessly and without acknowledgment; even
before the days of Lysons' *Environs of London,* which has become the
" Bible " for such writers. Here is what old Lysons himself had to say:
" The Hundred of Honeslow (now Isleworth Hundred) is mentioned in the
Conqueror's Survey. The hamlet of Hounslow is called in ancient records
singularitie of the corne. The raine of this especiall corne seemeth to
Hundeslawe and Hundeslowe. It has long been noted as a great thoroughfare, being situated on the principal western road. It stands in the parish
of Heston and Isleworth."

Not a very full account, perhaps, but though there is certainly a little
more the rest refers to other parts of our story. I notice that even Lysons
mentions the famous 120 inns—how they all love to quote that bit!

Contemporary with Lysons was Dr. David Hughson's *Circuit of London.*
I wonder if these two old topographers ever met on their rambles. It
would be an historic occasion ————— " Dr. Hughson, I presume! "

Hughson, however, had little to say about this place; beyond a notice
of the monastery and a few remarks about the ancient camps all he tells
us is " Hounslow stands on the edge of the heath of the same name." He
also adds that " in 1686 the King granted by his letters patent to John
Shales, his heirs and assigns, the privilege of holding upon Hounslow
Heath a daily market and a weekly market on Thursday."

Hounslow had its market—an institution which was of more importance
in medieval days than now—far earlier than this, for in 1296 a weekly
market was granted to the brethren of the Priory to be held on Wednesday
and an annual fair on the eve of the feast of the Holy Trinity to last a
week. A survival of this still exists.

Thorne, whose book bears the same title as Lysons' under a later date,
adds: " It is said that as many as 500 stage coaches passed through Hounslow daily and that 1,500 horses were kept in the town. The opening of
the railway destroyed the traffic, and Hounslow was for a while in a very
depressed condition. It has, however, quite recovered. Large numbers of
genteel houses have been built in and about it, and the place has now a good
local trade. But it is a dull place to visit. The town consists of a long mile
of characterless shops, many inns a commonplace Ch. and a Town Hall,

erected in 1857, and the immediate neighbourhood is flat, monotonous and uninteresting." Of course he tells us about the 120 inns, but in spite of that his account is hardly fair to Hounslow, even if its " Ch. " is commonplace architecturally —it was built at a dull period of ecclesiastical architecture. I am rather surprised at Thorne, usually so keen an observer, in what he said about the surrounding country. Flat it may be, and in its flatness perhaps a trifle monotonous to the casual passer-by, but uninteresting never; except to those who we are told are born at the rate of one a minute ! Yet Thorne was very far removed from that category—it must have been a mental lapse on his part.

Then comes Walford—w 10 owed more to Thorne than he himself knew —who, though he ignores the 120 inns, quotes the *Beauties of England and Wales* and thus saves the trouble of a separate entry from that interesting book. " The town of Hounslow," he writes, " consists mainly of a long uninteresting and monotonous street, with scarcely one picturesque or redeeming object on either side (this was written about 1883). As far back as 1650 it was noted for its numerous inns and ale-houses, and later on it became a great place for posting-houses." In *The Beauties of England and Wales* it is stated that " the chief dependence of the place is on the immense tide of road traffic, which rolls to and from the metropolis with surprising vehemence and bustle. As this hamlet is only one short stage from London the principal business of the town consists in providing relays of post-horses, and exchanges of horses for the coaches. The whole population seems on the wing of removal; and assuredly the main street of Hounslow is a place from which the examiner would wish to remove with all the celerity familiar to the spot.

The old inns of Hounslow could tell some wonderful yarns. I wish these had been collected before they were lost in the quicksands of the years. Space allows but for a brief outline of one of them. At The Old Nag's Head, in the High Street, there was formerly a large grandfather's clock, which was really the entrance to a secret chamber. Into this inn one night dashed Dick Turpin, hotly pursued by the Runners. The highwayman made at once for the clock—and vanished. The Runners peppered the clock with bullets, but apparently did not discover the hidden chamber, leaving Turpin free to mount Black Bess in the stableyard and gallop away over the Heath. The Bow Street Runners always appear so simple-minded in these stories— but, anyhow, the bullets were shown in the clock case for years as the " proof " of this episode!

" Being on the road to Windsor its street was often traversed by Royalty, from the days of the Tudors to those of Victoria. What statesmen, soldiers and philosophers have rolled along this road in their carriages. In the words of the poet:—

> " ' By Harley Swift invited comes to Court:
> And Harley, not ashamed his choice to own,
> Takes him to Windsor in his chaise alone.' "

These are the chief text-books for the rambler, though of course there are many others, such as the account of 1593 in *Speculum Britannae* : " Hounslow, or Hunslow, belongeth to two parishes, the north side of the streete to Heston and the south to Isleworth. There is a chappell of ease which belonged unto the freyerie there disolved. A faire house is erected where the friery was."

Most of the writers follow on with a mention of the Heath, whose wonderful history they usually dismiss in about fifty words—or less. Norden, however, says nothing about it at all, for the simple reason that its history then lay in the future. A typical entry concerning Hounslow is found in Harrison's *Survey of London and Adjacent Parts,* where he says: "This is a large village situated near ten miles from London, in the county of Middlesex. There was antiently a convent of begging friars in this village, but this is now totally demolished; and the place is only noted for having many inns.

"Here is a chapel of ease and a charity school; but not any of the buildings merit particular description. Hounslow Heath, which adjoins to the west end of the village, is very extensive and has been long noted on account of the many robberies committed on it. It is also a remarkable place for exposing the bodies of those malefactors who are sentenced to be hung in chains after their execution."

A more modern account in *Local History and Antiquities,* by John E. Morris and Humphrey Jordan, has a little more imagination in it, and it will be noticed that this places the number of horses kept there at a thousand more than the generally stated number. "Hounslow was the first stage out of London and through this place all coaches would pass, and would, moreover, stop there to change horses, of which there were 2,500 stabled here. In view of this it is no matter for surprise that many complaints were raised when coaching was superseded; towns that had been prosperous maintaining that they had been ruined. For it is not hard to understand that any country town which stabled so many animals, employed sufficient men to look after them, and supported inns at which there was the continual passage of travellers paying good prices for their entertainment, was likely to be in a very prosperous condition. About Hounslow there clings more of romance than is the case with any of the other stages on the western roads, for here Claude Duval, the Frenchman, who surely set the fashion in highwayman's manners, carried on his profitable business, until in 1670 his riding came to an end with a last journey in the hangman's cart."

In *Environs of London* (another book that has taken Lysons' title, this time in 1897) appears the following: "Hounslow is a fairly old place as places go. It is the *Hondeslawe* of the Domesday Book, so that it possesses a pedigree. Before the opening of the railway Hounslow had a most respectable posting business.

"The neighbouring heath was a very famous resort for highwaymen and of comparatively recent years it was no uncommon sight to see the bodies of rogues hanging in chains and dancing on nothing. Many a romance of the road has been written about Hounslow Heath, but the best adventures are probably unrecorded."

This account, even roughly analysed, is a curious one. What does the writer mean, in this case, by "as places go"? Hounslow Heath is far older than the *Domesday Book.* Then a "respectable" posting business has a strange sound, and as for the gibbets being there "in recent years" (writing in 1897) is more unaccountable still; they had been removed nearly a hundred years before that date; while the information that the history of Hounslow is not "sinister" can perhaps be doubted if applied metaphorically!

The writer goes on to speak of the "double bifurcation" of the roads at Hounslow in the days of the coaches; why "double," which surely

Photo lent by Middlesex Chronicle.

OLD BELL INN, HOUNSLOW.
Since re-built.

makes them four? He could hardly have meant the Whitton and Lampton Roads, which, in those days, were country lanes. I am in entire agreement with him, however, when he says that the best adventures on the Heath are unrecorded; this is probably quite true. In another chapter I have done a little to remedy this, from various sources, perhaps rather briefly, for if even half these stories were written up they would easily make a book by themselves, and those left out would make a sequel.

Nothing would be easier than to go on quoting these excerpts, but they are very similar, and though I found a certain amount of interest in them as a close student of Hounslow's history, the repetition might weary the general reader. One or two, however, are not without a quaint humour that gives them a distinction, such as that from *Magna Britannica* (of 1724) which contains rather negative history when it says: " Hounslow is remarkable for the Road through it and the Heath beside it "; while in another old book, dated two years later, the only " information " concerning Hounslow is a paragraph mentioning the charity loaf, referred to elsewhere.

In *Excursions*, by Rev. John Evans, a clergyman with a taste for rambling about 1818 and who left very entertaining notes of his intineraries, we read: " Hounslow, where we just stopped to change horses, is remarkable for its numerous inns. Immediately upon our entrance to the heath about a stone's throw from the road towards Whitton there is to be seen a wooden monument, shockingly marked by a *bloody hand* and *knife*, with an inscription. This was " The Bloody Post " referred to elsewhere.

" The sight of such an object instantly conjures up in the imagination all those cruelties which have been perpetrated on this secluded spot by wretches in the last stages of depravity. Of later years, however, the traveller has met with fewer interruptions, though we still hear, not infrequently, of robberies in that quarter during the winter season, a proof of which is exhibited by a gibbet near Bedfont, on which we saw the body of Haines, generally known as the ' wounded highwayman.' He was a large tall man; his irons were so constructed that his arms hung at some little distance from his body, by which means the hideous sight was rendered more terrific and impressive. The skirts of his coat waved in the wind, and suggested with full force the horrible idea of a fellow-creature deprived of the honours of sepulture, and consigned, with every mark of execration, to the grinning scorn of public infamy."

At the west end of the High Street at Hounslow, opposite Trinity Church was an old building formerly known as the Treaty House, from the fact that after the battle of Brentford a treaty was signed there by Lord Falkland and the Parliamentary General.

The building stood until the erection of the present Council House and Library in Treaty Road. A local resident, who was a boy at the time of the demolition of Treaty House, tells me that there lingers in his mind far more vividly than any historical associations a notice that was painted on the garden wall at the back:—

> " Here savage dogs roam loose at night;
> They never bark, but always bite!"

* * * * * *

Of modern Hounslow there is even less to say than in the past days; the few mentions of it are usually in the nature of terse comments, such as " a long uninteresting street," or words to that effect. To the casual

observer this may have a certain amount of truth, for after the coaching
days the town had a long spell of depression from which it is now fast
recovering owing to its rise as a residential centre, though this has had the
result rather of destroying its former old country town look. It has little
enough of that left now, but to the observant eye it is never uninteresting,
and even now I find a walk up the long length of its High Street worth
while, if only in looking for traces of its old inns.

Although there are a fair sprinkling of these left, perhaps a dozen or
so, there are still over a hundred to be accounted for. Some of these may
be recognised quite easily, converted into shops with merely a new front,
while others have been more drastically altered and sometimes rebuilt.
The best "clue," however, is the simple one of looking for an opening at
the side—often an archway—leading to a yard, and by a mild trespass the
backs of the houses can be seen, where their age is more apparent than in
front. These archways once led to inn-yards where the coach or post-
chaise had to pass the night while the travellers slept at the inn. In some
cases the old stabling is also still to be seen.

There are many such openings in Hounslow's High Street, and it is
searching for them and reconstructing mentally what the house was like
in its pristine state that makes a walk up its mile-length a matter of vivid
interest to those who would read, in bricks and mortar, its stories of
yesterday. I am glad to notice a memory of some of these stories at the
Coach and Horses on the main London Road, in a very good copy of an old
coaching picture, used as a signboard.

These are many, mostly in connection with the old inns and road
life. Some appear elsewhere in these pages, but one I was told recently
is not out of place here. It deals with one of the still existing inns—
which particular hostelry I do not know, as it might apply to several.
This inn has a bedroom with a "secret" exit into a yard, through which
Dick Turpin is said to have dodged the Bow Street Runners (incidentally
a story told of almost every inn in this district!). This room was once
shown, as a curiosity, to a modern commercial traveller, who expressed
himself so interested in this romantic chamber that he asked if he could
spend the night there. This he did—with the result that he left by the
secret exit early next morning without paying his bill. Now it is said that
the landlord requests any guest occupying this room to settle overnight.

References to Hounslow Town can be found in a good many books,
usually rather scrappy and not always flattering. Harper, in his Road
books, does not paint a very bright picture of the place, though we must
feel sympathy with his remarks concerning its spoilation by the builders
years ago—what would he say to-day? Then a journal of 1842 still further
depresses us when it says: "At the formerly flourishing village of Hounslow
so great is the general depreciation of property on account of the transfer
of the traffic to the railway that at one of the inns is an inscription, "New
Milk sold here," while another announces the profession of the landlord
as "Mending Boots." Further reference rather on the same theme, with
perhaps a little more about the Heath, can be read in *Recollections,* by the
Hon. Amelia Murray, written about twenty years later than the foregoing.
All accounts about this unlucky period in Hounslow's history are rather
depressing.

The "guide" books (so-called) are the biggest offenders against the
Hounslow district. To mention two only: The *A.A. Handbook* has no mention at all of the place, and *The Dunlop Guide* puts as the sole feature of

interest hereabouts the Barracks! No wonder people get a wrong impression of Hounslow and its vicinity.

If a nation that has no history is happy does this apply to a town? And if so did this make Hounslow a happy town in the eighteenth century? I rather doubt it; its proximity to the Heath may have had something to do with it. It was, I should imagine, rather a town of fear and relief. Those travellers who had the passing over that dreaded waste before them, and in those days it was a very real source of terror, would arrive in the town full of apprehension; and those who, the heath and its dangers behind, arrived at the comparative safety of Hounslow Town must have felt a sense of relief that their journey's end, as far as the heath was concerned, was safely reached.

*   *   *   *   *   *

Hounslow—its vested interests being wrapped up in horseflesh—violently opposed the "new-fangled" railway projects so successfully that the G.W.R., who had originally intended bringing the railway through the town, decided to take it through Southall, and left poor Hounslow more stranded than ever. We notice, however, that even in those early days of railways there was another Richmond in the field (or on the heath), for in Faulkener's *History of Brentford* we read: "Among the projected improvements (1845) of this neighbourhood may be mentioned the Hounslow Railway, projected to be constructed on the Atmospheric plan, which is proved to offer many advantages over steam for short distances. It is intended to carry this road through Brentford, Turnham Green, Hammersmith, Kensington and Knightsbridge, where it is to terminate within half a mile of Hyde Park Corner."

The chief mover in this was Samuel Clegg, an engineer, of whom we read: "He became much interested in railways, but was unfortunately too much fascinated with the atmospheric system, the failure of which as a practical plan of locomotion was a great blow to him."

C. G. Harper tells us rather a surprising thing when he says: "George Eliot anticipated the tube railway, for she once wrote ' Posterity may be shot like a bullet through a tube by atmospheric pressure.' " In which book she made this remark is not stated, but it is probable that she got the idea from the proposed Hounslow Railway.

Anyhow neither steam nor atmospherics touched Hounslow, one of the most pathetic instances—and there were many such in England—of an old coaching town killed by progress.

*   *   *   *   *   *

We must remember that the actual town of Hounslow once stopped by the church. A traveller in the eighteenth century could see before him from this point the open heath stretching away for miles. He would see one or two things in the foreground of this picture; there would be the Manor House, a large red brick building that stood on the fringe of the heath; there would be the turnpike-gate and the toll-house just before the Staines and Bath Roads branched off from the main London road; there would be one or two inns that had ventured beyond the town, notably the Bell, with the large elm trees by it, that were a landmark for miles around, and—most noticeable of all—there would be the lines of gibbets with their ghastly loads that stood between the first furlongs of the two heathen roads.

All these would he see, but beyond lay all that wild and desolate region of Hounslow Heath, whose very name struck terror into the heart of the wayfarer. The scene is changed now. The Bell (or its successor) is the only landmark left; all else is swept away into the limbo of half forgotten things; though it is preserved for us on canvas by George Morland. Of turnpike, toll-house, or gibbets there is not a sign; where the wild waste was visible we can see only houses and two roads going away into the distance.

Yet it is along these two roads, and all that surrounds them for many a mile, that I am going to ask you to accompany me to-day. There may not be much heath to see, but there are one or two other things that tell many a story of old romance, that go back even farther than the exciting "Stand and Deliver!" days, for we shall see things that were already ancient history when Claude Duval and Dick Turpin rode o' nights over the moonlit heath; but "memories too congenial food" (as Blackmore wrote of the exploits of Tom Faggus, the highwayman, in *Lorna Doone*); we shall also hear plenty of stories of these gallant (on paper) Knights of the Road as we traverse the actual scenes of their exploits.

Come then, over the Heath with me.

CHAPTER VIII.

Two Rivers of the Heath, and of the land through which they flow.

1. The River Crane.

THE study of all Middlesex rivers, which, if small, are more numerous than is generally supposed and really very little known, is interesting, and of these there are two which can be claimed as belonging specially to the Heath country. These are the Crane and the Exe, of which the former is the more important, as not only is it longer, but it flows directly across the old-time heath, whereas the other skirts it. The best account of the Crane was written in 1893, and allowing for the passage of years it is surprisingly up-to-date, for this little river has not altered a great deal in the interval, though naturally certain changes are noticeable.

This account is in *The Way about Middlesex*, that charming little book by H. S. Vaughan, who thus prefaces his description: " I may observe that the average tourist will find in this chapter little to interest him; but for the man who delights in a quiet lazy ramble by all sorts of short cuts and byways will see some unpretentious scenery upon a stream whose praises, I believe, have hitherto been unsung, and even unnoticed; for that man this description is intended, and by him alone will it be appreciated."

The writer's next words are very true: " ' The Crane? Never heard of it! ' I wonder how many will make the above remark. Yet there are a dozen views along its course well worth a picture. Among them is the lovely tree-fringed pool below the bridge at Hounslow Powder Mills, and it has this merit also of showing a number of cross-routes and lanes which could not otherwise be mentioned."

The author traces the whole course of the Crane, and we may as well follow him, as he has many fine descriptive passages, and as he specialises more on the lower portion of the river we shall not be led out of our way. He begins at the mouth, the proper way to explore a river. " It is at Isleworth that the Crane enters the Thames by two mouths (one artificial).

One in the centre of the old village, close to the church, and the other just above the eyot, north of the R.N. School at St. Margarets. The latter channel leaves the main one north of Twickenham Green, and winds across the fields to its outlet.

"The Crane rises near Headstone Farm, near Pinner; thence it follows a winding course. South of Ickenham it turns southward and is known as the Yeading Brook. Beyond here it dodges about among two big canals, the Paddington and the Grand Junction, passes through Cranford Park to Cranford Bridge, turns up again at Bedfont Powder Mills and those of Hounslow, and so comes down to Twickenham—by that time quite a respectable size.

"The ramble I now want to describe is chiefly concerned with the lower part from Isleworth to Cranford. Starting from the old church at Isleworth we pass up the narrow street to the bridge at the mill, and there get our first glimpse of the Crane, a somewhat prosiac one, but yet having an element of the picture about it. In the Mill-pool a barge with tanned sails is sometimes lying, and the dark water comes rushing down from under the gloomy mill building.

"We can follow the footpath to Twickenham Green till the handsome old red pile of Kneller Hall comes in sight among the trees, and the road to Whitton is crossed. Here for a short distance one has to take to the road till Fulwell Park is reached; turn aside at the footpath and soon some farm buildings are seen and our river makes one of its prettiest appearances in a little dell hemmed by trees. The old rusty mill-wheel, the tall poplars, the little cascade and rushing stream, and the red-tiled barns and farm waggons are among the elements of the picture."

We can make a pause here on paper as we should in a ramble; for it is a delightful spot, though the building estate in the park is not going to improve it. The view by Warren Farm and Hospital Bridge is worthy of Constable's brush—it is a real piece of old England—stream, meadows and trees. The name of Hospital Bridge has always intrigued me. Why is it so called? There is no hospital near, nor ever has been. Possibly it is a shortening of Hospitallers Bridge, proving that in medieval days the land hereabouts was owned by the Knights Hospitallers.

The Rev. R. S. Cobbett, in his *Memorials of Twickenham,* however, puts forward another theory when he says: "The bridge on the road leading out of the Hanworth Road to the new cemetery is to this day called Hospital Bridge, from the fact of its proximity to the Camp Hospital (of James II.'s army in 1688)." In spite of this ingenious view I like to think that my derivation with regard to the old Hospitallers is the more correct. Field hospitals were not at all common at that date; in fact, many hold that it is to Florence Nightingale we owe their introduction in the Crimean War. Anyhow, here are the two theories and in the absence of any proof the reader must choose.

"The path leads up past the farmhouse," continues the book, "on to the high land. Then one gets quite a notable view for this part of the world. Looking eastward the distant hills of Richmond are in sight, and the "Star and Garter" conspicuous. Towards the north-east is Kneller Hall, picturesquely rising from the dark woods round Whitton.

"Soon we strike across what is remnant of Hounslow Heath, the poor sandy nature of the soil is apparent, and the trees are largely firs. At the end of the road, past the gates of the Hounslow Powder Mills, we reach

our stream again, at what is perhaps the loveliest part of the course. The
dark channel flows smoothly down under the tall trees to the mills. A few
yards beyond you look over the bridge on to the backwater, with its
thickly massed trees, and patches of weed and water plants on the surface
break up the dark reflections in the quiet pool.   Without knowing the
stream one would hardly credit the Crane with producing such a charming
bit of scenery.   The road ahead goes to Hanworth Park, but we must
follow our stream to where it crosses the Hounslow Road to Staines; here
are several pretty views, notably that looking down the stream from
Babers Bridge. Bedfont Powder Mills are also surrounded by fine trees.
    " From this point there are two or three lanes and byways by which
the Bath Road, near Cranford Bridge, may be reached without going far
from the water. At Cranford there are some pretty views of the restful
kind. Rushes and willows reflected in quiet pools, patches of bright surface
weed, and here and there a group of lily leaves, or a clump of tall feathered
grasses. Above this point the stream runs through Cranford Park."
    On the whole this is as good an account of this typical little Middlesex
river as we can hope to get. Although it is true, as the author says, that the
Crane by Bedfont Powder Mills is sometimes called the Old River, it should
not be so named, for the Old River really ends at the confluence of the two
rivers. The Old River is so called to distinguish it from the New River
(not to be confused with *the* New River from Amwell) which flows not far
away, and cut (some say by Wolsey, some by Charles II., and some by
Elizabeth) to supply Hampton Court with water.
    The rivers of West Middlesex, both natural and artificial, are rather
confusing, especially as they are often, both rightly and wrongly, called by
different names when the same stream is meant. The Colne by Stanwell
and Staines Moors has several channels, some named and some not, while
the Crane is known as we have seen in part as Yeading Brook and
(wrongly) as the Old River. To make it a little harder still the genuine Old
River is often called the Duke's River, because it belongs to the Duke of
Northumberland, though originally called the Monks' River, as it was made
by them to supply Syon Monastery with water, or to feed their own
mill stream.   Then the New River is sometimes called the Cardinal's
River, sometimes the King's River and sometimes the Queen's River,
according to the different theories of its first cutting.
    Another theory, put forward by Mr. Herbert Gibbs, who has given a good
deal of study to the subject of Middlesex rivers, was that the Queen's River
was cut by Elizabeth to employ her soldiers in some useful work; and this
certainly may be the case. This little river, where it flows through Hampton,
is mentioned in one of Sir James Barrie's early books.
    The most popular name is still the Cardinal's River, for, although in
this case incorrect, his name seemed linked up with most things to do with
Hampton Court. Probably the truth on this perhaps not very vital point
is contained in Law's *Hampton Court,* where we find: " Though sometimes
called the Cardinal's River, the cutting of the canal from the Colne at
Longford over Hounslow Heath to Hampton Court was really done by
Charles I. in 1638. It is eleven miles long, and its real title is ' The King's
or Longford River.' " In Ryder's *Foedera* we get confirmation of this,
where we read: " 1638. Commissor to William, Lord Pagett, Francis, Lord
Cottington, and under-treasurer of the Exchequer, Sir Thos. Jermyn, vice-
chamberlain of the Household, and 15 others to make a new cut from the

Colnebrook river from Drayton Bridge over Hounslow Heath to fall into the Thames at Hampton Court." Again I wonder why all this labour was necessary for water, with the then unpolluted Thames flowing past their doors. The little river Exe that flows from Staines to Sunbury is also known as the Ash, the Ax, the Echel and the Echoal.

Those who would study this Riddle of the Rivers further should read the chapter on this topic in the *Middlesex* volume of the Cambridge County Geographies, where G. F. Bosworth has given an interesting account of these little waterways. In *London and Environs* (1811), by Rev. Harry Hunter, will be found an earlier description of the rivers, with a very good map of their courses. The information in the latter book is sometimes rather quaint (of course, there is the usual confusion between the Colne and the Crane); such as the interesting information: " On the Colne are oil mills which are confined to the making of oil." The author has many similar " surprises " in his pages!

All this, perhaps, explains the frequent mixing-up of the Crane and the Colne; for the former is often referred to as the Colne, yet they are some six miles apart at their nearest point. In the Middlesex section of Lambert's *Survey of London and Environs* (1800) we find: " The River Colne crosses Hounslow Heath, and on it are powder mills." This obviously should be the Crane, but a worse error is found in Beeton's *British Gazetteer*, which says: " Hounslow is on the Colne." It is not even on the Crane, which is two miles away; the Colne being about eight. There may, however, in this case be an explanation. Mr. Beeton was the husband of the famous cookery book writer, and if, as rumour has it, she first tried the recipes on him, perhaps he was suffering at the time of writing from such severe dyspepsia that he didn't care a damn if he put Hounslow on the Nile! Mr. Beeton died comparatively young, I believe. It is refreshing, however, to find that there *was* a Mr. Beeton. Who ever heard of Mr. Grundy or Mr. Malaprop?

*   *   *   *

Many writers confuse these two rivers from taking another's statement without verification; an easy, but often dangerous, method.

The best account of the Colne proper, and it is a delightful one, is in Thorne's *Rambles by Rivers*, that entertaining volume as rich in historical as in legendary lore. Here the story of this picturesque little river is traced from source to mouth, and in the account is woven much of interest concerning the country which lies on the Middlesex bank of the stream.

All the rivers in this part, of course, eventually reach Old Father Thames, which Mr. John Burns so truly called " Liquid History." Here there is no lack of books on various phases of its history; such as Murray's *Picturesque Tour of the Thames, The Book of the Thames* and many others, while in my own book *The Authors' Thames* I have dealt with its literary story. In all these books something—sometimes more and sometimes less— will be found of riverside Middlesex. In *On the Thames*, a study of the river in the reign of James I., by W. Cullery Gaze, and in F. V. Morley's interesting book on this river I'm afraid riverside Middlesex comes in the last category and is rather hurried over; a pity in two books otherwise so good. *The Tour of the Grand Junction Canal*, by J. Hassell (1819), with its wonderful colour plates, has also something of other Middlesex waterways.

There is a refreshing and unusual touch, however, in A. G. Linney's *Lure and Lore of London River*, for while writing of the Thames he finds time to describe—with a good deal of humour—a "voyage" up the mouth of the River Crane from Isleworth as far as this little river is navigable.

The Middlesex County Council are showing fine spirit and judgment in the matter of these small rivers. They have already acquired the Duke's River to save it from spoilation, and are making an attempt to save the Crane before it is too late.

I love out of the way stories, so I hope the reader will forgive a slight digression to relate a curious old custom of the riverside here, which I found in an old record, which stated: "Coke, the eminent lawyer, mentions a curious law once in use in Middlesex, for the punishment of one who stole lawfully marked swans. The bird was taken and hung by the beak from the roof of a house so that its feet just touched the ground. Wheat was then poured over the head of the swan until there was a pyramid of it from the floor sufficient to cover and hide the bird completely; this quantity of wheat was the fine paid by the culprit to the owner of the swan."

* * * * *

The Crane has its own modest little niche in literature and some of these accounts are certainly interesting. One of the earliest is that of the old topographer Leland, in his *Itinerary*, written about 1549, where he says: "There runneth a Land Water through the Hethe of Hundeslawe as a Drene to the whole Hethe, that is of great cumpace, and I passed by a bridge of Tymore over it." He does not give the stream a name, and the bridge was probably Babers Bridge on the Staines Road, one of the oldest spanning this river.

In Wilkes' poem *Hounslow Heath* he gives a description of the Crane as it flows past the mansion in Cranford Park, one of the most pleasant spots on its course:—

"Before the front a swelling river glides,
A lofty bridge bends o'er its rising sides,
A sinding vale the peaceful flood receives,
And here the stream its glassy bosom heaves."

Some years later in Pope's *History of Middlesex* we find a little about this stream, while in Middleton's *Agriculture of Middlesex* there is a most interesting account of the various rivers and canals that flow through the Hounslow Heath district. Nightingale, in 1816, calls this river the Carn.

In A. R. Hope Moncrieff's *Middlesex* there is a short but pleasing account of the Crane: "The Yeading Brook waters a stretch where itself seems the pleasantest feature. Here comes another of those odd blanks in the map of Middlesex, a flat of sodden green, looking wrapped in a November mist, through which loom snug farmhouses, but it is else so unpopulated that only one road runs across it. Bold explorers might find a touch of adventure in trespassing against notices which block approach to that devious brook, over a country of such agricultural note that it is not to be sneezed at unless by sufferers from hay fever. The Yeading Brook, further down promoted to the title of the Crane River, should have observance as the largest stream belonging to Middlesex. It rises in two forks on the slopes above Harrow, and after flowing right across the county has two mouths into the Thames, one with the by-name of Isleworth River."

These lines were penned some twenty-five years ago, and I fear by

SHEPPERTON CHURCH.

Drawn by Donald Maxwell
Drawing lent by Mr. Geoffrey Bles

**A NIGHT IMPRESSION OF
SUNBURY CHURCH.**

Drawn by Donald Maxwell
Drawing lent by Mr. Geoffrey Bles

ON OLD HOUNSLOW HEATH.

Drawn by Lucilla Maxwell from an 18th century picture

now some of those delightful blanks in our county's map are getting filled in, though a few are still there for ardent trespassers

Middlesex and Herts. Notes and Queries, usually accurate, slips up on this point, for we read there: " In 1718 there was a scheme proposed to draw water for London—another New River—from the Colne that drove Hounslow Powder Mills, but the scheme was found impracticable." This, of course, should again have been the Crane.

Clifford Harrison has written perhaps the most pleasing lines on this river, though even he makes the usual muddle about the names, but the title of the poem, *Fulwell Park,* settles beyond doubt of which river he writes, as the Colne does not flow within miles of that spot. The whole poem, found in his book *Lines in Pleasant Places,* is too long to quote in full, but the lines that matter are:—

" In Arcady, I think, is the address,
Not Middlesex. The Colne must rise, I'm sure,
Somewhere where Pan still hides from sight serene.
A Thames in miniature, it winds its way
Secure from public view. The very spot
Wherein to dream the livelong day!
And yet why dream in spot so fair? Ah, nay,
Open your eyes! Dream where you will, but not
                    Beside the Colne."

And yet enchanted day-dreams have been mine as I have lingered by those peaceful scenes of rare beauty that I have found—and learned to love—beside the *Crane.*

*   *   *   *   *

The mansion at Fulwell Park is mainly Georgian, though part of it dates back to the seventeenth century, when, as a smaller house, it was a hunting box of James II., probably at the time of the Hounslow camps, as the proximity of the Heath would make it a convenient spot.

In modern days it was, until recently, the home of another King— Manoel of Portugal—but by the time these words are in print Fulwell Park will not exist, that is in its pristine condition; more's the pity, for if any place cried out for salvation this estate did. Already laid out as a park it would have needed no conversion for public use. But it is gone now and the purse of a super-millionaire could not restore what has been destroyed; for the mellow hand of Time alone gave it such complete charm.

I paid a trespass to it just before its end and I felt like being at a funeral service. The hand of the vandal was already at work, and when I climbed through a window to explore the great empty mansion and heard my footsteps echo along the corridors and through the silent rooms I felt almost like a ghost myself, back from another age to visit its old haunts.

All was so still and silent in this great house, where two Kings have lived, that I should hardly have been surprised to meet either the spirit of a Jacobean courtier or a Portugese grandee, who would gibber at me in a strange tongue. I met no one, however; even the ghosts have deserted the unlucky old place.

The grounds are alike desolate. In one corner they are already building, and in another I came upon the Great Well—the Full Well that gives the estate and district its name. A huge brick circumference that looks dark and gaping beneath its old arched brick covering. This soon will probably be filled in, and its very site forgotten; it is probably older than the house itself.

The only thing that they have not been able to destroy is the river. It is a real beauty spot, and I hope the trees will be left on its banks, to let us still dream—with our backs to the nightmare—beside the Crane.

* * * * *

Now we are at Twickenham I should like to write more of it, for no town in the county has a more wonderful story in English Literature, but as it cannot be condensed into anything like the space at our disposal we must reluctantly leave it alone. Those interested will find three chapters on its literary history in *The Authors' Thames*.

There are, however, one or two curious items in its story that might find a place here; they are gathered in passing from various sources.

First of all it is strange to note how little R. S. Cobbett, in his wonderful book on Twickenham, has to say of so fine a place as Fulwell Park. There is one meagre notice only, which says: "Fulwell Lodge (late Park), the last house on the Hanworth Lodge, the seat of Sir W. Clay, Bart., and lately of his father, Sir William Clay, Bart., obtains its name from a spring of good water which exists on the estate. Mr. Dickason, father of the first Lady Clay, purchased it some years ago and left it to his daughter." And then there is a mention of it having been a hunting box, as we have seen, and that is all. My own notice of it has been brief enough, but that was in passing, whereas the former book was devoted entirely to Twickenham and its old houses.

In the earliest history of this town—that of Ironside—we read of the Great Frost of 1788, and how "when the thaw came suddenly and with a great noise, occasioned by the separation of the ice, it threw over the adjacent land as far as 100 feet from the river pieces of ice a ton in weight. Both sides of the river had the appearance of a rocky shore as far as the eye could reach and looked very awful." The last expression sounds quaint to modern ears, but the use of the word "awful" in this case is far nearer its truer meaning than as now generally used.

In the eighteenth century a vicar of Twickenham was named Du Val; but if he were any relation to a more famous bearer of this name, who also knew this district well, is more than I can say.

In Mid-Victorian days there lived in Twickenham two men who both had designs on the peace of the Pope; for the Rev. George Townsend went to Rome with the optimistic idea of trying to convert the Pope to Protestantism! Another man also went from this town about the same time with even more sinister ideas against the Pontiff, for he took with him a large knife with which he intended to cut the Pope's throat! The second man was put in an asylum before he could carry out his deed of blood—and the account quaintly tells us that *in honour of His Holiness* the would-be throat cutter thoughtfully put a new handle on his knife before he set out! But what happened to Mr. Townsend? I have never heard of a Protestant Pope, so presumably he did not succeed in his mission either—perhaps the Pope won, and Mr. Townsend became an R.C. instead!

In a small cottage on the Staines Road, not far from Twickenham Green, once lived Joanna Southcott, the mad woman who claimed to be an inspired prophetess, and imposed on many credulous people with her writings and preachings. Cobbett tells that as late as 1872 he found many adherents to her in the town, though she died in 1814.

In connection with Joanna I cannot resist a personal story which is not inappropriate perhaps. Not long ago I was the victim of an accident—a motor-cycle knocked me senseless. I came to in the ambulance, when the attendant kept worrying me to know if I were Church of England or not. Feeling half dead I suppose I was fed up with his persistence, and answered " My dear chap, what *does* it matter if I am A Believer in Joanna Southcott? " The attendant, never having heard of this worthy lady, subsided. The cream of the jest came next day in hospital, when the Matron said to me: " I hear you were delirious in the ambulance, for the attendant said that when he asked your religion you *started talking about some young lady!* "

Shades of Joanna!

2. The River Exe.

If you say " Do you know the Exe in Middlesex? " most people imagine it a riddle on the last letter, and when you explain that you mean a river they ask, rather pityingly, if you haven't made a mistake and mean Devonshire?

I do not. I mean Middlesex; for the Exe is a pleasant little river that flows across the south-west corner of the county, incidentally creating an island, which, following on the first idea, might be called " X Island," for so few know of it.

The Exe does not rise in the usual way but flows out of the Colne on the borders of Bucks, and enters the Thames at Sunbury Mead. There is no Exe Valley in Middlesex, but it is a very pleasant plain across which it winds. It starts on Staines Moor, crosses the old Roman road—the legions had to ford it—and then goes over Shortwood Common to Ashford Ford, and then on to Littleton, past the huge reservoir that dams and damns this charming old village. On through Littleton Park it flows, passing between the hamlets of Charlton and Shepperton Green, and on under Gaston and Hoo Bridges to Sunbury Mead. The latter bridge is now very civilised, but up to quite recently it was an old-fashioned wooden plank bridge, with a water-splash for vehicles.

In spite of the Exe being the smaller river the " story " on its banks is more varied than that of the Crane, for whereas the latter flowed right across the one-time heath, the former skirted it, and consequently touched more inhabited parts of the south-western corner of the county.

One of the few writers who has touched upon " Exe Island," though briefly, is the anonymous author of the *Chronicle of English Counties*, where he tells us: " To explore the peninsula cut off by the highway between Brentford and Staines we may take first a cross-country road to Ashford. The first cause of Ashford, the ford over the little river, once the Esk, no doubt, varies the dullness of the way; a pretty scene, with a planked bridge, and a run of water beneath, with reeds and water meads, and sometimes a water-hen splashing about, and all with a background of dark firs. Ashford itself comes next, with villas and cottages about the little church, and bigger houses scattered about it in the midst of lawns and gardens."

This is Ashford of 1886, hardly recognisable now, but even more strange is the writer's account of the next place: " Close by is a kind of wilderness, called Littleton, with gorse and thorn bushes, and swarming with rabbits, while some fine old trees give a dignity to the scene. Littleton looks interesting, and as if it had a history, but nobody seems to know anything, about it." I am afraid the writer could not have looked very far for information, for Littleton existed in Saxon days.

We can now look a little more closely at the various places the River Exe touches, or flows near, in its short course of some five miles as the crow flies, but rather more as the fish swims.

We have heard something in these pages of the lonely stretch of country known as Staines Moor, and it is just south of that portion whose name is reminiscent of a sermon—Furthermoor—that the Exe starts on its travels. Shortwood Common is a pleasant, well-watered spot that lies on the left of the main road, which it borders for some way and leads on to Ashford Ford, a cluster of houses that has increased of recent years. Ashford itself lies to the eastward, and if a part of Staines Moor reminds us of a sermon Ashford may well remind us of a hymn-book, for it is certainly ancient and modern.

It is a deceptive place at first glance; few towns hide their antiquity better. It has all the appearance of being modern, yet it is ancient. The chief reason for this false idea is that there is no old church, the keynote to most old places. There was a Saxon church here once, but it was demolished in 1796, though its successor's life was short, as in 1858 it was in turn pulled down to make room for the present structure.

Lysons reminds us that the name of the place " is written Exeforde in *Domesday*, in records of the 13th and 14th centuries Echelforde, or Echelsford, being so called from the ford over the little river Exe or Echel. When the survey was taken Robert, Earl of Mortain in Normandy and of Cornwall in England, held an estate in Ashford, which in the reign of Edward the Confessor was the property of Aluric, a servant of the Abbot of Chertsey, within the Manor of Staines; but the Earl made it an appendage of his Manor of Kennington (Kempton).

" The manor appears from a very early period till after the dissolution of the religious houses to have belonged to Staines, and King Edgar gave it with land at Echelsford to the Abbot of Westminster." More of this can be found in *The Antiquities of Westminster*. Finally the manor passed into possession of the Crown and was annexed to the " Honour of Hampton Court." Since then it has had many owners, after being given to a favourite of Queen Elizabeth.

There is nothing special about Ashford that calls for notice here, unless it is a few quaint bits from its parish registers. Here in the olden days certain sums were paid for the " Kyllynge of sparrowes and other vermin in ye churche," and a lady left " £7 a year to her dog with a reversion after its death to six poor old men."

I am glad to see that a Middlesex farm recently held its own, for at a Surrey Agricultural Show the prize, open to both counties, for the best kept farm was won by Messrs. W. and S. Curtis of Ashford, who were also successful for growing corn. A triumph for an " urban " county.

At Ashford I nearly fell into a trap. Not a pit digged by mine enemies, or even a man-trap through trespassing. The trap was on paper and due to not realising (as I ought to by this time) that things are not always what they seem.

I read in a book dated 1801 that " the present number of houses in Ashford, Middlesex, is 38. In the year 1548 there were in this parish 77 houslyng people." The latter statement I took to be, considering the date, an archaic way of saying that there were 77 householders. Yet, by some instinct, I was not quite satisfied; the " new " word was old enough to rouse suspicions. So I ferreted the thing out and proved my second thoughts to be correct. The quotation was taken, unacknowledged, from Lysons, who explains the real meaning of the word in this interesting note: " Howsel, or Housel, is the Eucharist—to housel is to receive the Eucharist—houslyng people are, therefore, communicants."

In *A Pilgrimage of the Thames,* by Donald Maxwell, will be found reference to Pontefract in Middlesex, and lest I am accused of stealing my brother's thunder a word will explain. Although we have both written topographical books for some years and have done much exploring together, we have never clashed up to now. On the River Exe, however, we did clash, not as rivals, but collaborators, for we went out hunting together and agreed to "share the bag." Among my contributions was the discovery about Pontefract, which he used in his book, and in return he has allowed me " full cribbing rights " of his theory regarding the river's name, and also (a little later) the humorous, but striking, description of Shepperton as the village of the Comic Opera, and the idyllic simile concerning the Shepherds and the Silent Pool.

First for Pontefract. Here again most people misunderstand and ask if I don't mean Yorkshire? Once again I say " No, I mean Middlesex." My authority in this case is the *Transactions of the London and Middlesex Archaelogical Society : 1860,* where appears:—

PONTEFRACT IN MIDDLESEX.

In a recent number of " Notes and Queries " are pointed out five documents of the year 1321, which are printed in Ryder's *Foedera* and that bear date " Teste Rege, apud Pontem Fractum super Thamis " or " A correspondent had expressed his opinion that Kingston Bridge was the ' Pomfret on the Thames,' but it is now stated that at the village of Shepperton-Ashford, about three miles from Sunbury and seven from Kingston, there is a place still known by the name of the Broken Bridge, or Broken Splash, and it is also stated that, about 20 years back, traces of a road laid on piles, running directly towards the Thames and crossing several small pieces of water on its way, but stopping at the brink of the river, could still be traced."

This is extraordinarily interesting and still another of those "unknown" bits of history in which this county abounds. Equally interesting is the account of the origin of the river's name in the *Pilgrimage* : " The explanation of this old name, Exe, that gives Exeford instead of Ashford in *Domesday* is simple. The Gaelic or Erse word for water is ' uisage,' and from this comes our word ' whisky.' All those river names—Esk, Ash, Usk and Exe, and the like—simply mean water, so at one time, no doubt, the waters of the Colne were known as Exe, and this one example is a survival of the old Celtic name (the same writer states that the Colne was probably so-called by the Romans as it had something to do with the ' river of the Colonia '). When Exeford began to be spelled as Ashford the purists were no doubt shocked at the Ford of the Ash crossing the River Exe, and so the river, too, became Ash to satisfy everybody who gloried in consistency."

After leaving Ashford the Exe skirts Laleham, one of the prettiest of Thames-side villages, which, like many another place, is suffering from that holy-horror, the estate developer, whose latest victim is Laleham House, the seat of a former Earl of Lucan, who was wounded in the charge of the Light Brigade; and also where a former Queen of Portugal lived in 1829. I am glad to find, however, that there is a chance of some of the finely wooded grounds being saved for the public.

It was once the seat of the Lonsdales, and here, in the eighteenth century, lived Sir James Lowther, who became first Earl of that name.

I was told recently of some excavations at Laleham House grounds where some old bricks and paving were dug up—"said to be the remains of Laleham Priory." *Was* there ever a Laleham Priory? I can find no trace of it. Lysons, Thorne and Walford, the usual "quick reference" sources, have no mention of it, nor have such learned authorities on the subject as Dugdale's *Monasticon Anglicanum,* Tanner's *Notitia Monastica,* or Stevens' *Ancient Monasteries, Abbeys and Priories.*

Lysons certainly says "The Abbot and Convent of Westminster had an exemplification of the privileges and liberties in Laleham in the year 1254," but this does not prove the existence of a Priory. We know, too, that the manor was once held by Estrild, a Nun. Possibly there may have been a Cell, out of which the imagination of the finder built his shadowy Priory. I should like "chapter and verse." I do not doubt for a moment that the finds are ancient, and the source from which I had this information is quite reliable, but if they were monastic it is curious that such authorities as I have mentioned ignore it.

Since writing the above lines—which may stand as a point of interest— I have solved this "mystery." There was no Laleham Priory, but there certainly were monastic buildings here. They belonged to Chertsey Abbey, and are referred to under that head. They consisted of a grange—or monastic farm—and a Monk's House, and it is doubtless the remains of these that were dug up here

Laleham has a quiet literary notoriety in connection with the Arnolds, father and son, schoolmaster and poet. The former was a resident here, and in his *Life of Arnold* Dean Stanley speaks of his love for this village: "Years after he left Laleham he retained his early affection for it,· and entertained a hope to return in his old age . . . . . after he would revisit it and delighted in showing his children his former haunts; in looking once again on his favourite views of the great plain of Middlesex—the lonely walks along the quiet banks of the Thames—the retired garden, with its wilderness of trees, behind the house and the churchyard with its family graves."

The house in which he lived has been demolished, but it was here that his son Matthew was born in 1822. Although the poet lived mostly at Cobham in Surrey he kept a kindly corner in his heart for his birthplace, and was buried here at his own wish, "near to," as he wrote, "the great road to Staines that runs through the flat, drained Middlesex plain, with its pollarded elms."

In *The Story of the Thames,* by J. E. Vincent, we find a good description of Dr. Arnold's life at Laleham, and the author adds: "The associations of this Middlesex village are precious to all English speaking men.'

William Watson wrote of his fellow poet who lies sleeping in this riverside village:—

"Lulled by the Thames, he sleeps, and not
               By Rotha's wave . . . .
And nigh to where his bones abide,
The Thames with its unruffled tide
Seems like his genius typified—
               Its strength, its grace,
Its lucid green, its sober pride, its tranquil pace.'

Frank Buckland, the naturalist, was a fellow pupil of Matthew Arnold at Laleham, at a school kept by the former's uncle. Very different types of writers were passing visitors here, and one of them wrote, during a river trip in a cumbersome craft called "The Ark": "The river was nearly new to me hereabouts, and much better than I expected, especially from Chertsey to Staines; it is full of strange character in many places—Laleham, for instance, with its enormous willows, and suggestions of old houses on the banks." He goes on to describe how he and his fellow voyager were chaffed by the idle river crowd. Probably no one among that jeering crowd had the least idea who the rowers were, or how cleverly they could use their skulls—if not their sculls—for the writer was William Morris and his companion William de Morgan.

Dr. Stukely in his *Itinerary* tells us that at Greenfield Common, to the north-east of the village, was one of Caesar's camps, after he had crossed the Thames, and where he received an embassy from the Londoners. There is little enough to be seen of it to-day; in fact, Brewer, in his *Beauties of England,* casts grave doubts on the theory, though Lysons, on the other hand, gives actual measurements. No one can solve the problem now, but there certainly was an encampment of some sort once. Possibly one of those thrown up by Theodosius. Whether British or Roman is perhaps doubtful, but another writer's record says: "Between Ashford and Laleham Roman coins have been dug up in quantities sufficient to make it probable that these level plains were once the site of a camp or station during the occupation of the Imperial Eagles." Another authority states that a Roman Temple once existed in Laleham, which, if we accept the Roman camp as a fact, is certainly probable.

In *The Ambulator* of 1811 we find recorded of Laleham: "The Thames narrows considerable here, and about the shallows the water is beautifully transparent. The tranquility of the scenery, the various objects gliding on the stream, and groups of cattle in the adjacent meadows, is all pleasing to the contemplative eye."

It is still possible to find such a picture in certain parts; though the contemplative eye is apt to get a few shocks, as in the case of the ghastly pylons that mar the beauty of the meadows. Wherever we see these hideous metal towers spoiling a fair countryside we are reminded of the hymn words, "Where every prospect pleases, and only man is vile." And he can be horribly vile at times.

Laleham is Leleham in *Domesday,* and it differs somewhat from most places mentioned as having certain of its lands held by "one Estrild, a nun"; women landowners, especially nuns, were rare in those days.

The mention of *Domesday* brings up a mild mystery that I have found here. What is the exact meaning of the name "Domesday Bushes" marked on an old map as being between Laleham and Shepperton? There is no mention of any particular bushes in the *Domesday* account, though a "meadow for seven ploughs" is referred to. I do not even remember if there are any bushes in the spot indicated (rather hard to fix accurately as the name straggles on the map) but I think there is a hedge of sorts. At the other end of Middlesex, at Southgate, there is the Domesday Tree still standing, but bushes would hardly be taken into account, except, perhaps, as a boundary.

I discovered locally that there are some fields at Shepperton still called "Dumsey Meadows," which seems to be an obvious corruption of the original word, and it is a remarkable case of the survival of ancient minor place names.

In that most interesting book, *The Thames Highway*, by F. S. Thacker, there is some mention of the " Dumsey Bushes."

Chronicles of English Counties speaks of this village in connection with another meadow: " Laleham is a nice little village, on a pleasant bend of the river, where the banks are shaded with ash and willow, and rows of elms. Here are old-fashioned red-brick houses with roomy gardens. Ponds and ducks abound, and ditches conduct the waters of the district in a primitive way towards the river. There is a rambling old church, very ancient, and a parsonage covered with syringa. Happy, too, is Laleham in that it has no history of definite character, though tradition speaks of a certain river meadow gained for the parish by the pious care of its inhabitants in burying a drowned person found on its banks."

Before leaving Laleham we may notice Thorne's slightly derogatory words, and their rather naive justification: " Laleham is a quiet commonplace, riverside village, with a few good old fashioned houses; the country is flat, and the broad meadows can hardly be deemed picturesque. But the scenery grows in favour with intelligent people." The only trouble is to find the latter.

Not far away is Feltham, tne Felteham of *Domesday*, and literally meaning the more picturesque name " The Field Village." It is another place that hides its past and with little to record of its present. A long straggling street with a green and a pond, with a few old fashioned houses and shops intermixed with the more modern ones—and you have Feltham.

The old church of St. Dunstan is a pleasing brick edifice with a tower and wooden spire, which superseded an older structure in 1802. Though not ancient it is always known as the " old " church to distinguish it from the new St. Catherine's near the station, whose tower is a landmark for miles.

In the old churchyard lies Ryland, the first engraver in the " dotted style." He was engraver to the King, when (as an old book informs us) he " executed the King and Queen with great skill." This fate overtook *him* in reality subsequently, for, as we read in *Tyburn Tree*, by Alfred Marks, that interestingly gruesome book of annals of this grim spot: " In 1783 William Wynne Ryland, executed at Tyburn for forgery. Ryland was an engraver of repute, in the manner of Bartolozzi. He is the subject of a careful study, perhaps too sympathetic, by Horace Bleackley, in his *Distinguished Victims of the Scaffold.* " Ryland had the " honour " of being almost the last to be hanged at Tyburn.

There died at Feltham in 1882 an old lady, one of the last survivors of the great school of actors to which belonged Mrs. Siddons, John Kemble, Edmund Kean and Mrs. Jordan. This was Frances Maris Kelly, who, born in 1790, trod the boards with the above, and was in Colman's company at the Haymarket as early as 1807.

In 1634 a terrible fire swept Feltham, which we are told " destroyed the manor-house of Lord Cottington, 13 dwelling houses and 16 barns, being almost the whole village." Were life and personal property saved there is one part of Feltham I should like to see burned down to-day, and that is a certain new street near the old church; I do not know the name, for after one devastating glance, which almost took my breath away, I always turn my head when passing. I think it is the most blatantly ugly

THE OLD CHURCH, FELTHAM, 1807.

Block lent by Middlesex Chronicle.

road in all Middlesex; and the builder who put it up (I will not insult architects by assuming one was employed) ought to be fined heavily—and then made to pull it down!

Near the old church there stood until recently a fine old farm with two white gables and a long tiled sloping roof. It was known as Blaize Farm, and I had admired it long before I discovered its history; in fact, it was by chance only that I found it had any. It was called "Nell Gwynne's Farm" locally, though beyond this no one seemed to know anything about it. The name of Sweet Nell, however, naturally suggests "Old Rowley," and on investigation what little I could discover associated this old farm with Charles II. in the days when Nell Gwynne was his quean.

Subsequently I found the following in the *Home Counties Magazine*: "In the Lord Chamberlain's records is a warrant dated at Hampton Court, July, 1666. 'These are to testify that by the command of the King I have taken the house called Greshams Farm, situated on Hounslow Heath, in the parish of Hampton in the County of Middlesex, for the use of the King's Majesty.' For what purpose did the King require this lonely house? "

Knowing Charles II. I will give the reader one guess. This may or may not have been Blaize Farm, for names can be altered, and Feltham in those days may have been included under Hampton. Of course Charles was a broad-minded man where the ladies were concerned, and may have needed *two* lonely farms!

That he knew the Heath is proved by a note in an old Gazetteer, which stated "Hounslow Heath was a Royal preserve as late as the end of the 16th century and used for falconry," the writer adding, with a touch of unconscious humour: "His Majesty King Charles II. was much attached to the Birds."

It is known that Nell Gwynne's sister married a highwayman, who no doubt when employed upon the Heath found Blaize Farm a convenient hiding place; so it is not impossible that on a visit to his sister-in-law the Knight of the Road met the King of the Realm. Perhaps they had a friendly drink together! Charles, with all his faults, was really a very human person.

I went down to Feltham specially to get a photograph of Blaize Farm, but I was a few days too late. To my disgust all I found was a heap of stones. I spent some hours in Feltham trying to obtain a photograph. Plenty were offered me of hideous new roads of ugly houses (probably with an aspidistra in every window). I am afraid I shocked one worthy shopkeeper with the warmth of my remarks when this happened for the fifth time! It is an amazing thing that a beautiful and historical old house like this should never have been photographed (as far as I could discover), when postcards of vile modern ones can be had by the thousand. *What* a comment on the modern mind!

Southville, once a hamlet north of Feltham, is now absorbed—one might almost say "sunk," so completely has it disappeared; but on all maps you will find it marked. Near the old church is "Feltham Hill." On the map, that is; but where is it in reality? The country round it is as flat as a pancake for two miles, save two artificial "bumps" one by the station and one at Hanworth Mount, so called by some humourist because of the remains of an old ice-house earthed over, and this may disappear any time! Blackmore in *Kit and Kitty* confuses us still more by describing children "rolling down Feltham Hill."

This has often caused me a mild wonder, though I had no explanation to offer; but a possible reason for this paradoxical name was given by an old lady resident, who ingeniously pointed out that there is a small brook separating the parishes of Feltham and Sunbury which was once known as Feltham Rill; and she suggests that the name in the course of years, and *vox populi,* has become corrupted. This is ingenious, but the real explanation of this name goes deeper than this and can be found in Sir Montagu Sharpe's *Middlesex,* where he writes of the Roman landmarks, including the *botontini,* or artificial mounds. One of these existed at Feltham, and it is from this that this " hill " and others derive their name.

Mystery hills seem popular hereabouts, for on the same map that showed me " Domesday Bushes " I found just north of Feltham a place marked " Bhudda Hills " (sometimes spelt " Buda "). Not only are there no hills here, but what on earth has this Oriental deity got to do with this village? Middlesex still preserves some of her mysteries; even to me, who has managed to ferret out (by diligent research aided by a little luck) a good many of them.

Some of these names we have noticed in passing and have guessed at their meanings, and some are most interesting. Here are a few more from old maps and other sources. Black Moor Hill, near Strawberry Hill, may be a memory of some bleak portion of the old Heath; Beavers Farm, a picturesque little place near the barracks, may recall a time when these little animals, once resident in England, lived on the banks of the Crane; Babe Bridge must be a corruption of Babers, and has no connection with children; Hanger Pits recalls an old woodland and not aeroplanes; Butchers Grove is the old Bath Road trotting ground for that fraternity; Maltmans Bridge is a memory of the old pack-horse trains; and we have Great Housen Close, an interesting survival of the old plural form.

Then there are Cuckoo Pound and Withygate Field by Staines; Coldharbour, of Roman origin, near Hayes; By-the-Ways near Hospital Bridge; and Gospel Oak, not far from Boston Manor.

On a map of 1635 is Crick Old Haven on the Bath Road, near which are Magpie Meadows, while at Bedfont is marked Hag's Lane—the last probably a corruption of Hog's Lane and having no connection with any old beldames of former days.

All these names have meanings, some are probably corruptions of ancient British or Roman names. All could probably be traced if time allowed. I have never discovered any " Devil names " in Middlesex, though often found in Surrey and Sussex. Why his Satanic Majesty avoided this county is more than I can say, unless, as regards the south-western part of it, he found the river mists and cold winds sweeping across the Heath in winter too much contrast with the Nether Regions; or he may have found the Heathens too pious for his machinations. A wiser head than mine must solve this riddle.

The lady already mentioned, finding I was interested, asked me into her sitting room. I did more than just step from the road into her house — I stepped from the twentieth century right back into the eighteenth. It was with pride and reverence she showed me her treasures, and wonderful they were. The room, she told me, had not been altered materially since 1787, when her great-aunt (I think) first came to live here. I can well believe it, for everything breathed of a more peaceful past. Delightful old coloured aquatints were on the walls; chairs, tables and cabinets were equally pleasing, even to one quaint piece of furniture known as a "coffin stool," that had been given to her aunt by a former vicar, and came from the older church. Another curio was an old copper beer-warmer, with a hook to go over the bars of the grate.

There was one ornament, however, in which Miss Wilkes took special pride, and as she showed it she remarked: "Now, I do not suppose you know what this is." It was then I made my second error in tact, for when she found I *did* know I saw a shadow of disappointment cross her kindly face for a second; I should have pleaded ignorance, as it would have pleased her to enlighten me. The article was a rushlight-holder that had been used by her family in former generations. People made many strange guesses, she said, as to its origin; one lady stoutly avering it to be a curling-tongs!

Altogether it was an afternoon that will linger in my mind for all time, that wonderful little glimpse into a fascinating yesterday. The whole room somehow reminded me strongly of *Cranford,* and she herself recalled a character from that sweet and gentle romance—I can pay her no higher compliment.

* * * * * *

We must return to the banks of the Exe, from which we have so pleasantly strayed. The next place ahead is Littleton, though all that can be seen as we approach is the huge wall of the reservoir—which, I believe, is the largest in the world, though it has overshadowed a charming village. By a mild trespass and the negotiation of some rather unpleasant spiked railings, this vast sheet of water can be viewed. I first saw it at twilight when the distant shore seemed an immense distance away. It was certainly impressive, and were it not for the high bank, which cuts off the view from below, it might even be a feature in the landscape—as at Ruislip. I hear that two more reservoirs are to be built at Littleton—isn't it swamped enough already?

I was told by someone away from the place that Littleton Church and village were submerged beneath the waters of the reservoir. This is naturally untrue, but I find that some cottages, a farm and a chapel were actually left when the waters were let in; in fact, my informant waxed most eloquent and gave me all sorts of impossible details concerning this, and with a little encouragement would, I think, have painted a graphic word picture of the terrified vicar and villagers fleeing before the engulfing flood.

Littleton is a delightful little place with a small green, which curiously enough lacks the inevitable village inn, but it is bordered on one side by some fine old houses, notably Littleton Farm, with its old farm yard, now rather civilised, and the old Manor House and Vicarage nearby.

Here is the account—notable in a technical publication—by the Metropolitan Water Board's brochure, which is written with far more imagination than most of such productions. It was published in 1925 when the reservoir was opened. "Contrary to rumour," it states, "the village of Littleton is not to be drowned out of existence. It is a pretty and sequestered spot and well justifies its name, for it is among the smallest of villages, itself the centre of one of the smallest Middlesex parishes. . . . The ground falls gradually towards the Thames, the higher and more northern parts being well wooded, with two stretches of common, known as Astlam and Littleton Commons. Although well within the suburban area

(I do not agree with this!) Littleton is practically unknown, being outside the beaten route of the great highways. The village itself is one of the least spoiled in the county. It is built entirely of red-brick and presents a cheerful and peaceful aspect. It centres round an interesting parish church, with a few houses scattered here and there. There is no village street and there is not, and never has been, any public house or shop in the parish, and the only trade represented is that of the blacksmith."

The red-brick church is one of the oldest and most beautiful in the county. It dates from 1135, and has a font said to have been there since that date. There are memorials to the Wood family, former lords of the manor, and some old flags of the Grenadier Guards. There is also a small stained glass window painted by Sir John Millais, who once had a summer home in the village.

This little churchyard is a beautiful and peaceful spot, rather marred, however, by one terribly incongruous and huge modern mausoleum quite out of keeping with its surroundings.

We are getting sadly used to finding the old mansions and parklands of Middlesex falling into the hands of the builder and seeing him do his horrid worst with them, that it comes as quite a shock—albeit a pleasant one this time—to discover an estate in which this process is reversed, and where, though it has changed hands and is no longer used for residential purposes, its old-world character is being preserved as far as possible, although the uses to which it is now being put are as poles asunder from those it has known since medieval days. In fact its two stories are both romantic, and from their very difference we might almost call the history of this estate " The Romance of Two Worlds."

The estate in question is Littleton Park; and it will be best to deal with its " dual personalities " separately. First its ancient history. It is not mentioned in *Domesday,* and Lysons states that the first owner of the manor was Sir Guy de Bryen in 1350. He was Standard-Bearer to Edward III. at the taking of Calais in 1347, and apparently received this estate as a reward for gallant service; for the King granted him " free warren in his demesne lands at Littleton."

In 1372 Sir Guy gave the advowson of the church to the Priory of Hounslow; and it is interesting to note that the rent of the whole estate in the Middle Ages was one pound of pepper annually. Perhaps the best way to learn concisely the story of the various hands through which these lands have passed would be a consultation of the " History Board " in the Great Hall of the present mansion, since it is the only one of its kind I have ever seen and owes its origin, I believe, to Sir Edward Nicholl, a former owner. The details on this board are too long to quote here, but for those who cannot visit the house a full copy of it can be found in *The Life of Sir Edward Nicholl,* by T. C. Wignall.

Another good account of Littleton and its descent as a manor will be found in the *Victoria County History of Middlesex,* Volume Two. It is hoped one day that volume one will be written, for if every account is as good as this it will be of the greatest use to students of this county's history. It was written, of course, in pre-war days, but this makes little difference to the description, luckily.

The "History Board" just mentioned is so complete that there is nothing to add about the former owners of the estate. I hate to be too critical over the compilation, obviously a work that entailed research and trouble, but I should like to know (in view of Lysons' remarks, which are usually most accurate) whence the early history is derived. The compiler assumes Littleton to have belonged to the Manor of Laleham, though there is no actual evidence of this; its lands might easily have been part of Charlton or Shepperton, both *Domesday* manors nearer to Littleton.

That Littleton existed in Saxon days is proved by its name. Again Lysons is my authority, for he tells us: "In ancient records this place is called Lytlyngton, Litlington and Littleton. *Litling* is the Saxon word for infant, and was used, it is probable, to express anything small or diminutive."

Walford describes Littleton Park as "a magnificent mansion standing in a pleasant but level park. . . . . The house was of the Dutch type, reminding one of Kensington Palace. It contained some fine pictures, which perished in a fire (in 1874), including Hogarth's 'Actors dressing in a barn.'" The original park was much larger than at present, some 600 acres compared with about 60, and the house was built in the reign of William III., said to be by the same workmen then employed in erecting King William's Buildings at Hampton Court. This seems feasible, as the Thomas Wood of that time was Ranger there. Sir Christopher Wren was said to have assisted in the design of the house.

King Edward VII., when Prince of Wales, was often a visitor here as the guest of General Wood, but a more frequent Royal visitor was William IV., and in a summer house by the river—a typical "period" building—is an urn (the sort you see in old prints usually with a languishing female leaning against it) with the inscription:—

> "This urn is placed by Lady Caroline Wood
> to commemorate the last visit of King
> William IV. to these grounds.
> Anno Domini 1836."

There is another building near the reservoir bank known as "The Pineapple Tower" belonging to those times, but if erected in honour of the same monarch I cannot say; and still another one brought here from Buckingham Palace more recently.

The River Exe is here widened into a lake, and very effective it is, with its statue of Father Thames in mid-stream and its wooded islands.

The lands of the estate are especially fine, with some beautiful trees; they have all the characteristics of an old English park. It is an ideal place to spend an idle busy day, as I did recently by the courtesy of the present owners, for here is plenty of "such stuff as dreams are made on" to aid the waking visions.

The modern house dates from the fire just mentioned, except one corner which survived; but it is a pleasing red-brick structure, set by a really wonderful lawn, to which an ancient cedar, said to be 300 years old, lends an added dignity. The main hall may be called baronial without exaggeration; it is a splendid place, and has its own story to tell, for the fine oak ceiling came from the old House of Commons, and the marbles in the vestibule from Westminster Abbey. These depict the "Death of Nelson" and the "Battle of Waterloo." How these came to be here is a mystery, and several "hints" I am told have been made to former owners as to their return; but surely the Abbey is groaning beneath enough marble (especially pear-shaped worthies) without coveting these !

In this hall are some stags' heads shot on the estate, for the reservoir covers the old deer park. Although no deer roam the estate now it is not without wild life; hares can be seen in plenty, while quite recently a vixen and her cubs were discovered on the reservoir bank.

Hounds were once kept here, in connection with which a good story is told. During the Peninsular War the Duke of Wellington sent for some hounds so that his officers could get some hunting, and it was from Littleton that the pack was sent out. Unfortunately on the first run the fox over-ran the enemy's lines with the hounds in full cry, when the latter were promptly captured by the French. This recalls Conan Doyle's delightful story " How the Brigadier slew the Fox " in *Brigadier Gerard*; and it is probable that it was from this Littleton pack that the idea originated.

To return to the interior of the mansion, so full of interest. One of the many things to be seen there is actually built into the structure, and that is the Robing Room used by King Edward VII. at his coronation at Westminster Abbey. What interested me more, however, was the Deed Box, not old in itself but with precious contents. Here are stored the deeds of the estate from 1373 up to the present time. To read all these word for word would mean a deep knowledge of old Latin and medieval English, though it was fascinating to pick words out here and there, and to admire the wonderful work of these old scriveners, and the great seals attached to many of the parchments yellow with age. On the Deed Box is a reference to the Manor of Astlam, once a sub-manor to Littleton, whose very name seems submerged with its lands beneath the waters of the great reservoir. In old maps there are some buildings marked " Astlam " hereabouts, though absent from modern ones, but if they were the remains of an old manor house or merely farm buildings is uncertain; very likely the former descended to the later, as is often the case. Anyhow the calm waters of the " inland sea " of Middlesex must keep its secret. I daresay it *could* be discovered by a diver—into old records, not beneath the waters—but it would be a long job.

A visitor to Littleton Park will notice an unusual thing in the gardens in front of the mansion, and that is railway lines on most of the paths and two " tunnels." These are the remains of the famous model railway, made to carry passengers, built here by Sir Edward Nicholl, and which delighted so many youngsters. The miniature rolling-stock is now to be seen at Southsea.

* * * * * *

The full story of the modern Littleton Park, or " Sound City," to give it its professional name, cannot be told here, but it is a marvellous one. When I trespassed in it I was " captured " by two of the directors—Mr. Norman Loudon and Mr. M. Bryant—who very sportingly gave me permission to roam where I liked; and I have not spent a more entertaining day for a long time.

In addition to the scenic beauties already briefly described it is intensely interesting to see the technical side of film production; for here and there one came across a " street " one plank thick, or a rural " cottage " where you walked through the front door to nothing! Though what interested me most was the " Lists," where a medieval tournament scene had recently been filmed.

There was one strange coincidence in connection with the former owner of the estate—Sir Guy de Bryen—and that was that he was an ancestor of Mr. Bryant, the director mentioned, whose name is derived from the earlier form. Until he came to look through the deeds of the estate he was not aware that his distinguished forebear had once owned it. Mr. Bryant's crest—a flag and a staff—is a reminder of the standard borne by Sir Guy at Calais.

* * * * * *

Before the River Exe flows through the meadows, and by two picturesque (except to motors) splashes on to Shepperton, it skirts the hamlet of Charlton. Although Domesday accounts are very similar in this case, it may be interesting to quote part of it; for the reason that so small (and then even smaller) a place should have been given such prominence. The Domesday Surveyors were certainly thorough, especially in this quiet corner of Middlesex, which almost seemed better known then than it is now!

Here is Lysons' account, incorporating the older one, somewhat condensed: " Charlton, anciently called Cerdertone and Cherdyngton, is thus described. Roger de Rames holds the manor of Cerdertone in the hundred of Spelthorne. The land is four carucates and the villans keep one plough. There is a bordar who has eight acres and six slaves. There is pasture for the cattle of the manor. The annual value is 30s. Two brothers held it, one a servant of Archbishop Stigand and the other of the Earl of Levin. The manor was given at an early period to the Prior of Merton and became vested in the Crown in 1538."

Charlton to-day is a quiet, sleepy little place, with a small but picturesque village street, with the usual sprinkling of cottages, some larger houses, such as Charlton Court and Charlton House, three delightful old farms, and the pretty little whitewashed and thatched inn, " The Harrow "; all lying amidst pleasant pastoral country.

Shepperton, like many very old places, has had varied names. In *Domesday* it was Scepertone, but earlier it bore the Saxon name of Sceapheard-ton, and later Scepertune, all of which mean " a habitation of the Shepherds." Yet what pastoral records it has refer to cows and not sheep, for in bygone days there was a curious old law in force here known as Cow Farrens, by which the common pasture lands were divided among 117 inhabitants, each of whom was allowed to keep one cow and no more, at the expense of the community.

It is still a quiet, and in these days a fairly peaceful, place, though it wakes up a little during the river season. The village " square " down by the river is most pleasing, even the new petrol station has been designed with taste and is not the eyesore that might be imagined. At each side two inns face one another—The Anchor and The King's Head—but the picture is really made up by the fine old church. It is partly sixteenth century, and has a curious outside staircase to the gallery. By a coincidence—or was it intention?—Chilvers Coton Church, in Warwickshire, which in George Eliot's *Scenes of Clerical Life* is " Shepperton Church," has a similar staircase.

In this Middlesex churchyard is buried the infant daughter of Thomas Love Peacock, the novelist. The epitaph is from a poem by her father, beginning " Long night succeeds thy little day." It is beautiful by its simplicity and far better than most verses seen on tombstones. Peacock lived for some years at Elm Bank on Halliford Green, where he wrote, among others, those curious novels *Headlong Hall* and *Nightmare Abbey*.

Vine Cottage, also overlooking the Green, was for some time the home of George Meredith, whose first wife was Peacock's daughter.

Another author connected with Shepperton was the Rev. John Mason

Neale, who wrote the famous hymn " Jerusalem the Golden " and many others. He spent his boyhood under the care of the rector here, and later, in 1844, he wrote while a guest at the rectory his historical novel *Shepperton Manor,* a picture of the English Church in the seventeenth century. The scene of much of the story is laid here and the " clues " can easily be traced. The book opens with a pleasant description, which though some ninety years have passed, is not entirely inapplicable to-day. " The pretty village of Shepperton," he wrote, " lies at the extreme verge of the county of Middlesex. Time has indeed changed it since the period at which our tale commences—the summer of 1616. Now the side of the river is lined with a succession of villas, with their green lawns and trim gravel walks; substantial houses of brick occupy the place of the thatched cottages which preceded them; a broad highway has replaced the village lane; country character has yielded to the effects of the vicinity of the metropolis; and most of all the church has suffered from the improvements of modern times.

" Yet, sooth to say, Shepperton has beauties still, and though they might escape the notice of the casual traveller, the inhabitants may well pride themselves on the broad bend of their clear river; the green meadows beyond, and the thick woods of Oatlands on the horizon; or the breezy range with its ancient Domesday Bushes, and the singular beauty of the elm-shaded lanes. At the time of which we write the village, though hardly eighteen miles from London, was completely secluded from the world, and notwithstanding the nearness of Hampton Court."

It will be seen that Neale offers no explanation of the name Domesday Bushes, though the one already given is, I think, the correct one. It is said that the rather highbrow joke between two members of the Oxford Movement took place in Shepperton Rectory, when Keble was visiting Neale. The latter was said to have known twenty languages, and on this occasion he placed before his fellow hymn-writer one of his (Keble's) own hymns, but in Latin, with the remark, " Why, Keble, you told me that *The Christian Year* was entirely original!" The other professed himself utterly confounded, until Neale owned up to having just turned it into Latin himself.

Again we notice from a mention of a priest that a church stood here in Saxon days, though no trace of it remains. Walford has some remarks on this village and mentions the old rectory which is one of the most pleasant features of the square. " This is a most substantial red-brick building," he says, " with projecting beams and a picturesque roof. Before it is a small square, now gravelled, but which was once doubtless a village green."

Here we can notice the account of this place in *A Pilgrimage of the Thames,* already mentioned: " Leaving the River Exe," writes the artist-author of that book, " we come to Shepperton. The effect is sunny, and I pull up, all standing, to see the most realistic stage-setting ever made. I did not know before where scenic artists got their inspiration. Now I know. It is at Shepperton. This place must be the original of all those jolly comic opera scenes in the first act, when the curtain goes up and we " discover " an old village church with a village green in front of it, and a picturesque inn right front and another right left, and a right centre entrance for the trooping in of the village lads and lasses.

" The landlord, large in circumference, will stand outside The King's Head, beaming across the sunlit road to his friendly rival at The Anchor opposite, while a couple of sailors, complete with kit-bags, will be seen entertaining two village worthies to copious draughts of ale. The hero

LITTLETON PARK FROM THE AIR.

Photo by Sound City Film Studios

RIVER EXE IN LITTLETON PARK.

Photo by Sound City Film Studios

with high tenor voice and blue eyes, will enter from the right wing by the post-office, and exclaim, 'Ah, the old place. The same old tree,' etc.

"Meanwhile we see the man who has tried to supplant him in the affections of the squire's daughter standing with folded arms in the shadow (back left) with a sardonic smile on his face. I see it all now. It is as clear as daylight. These pleasant conventions are all based on Shepperton. If you doubt me, look at the picture. That I can guarantee is true enough; yet is it not indeed 'Scene I.: The village of Hog's Norton' ? "

Before the builder had taken toll of the green expanse of this level plain, Shepperton must have been set on the border of a vast region of pasture, in which meandered " a full-fed river winding slow, by cattle on an endless plain." It was the Town of the Shepherds. Its ancient church is dedicated to St. Nicholas, the friend of sailors. Even to-day an atmosphere of primitive things and simple pleasures pervades this riverside haunt. There is a piece of water, hard by the church, known as the Silent Pool. If there is any shepherd left in the pastures of the Exe, he can say with truth: " He leadeth me beside the still waters."

The most famous rector here was William Grocyn, the Greek scholar, in 1504, and according to Newcourt's *Repertorium* he was visited here by Erasmus. Another parson who entertained many famous men here was the Rev. Lewis Atterbury—rector from 1707 to 1731, a brother of Bishop Atterbury, the friend of Swift and Pope.

In a quaint book named *Social Gleanings* there is a curious little story of a visitor to the village in 1796: " The late Mr. Elwes, of Kempton Park, was in the habit of paying an annual visit to the Rev. Mr. Hubbard, Rector of Shepperton, and there was a peculiarity about this visit that is worth recording. The visitor was stone blind, both his carriage horses were stone blind, and his coachman was a Cyclops, having only one eye."

Many interesting finds have been made at Shepperton. In 1812 Joseph Boydell dug up an ancient British dug-out, hewn out of solid oak, and near it were stags' antlers and wild boars' tusks, which give a glimpse of the very early days of this district. Since then many British, Saxon and Roman articles have been found. One account states that a gold vase was dug up here, from a supposed Roman cemetery.

In an interesting and sometimes quaint old book of 1841, *The Banks of the Thames,* it is said that Shepperton and the water-courses of South-west Middlesex were the places Walton had in mind when he wrote his poem *The Anglers' Guide,* beginning:

" I in these flowery meads would be,
These crystal streams should solace me,
To whose harmonious bubbling noise
I with my angle would rejoice.

In the same book appears a curious paragraph: " It has been stated, but on what grounds I do not know, that Walton (the town) was formerly in the County of Middlesex, but that three or four hundred years ago the old channel of the Thames was changed by an inundation, by which also a church was destroyed." I know this part is liable to floods at times, but surely if there were one serious enough (and comparatively recently as history goes) to destroy a church and change a county boundary, some record of it would be noted. The " county exchange " would seem a habit down here, for if at Shepperton we find a piece of Surrey straying into Middlesex, at Laleham the position is reversed, for a piece of Middlesex crosses the

river into Surrey, as a field known as Laleham Burwash, though on the
southern bank, was formerly counted as being in the northern county.

The best explanation of this "mystery" will be found in Sir Montagu
Sharpe's *Middlesex*. It concerns an inundation much earlier than the other
writer mentions (probably in the tenth century).

Recently the peace of Shepperton was disturbed by two ghosts, or so
my news-cutting book says. They are both from *The Daily Mirror*, and the
first is related by Mrs. Dick Turpin—a suitable name for these parts—of
The Anchor Hotel. Here are this lady's own words: "I was awakened at
midnight by a loud crash. Thinking it was a motor accident I looked out
of the window. I saw an aeroplane, silent and silvery, almost as if it
were lighted up, flashing through the sky towards the ground."

Others also claim to have seen the phantom plane; one man who saw
it disappear into a lake was so certain about it that he had it dredged the
next day, but found nothing. Superstitious residents declare this to be the
ghost of a plane that crashed some years ago, when two airmen were killed.

The other ghost is an aquatic one, and thus described by the one who
saw it: "In 1928 a friend of mine died at Shepperton on Christmas Eve.
It was his habit to cross to the island every night at ten o'clock. A year
after he died I was walking with others along the towpath, when I saw a
ghost of a man in a boat. Before I spoke my companions exclaimed 'Did
you see that boat?' At that time the river was in flood and it would have
been impossible for a live man to have rowed over to the island. We all
agreed that we had seen the ghost of the dead man."

In Mrs. J. H. Riddell's *A Terrible Vengeance* we meet a Shepperton
ghost of fiction. It is quite a good "spooky" story and not too conventional, but what interested me more was the wide knowledge the writer
shows of this district. She mentions "Dumsey Deep" off Dumsey Meadows
—of which we have already heard—and here is a paragraph, written perhaps forty years ago, but which might apply in a lesser degree to the
present day, and in winter-time it is almost still true to life: "Hard would
it be, indeed, so near life, railways, civilisation and London, to find a more
lonely stretch of country, when twilight visits the landscape and darkness
comes brooding down over the Middlesex shore, than the path which winds
along the river from Shepperton Lock to Chertsey Bridge. Even at high
noon for months together it is desolate beyond description—silent, save for
the rippling and sobbing of the currents, the wash of the stream, the sway-
ing of the osiers, or the noise made by a bird or rat."

Something of this isolation is hinted at in Blackmore's *Kit and Kitty*
(of which more anon), when the writer tells us (as late as 1860) of a man
at Woking Station anxious to get a conveyance to drive him to Shepperton
(about six miles), but he has great trouble to find anyone who has ever
heard of Shepperton, so isolated was it in those days. When he did find a
vehicle the driver, when asked to go to Shepperton, said he "did not like
going into such unknown places."

Mrs. Riddell's story begins outside the Ship Inn, Lower Halliford,
and wanders through Laleham to Staines, though the main part of it deals
with Shepperton itself; some modernists might term it an old-fashioned
tale, but that, in a ghost story, is not always a detriment.

About a mile from Shepperton is the little cluster of riverside houses
round The Ship Inn, marked on an old map as Hawford, but now called
Halliford. This again is notable for the many changes of name, though not

mentioned in *Domesday,* like its smaller neighbour. Dart, in his *Antiquities of Westminster Abbey,* says King Edgar gave lands at Haleghfort in Middlesex to the Abbey. It is also spelt in old documents Halgford, Halughford, Hallowford and Hallford. I read recently in a book that ought to have known better that "The Priory of Halliwell in Middlesex" refers to Halliford. This is incorrect, that Priory being near Shoreditch.

This Manor has had many owners, including a son of King Stephen, Queen Elizabeth, and Queens Henrietta Maria and Catherine of Braganza, wives of Charles I. and II. respectively.

Reverting to the name it will be noticed that though the prefix changes the word "ford" remains the same ("fort" in this case having the same meaning), and this has given it what fame it possesses, for here were the famous Coway Stakes, one of the much disputed crossings of the Thames by Julius Caesar.

For those who wish to hear more of the Coway Stakes reference is advised to Bede's *Ecclesiastical History,* Geoffrey of Monmouth's *History of the Kings of Britain,* and Manning and Bray's *Surrey.* Yet in spite of all this historical evidence there are still those who hold to the simple explanation that the word Coway should be taken quite literally as "Cow Way," or where the shallows of the river were used in former days as a ford for cattle. Thorne, however, puts forward another ingenious theory: "It should be noticed that the stream from Littleton (the River Exe) flows into the Thames *between* Upper and Lower Halliford, and though now of little consequence, it may of old have formed a sort of creek, fordable near the present Hoo Bridge, and Halliford would then belong to the same class of riverside names as Brentford and Deptford." Brentford, yes; but Thorne has caught himself napping here, for a reference to his own words earlier in his own book would have told us that Deptford does *not* mean "Deep Ford" (over the Ravensbourne, as the former over the Brent), but "Deep Fiord" or harbour, a name surviving from Viking days.

The lock at Shepperton is said to be the original of Plashwater Mill Lock in *Our Mutual Friend,* and thus described by Dickens: "The Lock looked tranquil and pretty on an evening in summer time. A soft air stirred the leaves of the fresh green trees, and passed a smooth shadow on the river and like a smooth shadow over the yielding grass. The voice of the falling water, like the voices of the sea and the wind, was an outer memory to a contemplative listener." It is the place of two tragic happenings in the novel, where Wrayburn is attacked and his body thrown for dead into the river, and the ghastly scene at the end, where Riderhood and Headstone come by their deaths.

"The distance mentioned by Riderhood," points out C. Fox Smith in her little guide, *The Thames,* "agrees fairly well with Shepperton. Moreover, the allusion to the posts along the towpath with the sword of St. Paul —not, as Dickens has it, following the popular error, 'The dagger that killed Wat Tyler'—seems to fix the place definitely as somewhere on the London side of Staines."

Past the Ship Inn we reach Halliford Green, which has still an unspoiled rural look and some picturesque old houses.

Just beyond this green is Hoo Bridge, across which we pass over the Exe for the last time, for near here it flows into the Thames at Sunbury Mead. The name of the picturesque old house near—Watersplash Farm— tells us what was here until recently.

On Gaston Bridge, over the same river a little farther up, there was until recently (when it was removed for repairs) a notice, some hundred years old, that stated "Anyone damaging this bridge will be liable to penal servitude for life." Just the thing for initial-carving fiends!

Sunbury is a pleasant old-world place, with some fine old houses. In fact it is the best place I know round London to study eighteenth century domestic architecture; and many an hour have I spent in that fascinating occupation.

These fine houses are fast disappearing to my intense regret, and every time I visit Sunbury I have some trepidation lest I shall witness the passing of an old friend. I remember once reaching one particularly fine old place to find it half down, and a drain being cut across an old-world garden. Again I am afraid the warmth of my comments shocked even the old watchman! That this wonderful pleasuance, which I have often peopled with creatures of my imagination—in silk brocade, flowered satin, powder and patches, and all the eighteenth century panoply—should be covered with undesirable villainous residences made my blood boil. Would that the ghosts of those old dream-folk of mine come to a real spectral life (to be slightly Irish) and scare the life out of Jerry the Builder.

In *Domesday* it is named Suneburie, and Lysons adds that "in ancient records this place is called Sunnabyri, composed of two Saxon words, *sunna* the sun, and *byri* a town, and may be supposed to denote a place exposed to the sun."

Sunbury in bygone times seems to have been noted for linguists, as in 1590 the manor was demised by Queen Elizabeth to Charles Yetswert, "secretary of the French tongue"; while in an earlier church there was a monument to Daniel Rogers, Clerk of the Council to Queen Elizabeth, described as a "man of excellent learnyng and having a goode knowledge of toongs, and often emploied in ambassage."

A quaint bequest is worth recording:

> "November the first day 1636. I do give unto the Vicar and church-wardens the white mare and mare colt with a white star in the forehead, for the use of the poor of the said parish of Sunbury for ever. I appoint the good man Piper the elder, and George Blundell, to see that this be done. And if the churchwardens shall be negligent and do not amend after reasonable warning, then I do give the said Piper and Blundell leave to sell them, and give the money to the poor.
>
> Jeremy Norcrosse."

Unfortunately no further details are to hand, and we are left in doubt if the good man and his fellow trustee were forced to sell the church-wardens, and the market price of these worthies—for so a literal reading of the terms would mean.

Whatever trouble this white mare may have brought about, an animal of a more extraordinary colour caused some litigation a little earlier; for in Elizabethan times a Sunbury man was charged at the Middlesex Sessions with stealing a "blewe cowe." Was this the remote ancestor of the famous purple cow, noted for never having been seen?

Sunbury has a few quiet niches in English Literature; and we have already noticed Dickens' mention of it in *Oliver Twist;* but it is curious to find *The Royal Thames Guide* stating that Sykes and Oliver *slept* in Sunbury churchyard. A glance at the text makes it perfectly clear that they merely passed it on their way.

It is R. D. Blackmore who has the most to say of Sunbury in his interesting novel *Kit and Kitty: A story of West Middlesex:* " My uncle possessed an ancient garden, which once belonged to a monastery " — Blackmore apparently accepts the erroneous theory of Kempton Park once having been a religious house, though it never was—" and the times being better than now he made a fair living. We lived in an ancient cottage in the fine old village of Sunbury. Our window looked out upon the Thames."

Here are two more extracts, which show Blackmore's close knowledge of the district. The period of the novel is 1860, and this vivid glimpse of an even earlier Sunbury—in Regency days—is given: "When I was a young man there used to be a lot of talk about the two handsome Miss Coldpeppers, of the Manor Hall. They deserved the name they went by in London, ' The Two Bright Suns of Sunbury.'

" There used to be a lot of coaches running, not so much through Sunbury, which lay to one side of the road, though some used to pass here on the way to Chertsey; and there was tootle-tootle along father's walls three or four times a day. But most of them went further back, along the Staines and Windsor Road, where the noise was something wonderful. Lots of young sparks, bucks, dandies and Corinthians used to come down by the coaches then.

The second extract is of an entirely different nature, and gives a glimpse of wintry conditions hereabouts: " The snow must have been ten inches deep on the level, and as many feet in the drifts, for a strong wind urged it fiercely. When I came to the Bear at Hanworth, an old-established and good hotel, the principal entrance was snowed up, from the sweep of the roads that met there, for every road running east and west was like a cannon exploding snow. But I went in by the little door round the corner, and finding only the barman there, for all the neighbours had been glad to get home while they could, I contrived, with some trouble, to ask for a glass of hot brandy and water." Then follows a graphic account of how Kit tried to reach Sunbury, but was completely lost and only rescued, half dead, the next morning by his Scotch terrier, who tracked him.

Blackmore was a great lover of this county and there are still luckily left in these parts some of those trees which caused him to write " The glory of Middlesex is its noble elms."

This part of Middlesex is, in a way, Blackmore's " homeland," for besides having once been classical master at Wellesley House School (now the Police Orphanage) at Strawberry Hill, he lived for over forty years at Gomer House, Teddington, where he wrote *Lorna Doone,* though nearly everyone thinks it was written in Devonshire. So often has my word been doubted on this point and so often have I been told (with the dogmatism of ignorance) that I was talking nonsense, that I wrote to his niece for confirmation, and I have in my possession her reply, in which she says that it is perfectly true that every word of that famous romance was written in Middlesex.

I have other evidence, of a less authoritative though more original nature, for I discovered an old man who used to work in Blackmore's market-garden—for he took his fruit-growing as seriously as his writing. This old labourer told me many interesting things about the famour author-gardener, and added, almost as an afterthought, " Do you know, sir, that

Mr. Blackmore 'e wrote a book as well as kep a market-garden." I said I
had heard something to this effect. " Oh, yes, sir," went on my informant,
" it's true enough, 'e *did* write a book. Why, when I used to go up to the
'ouse for orders *I often catched 'im at it!"*

One reminiscence brings up another, and I can recall as a schoolboy,
after I first fell in love with Lorna, that I rode down to Teddington to see
the house where it was penned, of which I was told. I can remember, too,
how I climbed a tree overlooking the garden, and saw an old gentleman
with a fringe of white whisker, sitting in a chair reading. My first and
only glimpse, full of boyish hero-worship that has grown rather than
diminished with the years, of R. D. Blackmore, though I was not lucky
enough, like my old friend, " to catch him at it!" This was in the evening
of his days, but in my vivid storehouse of memories that picture will never
fade.   *   *   *   *   *

William Morris has a little about Sunbury, but nothing specially
quotable; while an author of a different stamp was once a resident at
Kenton Court, a house facing Kempton Park Racecourse—Guy Boothby,
who wrote *Dr. Nikola* and *The Beautiful White Devil.*

Gilbert White, in his *Selbourne,* has written of the birds found on the
river at Sunbury (a chance for humourists here!), though he does not tell
us much else about the place. Anthony Trollope was at school here, and
a little of this district can be found in his novel *The Three Clerks..*

In Thomas Miller's *Country Life* can be read something of the old-
time Middlesex industry of osier-cutting, for which Sunbury was once
noted. Theodore Hook has laid the scene of one of " ludicrous adventures "
at Sunbury (in his *Sayings and Doings).* Another resident in the village
was Leslie Ward, the famous cartoonist, better known as " Spy."

It was the name The Flower Pot, the inn in the High Street, that
suggested to Hook this practical joke. There resided in the village (circa
1820), in a large house, an elderly bachelor of eccentric disposition whose
ruling passion was his garden. This was decorated with a profusion of
ornaments in the height of suburban fashion—and facing the entrance
was a huge vase filled with a flaming cluster of plants.

Here one afternoon Hook pulled up his horse and rang the bell, and
when the gardener answered it he ordered him to take the animal to the
stable, and have it fed and groomed. Hook then walked into the hall, and
ringing the bell in passing, went on into the dining room, where he threw
himself on to a sofa. A maid-servant appeared at the summons. " Bring
me a brandy and water," he said. " La, sir," cried the astonished girl.

Soon after the owner of the house—a Mr. Maire—made his appearance.
" The rules of your establishment are a little inconvenient to travellers,"
said Hook, " I am still waiting for the brandy; and let me know what you
have for dinner."

" The old gentleman was speechless," the story continues, " his face
purpled, and he seemed in peril of choking with indignation. ' Why, the
fellow's drunk,' cried Theodore, " at this time of day. I shall feel it my
duty, sir, to lay a statement before the bench.' Mr. Maire rang the bell
and ordered his servants to turn the impudent scoundrel out. This led to
an explanation. Nothing could exceed Mr. Hook's regret; what apology
could he make? He was a stranger to Sunbury, and he had been directed
to ' The Flower Pot ' and on seeing what he imagined to be a gigantic
representation of the sign he had entered.

" This was the unkindest cut of all. To hear his pet vase—the envy of all Sunbury—likened to an alehouse sign was an humiliation."

I have often wondered, as I have roamed round Sunbury, which of the many old-fashioned gardens that please the eye formerly contained that gigantic flower pot, if it ever existed. I once told a man with whom I got into talk in the village, the trend of my thoughts and part of the story, but I am afraid it was not one of my successes in imparting even such pseudo-historical information, for my hearer obviously imagined that my rambles in search of a huge semi-mythical giant vase were the result of over-indulgence at the real Flower Pot. Others whom I have asked (knowing perfectly well they did not!) if they had ever heard of this big flower pot merely directed me to the inn.

In *The Taverns of Old England* H. P. Maskell puts forward a serious explanation of the name of this inn: " The painting of the Annunciation brought the Gospel message to every passer-by; but at last came the time of the Puritan ascendancy and a starving out of ideals. The figure of Our Lady was blackened out as idolatrous; sometimes the Puritan was not even satisfied about the Angel and so blackened him out as well; leaving only the vase of lilies. Thus it came about that this inn acquired the name of the Flower Pot."

In *The Adventures of Mr. Ledbury* Albert Smith has some delightful descriptions of Sunbury in the " forties." It is thinly disguised as " Clump-ley," but easy to identify from the clues given. " It was pleasantly situated," he writes, " on the banks of the Thames, under a score of miles from London, and during the summer formed a place of resort for numbers of gentlemen who thought the extreme of earthly happiness was sitting in a punt all day watching a bit of painted cork float on the water." A " sport " not un-known in Sunbury to-day, but the author's descriptions of the old village are charming and worth reading. I wish space allowed for quotation.

There is an episode of a haunted house at Sunbury, extremely uncon-vincing, but which, if handled better, might have been fairly effective, in *Three Women in One Boat*, by Constance MacEwen. This book is not a great work, a feeble imitation of Jerome's Thames epic, and the humour of the female version is flat in comparison.

* * * * * *

I wonder how many visitors to Kempton Park on race days know (or would care two straws if they did) that they tread on historic ground, and that the spot was once a Palace of the Kings of England? Historic land-marks have a strange way of getting swamped.

Although Kempton Park was the home of early British kings, the first documentary evidence of its existence is in *Domesday,* where it is called Chenetone; and it had several other names, including Col Kenyngton, Cold Kennyngton, Cold Kenton, before settling down to its present desigation. The *Domesday* account reads: " Robert the Earl holds the manor of Chene-tone in the hundred of Spelthorne, which is rated at five hides. There is pasture for cattle of the manor and eight acres of vineyard. The value is 4l. per annum. In the reign of Edward the Confessor it was the property of Wlward Wit, the King's Thane."

Lysons has some notes about this estate, and tells us " The Earl of Cornwall was succeeded in his title by his son William, who being in rebellion against Henry I., and having quitted the Kingdom, the King seized his estates in the year 1104. This manor in consequence became

vested in the Crown, and the manor-house was made a Royal Palace. It must
be observed that where Kennington occurs in the Royal Charters it has
hitherto, I believe, been always understood of Kennington, near Lambeth,
where also was a Palace. There is a charter of Edward II., dated from Kennington in 1309, at which time Kennington, in Surrey, was in the possession
of John, Earl of Surrey.   It is probable that many of the earlier charters,
dated from Kennington, were signed at Kennington in Middlesex."

This is intensely interesting, and gives credence to the story that it
was at Kennington Palace, Middlesex, that King Hardicanute, son of
Canute, fell dead at the wedding feast, and *not* at Kennington, near
London.

Some chroniclers state that Kempton Park was also once a monastery,
but I can discover no trace of this at all; in fact Lysons clearly states:
" I cannot find that even tradition has preserved the memory of the palace
which once stood in Kempton Park to have been the remains of a religious
house; of whose existence there are no proofs from history or record."

" The existence of the palace " continues Lysons " is proved by the
following document, being an Inquisition taken by the order of Edward III,
transalated from the original, which is among the records at The Tower
of London."

Here is an epitome of it:

"The Return to a Writ to enquire into the state of
the Palace and Park of Kenyngton in Middlesex: 1331.

" An Inquisition taken at Kenyngton on Saturday following the feast
of the Conversion of St. Paul.

"The Jury do say upon their oaths that the dilapidations in
the Great Hall, and in the pantry and buttry, and they estimate
the repairs at 4l. 6. 8d.   Item: the chamber at the west end is out
of repair and the chimney likely to fall down unless repaired at the
expense of 10 marks. Item: The Great Chamber, with the chapel
and wardrobe, are much out of repair, expense 10 marks.   Item:
The Queen's Chamber is out of repair, expense 13 marks.   Item:
The repairs of the chamber called Aleye, which must have new
beams at 30s. Item: The house called Aumerye is so ruinous that
it threatens to fall, expense 10 marks.   Item: The dresser in the
Great Hall is entirely broken, 40s.   Item: Repairs to the Guard
Chamber beyond the gates, 100s.   Item: Repairs to the farm-house
next the granary, 10s."

It is probable that after this date Kennington Palace was never again
used as a Royal residence.

In 1446 a " Protection " was granted to " the tenant of the Royal Manor
of Colde Kenton that nought of his goods or chattels, corn, hay or carriages
should be seized for the King's use during the space of ten years," and in
1461 the custody of this manor was granted to Christopher Warter, and in
1558 " the manor of Col Kennington, alias Kempton, was granted to Anne,
Duchess of Somerset, widow of the Protector, to be held in fealty for life."

Kempton has even a slight connection with Literature, for in Lord
Shaftesbury's *Diary* he mentions how he used to visit his relative Carew
Raleigh (son of Sir Walter) at his seat of Kempton Park.   Later the estate
passed into the hands of the family of Thomas Killigrew, the dramatist,
while a still later owner was Sir John Chardin, the Eastern traveller, who
wrote his *Travels in Persia and East Indies* here.

OLD HESTON MILL. *Block lent by Middlesex Chronicle*
Now demolished, it was here that
Queen Elizabeth's corn was ground.

OLD FELTHAM VILLAGE. *Block lent by Middlesex Chronicle*

In Mrs. J. H. Riddell's story, *An Evening's Experience*, the scene is laid at Kempton Park (as a racecourse) and there are several local touches in the tale, while its story (as a residence) is also told in *The Banks of the Thames,* where it says, among other details, that " Kempton Park contains an extensive mansion built in the Gothic style by the late Mr. Hill, proprietor of the Gunpowder Mills on Hounslow Heath."

The best book on this estate, however, is *A Garden of Eden: Kempton Park Once upon a Time,* by Edith A. Barnett, the daughter of the late private owner of the manor. It is a delightful work, hard to place definitely. A little topography, a little history, a little legend, a few character studies, and more fantasy than any of them.

No book is more quotable, and reading it again after a recent exploration of the place I can pick up many clues. Here is one: " The Ruins where the children used to play are mentioned as the remains of a pinnacled mansion behind the orchard, and tales were told of a house that was never completed." You will hear, later on, my " discovery " of what is still left of it.

Here is another: " They (the residents) heard say that theirs was the finest garden in Middlesex, but this they thought poor praise, because they thought it the finest in the kingdom."

The country round Kempton at the period of this book must have been lonely, from the glimpse we get of it about the seventies of last century. " The lanes wound through a strange, uninhabited country, and how they came to be as they were, so near London, nobody seems to know. There were miles of lovely, interlacing lanes through which the public seldom passed, and where gipsies used to camp. In these lanes a dangerous tramp might be met, or creatures more shadowy, yet more fearful, for there were legends of haunting by a ghost of a murdered woman."

There are delightful glimpses, too, of the old village life in Sunbury in the mid-nineteenth century, for in 1850 the following amusing episode happened in the church by the river: " There was discontent among the gentry because the lunatics from the asylum sat in front. One day a gentleman sat in the vicarage pew, and he had large warts or wens, on his bald head. Suddenly, in the midst of the sermon a hoarse ' whisper ' was heard, ' Why don't you cut 'em off?' It was one of the lunatics, and people pretended to take no notice. ' Why *don't* you cut 'em off?" repeated the village idiot. The congregation gasped, and there was dead silence, to be broken by the same voice, ' I say, why don't you cut 'em off; they would make capital bait for gudgeon!' After that the lunatics *were* moved to a less conspicuous position."

Some of the pen-pictures of the old folk have a touch of *Cranford* about them; space will allow only one here, but it is a gem. " Old Mrs. Robert was a spare old woman with thick features and a face all on one side. But she had been a celebrated beauty. Nobody could have guessed it, and she was too modest to say so: but she had an ingenious mind. ' My twin sister,' she observed carelessly, ' was the most beautiful girl in Brighton, and I was her exact image; no one knew the difference between us!' . . . Old Mrs. Robert had a romantic history. A wicked baronet had sworn to marry her, and had given her a ring; yet here she was, married to a mere commoner, and living in poverty and perpetual discontent. Her discontent was so high that it almost edged itself among her virtues, and no one in her company could forget that she was used to something better. Was a chicken sent her she fiercely reproved the unrighteous donor, who must have intended her to stay home from church to cook it. Was the next bird brought roasted, then she was sure she had no taste for so much cold meat. When she had a pudding sent her she picked out all the lumps of suet and kept them on a plate, to show how the cook had wished to be the death of her in order to save herself trouble in chopping.

"We once made her a superlative jelly, which set proudly. Mrs. Robert found it passable only when it was warmed up and drunk out of a tea-cup! She had grand manners, even when she meant to be rude. When Mrs. Miller (an old crony) and her society became distasteful she would turn her back squarely on that lady; but she always said politely, 'You'll excuse me turning my back, Mrs. Miller.' And Mrs. Miller replied, 'Don't mention it, Mrs. Robert, I prefer it to your face.' All the while they knew they must face each other over the tea table, neither wishing to demean herself by descending to tea in the kitchen, or leaving before the meal."

*   *   *   *   *   *

One account of Kempton Park, shortly before it was sold for its present use, tells us, "Despite the felling of many of the venerable forest trees by which the park was thickly adorned, and the demesne despoiled of much of its beauty, Kempton Park has still some fine pollarded-oaks. It is about 500 acres in extent, and is bounded by a little stream."

Kempton Park House at the beginning of the nineteenth century appears to have been a kind of rival to Strawberry Hill. Writing in 1816 Brewer thus describes it, in the *Beauties of England:* "The present mansion of Kempton is an imitation of the Gothic style, different parts of which were executed by subsequent owners. Indeed, it is evident that the whole as constructed was intended as a single design. The building is extensive, but has, on the exterior, all the gloom of the ancient English style, without any of those graces which were sometimes produced by genius in entire disdain of rule. Yet ample use is made of what is termed the Gothic; even the stables and greenhouses have embattled parapets, and the garden is entered by a pointed and embattled gateway. The interior of the mansion is not yet finished, but many of the rooms have an air of comfort."

A later account says, "The present house is a good substantial mansion of the ordinary type." There are no traces visible of the ancient palace.

I was under the impression, as I imagine were any who had ever given a thought to the matter, that the old mansion of Kempton Park and the ruins had disappeared. I was agreeably surprised, however, to discover upon a happy trespass, that not only is the old manor house of the Barnett's standing, but that some of the old castellated stabling is still in use. The old tower is gone, but only within living memory, though if this were part of the old palace (which is very unlikely) or only of the "castle" I am not sure. An estate worker, who had lived here for many years, informed me that it was "terrible old," but he also said that the stabling (which is obviously part of the sham-Gothic structure of 1816) dated from the time of Queen Elizabeth. The old man took great pride in showing me an "open-air pulpit," which I hadn't the heart to tell him was merely a saint's niche, minus the figure; it seemed a shame to damp his ardour for antiquity, and his love for history. Of the latter he certainly had a good deal, for he told me that the Black Prince once signed a charter here, which was pretty near, for the signer was Edward II., grandfather of the sombre armoured warrior.

The old man also told me that the building had been "a chapel of Queen Elizabeth," and that there had been a font here at one time, and added the interesting information that this proved it to be old, as "Protestants don't have fonts!" I presume he was muddling it up with stoups, and also rather vaguely mixing up the Virgin Queen with the "Bloody" sister as an ardent Roman Catholic. Anyhow this "Gothic" stable makes a most picturesque vista, with its clock tower and pinnacles above the belt of trees.

A talk with Mr. Walter Hyde, the Secretary of Kempton Park, who lives in the Manor House, led back to the real history of the place as already narrated; and he courteously gave me permission to explore his private grounds. A very delightful old house is this old manor; the last occupier (before the racecourse was made) was the father of the authoress of *A Garden of Eden*. The back of the house is much older than the front (which is early nineteenth century) and was built, I was told, at the same time as Hampton Court.

I think the farmyard, with its quaint ancient granary and high-gabled old barn, pleased me most—it was all a surprise, this rural picture, where I least expected it. When I "discovered" this pleasant oasis behind the tall trees in one corner of the course it gave me a shock I would like to experience again; it is usually the other way about, to go to see a place you think imagine is still existent, and to find it gone. So to go to a place you think is gone and find it still there, with all its old-fashioned charm undisturbed, was a refreshing surprise.

I am afraid, however, that most visitors to Kempton Park to-day care little enough about its history—the result of the 1330 Inquisition moves them less than the result of the 3-30!

* * * * * *

Beyond Sunbury is Hampton, with its memories of David Garrick, who lived here for many years, and numbered among his visitors Dr. Johnson and other famous folk of that day.

Hampton might be described as "picturesque in patches." There are some good old houses left and the waterside by the church is pleasant; but I'm afraid parts of the place have been rather over water-worked.

We are, however, without intending it, getting back to our Heath, for Lysons tells us: "There is a large common at Hampton, computed at about 1,000 acres, adjoining Hounslow-heath, of which indeed it appears to form a part." There is no Hampton Common now; but formerly it was where Hampton Hill adjoins Fulwell.

So ends our exploration of the River Exe, and that district, so rich in varied history, through which it flows. In one or two cases we may have strayed a mile or so beyond the confines of the Heath, extensive as it once was, but the highwaymen themselves were probably no respectors of parish boundaries.

CHAPTER IX.

The Roads that lead over the Heath.

I. Some Glimpses of their Picturesque Past.

HOUNSLOW owes its existence to the same cause as the Heath owes its fame—the Roads. Had it not been for these the town would never have come into being, or the Heath attracted the Knights of the Road who gave it notoriety; for no wayfarers—no highwaymen.

The history of all roads is interesting, and the Staines Road over the Heath is no exception; for of the two great highways traversing this region the Bath Road is comparatively modern.

The first makers of the Staines Road as a way worthy of the name were the Romans, though its early name of the Via Trinobantes points to the existence of a previous thoroughfare, probably an ancient British trackway across the wilds. " These old trackways were not paved and gravelled," Sir Montagu Sharpe reminds us, " but had a basis of turf, and those which were found convenient were extended and enlarged by the Romans."

The Romans made this road, one of the earliest stane (or stone) streets that cross England, over the marshland to Pontes (Staines), even then a township of importance.

This road has had many names; we find traces of five on different maps: Staines Road—via Trinobantes—Thamesis Street—via Imperia and via Militaria: while there was probably another linking it up with Pontes itself.

There was a Roman Camp at Kings Arbour on the Bath Road, but this does not necessarily destroy the theory (though it is a fact) of the Staines Road being the older, for this camp was probably in existence before the Romans made the road over the Heath; and it is probable that there may have been at Hounslow—possibly towards Brentford—a mansio, or inn, for the changing of the chariot horses. No trace of it exists, but there were such places on all Roman roads.

To those who would read more of the ancient roads in this part of the country I would recommend Sir Montagu Sharpe's book *Antiquities of Middlesex*—as deeply learned as it is brilliantly imaginative.

In early days the history of the Staines Road was much like that of any other road in England; it echoed the tramp of the Roman legions and saw much of the picturesque road life of medieval days, the most vivid account of which is written by a Frenchman, J. J. de Jusserand, in his wonderful work, *English Wayfaring Life in the Middle Ages*.

That there were robbers on the road in those days I have no doubt; villainy is as old as the hills (or the plains), but it was not until after the Peace of Ryswick in 1697, when so many disbanded soldiers—both officers and men—were forced to take to the highway for a living; they went " on the road " as to-day old soldiers go " on the dole "—a bitter commentary on a nation's " gratitude."

After the Romans left our shores we neglected the fine roads they made and those round Hounslow town became—and for centuries stayed—as bad as any in the kingdom. In *Her Majesty's Mails* (1865), William Lewin's book on the G.P.O., there is something of roads in this part. In 1703 it often took six hours to go nine miles, and Prince George of Denmark actually took this time on an official journey; the writer adding, not without a touch of unconscious humour, that " his highness made no stop during the journey except when overturned or stuck in the mud."

Twenty years after this the road between London and Brentford was considered a good road, yet in 1727 George II. and Queen Caroline took a whole night travelling between Kew and London; and on one occasion they were overturned, and both pitched into a quagmire!

In the following word-pictures taken from various books we can trace much of the life on and around the two great roads over the Heath in the eighteenth century.

In spite of such reminders of the " real thing " I'm afraid the romantic side of the old coaching days, seen through the vista of years, is apt sometimes still to blind our eyes to the realities of olden road travel. That there were inconveniences is undeniable, and the following account, from a journal of 1780 (a comparatively late date in the history of coaching, when much of the hardships of earlier travel were supposed to have been remedied), of a journey from London to Bath, is but another bit of evidence.

" The getting up to the coach-top alone was at the risk of one's life; and when I was up I was obliged to sit at the corner of the coach with only a small handle to hold on by. I sat nearest the wheel and the moment we set off I fancied I saw certain death before me.

" The machine rolled along with prodigious rapidity over the stones till we got clear of London and so on along the western road through the narrow Brentford street and on through Hounslow and over its wide Heath, where luckily we met with no stoppage from highwaymen."

It goes on to relate how the traveller, in fear of falling off the top, manages to take refuge in the basket behind. Here, however, he was even worse off, for " all the boxes, hob-nailed and copper fastened, began to dance around me; everything in the basket seemed to be alive, and every moment I received such violent blows that I thought my last hour had come."

A brighter picture is drawn by Washington Irving in describing a coach journey, some forty years later it is true: " A stage coach carries animation always as it whirls along. The horn, sounded at the entrance of a village, produces a general bustle."

In de Quincey's " Going Down with Victory " (a section of *The English Mail Coach)* there is a fine description of the mail coaches as news bearers, and how, at the time of a victory, coachmen, guards, horses and vehicles were " all dressed in laurels and flowers, oak-leaves and ribbons." What a wonderful movement is there in the description of the setting off of these coaches from London, which begins: " Can these be horses that pound off with the action and gestures of leopards? What stir!—what a thundering of wheels!—what a tramping of hoofs!—what a sounding of trumpets!— what farewell cheers—a fiery arrow seems to be let loose. Even the dreaded Hounslow Heath would have no terrors for them; for the boldest highwayman would hesitate to attack such a coach, with its very wide-awake crew.

Every village was out to cheer; waking up in the middle of the night rather than miss the spectacle. " In these days of cheap postage and newspapers it may be difficult to comprehend the intense interest," says the author of *Her Majesty's Mails,* "centring in the appearance of the mail coach on any of the lines of the road."

It was not only war tidings that were disseminated by the coaches, news of "Domestic and political events were just as eagerly wanted by country folk," as Harriet Martineau reminds us in her *Thirty Years Peace:* "During the trial of Queen Caroline (1820) crowds stood waiting for news of the trial, which was shouted to them as the coach passed."

In Nimrod's fascinating book, *The Chace, the Turf and the Road,* there is an account, half humorous and half contrasting, of a Rip Van Winkle of the Roads, an old gentleman supposed to have fallen asleep in 1742 in the times of the heavy lumbering coaches and awakened in 1836—when coaching was at its best.

He is waiting in Piccadilly: "'What coach, your honour?' says a ruffianly looking fellow, much like those who lived a hundred years back. 'I wish to go to Exeter,' replies the old gentleman, mildly. 'Just in time, your honour, here she comes—them there grey horses.' 'Don't be in a hurry,' observes the stranger, 'that's a gentleman's carriage!' 'It ain't!' says the cad, 'it's the Comet, and you must be as quick as lightning.'

"In five minutes the coach arrived at Hyde Park Gate; but long before it got there, the worthy gentleman of 1742 is set down by his fellow-passengers as either cracked or from the backwoods of America.

"In five minutes under the hour the Comet arrives at Hounslow, to the delight of our friend, who waxed hungry, not having broken his fast. 'Just fifty-five minutes and thirty-seven seconds,' says he, 'from the time we left London!—wonderful travelling, gentlemen, but much too fast to be safe. However, we have arrived at a good-looking house; and now, waiter, I hope you have for breakf——.' Before the word, however, could be pronounced the worthy old gentleman's head struck the back of the coach by a jerk—which he could not account for (the fact was, three of the four fresh horses were bolters)—and the waiter, the inn, and indeed Hounslow itself disappeared in the twinkling of an eye. Never did such a succession of doors, windows and window-shutters pass so quickly in review. 'My dear sir,' said he, 'you told me we were to change horses at Hounslow? Surely they are not so inhuman as to drive these animals another stage at this rate.' 'Change horses, sir,' says the proprietor. 'Why we changed them whilst you were putting on your spectacles."

"The Heath is safely crossed—highwaymen in 1836 were getting scarce —and there is another change of horses at Staines, and once more the old gentleman is astonished at the excellent condition of the roads, which in his day were often little more than deep-rutted tracks of mud. 'What has effected all this improvement in your paving?' he asks. 'An American called McAdam,' was the reply, 'but the coachmen call him the Colossus of Roads.' "

The coach has now galloped out of this book and we must reluctantly watch it disappear down the highway in a cloud of dust.

Readers of *Tom Brown's Schooldays* will remember that chapter, "The Stage Coach," which has many vivid touches that bring to the mind glimpses of the old sporting prints. The early scenes are laid on the Bath Road and the coach must have passed over Hounslow Heath.

What a fine imaginative touch there is about this writing, when Thomas Hughes tells us of "the dark ride on the top of the Tally-ho coach. Then you knew what cold was; but it had its pleasures.

First there was the consciousness of silent endurance, so dear to every Englishman—of standing out against something and not giving in. There was the music of the rattling harness, and the ring of the horses' feet on the hard road, and the glare of the two bright lamps through the steaming hoar-frost over the leader's ears into the darkness.

" Where can the sunrise be seen in perfection but from a coach roof. . . . And now the dawn breaks as the coach pulls up at a little roadside inn with huge stables behind. There is a bright fire gleaming through the red curtains of the bar window, and the door is open.

We need not follow them into the inn (temptation to loiter in inns has sometimes to be resisted on paper as well as on the road), but wait for them to come out. " Time's up." Toot-toot-tootle-too goes the horn and away they are again.

" And now they begin to see the early life of the countryside: a market cart or two, men in smock frocks going to their work pipe in mouth, a whiff of which is no bad smell this bright morning. The sun gets up and the mist shines like a silver gauze. They pass the hounds jogging along to a meet; the huntsman exchanges greetings with the coachman. Now they pull up at a lodge and take on board a well-muffled-up sportsman, with his meet; the huntsman exchanges greetings with the coachman."

And in these delightful surroundings, alike romantic and practical, we must once more leave our travellers, perhaps not without a touch of envy!

In Rev. P. H. Ditchfield's *English Villages* the author writes of these old inns, which, he says, " have a great history." And as regards those about Hounslow: " Sometimes a gentleman would ride to an inn door on a beautiful, fleet-looking steed, and receive a hearty welcome from the landlord; but the pistols in his belt looked ominous, and presently some soldiers would steal noiselessly into the inn where the gentleman was refreshing himself, and there would be heard sounds of vigorous fighting; and often, in some wonderful way, Claude Duval, or the noted Dick, would fight his way out, whistle to his steed, and jump into the saddle, and ride away from his less nimble pursuers."

In *English Wayfaring Life,* a book that generalises more than specialises on any particular highway, are some real gems from medieval times, witness this conversation between a traveller and an inn-keeper, taken from a fourteenth century manual. " The servant, sent forward to engage the room, utters the hope ' that there are no fleas, nor bugs, nor other vermin.' ' No, sir, please God,' replies the host, ' for I make bold that you shall be well and comfortably lodged here—save that there is a great peck of rats and mice.' "

Further on there is a conversation, at another hostelry, between two travellers: " William, undress and wash your legs, and then dry them with a cloth, and rub them well for the love of the fleas, that they may not leap on your legs, for there is a peck of them lying in the dust under the rushes. Hi! the fleas bite me so! and do me great harm, for I have scratched my shoulders till the blood flows."

Again the vistas of years play their part in the description of the old stage-coachman, drawn with so romantic a touch by Washington Irving in " The Stage Coach," a chapter of his wonderful *Christmas at Bracebridge Hall,* a delightful picture of old England, by an American:—

" Whenever an English stage-coachman may be seen, he cannot be mistaken for one of any other craft. He has commonly a broad, full face, curiously mottled with red; he is swelled into jolly dimensions by frequent potations of malt liquors, and his bulk is increased by a multiplicity of coats. He wears a broad-brimmed, low-crowned hat; a huge coloured handkerchief about his neck; and has in summer time a large bouquet of flowers in his buttonhole, the present, most probably, of some enamoured country lass. His waistcoat is commonly of some light colour, striped, and his small-clothes extend far below his knees, to meet a pair of jockey boots." A picturesque type that the Bath and Exeter Roads must often have seen.

The other side of the picture is given by a writer I can acknowledge by initials only for " C.H.L." writing in *The Autocar,* June 13th, 1930, gives a striking picture in his " Road Hogs of the Past " concerning a few of the perils of travelling in the good old days.

" Without some knowledge of the past it is impossible," he says, " for critics of modern travelling to judge whether or not our roads are safer now than they used to be. Admittedly we have no highwaymen now, and traffic is denser, but the good old days were not entirely good.

" When coaches travelled there were road hogs just as there are now. The road hogs then were the coach guards, who thought nothing of shooting off their pistols in the faces of passing horses to frighten them, and they used to use their whips on passers-by.

" When the reign of the coachman came to an end and mechanically driven coaches were introduced, opposition was forthcoming. A century ago Gurney ran several steam-carriages; but to stop this the authorities placed ridges of stone eighteen inches deep across the road, crippling horse traffic as well, and put tolls on the horseless vehicles at as many pounds as shillings were charged for horse-drawn vehicles.

" In 1846 Scott Russell operated a fleet of horseless vehicles. But when the road trustees saw that the venture was a success they also sank ridges of stone across the roads. The steam coaches ploughed through these, whereupon the height of the stone was increased, so much so that horse-drawn coaches had to travel by a different route. Still the steam coaches negotiated the obstacles, until one day the excessive strain caused the wheel of a coach to break and the boiler exploded."

Here, also, is contemporary evidence of the road hogs (on a western road, too) of former days in the following extract from *The Weekly Register* in 1733. The owners of the Hackney coaches used to pay their drivers to upset private chaises, apparently with a view to increase Hackney coach hire as safer.

" Even the miserable shrieks of women and children not being sufficient to deter the villains. I heard a driver of a Hackney coach with four horses give an account of a hard chase he gave a two-horse chaise which was going with a gentleman and three ladies to Windsor. They had passed through Hounslow and had come between Longford and Colnbrook.

" He whipped up for dear blood and went on after them till they came to a narrow road, when he gave his horses a jerk, and came with such violence upon them that he knocked their chaise over. He said the cries of the women were so loud that they might be heard in Piccadilly (sixteen miles); there being nobody near he got clear off, and as his own passenger was blind, safe from evidence.

" Their intolerable behaviour has rendered them so odious that there is more joy seen for an Hackney-coachman's going to the gallows than for a dozen highwaymen."

ALBERMARLE HOUSE, CADET ACADEMY, HOUNSLOW, 1800.

Block lent by Middlesex Chronicle

ALBERMARLE HOUSE IN THE
WHITMARSH RIOTS, 1882.

Block lent by Middlesex Chronicle

Comparisons may be odious, but they are often interesting. In Hone's *Table Book*—published in 1827—is a coaching item that gives me food for thought. This was it:

"STAGE COACH ADVENTURES.

"INSIDE.—Crammed full of passengers—three fat, fusty old men— a young mother and a sick child—a cross old maid—a poll parrot—a bag of red herrings—and a snarling lap dog. Awake out of a nap with the cramp in one leg and the other in a lady's band box—getting out in the dark at the half-way house, in the hurry stepping into the return coach and finding yourself next morning at the very spot you had started from—asthmatic old woman and child with the measles—window closed in consequence— pay the coachman and drop a piece of gold in the straw—not to be found— fell through a crevice—Coachman says 'He'll find it '—can't—get out your- self—gone—picked up by the ostler—Coach off for next stage.

"OUTSIDE.—Your eye cut out by the clumsy coachman's whip—hat blown into a pond—seated between two apprehended murderers in irons— a drunken fellow half asleep falls off the Coach—and in attempting to save himself drags you along with him in the mud—musical guard, and driver horn mad—turned over—one leg under a bale of cotton—the other under the coach—head in hamper of wine—lots of broken bottles *versus* broken heads—send for surgeon—wounds dressed."

Did Dickens get the idea for Mr. Jingle's way of speech from this? The style is the same. *Pickwick Papers* was published in 1837—ten years after the *Table Book*.

Probably the finest book on the old roads of England is W. Outram Tristram's wonderful romance—for it *is* a romance, though not a novel— *Coaching Days and Coaching Ways*, with its equally delightful illustrations —Herbert Railton being responsible for those old inns and houses, many of which are happily still left, and Herbert Thomson for the vivid reconstruc- tion of those old-time scenes of coaching and road life that have now passed into the realm of picturesque memory. Tristram says:

"I shall try to get some glimpses of life when men began to travel. I shall show our ancestors busy at eating and drinking, quarrelling, delivering up their purses, grumbling over their bills—a motley crowd of kings, queens, statesmen, highwaymen, generals, poets, wits, fine ladies and coachmen.

"I shall picture these worthies on the road and off it, snowed up, in peril from the great waters, starting from the posting houses, alighting at the inns for which England was once famous, with their broad corridors, their four-posted beds hung with silk, their sheets smelling of lavender, their choice crockery and wines.

"Here, too, I shall hope to call up some ghostly figures who lived near the road or posted down it before Fate sent them posting to Hades."

This classic of the road is a real travellers' joy, so vivid and animated that even an armchair traveller can feel the thrill of old-time travel over the old roads in those magic pages.

Tristram, of course, deals with the Bath and the Exeter (or the Staines, in our part) Road separately, as he follows their course naturally much farther than we do here, for we shall end at Colnbrook and Staines. He quotes an old Road Bill of 1670:

" FLYING MACHINE.

" All those desirous to pass from London to Bath, or any other place
on this Road, let them repair to the Bell Savage on Ludgate Hill
and the White Lion at Bath, at both which places they may be
received in a Stage Coach every Monday, Wednesday and Friday,.
which performs the whole journey in Three Days (if God permit)
and sets forth at five in the morning."

Of course the dangerous " flying " speed of 106 miles in three days was
by 1830 reduced to fourteen hours.   To-day a car could easily do this in
three, and a fast aeroplane in half an hour.

It is not often that Tristram is in error and it is with diffidence I correct
him, but in the days to which the following paragraph refers Cranford was
in the centre of the Heath and not beyond it, for it then extended to
Colnbrook.

" This Hounslow Heath which the Flying Machine has now left behind
it," he writes, " that creaking, mud-covered old caravan is now drawn up
outside the Inn at Cranford, the horses are in the stable feeding, the guard
and coachman in the snug bar lying about their heroic resistance to six
highwaymen—the Hounslow Heath, which the Flying Machine has left
behind it, holds a prominent place in all periods in the ' Annals of the
Road.' "

In the foregoing account I always assume somehow that the " Inn at
Cranford " was the old Berkeley Arms.   Here is a short quotation from the
same writer that mentions the opposite hostelry: " After leaving Cranford
Bridge with its White Hart Inn, the memory of which is in the nostrils of
old stage coachmen as a sweet smelling savour, the Bath Road runs through
flat pastoral country, past Sipson Green, where at ' The Magpies ' post horses
could be procured, past Longford, till it reaches Colnbrook."

In a most interesting book, by Archibald Robertson, in 1792, and which
bears the cumbersome title *A Topographical Survey of the Great Road from
London to Bath,* the author reminds us that " the road from London to
Hounslow runs nearly on a level; the country on the left imperceptibly de-
clining to the Thames. The grounds on each side are chiefly occupied by gardens, nurseries and orchards, with an almost continuous chain of buildings of
various dimensions and appearances, extending for more than eight miles
from the metropolis. . . . Beyond Brentford, towards Hounslow, the
country is diversified by cultivation, ornamented villas and woody scenery.

" A little beyond Hounslow the Bath Road branches off the Great
Western Road in a north-west direction, along the skirts of Hounslow Heath.
This waste is a dead flat, of great extent and having little variety; the weary
traveller wishes to hasten speedily from it.   The scene is indeed a little
changed by the intervention of some wood and cultivated land taken from
the common near Cranford Bridge, beyond which it again assumes its dreary
aspect, extending to the 14-milestone."

That it was not always " plain sailing " in journeys over the Heath,
apart from highwaymen, is shown by this account: " The Exeter Fly is
standing before The Pigeons at Brentford, refreshed as to men and horses.
The talk among the passengers is of Hounslow Heath; the ladies fearing
the highwaymen.   The Coach now begins to jolt unspeakably and soon
enters the town of Hounslow.

" Here they are advised by the landlord of The George not to go
forward, as the Bath Flying Machine up to town has been snowed up beyond

Colnbrook, and six beds at The George are aired and empty. As sole answer to this appeal the coachman calls for more brandy, and two more horses, to take them over the Heath, and the Fly leaves Hounslow.

"The first thing to be seen on the notorious Heath is the Salisbury Fly in a terrific snowdrift. The driver of the Exeter Fly observes this catastrophe, but he regards it purely as a landmark, and majestically avoids the pit into which his less fortunate brother has fallen.

"When the Coach draws up before The Bush at Staines the Exeter Fly has taken nearly three hours to come the seven miles from Hounslow."

Fog, as well as snow, was another enemy to be feared in crossing the Heath. Here is an account by C. Ward (quoted by Tristram) of some thick weather in 1840: "We had to be escorted out of London by torches; seven or eight mails following one after the other, the guard of the foremost lighting the one following, took three hours to do the nine miles to Hounslow. We found the Exeter mail in a ditch on the Heath; they had fallen down a steep embankment into the mud and water."

The same writer speaks further of the fogs here: "Coachmen always greeted each other, and I was once passing a Mail and gave the wonted salute. A coachman named Downs was driving the Stroud mail. He recognised my voice, and said 'Charley, what are you doing on my road?' It was he, however, who had made the mistake: he had taken the Staines instead of the Slough Road out of Hounslow."

Here is another pen picture on the same indistinct topic from *Coaching and Anecdotes of the Road,* by Lord William Lennox; the date of the incident is the early nineteenth century: "I was on the box-seat of the coach and after passing Cranford Bridge a dense 'pea-soup' fog set in. 'I don't half like this,' said Moody (the driver). 'If I can only manage to get safe to Hounslow I'll have the lamps lit.' In those days lucifer matches were unknown, so to get a light from the passengers was impossible. Scarcely had my box companion uttered these words when we were upset in a ditch.

"After some trouble things were put to rights, happily no one being severely injured. Thinking it more than probable that if we attempted to go on our journey without lamps we should meet with another mishap, I got a labourer who came to our assistance to walk to the Travellers' Friend and borrow two lanthornes. So with the aid of our own lamps and the above lamps we managed to reach Hounslow in safety. From Hounslow to London we had the same difficulties to contend against."

The young Corinthian bloods—or Regency bucks—often aspired to drive the stage coaches, with varied success, as a contemporary account reminds us: "The Bath coach was bowling along the Western Road toward London, a much be-caped Jehu on the box, who had, for the time being, surrendered the reins to a young gentleman beside him. The youth was fashionably dressed, and his narrow face wore a rakish expression, which was enhanced by his manner of wearing a hat like a truncated cone with a curled brim. Pride went before a fall, for: "All at once the coach lurched heavily to one side and toppled over. The off-leader had shied at a white milestone and the whole machine was hurled off its balance into the hedgerow. From within the coach proceeded the sound of feminine screams," and in the rescue of the fair we must leave the brave.

To choose a final example from so rich a store is hard, but perhaps Blackmore's little paragraph (from *Kit and Kitty)* will do as well as another. It tells us of an amateur whip to whom silence was more cerulean than golden! " The Hon. Tom Bulwrag used to drive the Windsor Coach from London to Hounslow; for the passengers could stand him while the stones and air were noisy; but there he was forced to get down from the box, for nothing that lived, neither man nor horse, could endure this gentleman's language when there was enough silence to hear it."

* * * * * *

I shall make no attempt to write a history of the inns either of Hounslow or those in the vicinity.

But what a topic to tempt a writer! What romance lurks in the very memories of the vanished " glories ' of such places; what stories of coaches, post-chaises, eloping lovers, or rubicund hosts and pretty mob-capped chambermaids, of highwaymen and ostlers, and of the dozens of other types that made up those vivid scenes.

Here, for instance, is a delightful vignette; a humorous interlude of the earlier Great West Road: " Brentford is seven miles from Hyde Park Corner, and is a noted town in the opinion of some experts, though others, I observe, prefer to describe it as a filthy place. The Pigeons was, at any rate in the old coaching days, a noted inn for post-horses, two of whom, tired of life and the vile paving stones which adorned the streets, tried to drown themselves in the Grand Canal, in the decorous company of a clergyman who was seated in the chaise with twelve volumes of sermons, two maiden daughters, and their aunt. On being recovered from the waters the clergyman sought his sermons wildly, and when he found they had gone to improve the fishes he lifted up his voice and said the strangest things. He told one of his daughters that he could better have spared her aunt, and spoke in monosyllables to the post-boy, who was duly discovered to be drunk."

A final word-cameo from Washington Irving, a perfect picture of a roadside inn of bygone days, and though no special one is mentioned it always brings again to my mind a vivid glimpse of the *old* Berkeley Arms at Cranford Bridge. Who can say that this old inn was not its prototype? That Irving knew the Western Road out of London we can tell from his writings, and I can hardly imagine him passing by so delightful a place as this now sadly lamented hostelry that breathed the very spirit of the past.

" In the evening we reached a village where I had determined to pass the night. As we drove into the great gateway of the inn I saw on one side the light of a rousing kitchen fire beaming through a window. I entered, and again advanced. It was the kitchen of an English inn, spacious, hung round with copper and tin vessels highly polished and decorated with a Christmas green. Hams and flitches of bacon suspended from the ceiling; a smoke jack made its ceaseless clanking beside the fireplace, and a clock ticked in one corner.

" A well-scoured deal table extended along one side of the kitchen, with a cold round of beef, over which two foaming tankards of ale seemed mounting guard. Travellers were preparing to attack this stout repast, while others sat smoking and gossiping over their ale on two high-backed settles beside the fire. Trim housemaids were hurrying backwards and forwards under the directions of a fresh, bustling landlady."

Gone now, alas, is the fine old Berkeley Arms—but its memory lingers. I shall never forget the shock I had (though I knew it was coming) when having left it one day, I returned only the next week to find a heap of bricks in its place. Another link with the old English road life snapped.

In addition to those mentioned, many books deal with these roads, among which may be mentioned in passing Thomas Codrington's *Roman Roads in Britain,* B. C. A. Windle's *The Romans in Britain,* and J. W. Gregory's comprehensive work, *The Story of the Roads,* while W. J. Loftie, in his *London* (Historic Towns Series), has something to say on the subject and makes the remark as to how little known is the history of some of these Middlesex roads even to-day. Very true of the whole county, I am afraid.

II. Up and Down the Great Heathen Roads To-day.

That portion of the old turnpike road to Exeter running between Hounslow and Staines—now known as the Staines Road—is much changed since the coachmen "fanned their cattle over the flat," though, aided by imagination and memories, a journey along it to-day is not quite without interest, if it lacks the excitement of yesterday.

In some parts the countryside has really altered very little since its earlier days, and here and there we find inns and houses that skirted the Heath-road quite the same now, save that in these days of changed traffic many of the former have been put to other uses, though it is usually fairly easy to pick them out; for an inn turned into house always retains, unless entirely refronted, some " clue " that tells of its pristine usage; an old sign, or the place for it, the remains of a water-trough, an obvious tap-room window are the most common, though others can often be discovered.

Five roads now meet at the Bell Inn, but though formerly the old Toll Gate stood rather eastwards of the present bifurcation of the two old coach roads—for the Heath once extended as far as the Church—and hereabouts stood the old Hounslow Turnpike, the scene of so much activity, though the chief " sight " here was the line of gibbets that stood, each with its ghastly burden, between the two roads. This was a sight indeed, one to which gentlemen of the " quality " brought their lady friends, and apprentice lads their lasses for a Sunday outing, as an old print in *The Newgate Calendar* shows.

In *Where Traditions Linger*—a volume of fragrant memories—Alan Fea writes of this part in his chapter " Across South-west Middlesex." He is one of the few writers who realises that in Middlesex—the most " Home " of all the Home Counties—traditions lurk so thickly, usually unnoticed, it is true, by the casual passer-by, and generally completely ignored by writers of books dealing with old England.

The author writes of " The Bell Inn "—rebuilt since the coaching days— " the quaint litle roadside inn The Bell." " The last house out of London before crossing Hounslow Heath—has vanished. By the swinging sign of the bell, cut to shape and suspended from its massive framework, two ancient trees preserved the tradition that ' Dick ' used occasionally, when pursued, to conceal himself in their leafy branches.

" Wayfarers accustomed to lodge there handed down the story that it was no uncommon thing at night, in looking across the expanse now covered with bricks and mortar, to see and hear the flash and report of firearms, speaking only too plainly of a ' hold-up ' by some of the lawless gang."

Just past The Bell, where The Alcazar now stands, was Albemarle House, the scene of the famous Hounslow Riots of some fifty years ago, which are still talked of by the older inhabitants of the town. The story can be told briefly. In 1883 Dr. Whitmarsh and Dr. Edwardes were partners in Hounslow. The latter was the victim of a baseless slander by a working woman, which so preyed on his mind that he committed suicide, and in a note he left he accused his partner of siding against him with the idea of driving him away from the place so that he (Whitmarsh) might retain most of the purchase money paid for the share in the practice. Edwardes was a popular man and public feeling ran high against Whitmarsh. His effigy was burned before his house, the windows of which were broken with stones.   Scenes of wildest rioting took place, and had the unpopular doctor appeared he would undoubtedly have been lynched. Large forces of police were drafted into Hounslow and the military were held in readiness. The event became notorious all over England and brought Hounslow into an unenviable limelight.

Albemarle House, one of the old mansions on the fringe of the Heath, was formerly a boys' school, to which reference has been made elsewhere.

On the same side of the road was once the Hounslow Race Course, now long since swept away, but mentioned in Wilkes' verses, while Pinkerton, the annotator of this poem, has a paragraph: " The site of this race course is clearly laid down on Rocque's map of Middlesex. It is on the left of the Staines Road, a short distance from The Bell public-house. Many notices of the races at Hounslow are found in the newspapers of the last century."

The names of the inns just beyond give us a clue to what lies just off the road here. The Duke of Wellington, The Light Horse Inn and The Huzzar all point to the vicinity of the Barracks.

Crossing the road again we come to what is perhaps the most inter-esting part of the road—the only piece of the old Hounslow Heath *in situ*. It is some 300 acres, formerly the drilling ground of the Barracks, but now seemingly little used. It appears, anyhow, to have " gone native " again and the public wander at will over it. The gaunt firs to the right and the bushy ground that lies towards the Hanworth Road are very similar to what I imagine most of the Heath was formerly.

The last use this place was put to was as a military flying ground during the War, and subsequently I can remember the squat light houses erected for civic aviation—but somehow, about 1920 all activities stopped.

Near here once stood the old Toll House (removed from its original position at the junction of the two roads), but this interesting little struc-ture has recently been demolished to make room for new buildings. It is a thousand pities that such a link with Hounslow's old-time road life were not re-erected in one of the public parks; surely such a romantic relic was worth saving.

A little further on—on both sides of the road—we see what might be described as the Curse of Middlesex—the gravel pits, with their noisy, clanking machines; ugly to eye and ear alike.   The richness of the undersoil here is to be regretted—from all points of view save that of the owner!

Here, where the River Crane is crossed by Baber's Bridge, are more derelict Powder Mills, not unpicturesquely set on the wooded banks of the stream, although not the original mills of the Heath—which are on the Hanworth Road and described elsewhere. These Staines Road buildings date from the eighteenth century and have no doubt played their parts in the big bangs. It was at Baber's Bridge that the seventeenth century sword works were situated, on the other side of the highway from the Powder Mills.

There are one or two picturesque old country residences on this stretch of the road, notably the red brick house known as St. Bridget's; Spelthorne St. Mary (now turned into flats), an ivy-clad building with fine grounds, and a white house called Holmwood with its fine old gates. On the other side of the road is a little house that always rather puzzled me. It is—or was—obviously a lodge, and there is an overgrown drive running down by one side of it—but the drive " tails off " into a field and leads to nowhere. I often wondered if there was ever a country mansion there, since demolished, and the site overgrown, or if, the lodge built, the owner was " frightened off " the development of his estate by the evil character this Heath country formerly bore. I did not even know the name of this " lost house "; perhaps it was The White House, a name popular on these two roads, for I find three, but they are really quite easy to distinguish; one is blue, another yellow, and the third a yellow-blue! I have since ascertained it was one of the old lodges to the Powder Mills—so much for my romantic story!

We have now reached The Black Dog Inn, just beyond which the road is carried over the Cardinal's River; and we pass Bedfont village.

A little way past here, by the Royal Oak Inn, the Great West Road enters obliquely into the old road. The bank of Stanwell Reservoir lines the road to the right, in the shadow of which The New Inn Kennels are picturesquely situated. The New Inn itself, like many things bearing this name, was very old; its site is now occupied by a garage.

On the left we are in Ashford parish, which lies beyond the fields behind the Stag and Hounds and Hengrove Farm, which soon give way to Shortwood Common, a picturesque spot with its reed-fringed ponds.

Opposite here is The Crooked Billet Inn, mentioned in Blackmore's *Kit and Kitty,* and so we arrive over the bridge spanning a branch of the Colne into " practical, historical Staines," as one old writer describes it.

Turning off the main road, our way lies past Duncroft Hall and Yeoveney Farm over Staines Moor, through the village of Poyle, to join the Bath Road by The Punch Bowl Inn, whence we shall make our way back to Hounslow.

The first thing we see is a cottage facing the inn, which now looks peaceful enough, but it has an eventful history—it is the original toll-house of the Colnbrook Turnpike Gate—the last gate of this stretch of Heathen road, as Hounslow was the first.

The Bath Road is modern compared with the Roman Highway to Staines, for in the olden maps the former is not marked at all in its present state and it was of little importance until a shorter way was wanted to Bath. Its history, however, especially with regard to highwaymen, is equally interesting, for many a fat purse or casket of jewels did the night-riders take from the " quality " on their way to or returning from the realms of Beau Nash.

Colnbrook, the bi-county town, lies behind us and ahead is Longford, a picturesque, sleepy, old-world village, with some fine old houses.

The numerous branches of the Colne mostly pass through or near Longford, and again I wonder why the road bridge over one of these streams is marked on some maps as Mad Bridge; local inquiry failed to furnish any legend to account for this. Is it a corruption of " Mid Bridge "? There are many water courses here and this might well be the middle one.

Longford, one of the most picturesque roadside villages in the county, is now a quiet, sleepy place, though busy enough in coaching days, chiefly from post-chaises that needed fresh horses.

The village is now much the same as it was then: a few cottages, a farm or two abutting on the main road, and a couple or so inns and no church. Thorne sums it up fairly concisely when he says "Longford is the largest collection of houses in the parish (of Harmondsworth), including three roadside inns. Here the Bath Road is carried over the Colne by King's Bridge, which occupies the place of the *long ford* to which the hamlet owes its name. The fishery here is in good report among anglers, as is also The King's Head Inn." Walford is not much more eloquent: "Longford is a hamlet in this parish on the way to Slough. It takes its name from its situations on the branch of the River Colne, which supplies Hampton Court with water and is crossed by the Queen's Bridge.

Longford has little history, and though a pleasant enough lingering place in reality, need not detain us long on paper. It is mentioned in Charlotte Yonge's *Love and Life,* an eighteenth century story. Describing a coach journey from the west to London the author writes: "They slept at a poor little inn at Longford, rather than cross Hounslow Heath in the evening, and there heard all the last achievements of the thieves, so that in crossing the next day they looked to see a masked highwayman."

The "poor little inn" must have been The White Horse, now a picturesque-looking house certainly belying the disparaging adjective, whatever it may have been then; it could hardly have been The Peggy Bedford, then in the zenith of its fame, which lies ahead.

Its real name is The King's Head, but was always known by the name of a former landlady of coaching days. It was one of the most famous houses of call on the Bath Road. When exactly it was first built is uncertain; on the back wall is a tablet of 1691, which dates most of the present structure.

For some time after the erection of a new and modern road-house, bearing the old name, at the end of the Colnbrook by-pass road the old house lay empty and forlorn, though newly painted, which made it look all the more bizarre. It was left as the prey of the hooligan, every window almost was broken and many doors wrenched off. If ever a ghostly coach passed through the village the spectre occupants must have sighed to see the once famous old inn in such sorry plight.

One thing I discovered on an exploration of this gaudily painted shell was that all the timbering outside was a fake; as one passed on the road it looked genuine enough, but a closer examination showed the fraud; it would have been better without it, though I have my fears as to the long existence of this old inn—more's the pity. I was glad to notice an old thatcher working on a barn opposite instead of seeing it being re-roofed with corrugated iron—to see old customs being observed in a changing world is a tonic.

Since my exploration of this old inn the recent fire has rendered it more desolate than ever; it is now but a burned-out shell, and probably will not survive long. I was surprised to find that Peggy Bedford, the famous landlady, died only as recently as 1859. It was always her boast that she nursed the Prince of Wales (Edward VII.) as a longclothes baby when Queen Victoria stopped at the inn.

The original Peggy Bedford was said to be 700 years old, and the shop opposite, once part of the stables of the inn, is reputed to be of the same age. I am indebted to Mrs. Neal, who keeps this shop, for many interesting details of Peggy Bedford herself, for Mrs. Neal's mother was a personal friend of the famous old landlady.

TWO BRIDGES FARM AND THE DUKE'S RIVER, BEDFONT.

" THE KING'S COTTAGE," HATTON.

What is left of the inn after the fire is now being restored and added to, which is a good thing. I should be sorry to see it disappear into the realms of memory only, like so many old houses hereabouts.

I read that Hawkins and Simpson, the two highwaymen who were notorious for their many robberies of the Bath Mail, were gibbetted in Longford in 1722, and one evening as I was vaguely wondering whereabouts this place of grisly memory might have been I had a mild thrill of another sort. It was just as twilight was deepening into night, and going up a small side road I came across Island House, built, as its name implies, between two streams. It is (at night anyhow) a mysterious place in the deep shadows of some large trees, with large iron gates to keep curious tramps such as myself at a distance. As I watched a white figure—either girl or ghost—emerged from the bushes and glided across the path and over the lawn, to disappear, in true wraith fashion, into more bushes at the other side. Yet I heard no sound whatever! The prosaic will say she wore rubber shoes and thus destroy my only chance of ever seeing a ghost! The setting was certainly ideal; if I ever want to write a ghost or mystery story I could do worse than lay the scene of weird happenings here. *The Secret of Island House* has a " thriller " sound!

In an old book of 1792, *A Topographical Survey of the Great Road from London to Bath,* by Archibald Robinson, he writes: " Passing through the pretty village of Longford the road becomes more pleasant, accidental glances of the stately towers of Windsor Castle are obtained, and, though not distinctly seen, they contribute to cheer the mind after the dreary scene that has been described." There is a fine old print in this book of Island House, though with rather less wooded surroundings than now.

Longford is a good place for dreams—and I must confess that I have often seen, in imagination, a coach swinging through that old village street —one of the most perfect settings for such daylight visions in the whole county. I made the fatal mistake of trying to explain this to a very conventional friend. He called it " sheer waste of time." Yet he'll spend hours at bridge! Ye gods! I remember once I said to him, " For goodness sake wake up and dream." " But you *can't* do that," was his fatuous reply! Well, I suppose *he* couldn't! Yet I have often done so in Longford.

Just beyond here, where the Colnbrook by-pass branches off from the old coach road, is the new Peggy Bedford Inn, about which I can get up little enthusiasm. Not that there is anything particularly wrong with it; it has its full quota of petrol pumps to " improve " the landscape; but I can never quite forgive it for having ousted its older sister from pride of place.

Standing at this parting of the ways the most picturesque thing in the landscape is the bell-tower of Harmondsworth Church above the tree tops in the middle distance, to which there is a field-path.

The next inn is The Old Magpies, with its thatched roof. This is probably the oldest house now existing on these two main roads over Hounslow Heath. Every time I pass I fear to find that the hand of some vandal restorer has been laid on its time-honoured walls and hoary thatch.

It was in the quaint bar-parlour of this delightful old inn, when I was listening to some " true " stories related by an ancient rustic, that I heard of an underground passage supposed to run from here to The Green Man at Hatton, along which one night, when pursued by the Runners, Dick Turpin and Black Bess made their escape! This is the first time I have heard of a *mounted* highwayman " going by Tube."

It is worth turning off the highway here and going down the Sipson Road a hundred yards to look at Sipson House, one of the finest examples of an eighteenth century farmhouse in the county.

A little way beyond, past the blacksmith's that has now descended into a garage, is another Magpies Inn, an eighteenth century building, interesting enough it its own way as an old coaching house, but not to be compared with the other one; two inns so near bearing practically the same name must have led to a certain amount of confusion when the road was a busy coaching highway.

There are plenty of smaller inns in this road, but none of any note until we come to The Coach and Horses at Harlington Corner, with its newly-painted sign that is very pleasing. A typical eighteenth century hostelry, its storied past must have witnessed more romantic scenes than the endless stream of motors that it sees now, to say nothing of the hideous new greyhound racing track that has been erected near, nor can the derelict car dump opposite be anything but a terrible eyesore.

But worse is ahead, for at Cranford Bridge the fine old eighteenth century coaching inn The Berkeley Arms has recently been razed to the ground; this old place had a " Highwayman's Room " in the roof and very wonderful associations with a more picturesque age. Opposite the old building of Cranford Hall stands desolate and forlorn, with its fine old-world and walled garden laid bare. I suppose soon it will go the way of all such places on a main road near London. Once these relics of the past are gone nothing can ever bring them back. Are there no other people in the world but motorists? Have saner folk who love old England and hate to see it ruined no right to have their opinions considered?

The White Hart Inn is still left—in the eighteenth century the place of call for waggoners (the " quality " used The Berkeley Arms).

We now cross the Crane, a pretty little stretch of river at this point, where the two most interesting " sights " are the blacksmith's forge and the fine oak avenue on the left leading to Cranford village. This view has lately been sadly marred by the erection of the new Berkeley Arms, an extraordinary building, quite un-English and totally out of keeping on this old coach road. What style of architecture it is impossible to tell; it is reminiscent of a German baron's castle as it must have looked when it was brand new in medieval days.

Almost opposite is a fine old country house—Meadowbank. Again, how long will it survive the devastating hand of Progress?

By the Great West Road is The Travellers' Friend, an old house, as eighteenth century records tell, but entirely rebuilt.

We are now on the home stretch back to Hounslow Town and the country is giving place to suburbia, but on the left it is worth while to look at Vicarage Farm, but admiration for this typical old Middlesex farm is tempered with sadness; it is doomed.

Just past here is the new railway station, and a little further on is St. Paul's Church, a modern tall-spired building. There are one or two small inns and we are at the end of the road, though the eighteenth century Clipstone House (now a Public Health Department) is worth passing notice, for in the old days it stood right on the open Heath and another witness of stirring times round about the turnpike gate—for we are now back opposite The Bell, whence we set out to see something of these old Heathen roads as they are in these rapidly changing modern times.

A great deal of what might be called General Information has been written in various books, usually in passing, about these two highroads over the Heath. Harper's two books have been mentioned as we went along, and very wonderful books they are, too. I like his comment as he stands at the junction of the two roads: "We stand upon highways famed in song and story—not merely the flat uninteresting roads some think them."

In John Norden's *An Intended Guyde for English Travailers,* written in 1625, there is a delightful footnote on *every* page, "Beere with defectes." A splendid motto for topographers. To be candid, this injunction is certainly necessary in Norden's book, for it is rather inaccurate.

In 1754 the roads over Hounslow Heath were reported before a Parliamentary Committee to be "only two feet in mud"; this was considered rather good, compared with some of the smaller English roads at that time.

In *London's Countryside,* by Edric Holmes, there is a chapter "On Western Roads," and though dealing in part with South-west Middlesex, it has nothing at all to say of the associations or memories of Hounslow and its Heath.

To close this section—though there are many more—I should like to mention two books that pleased me. The first is *The Highways and Byways of England,* by T. W. Wilkinson (though having no connection with the well-known series of a similar name). This book is full of vivid pictures, both for mind and eye, and should be read by everyone interested in the subject of highways. In it is something of the old roads of Middlesex, though not a great deal of the Bath and Staines Roads over the Heath, except by implication, and of course a few highwaymen ride across its pages.

It deals in the main with the historical side, from the old British trackways up to the modern road. There is one sin of omission, however; it has no index, and a book so full of place-names and facts never needed one more.

I find I cannot resist one short quotation, and that is of some quaint information on the state of the seventeenth and eighteenth century roads: "Trees in those days (1637) were conveyed on a tug, drawn by twenty-two oxen, and as they had to be left in the mire when the rains began it took *two or three years* to get from Tonbridge to Chatham" (15 miles).

A hundred years later things were not much better, for the writer adds this quaint piece of information concerning a neighbouring shire: "Transport was particularly difficult on the Sussex clay, which had an evil reputation for centuries. As late as 1751 Dr. Burton suggested that all the animals, including the women (sic!) in that county were long-legged, owing to the difficulty of pulling their feet out of so much mud, which strengthened the muscles and loosened the bones." This must be a leg-pull!

Then there is *The Roads of England,* by R. M. C. Anderson, a fascinating book for all who love road life and road lore. Again this takes us from the earliest days up to the present, and coaches and highwaymen play their proper parts in the right place. This book is a rich field; browse in it; it will carry you on many an imaginary journey along the English roads of yesterday.

*　　*　　*　　*　　*　　*

Nothing would be easier than to compile a list of books that touch upon these western roads over the Heath, but space will not allow more than a brief mention of some in passing. There is Mark Searle's monumental work, *Turnpikes and Toll-Bars,* where we find a fascinating chapter on

Middlesex Toll-Gates, including Hounslow and Bedfont, which records
many incidents that took place here, while the chapter on highwaymen is
full of anecdotes and has some really fine old pictures.

Southey, in 1796, wrote to a friend in verse describing a coach journey
along the Bath Road, in which he expressed surprise that there was no
breakdown, which even at that comparatively late period of the coaching
era, was apparently fully expected.

Of great local interest is Mr. Lynwood Palmer's fine article (in *English
Life), The Great West Road a Hundred Years Ago.*

Those who would learn more of the Roman roads in these parts should
consult for further information *Roman Roads in Britain,* by Thomas
Codrington, and *Roman Roads,* by Forbes and Burmeister, both as excellent
as they are informative; while no student of road-lore should miss that
splendid bibliography of this subject, *Road Books of Great Britain,* by Sir
H. G. Fordham.

What can I say of the new Great West Road—that is, printable things?
—though I am afraid I have said a good deal about it in another way. I
can only repeat that this arterial horror sears the face of rural Middlesex,
or what was once so. We have seen how the brontosaurus roamed these
parts in bygone ages. More murderous things rush along this new road
to-day, things which for sheer killing make the old Bronto a family pet.
I am told the average is a death a day on the Great West Road. And
nothing is done about it—as usual.

Since I wrote the above I have seen in *The Long Journey,* by Laurence
Housman and C. H. K. Marten, this sentence: " Most people would say that
our highroads are safe now (sic!), but they would be quite mistaken. For
while in the old days a few people here and there were killed by highwaymen, now, with our furious driving of cars, we kill hundreds. And nobody
is hanged for it!" So it seems that others share my views.

A strange thing happened to me recently on the Great West Road. A
motorist speeded round a corner on his wrong side, and when I told
him what I thought of him (he nearly knocked me off my bicycle) he
stopped and came back. I expected the usual discourtesies motorists generally have for mere cyclists, and was getting ready for a " spot of Lower
Deck," when he took the wind out of my sails by *apologising!* I nearly
fainted, but it gives me pleasure to record that there is at least one Gentleman of the Road still left on the King's Highway.

My remedy is a drastic one. Hang a motorist for murder! Give him
a fair trial, like any other murderer, but if he is proved guilty then he
should pay the penalty.

In one year motors have killed more people in these parts than the
highwaymen killed in two hundred years. A gibbet, duly loaded, by the
side of the Great West Road to-day would be more effective, I think, in
stopping these murders than some quite inadequate fine. A writer a short
time ago described this road as one of the Seven Wonders of London. I
should call it one of the Seven Horrors of England—a Road of Blood and
Ugliness.

In spite of its short time in existence the Great West Road has figured
in a novel, *The Terrible People,* by Edgar Wallace. The interest for us lies
in the chapters dealing directly with this road, which are in its quite early
days, for where factories now loom is described as fields. Instead of the
usual old house of mystery, beloved by novelists, the scene here takes place

in a brand new villa. There are several clues in the book to prove that the author knew the road well, little touches that the ordinary reader might miss, but which are there in reality, mostly round that part where the new road crosses the old Hounslow-Bath Road and becomes the Great South-West Road to Staines.

Another modern book in which the roads round Hounslow figure in a motoring smash is J. Russell Warren's " thriller," *Half a Clue.*

CHAPTER X.
Coaching.
When the merry notes of a yard of tin woke the echoes of the Heath.

IF the great roads over the Heath made its history, the coaches made these highways necessary. From the lumbering broad-wheeled vehicles that ploughed through the mud and bumped over the pot-holes of the so-called roads of the early seventeenth century, up to the light, fast coaches that ran swiftly over McAdamised surfaces up to the third decade of the nineteenth—the Golden Age of Coaching—an endless procession has passed along these two historic highways. In addition to the coaches there might also be added the numberless post-chaises, curricles, barouches, phaetons, whiskies, tilburies, gigs, and many another now almost forgotten vehicle of the Regency days.

It is not proposed here to attempt anything that approaches a history of coaching, even though confined to the itinerary of this volume; rather I hope to quote a few books that deal with the subject, to tell a few stories, and to leave the rest to the readers' imagination.

No finer book on the old road days exists than the immortal *Coaching Days and Coaching Ways.* This will crop up in various places as we pass along, and it is essentially a book that every lover of the road should keep on a handy shelf, for no volume will bear dipping into more.

* * * * * *

Some of the most imaginative vignettes of the old Hounslow coaching days have been written by Lynwood Palmer, the artist, and a resident of Heston. These are not (as far as I know) in book form, though they ought to be. I found them among some cuttings from *The Morning Post* of 1925. " Old landmarks," he writes, " have mostly disappeared; there is little left to record the scene of one hundred years ago, with the glory of the Heath and its magnificent sunsets and fine air.

" It was a remarkable sight to watch the night mails leaving Hounslow. Five shining lamps on each coach, horses being hurriedly put to, the coachmen giving sharp orders, and then they were off through the gates, which were flung open at the sound of three mellow notes from the mail horn.

" There were also the celebrated fast coaches—let us watch the Comet —London and Exeter—coming up the rise into Hounslow. The merry notes of the coach horn announce her approach, the change of horses is waiting, before she stops her leaders are off and walk unaccompanied to the stables. The stage from Hyde Park Corner has been performed in 35 minutes 36 seconds. A young man pokes his head outside the window and asks if he can get breakfast here. ' Yes, sir, if you can eat it while I count thirty,'

And here are two contrasts of road travel, imaginatively told by the same writer. On one side: "The rich nobleman travelled with his four-horsed carriage, or Briske, the postillions clad in jackets either scarlet, yellow or blue (according to the inn they belonged to or changed at), small square white beaver hats with felt brims, white Guernsey breeches, and top boots." And the other: "Wonderful were the heavy stage-waggons, with huge broad wheels and vast covered tops, protecting both travellers and merchandise, the only means of transport for the poor, and drawn by a team of twelve horses, each with a bell on the top of the bridle.

The term "Flying Coach" as used in the seventeenth century is misleading at first. In those days the ordinary coaches bowled along at about four miles an hour, which was considered good, but the *flying* coaches actually dashed along at the breakneck speed of *five* miles an hour.

No place in England witnessed more different types of vehicles and animals in the old days than the High Street of "Coachopolis," as Hounslow might have been termed. Yet there was one type of the latter of which Hounslow would not see many, and that was a Cock Horse, for this animal was not merely a fabulous beast kept solely for riding to Banbury Cross (as I imagined in my childhood's days), but an animal of practical utility. It was one used to help vehicles up hills, and that is why the flat of Hounslow would have no use for such.

In connection with the famous rhyme I heard an ingenious theory lately that throws new light upon it; I read that the line

"To see a fine lady ride on a white horse"

should read

"To see a Fiennes lady ride on a white horse."

Fiennes being the family name of the Lords Say and Sele, of Broughton Castle, Banbury, and as such a Fiennes lady would be a person of distinction, especially in the old days when this rhyme had birth, before these democratically-levelled times. The connection with Hounslow Heath may be slight, but it exists, for in the seventeenth century Lord Say and Sele lived at Stanwell Place, and I have no doubt many Fiennes ladies used to ride over the Heath, though why they should ride Cock Horses instead of ordinary saddle horses is a mild mystery I cannot fathom for you. But I think I would rather this idea were not true—after all, I have loved the "fine lady" since such very tender years that I would fain remain true to her memory.

The Duke of Beaufort, in the Badminton volume, *Driving,* gives a vivid picture of the old post boys—invariably men despite the name—whom he says "Were as picturesque a feature of old-time road travel as the driver or guard of the mail coaches; in fact they were more numerous, for "posting" —i.e., hiring a private vehicle which changed horses at various points—was the quickest way of travel for those who could afford it. Each stage had a certain number of regular post boys, and so many cads—the latter being a sort of understudy to the former, though how he came by his name, which had no connection with the modern word, is a mystery.

The Duke has a good description of the former: "Post boys were neatly dressed, they all wore beaver hats, generally white. . . . One old post boy was well known on the western roads, he had a yellow jacket and a very red face. It did not signify at what time of the year he drove you, he always had a yellow flower in his mouth, and in the yellow jacket he always had a red flower. Another celebrated post boy once drove Lord Fitzroy Somerset from London to The George Inn, at Hounslow. Whilst they were changing horses the old ostler approached Lord Fitzroy and said, "Old Tippoo brought you down, my lord, I see. He is a rare judge of his company, he is —rattled you down in forty-five minutes. Why, if it had been an old lady he had been driving he would have taken an hour and forty-five toddling her down!" Tippoo's father was a nigger, and he was marked with the tar brush.

Those who like to learn their history from fiction—not a bad way—will find interest in the story *The Post Boy's Hand Horse*, by H. S. Orpen.

Rev. P. H. Ditchfield, always a pleasant writer on customs and scenes past and gone, in his *English Villages* tells us: "The old village inn, sometimes with its curiously painted signboard, has its own story to tell of the old coaching days, and of the great people who used to travel along the main roads, and were sometimes snowed up in a drift below The Old Magpies at Harlington, near Hounslow, or some other old inn hereabouts."

Captain Malet's *Annals of the Road* has two chapters on "The Great Western Road," both of which deal in passing with the highways over the Heath, and he tells many anecdotes. Lord William Lennox, in his *Coaching* (1876) also has many stories, some concerning this part of the King's Highway over the Heath. "In 1827, as the Salisbury coach was on its way to London, the fog was so thick that the driver could not see his way, and on entering Bedfont, near Hounslow, the horses went off the road into the pond called the King's Water, dragging the coach along with them."

From tragedy Lord William turns to comedy, which jostle each other on the road as in life, and tells us of the Oxford coach stopping at an inn at Hounslow; the vehicle was crowded with undergraduates and when passengers tried to enter the cry was "Full up!" till a demure and pretty girl went to the coach door and asked shyly, "Have you not room for just *one* more?" "Yes, yes," they cried, in this case, "come in; plenty of room." The maid thanked them with a sweet smile, and turning to an old man behind her said, "Get in, grandfather, these gentlemen have kindly made room!"

In the boisterous days of the Regency bucks coach racing was a favourite pastime, and here are two accounts, the latter proving that professional whips were not any more immune from the temptation to indulge in this sport than the amateurs. The first is dated 1810, and reads: "Last Thursday the Exeter Mail, with four beautiful greys driven by Mr. Cave Brown, of the Dragoons, for a bet of 500 guineas, raced against the Bath Mail, driven by Mr. Chichester, with four capital blacks, the first to reach Colnbrook turnpike to be the winner. The bet was won by Mr. Brown, who drove the sixteen miles in one hour fourteen minutes."

Tragic results followed the attempt, eight years later, of two stage coach drivers to copy the methods of the Corinthians, for we read: "Following an accident by the overturning of the Bath Stage, by which a passenger lost his life, a verdict of manslaughter was given against Thomas Parwell, the driver, and also against William Butler, the driver of the Exeter Mail. It was proved on evidence that they were racing against each other in a furious manner on the road from Brentford to Hounslow."

In Reyardson's *Down the Road,* a book of coaching reminiscences, other sports of the highway are mentioned, among which we find the rather mysterious entry concerning what the author calls "The Road Game." "The coachman for instance," he writes, "and the person beside him would play this game, tossing up for choice of the side of the road. A donkey counted seven, a pig one, a black sheep one, a magpie one, a grey horse five; and there was one thing by which game might be got at once, but it was connected with what I cannot venture to describe; it was a very rare occurrence, and only once did I see this feat performed, and it elicited a shout, ' Game, by Jove!' "

Some of the best descriptions of the old coachmen, good and bad, who drove the stages on the western roads, are found in *The Romany Rye* and *Lavengro,* especially the former, where that vivid account appears of the fight in the inn yard between the bullying " bang-up coachman " and the little engraver, in which the latter springs a surprise by defeating his bigger rival and then modestly explains how he had been trained in the fistic art by the famous pugilist Broughton.

Of the many books written on the historical side of road travel one of the best is Hilaire Belloc's *Highways and Vehicles,* with its wealth of illustration, to gaze at which is to visualise the various types that must all have passed over the Heath roads at one time or another. Another book on the road that cannot be neglected by any student of the topic is *The Story of the King's Highway,* by Sidney and Beatrice Webb. It is somewhat legal in tone, but it is a wonderful mine of information, with very full appendices.

The last official mail coach to cross Hounslow Heath was the London to Plymouth Stage in 1847; though this does not mean that none has passed since, for many private coaches continued to run after this date, especially during the Coaching Revival in the 'seventies of last century, and even later, for not long ago I stood by Sion Hill Farm on the Great West Road and watched the old Berkeley Coach change horses—it was a sight that cheered me, even though it took place to the echo of passing motor horns.

Something of the same thoughts must have come to Stanley Weyman when he wrote in his novel, *The Castle Inn:* " To-day the old Bath Road is silent, or echoes only the fierce note of the cyclist's bell. The coaches and curricles, wigs and hoops, holstered saddles and carrier's wagons are gone with the beaux and fine ladies whose environment they were." Yet neither the bell nor the horn are as musical as the old coach guard's yard o' tin.

*   *   *   *   *   *

Books on coaching, or those that deal with it incidentally, are almost endless, and it would be possible to quote from them *ad infinitum.* For instance, in that interesting book *Under Five Reigns,* Lady Dorothy Nevill has several first-hand glimpses of old-time road travel, while in a book full of picturesque detail of eighteenth century days—Henry Mackenzie's *Man of Feeling*—there is an amusing chapter of a stage coach journey on the western road out of London, though the travellers apparently manage to traverse the Heath unmolested.

In *The Pleasing Instructor* for 1784, one of those quaint old books beloved of our great-grandfathers that contain essays and letters on every subject under the sun, is an account of a coach journey, in the course of which the vehicle passes over Hounslow Heath, but the writer is so engrossed with describing his fellow-passengers, especially a pretty Quakeress with whom he seems to have been enamoured, that he quite forgets his promise, made at the commencement of his paper, to tell us of an adventure which befel on the Heath.

Road travel, both amateur and professional, formed the subject of many magazine articles in those days, and the following from *The Ladies'*

"BESIDE THE STILL WATERS."
The River Colne near Harmondsworth.

**A TYPICAL HEATH FARMHOUSE
OF THE 18th CENTURY.**

**" THE GOTHIC STABLES,"
KEMPTON PARK.**

Photo by the Author

COURSING ON HOUNSLOW HEATH, 1860.

Magazine for 1772 is typical of many. It is entitled *A Sentimental Journey,* by A Lady (an imitation of Sterne). " While I was making reflections my companion was contemplating the road over Hounslow Heath we had already passed and that which lay ahead. Among other things I have observed (said she) in the midst of this populous country what a number of heaths such as this are still uncultivated. Most of the heaths as they now lie are generally famous for robbers, such as this one of Hounslow.

This conversation took place in a postchaise, in which these ladies drove about the country (apparently without escort or mishap in these dangerous days for travellers) and amused themselves by reflections, moral and otherwise, on what they saw by telling each other stories apropos of anything, or nothing. It is a quaint account, mostly rambling discourses, but with some interesting and amusing bits. Apparently the waste lands of Hounslow turned their thoughts upon serious matters, for one lady relates a tragic story of these parts, which might be called " A Winter's Tale of Hounslow Heath," for it concerns an unlucky traveller walking to Staines, who was frozen to death on the Heath. It also has some pleasing touches of life in the old Hounslow inns, and of the welcome to travellers, which bring to mind Shenstone's well-known lines anent Life's Dull Round and the warmest welcome at an inn.

Coaching stories are legion, and many bear a strong family likeness, such as that in which the traveller relates how he came up from Bristol and every passenger except himself was dead and frozen; and the one when the traveller tells how he pushed his way into a coach in the dark (for lights inside were then unknown) and apologised for stumbling over the other passengers, and then his hand, touching something cold and clammy, he withdrew it, to find, to his horror, that it was covered with blood—and that every passenger inside was a corpse! In both cases the passengers were turkeys for the London market.

Then there is a similar story, but with the horror real instead of imaginary. There was a traveller in the Exeter coach who entered en route and spent an hour in a fruitless attempt to start a conversation with two fellow-passengers, dimly seen in the opposite corner. Concluding they were asleep he also composed himself for slumber. Awakened in the dim dawn by the coach stopping at an inn, the traveller hospitably invited his neighbours opposite to join him at breakfast. Again silence, and when he complained to the coachman of the surly dispositions of his travelling companions the Jehu replied, " Well, sir, it would have been a wonder if they *had* answered you; they was both hanged yesterday for highway robbery, and we are taking up the corpses to London for the surgeons to cut up!"

Nothing would be easier than to compile a bibliography of coaching books, of which there are so many, and most of them, judging by the ones I have read, mention Hounslow Heath at some time or another. A mere list, however, will avail us little here, though a few may be given.

There is E. D. Cummings' *Coaching Days and Ways,* good but slight, but with good coloured pictures by G. D. Armour, though why the author took a title so near a more famous book on the same subject seems strange. It is not usual to associate the name of Andrew Carnegie with anything but steel and libraries, yet he wrote *An American Four-in-Hand in England;* while Stanley Harris' *The Coaching Age* has fine pictures.

There is a type of book, too, that is different from the above, and that is the one written by an old professional " Whip," such as Thomas Cross, who wrote *The Autobiography of a Coachman,* a book having some of the best type of this kind of picture I have ever seen, and Moses Nobbs' *Old Coaching Days.*   Between these two categories is the book of the semi-professional coachman, such as E. Corbett's *Old Coachman's Chatter.*

These books deal with the subject from the driver's point of view, though most books of this nature are more general, such as Violet Wilson's *The Coaching Era,* which is full of anecdote; and still another type are ones like Mrs. Manley's volume, written in 1725, where we get these stories first hand.   Her book is entitled *A Stage Coach Journey to Exeter: Describing the Humours of the Road, with the characters and adventures of the company.*   It is very quaint and most amusing reading.

Literary research always brings surprises, but I must confess to an extra mild wonder when I found that a writer named Adolphus Trollope had not only written a good deal on the old coaching days, especially on the Exeter Road, but was also the author of *thirty-seven* other books.   And I had never heard of him, nor has anybody else I have asked up to now, for his works are quite forgotten, and whatever fame he may have had in his day swamped by his famous brother, Anthony.

Examples of this type of book must end somewhere, and my choice to finish this chapter is *Essays and Fragments,* by Jacob Stanley, which has a spirited account of a coach journey, full of character studies of a refreshing nature, and ends with this illuminating passage: " When I arrived at the last stage I was not a little surprised to find that many of my fellow-passengers were persons so very different from what I had supposed.   One gentleman, whom I had considered a plain country farmer, I found was none other than Sir John ——.   A second, whom I supposed to be a rich esquire, was met by a barber's boy with ' Master, Miss S. has been waiting this half-hour to have her hair dressed, and to inquire if you have brought her mamma's wig.'   A middle-aged gentleman, who had passed for a bachelor, and who on several occasions had attempted to take improper liberties with the female passengers, was met by his wife and four fine children.   And a female, who from her appearance and a number of rings which glittered on both hands might have been an heiress, was, as soon as the coach stopped, accosted by an old washerwoman with ' Ah, Bett, my child, how are you?' "

It may be mentioned that the ominous sounding " improper liberties with females " taken by the supposed bachelor, is explained as " offering his umbrella to two maiden ladies during a shower, without a formal introduction."   They were certainly quite nice to know in 1829.

" On leaving the coach," the account continues, " I put a piece of silver into the hand of the coachman, and complimented him on the uniform civility which he had manifested to all passengers during the several stages he had driven us.   ' Sir,' replied he, ' I am always civil, for my poor old mother taught me that *honey catches more flies than vinegar.*' ' Ah,' I said to myself, ' thy civility is the offspring of selfishness.' "

Again may I add a personal note concerning this book.   It was written by my great-grandfather!   In a sense it exposes me, for it had rested on an obscure bookshelf among a lot of " odd junk," forgotten by all of us; and the other day I happened to open it quite by chance—perhaps it sent me a telepathic message—and there was this delightful essay on the old coaching days.   " What's nearest the eye is hardest to see " seems to have been true of our family bookshelf, as it is of Middlesex generally.

CHAPTER XI.

How some obscure verses inspired a world-famous poem.

WHEN I said that there was no book on this countryside I had not forgotten the Rev. Wetenhall Wilkes' poem *Hounslow Heath*. Though subsequently published in annotated form some hundred and twenty years later, the poem can hardly be termed a history.

In the British Museum it has no separate existence, being bound up in a collection of contemporary minor poems. Practically every account of the district that deigns to mention this poem at all—most ignore it—has a sneering word for it; it is contemptuously referred to as "poor stuff," "mediocre," or some such slighting remark, and left at that. Without claiming it as a great poem, it is certainly far better than is generally described; it has a vivid topographical interest and its pastoral touch is pleasing.

It is dedicated to the Duke of A - - - ll. This is Argyll, who lived at Whitton, though why it was necessary to put in the dashes in this case is hard to understand; there was no chance of libel; but they loved that kind of thing in the eighteenth century. Why, in a magazine of 1764 there is actually a page headed " B - - k Reviews "—*and no clues given!*

I must begin by contradicting myself slightly. This dedication (which appeared only in the Second Edition) is in verse, and *is* pretty poor stuff. turgid and sycophantic.

Space forbids the quoting of the whole poem, though, as the only one written on the Heath it is of undoubted value. Other extracts appear elsewhere, but we will take the parts of the poem separately as regards places. The author begins with an appeal to the Muses:

"Assist, ye sacred Nine, the sports rehearse
Of *Hounslow Heath*—a word not seen in verse;
Hounslow—unknown to all the tuneful throng,
A place ne'er mentioned in descriptive song;
Pure is the air, the prospects unconfin'd;
And various are the sports t'unbend the mind.
Shall ancient *Hounslow* then be lost to fame,
And dull oblivion desecrate the name?
No—from the Nine we this advice receive,
That in their records *Hounslow's* name shall live."

Then follows a somewhat closer description of the Heath, in which appear the lines:

"Hail, happy scene, secure from factious noise,
From pomp, from cares, from all delusive joys;
From all expensive criminal intrigues,
From levee, court and drawing-room fatigues;
Where verdant lawns fill up the space between,
And beauteous seats adorn th' extensive green;
Where soaring larks awake the dewy plains,
And tempt the Muse to sing the rural scenes;
Where wilds present a wide extended view,
Far as the circling eyesight can pursue."

Perhaps a captious critic might argue that being robbed by a highwayman *was* an "expensive criminal intrigue," and that James II. found his Heath Camp, which so disappointed him, a "delusive joy"!

So much for the Heath *in situ;* later on the writer begins to specialise:

Convey me, goddess, to the western end
Of *Hounslow Town*—to see a worthy friend.'

Then we are led to see some of the "beauteous seats" mentioned, as we read on:

"Four large patrician elms behind the town
(True as a beacon to the trav'ler known),
Their lofty boughs with ancient pride display,
And to fair *Whitton* point the cheerful way.
Whitton demands her verse—the Nine conspire,
To swell my numbers with poetic fire."

Not that we hear any real particulars about Whitton, for all the space is taken up with panegyrics about the mysterious Duke of A - - - ll!

As we move westward, however, we hear of another estate on the Heath:

"Two miles from *Hounslow*, tow'rds the west is plac'd,
With all the beauties of retirement grac'd,
A grand and rural seat in Berkeley fam'd,
Gay *Crantford's* Castle by the Muses nam'd."

Two things are puzzling about these lines: why the "t" thrust in the middle of the name, and why "Castle"?

Crantford Field—again the "t"—is mentioned later on in connection with hunting, of which the poem has a good deal to say, in language surprisingly technical for a parson, but this is dealt with elsewhere. Botany of the Heath also occupies some space, but more interesting are the glimpses of pastoral life, which are almost elegiac. Here are two of Wilkes' rather pleasing country pen-pictures of Mary and Hodge, whom a footnote informs us represent any farmer or shepherd and his wife:

"Mary, well harden'd to the morning air,
Now with delight surveys her feather'd care.
With early thrift she tends her home-bred flock
Of cackling pullets round the crested cock;
The ducks and geese upon the liquid plain,
Move slow before their downy, chirping train."

And here is the "companion picture":

"When night's involving shade bids Hodge repair
Homeward, from penning up his fleecy care;
He drinks his pot of home-brew'd ale, and smokes
A cheerful pipe—tells twenty merry jokes;
And lives as pleasantly as richer folks.
His little children climb, in sweet amaze,
About his neck . . ."

These lines are reminiscent of George Morland's pictures, which as our highbrow friends would put it, is not a bad reaction.

There are two extraordinary omissions in Wilkes' verses. One is mentioned by Pinkerton — that "the writer does not allude to any of the camps in his poem; not even to a camp that was formed in 1740, just a few years before he wrote." This is certainly strange, but not so much so, I think, as the second omission which the annotater misses—Wilkes makes no mention of those who made the Heath famous—The Highwaymen! This is strange, for at that time, not ten years after Dick Turpin was hanged, the Heath was in its full blaze of "glory" with regard to the Gentlemen of the Road, some of whom our poet, in his wanderings over the Heath musing over its beauties, can hardly have escaped meeting, though perhaps he was not affluent-looking enough to have aroused their professional attention.

And the gibbets?—the chief "lines" of these were in full view as the reverend gentleman stood at his church door and gazed over the Heath, which then extended almost up to the precincts of the sacred building. The omission is probably deliberate. Possibly he did not wish to sully the fair pages of his beloved Heath with so dark a shadow.

There was an earlier poem, also entitled *Hounslow Heath,* published in 1686, in *Poems on the Affairs of State,* but it is merely a political effusion and not about the Heath at all. It is an attack on James II. at the time of one of the camps.

* * * * * *

Comparison, if sometimes odious, is also sometimes startling; so now for a little criticism of Wilkes' poem and a surprise. Pinkerton has accused Wilkes of "cribbing" from Thomson's *The Seasons* in one place. Here are the two extracts. Thomson wrote:

> "Rous'd by the cock, the soon-clad shepherd leaves
> His mossy cottage, where with Peace he dwells;
> And from the crowded fold, in order drives
> His flock, to taste the verdure of the morn."

While these are the lines of Wilkes:

> "Rous'd by the cock, the soon-drest shepherd leaves
> His peaceful cottage—and to pasture drives
> His folds, to taste the verdure of the morn;
> And farmers rise to guard their ripening corn."

There is certainly some resemblance, especially in two lines; but I do not think Wilkes did much to harm the reputation of *The Seasons,* written some twenty years earlier. There is another charge of "cribbing," however, on which Pinkerton has not commented, nor anyone else, and the onus this time is not on Wilkes, but on one more famous even than Thomson.

In Wilkes' poem we find the line:

> "The white-wing'd plover wheels her sounding flight"

which was written in 1747. Now in 1751 Gray's *Elegy* was published, and contained the line:

> "Save where the beetle wheels his droning flight."

So Wilkes' obscure and practically forgotten poem was published three years before Gray's world-famous one. Did Gray "crib" from Wilkes? The mystery can never be cleared up now.

Anyhow, it is distinctly a feather in the much-moulted cap of the despised Wilkes that so great a poet should have even thought it worth while to paraphrase (we will not say "crib") one of the lines of this obscure poem, which Gray almost certainly did.

Laurie Magnus, in his *Dictionary of European Literature* (a wonderful piece of research work), mentions the chief influences that affected Gray in the writing of the *Elegy,* and while Chaucer, Spenser, Shakespeare and

Milton are all given their due tribute, not a word is said about Wilkes, or his despised poem.

*   *   *   *   *   *

The first edition of *Hounslow Heath* appeared in 1747, but it is the second edition of the following year that is usually quoted.

The poem has been saved from complete oblivion by the edition of 1870, published in aid of the funds for Hounslow Church. To this edition William Pinkerton, F.S.A., has contributed a very fine series of notes, to which I have been indebted for several interesting facts concerning the district.

There is a contemporary review of this edition in *Notes and Queries* (1870), which contains the usual silly sneer about the poem: "This curious little reprint well deserves the attention of Middlesex collectors—not because the impression is limited to 100 copies, not for the poem, which, as Mr. Pinkerton justly remarks, is 'of a very mediocre description,' but for the curious notes, full of interesting local history."

Little seems to be known of the Rev. Mr. Wilkes, and what is may be found in Pinkerton's introduction. "I have a book entitled *An Essay on the Existence of a God,*" he writes, "by Wetenhall Wilkes, Sub.Gra.,Belfast, 1730. And I was much surprised at meeting with the same man again as Minister of the Chapel at Hounslow, and author of a poem called *Hounslow Heath,* at the end of which he acknowledges the authorship of the *Essay.* The poem is of a very mediocre description."

"About Wilkes' work," he continues, "I know almost nothing; there is a short *Essay on the Resurrection* at the end of the above-mentioned essay and an introduction to it, dated 'Carrickfergus, 1729.' Probably he was curate there.... He did not stay long at Hounslow, for I see by the *Gentleman's Magazine* that he was preferred to the Rectory of South Summer Court, in Lincolnshire, in April, 1750, where he did not live a year, having died, according to Musgrave's MS. *Obituary,* on March 25th, 1751.

So much for the author of the only poem inspired by our Heath, for to this account there is nothing to be added. This mild little clergyman (there is no authority for saying that he was either mild by nature or short in stature, but so I always imagine him) had no connection as far as can be ascertained with the fiery demagogue John Wilkes, who ran the notorious *North Briton,* and caused so much excitement in the Middlesex election some few years later; yet both left, under the same surname, their mark on the county's history.

John Wilkes, "witty, resourceful, but unprincipled and profligate," had little to do with the Heath, though in Whitehead's verse we read:

"Now nearer town and all agog,
They knew dear London by its fog.
Bridges they cross, through lanes they wind,
Leave Hounslow's dangerous Heath behind,
Through Brentford win a passage free
By shouting 'Wilkes and Liberty!'"

To the Rev. Mr. Wetenhall Wilkes, however, his poem was the one "great adventure" of his otherwise uneventful life, and it is *his* spirit, rather than that of his more notorious namesake, that one should meet at night in a poetical perambulation of the fields and lanes that once formed his simple, but happy, hunting ground in search of the Muse. I have never met Mr. Wilkes' ghost there yet, as I have ridden these lanes at night, but I should not mind much if I did; I fancy it would be a very gentle spectre!

CHAPTER XII.

When Hounslow Heath resounded to the tramp of armed men.

"THE Heath has a great history, peculiarly its own, as a place for the mustering and encamping of the large armies formerly raised in England. Its contiguity to London, and its position on the way to Staines Bridge, then the only one on the river besides London Bridge, and the direct road to Portsmouth, the usual place of embarkation, made it highly eligible for mustering the armies employed by the kings of England to enforce their claims to the throne of France." Thus writes Pinkerton, though the military history of the Heath began at a much earlier age than medieval days; it is impossible to date its first camp.

It was probably an Ancient British stronghold, for the Roman camps, were certainly not the first gatherings of armed men here. Of these early military displays, however, we have only conjecture to guide us.

The first assembly of troops on the Heath for which we have direct authority was in 1215, when it was the scene of a magnificent spectacle shortly after King John had sealed the Magna Carta. Here it was that the Barons arranged a great tournament in honour of their achievement. Originally they had decided to meet at Stamford, but fearing the King might make an attempt to seize London, they thought it better to assemble nearer the capital. We read in Dugdale's *Baronage* how Robert Fitzwalter, the leader of the Barons, wrote to William de Albini saying that he had been forewarned that there was treachery afoot, and adding there would be a "tournament near London, in Staines Wood and at the town of Hounslow," and intimated that he should come with "horse and arms that he might obtain such honour." The chief prize for which the knights contended was a bear, which had been presented by a certain "faire ladye."

The next meeting of importance on the Heath was two years later, soon after John had summoned the French to his aid. There is a patent among the records of the Tower of London, dated 1217, which grants safe conduct to four peers and twenty knights of Louis, the Dauphin of France, to go to "Hundeslawe" to hold a conference with a like number of English nobles and knights.

In 1267, as we learn from Holinshed's *Chronicles,* the "Red Earl"—Gilbert de Clare, Earl of Hertford and Gloucester—being at the head of the Londoners, then in a state of rebellion, assembled his troops at Hounslow, where it was his intention to give battle to King Henry III., but fearing that the contest would prove unequal he retreated before the arrival of the royal forces.

There is now a long gap before Hounslow is again connected with military matters of any moment, which brings us to the seventeenth century, the most notable epoch in the history of armed forces on the Heath.

In 1628 Charles I. reviewed his troops of horse here; though of little importance historically, it is significant, in the light of subsequent events, to read that there was general discontent among the soldiers on this occasion. It was in this year that the King was forced to give his consent to the Petition of Right.

In 1642—the year the Civil War began—was fought the Battle of Brentford, in connection with which Hounslow Heath seems to have been a place of assembly for both armies, before and after the battle.

Here is an eye-witness account of this engagement, most of which, except the skirmishes round the street barricades, was fought in Syon Park. It was written by an officer in the Royalist army: " One Saturday very early we marched from Ashford, and at Hounslow Heath all the King's forces met, expecting a battaile, but none offered: on still we went to Hounslowe towne, thence to Brainforde, where unexpectedly we were encountered by two or three regiments of theirs, who had made some small barricadoes at the end of the first towne called New Brainford. The van of our army being about 1,000 musketeers answered their shot soe bitterly that within an hour or less they forsooke their worke in that place, and fled up to another which they had raised betwixt the two townes.   My colonel's regiment was brought to assault, whose happy honour it was (assisted by God, and a new piece of canon newly come up) to drive them from that worke too. . . .   Then we, thinking all had been done for that night, two of our regiments passed up through the old towne, but they were encountered by a fresh onset, which scattered like the rest after a short conflict, and fled away towards Hammersmith, and we were left masters of the towne. That night we lay in the cold fields."

Then follows the most interesting part—a " Naval " engagement off Syon Park. There were certainly fights on the river in Danish days, but this was the only one so high up and in which artillery was used. " The next morning early," continues the narrator, " we were startled afresh by the loud music of some canon, which proved to be some 14 barges of theirs, who, with 13 ordnance and 600 men, attempted very indiscreetly to pass up (sic) the river from Kingston, by the towne where we lay, for London; but being discovered, what from the bancke and from Sion House, where we had placed some four musketeers, we sunk four or five of their vessels with the canons in them, took the rest, and 8 pieces in them, for our breakfast."

The identity of the writer of this vivid account is not known; it was in a personal letter signed " M.S." The original is in the Ashmole Museum at Oxford.

An interesting sidelight on the remark re the King's pardon is found in Clarendon's *History,* where we read that " the Parliamentarian soldiers taken prisoners by the King's army at Brentford were discharged on their simple promise not to take up arms again; but that the Puritan camp chaplains declared that they were not bound by such an oath, and absolved them from the necessity of keeping it." What sportsmen!

There are several points about this battle that have a slight bearing on literature; one was the capture of the notorious John Lilburn, the author whose pamphlets seemed to land him in trouble from both sides; and the statement of John Evelyn, the diarist, who says: " 12th Nov., 1642, was the Battle of Brentford surprisingly fought, and to the great consternation of the Citty had his Majesty persu'd his advantage (as 'twas believed he would).   I came in with my horse and arms juste at the retreat, but was not permitted to stay longer than the 15th by reason of the Army's marching to Glocester."

A brief mention of this battle is made by Scott in *Woodstock,* though perhaps the most interesting of all is contained in *King and Commonwealth,* by R. M. Cordery and J. S. Philpots, where it is stated that when John

HOLY TRINITY CHURCH, HOUNSLOW, 1829.

Block lent by Middlesex Chronicle

Milton wrote his sonnet " When the Assault was intended to the City "
on this battle, and which begins:

> " Captain or Colonel, or Knight in Arms,
>   Whose chance on these defenceless doors may seize "

he pinned it to his front door when the news reached London that the
fight was in progress. It is a little difficult to see why Milton did this;
it could hardly have been a pean of triumph, for his side lost. Advertising,
even for poets, was embryonic, so it must have been either in the nature of
a warning, a " News bulletin," or a " Stop Press " notice of the tide of events.

A good reflex of these troublous times, as they affected the poet, can
be found in David Masson's *Life of Milton.*

In *Memoirs of Troublous Times,* one of those books by Emma Marshall,
in which history and fiction are blended, we find mention of the battle:
" As soon as we reached the city we found the inhabitants all in arms, and
nothing to be heard but drums, trumpets and the clattering of arms. People
on all sides crying, ' Arm, arm, for the enemy is near the city ! ' which
proved to be that bloody fight between the Parliament and the King at
Hounslow Heath," though strictly speaking the Heath was the scene only
of after-battle skirmishes and encampments. In the same book appear
John Lilburne, and Sir William Waller, who later lived at Osterley Park.

A description of this battle is found in Defoe's *Memoirs of a Cavalier,*
mentioning a manoeuvre, absent from most accounts, of a detour by the
Royal troops through Osterley Park to attack the enemy from the north. It
is said that Charles I. watched the progress of the fight from the grounds
of Boston House, Brentford.

After the defeat of the Roundheads the King's army fell back upon
the Heath, fighting a rearguard cavalry action. According to some accounts
they entrenched themselves here, but it could not have been for long, as
the Earl of Essex and the Parliamentarian troops soon afterwards encamped
on the same ground, and in the following year, when Essex was about to
raise the siege of Gloucester, the rendezvous for the army was again
appointed for this place.

It was in 1647, however, that the chief gathering of the Parliament
troops was held here, of which Clarendon writes: " When Charles I. was a
prisoner at Hampton Court Fairfax appointed a general rendezvous for
the whole of the Parliamentary Army upon Hounslow Heath, when there
appeared 20,000 foot and horse, with a train of artillery and all other
provisions proportionable; upon which occasion the Speakers of both
Houses of Parliament and several members were present." *The Perfect
Diurnal* adds to this: " There were present the Earls of Northumberland,
Salisbury and Kent, Lord Grey of Wark, Lords Howard, Wharton, Say and
Sele, Mulgrave, and others. The whole army was drawn up in battalions,
near a mile and a half in length. . . . Having viewed the army they
took leave of the General, and some went to the Earl of Northumberland's
at Syon, and others to Lord Say and Sele's at Stanwell." After the review
the army was quartered at Hounslow and the adjacent villages.

The assembly of the army here in 1678 had no political significance; it
was merely a review, in spite of Evelyn's comment, who again comes into
the picture, not as a would-be combatant this time, but as a spectator:
" Returned with my Lord Chamberlaine from Windsor by Hounslow Heath,
where we saw the new-raised army encamped, designed against France, in

pretence at least, but which gave umbrage to Parliament. His Majesty and world of company were in the field and the whole army in battalia, a very glorious sight. Now were brought into service a new sort of soldiers called Grenadiers, who were dextrous in flinging hand grenades, every one having a pouch full; they had furred caps, with coped crowns like Janizaries, which made them look very fierce, and some had long hoods hanging down behind as we picture fools. Their clothing being likewise piebald yellow and red."

This brings us to the three Heath camps of James II., which play an important part in history, especially the last. The beginning of it all was half political and half religious, perhaps rather more of the latter. The infringement of the Test Act was the spark that lit the flames of discontent, which, as J. R. Green points out in his *Short History,* "would have startled a wiser man into prudence, but James prided himself on an obstinacy which never gave way and on the reckless violence of his procedure. A riot which took place on the opening of a fresh Roman Catholic chapel in the City was followed by the establishment of a camp of 13,000 men at Hounslow to overawe the capital."

Macaulay has even more to say. "The King resolved not to yield," he writes. "He formed a camp on Hounslow Heath, and collected there, within a circumference of about two miles and a half, fourteen battalions of foot and thirty-two squadron of horse, amounting to thirteen thousand fighting men. Twenty-six pieces of artillery, and many wains laden with arms and ammunition were dragged from the Tower through the City to Hounslow. The Londoners saw this great force assembled in their neighbourhood with a terror which familiarity soon diminished. A visit to Hounslow became their favourite amusement on holidays. The camp presented the appearance of a vast fair. Mingled with the musketeers and dragoons, a multitude of fine gentlemen and ladies from Soho Square, sharpers and painted women from Whitefriars, invalids in Sedans, monks in hoods and gowns, lacqueys in rich liveries, pedlars, orange girls, mischievous apprentices and gaping clowns was constantly passing through the long lanes of tents. From some pavilions were heard the noises of drunken revelry, from others the curses of gamblers. In truth the place was merely a gay suburb of the capital. The King, as was amply proved two years later, had greatly miscalculated. He had forgotten that vicinity operates in more ways than one. He had hoped that his army would overawe London: but the result of his policy was that the feelings and opinions of London took complete possession of the army."

Almost every historian of note has some mention of these camps; here is a typical one, that of Hume in his *History of England:* "Ever since Monmouth's rebellion the King had, every summer, encamped his army on Hounslow-heath and so overawed the mutinous people. The few converts whom the priests had made were treated with such contempt and ignominy as deterred every one from following the example. Even the Irish officers, whom the King introduced into the army, served rather, from the aversion borne to them, to weaken his interest among them." Then follows that incident which again is practically always mentioned—the joy of the troops at the acquittal of the Seven Bishops and James' remarks thereon.

One of the minor "heroes"—or "martyrs"—of this camp was Samuel Johnson. Not the bulky Doctor of some years later, but a Church of England clergyman. He was the victim of the religious bigotry of James

II., who encouraged his Roman Catholic priests to move freely among the troops to spread his propaganda, both verbal and written, which led to results far different from those intended.

Macaulay gives us some details of the "literary" value of these: "It was impossible for any intelligent Roman Catholic to deny that the champions of his Church were completely overmatched. The ablest of them would not, on the other side, have been considered as of the third rate. Many of them, even when they had something to say, knew not how to say it. They had been excluded from English schools and had passed their lives on the Continent, and were almost unlearned in their mother tongue. When they preached their outlandish accent moved the derision of the audience. They spelt like washerwomen."

The historian quotes several of their effusions; here is one, supposed to be a description of Protestants! "Peter signifies an inexpugnable rock, able to evacuate all the plots of hell's divan, and naufragate all the lurid designs of empoisned heretics." What it all means I have no idea, probably the writer had not much more!

So angry was James that the soldiers, instead of at once changing to his religion through this balderdash, merely laughed, that when Johnson wrote a pamphlet, *An Humble Address to all Protestants in the Present Army*, in answer to these strange effusions, the King had him cast into prison for "inciting to rebellion," and whipped at the cart's tail. The unhappy clergyman, who met his punishment with great bravery, did not suffer in vain, for after this act of brutal injustice the Roman priests met with scant courtesy as they still tried, by the King's orders, to convert the troops to their own faith.

"The victim," runs one account of this unhappy event, "bore it with the spirit of a martyr, observing afterwards that the text of Scripture, 'He endureth the Cross, despising the shame,' so supported him in his bitter journey that had it not seemed vain glory he would have sung a Psalm while the executioner was doing his office." The writer of this account (a contemporary one) waxes wrath at "the striking cruelty and gross insult to a clergyman of the glorious Church of England by the followers of the *Foreign* Church, the accursed and Bloudie Papists from Rome." There is quite a "Buy British" flavour about this comment!

In the Guildhall Library, London, there are three views of the camp. One is entitled "An Exact Prospect of the King's Forces encamped on Hounslow Heath, 1686." Another is "The Camp on Hounslow Heath, 1686," and the third (undated but probably 1688) "The Prospect of the Royal Army encamped on Hounslow Heath."

The camp of 1687 did not differ materially from that of the previous year, but the one of 1688 is the most important of all.

The Revolution of 1688, by Richard Heath, which deals chiefly with the religious side of the affair, speaks of the wonder of the citizens at the crowd of foreign priests brought into London by James, and adds: "Riots broke out and the train-bands sent to suppress them cried out, 'We cannot in conscience fight for popery,' upon which the King, determined to have his own way, formed a camp at Hounslow." This seems to have grown into a habit with James II., but this one failed, as the others had done, in frightening the people of London.

The Antiquarian Repertory has a full description of the army of James II, as encamped here, with a list of the officers, number of men and method of laying out the camp; even the different uniforms are specified in detail. This is culled from contemporary documents, in which the camp figures a good deal. Two points about this account are interesting; the first is the spelling of "center" in the modern American way, another proof that many of their "modern" spellings are our discarded ones, and the other was that the Quartermaster-General was a Colonel Maxwell—so apparently I am not the first of that name to go a-wandering on the Heath!

Again sidelights, as they so often do, prove illuminating, and here is one that gives us a curious glimpse of life in that camp. It is in *The Gentleman's Magazine* for 1804, in an article on the old Trinity Chapel in Conduit Street, off Oxford Street. The history of this chapel is extraordinary for such a building. "It was," says this article, "originally a Royal private chapel of King James II., *and moved on wheels,* wherein he had Mass performed when he assembled his army upon Hounslow Heath, previous to his Abdication. It stood upon Conduit Mead."

The caravan-chapel rather intrigued me and I tried to discover more about it: I was more successful than I thought to be, for I found that several other writers have mentioned it.   Patterson, in a scarce book entitled *Pietas Londoniensis,* speaks of it as "the relick of that famous *Portatile, or Moving Tabernacle,* originally erected by James II. when he was encamped with his army on Hounslow Heath, where he had Mass constantly performed in it; but since that time has been refounded here as a Chapel of Ease for the use of the district of St. Martin's-in-the-Fields."

Hume has a passing reference to it and the failure of the King to make the soldiers use it, while Pennant, in his *History of London,* tells us: "It was originally built of wood by James II. for private Mass and was conveyed on wheels attendant on its Royal master's excursions. Among other places it visited was Hounslow Heath, where it rested for a long time after James' Abdication and the Revolution as a melancholy memorial of that monarch's weakness and infatuation."

This strange chapel was eventually rebuilt in a more permanent form in brick and stood for many years in Conduit Street.

*   *   *   *   *

Evelyn has not much to say about the 1686 camp beyond mentioning: "The camp was again pitch'd at Hounslow, the commanders profusly vying in the expence and magnificane of their tents," and continuing with a note about the weather: "Such storms, raine and foul weather, seldom seen at this time of year. The camp from sicknesse and other inconveniences of the climate forc'd to retire to quarters; the storms being succeede by excessive heat, many grew sick. Great feasting there, especially in Lord Dumbarton's quarters. There were many jealousies and discourses of what was the meaning of this incampment." Curiously enough he has even less to say of the most famous camp of all in 1688, contenting himself with a simple line, "The camp now begun at Hounslow, but the nation was in high discontent."

These camps attracted the ballad writers on both sides.   The most popular is the satire—mild for that outspoken age—against the unpopular King:

> "Near Hampton Court there lies a Common,
>   Unknown to neither man nor woman;
>   The Heath of Hounslow it is styled;
>   Which never was with blood defiled,

Though it has been of war the seat
Now three campaigns almost complete.
" Here you may see great James the Second
(The greatest of our Kings he's reckoned),
A hero of such high renown
Whole nations tremble at his frown;
And when he smiles men die away
In transports of excessive joy."

Another touches on the festive side of the camp (which so annoyed the King). Here is one verse:

" I liked the place beyond expressing,
I ne'er saw camp so fine.
And not a maid in plainest dressing
But might taste a glass of wine!"

There is another, in a little volume *Poems on the Affairs of State,* from the Pepysian Collection, written one would imagine by a sycophant of the King. It is entitled *Hounslow Heath,* and begins:

" Now pause and view the Army Royal,
Composed of valiant souls and loyal
Not raised (as ill men say) to hurt ye,
But to defend ye and convert ye."

   *   *   *   *   *   *

The author of *As the Crow Flies* tells us: " There is a pretty tradition of Hounslow which addresses itself to the human heart. During those cruel wars that brought the King's army and the Parliamentarians alternately to encamp on Hounslow Heath, one Mr. George Trevelyn, a Cavalier gentleman of Somerset, and suspected of plotting against Cromwell, was seized by Puritan soldiers, and sent to the Tower. His property was destroyed and every horse driven off that could mount a dragoon, or drag a cannon. They left the old house ransacked and rode off singing their sullen Psalms.

" Heaven and earth were moved for Trevelyn's release by his devoted wife, but Cromwell, bent on breaking such stubborn spirits, would not listen to less ransom than two thousand pounds. But where to find it? The faithful steward racked his brains, and the poor wife prayed in her great need. Farms were sold, old oaks felled and heirlooms went to the Jews. The difficulty was how to get the gold to London, and escape the highwaymen of Hounslow Heath. At last she had a thought; she had heard of the rough roads where strong oxen had pulled the coaches through the sloughs and ruts. The horses were gone, but the oxen were harnessed to the family coach, and, accompanied by the old steward, she started, and took twenty-eight days on the journey."

The ransom was accepted, and then the narrative can be followed to its tragic close: " The wife flew into the arms of her free husband; but she sickened of small-pox at Hounslow—the first halting place for the swift homeward horses as it had been the last for the slow oxen—and she died breathing the name which had been the watchword of her devotion. She was buried at Hounslow, on the site of the home of the old Brotherhood of the Trinity, who had devoted their lives to the redeeming of captives; and in the church a simple tablet exists to her memory." A grim jest of fate, this. Anxiety—a terrible journey—success—and then death.

It was the acquittal of the Seven Bishops that caused not only the break-up of the Hounslow camp, but of James's kingdom as well. Macaulay gives a slight, but vivid, word-picture of the last scene of all: "The King had that morning visited the camp on Hounslow Heath. Sunderland instantly sent a courier thither with the news. James was in Lord Faversham's tent when the express arrived. He was greatly distressed and exclaimed in French, "So much the worse for them." He soon set out for London. While he was present respect prevented the soldiers from giving a loose rein to their feeling, but he had scarcely quitted the camp when he heard a great shouting behind him. He was surprised and asked what the uproar meant. "Nothing," was the answer, "the soldiers are glad that the Bishops are acquitted." "Do you call that nothing?" said James, and then he repeated, "So much the worse for them."

Dickens, in his *Child's History of England*, speaks of the shout that went up at Westminster at the acquittal as spreading over England: "It passed on among the people away to Temple Bar, and away again to the Tower. It did not pass only to the east, but to the west too, until it reached the camp at Hounslow, where the fifteen thousand soldiers took it up."

In *Sieges of London* (a magazine article) is a statement: "There arose a rumour that Faversham's Irish troops were marching from Hounslow on London to take the city and massacre the protestants. The City sprang to arms, the chief streets were barricaded and all travellers were stopped and questioned. The Irish Panic died down as quickly as it had arisen."

The fact that Lord Faversham, the Commander in Chief of the British Army, was a Frenchman did not make him any the more popular. It is surprising to find, however, that he was nominally a Protestant, though Burnet in his *History of my own Times* hints that James had secretly converted him to the Romish faith, which, knowing James, is more than likely. Faversham was the general who is said to have won the Battle of Sedgemoor by staying in bed. It is a fact that he had to be awakened to get down to the battlefield in time.

It was the end of the camp, for Macaulay adds: "Nowhere had the news of the acquittal been received with more clamorous delight than at Hounslow Heath," while Lutteral's *Diary* contains the comment: "In truth, the great force which the King had collected at Hounslow for the purpose of overawing his mutinous capital had become more mutinous than the capital itself, and was dreaded by the Court more than the citizens. Early in August, therefore, the camp was broken up."

Of the aftermath G. E. Bate pictures the state of things in the district when he writes: "James had played and lost, and the great men of England sent an invitation to William of Orange to come and help them. He landed at Torbay and marched on London. James fled and Faversham disbanded the soldiers without disarming them, and thus set them loose to prey upon the country. There were tumults among them, and one's imagination can picture the scenes in Hounslow, when thousands of men, armed, but without discipline or order, walked into the town." Meanwhile William and his Dutch troops, in a hurry to seize the Crown, dashed through Hounslow and on to London, the only time the Heath ever saw "The Flying Dutchman."

Even if the London citizens lost their fair ground I do not imagine that the countryfolk were altogether sorry to see the last of James's army. I wonder if there is any truth in the story that the Rose and Crown Inn at Hounslow gained its second title from the King staying there?

James II. was one of the worst kings that ever sat on the throne; a bigot, more priest-ridden than the most ignorant Irish peasant, and who had not enough sense to see the stupid mistake it was to try and overawe London by military force.   In character judging, as in other ways, little things mean a lot, and there is wit, wisdom and truth in the remark of Catherine Sedley, a favourite of James II., who could not understand the King's infatuation: " It cannot be my beauty, for he must see that I have none; and it cannot be my wit, for he has not enough to know that I have any." If James II. had possessed a sense of humour he might also have had a sense of proportion—and English history might have been different.

Well, we must not kick him when he is down, but try and think of his one sensible act.   He at least realised that an island kingdom must have a strong fleet, and he did his best to improve the Navy.   So let us not remember James by his many faults, but by his one virtue.

The only later camp having any real significance was that of 1690, when the King of France was helping ex-King James in an attempt to regain his throne, and the army was raised to repel any attack, and again encamped on the Heath, on the same spot where another army was encamped who failed to keep the crown on his head.   Some might see a Divine justice in this.   The troops on this second occasion were reviewed by Queen Mary and Marlborough, the newly-appointed Commander-in-Chief.   In Winston Churchill's notable book, *Marlborough*, there is mention of these Heath camps.

The next one of any note was that of 1740, and this seems to have been an elaborate affair.   The Dukes of Cumberland and Marlborough and the Earl of Albemarle and Sir Charles Wills were the chief commanders, and the journals of the day often refer to it.   Here is one such paragraph, chiefly notable for its contrasting items: " It having been represented to His Majesty that the troops on the Heath cannot support themselves on their pay, orders are given that an allowance of a pound and a half of bread per day be delivered to each private sentinel, for which they are to pay no more than five farthings. . . . The baggage and furniture belonging to his Royal Highness the Duke of Cumberland was carried from St. James's to Hounslow, and yesterday he gave a grand entertainment to the officers.   Great quantities of wine were sent down.   His Highness's tent is a magnificent one, containing several rooms."

Two more items follow of a totally different nature: " On Sunday night two soldiers strayed out of the camp at Hounslow into a farmer's ground, with a design to make free with his sheep, but the former's servant shot one of them through the back so that he instantly died." Another item appeared: " The soldier shot near Hounslow in a sheep robbery and committed by Justice Clitheroe to Newgate, is much amended since his commitment and is in a fair way to the gallows."

So popular was this particular camp that it is said that on one Sunday it had no less than 20,000 visitors, many of whom came by water to Isleworth.   Nor did public interest end here; an opportunity was given to those who stayed at home to visit it " by proxy," as it were, for in the *Daily Advertiser* appeared the announcement:

" To be seen, at One Shilling each Person, at the Swan at the bottom of Hay Hill, Dover Street.

" The Whole Prospect of the Camp at HOUNSLOW HEATH, representing in proper order, both Horse and Foot, every Officer in his Proper Post, with the Liveries and Colours in the nicest distinction, representing Life nearer than anything of that kind hitherto invented.   The Train of Artillery in its proper Decorum."

There is one little item, from an eighteenth century journal, which is not without interest, in view of the prize competition money, free insurance and other benefits given by modern papers. It reads: " Hounslow Heath was the scene of an interesting experiment made recently in training a company of young soldiers at the expense of *The Spectator* and its readers." Those further interested in military subjects should refer to the article, " The Battlefields of Middlesex," in that fascinating volume, *The Memorials of Middlesex*, edited by J. Tavenor Perry.

Little remains to relate here of the history of the armed forces on the Heath, for of its modern military annals this is not the place to deal. The Cavalry Barracks were built in 1793 and the Infantry in 1875.

In Evans' *Excursions* (1818) he says rather quaintly: " In 1793 the barracks were built on the extremity of the Heath nearest Colnbrook, capable of containing 400 men, who, in general, behave." What he means by " nearest Colnbrook " I have no idea, for they are at the very opposite extremity of the Heath.

We have already noticed that the 300 acres of land, usually referred to as the Heath, is all that is left of 6,000. This smaller area was first laid out as a drilling and review ground in 1818, though some parts of it are still wild enough to help us visualise what this vast expanse of scrubby waste-land must have been like before the Enclosure Acts turned it into farmland.

* * * * * *

In *Forty Years On*, that interesting book of reminiscences by Lord Ernest Hamilton, there is a chapter entitled " Hounslow," which gives us a picture of a cavalry officer's life in these barracks, but what is more unusual, he also gives an account of that mysterious semi-legendary figure, Spring-Heeled Jack, carrying on his antics on Hounslow Heath. This is the nearest real evidence I can produce of a ghost on the Heath, though our light-footed friend was flesh and blood all right.

In Samuel Foote's play, *The Mayor of Garrat,* written in 1784, there is a delightful satire on the Militia of that day, in which is described the " Battle " of Hounslow Heath. It is related by " Justice Sturgeon, fish-monger from Brentford and Major of the Middlesex Militia." It was during the army manoeuvres, and the gallant major relates: " Why, there was our last expedition to Hounslow. In order to get our men in good spirits we were quartered at Thistleworth the evening before. At day-break our regiment formed at Hounslow town's end. On we marched in high spirits to attack the gibbet where Gardel is hanging, but turning down a narrow lane to the left in order to possess a pig-stye that we might take the gallows in flank, who should come up but a drove of fat oxen.

" The drums beat in front, the dogs barked in the rear, the oxen set up a gallop; on they came thundering upon us; through our ranks in an instant, and threw the whole corps into confusion. The major's horse took to its heels and away he scoured over the Heath; and that gallant com-mander (Major Molasses) plunged into a gravel-pit by the Powder Mills." To make matters worse some of the officers (Captain Cucumber, Lieutenant Patty-Pan and Ensign Tripe) were stopped by the turnpike and robbed by a footpad.

In Charles T. Gatty's *Mary Davies and the Manor of Ebury* there is a chapter, " Hounslow Heath." The connection with this book and the Heath is explained by a paragraph in *The English Baronage* for 1741, where it is stated that Sir Thomas Grosvenor was offered by James a peerage and a

THE OLD TOLL GATE. HOUNSLOW.
Junction of Bath and Staines Roads.

Block lent by Middlesex Chronicle

Block lent by Middlesex Chronicle

WHERE THE OLD TOLL GATES STOOD.
Neal's Corner to-day.

high command at Hounslow Camp if he would side with him in the growing discontent. Sir Thomas refused the bribe—he probably saw what was coming more clearly than the bigoted monarch.

Odd pieces of information about the Hounslow Camps crop up in all sorts of places; here are two from that veritable mine of information (for those who have the time and patience to search) *The Calendar of State Papers.* They are both for the year 1697. The first is "A Petition from the Innholders of Middlesex who have quartered on them several Regiment Horse from Hounslow Camp, complaining of their payment in lottery tickets." The second is a note concerning "the furnishing of the King's bedchamber for his house at Hounslow." No clue is given by which we can now identify which house this was.

In *Old Cavalry Stations,* by B. Granville Baker, we hear something of military Hounslow; and how the fogs of the Thames Valley prevented the Heath being turned from a military air station to a big civil airport is related in *By Air,* by Sir Harry Britton, though since this was written other airports have sprung up near, who do not worry about the fogs, which I do not think are any more prevalent here than at Croydon, which took Hounslow's place, for which we should be glad, for it would have meant the end of what remnant of the Heath we have got left.

Hounslow's air history, if short, is memorable in civil aviation, for it was from the Heath that the first commercial 'plane flew to Paris in 1919, and at Hounslow was established the first Air Customs House in England. Brief as its life was Hounslow Airport had time to get into fiction, for it plays a part in William le Queux's mystery story, *The Fifth Finger.*

The Diamond Jubilee of 1897 is to me but a faint boyhood's memory, but Hounslow Heath at that time was a place I should much like to have seen, for here were camped sections from every regiment in the British Army, and I am told by those who remember it that though they marched to London at three a.m., the streets were lined with people, who had waited up all night to see this unique spectacle.

The Aldershot Tattoo of this year had an episode representing the great camp on Hounslow Heath in 1686, including a review of the troops by James II. It was interesting to notice that the fair-ground, so vividly described by Macaulay, was faithfully represented.

There is little space left for personalities, but I have a note in my collection that may be of interest to the effect: "Roger Tichborne was in the Carabineers stationed at Hounslow Barracks. His Colonel, Constance, who lived on the Bath Road, was of the opinion that the Claimant, Arthur Orton, *was* really Roger Tichborne. Orton invariably stopped at the Red Lion, Hounslow, when on his way down to Staines for duck-shooting."

* * * * * *

Hounslow's military fame began very early, for we have seen elsewhere how the gunpowder for the first cannon ever used in a battle—at Crecy in 1346—was made on the Heath. In General Wrottesley's interesting book, *Crecy and Calais* we find no actual mention of the Hounslow-made powder, though there is a brief mention of the cannon themselves. We can imagine some die-hard old knights exclaiming: "These new-fangled inventions are ruining the army, sir! What is wrong with the good old longbow?" The "five portable guns" at Crecy are here referred to as the "Artillarii," and the men who served them as the "Gunnatores," but they were of little

account and played no very serious part in the fight, the brunt of which
was borne by the English bowmen.

In a medieval chronicle we read: "At the battaile of Crecy sixty yeomen-
archers from the Countie of Mydllesex did fight in ye Kynge's army on that
bloudie fielde." Among those appointed to " warn and choose " the archers
of this county for the King's service were John de Cherlton and William
de Langford; surnames little altered from the present Charlton and Longford.

Whenever I stand beneath the great yew trees in many a Middlesex
churchyard—such as Harlington or Cranford—I often wonder if the bows
of any of those gallant sixty were once growing on the trunks above me.
And were there any of these Middlesex archers among the Bowmen of
Mons? Perhaps Arthur Machen can tell us this.

Resting one day beneath the Cranford yew I tried to picture those old
yeomen leaving their native shire to fight on foreign soil, and the following
verses came into my mind—a glimpse of mediaeval Middlesex—which I
have called

THE SIXTY ARCHERS.

The bows that bent on Creçy's field
  Were grown on English ground;
No yews so resilient—so tough—
  In all the world around.

Some trees still stand in Middlesex
  Beside her churches grey,
That gave those yard-long arrows force
  To win that bloody fray.

The giant yew of Harlington,
  Or that by Cranford's fane,
May well have helped the English arms
  To victory again.

So we who roam the shire to-day
  Should give a dreamer's thought
To those stout yeomen-archers who
  For Middlesex once fought.

From Stanwell Moor, from Harrow Hills,
  From Hounslow Heath they bore;
The forest glades encircling Staines
  Sent forth their sons to war.

To-day thrice sixty thousand men
  The shire's torch keep aglow,
To echoes of the bowstring's twang
  Dim centuries ago.

CHAPTER XIII.

An echo of an old hunting-horn; and other bygone sports of the Heath.

IN the eighteenth century, in spite of its ominous reputation, Hounslow Heath was one of the best-known places for field-sports in the Home Counties; these included racing, hunting, hawking and shooting, none of which has survived in this locality to the present day.

From the earliest days up to the disafforestation the Heath had been a Royal chase, and strictly preserved for the King's use; here were stags and wild boars, to hunt which a special pack of hounds were kept. The popularity of the Heath as a hunting ground was partly because of its position almost equi-distant from London and Windsor.

In the seventeenth century hawking, though not so extensive as in the middle ages, had a great " boom " as a fashionable pastime, and the Heath was again a favourite place for this sport, and the swooping wings of the falcon were often seen in these parts. Old records contain mentions of hawking on the Heath; for instance, to mention one only, we find in the *Papers of Henry VIII.* the following: " 1521. Accounts of the Duke of Buckingham. To the King's falconsers, showing my Lord game with their hawks, between Colbroke and Houndeslowe. 6s. 8d."; while in *Notes on Hawking* there are several mentions of these parts. " Amongst the English monarchs who delighted in hawking," runs the account, " the most enthusiastic was James I., and ' Hawking at the brook,' i.e., at wildfowl, such as ducks, teal and widgeon, was one of that Royal Nimrod's prime diversions, so much so that he would often rise abruptly from the council-table saying ' that he had worked long enough and would fain go see his hawk fly a mallard at the brook.' More than once when confined to his bed with gout, he insists on being carried in a litter for the same purpose. The western part of the Heath by Hounslow, with its many water courses, was often chosen for the sport." Charles II. was also a keen follower of hawking, as well as other forms of hunting, and came to the Heath for that purpose a good deal. During his reign (1669) we read in the *Calendar of State Papers* of an " Appointment of Keeper of His Majesty's Game within the Honour of Hampton Court, Hounslow Heath and the woods and grounds from Staines Bridge to Brentford Bridge." Another entry from the same source and date reads: " An appointment of a Conservator of all Watres belonging to the Honour of Hampton Court, running from Longford through Hounslow Heath, and falling into the Thames, of all breaches and overflowings of the same, and of all fishing and fowling thereon."

In the eighteenth century, the red deer and wild boars having disappeared with the hawks, the Heath was a favourite place for stag and fox hunting, as we know them to-day, and much patronised by the Royal family, as extracts from the newspapers of the day prove. Here are three typical ones, from *The Evening Post*, 1734:

> August.—" Yesterday their Majesties the Prince of Wales and the eldest Princesses went to Hounslow Heath, where a stag afforded them a pleasant chase for several hours. Their Majesties followed

as far as Harrow-on-the-Hill and then back to Kensington, which they did without their attendants having lost them in the chase."

September.—" On Saturday morning their Majesties went again to Hounslow Heath, where a stag was turned out, which was killed near Canons, the seat of His Grace the Duke of Chandos."

September.—" Yesterday their Majesties went to Hounslow Heath, when the stag ran directly to Staines, but being turned back to Brentford, where he crossed the Thames, and re-crossing at Hampton, ran through Staines and was finally killed near Windsor."

In *The Book of the Court,* a collection of anecdotes of the period, there is one of an amusing incident in connection with the Royal hunting on the Heath. "Many years since," it says, " a man named Feltham rented Hampton Court Bridge. One morning the Royal hunt came across Hounslow Heath (in those days extending to Hampton Common, now Hampton Hill) to the bridge, where the stag swam across. The hounds passed the gate without ceremony, followed by a large company crying ' The King.' Feltham opened his gate, and closed it when they had gone through without paying, when a more numerous party came up vociferating more loudly ' The King.' Feltham stood with the gate in his hand, though menaced with horse whips. ' Hang me, if I open my gate again, till I see your money. I've let King George through, God bless him, and I know of no other king in England; if you have brought the King of France, hang me if I let him through without paying!' Suddenly the King himself appeared; Feltham made his reverence and opened the gate. On His Majesty enquiring the cause of the delay he at once sent back an equerry to give the old man a guinea. Soon afterwards George III. was crossing the bridge in his carriage, when he pulled down the window, and laughing heartily, said to the toll-keeper, ' No fear of the King of France coming to-day, eh, Feltham. What! What!' "

It would appear that the hounds from the Heath often made their way to Hampton Court, as mention of the same happening is found in Ernest Law's *History of Hampton Court,* and in Lord Hervey's *Memoirs* the hounds on the green here are referred to again.

Hunting on Hounslow Heath at its best, however, is inseparably associated with the Berkeleys, who kept the hounds at Cranford House for many years. There is no lack of evidence of this in many sporting books, and in *Records of the Chase* we read: " The fifth Earl of Berkeley, who was born in 1745, hunted an extensive country for some years, distinguished by the title of the Old Berkeley. His lordship had kennels at Cranford, his seat in Middlesex, and another at Gerrards Cross, in Bucks, as well as others away from the vicinity of London. . . . The Hon. Morton, and his brother the Hon. Grantley Berkeley kept a pack of harriers at the family seat at Cranford, but they were soon converted to staghounds. It was a truly aristocratic establishment. The earl hunted them and Mr. Grantley whipped them in. They wore the orange plush or ancient tawny coats of the Berkeley family, with black velvet caps. They continued about twelve years, and afforded abundant sport at Hounslow Heath."

Mention of this is found in Grantley Berkeley's *Life and Recollections* and *Reminiscences of a Huntsman.* In the latter book is the description of the famous incident of the humorous result of a stag-hunt which began somewhere near Hounslow Heath, *but finished up at the British Museum!*

Incredible as it may sound, this is true, and it happened not much more than a hundred years ago—about 1823. It appears that the stag actually got as far as Regents Park, and made its way to Bloomsbury, to Montague Street, adjoining the Museum. When the hunt were trying to capture the stag, which had taken refuge on the doorsteps of a house, the occupier, a choleric old gentleman, appeared at the front window and ordered Berkeley (having mistaken the huntsman's clothes for those of a showman) to take his performing animal away or he would call the Beadle! There is a delightful illustration, by John Leech, of this incident.

The *Recollections* are full of glimpses of the country round Cranford, only natural in a place so intimately connected with the author's family. "Previous to my purchasing a house adjoining the park at Cranford," he writes, "my sojourn was the Old Cranford Bridge Inn (the recently-demolished Berkeley Arms). The neighbourhood of Hampton Court and Twickenham were very gay. I was president of the Duke of Clarence's Cricket Club, and there were balls and parties without end. The hours I kept not according to those of my mother, it suited me well to live at the inn, and a jolly life it was."

"On hunting days," the writer continues, "some amusing things happened. Mr. Gunter, the renowned pastrycook, was one day mounted on a frisky horse. 'Mr. Gunter,' remarked Lord Alvanley, 'that's a fine horse you are on.' 'Yes, he is, my lord,' replied Gunter, 'but he's so hot I can hardly hold him.' 'Why the devil don't you ice him, then?' rejoined his lordship. Gunter looked as if he did not like the suggestion."

The Victoria County History of Middlesex has mention of the hunting here and quotes several incidents from Berkeley's books. "Owing to the proximity of London," it states, "the runs were sometimes attended with amazing results, such as the one in which the stag from Hounslow Heath headed for Twickenham, Isleworth and Brentford. Of this run Lord Alvanley is reported to have said, 'Devilish good run; but the asparagus beds were awfully heavy and the glass was up to one's hocks; the only thing wanted was a landing-net, for the deer got into the Thames and Berkeley could not get him ashore!'"

On another occasion the stag was run from the Heath and brought to bay in Lady Mary Hussey's drawing room at Hillingdon; and on a third it entered the kitchen of a house, the wrathful owner of which said in reply to Berkeley's apologies, "Your stag, sir, not content with walking through every office, has been in my drawing room, sir, whence he proceeded upstairs to the nursery, and damme, sir, he's now in Mrs. Blank's boudoir!"

There is also mention of shooting and poaching in his books, though to a less extent, and a little about pugilism; in fact Gentleman Jackson, the former Champion of England, figures in his pages.

Mr. Armytage's book, *By the Clock of St. James's* (of which more elsewhere), there is a paragraph of interest to the present chapter. "Cranford House to me," he writes, "always recalls stories of the Bloods of my first few years, of the hunting field, of boxing, of cock-fighting, of poaching battles, fishing, shooting and other pursuits; of hard swearing and hard drinking; with more than a whisper of the knights of the road who infested Hounslow Heath very nearly until the days when the curtain of my own existence was rung up."

In Wilkes' poem *Hounslow Heath* will be found a good deal of information, and rather flamboyant description, of the hounds that hunted over

these lands, but far more interesting verses still, I think, are those recently
discovered in the stables at Cranford House, painted on a board, and which
by the courtesy of Mr. Sadler, the Bailiff, I was able to copy. Part of the
stables, of course, were once the actual kennels of the Cranford Staghounds.
"RALLYMAN.
"A favourite staghound died on Friday, 28th January, 1825,
in his sixth season.
" On reaching the kennel sad news met my ear,
And caus'd, though I own it, my shedding a tear.
The words were most homely, sincere but confus'd,
Yet render them better, the subject abus'd.
Said Butler poor Rallyman's gone, sir, at last,
'Tis pity, no help for't, I may be downcast.
But, sir, I've a favour, 'tis one I must crave,
Give a rattling ' View Halloa ' thrice over his grave,
And unless at that warning he lifts up his head,
You may fairly conclude that poor Rallyman's dead.
Alas, it was given—poor Rally ne'er mov'd,
And dark fell the earth on the Hound that I lov'd.
He that oft hit the scent is himself hit at last,
And stern Death with true aim has now made a sure cast.
Fare thee well, then, dear Rallyman, oft in the chase
I shall miss thy loud challenge and good-humour'd face."
The verses are said to have been written by Grantley Berkeley.

     *   *   *   *   *   *

The Racecourse at Hounslow was a popular place in the eighteenth
century. It is marked on Rocque's map of the county (1754) as "The
Horse Course" and covered 254 acres. It was on the left of the Staines
Road (going west), a little past The Bell Inn, and must have been partly
on the ground now occupied by Spooners' Nurseries. In this map are
marked "Hounslow Wells," at the back of the Racecourse. Though little
seems to be known of them, they were chalybeate wells in the eighteenth
century, though they never attained much fashionable notoriety, as many
such did. In the garden of a house still called "The Wells" in Hibernia
Road is a depression in the ground said to mark the original site of the well.

Newspapers of the period contain many references to this course; in a
typical one in *The Evening Post,* 1734, we read: " On Thursday last seven
horses started at the races at Hounslow Heath. They ran three heats ";
and again in the same year: " On Friday five horses started for a Purse of
£20, and the Lord Anne Hamilton's mare, who was entered at the post, won
the Prize." Lord Anne was a curious example of a feminine name being
given to a man; he was called after Queen Anne. There was, however, a
King of the East Angles called Anna (c. A.D. 670).

This Racecourse is mentioned in Wilkes' poem:
" Near to the town, behold a spacious course,
The scene of trial for the sportive horse.
With tall white posts of ample circuits grac'd,
Of equal size at proper distance plac'd."

A rather curious sidelight on eighteenth century prize-fighting concerning this Racecourse occurs in a paragraph in *Knuckles and Gloves,* by
Bohun Lynch: " Slack, a butcher by trade, one day at Hounslow Races had
" words " with the champion (John Broughton), who laid about him with

a horse whip. Thereupon Slack challenged Broughton and the fight took place at the Amphitheatre on April 10th, 1750. The fight was won by Slack."

When this Racecourse was given up is uncertain, but Berkeley has no mention of it, and he would hardly have missed out such a thing, so it is to be presumed that it disappeared before his day.

I find, as usual, several interesting items among my notes of old-time Hounslow sports, of which there is not space here beyond passing mention; such as Cock Fights at the old George Inn in the High Street; Bull Baiting at another Hounslow inn, and Throwing at Cocks at Heston. In the *Pell Records* for 1607 we find a note: "To the Treasurer of our Exchequer, Greeting, whereas we have appointed a Dove-house to be built in Hounslow Heath for the better breeding and preservation of wild fowl."

We can conclude this brief account of the old-time Heathen sports with a note of a more modern one, for if the spot saw the "death" of some old sports, it witnessed the "birth" of another, for on Hounslow Heath the first game of polo was played in England. *The Victoria County History* reads: "Polo was instituted at a match played at Hounslow between the 10th Hussars, who introduced the game into this country from India, and the 9th Lancers." Middlesex, therefore, may claim the credit of having been instrumental in bringing the game into notice, and the county has ever since maintained the leading position it thus acquired."

No date of this historic match is given, but it was probably just before the Polo Club was formed in 1872.

CHAPTER XIV.

The High Toby — "Stand and Deliver."

ON several occasions in the making of this book I have been tempted to comment on the same thing, and that is how the particular theme in hand would fill a book by itself. On each occasion this has been true enough, but, perhaps, brought most forcibly to mind in the case of the Highwaymen of Hounslow Heath.

In this chapter it is proposed to deal with highwaymen in general, as in other pages can be found the more personal side of these knights of the road.

What the mere mention of the name Hounslow Heath meant in the eighteenth century to travellers on the western road is summed up in C. G. Harper's *The Bath Road,* when he says: "The passengers by the Bath Flying Machine grew at this point a shade paler. They generally expected to be robbed on Hounslow Heath and their expectations were almost invariably realised by the gentlemen in cocked hats and crepe masks, as the flower of the highwaymen practised on the Heath."

Macaulay, in his *History of England,* devotes a good deal of space, for such a work, to this subject in the chapter "The State of England in 1685." "Travellers," he writes, "unless they were numerous and well armed, ran considerable risk of being stopped and plundered. The mounted highwayman, a marauder known to our generation only from books, was to be found on every main road. The waste tracks which lay on the great routes near London were especially haunted by them, such as Hounslow Heath."

"It was necessary to the success and even to the safety of the highway-

man that he should be a bold and skilful rider, and that his manner and
appearance should be such as suited the master of a fine horse.   Sometimes, indeed, the highwayman was a man of good family and education.
A romantic interest, therefore, attached, and perhaps still attaches, to the
names of the freebooters of this class.   The vulgar eagerly drank in the
tales of their ferocity and audacity, of their occasional acts of generosity
and good nature, of their amours and their miraculous escapes."

This mention of the highwayman being a man of good birth has been
the keynote of many romantic tales; of heirs defrauded from their estates,
or those who had lost all at the gaming tables; and while most of these
stories can be regarded as pure fiction, certain of them at least might be
founded on fact, if embellished later.

In *Narratives from the Courts of Justice,* by Peter Burke, an authentic
case is recorded, without giving names, under the heading " A Highwayman
of Rank," and runs as follows: " An extraordinary affair happened during
the reign of the second George in the family of a Buckinghamshire baronet.
A gentleman had been on a visit to him and was to proceed on his journey
to London alone on horseback, and just as he was starting the groom
contrived to whisper this warning, ' Sir, see if your pistols be loaded as
soon as you are gone beyond this domain.' The traveller so, and to his
surprise found that his charges had been drawn.   He at once reloaded, and
it was almost dark when he reached Hounslow Heath, and here he was
stopped by a masked highwayman, who rode up to him and levelled a pistol
at his head.   The gentleman fired instantly in self-defence and his assailant
fell   dead."   On   taking   the   mask   from   the   bleeding   corpse   of
the robber, to his horror he discovered him to be the son of his late host.

Possibly it was this incident that caused Swift to write his scathing
satire on the men selected for Irish Bishoprics, wherein he declared that
most excellent and moral men are always selected for these posts, but adds:
" It unfortunately has uniformly happened, however, that as these worthy
divines crossed Hounslow Heath on their road to Ireland to take possession
of their bishopricks, they have been regularly robbed and murdered by the
highwaymen frequenting the Common, who seize upon their robes and
patents, come over to Ireland, and are consecrated in their stead."

Bishops seem to have had a good deal to do with the Heath, usually
unluckily to themselves, for, apart from the famous Seven Bishops, whose
real connection and supposed adventures here we have heard in another
chapter, as we have also of an alleged Highwayman-Bishop, here is
another case, from a newspaper of 1751: " On Monday about noon the
Bishop of Hereford, passing over Hounslow Heath in his coach and six, was
attacked by two mounted highwaymen, who robbed his Lordship and his
company of their money and watches, and then made off hastily across the
Heath towards the road to Staines."

In *The Story of a Feather,* Douglas Jerrold's rather curious book, we
find a further mention on this theme, when he says: " Some declared that
one of Mrs. Crumpet's lodgers had murdered a Bishop on Hounslow Heath,
and with a heathenish contempt of religion had pawned the dead man's
canonicals." No further details being given of this affair it is impossible
to link it up with any of the incidents mentioned here.

There is still another story told of a Bishop and an Irish highwayman,
with a different ending, when the latter at least lived up to his national
characteristic.   Whether this took place on Hounslow Heath is uncertain;

OLD HOUNSLOW POST BOY. 18th CENTURY.

Print lent by Mr. Harold Groom

no place is mentioned, but it seems that his Lordship's chaise was stopped with the usual result. The Bishop could tell from the speech of his attacker that he had recently come from Erin's Isle, and when the "business" was concluded the robber finished up by compelling the Bishop to change his good broadcloth coat for his own tattered garment. It being a cold night, the prelate was forced to wear the none-too-clean coat of the highwayman, but on reaching his journey's end he took it off with disgust and threw it in a corner. To his surprise he heard a jingling noise, and on examination he found in the pockets not only his own watch and purse, but in addition a canvas bag containing thirty guineas! Let us hope that his Lordship duly used the latter sum in aid of those in moral peril in his See!

Another historian who did not neglect to mention the highwaymen was Justin McCarthy. Indeed what writer could who wished to give a true reflex of life in those days, for the knights of the road were part and parcel of everyday existence. In his *History of Our Own Times* he writes: "The highwayman, that familiar figure in the romance and life of our grandfathers, has of late years disappeared altogether, and is even fading out of the romance of modern days. Of course the romantic writer made the most out of the highwaymen."

It is not fiction writers only who tried to glorify the highway robber, for no less an author than De Quincy has endeavoured to throw a *couleur de rose* over the ideal highwayman: "He followed a literal profession, one which required more accomplishments than either the bar or the pulpit, since it presumed a bountiful endowment of qualifications—strength, health, agility and excellent horsemanship, intrepidity of the first order, presence of mind, courtesy, and a general ambidexterity of powers for facing all accidents and for turning to good account all unlooked-for contingencies." The writer adds that he considers "the finest men in England, physically speaking, throughout the last century, the very noblest specimens of man, considered as an animal, were the mounted robbers who cultivated their profession of the great roads. When every traveller carried firearms the mounted robber lived in an element of danger and adventurous gallantry." To which Dutton Cook adds: "If to courage, address, promptitude of decision be added courtesy and a spirit of forebearing generosity, he seemed to be almost a man who merited public encouragement."

Indeed De Quincy seems to think that a shade of disgrace had fallen upon England in a previous generation, inasmuch as the championship of the road had passed for a time into the hands of a Frenchman—Claude Duval.

In considering the opinion of authors on this topic that of Dr. Johnson cannot be ignored, for Boswell tells us (under the date 1778) how "He (Johnson) talked of going to Streatham that night. Taylor: 'You'll be robbed if you do, or you must shoot a highwayman. Now I would rather be robbed than do that.' Johnson: 'But I would rather shoot him in the instant when he is attempting to rob me than afterwards swear against him at the Old Bailey, to take his life after he had robbed me. I am surer I am right in the one case than in the other. I may be mistaken as to the man when I swear; I cannot be mistaken if I shoot him in the act. Besides, we feel less reluctance to take away a man's life when we are heated by the injury than to do it at a distance of time by an oath, after we have cooled.' Boswell: 'So, sir, you would rather act from the motive of private passion than that of public advantage.' Johnson: 'Nay, sir, when I shoot the highwayman I act from both . . . for, perhaps, one may, a year afterwards, hang himself from meanness for having shot a highwayman.' Boswell: ' Then, sir, you would not shoot him?' Johnson: ' But I might be vexed afterwards for that too.' "

The opinion of another notable author is that of Hazlitt in his spirited essay *The Fight:* " Even a highwayman in the way of trade may blow out your brains, but if he uses foul language at the same time, I should say he was no gentleman."

In John Ashton's *Social Life in the Reign of Queen Anne* we get some glimpses of these gentry: " Their personal appearance, which was not the gold-laced costume of the penny dreadfuls, is given in an advertisement: Stolen by two highwaymen, one in a light-coloured coat with a light-coloured wig, and the other in a light coat trimmed with black button-holes and dark brown hair." Black button-holes and dark brown hair seem something new in trimmings!

Here is another from the same source, where again the rather vague wording might be mis-read: " Advertisements frequently occur of men being taken up on suspicion of being highwaymen, and one account states ' There is now in custody in Newgate a middle-sized man, aged 40, having a High Bridge Nose, a thin Visage and pale Complexion. He was caught on August 25th and supposed to have committed divers Robberies on the Highway, he having in his Pockets a brace of loaded pistols, a Mask with strings and a black jet Mare.' " Circumstance is certainly strong against this gentleman, but what I should like to have seen, however, would be the highwayman taking his mare out of his pocket, which, if we read the notice literally, seems what he did!

Two points of view on the highwayman question are touched upon in *Famous Flights from Justice*, by Charles Kingston, where we read: " There is something exciting in a fight against odds, and all its resources; the penalty of failure being death it is only natural that the contest should engender excitement. That is why many notorious criminals have become quasi-historical characters and have been objects of sympathy entirely out of place. Dick Turpin was a thief and a murderer who ought to be branded as infamous for all time, but legend has busied itself with his name, and if not actually a hero, he is at any rate a personage."

Here is another side of the picture which shows that in his own day, however, the highwayman did not receive popular sympathy, whatever may be thought of him after a lapse of years. Again John Ashton is quoted, " In 1712 a miller was attacked by a highwayman who fired twice, but missed. The miller, judging that he had expended his ammunition, closed with him, knocked him off his horse, and then beat him senseless with his cudgel. He then dragged him to a tree and hanged him with his own belt. For this the miller was tried and acquitted.

In that interesting book *Polly Peacham,* by Charles E. Pearce, there is a sentence which reflects the *public* opinion of the times concerning these knights of the road: " Macheath, after all, was the character which appealed to the pit and gallery. The Dashing Highwayman of real life was not an unpopular character with the people. If he got his money by questionable means he spent it freely, and his daring imparted a romance to his deeds. Highwaymen were not all ruffianly Dick Turpins. They came from all classes, and being eased of one's purse by somebody who had the manners of a gentleman may have softened the offence. At any rate as a rule he robbed only the well-to-do, and this went for much in the opinion of an eighteenth century mob."

In those articles *The Crow Flies,* which we have met elsewhere, we find the paragraph: " It is interesting to note that the first suggestion of Gay's *Beggar's Opera* was a remark of Swift's, as he sat with his friends one day at Pope's Villa at Twickenham. Hounslow Heath then spread within a quarter of a mile of Twickenham, Pope must often have seen flying highwaymen chase past his door. Fielding, writing in 1775 (a misprint, Fielding died in 1754) does not say much for the Hounslow population at that time. He describes a captain of the Guards who, being robbed on the Heath, as soon as the robber left, unharnessed a horse, mounted it, and pursued the fellow at noon-day through Hounslow Town, shouting ' Highwayman!' but no one joined in the pursuit!" Such a scene, however, was certainly no novelty to the Hounslow folk of those times.

Paul Clifford contains much of the doings of the knights of the road, for in addition to Paul himself—" the highwayman redeemed by love "—we find two other notable night-riders, Gentleman George and Fighting Attie, and of the latter Lytton says: " When he dies the road will have lost a great man, whose foot was rarely out of the stirrup, and whose clear head guided a bold hand. His words were few, his actions many. He was the " Spartan of Tobymen."

It is hardly to be expected that the entertaining gossip Horace Walpole should be silent on this topic; in fact it is this sometimes (for a man, anyhow) petty trait in his nature rather than any greatness of character that makes his *Letters* so true a mirror of the small things of his day. In 1771 he writes: " Our roads are so infested by highwaymen that it is dangerous stirring out almost by day. Lady Hertford was attacked on Hounslow Heath at three in the afternoon." He relates also how once he saw a highwayman dash past his window at Strawberry Hill. In 1781 he was himself the victim of an attack, of which he has left an account in a letter to the Countess of Ossory: " Lady Browne and I were going to the Duchess of Montrose at seven o'clock. The evening was very dark, and in the lane under her park-palings a black figure on horseback passed the chaise. I suspected it was a highwayman, and so did Lady Browne.

" I had the presence of mind to stuff my watch under my arm. He said, " Your purses and watches.' I gave him my purse; it had nine guineas. It was so dark that I could not see his hand, but I felt him take it. He then asked for Lady Browne's purse, and said, ' Don't be frightened, I will not hurt you.' She gave it to him and was going to add her watch, but he said ' I am much obliged to you. Good-night,' pulled off his hat and rode away."

It is amazing how careless some writers can be, for the author of an article, " Coaching Days," in an old magazine (though of 1886 only) quotes this incident verbatim from Horace Walpole, but informs his readers that it is related " by *Lady* Walpole in her Letters!"

In the eighteenth century Hounslow Heath, and especially its chief heroes Turpin and Duval, certainly set the standard to which comparison was frequently made in later days, such as the title of an article in Chambers' *Popular Literature* on " The Turpins of the Antipodes," by which bushrangers were meant, and in *Chambers' Journal* a similar article appears on " A Queensland Dick Turpin." In *All the Year Round* is the story of Freney, the " Irish Claude Duval," though the brutal methods of the Hibernian robber bear no resemblance to those of the French road-knight.

Vidocq, another famous French criminal, is often called "The French Jonathan Wild," and we have heard elsewhere the comparison between another Irish highwayman—Brennan of the Moor—and Dick Turpin.

A similar comparison with a French robber and Claude Duval is found in *The Mystery of the Rue du Pot-de-Fer,* a story founded on history by W. Bayford Harrison of a knight of the road with a dual personality—exquisite by day and highwayman by night.

Still another comparison is found in an article on "The Road Agents of the Wild West," which says: "Evidently these stage-robbers of our day had read of the gallantry of Dick Turpin and Claude Duval in their treatment of ladies, for it was no unusual occurrence for these modern knights of the stage-road to demand a kiss in consideration of allowing lady passengers to pass without loss of jewellery."

In Blanch's *History of Camberwell* we read: "At the commencement of the present century Sydenham Hill had a reputation somewhat similar to Hounslow Heath," while in places even farther afield the same comparisons are made, for in *Travels in Asia Minor* the writer, in describing some native robbers who had been hanged on a tree, adds: "These bodies reminded me strongly of the stories my father used to tell of his young days, when on crossing Hounslow Heath he had seen the bodies of highwaymen hanging in chains from the gibbets."

To revert, before we pass on to foreign highwaymen there will be found in Anthony Hope's *The Heart of Princess Osra* a story, "The Courtesy of Christian the Highwayman," of a foreign road-knight who is compared with an English one.

We see the other side of this picture in a French account of English highwaymen in 1726 in *A Foreign View of England in the Reigns of George I. and II.,* by Cesar De Saussure, an interesting series of contemporary letters, being a foreigner's impressions of eighteenth century England. "English highwaymen," he writes, "are generally well mounted; one will stop a coach containing seven travellers, with one hand he will present a pistol, with the other his hat, asking the unfortunate passengers for their money or their lives."

Another foreign view of English road-knights is that of a learned Frenchman who also visited our shores in the eighteenth century, and left some amusing comments in his *Letters* concerning English highwaymen, for whom he confesses admiration, which, he adds, was shared by the English themselves. "I continually meet Englishmen," he writes, "who were not less vain in boasting of the success of their highwaymen than of the bravery of their troops. Tales of their cunning and generosity were in the mouths of everybody, and a noted thief was a kind of hero."

The state of things in 1737, two years before Turpin's death and before the official foundation of the Bow Street Runners, is shown in these pages —by the Abbe le Blanc—who continues: "It is usual in travelling to put a dozen guineas in a separate pocket as a tribute to the first that comes to demand them; the right of passport which custom has established here in favour of the robbers, who are almost the only highway surveyors in England. The English call these fellows the 'Gentlemen of the Road,' the Government letting them exercise their jurisdiction without any great molestation."

Then follows the most amazing paragraph, perhaps, of all, and shows a state of lawlessness in those days almost unbelievable: "About fifteen years ago these highway robbers, with a view of maintaining their rights, fixed up papers on the doors of rich people in and about London expressly forbidding all persons, of whatsoever quality, from going out of town without ten guineas and a watch on the pain of death."

Referring back for a moment to the first of these two Frenchmen's books, I should like to make a slight digression, and quote another passage of interest with regard to this district. "Now let us go across the river into Middlesex," he writes. "In order to do this we need only leave Kingston and go over a fine wooden bridge and find ourselves at Hampton Town." (This should be Hampton Wick, unless of course he meant Hampton Court Bridge; there never was a bridge at Hampton.) He calls his journey "A tour through Middlesex," but after leaving Hampton Court he merely passes along the Middlesex bank of the Thames, through Isleworth, Brentford, Chiswick, Fulham, Chelsea and Hammersmith, and seems under the humorous idea that he has seen all there is to see in the county! He is certainly full of praise for the picturesque villages and fine country houses he saw on this itinerary, which he fondly imagines is all there is to be seen in the whole county. It seems that the Middlesex of two hundred years ago was almost as "unknown" as it is to-day.

* * * * * *

To return to the highwaymen. Stories of their doings on the Heath crop up in all sorts of likely and unlikely places, and I have often found them when on quite a different quest in old books and documents. For instance the *Historical MSS. Commission re Middlesex* for 1738 has an entry concerning "A Ladye of Qualitie," who writes how she had "arrived quite safe at Colnbrook, but escaped being robbed on Hounslow Heath most narrowly. The Bath Coach, not forty yards before me, was stopped and robbed."

Walford tells the story of The Itinerant Tailor and the Highwayman: "Notwithstanding the bold front which the highwayman assumed he was often outwitted. 'Stand and deliver!' were the words addressed to a tailor travelling on foot over Hounslow Heath, by a mounted highwayman, whose pistols looked dangerous. 'I'll do that with pleasure,' was the reply, and at the same time handing over a purse which looked well stocked. 'But,' continued the tailor, 'suppose you do me a favour in return. My friends would laugh at me were I to go home and tell them I was robbed with as much patience as a lamb; suppose you fire your two bull-dogs through the crown of my hat, it will then look like a show of resistance.' His request was granted, but hardly had the smoke blown away when the tailor pulled out an old horse-pistol and in his turn politely requested the thunder-struck highwayman to give up everything of value, including his pistols."

This one, from a magazine of 1781, is not without humour, with a "Leave it to the Navy" flavour. "The Sailor and the Highwayman: One of the Bristol stages on its way to London was stopped when crossing the heath near Hounslow. The knight of the road proceeded to exercise his employment on a Jack Tar passenger, who, waking out of a sleep, demanded what he wanted. 'Your money,' replied the son of plunder. 'You shan't have it,' replied Jack. 'Then,' said the robber, 'I'll blow your brains out.' 'Blow away then, you —— landlubber,' cried Jack, squirting tobacco juice out of his mouth, 'I may as well be without brains as without money; drive on, coachman.' The highwayman was so much amused at the Tar's wit that he bade him a ' safe voyage ' and rode away."

Macaulay, writing of the year 1698, says: " On Hounslow Heath a company of horsemen, with masks on their faces, waited for the great people who had been to pay respect to the King at Windsor. Lord Ossulton escaped with the loss of two horses. The Duke of St. Alban's, with the help of his servants, beat off the assailants. His brother, the Duke of Northumberland, less strongly guarded, fell into their hands. They stopped thirty or forty coaches, and rode off with a great booty in guineas, watches and jewellery. So great indeed was the menace for a time it was necessary for the cavalry to patrol these Middlesex roads every evening."

The following account, in the *Records of the Middlesex Sessions* for 1650, is worth notice for its phraseology, for the highwaymen are termed :" gentlemen " and their victim " a man ": " A True Bill was returned at Heston in a certain place call'd Honesloweheathe, Co. Midd., against John Seynlgar, alias Sellinger, John Carrowe and William Hulton, all of London, gentlemen, for wounding and robbing a man called Phillpott on the highway."

Although it is impossible now to identify many spots on the Heath where famous crimes were committed. except in a few cases where landmarks, such as inns, are mentioned, there is one spot of gruesome memory that can be fixed with accuracy. That is where the gibbets were once situated at the junction of the Bath and Staines Roads, where they meet the main London Road, which has gradually extended westward a little beyond the spot where the old Toll-Gate once stood on the open Heath.

As late as 1899, when the tramlines were being laid, remains of these old gibbet posts were dug up. At one time these " trees " with their ghastly " fruit " lined both sides of the roads in this spot, and here the malefactors who were " turned off " at Tyburn and elsewhere were brought to hang in chains, till their skeletons rotted away, with the idea that they would be an object lesson to other evil doers.

In some verses entitled *The New Raparees* of 1691 we find the lines:
" As often upon Hounslow Heath
Have seen a felon long since put to death,
Hang, crackling in the sun his parchment skin,
Which to his ears had shrivell'd up his chin."

I have seen this verse quoted of other heaths round London where gibbets also existed—such as Hampstead, Putney, or " bleak Black Heath." In those days it was probably an equally common sight on them all, as newspaper paragraphs testify, of which the following are typical of many:

" 1751. Robert Bryant,who was executed at Tyburn for the murder of his wife, was carried to hang in chains on Hounslow Heath."

" 1784. Yesterday morning the body of Thomas Clarke, who was executed at Tyburn, was conveyed to Hounslow Heath to be hung in chains, with his accomplice Haines."

Usually it was the custom wherever the malefactor might be executed to take the body to hang in chains on the scene of his crime, though no doubt if the supply ran short Tyburn supplied the deficiency " from stock " to a popular gibbetting ground, though Hounslow Heath was more likely to be overstocked than otherwise. As far as I know there never was a gallows —quite different from a gibbet—on Hounslow Heath.

When I write " a popular gibbetting ground " it is no figure of speech, but an actual thing, for such places were always one of the " sights," and in *The Newgate Calendar* there is a well-known print of the times, showing gentlemen and ladies riding and walking by the Hounslow gibbets sight-seeing. They were the "pictures" of those days.

Pinkerton, in his notes on Wilkes' poem, *Hounslow Heath*, comments on this. "Though Hounslow Heath," he says, "was a noted place for highwaymen, many persons were brought there and gibbetted whose crimes and punishments had taken place at distant places. Thus, one Theodore Gardelle, a native of Geneva, and an artist, who committed a horrible murder on his landlady, and attempted to dispose of the body under revolting circumstances, was hanged in the Haymarket, close to Panton Street. The body was hung in chains on Hounslow Heath."

How common a sight this was we have evidence from many sources. In a country clergyman's diary of 1761 we read: "Set off for London at six in the morning. We met nothing extraordinary on the way. We saw half a dozen gibbets within a pistol shot of each other on Hounslow Heath, which, however, we passed over safely, though two post-chaises were robbed on that spot half an hour before." It is significant of the everyday sights of the period on the Heath that six gibbets are said to be "nothing extraordinary."

In Charles Knight's *Passages of a Working Life* we read: "In 1804, as I was riding home from school over Hounslow Heath the man who accompanied me proposed to show me something curious. Between the two roads, near a clump of firs, was a gibbet on which hung two bodies in chains. The chains rattled, the iron plates scarcely kept the gibbet together, and the rags of the highwaymen displayed their horrible skeletons. This was a holiday sight for a schoolboy sixty years ago!"

Two years later Cyrus Redding writes: "It was a cold night when I passed the gibbets on Hounslow Heath about midnight. All the coaches had guards and ours prepared his pistols and blunderbuss soon after we left Reading; a paradoxical mark that we were approaching the more civilised part of the kingdom."

Crabb Robinson, writing in his *Diary* under the date 1819, says he was assured by his old coachman that when he was a boy "the road beyond Hounslow was literally lined with gibbets, on which were in irons the carcasses of malefactors blacking in the sun."

In Rocque's Map of Middlesex in 1754 these gibbets are clearly marked (each complete with a body!) as standing on the spot mentioned.

Facing here in the old days was an old mansion called Albemarle House, for some time a boys' school and known as Hounslow Academy. There is an engraving of it in 1804, when all England was in arms to resist the threatened invasion of Napoleon, and the picture represents a large playground in the rear of the building, where the boys are drilling as volunteers. One writer points out that it was no doubt then considered good for the boys always to have the "humanising spectacle of the gibbets in front of their eyes!"

Indeed they were not allowed to forget them, for in *The Asylum of Fugitive Pieces* of 1785 we find the edifying item:

"Familiar Verses Addressed to the Young Gentlemen
at Hounslow Academy.

"Take notice, roguelings, I prohibit
Your walking underneath yon gibbet;
Have you not heard, my little ones,
Of Raw Head and Bloody Bones?
How do you know but that there fellow
May step down quick and up you swallow?"

The writer quoted above laments the effects of this rhyme upon the
" susceptibilities and morals of tender youth," but I think it was equally
dangerous to their studies in poetry and grammar! The verse is said to
have been written by a master at the school—the Mathematical Master we
can only hope!

One historian has written: " Whilst the general spirit of the eighteenth
century was essentially bluff and lighthearted, there was a certain ferocity
about life which made folk think little of what would seem dreadful to-day."
This is typified by an extract from an old book dealing with contemporary
life in the middle of the century in question. The writer was describing
how he once got lost on Hounslow Heath in a fog, and how it seemed that
he might be in some foreign land for all the signs of life or human habitation he could find; which was probably true enough, for the Heath then
was a lonely and desolate waste indeed. He adds with a touch of grim
humour, quite unconscious: " After having walked for hours without finding
human trace, to my comfort and delight I saw a man hanging upon a
gibbet; my pleasure at this cheering prospect was unexpressible, for it convinced me I was once more approaching a *civilised community!*"

The Hounslow Heath gibbets were eventually removed as they were an
offence to the Royal Family, who passed this way to Windsor. The exact
date of their demolition is uncertain, but it was probably about 1809;
anyhow, when Hughson wrote his *Circuit of London* in that year they were
gone.

*   *   *   *   *   *

George Borrow, in *Romany Rye,* that wonderful book that reflects so
much of the English roads about 1825, though written later, tells the story
of the old ostler: " Among the places he had served was a small inn at
Hounslow, much frequented by highwaymen, whose exploits he was fond
of narrating, especially those of Jerry Abershaw, who, he said, was a capital
rider. . . . My old friend would add that good rider as Abershaw was
he was inferior to Robert Ferguson, generally called Galloping Dick.

" I learned that both were capital customers at the Hounslow inn and
that he had frequently drank with them. He said that no man could desire
more jolly companions over a glass of 'summat,' but that upon the road
it was anything but desirable to meet them; there they were terrible."

The ostler's opinions on highwaymen are worth reading, though too
long to quote, and he says that the inn at Hounslow (unfortunately not
mentioned by name) was now closed, so it can never be identified. The
main interest, however, in the above extract is that it definitely associates
the notorious Jerry with Hounslow Heath, for he is nearly always depicted
as operating on the rival waste of Putney. He also figures in *Lavengro*—
but as a ghost only.

A very favourite story of the old writers and told of many places,
Hounslow Heath often being that chosen, is that of the two travellers,
one of whom confesses to money hidden in a boot (or some such place),
and when attacked by robbers this fact is disclosed by his companion to
the highwaymen. Upon natural indignation being subsequently shown at
this treachery, the informer explains that he did this to prevent them both
being searched, as he himself had a much larger sum hidden in (say) his
hat, from which he compensates his companion for his loss. This is quite
a " hardy annual " among highwaymen yarns, with variations.

In *On the Track of the Mail Coach,* by F. E. Baines, there is a good

CLAUDE DUVAL ON HOUNSLOW
HEATH.
I.: The Invitation.

II.: The Dance.

DICK TURPIN AND TOM KING STOPPING THE ROYAL MAIL ON HOUNSLOW HEATH.

From an old coloured print

BROAD-WHEELED WAGGON, 1801.
Note similarity of wheels to modern balloon tyres.

From an old print

story of a man who bought a horse cheap in London. When he was returning home over Hounslow Heath all went well until he observed another horseman approaching. The horse at once sidled up to the newcomer as though he would ride him down, and behaved in so menacing a way that the stranger promptly produced his purse. Explanations and apologies followed. Soon a post-chaise drew near; again the sidling process was gone through. Now, however, blunderbusses were thrust through the window and threats were used that if the alarmed rider did not draw off the inmates would fire at him. At Colnbrook the rider sold the horse, not wishing further to own a steed so well acquainted with the habits of the knights of the road. The weak part of this story is this—would a highwayman have wished to dispose of a steed so well trained in the niceties of the profession?

" There was seldom great daring in the robberies of the highwaymen," writes " The Crow " (Walter Thornbury). " They were but poor humbugs. They had houses of intelligence; they had ostlers, drivers of waggons, innkeepers and many others in their pay. They did not attack armed travellers if they could help it, except by force of numbers or by surprise. Wild drinking and gambling were the desperate reactions from their dangers. Then came the gallops, the flying over gates and brooks, to get by moonlight to Hounslow; every bridle path and field and hedge, of which every highwayman was familiar, was used by them to advantage.

" In the reign of William and Mary Hounslow trembled at the name of Whitney, who, like his successor Turpin, began life as a butcher. The best story told of him is when he plundered a gentleman named Long, upon the Heath, of a hundred pounds in silver. The traveller begged for just enough money to be returned to pay his expenses on the road. To this Whitney agreed and opened the bag, but when the gentleman drew out a brimming handful, far more than was stipulated, the professional thief was quite shocked and exclaimed sadly, ' Why, I thought you would have had more conscience, sir,!'

" John Hawkins, one of the wretches that fed the Hounslow crows in 1722, was the greatest robber of mail coaches on record. He stole the bags of five in one morning. He used to go to the Three Pigeons in Brentford, then ride on about six in the evening to the Post House at Hounslow or Colnbrook, and enquire at what hour the mails were due."

In the *Midddlesex County Records* are some quaint extracts concerning highwaymen round Hounslow, rather earlier than most of such items. Here are a few:

" 1294. Pardon at the instance of the Earl of Cornwall to three persons, Hugh and Stephen le Whyte and Richard le Breunere, charged with the death of William Donegal on Hundeslowhethe."

" 1585. Joan Barringer, of Houndeslowe, practised the detestable arts of withcraft against Rose Edlyn with the intention of murdering her. The said Rose languished from the effects of the said diabolical practise that she did die."

" 1602. On the highway at Howneslow, Co. Middx., Francis Kimber (a Gentleman of London), assaulted Wm. Peverell with a certain instrument called a pistol, which he, the said Francis, with his right hand pointed at the said William's beast and put him into great fear and terror."

" 1620. A True Bill was returned that at a common inne called the Maidenhead in Hounslowe John Starre and William Walter, Yomen of

Hounslowe, cheated and defeated Matthew Foster of 44s. in playing a certain game of cardes called ' Thy carde and my carde.' "

" 1674. A great and horrible murder on Hounslow Heath; being a full and true relation how a woman's brains were knocked out with her own patten, rob'd and her throat cut."

More intriguing, however is an entry which, though it does not actually concern Hounslow, contains a name in later years to be famous on the Heath:

" 1602. There was to-day taken one Bartholomew Turpin, a Highway Man."

Was he any relation, I wonder, to Dick of that ilk? Though a definite relationship is claimed some years later, for in 1771 one John Joseph Defoe was hanged at Tyburn for highway robbery. Records state him to have been a grandson of the author of *Robinson Crusoe*.

In *Machyn's Diary* of a few years earlier we find some very quaint little bits of information concerning the Heath. It was written in the good old spell-as-you-please days.

" 1552. The xxj day of Desember rod to Tyborne to be hanged for a robery done on Honsley heath, iij talmen and a lake." (Three tall men and a lacquey, a modern " translation " gives it.)

" 1556. The ij day of Marche rod from the Towre my lord Sturton with Ser Robert Oxenbryge, the leyff-tenantt, and iiij of my lordes servandes, with serten of the gard, through London, and so to Honsley, and ther they lay alle nyght at the Seyne of the Angell and the morrow after to Staynes."

Here is an account, from a newspaper of 1817, that at first seems irrelevant, but has a distinct bearing on the present subject: " Most Atrocious Murder! We have to record a deed perpetrated at Theddlethorpe, in Lincolnshire, so sanguinary in its nature and so horrible in its circumstances that we could almost wish ourselves of a different species from the diabolical and inhuman wretches who were capable of committing it."

The murder of an old couple in a lonely cottage is reported in bloody detail and at great length. Here are some of the milder passages—the comments are mine! " The victims were most bloodily murdered by some horrible monsters in human shape, who entered the house by the back way for their bloody purpose. The dead bodies were discovered by some workmen, who, after observing large quantities of blood streaming through the ceiling, thought that something might be amiss. (You know my methods, my dear Watson!) On going to the bedchambers they beheld the appalling spectacle of the mangled corpse of the housekeeper placed in a sitting posture upon the floor against the wall, and in the other room the still more terrific object of her old master, lying dead on the floor.

" Upon the arrival of the coroner to view the bloody scene of carnage, where the bodies exhibited marks of the most sanguinary barbarity, the officer of the law expressed the opinion that a most horrid double murder had been done." (What a wonderful man you are, Holmes. How *do* you tell these things so quickly?) Then follows a detailed description of all the wounds; it is not pleasant reading, but it is graphic and makes the modern *Police Budget* seem anaemic stuff! What connects it with this book is the remark that says: " Some think this crime the work of a band of footpads, lately operating on Hounslow Heath, who have been driven away from that locality by the Runners and have sought fresh places for their wickedness."

This statement is remarkable in several ways; the date was towards the end of our Heath's "glory," and news travelled slowly then. Besides Theddlethorpe is some 150 miles from Hounslow, a long distance for footpads to travel to seek new unhappy hunting grounds, whatever mounted highwaymen might do. This last piece of information seems a flight of fancy—a case of "Give a Heath a bad name!"

These old newspapers had a quaintness missed in these more sophisticated days. Here is an item of 1810: "Last night about twelve o'clock three highwaymen attempted to stop the Armed Post Rider near Hounslow. The Rider escaped with the Bags safely, after a fierce fight with the would-be robbers." The following is a full description of the robbers as given by the Rider: "One a Tall man of 5 foot 11½ inches, wearing a long straight cut drab coat, trowsers of the same colour, complexion dark, about forty years of age. Another about 5 foot 6 inches, in a short blue single-breasted coat, light coloured stockings and neckcloth and breeches; the third the same height within an inch, in a drab single-breasted coat, breeches and light stockings, both fair of complexion, and about thirty years of age." The Rider must have been a very observant man to notice so much detail about his attackers while fighting them in the darkness.

A good highwayman story of an entirely different kind is W. M. Thackeray's little-known book *Catherine*. It is really a satire written, so the preface states, "to counteract the injurious influence of some popular fiction of the day, which made heroes of highwaymen, and created a false sympathy for the criminal." It is really a most interesting eighteenth century story, in which "the famous highwayman Captain Macshane" (fictious, of course) appears, and many of his adventures take place on the roads of Middlesex.

*   *   *   *   *   *

Some writers on Hounslow tantalise and rouse our curiosity without satisfying our wish for topographical details. This paragraph from an anonymous writer in an old magazine is one in point: "The great highway to the west of England has provided many incidents upon which novelists could found romances. It is not unnatural, therefore, that some of the old buildings which bordered the road, the posting inns, and even some of the ancient manor houses, should have their stories of Dick Turpin, Claude Duval, and the like. Set some distance from the main highway across Hounslow Heath there stood until comparatively recently an old dwelling, half farmhouse, half inn, which was, like many others hereabouts, reputed to have been the resort of highwaymen working the Western Roads. When it was demolished, cunningly placed behind the panelling was a cavity in the wall, which, when opened, showed a gruesome sight. Propped up against the wall, half sitting, half kneeling, was the skeleton of a man dressed in the riding attire of about 1780, with a pistol in his belt and another on the floor by him. The latter had been discharged, and part of the man's skull was blown away. Fallen from the pocket of his now rotten coat were two gold watches, some rings, and a score of guineas dated 1776.

"The story is easily read. Here evidently was all that remained of some bold gentleman of the road, who for some reason had in a fit of despair, or because he had been left to starve, blown out his brains. We learned the old house had for many years borne the reputation of being haunted by a highwayman's ghost, the troubled spirit of one known as

'Black Will.' Now the mystery was solved, and the mortal remains of poor Will, trapped at last by fate, were brought to light."

In spite of the writer's statement that the mystery was solved, for us it has only begun. The extract was undated; is it fact or fiction? Where was this house and who was Black Will? *The Newgate Calendar* cannot tell us.

Probably the most amazing record of highwaymen is one we can read in *The Bath Road*. It seems that in the first quarter of the eighteenth century Everitt and Williams, " two professors of the art of robbery on the highway, entered into a verbal agreement to work together on the roads near London, and to share the results equally. They did extensive business on Finchley Common and Hounslow Heath, but when the time came to settle accounts Mr. Joseph Williams (a Welshman!) could not be induced by his partner to give a statement or pay up. Thereupon, in 1725, the aggrieved Mr. Everitt actually brought an action-at-law against him. He filed a Bill in Equity in the Court of Chancery, which recited the entry into partnership, and how they had done ' business ' to the amount of £2,000.

" The Court resented this action and dismissed it. The plaintiff's lawyers were fined £50 for contempt, and his counsel had to pay costs. It is even more amazing that these self-confessed highwaymen, who openly owned that they had ' dealt with several gentlemen for divers watches, rings, swords, cloths, saddles and horses ' on profitable terms, were not arrested, but they were allowed to go free. It was not for long, however, as both were hanged soon after for other robberies." This case was mentioned before Mr. Justice Darling in 1920, when he refused to believe it other than a joke; but it was proved a fact by the Record Office.

It is hard to end this chapter, so thickly do these stories crowd one another. There is that of Mr. Nutthal, solicitor to the Earl of Chatham, who is said to have died of fright on Hounslow Heath when a highwayman fired at him, though the bullet went wide.

Sometimes, however, the highwaymen got some shocks, as in the case of one who rode up to a coach on the Heath and ordered the occupant to alight. The passenger obeyed at once, and when the robber set eyes on him the knight of the road nearly fainted, and then fled as if the devil were after him! *The passenger was eight feet seven inches in height.* It was Patrick Cotter, the Irish Giant, who was the tallest man ever born in the British Isles.

A shock of a milder sort for the highwayman is told in the following story: " A coach, bowling across Hounslow Heath in June, 1741, pulled up sharp. A masked man covered the coachman with his pistol. Three little heads bobbed out of the window, and disappeared as a frantic attendant clutched her charges. ' Who are these pretty dears?' asked the highwayman. ' The grandchildren of your King,' came the quavering reply from the nursemaid. So they were, sure enough: the young family of Frederick, Prince of Wales, travelling from Epsom to Windsor. The boy was Prince George, aged five (one day to reign as George III.—was ever another monarch held up by gentlemen of the road?).

" ' God bless them!' cried the loyal highwayman, and doffed his hat. ' Let 'em pass, mate,' he added to his companion. But they rifled the coach behind, where the under-nurses were huddled." Loyalty was all very well, they evidently thought, but business was business on the Heath, after all!

Recently I saw in a cottage garden near Hounslow, on that part of the country that had once been the Heath, a scarecrow. Not that there was anything unusual in that, but I wondered if the way it was displayed was by chance or design. Probably the former, but it looked ominous, for instead of being stuck on a pole in the ground in the ordinary way, it was hanging by the neck from the bough of a tree. It looked mighty like one of the highwaymen of old suspended on a gibbet!

Eric Partridge's *Highwaymen* and Arthur L. Hayward's *Book of Highwaymen* are both books no student of this subject should miss. The latter has written a good condensed edition for boys, in which we find the paragraph: "Hounslow Heath was a sinister place in the olden days; a great wilderness of furze bushes and grassy mounds, interspersed with swamps, and tracks little known to honest men. For the Gentlemen of the Road it was the finest hunting ground in England."

In *The Story of the Roads,* by C. H. Hartmann, we hear a good deal of the Heath; here are two typical extracts: "Owing to the great number of travellers in the vicinity of London, the favourite haunts of highwaymen were the lonelier spots on the main roads out of town. In 1636 so much alarm had been caused by the frequency of highway robberies on Hounslow Heath and the roads about Staines that the Privy Council ordered that a special campaign should be carried out against robbers in these parts. The method advocated was that the highwaymen should be entrapped by sending out a decoy horseman of affluent appearance, followed at a suitable distance by armed patrols." "In the eighteenth century the roads were infested with highwaymen, cut-purses and pick-pockets, their favourite haunts being the lonely stretches of common such as Hounslow Heath."

*   *   *   *   *   *

We must end this chapter, however, on a serious note, as befits the subject, and Borrow's "epitaph," in *The Romany Rye,* on the passing of The High Toby is more than serious—it is almost pathetic: "Finding the old ostler so well acquainted with the history of highwaymen, and taking an interest in the subject myself, I asked him how it was that the trade of the highwayman had become extinct in England. Whereupon he told me that many causes had contributed to that result, the chief of which were the following: the refusal to license houses which were known to afford shelter to highwaymen, which, amongst others, had caused the inn at Hounslow to be closed; the inclosure of many a wild heath on which they were in the habit of lurking; and particularly the establishing in the neighbourhood of London of a well-armed mounted patrol, who rode the highwaymen down, and hanged them without ceremony."

"*Sic Transit*——."

CHAPTER XV.

"Bloody News from Hounslow Heath."

THE above heading, from an actual paragraph in a newspaper of 1751, was enough to send a shudder of apprehension through travellers to be on the western road out of London in those days, when those were considered lucky who crossed the dreaded Heath unmolested.

The terrors of Hounslow Heath occupied the public mind a good deal then, and those who stayed safely at home liked to read of the perils of travel; these news items were the "thrillers" of a bygone age, and if the news were gory so much the better—human nature was much the same then as now. Nor were these sensation lovers disappointed, and used as I am to the surprises of research when fishing in the sea of print, I must confess to wonder in finding so many mentions of Hounslow Heath in the old newspapers and journals since the days when Defoe started *The Review* in 1704, which was the first newspaper as we know them to-day, though several news sheets existed in the seventeenth century. By far the largest crop, however, come from the later eighteenth century journals, of which period one historian states "It is literally true that not one single number of any London newspaper of this period was without reports of outrages by highwaymen," and it is equally true that a very large proportion of these took place on Hounslow Heath.

A full list of magazines and newspapers consulted would make this chapter mostly names, but the more important ones will be found in the Bibliography. Many of these titles are the same as those existing to-day, but with the exception of *The Times* and *The Morning Post* have no connection. The number of forgotten journals is amazing, such as *Le Journal de Middlesex* of 1791, entirely in French, for some mysterious reason, though printed and circulated in London.

I have put the dates of the extracts as a matter of interest, and when the heading is in italics it is the original one; but as these paragraphs were usually without headings I have, in most cases, supplied them myself, for uniformity—or as a passing comment! The first one, giving this chapter its title, reads:

1751.   *BLOODY NEWS FROM HOUNSLOW HEATH.*

"On Wednesday night there was committed on Hounslow Heath a nasty crime. As a gentleman was riding near Bedfont he was attacked by two desperate highway-men, who demanded his money.   Upon the gentleman offering resistance the ruffians attacked him with pistols and swords and left him, after robbing him, sorely hurt to die of his wounds. He was found next morning by a farm labourer, and carried to the Black Dog. The villains who did this horrid and bloody deed have not yet been caught."

Similar accounts appear in almost endless succession, in which tragedy, comedy and romance mingle.   Here are a few:

1750.   A " TOPOGRAPHICAL " HIGHWAYMAN.

It was the custom of some Gentlemen of the Road to frequent one particular spot for their " business." This could not be said of Peter Finloryer, a Highwayman hanged in 1750, for an old magazine account is notable for the different places round London he honoured with his attentions. His knowledge of the environs of London as far as the best spots in which to play the High Toby must have almost earned him the title of "The Lysons of the Highway." Here is the account of his "topographical" activities: "Some time since Finloryer robbed a gentleman on Shooters Hill. He next robbed two gentlemen near the Green Man at Dulwich. Two more he robbed in a post-chaise near Sydenham. He robbed a coach near Eltham Church, and then robbed a gentleman on Hounslow Heath. He then robbed a gentleman in a one-horse chaise within a hundred yards of Hounslow Turnpike. That same night, in coming towards London he robbed a gentleman near Kensington Turnpike. He committed several robberies near The Whale-bone, within two miles of Romford, on the Essex Road, and many on Putney Heath, Barnes Common and Wandsworth Common. He next went to Woolwich and robbed a gentleman there, and next day was seen at Dartford. He was pursued to Epping Forest, where he escaped again to Finchley Common and to Hounslow Heath again."

1751.   GOOD SAMARITAN AND HIGHWAYMAN!

"Thomas Jackson was indicted for assaulting George Brookes on the King's Highway and robbing him. George Brookes deposed that as he was riding over Hounslow Heath his horse slipped and he fell down, but the prisoner, coming by, help'd him (he being lame) up on his horse; that the prisoner then walk'd by his side for about two miles, when he on a sudden said, ' *Old gentleman, you must now come down,*' and then pulled him off his horse and took a purse out of his pocket, and left him on the ground, where he lay some time, as he was unable to help himself."

1751.   THE WALLET AND THE CARPENTER.

"On Saturday night last a gentleman was robbed of his wallet on Hounslow Heath by a single highwayman with a crepe on his face. A journeyman-carpenter, with a bag of tools on his shoulder, seeing the action, told the gentleman if he would lend him his horse he would pursue and take him, to which the gentleman consented. The carpenter came up with the highwayman near the Toll-gate and with the butt-end of the whip knocked him off his horse and secured the wallet."

1751.   A "BATTLE" ON THE HEATH.

"On Thursday last Mr. Thomas Vincent was returning from London to Windsor in his coach with his lady, and about a mile from Colnbrook Turnpike, near Hounslow Heath, they saw at some distance a highwayman rob a young gentleman, but upon seeing the coach he rode off without taking any money; when the gentleman coming up and confirming it, Mr. Vincent got out of his coach, and mounting a led horse with pistols, he with two of his servants (one of whom was armed with a musket) pursued the fellow, and overtaking him in less than two miles, he dismounted and stood upon his defence; they likewise quitted their horses, and advancing towards him, he fired a short fusil at the servant with the gun, but the ball missing him, the servant returned the fire, though without effect. The highwayman then ran up to the servant and shot off a pistol close to his head; but he in the scuffle putting it aside with his arm, it providentially did him no injury; upon which the servant knocked the villain down with the butt-end of his musket, and secured him. Besides the Fusil, he was armed with a Brace of Screw Barrel Pistols and a Cutlass."

1751.   THE CLUE OF THE LAME HORSE.

" A few days since a young man of about twenty-six years of age came
to the White Hart at Cranford and put up his horse, which he had rode
very hard, and shoulder-slipp'd.   A farrier blooded and oiled him, and he
would have hired another in the neighbourhood, but could not, upon which
he said he would stay all night, but found means to steal his horse out of
the stable, and went off without paying his reckoning, and went immediately and robbed a Higgler of five shillings near Colnbrook and a gentleman's
servant near Longford.   He was dressed in a coat with a broad cape, and
mounted on a tall black horse very lame."

1761.   THE GENERAL'S BIRDS!

" General Napier was last week robb'd on Hounslow Heath of a painted
Silk Neglegée and two Petticoats, with a pattern of flowers and leaves in
gold and silver, with butterflies painted thereon and some birds."

[Why the gallant general was travelling with such luggage is not
explained—unless, of course, the last two words of the paragraph are meant
as a subtle clue!]

1761   *A WRONG SHOT.*

" A highwayman having committed several robberies on the Hounslow
road, the Western stages have employed a guard to attend them till daylight, when they generally think themselves safe; but this day two thief-
takers, in hopes of entrapping the highwayman for the sake of the reward,
set out early in the morning, with a view of being attacked by the highwayman at the usual place.   When they had got to the middle of Hounslow
Heath they passed a stage coach, and observing the guard riding towards
the vehicle with fire-arms, concluded him to be the highwayman of whom
they were in pursuit, and firing a blunderbus at him flattened his arm in
a terrible manner and killed a servant who rode upon the top of the stage."

1763.   *A BATH ROAD TRAGEDY.*

" A desperate highwayman, not above eighteen, after robbing several
people on the Bath Road, met a man returning from market near Hounslow, with a boy before him, who, making some demur in delivering his
watch, the villain pulled out a pistol and shot him dead.   Having been soon
after apprehended at a blacksmith's on suspicion, and in his examination
confronted by one who he had robbed, he pulled out a knife and cut his
throat, though not effectually enough to escape the gallows."

1765.   A JEKYLL AND HYDE OF THE HIGHWAY.

" Thomas Wilson, who guarded the Bristol Mail, was hanged for robbing
the Bath stage waggon on the highway as it crossed the Heath near
Hounslow."

1766.   QUITE THE LADY.

" A few nights ago, among the passengers that were going in the stage
from Bath to London, were two heavily-veiled females that had taken outside places.   As they were climbing into their seats it was observed that one
of them had men's shoes and stockings on, and upon further search
breeches were also discovered; this consequently alarming the company,
the person thus disguised was taken into custody.   The next day he was
brought before a magistrate, and upon a strict examination into matters
it appeared that he was a respectable tradesman who, having cash and
bills to a large amount on him, thus disguised himself to escape the too
urgent notice of the ' Travelling Collectors ' on Hounslow Heath and other
places."

A GIBBET ON HOUNSLOW HEATH.

1767. THE CHURCH MILITANT.

" On Wednesday last Captain Maynard was robbed by a single highwayman by the Hounslow Turnpike of twenty-one guineas. After he was robbed the Captain went back to Hounslow town, where he procured two post-horses and a post-boy and went in pursuit of the highwayman, and came up with him near Bedfont, engaged in a tussle with a clergyman whom he was attempting to rob. When the help arrived the parson valiantly assisted in the capture of the robber."

1773. UNLUCKY 13!

" Among those who missed the gallows was the noted Sixteen-string Jack, for robbing a gentleman on Hounslow Heath of his watch and seven guineas, who now for the twelfth time escaped that justice which has so long awaited him."

Jack Rann finally hanged—the *thirteenth* time—on November 30th, 1774.

1775. A TRAGIC MIX-UP.

" A poor fellow was shot dead by the guard of the Exeter coach near Bedfont on suspicion of his being a highwayman, but on examination they could find no firearms, nor any powder or ball, nor any money in his pocket. He had only a pair of gloves, an apple, and a watch. His horse had saddle-bags, in which they found two clean shirts.

" At the coroner's inquest it appeared he was a hairdresser in King Street, Westminster, and it is said, being in liquor, and got entangled among the coach-horses, and calling out to the driver to stop, upon which the guard too hastily fired."

1776. CAMOUFLAGE.

" The Bath stage was attempted to be robbed near Colnbrook by a single highwayman, but the guard fired a blunderbuss and lodged two slugs in his forehead. After he was dead it was found that he had no firearms about him, but made use of a candlestick instead of a pistol."

1776. " UP GUARDS AND AT 'EM!"

" The Exeter stage was this morning attacked on Hounslow Heath by seven highwaymen; the guard behaved with great bravery and shot dead two of the villains, when the Bath stage happening to come along the guard of that coach went to his comrade's assistance and shot other of the robbers, whereupon the rest rode away, for having exhausted their pistols they had naught but vile oaths to fire off at the brave guards."

1780. SHERLOCK HOLMES AGAIN!

" A banker of London seeing one-half of a £10 note joined to the half of a £20 note had a suspicion that something was wrong. So it proved, and it was finally traced to a tradesman, who said he had been given it by a fellow who has now been arrested for robbing the mail. To this he has confessed, and it seems was too ignorant to be able to read, and so joined the wrong notes that had got torn in the struggle."

1803. A HARSH ANSWER TURNETH AWAY A THIEF.

" Yesterday evening as Mr. Pincett, of Clerkenwell, with his wife, was passing over Hounslow Heath on his way to Staines, he was stopped by a highwayman, who produced a pistol and demanded his money with an oath. Mr. Pincett said he would see the fellow in hell before he would be robbed, and when the highwayman, angered by this, tried to get his pistol, Mr. Pincett jumped out of the chaise and seized hold of the highwayman's

leg, nearly pulling him off his horse. Upon which the highwayman struggled
and spurred his horse till the animal rearing, Mr. Pincett was forced to
let go. The robber, however, as soon as he had gained his balance rode off
at once towards Bedfont, for in his struggle he had dropp'd his pistol, which
Mr. Pincett picked up and discharg'd at the flying villain!"

1811.   **THE KISSING HIGHWAYMAN.**

" An extraordinary robbery was committed on Thursday on Hounslow
Heath by a highwayman who stopped the coach of Dr. Morris, in which
were himself and the two Miss Somervilles. The fellow swore he would
stab Dr. Morris if he made the least resistance; he gave him two five-pound
notes. The ladies were much agitated lest the fellow should commit some
barbarity and held their money out, begging he would take it and go, but
to their surprise he replied by saying, ' Nay, ladies, don't be frightened, I
never did the least injury to a woman and never will. D—n me, keep your
money, all I ask is a kiss from you apiece.

" The ladies had no chance but to comply with this bold demand, whereupon the highwayman raised his hat very civilly and took his leave. He
was mounted on a fine horse, and well dressed, and spoke with an Irish
accent."

CHAPTER XVI.

The Low Toby—of Lesser Rogues but Greater Vagabonds.

WHY is it that the masked highwayman, riding over the moonlit
Heath with pistol in hand and mounted on a fine horse, will
always remain a figure of romance—however prosaic we may think
ourselves—while the footpad, sneaking in the shadows grasping
his cudgel, earns only our contempt as a sorry ruffian? Yet take the highwayman off his horse and he was just as big a rascal.

The answer then, is not to do with the man—it is the horse. Even so
famous a robber and thief as Jack Shepperd, who was more house-breaker
than " knight of the road," has not a quarter of the imaginative appeal of
Dick Turpin on Black Bess, or Claude Duval riding up to the coach on the
Heath to invite the fair lady to dance.

Yes, undoubtedly it is the horse that has earned for the High Tobyman
the place he holds in our imaginative memories and in the pages of count-
less books.

The records of Hounslow Heath, however, contain almost as many
references to the less picturesque villain, who probably outnumbered the
mounted men. The only " capital " a footpad required to commence his
business career was a stout cudgel, whereas the highwayman proper not
only had to possess a horse, but find accommodation—the more secret the
better—for his nobler and innocent partner in crime.

Here, then, are some newspaper and magazine stories of the lesser
" Gentlemen of the Night," and one or two other incidents.

1741.   **A NEW METHOD OF ROBBING.**

" There has of late been a new method of robbing put in practice. The
method was this: Three men well armed, pretending to be Bow Street
Runners, came to the house of a gentleman of Harlington, near Hounslow-

heath, saying that they had word that some highway robbers were hiding
in the house, and had hidden their booty there after a robbery on the
Heath. The maidservant being afraid to oppose legal authority, immediately admitted them, and two of them went to the bedchambers, whilst the
other demanded the keys of the cellar and other rooms in the house; and
the servant being obliged to attend this last, his companions broke open
drawers and took a large quantity of silk and everything else that was
valuable, including twenty pounds' worth of plate; after which the three
fellows went off with their booty undiscovered, pretending to the servant
they had found many articles stolen by the highway robbers. When the
owner came home he found his bedchamber stript; whereupon he went to
the office of the Runners, but was told that no officers had been sent to
search his house " — and this account ends with a touch worthy of Dr.
Watson at his best—" from whence it at last appeared to them after due
consideration that all this was but an invention of rogues, in order to get
in and rob the house!"

1750.   THE DANDY FOOTPAD

" On Saturday evening last a footman was robbed on Hounslow Heath
in the following manner. As soon as he had got over a stile he saw a
gentleman-like person with ruffles, etc., and a laced coat, stooping and
looking on the ground as if he had lost something. The footman civilly
asked if he could assist him, whereupon the man presented a pistol ready
cock'd to his head and with many imprecations declared that if he did not
deliver his money he would blow his —— brains out; whereupon the footman concluded that he was no gentleman and delivered up his money."

1750.   A WITCH ON HOUNSLOW HEATH.

" Last Tuesday some peasantry near Bedfont were inflamed against an
old woman who lived in a hut, ruinous in condition, near a coppice upon the
Heath. They would have mishandled her, declaring she was a witch and
did possess an evil eye, wherefrom their sheep and cattle died; but upon
some gentlemen of the neighbourhood coming up on horseback and
discerning that she had inhabited that hut for many years, as all knew,
and was quite harmless, her only crime being that she did sometimes beg,
whereupon the people left her in peace and her want was relieved by a gift
of money from the gentlemen."

1751.   BEWARE OF MAN TRAPS!

" Last Sunday a gentleman riding through a wood on Hounslow Heath
overtook a buxom young woman, who asking charity of him, he told her
he would make her a present on condition she would give him a kiss, which
she, after a seeming reluctance, consented to, and proposed going down a
path that led into the middle of the wood to be free from prying eyes. The
gentleman followed her a considerable way, when he dismounted and tied
his horse to a tree. He then claimed her promise; but before he could
execute his gallant intention a lusty, ragged fellow appeared, who said the
woman was his wife and demanded his money, which the gentleman gave
him, not thinking it prudent to dispute with him."

1754.   A CUNNING—BUT CHILLY—ROGUE.

" Last week in the road from Hounslow to Colnbrook turnpike a man
was found quite naked, tied to a tree, who being unbound by some
passengers travelling that way and carried to a house in the neighbourhood, declared that he had met with three rogues, who after having

plundered and stripped him, left him bound hands and feet. Some kind persons, pitying his condition, gave him money. But it has proved to be very ill applied, for as soon as the fellow had got good cloaths upon his back, and money in his pocket, he removed to other quarters; and it has since been discovered that he got two of his confederates to bind him in that manner in order to trick good-natured people out of their money, which he knew to be less hazardous, and perhaps thought less criminal, than robbery on the highway "—but also rather more chilly in February!

1756.   THE GOOD SAMARITAN OF HOUNSLOW HEATH.

" A few days ago as the Rev. Mr. Thomson was passing over the Heath near Hounslow he was assaulted by two ruffians on foot, who pulled him off his horse and took out of his pockets a Common Prayer Book, a guinea, some silver, and a ring off his finger, his hat and wig; and then tied him by the neck to a stump and left him. The robbery was done at nine o'clock in the morning, and the unhappy Divine continued bound till five in the afternoon, when he was released by a poor shepherd who chanced to come by and, like the Good Samaritan, carried the clergyman to his hut and gave him what refreshment his cottage afforded; he afterwards sought his horse and wished him a good journey, desiring him to remember John Wilson, the poor shepherd, in his prayers."

1760.   " SHE STOOPS TO CONQUER."

"Last evening, as a gentleman was alighting from a coach at a Hounslow inn, a respectable young woman (now supposed to be one of a gang) fell down as though in a fit at his feet, by which the gentleman fell over her, when others (of the same gang) very kindly came to their assistance, some to the young woman and some to the gentleman, and got them upon their feet, whereupon the young woman declared she had but tripped and all ended in laughter at the mishap; till, on going into the inn, the gentleman's laughter turned to anger when he missed his watch and his purse!"

1761.   SWEARING BY NUMBERS!

" A few evenings ago, as some gentlemen were drinking at a tavern on the Bath Road near Hounslow, one of them swore so terribly that a person in the company at last took cognisance of them and tore a piece from a newspaper every time he swore, to the amount of exactly 100; the next day he was carried before a magistrate, who thinking he had degraded himself to the lowest dregs of humanity, fined him one shilling for each oath."

1762.   " WHERE THERE'S A WILL——."

" A young lady of fortune, who had eloped the evening before, was overtaken this side of Colnbrook turnpike, concealed in a hearse, on her way to Gretna Green, in Scotland, her lover acting the part of the coachman, in the disguise of an undertaker."

1762.   THE JACKDAW OF — HOUNSLOW.

" A table spoon and a small spoon having been missed from an inn at Hounslow, a servant girl was taken into custody on suspicion of stealing, but the third day after her confinement a jackdaw who lived at the inn was seen to carry a tea spoon to the bottom of the yard and bury it in a straw stack, where upon search all the missing spoons were found, on which the girl was discharged."

1764.   " ALL THE NICE GIRLS——!"

" At the Middlesex Sessions a young woman was tried for stealing seven guineas from a sailor she met in a stage-coach at Hounslow. The proof not being sufficient and the evidence of the sailor very favourable, she was acquitted; upon which the prosecutor caught her in his arms and eagerly kissed her, swearing it was damned cruel to keep all, but that she was welcome to half. The smacks were so hearty and loud that the court could not help smiling at the oddity."

1769.　"WHAT A WONDERFUL MAN YOU ARE, HOLMES!

" A mysterious affair has come to light on Hounslow Heath, for several pieces of a dead body have been seen floating on a pond there, which, being dragged, produced the rest of the body. The authorities have concluded that there had been a murder hereabouts!"

1773.　　　A MEMORY OF HOUNSLOW SPA.

" Some time ago a person filled a tea kettle with a particular water from a well on the borders of Hounslow Heath towards Hampton Common, which entirely destroyed the crust formed by other waters, leaving the tea kettle quite clean to the tin. This water has since been tried on gravel from the human body, and it totally eats it up, and is supposed to answer all the desired effects on stone in human bodies. Experiments are now being made by eminent doctors, and there is great probability of them having the desired success."

1774.　　　A NIGHT OF THE GARTER.

" In May last Mr. Wilson, a merchant, had three threatening letters sent to him at his country house near Hounslow, charging him to leave a certain sum of money at a place appointed, on pain of death, and having his house burnt, etc., to which he paid no regard. On the last day of that month he came from his said house early in the morning, leaving only his maid at home, who locked the street door as soon as he had gone; and having occasion to go into the garden, she likewise locked the back door and took the key with her. She perceived three men and a woman get over the wall into the garden, having their faces covered with crepes, who all went to the back door and endeavoured to open it, which not being able to effect, they came directly towards her, upon which she was so faithful to her master as to throw the key down the well.

" Accordingly, when they found what she had done, they were so much exasperated that they took the poor girl's garters off and hanged her up by the neck; but her lamentable shrieks while they were committing this barbarity alarmed some of the neighbours, who came time enough to save her life by cutting her down, but not to secure any of the gang, who had all got clear off."

1774.　　　"WIND (UP) ON THE HEATH, BROTHER."

" A few days ago a gentleman of Hounslow was shooting with some friends on the Heath, when his dogs took to a wood, where all of a sudden they were heard growling and snarling. The sportsmen soon came up with them, and found them devouring half a sheep, perceiving, at the same time, footprints nearby. They followed the traces to a tent made with boughs and old blankets; in this the other half of the sheep was hanging.

" The sportsmen hastened to the next village and alarmed the neighbourhood, when some labourers armed with cudgels came back with them to capture the gipsy sheep-stealers. At the sight of the crowd the gipsies became much alarmed and fled in terror."

1776. THEY HAD NO "PICTURES" THEN, BUT——!

"This day Sir John Fielding informed the Bench of Justices that he had written to Mr. David Garrick concerning the impropriety of performing the 'Beggar's Opera,' which never was presented on the stage without creating an additional number of real thieves and highwaymen—as witness the increased robberies on Hounslow and Hampstead Heaths, Finchley and Wimbledon Commons, and other open spaces round London."

1777. THE BOWMEN OF HOUNSLOW.

"A bow and a quiver, much decayed, were recently dug up in a wood on the edge of the Heath of Hounslow toward Staines side. They are supposed to have lain there many centuries and to have once belonged to foresters who dwelt in the Great Warren of Staines, once a Royal Forest."

1797. A THRILLER—BY AN 18th CENTURY EDGAR WALLACE!

"The following diabolical scheme to take away the life of a young female was, by the interposition of Providence, prevented during the last week in Middlesex. As the driver of a stage waggon was going along a road near Hanworth Park about twelve o'clock at night he perceived a light in a field adjoining the road, and curiosity having been excited he unfastened his mastiff dog and proceeded to the spot, where he found a man digging a hole in the ground. The waggoner accosted him familiarly, but the man angrily informed him he had nothing to do with him or his business. He had not proceeded far on the road when he met a young female with a bundle, and he also questioned her, without receiving any satisfactory answer. The curiosity of the waggoner was on its full stretch, when he saw the young woman cross to the footpath which led to the man in the field; he again untied his dog and followed her. She went to the man, where, after a short conversation, he drew a knife from his pocket and exclaimed: '*I have prepared your grave, and you must die!.*'

"The waggoner then rushed on the man, and the mastiff seized him, when the waggoner bound him and conveyed him to safe custody, as well as the female, who wished to depart. The man has been committed for trial. The woman was a maid-servant at a farm and had met the man, a rustic, by appointment. He said he was going to take her away and marry her, so she left her situation and had £70 in her possession; and it is thought the villain had induced her to rob her master and then intended to kill her for the money."

1801. IT'S DOGGED AS DOES IT!

"When a gentleman and his dog—a big mastiff—were walking over the Heath, the former was stopp'd by a footpad near the Hounslow turnpike. The fellow demanded his purse, not seeing the dog, who was among the bushes. Whereupon the gentleman gave a whistle and an order to the animal, who had been trained as a guard-dog. Whereupon it attacked the footpad ferociously, biting him in several places. The dog, at his master's word, guarded the fellow till he was handed over to the watch."

1803. SWEENY TODD OF HOUNSLOW TOWN.

"A miscreant who projected a horrible affair has just been arrested at Hounslow. He had hired an old stable having an entrance from the street; in this he dug a pit six feet square and twenty in depth. This was covered by planks, supported at one end by a slender thread and covered with straw. It is thought he intended to lure the poorer class of traveller into this stable on some pretext and then when they had fallen into a pit set fire to some straw to suffocate them and then to rob them. He actually had digged a grave in one corner of the stable. He lured a poor pedlar into the stable and on his falling into the pit the villain tried to set fire to the straw, but affrighted by the man's loud cries he fled. The pedlar was extricated by the neighbours with little injury. The villain was arrested and it is thought he is mad to try and carry out in a town a scheme so diabolical."

1804. *NOW* THEY CALL IT "KLEPTOMANIA."

"A man said to possess property to the amount of nearly £20,000 was lately found guilty of stealing a joint of beef from an inn at Hounslow and sentenced to be whipt."

1805. THE GHOSTLY PEGASUS!

"A fellow arrested as a vagrant and thought to be frequenting the Heath for no good purpose was taken by the watch in Hounslow last night, and told them an incoherent story of a ghost in the shape of a horse that had inticed him into stable, where it kicked him till it drew blood and then flew into the sky. The fellow was found to be in liquor."

1807. "AN UNPARALLELED ATROCITY—ONE HANDKERCHIEF!"

"During the trial of two footpads for a robbery on Hounslow Heath, a circumstance of most unparalleled atrocity took place. One of the prisoners at the bar actually picked the pocket of the turnkey of his handkerchief, but being detected restored it with the most careless indifference. The court were horror-struck."

1810. SIR GALAHAD OF HOUNSLOW HEATH.

"As a dragoon stationed at Hounslow Barracks was returning from duty over the Heath his attention was arrested by the cries of some person in distress, which induced him to ride to the spot from whence they proceeded, where his humanity was shocked on beholding a woman tied to a tree, with the tears which her situation and suffering had produced actually frozen to her cheeks, and, horrid to relate, quite naked, having been stripped and robbed of every article of dress by two villains, who left her in that deplorable condition.

"The dragoon cut the cords that bound her hands and feet to the tree, and having in some measure restored to her the use of her limbs by rubbing them, wrapped her up in his cloak and proceeded to an inn, and as he was conducting the shivering object of his care into the house she looked through the kitchen window and suddenly shrank back, and in a faint voice exclaimed, 'There are the two men that robbed me and used me so cruelly.' The soldier in consequence entered the kitchen, and in his rage beat both the villains senseless and then secured them with ropes to be carried before a magistrate on the next day."

[The rogues, the record states, were transported for seven years, but it is silent as to whether the gallant soldier married the damsel in distress whom he met at such an opportune (if awkward) moment.]

1819. A BLACK GUARD.

"A man of colour, dressed in livery, who said he was a guard to Lady Lyle's coach, was charged with a highway robbery. A post-chaise driver stated that the fellow was seen riding behind the chaise, and on being ordered off he asked the driver to take him over Hounslow Heath for 1s. 6d. The chaise having set down its passengers and being on its return journey to London, this was agreed to, but at a lonely spot the black man called to the chaise to stop, whereupon he presented a pistol at the driver and robbed him of his money. Then under threats of instant death he made the driver dismount from his dicky and unharness one of the horses, on which the negro mounted and rode off at top speed. He was caught next day, however, at the Pack Horse at Turnham Green."

1785.   A TERRIBLE ALTERNATIVE.

"A gentleman crossing Hounslow Heath was accosted by a middle-aged, shabby fellow, who asked for a sixpence; this being thought so odd a demand it was refused; the man followed, repeating his request, when all at once he sighed deeply and, assuming a look of melancholy, exclaimed, 'Well, sir, I shall trouble you no more, but that small sum would have saved me from what I am now forced to do.' Then he walked dejectedly away. The gentleman relented. 'This poor creature,' he said to himself, 'is about to do something desperate.' The beggar was called back, and upon being handed the sixpence was asked the meaning of what he said. 'Why, truly, master,' answered the cunning rogue, 'I've been begging all day to so little purpose that unless your charity had saved me from it I should have been forced to *work!*'"

1778.   THE BITERS BIT!

"On Wednesday night the carriage of Mr. Riley, an apothecary of London, was stopped on Hounslow Heath by five footpads, who, seeing a box in the carriage, stole it and got away. The box contained mercurial pills, lozenges and medicated sugar plumbs, etc., of which the thieves fed so plentifully, thinking them to be sweetmeats, that they found themselves strangely affected, and were eventually caught by the Runners in a wood, where they were found, from the large doses they had swallowed, in as wretched a condition as ever were a nest of poisoned rats."

    *   *   *   *   *   *

Hounslow Heath was a great place for duels, though their stories have not survived, save in two instances. In 1606 there is a record of two lawyers who fought and killed each other here in a wild part of the Heath.

The other case was three years earlier, when Sir John Townsend fought a duel with Sir Matthew Brown, with sword and pistol, on horseback —an unusual method for those days. Both knights were badly wounded in a fierce encounter, Sir Matthew dying on the spot and Sir John soon after.

There are those who hold—perhaps rightly—that scandal-mongering is a greater crime than robbery, and the former crime shows also in the annals of Hounslow. Less than a hundred years ago there appeared some amazing paragraphs in the public Press concerning this town and actually mentioning by name residents well known at the time. Here are a few extracts:

"1839. Hounslow. Bo-Peep advises Mrs. Stevens not to allow her daughter to walk up the Staines Road looking after the soldiers. Shun Miss Johnson, my fair nymph.

"Bo-Peep wishes to know why Mrs. C. Chandler only shows her face out of a night. Is her darling afraid he will lose her? You need not be afraid, Charley, she is no 'tit-bit.'

"Bo-Peep wishes to know who that pretty girl was which Vallie, the sailor, had in a ditch down Irish Lane the other night. You had better look out, my boy, and take her a little farther abroad."

"1839. Bo-Peep wishes to know why old Bluegard does not keep his daughters at home, instead of letting them perambulate the streets so late at night without either bonnet or shawl on!"

1838.   PAUL PRY AND BO-PEEP.

"There is no harm in Lane the baker going to visit the fat girl at the butcher's shop, but it would be as well if he paid more attention to his home and not endeavour to break the heart of a too-confiding girl up the Bath Road. Beware and tremble.

"There is no harm in Miss Polly Goatly having a sweetheart, but she should choose the bye-lanes for billing and cooing with the Linge boy wot sports the pilot coat."

＊　＊　＊　＊　＊

The foregoing stories will show how plentiful and varied were the activities of the footpad and other criminals of bygone days, but I have kept the cream of such stories to the last (forgetting chronology)—two of them, one unconsciously humorous and one tragic.

The first is taken from a source that might be considered barren of such exciting incidents—no less than *The Political State of Britain* for 1731. In the mention of a slighlty earlier criminal report I came across this gem. It is an account of a would-be incendiary, who, seemingly, kept his operations to the lonely Hounslow Heath district. The report is incomplete, but it is certainly amusing—anyhow, to-day—for it chiefly concerns itself with the letters written by a potential committer of arson, one Joshua Hitch. who, it tells us, was "an apothecary by trade whose villainous actions were proved full against him."

Joshua certainly wielded a pretty pen; this was his first letter to his intended victim: "To Mr. Goodman Bailey at Longford, near Hounslow in Middlesex. Sir,—This with my service to you and I desire you'l of all love, lay me £30 at the Bottom of the Post next to your Barn a *Friday* night by Eight of the Clock, or if you do not, I'll burn your Houses to Ashes G—— d—— your Blood, and G—— d—— you, Sir, if you watch or declare the Secret to any Body d—— by Blood if Death shall not be your Portion. The D——l take you, lay it at the post, and in a month I'll lay it for you there again, and G—— d—— you if you don't, I'll burn your house and farm to the Ground, and kill you upon sight, *et cetera*. Keep this to yourself a Secret, it will be better for you Night and Day, G—— d—— you."

Had not Joshua Hitch written "of all love" one might have imagined the gentleman to have been annoyed; but anyhow he was distinctly peeved at his modest request not having been granted, as four days later he wrote another charming epistle to the same man, which ran: "Sir,—G—— d—— your Blood, I wonder you did not lay the £30 as I did write to you, but G—— d—— your Soul to H——l if I don't burn your House to the ground. G—— d—— your body if I don't kill you on the spot if you don't lay £30 at the Bottom of the last Post over against barn, and d—— your Blood if you declare your mind to any Body, or set any watch, for G—— d—— your Body I will burn your house in a week's time and all that belongs to you if you don't lay it by next *Saturday* night by seven o'clock, for I was there before and could not find it, and d—— my Blood if I don't lay it there in a month's time at the same hour. G—— d—— your Body to H—— if you deceive me, I'll be as good as my word, but if you lay it there I'll be yours to command and when you please."

Now I think that last sentence was very handsome of Joshua, for he obviously wrote in a spirit of pained disappointment. Something seems to have gone "agley" with his best-laid scheme and he never got either the money or his bonfire. The exact particulars of his capture are not given.

Joshua was really an ill-used man, for though the indictment took him to task for his "wicked and wanton naughtie words writ in his letters," I

think he showed great restraint by using dashes! Though a potential
incendiary and a would-be murderer, Joshua never forgot he was a gentleman! By the way, how do you "kill upon sight, *et cetera*"? Joshua never
lived to tell us; he was duly hanged, and, though I have no evidence of the
fact, it is probable, after the pleasant custom of that time, his body hung
in chains on the scene of his crime, i.e., Hounslow Heath. Perhaps his
ghost will one day tell the secret of that mysterious "*et cetera*" to some
ardent Spiritualist wandering amid the crowded shades that must surely
invisibly jostle each other on the site of those old gibbets that once lined
the western road.

*   *   *   *   *   *

The last example deals with the most famous crime ever committed by
footpads anywhere, which incidentally took place on the Heath. It happened in 1802 and caused a tremendous sensation at the time, with its even
more tragic aftermath. Here is an account, abridged from a contemporary
journal, of the sordid affair.

"November 6th, 1802. Murdered on Hounslow Heath, Mr. J. C. Steel,
of Catherine Street, Strand, lavender-water vendor to the Prince of Wales.
His body was not discovered until the 10th.

"Mr. Steel had purchased a piece of the Feltham enclosure on Hounds-
low Heath, and built a house on it to retire to, and had laid out some acres
of plantation of lavender and erected a distil house. The day preceding the
murder the deceased had gone down to prepare his house for the reception
of Mrs. Steel, who was to have gone down the ensuing week. On the evening of the murder the deceased left his house to return to London. about
seven o'clock, much against the persuasion of his domestics, having
borrowed a great coat and taken with him his cane, with a sword in it,
which he thought would protect him, and that there was no danger, as it
was very moonlight.

"In about a quarter of an hour it is supposed the deceased reached the
fatal spot, but nothing was heard respecting him till the 9th, when upon
a relation going from town to enquire, as he had not returned home to
London, and finding he had left his house for that purpose on the 6th in
the evening, and upon a number of persons offering their services to
examine the Heath, the body was found near the second clump of trees on
the right side of the road going from Hounslow, nearly covered with dirt
and the great coat was found in a pit on the other side of the road, covered
over with grass.

"It is supposed he recovered from this, got up and ran towards the
barracks for assistance, as about forty yards from the road, in that direction, was discovered a great quantity of blood, where it is believed the
persons overtook him and knocked him down with a very heavy bludgeon
found near the spot bloody, and with which, there is no doubt, the deceased
received other dreadful blows on the head, which had bared the skull and
fractured it in several places, and here, it is supposed, they left him for
some time from an alarm, probably of some persons appearing on the road,
and from thence, it was evident, they afterwards dragged him to the spot
where the body was found buried. Previous to covering over the body, it
appeared, his pockets were turned out and his hat, stockings, half-boots
and sword-cane taken away. Upon further examining the Heath, it
appeared that the bludgeon found near the deceased had been cut from
the stump of a beech-tree in a clump of trees near where the body was
found.

"The utmost diligence was used in the examination of every person who could be found to have passed the Heath and to have been near the spot on the day of the murder. The only property taken from the deceased, as near as can be ascertained, was a small sum of money, not amounting to a guinea, which, he said at the time he left his house, was sufficient to take him to London, and which, of course, will not enable the offenders to escape from the country.

For four years the murderers managed to elude justice, but the long arm of the law reached them in 1806; there were three of them, Holloway, Haggerty and Hansfield. The latter turned King's Evidence, and the last two entries bring this affair to its horrible close:

"1807. February 20th. This day, Holloway and Haggarty were tried for the murder of Mr. Steel. The evidence of Hansfield, the accomplice, was clear and decisive. Holloway killed Mr. Steel by beating him on the head with a bludgeon. After a long investigation the jury returned a verdict of Guilty."

"1807. Monday, February 23rd. This morning Holloway and Haggarty were executed before Newgate, pursuant to their sentence. To the last, the murderers of Mr. Steel persisted in their innocence. It is with pain we record the melancholy circumstance which followed from the curiosity which the execution excited. Twenty thousand persons, at least, were supposed to be present. Owing to the immense pressure of the crowd, some fell, and others tumbled over them, till there were two or three heaps of persons in this situation, all struggling with each other to extricate themselves. It was fully half an hour before effective assistance could be given. Besides several persons who were taken away in carts desperately hurt, the following is the statement of the killed: 24 men—3 women—2 boys." In addition many more were injured.—Yes, our ancestors took their "pleasures" quite strenuously.

CHAPTER XVII.

The "Heroes" of the Heath.

IN *The Newgate Calendar* are one thousand eight hundred biographies of famous malefactors from the reign of Henry II. up to mid-Victorian days.

It is not proposed to quote from the chronicles of all of them here, even if space allowed, for some were naturally unconnected with this district, nor is it possible to say how many actually roamed our Heath on evil bent, but during the seventeenth and eightenth centuries the proportion was large; a spot so convenient to London, and on the Great Western Road, where all the fashionable world passed to Bath, to mention one place only, could be neglected by no highwayman with an eye to business.

My authorities for these stories, in addition to the *Calendar,* are the well-known works on highwaymen of Captain Johnson, Alexander Smith and Charles Whitehead. Here, as in other parts of this book, I am also indebted to the old journals and newspapers of the period, and to the many other books of which mention will be found throughout the present volume.

We might begin our Gallery of Road Rogues with a distinguished name —for Sir John Popham (1531—1607) filled the dual role of highwayman and Lord Chief Justice of England—though not at the same time!

One early account of his activities tells us with a subtle, but unconscious, humour that when he married, at the age of twenty, a "respectably inclined wife" she persuaded him to desert the former habits and to study law, saying that "he could, with application, make as much money by the law as by highway robbery!" He was president at the trials of both Sir Walter Raleigh and Guy Fawkes.

No writer of Penny Dreadfuls ever conceived the idea of making his hero fill two such different roles as a knight of the road and chief lawgiver in the land; in fact I have been accused of inventing this for effect. As usual people will believe any extravagant lie and reject the truth; but doubters can find the authentic history of this strange dual personality in Campbell's *Lives of the Chief Justices*, Lloyd's *State Worthies*, and Aubrey's *Letters by Eminent Persons*. In the last book we find the illuminating paragraph: "In his youthful days Popham was a stout and skilful man at sword and buckler as any in that age, and wild enough in his recreations, consorting with profligate companions, and wont to take purses with them on the highway." The old writers seemed determined to include him as a "worthy" (in spite of his early unworthiness), for in the more famous *Worthies of England* Fuller tells us how Popham, "though once a knight of the road, himself advised James I. to be more sparing of his pardons to highwaymen and cut-purses." This fact is also mentioned by Dr. Donne in his poetical epistle to Ben Jonson.

It is related that on one occasion when Popham sat in judgment on one of his former companions he took advantage of the retirement of the jury to ask the culprit questions touching their early associates. "All the villains are hanged, my lord," replied the prisoner, "except you and me!"

As is natural, the names of certain persons stand out in this chronicle, and, to use a modern phrase for old-timers, we might speak of "The Big Five" among the crowds of highwaymen whose ghosts jostle the heathen roads. These five, in a rough order of importance, are: Dick Turpin, Claude Duval, Sixteen-string Jack (Thomas Rann), Galloping Dick (Richard Ferguson), and Jerry Abershawe. Then might follow the second batch, which could include William Nevison, Tom King, James McLean, and "Captain" Hind; with a third list which will contain mention of some known better by their nicknames than by their real ones, such as "The Golden Farmer," "Old Mob," "Mull Sack," and "Blueskin."

Then as a finale we shall hear a little of the famous highwaywoman Moll Cutpurse. There were, of course, other female robbers on the highway, but we have no space to deal with them here, and Moll will have to represent the fair sex in these accounts.

We have, of course, missed out many in these notes, some of whom have interest in this district; for instance, there was Thomas Gray, who played the High Toby over the Heath in the seventeenth century and finished up with the unusual end, for a highwayman, of marrying an heiress instead of dangling at the end of a rope.

* * * * *

In the edition known as The Complete Newgate Calendar, so ably edited by J. L. Rayner and G. T. Crook, there is, in the Preface, the following sentence: "Deep back as these lives take us into our national existence, it is extraordinary how nearly they are linked to our own times. Though it seems hardly credible, there is still living in an institution near Liverpool a woman who remembers, as a child, peeping out of a stage-coach and seeing the passengers robbed by highwaymen. Mrs. Janet Ann Newberry is her name, and she is only 102. We dedicate this work to her."

This was written in 1924, and if the old lady is still alive I do not know, though ten years later—in the present year of grace 1934—I have actually shaken hands with an old man who, as a youngster, once spoke to a highwayman of Hounslow Heath. This happened at Cranford, and a most interesting yarn he told me over a friendly glass of beer and a pipe at a wayside inn. It would take too long to tell the full story here, and to cut it would be to spoil it, but elsewhere I have related the whole incident, together with the yarn, that is a real link with the old highwaymen.

"THE BIG FIVE."
DICK TURPIN.

The two things by which Dick Turpin. is best known are both at variance with the truth.

The first is that the *Newgate Calendar* has no mention of him ever having been on Hounslow Heath! Yet we know from many other equally authentic sources that he was often there.

The second strange thing about him is that the incident upon which his fame rests—the Ride to York—was a complete myth and he never performed the feat at all; it was merely the invention of Harrison Ainsworth in *Rookwood,* written in 1834, nearly a hundred years after the highwayman's hanging.

It was first believed, but the truth came out eventually. and the cne who did the most to "scotch" a story still thought true by many was no less a person than Macaulay, who always took an interest in highwaymen, as his *History* proves. In Timbs' *Romance of London* we read: "It is doubtful if Turpin ever performed this journey at all"—the gradual stripping of the glamour off a popular hero is noticeable.—"Lord Macaulay had no faith in the story. He was dining one day at the Marquis of Landsdowne's; the subject of Turpin's ride was started, and the old story of the marvellous feat was alluded to, when Macaulay astonished the company by assuring them that the entire tale was false; that it was founded on a tradition several hundred years old; that, like the same anecdote fathered on different men in succeeding generations, it was only told of Turpin because he succeeded the original hero in the public taste; and that if any of the company chose to go with him to his library he would prove to them the truth of what he had stated in black and white, a favourite pjhrase with Lord Macaulay." I wonder if anyone accepted this invitation —what a chance.

Though she never bore her master to York—at least in one night— Black Bess is said to have been a real horse. I once read her pedigree, whether authentic or not I do not know, which stated that she had Arab blood in her veins. She must often have galloped over Hounslow Heath and through the sleeping villages of the surrounding countryside.

Many were the songs sung to the praise of this famous mare; here is one typical verse from an old ballad of the period:

> " Then one halloo, boys, one loud cheering halloo!
> To the swiftest of coursers, the gallant, the true!
> For the sportsmen unborn shall the memory bless
> Of the horse of the highwayman, bonny Black Bess."

In fact, the famous mare's name figures in most of the numerous verses on Dick Turpin; such as that in *The Chapter of Highwaymen:*

> " Nor did highwayman ever before possess,
> For ease, for security, danger, distress,
> Such a mare as Dick Turpin's Black Bess, Black Bess,
> Which nobody can deny."

*　　*　　*　　*　　*　　*

Turpin was born in 1706, the son of a farmer, at Hempstead in Essex. He was apprenticed to a butcher at Whitechapel, where he got into bad company. When he started in business on his own account he found it more paying to steal the beasts than to buy them. He proceeded from bad to worse, and nearly every iniquity is laid to his charge. For a time he was the terror of every traveller on Hounslow Heath and Epping Forest; at the latter place he had his hiding hole, known as Turpin's Cave. Certain relics said to have belonged to the famous highwayman can still be seen at " Turpin's Cave," a small inn on the reputed site of the real " Cave."

When matters got too hot in the neighbourhood of London he fled to Yorkshire, where he took the name of John Palmer. He continued highway robbery and horse-stealing and for some time evaded detection. Eventually he was arrested on a charge of horse-stealing and lodged in York Castle. There was then no suspicion that John Palmer was the notorious Dick Turpin, and it is possible that this fact would never have come out had he not written to his brother asking for help, the letter concluding: " For Heaven's sake, dear brother, do not neglect me; you well know what I mean when I say I am yours, John Palmer." The letter led to his identification in a curious way. His brother declined to pay the postage (which in those days was paid by the receiver) and the letter was returned to the local post office, where it was seen by the village schoolmaster, who recognised the writing of his old pupil—Richard Turpin. The letter was taken to a magistrate, who communicated with the authorities at York. Subsequently the schoolmaster identified the prisoner, John Palmer the horse thief, as the famous Dick Turpin the highwayman. He was executed at York on April 10th, 1739. He was buried in the churchyard of St. George's. His mourners were supposed to watch the grave, but the body was stolen and subsequently found in a doctor's garden. It was re-buried in the same grave, but this time in quick-lime to avoid further disturbance.

The stories—of which boys' journals are the chief sources—which make Turpin a wronged heir, anxious (for some unexplained reason) to right the world, may be dismissed as pure fiction.

I discovered an interesting story of Turpin in an American magazine, *The New York Mirror* for 1837. Some curious news comes from America at times, but this is the first occasion I have found an English highwayman story that was new to me, from that source:

" I chanced to stumble upon an ancient tavern in a village on Long Island. In the inn hung an engraving representing two horsemen facing each other. One, a bold, dashing, gentlemanly fellow, was seated on a horse rearing upright. The second horseman, stretching over the neck of his nag, appeared in the act of discharging a pistol.

" What historical event this commemorated I could not conjecture. My horse was brought by an old hostler—a Yorkshire man, he told me.

" ' Do you know what that picture in the parlour represents?' ' What, zur, the one wi' the men and horses? That be the robbery of Captain Stanley by Richard Turpin, the great highwayman, on Hounslow Heath,' responded the hostler, raising his hat, as one is apt to do at the mention of a celebrated man. ' Why,' said I, ' he was the prince of highwaymen, and worthy of his mare.' ' Did you ever hear, zir,' asked the ostler, ' that before she died Black Bess were as white as driven snow?' ' No, I never did,' I replied. ' It's true as the Bible, zir,' replied the ostler."

Dick Turpin's name crops up so often that it is impossible to keep track of all the places, often quite unexpected, where mention of him is to be found. Often his name is used merely in a comparative way, but this, at least, proves the hold it had upon the popular imagination.

For instance, in Edgar Wallace's *The Worst Man in the World* he writes: " One has heard a great deal about the romance of crime. But a great deal of romance is sheer imagination. Men like Dick Turpin have been exalted by imaginative novelists into the character of something chivalrous and splendid. Dick Turpin was a horse thief, and a coarse, illiterate boor. The glamour of his ride to York on ' bonny Black Bess ' is chiefly remarkable for the fact that he never did ride to York, but to Lincoln." I have never heard of the " Ride to Lincoln."

Another modern writer who mentions Turpin is Arthur Beverley Baxter in " Merrie Gentlemen " (Chamber's Journal, Christmas 1919): A " Ghost " Highwayman Story. Here Dick Turpin is made with a *beard!* Of course, there is no logical reason why a highwayman should *not* have a beard, but somehow it doesn't seem to fit. A pirate, yes, but not a knight of the road.

Mentions of Turpin in this way cannot help being " scrappy," and I make no apology for jumping quickly from one story to another. So we come, haphazard, to the immortal *Rookwood*, of which he is the hero. Even though hard fact has killed the truth, it has not shattered the romance of that ride to York! I love every word of Ainsworth's description of that swift dash on the gallant black mare. May I never be too old in mind to feel the thrill of galloping hooves that fly through the night on the Great North Road. Fiction or truth matter not as we read on—the spirit of the road is there—a vivid word picture of days that have gone, that moves forward in every line as Bess carries her master to the northern city.

Even if we have robbed Ainsworth of the truth concerning his hero it is not quite " playing the game," surely, to try and rob him of the credit of writing it; but it is stated in Brewer's *Reader's Handbook* that " The powerful description of Dick Turpin's Ride to York, in *Rookwood,* was really written by William Maginn, and not Ainsworth." I do not believe it; why should Ainsworth have called in Maginn? The latter could write well, but the touch of the York ride is truly Ainsworth.

*   *   *   *   *   *

A learned Frenchman, the Abbé le Blanc, in his *Letters,* quotes several anecdotes of Turpin (probably not true!), for, he relates:" I am considerably entertained with stories of how, when he robbed gentlemen, he would generously leave them enough to continue their journey. Turpin once stopped a man he knew to be rich, but not finding more than six guineas on him, he entreated him in the most affable manner never to come so ill-provided; adding that if he fell in with him again and he had no more than such a paltry sum he would give him a good licking." Was schoolboy slang good English in those days, or was it a Frenchman's love for " idiom "?

Another story told to the Abbé by one of Turpin's admirers was of a robbery near a racecourse—perhaps that of Hounslow, which was in vogue at the time. " Here Turpin and his victim met," runs the account, " when the latter boasted that he would win some of his money back in an honest way. Turpin offered to bet with him on a favourite horse, and the other accepted the wager with as good a grace as he could have done from the best gentleman in England. Turpin lost the bet and paid it immediately, and was so smitten with the generous behaviour of the gentleman that he told him how deeply he regretted that the trifling affair which had happened between them did not permit them to drink together. The narrator of this anecdote was quite proud that England was the birthplace of such a highwayman."

It is amusing to find a highwayman so strict on a matter of etiquette, which apparently allowed robber and victim to bet with each other, yet not to drink together.

The "Ride to York" story dies hard. We find Grantley Berkeley, in his *Life*, writing in a chapter called "Highwaymen and Ghosts" (and if ·*that* title won't please the romantically minded, what will?): "It is not necessary to remind the reader of the alleged exploits of Dick Turpin; no good book ever had the circulation which the history of that worthy obtained; in truth, the colporteurs of the last generation could scarcely find enough copies to supply the demand. The fascination of the subject was put to a profitable use by a modern novelist, who made a large literary capital out of his ride to York; a modern dramatist seized upon his capabilities for Astley's Amphitheatre; and even introduced not only the hero and the favourite steed, but the fabulous scene of the horse swallowing a rump-steak as a refresher."

Omnibus volumes would seem to be no new thing, for in *Black Bess, or The Knight of the Road,* published in 1868, there were over 2,000 closely-printed pages—and double columns at that. They were stout readers in those days, and it was originally issued in penny numbers. It is an extraordinary work and its chronology is terrible; Claude Duval and Rann, despite over a hundred years separating them, are made contemporaries, and then, after a complaint from a reader apparently, the author explains that he meant the *nephew* of the famous Claude! Then in the middle of the story the author breaks off to complain bitterly about the piracy of his book. The illustrations are a joy—strong meat if crude in representation.

Thomas Seccombe, writing in *The Essex Review* (the county of Turpin's birth), says: "The stories of all the highwaymen have been concentrated into a halo round this illustrious head. St. Turpin is the sweetest saint in the Newgate Calendar. Every schoolboy in particular is a devout believer in Gentleman Dick, and the belief symbolises two very fine things: jumping five-barred gates, and the love of a gallant rider for a gallant steed. Let the legend grow! It is one of the big verities of Fiction which is so far greater and stronger than the Truth! On clear nights, when the road winds upwards through dark copse and hollow to the dry and bracing upland, and spectral gates reflect white light from the moon, my belief in Dick Turpin far outweighs my incredulity. I see the gallant outlaw dashing across the open, I hear the regular tlot-a-tlap of his horse's hooves; I see the smoky breath of Black Bess, and watch the curve of her flanks as she stretches herself on the level turf. Forgotten are Thackeray and his cynical carpings; I am heart and soul with Harrison Ainsworth. I cheer onward his gallant robbers and execrate the dastardly pack of his pursuers.
'Hurrah! o'er Hounslow Heath to roam,
Hurrah for the stilly hour!'"

As a last example there will be found in a book entitled *Extraordinary*

A HOLD-UP BY HIGHWAYMEN.

Pictured by George Cruickshank

Popular Delusions, by Dr. Charles Mackay, the sentence: "Turpin's wondrous ride from London to York has endeared him to the imagination of millions, and his proud bearing upon the scaffold at Tyburn is looked upon as a virtuous action."

This account has an unconscious humour in a book on *Delusions,* in the view of Turpin never having ridden to York (which a man of Dr. Mackay's knowledge must surely have known), and the highwayman was not hanged at Tyburn at all.

Even the stories of the actual circumstance of the theft which led to his capture vary; horse-stealing is generally stated as the cause, but in one account it says it was because of the shooting of a barn-door fowl at an inn in a drunken frolic after a shooting party.

Anyhow, horse or fowl, it was a poor enough *finale* for one who often had held up stage-coaches on Hounslow Heath and the mention of whose name was a matter of apprehension to travellers. History or legend do not record the fate of Black Bess; for her death on the road naturally could not have occurred, as Ainsworth described it.

Harper, in his *Half-hours with the Highwaymen,* declares Black Bess to be a myth, but much as I admire that book I do not agree with this statement, though many tales about her may be pure fiction. It is curious that the D.N.B. has no mention of Turpin, though it deals with highwaymen of less fame, such as Hind and Nevison. Nor has the famous highwayman, though his memory is still green there, any lasting memorial in Hounslow, save a lane bearing the local name of "Dick Turpin's Walk," off Wellington Road South. Whether this has a connection with any special incident in his career I do not know.

CLAUDE DUVAL.

This French highwayman, who gained fame on English roads, was born in Normandy in 1643. "He was brought up in the Catholic faith," we read, "and received a fair education." He had at least a reputation of courtesy and politeness towards his victims. Unlike Dick Turpin, whose chief adventure is purely imaginary, the episode that gave Duval lasting fame is an actual fact, proved by documentary evidence; and since it occurred on Hounslow Heath warrants mention here. This is the famous incident of the dance on the moonlit Heath with the fair lady whose coach he had stopped.

In *The Memoirs of Monsieur Duval* (1670), an entertaining volume with the interesting, if long, sub-title: *Being the History of his Life and Death: whereunto are annexed his Last Speech and Epitaph; intended as a Severe Reflection on the too great fondness of English Ladies towards French Footmen, which it too common a complaint,* we read of this the most famous happening on our Heath. "Mons. Duval," runs this account, "with his squadron, overtakes upon the Heath of Hounslow a coach in which was a knight and his lady.

"The lady, to show that she was not afraid, takes a flagelot out of her pocket and plays. Duval takes the hint, plays also, and excellently well upon a flagelot of his own, and in this posture he rides up to the coach-side. 'Sir, says he to the person in the coach, 'your lady plays excellently, and I doubt not but that she dances as well: Will you please to walk out and let me have the honour to dance one Courante with her upon the Heath?' 'Sir,' said the person in the coach, 'I dare not deny anything to one of your quality and good mind. You seem a gentleman and your request is very reasonable.' Which said, out comes the knight, Duval leaps lightly off his horse and hands out the lady. They danced, and here it was that Duval performed marvels; the best masters in London not being able to show such footing as he did in his great French riding boots.

"The dancing being over, he waits on the lady to her coach. As the knight was going in, says Duval to him, 'Sir, you have forgot to pay the musick.' 'No, I have not,' replies the knight; and putting his hand under the seat of the coach, pulls out a hundred pounds in a bag and delivers it to him, which Duval took with a very good grace and courteously answered, ' Sir, you shall have no cause to repent this liberality of yours."

This account, published soon after Duval's death, seems to have been the branch upon which all similar ones are grafted, for in Johnson's *Lives of the Highwaymen* we find almost the identical story, except that the capitals are not sprinkled about with such fine abandon.

It was Leigh Hunt who remarked that Duval's dance was " an eternal feather in the cap of highway gentility."

The stories of Duval are almost as plentiful as those of Turpin, though the French rogue has never quite supplanted the English one in popular favour—we like to be British even to our highwaymen.

Duval was finally captured in a drunken brawl and committed to Newgate and executed at Tyburn in his twenty-seventh year (1670). " So much had his gallantries and handsome figure," we read, " rendered him the favourite of the fair sex that many a bright eye was dimmed at his funeral; and his actions and death were celebrated by the immortal author of *Hudibras*." Butler's verses have the grandiose title of *A Pindarick Ode on the Happy Memory of the most renowned Duval.*

Of course, Duval was the hero of ballads galore, of which the following verse from one of them is typical:

> " When I was mounted on my steed,
> I thought myself a man indeed;
> With pistol cock'd and glittering sword,
> Stand and deliver was the word
> Which makes me now lament to say,
> Pity the fall of the great Duval,
> Well aday!"

It is hard to realise in these supposedly more matter of fact days the stir that the death of the highwayman caused, especially among the womenkind, of whom it is stated that " abundance of ladies, and those not of the meanest quality, visited him in prison, and interceded for his pardon, and not a few accompanied him to the gallows, with swollen eyes and blubbered cheeks under their vizards." But I suppose many women will make just as big fools of themselves over some conceited and insipid ass who calls himself a " film star " in these more " enlightened " days.

In *Groans from Newgate*, an old Broadside of 1677, we read:

> " When brisk Duval, that French Latroon,
> Received reward of Picaroon,
> And put poor Ladies in a swoon."

This will be found in *Broadside Elegies*, a most interesting collection by John W. Draper.

Duval's epitaph was typical, part of it read:

> " Here lies Duval, reader, if male thou art,
> Look to thy purse; if female to thy heart.

One would not expect to find romance in a publication generally considered so "dry as dust" as a Government Blue Book, usually filled with statistics which mean anything or nothing (more often the latter!). Yet I have got so used to finding the romantic in even more unlikely places that I was more pleased than surprised to find a Blue Book, with the not very exciting title *Minutes of Evidence and Appendix of the Royal Commission on Public Records,* that was not only intensely interesting in those parts that dealt with the preservation of the Records for the County of Middlesex, but also to find one item that had a touch of romance. By the evidence it seems that there were two highwaymen by the name of Duval, said to be brothers.

Here is the quotation from the Blue Book (Royal Commission on Public Records, 1914): "At the Middlesex Sessions held on the 14th day of January, 1670, Claude Duval appeared at the Sessions charged with robbery on the King's Highway and with stealing the horse and goods of Viscount Grandison, and with the murder of Thomas Tirrell. At the same time as Claude Duval was convicted, a certain Louis Duval was found guilty of a robbery on the highway. Like his better-known brother he paid the penalty of his crimes upon the scaffold."

Duval is also a "hero" in a book of quite another kind, a novel entitled *Whitefriars: Or The Days of Charles II.,* by Emma Robinson; though the portrait is drawn more from fancy than fact. This novel was dramatised by W. T. Townsend, and has a scene "Hounslow Heath by Moonlight." When it is mentioned that another scene is "The Haunted Room in the Lone House" it is not hard to guess that it was one of those lurid melodramas beloved of our great-grandparents.

There is an account written of Duval by no less a person than Titus Oates, in which we find the following illuminating statement: "It is true Duval was a man of singular parts and learning, only he could neither read nor write." After that, there is no more to be said!

In *The Bon Gaultier Ballads* are some verses "The Death of Duval," one of which will have to suffice here:

"With step majestic to the cart advances
    The dauntless Claude, and springs into his seat.
He feels that on him now are forced the glances
    Of many a Briton bold and maiden sweet,
    Whose hearts responsive to his glories beat.
In him the honour of ' The Road ' is centred,
    And all the hero's fire into his bosom entered."

The fame of Duval still lingers, and in a recent newspaper article by Philip Macer-Wright we read: "In the reign of Charles II. there was a fierce crop of highway robberies on Hounslow Heath and on the roads about Staines. To stem it the plan was conceived of sending out decoys, of opulent mien, followed at a judicious interval by armed patrols. Claude Duval was the outstanding figure of the period and Captain James Allen the conspicuous highwayman catcher." It shows how serious was the highwayman menace when we read that at this period a new office was established, especially to deal with the keeping down of highway robbers, to which was given the important title of "Marshal of England."

*   *   *   *   *   *

I believe those who like to take their pleasures morbidly can still see the skeleton of the famous Claude in the Surgeons Hall Museum. I have never

seen them myself, nor do I want to. I prefer to think of the gallant (in
fiction!) highwayman in the saddle, and the sight of his mouldering bones
(even if preserved) would somehow destroy the memory of that famous
Courante on Hounslow's moonlit Heath.

JERRY ABERSHAWE.

In the last decades of the eighteenth century no highwayman round
London was more famous than Louis Jeremiah Avershawe, better known
by his nom-de-rue of Jerry Abershawe.   Another variation of his name,
intentional this time, was to Jemmy Abercaw, under which and the thinnest
of disguises he appears as the hero of Bernard Cape's novel of that name.

Jerry Abershawe was probably born in 1773 at Kingston, and took to
the road early, for he was but twenty-two when he was hanged. At seventeen we find him "captain" of a gang of highwaymen who infested the
roads between London, Wimbledon and Kingston. Although often using
the Green Man Inn at Putney Heath, his real headquarters were at the
Bald Faced Stag, another inn on the heath, but nearer Kingston.

Both these buildings still remain, the former still as an inn and the
latter now used for business purposes (the office of the K.L.G. Plug Company). At the end of the eighteenth century these inns were in the wilds
of the country, especially the Bald Faced Stag, which stands upon the roadside close to the Beverley Brook and not far from Coombe Woods.   In
Abershawe's day these woods were more extensive and made excellent cover.
Within an easy ride of London and handy for the adjacent roads, no better
hiding place was wished for by the highwayman and his associates.

If, however, the Bow Street Runners got too active in his own haunts
the active Jerry used to slip across the river and spend a few quiet days and
active nights on Hounslow Heath. This was easy for a well-mounted man;
in fact he could quite easily, had he wished it, have carried on his
"business" at both the Surrey and Middlesex Heaths on the same night.
All he had to do was to ride through Kingston from Putney Heath, make
his way through Teddington to Twickenham Common, which in those days
touched Hounslow Heath.

There is a good account of Jerry Abershawe in *London Stories,* which
relates the tale of the Putney doctor's visit to the Bald Faced Stag where
the highwayman lay sick. Some of Abershawe's men were doubtless in the
saddle that night for when the doctor was taking his leave Jerry offered
to send a "friend" as an escort. "I thank you," replied Dr. Roots, who
had no idea of his patient's identity, "but I fear no man on the road; no,
not even Jerry Abershawe himself." This was the pill that cured Jerry, and
he remembered and often repeated the doctor's testimony to his eminence.

Abershawe was taken by the Runners at a Southwark inn after a
violent struggle in January, 1795. Justice in this case showed no undue
haste, but on August 3rd he fared to the "Three-legged Stool" on Kennington Common. A highwayman's vanity sustained him to the scaffold. Jerry
appeared in the cart beside Jack Ketch with his shirt thrown open and a
flower in his mouth. In a pamphlet on his career published soon after his
execution and entitled *Hardened Villainy Displayed,* he is described as a
"good-looking young man."

One account concerns itself chiefly with his trial and is rather prosy,
though the story of his last days in prison redeem it somewhat, for "Artist
Highwaymen" are rare!—"Having some black cherries in prison he amused
himself with painting, on the white walls of his cell, sketches of his robberies,

representing him running up to the horses' heads of a post-chaise, presenting a pistol at the driver."

Even after his death Abershawe was famous, for an account states that " On the Sunday following his execution London was like a deserted city: hundreds of thousands went to see him hanging in chains. Later he was long on view, similarly festooned, at Putney Bottom." In Marryat's novel *Jacob Faithful* we read of the two poachers hiding in the bushes at this spot who are startled by a weird noise overhead, which proved to be " Jerry Abershawe, who had been hung in chains, and the unearthly sound was the creaking of the rusty iron as the body swung to and fro."

Jerry Abershawe is honoured with a notice of nearly two columns in so serious a publication as *The Dictionary of National Biography.*

GALLOPING DICK. (Richard Ferguson).

Ferguson began life as a postilion, and became a fine rider and an acknowledged expert on things equestrian. He made the acquaintance of the notorious Jerry Abershawe, then at the height of his fame. Ferguson was then driving post-chaises on the roads round London and eventually they entered into partnership; Ferguson's share being to supply the highwayman with information regarding his passengers.

" At length," runs the account in the *Calendar,* " Ferguson lost his place and consequently his knowledge respecting travellers, and he was obliged to go on the road. Still keeping up his association with Abershawe, Ferguson became himself remarkably successful as a highwayman. He triumphantly asserted that he would gallop a horse with any man in England." From this incident apparently arose his nickname.

After Abershawe's execution Dick varied highway robbery with honest work, for, the *Calendar* goes on: " He drove post-chaises between Hounslow and London, and notwithstanding he passed by his old companion Abershawe, where he hung in irons, it had no effect in altering his morals."

Here, I am afraid, the *Calendar* is at fault; Abershawe was gibbeted at Putney Bottom and nowhere near the Hounslow-London Road. It was even in a different county and in those days, when Thames bridges were few, it would have been unlikely he would go twice as far on the journey.

Eventually Dick took to the road exclusively and was finally apprehended and hanged at Aylesbury in 1800; though where he was gibbeted I do not know.

Over Ferguson's end the *Calendar* indulges in a little moralising: " When he found himself left for execution he seriously prepared for his end, and when he came to the fatal tree met his fate with resolution, inspired by the firm hopes of the pardon of his transgressions, through the merits of his Blessed Redeemer. Galloping Dick took a hasty road to perdition. Happy had it been for him had he chosen the safe part of virtue, and run a good race."

The last words might have been differently put, I think; he certainly ran a good race literally, as his nickname implies, if not metaphorically.

Galloping Dick—chiefly by the romantic sound of his nom-de-rue, I think—has appeared in fiction and memoirs, though not to the same extent as Turpin or Duval. In Marriott Watson's *The High Toby* there is certainly a highwayman-hero called Galloping Dick, but his surname is given as Ryder—possibly the character is founded on Ferguson. In Ralph Nevill's *The Merry Past* there will be found the story of this highwayman and the lawyer; while in an old magazine I came across a story by an anonymous author entitled *Galloping Dick*. This is of the supposed ghost of the highwayman and how "his unlaid spirit became by time and tradition an evil power haunting the heath." It is a story that disappoints ere it finishes; it has just escaped being really good, and the author is out in his dates by over a hundred years!

An account of this highwayman was written by Camden Pelham in 1863, but it does not add much to the existing knowledge of him.

SIXTEEN-STRING JACK (John Rann).

"John Rann was an impudent and arrogant self-created gentleman." So begins the account of this unworthy in the *Calendar*. Like Ferguson he rose to be the driver of a post-chaise and it was at this period of his career that he earned the curious nickname of "Sixteen-String Jack" which clung to him for the rest of his life—and after; for he is remembered by this far more than by his real name. The reason was because he wore breeches with eight strings at each knee.

Bad luck attended him at first, for we read: "Soon after starting his evil career he was arrested for robbing John Devall near the nine milestone on the Hounslow Road." Rann's reply to Sir John Fielding, the magistrate, who asked if he could offer anything in his defence, was characteristic, if ungrammatical: "I knows no more of the matter than you do, nor half so much neither." He was acquitted for want of evidence.

Rann, always a dandy, loved vain display; for the Sunday following his acquittal he appeared as Bagnigge Wells in a scarlet coat, tambour waistcoat, white silk stockings, and a laced hat, and publicly declared himself to be "Sixteen-String Jack, the Highwayman"; and soon after this he appeared at Barnet Races dressed in a most elegant sporting style, his waistcoat being blue trimmed with silver; and he was followed by hundreds of people "who were eager to gratify their curiosity by the sight of a man who was so much the subject of public conversation."

Shortly before he was capitally convicted Rann attended an execution at Tyburn, and getting within the ring formed by the constables round the gallows, desired that he might be permitted to stand there; for he remarked, not without a touch of grim humour, "perhaps it is proper I should be a spectator on this occasion."

Soon after Rann was captured after robbing Dr. Bell, Chaplain to Princess Amelia, at Gunnersbury Park. All he got was one shilling and sixpence and for these he was hanged.

Rann, always a ladies' man, the night before his execution had seven girls to sup with him in his cell; when we read "The company was remarkably cheerful, nor was Rann less joyful than his companions."

Even on the scaffold at Tyburn Rann's love of finery was evident, for he wore a new suit of pea-green cloth, a ruffled shirt, and his breeches were, on this occasion, adorned with the usual sixteen strings—*but this time they were of silver!*

Rann was hanged on November 30th, 1774; though in a novel *The Dark Lady*, in which Rann is one of the minor heroes, it states, quite wrongly, that he was transported in 1816.

In J. T. Smith's book of interesting reminiscences, *Nollekins and his Times*, he records how he was led, as a boy, by his father's playfellow, Joseph Nollekins, to the end of John Street, to see the notorious terror of the King's Highway, Rann, on his way to execution..

Rann's unofficial epitaph has been written by no less a person than

Dr. Johnson, for in the famous *Life* Boswell tells us: "Dr. Johnson said that Gray's poetry towered above the ordinary run of verse, as Sixteen-String-Jack above the ordinary foodpad."

THE SECOND STRING.
WILLIAM NEVISON.

When Dick Turpin was dethroned by Lord Macaulay from the "heroship" of the York ride folk began to look about for the real night rider of the Great North Road, for undoubtedly the feat *was* performed.

The mantle seems to have fallen on William Nevison, though why, I have no idea, for there is not a scrap of real evidence that he was the man. The *Calendar* certainly has no hint of it, nor can I find in other records any statement of *fact* that gives him this distinction.

He was an ingenious rogue all the same, and the only "Ghostly Highwayman" of whom I have heard. The supernatural adventures of Nevison came out in this way:—"He was committed to jail, where he was so strongly ironed that he could scarce stir; yet by a cunning stratagem he procured his release. Feigning illness, he sent for three trusty friends, one of whom was a physician, who gave out that he was sick of a pestilential fever, and that unless he had fresh air he would die and infect the whole jail. Hereupon the jailers took off his fetters and removed him to a room by himself. In the meantime a nurse was provided and his physician came every day, who gave out that his infection was contagious, and that there was no hope. They painted his face and hands with blue spots, as are forerunners of death in the plague. Then the physician prepared some strong spirits which made the 'patient' sleep heavily for some hours, and gave out that he was dead. Hereupon his friends demanded his body, bringing a coffin.

"The jailer, as customary, ordered a jury to examine the cause of death, who, fearing the contagion, stayed not long to consider, but having viewed him, seeing the spots, his eyes set and his jaws muffled, they brought in a verdict that he died of plague; he was put in the coffin and carried off."

Now comes the "spooky" part, for he soon took to the road again, and meeting several of his old "customers," the carriers whom he used to rob regularly, they were all "strangely surprised to see what they took to be the ghost of Mr. Nevison, who beyond all doubt had died of the plague." Nevison found this a good paying "line," for the terror nis supernatural appearance caused made robbing easier. In some way "the cheat was detected and the said jailer was ordered to fetch him in, at his peril; whereupon great search was made for him in all places." The "ghost," however, as all well brought up spectres do on occasions, vanished.

The "ghost," now solid flesh again, managed to evade the law for some years, but the usual end came at last—he swung at the end of a rope at York in 1684, aged forty-five.

Mr. Henry Nevinson, the famous writer, claims descent from this highwayman, for in a recent newspaper article, he wrote "Though I have some notable ancestors, I am truly proud of only one of them—Nevinson, the highwayman, who rode Black Bess from London to York—no, it was not Dick Turpin." Nor was it Nevison (the D.N.B. gives the "n" as an alternative), I'm afraid; who certainly never rode the famous black mare. As a matter of fact, if Nevison *had* ridden Black Bess she would have been *over fifty years old* when Dick Turpin bestrode her; which, even leaving out the ride to York, is not a bad age for such strenuous work as that on the highway.

Of course there are others who "vote" for Nevison; one of these is
Charles G. Harper in his interesting book *Old Inns of Old England,* where
he writes: "Nevison was the man who really did ride to York in one day.
He achieved the feat, and established the celebrated alibi by it, in 1676,
before Turpin was born."

In my cutting-book is an account (*The People,* 1912) recording the
death of a Yorkshire woman of ninety-eight. It states that as a girl (let us
assume about twelve) she was "warned against being on the roads at night
in case she met Ben (sic) Nevison, the highwayman, who rode to York
instead of Dick Turpin." Leaving out this spurious claim, and that his
name was William, Nevison, as we have seen, was hanged in 1684, which,
is she *were* thus warned, would make her about *240 years old* at her death.

Such is the "tosh" about highwaymen dished up by newspapers—a
glance at the dates in the *Calendar* would have corrected this. His name
was certainly not Ben, though the *Calendar* and the *D.N.B.* do not agree
about it; the former gives it as William, and latter as John. The *D.N.B.*
says of Nevison: "A tradition noticed by Macaulay represents Nevison as
the real hero of the ride from London to York, popularly attributed to
Turpin." I'm afraid the *D.N.B.* is quite wrong; Macaulay does nothing of
the kind—he certainly mentions Nevison, but says not a word about the
ride to York, nor does he even mention Turpin, though he relates the
famous story of Duval and the lady dancing on Hounslow Heath.

Nevison is the hero of George Edgar's highwaymen novel *Swift Nicks of
the North Road,* in which the author accepts the ride story as Nevison's
"copywright" without going into the pros and cons of the matter at all.

TOM KING.

Tom King is chiefly remembered from his association with, and his
accidental death at the hands of, his partner on the highway—Dick Turpin
—and among the many stories of their exploits together the two best known
are the first and the last—their meeting and their tragic parting. "One
day Turpin saw a substantial-looking gentleman upon the road before him,
so up he rode and, presenting his pistol, called upon the stranger to stand
and deliver. But King fell a-laughing," says the paper-covered history that
speaks of this. 'What, dog eat dog? Come, Brother Turpin, if you don't
know me, why, I know you, and would be glad of your company.'"

This was the beginning of their "business" friendship and they robbed
together for some time, but at last Nemesis overtook them.

"They often ventured abroad in some disguise, as the smock-frock of a
waggoner. It was in such disguise that they once overtook near to the sign
of the Green Man (which particular Green Man Inn this is not specified;
for there are many round London; the best known are Hatton, on Hounslow Heath, Epping Forest, Dulwich Common—now the Grove Hotel,—and
Putney Heath) in an outlying suburb of London, a Mr. Major, owner of the
one-time famous race-horse White Stocking. The day was foggy, so,
though but a few yards from the inn, Dick set a pistol against Mr. Major's
head, and ordered him to stand and deliver. He took from him his whip,
and silver spurs, and then, being a judge of horseflesh, bade him dismount.
Vaulting in to the saddle and putting spurs to the animal he dashed away."

What happened to Tom King the account does not state, but apparently
he made good his escape also, for he figures in the ending to this story; for
the horse led to the final tragedy: "White Stocking was too famous to be
spirited away like a parson's cob, and Mr. Major got news of such an

ROBBING OF LORD EGLINTON ON HOUNSLOW HEATH, 1750.

From the Newgate Calendar

GIBBETS ON HOUNSLOW HEATH AS A SPECTACLE.

From the Newgate Calendar

MURDER OF MR. J. C. STEEL ON HOUNSLOW HEATH.

From the Newgate Calendar

DICK TURPIN LEAPS THE TOLL GATE.

Lent by Mr. Barry Ono and Mr. Joseph Parks

animal having been seen about. He lay in wait, with a Mr. Baynes, and by-and-by up comes Tom King to get his friend Dick's horse. Out rushed the two men upon him, but King, ever quick and ready, instantly drew a pistol and fired at Baynes. Luckily it flashed in the pan, and before he could draw another he was seized and overpowered. Turpin now came riding up to his friend's help. ' Shoot him, Dick,' cried King.

" Turpin fired but though he missed his aim both balls struck King, who cried out ' You've killed me, Dick. Save yourself while you can.' Then Turpin wheeled his horse and rode away, leaving his friend wounded and in the hands of the law. King died of his wounds."

Turpin certainly does not figure as much of a " hero " in this episode—to wound his friend and ride away may have allowed him to rob another day—but was it cricket ?

Curiously enough the *Calendar* has no entry about Tom King.

JAMES McLEAN.

Press agents, as we now know them, were evils unknown, as such, in the 18th century and yet a famous highwayman had one in everything but name, and that " Press agent " was no less a person than the famous gossip Horace Walpole in his *Letters*.

It started with Walpole being robbed in 1749, when he was nearly killed. " One night in the beginning of November, 1749," he wrote, " as I was returning from Holland House I was attacked by two highwaymen in Hyde Park, and the pistol of one of them going off accidentally razed the skin under my eye. The ball went through the top of the chariot, and, if I had sat on the left side, must have gone through my head."

The firer of the pistol was James McLean, known as " The Gentleman Highwayman," and strangely enough this narrow escape, instead of bittering Walpole against his antagonist, had the opposite effect, for the Gossip took a strong interest in this Knight of the Road and wrote to all and sundry of the doings of the man who nearly shot him.

Soon after this episode Walpole writes: " McLean had a quarrel at Bowling Green House at Putney with an officer whom he had challenged for disputing his rank."

Later Walpole writes again: " My friend McLean is still the fashion; have not I reason to call him my friend? He says if the pistol had shot me he had another for himself."

Apparently it was this incident—though no name is mentioned—that is referred to by a writer in *The World* in 1754: " An acquaintance of mine was robbed a few years ago, and very near shot through the head by the going off of the pistol of the accomplished McLean; yet the whole affair was conducted with the greatest good breeding on both sides. The highwayman even offered to meet his victim at Tyburn at midnight so that he could *purchase again* his lost property."

Three weeks after McLean was captured, not on the highway amid a burst of " glory," but in the unromantic act of pawning a stolen waistcoat.

" Walpole's " press agency " for this malefactor seems to have influenced some of his contemporary authors, for we find Grey—of the *Elegy* fame—writing in his poem *The Long Story* :—

> " A sudden fit of ague shook him;
> He stood as mute as poor McLean,"

and in the same year Soame Jenyns wrote a poem entitled *The Modern Fine*

Lady, where he says: " Some of the brightest eyes were at this time in tears for one McLean, condemned for robbery on the highway."

On one occasion McLean stopped the coach of Lord Eglinton on Hounslow Heath and among the booty he got was a blunderbuss, which seems to have become famous, for Walpole specially mentions it, and Timbs in a brief resume of the highwayman's life also refers to it: " McLean took an odd booty from the Scotch earl, a blunderbuss," and again: " McLean's history is very particular, for he confesses everything, and is so little of a hero that he cries and bays and if Lord Eglinton had been in any luck he might have robbed him of his own blunderbuss."

McLean's father was an Irish Dean, one brother a Calvinist minister, and another an Anglican clergyman, while the highwayman himself was originally a grocer in Welbeck Street, for the reverend author assures us the religious principles of the malefactor were " most satisfactory." He was but twenty-six when he was hanged, and his skeleton appears in Hogarth's picture showing the interior of Surgeon's Hall in the " Stages of Cruelty " series.

" CAPTAIN " JAMES HIND.

Although the title of Captain is usually given to this highwayman there is little evidence that he was entitled to it. It is true he fought for the Royal Cause at the Battle of Worcester, but he was known as Captain long before this.

He was originally a butcher in Oxfordshire, but, coming to London to seek a better fortune, found a worse fate. His early history is much as many others; falling into bad company he lost what little money he had— and then took to the road to remedy his reverses.

He is chiefly notable for his antagonism to the Puritans, a result of his strong Royalist principles and he even once attempted to stop the coach of Oliver Cromwell, but was unsuccessful, though others of his victims were Hugh Peters, Bradshaw, and Colonel Harrison, all famous regicides. Our interest in Hind lies round Hanworth, for this heath village seems to have been his pet territory.

One victim was Thomas Killigrew, and the story was told in his day as a good joke against him, though perhaps not particularly witty according to modern ideas. " One day," runs the account, " when Thomas Killigrew, fool to King Charles II., was visiting friends in the neighbourhood of his birthplace, Hanworth, a village on the Heath, near Hounslow, he was stopped by a highwayman, who addressed him in the usual phraseology ' Stand and deliver.' ' Are you in *ernest,* my friend,' asked the wit. ' That I am,' replied the knight of the road (who according to the story seems to have known the identity of his victim—a little unlikely) ' for tho' you can live by jesting, I can't.' Killigrew found it was no jest which cost him twenty guineas."

It was here, too, that Hind met Bradshaw, who occupied Hanworth Park during the Commonwealth. Hind seems to have fared better than on his further attempts to plunder a regicide: " One day Captain Hind was riding upon Hounslow Heath when he met the coach of Sergeant Bradshaw, that arch-traitor, who passed sentence on the King, Bradshaw being on his way to his country seat at Hanworth. Hind rode up and demanded Bradshaw's money, who, supposing that his name would convey terror, informed him who he was. Quoth Hind: ' I neither fear you nor any king-killing villain alive. I have now as much power over you as you lately had over the king, but thou art unworthy to die by any hands but those of the common hangman.'

" Bradshaw began to perceive that the case was not now with him, as it was at Westminster Hall, supported by the strength of rebellion. To save a miserable life, the Sergeant pulled out that which he valued next to it, and presented the Captain with a purse full of Jacobuses." This extraordinary highwayman, though having got the money, was still not tired of preaching and at once began a sermon on the evils of wealth.

It terminates thus: " The Captain, having finished his panegyric upon the glittering metal, addressed the Sergeant, saying ' You and your infernal crew have a long while to live on, in a career of blood and impiety, falsely pretending that zeal for the Lord of Hosts has been your motive. I will, however, for this time, stop your race in a literal sense of the word.' With that he left Bradshaw to cool his heels upon the heath and to ponder upon the lessons he had received."

After such a flow of eloquence on the part of this loyal but loquacious highwayman, the conventional " Stand and deliver " of others of his kind would sound almost epigrammatic. . .

* * * *

All his loyalty to the Cause did not save the life of the Royalist Highwayman, though he had the " honour " of being taken before the Speaker of the House of Commons, for his charge seems to have been the mixed one of treason against the state, murder, and highway robbery. He was finally executed at Worcester in 1652.

One who signed himself " A Poet of his Own Time " wrote a set of verses *To the Memory of Captain Hind,* too long to quote, in which Hind is compared with Caesar, though why is a little obscure.

He has two columns in the *Dictionary of National Biography,* where there is a bibliography of the literature connected with him, including one of the *Roxburghe Ballads,* and a play in which he is the hero, described as " an excellent comedy," *The Prince of Prigg's Revels*; while an old chapbook, vividly illustrated, bears the title *The Merry Life and Mad Exploits of Capt. James Hind, the Great Robber of England.*

CAPTAIN DUDLEY.

I do not know if " the old school tie " tradition that we hear so much about these days held good in highwayman times, and when members of well-known public-schools met they metaphorically fell on each other's necks in the approved fashion with murmurs anent the " old school cravat " (as it would be in those days, I suppose).

If so some touching scenes must have been witnessed on Hounslow Heath when the Old Pauline Knight of the Road met some of his dear old pals. For Richard Dudley was educated at St. Paul's School.

It is true he ran away from school after robbing his father, who, when he caught his errant son, sent him on board a man-of-war, in which, we are told, "he sailed up the Straits, and behaved gallantly in several actions." Upon his arrival in England he left the ship and took to the road, after robbing the house of an admiral (just to keep up the nautical flavour, apparently), but he was caught and sentenced to death. Family influence (and a few bribes, probably, as well) secured his reprieve and obtained a commission in the army for him, where he remained for a couple of years, when he took to the road once more.

At Hounslow Heath he met with a farmer, robbed him, seized his

horse, and set forward in quest of new spoils. This was a fortunate day, for
Dudley had not proceeded far on the Heath when a gentleman, well dressed
and better mounted than the former, made his appearance. He was commanded to surrender. Dudley led him aside in a secret thicket, exchanged
clothes and horse, and rifled his pockets. Arrived in London his old associates were glad to see their friend (and the old school cravat, no doubt),
whom they elected as their captain.

There is one more adventure on the Heath, not without a touch of
humour. "The profligate Dudley," we read, "soon hastened to join his old
companions. Exulting to see their captain again they redoubled their activity
and committed all manner of depredations. Among other adventures they
robbed a nobleman on Hounslow Heath of £1,500, after a severe engagement
with his servants, who had their horses shot under them.   They next
directed their course along the West Country road, and, having robbed a
parson, enjoined him, under the most terrible threatening, to preach a
sermon in praise of highway robbery. He was forced to comply, and, the
sermon being ended, they returned his money, and gave him four shillings
to drink their health."

Dudley had a strange sense of humour, for there is an amusing account
of how he once robbed a pompous Justice of the Peace and afterwards tied
him backwards on the back of a stray ass, who solemnly carried his worship
into the nearest Assize Town to the great joy and amusement of the popu-
lace, with whom he was far from popular.

Dudley also tried for high game, once robbing General Monk, who
caused such a hue and cry to be raised that the highwayman was forced
to fly to France for a time to hide. The *Calendar* states that he was a confederate of Swiftnecks (though, as we have noted elsewhere, it says nothing
about that worthy), and concludes with the paragraph: "At last Dudley,
attempting to rob the Duke of Lauderdale when riding over Hounslow
Heath, was conquered in his enterprise and committed to Newgate; and
when he came to trial about 80 indictments were preferred against him in
the County of Middlesex alone. Then receiving sentence of death (though
intercession was made for him to King Charles) he was hanged at Tyburn
in 1681, aged forty-six."

HAWKINS AND SIMPSON.

The annals of the road contain mention of "twin" highwaymen, Hawkins and Simpson, who are practically always spoken of together—for they
lived, robbed, and swung in each other's company. Their careers are interesting as Hounslow Heath figures largely in their short but eventful history.
Here is an account of it, as told in *All the Year Round.*

Speaking of highwaymen the writer says: "Let us sketch two more
of these pests of the eighteenth century. In April, 1722 the Bristol mail boy
was stopped near Colnbrook by two mounted highwaymen named Hawkins
and Simpson. The robbers had handkerchiefs in their mouths, and pulled
their wigs over their faces. A rogue on a chestnut horse held a pistol to
the boy's head. He asked him if he was the lad who swore against Child
(a highwayman who had been hung for robbing the same mail). He said
he had not; he'd only been a postboy a little while, and had never been
robbed.

"'Why, then, you must be robbed now; we will be revenged upon somebody.' They cut the bridles, turned one horse loose and rode off on the
other, leaving the lads bound back to back, tied to a tree. After a great

deal of struggling the lads got loose from the tree, but not from each other, so they shambled back to an inn at Lengford (presumably Longford).

" The two highwaymen had ridden off from the Harmondsworth Lane, and taken the bags to Hounslow Heath, and going down a by-road, searched the bags and threw the refuse over the hedge."

The two highwaymen continued to act in company and specialised in the stopping of mail-coaches or post-boys; in fact, they often boasted that they had stopped as many as ten of the former in one day.

Hawkins was known as a local man long before he took to the highway; he was the son of a Staines farmer and served at the bar for a time at the Red Lion Inn, Hounslow.

The usual end came at last in 1722; and their bodies were duly gibbetted on Hounslow Heath, the scene of practically all their robberies.

NICKNAMES.

THE GOLDEN FARMER.

The ways of highwaymen did not, as a rule, show much subtlety; their methods were similar, with a few exceptions, just as the alleged doings of conventional ghosts bear a strong likeness.

The usual ride over a moonlit heath—the wait in the shadow of the old oak for the approach of the coach or post-chaise—" Stand and deliver! " —the robbery—and then away, hell for leather, ere the Runners came.

This, in effect, is the " plot " of most highwaymen yarns, even if other incidents are interwoven. Therefore it is refreshing to hear of a Knight of the Road showing originality, and who may be counted among the first " crooks " (to use a modern name for an old-world " hero ") to adopt a dual personality.

This was William Davis, a Welshman, who lived at Sudbury (not the Middlesex Sudbury, as some accounts state, but in Gloucestershire)), where he was married and had eighteen children. He worked hard on his farm also, and obtained the nickname of " The Golden Farmer," from his habit of paying for everything in gold.

At the same time, on many a heath and common far away from the peaceful farm, a highwayman was gaining notoriety for his curious methods —he would never touch jewellery, but took only gold. For some time no one suspected it as curious that these robberies always took place when the Golden Farmer was away from home attending " markets." Several of these took him as far away as Hounslow Heath, Enfield Chase, or Putney Heath. When he had collected as many guineas as he could, off he would jog to the West Country, perhaps doing a little " business " on the Bath Road en route, and lead an honest life for a time on his farm.

Beyond his dual personality the stories told of Davis do not differ from many another road-knight on Hounslow Heath, where many of his adventures took place; except, perhaps, the story of how, having just paid the rent for the farm to a grasping landlord, the Golden Farmer-Highwayman did some quick change work and got his money back ere the landlord reached home—and gave him a lecture on greed and compassion into the bargain!

After many years of success suspicion was aroused which finally led to detection; and the local sleuths at last came to the conclusion that one who always robbed and paid in gold might be connected. He was eventually arrested, and duly ended his life on the gallows.

In Harper's highwayman book there is quoted an old ballad, of eight
verses, on the Golden Farmer, but it is poorer stuff than even the average
of such rhymes (and the literary style is not high) and not worth quoting.
The Golden Farmer also figures in *Captain Jacobus,* a 17th century novel,
by L. Cope Cornford, which has a good deal in it about the Western roads.

OLD   MOB.

Simpson seems a popular name for highwaymen, for Thomas Simpson
is the third (see Jonathan Simpson and Hawkins and Simpson) of whom
we have record, though he is always known by his nickname of Old Mob.

The strangest thing about him is that he continued to " work " the
roads long after he had become a grandfather—when most highwaymen
were swinging at the end of a rope under thirty.

He was a rogue with a ready tongue, and one or two adventures are
related about him which differ from the conventional " type."   Once when
he robbed a lawyer, who had successfully appeared against him, of the very
money he (Old Mob) had been forced to pay him, he even beat the lawyer
at his own game of arguing in addition!

" Another time Old Mob attacked the Bath stage on Hounslow Heath,
with only one lady within.   She said she was a poor widow who had just
lost her husband.   " And is this any argument why I should lose my booty,"
asked Old Mob.   " Your tears, madam, can't move me; for I remember the
old proverb—' The end of a husband is a widow's tears, and the end of those
tears is another husband.' "

According to one account he recited to her " a story in verse," presumably his own composition; this earning the distinction of " The Poetical
Highwayman."   It is a strange effusion, but too long to quote; those interested will find it given in full in the *Calendar.*

Those he robbed included an astrologer, and once a quack-medicine
seller, who rejoiced in the curious name of Cornelius-á-Tieburgh, but whom
Old Mob renamed Theophrastus Bombasustus (for some occult reason), and
after giving the quack a moral lecture on the evils of selling his noisome
mixtures to the detriment of his " patients," took the " doctor's " portman-
teaux.   On examination the bag was found to contain twenty-five pounds
in money, and " all the instruments and implements of quakery."

His next victim was a personage of different type—whether up or down
in the scale is problematical, in spite of her being a duchess.   It was the
Duchess of Portsmouth, a lady of very easy virtue.   The fiery French-
woman indignantly demanded if he knew who she was— Old Mob's reply
was rude and to the point and he went on in his usual moral strain: " A
gentleman-collector upon the highway, madam, is a greater man and more
absolute than His Majesty is at Court.   You may say now, madam, that a
single highwayman has exercised his authority where Charles the Second
of England has begged a favour."

Her Grace told him he was an insolent fellow and she would give him
nothing, adding, " Touch me if you dare."   " Madam, that naughty French
spirit will do you no good here; I am an English freebooter, and I insist
upon it, as my native right, to seize all foreign commodities.   I am the
king on Hounslow Heath, madam, and I have use for money as well as the
other King.   The public pay for his follies, and so he must pay for mine."
Old Mob threatened her with his pistol; she cried for quarter, and delivered
her purse and jewellery.

The only other victim of Old Mob with whom we need concern our-

selves was no less a person than the infamous Judge Jeffries. The highwayman rode up to the coach and demanded his money. Jeffries, thinking
that his name would strike terror, disclosed his identity. This had no
frightening effect on Old Mob; he merely doubled the length of the usual
moral lecture "with which he usually robbed his victims," and then,
"thundering forth a volley of oaths, and presenting a pistol to the judge's
breast, threatened him with instant death unless he surrendered his money.
Perceiving that his authority was of no consequence on the heath he
delivered his purse." It was a pity, perhaps, that the lesser rogue withheld
his fire.

Old Mob came to the usual end; he was apprehended, presented with
thirty-six indictments, of which thirty-two were proved, and he was
executed at Tyburn in 1690, at an advanced age for a Knight of the Road.

MUL-SACK.

Mul-Sack (John Cottington) began his career, as many highwaymen did, as a pickpocket. Even in this humble profession,
however, he flew at high game, as the *Calendar* tells us: "We
are informed that before Mul-Sack left off his trade he was once
so impudent as to attempt the pocket of Cromwell himself, and
the danger he then ran of being detected was the occasion of his
leaving this secret sort of knavery and taking to the highway, in company
with one Tom Cheney . . . . These two fellows had the courage and confidence to set upon Colonel Hewson, a great man in those times, and one who
had been advanced from a cobbler to the dignity he then enjoyed merely
because his conscience was according to the measure of that time; that is
very large, or, if you please, very small, which expressions the witty author
of *Hudibras* tells us, signify the same thing.

"The Colonel's regiment was then marching to Hounslow, and he not
so far before it, but some of the troopers saw the action of our bravoes.
Nobody can doubt but they were soon pursued; yet by the help of a good
horse Mul-Sack got away."

His companion was less lucky and was captured—with the usual result.
The same fate overtook Mul-Sack's next partner, described as "Mr. Horne,
formerly a captain in the army." This gentleman shared the same fate as
Cheney and so Cottington was left alone again. "This time," we read, "he
was resolved to try his fortune alone, and he several times practised his
calling upon Members of Parliament, who were then almost the only men
in the nation worth robbing, they have plundered everybody also and
gotten the wealth of England into their own hands."

He was finally captured, however, after a run of luck, which still held
apparently, for he managed to "baffle the evidence" (another account says
he bribed the jury, which is more probable), and he was acquitted.

Soon after this, to escape the results of shooting a victim on the highway, he was forced to fly overseas, and "got himself introduced in the
Court of King Charles II., then in exile. He got so much intelligence here
that he ventured home again, upon a presumption of obtaining pardon
from Oliver Cromwell as a reward to what he could discover of the King's
affairs. Accordingly he applied himself to the usurper, confessed his crime,
and made promises, upon the performance of which Cromwell assured him
of his life. But whether he could not be as good as his word, or whether
the Protector thought such an abandoned wretch utterly unfit to live, so it
was that he was apprehended, condemned, and executed in Smithfield

Grounds in April, 1685, being forty-five years of age."

The *Calendar*, from which this is quoted, seems adrift here, either in facts or dates. Cromwell died in 1658—and Mul-Sack was not hanged (if this date is correct) until *twenty-seven years after*. In those days when highwaymen had short shift this seems impossible. The derivation of his nickname was from his favourite drink.

BLUESKIN.

Joseph Blake, always known as Blueskin in the Penny Dreadfuls, is generally pictured as a close companion of Dick Turpin; and though the Dreadfuls often mix up dates badly and class men together whom death has separated by fifty years or more, in this case the dates *do* agree, although the *Calendar* has no mention of this particular companionship.

We know Blake to have been the associate of Jack Sheppard (throughout his career there is no evidence of Jack Sheppard ever having committed a murder—a rare omission for an eighteenth century criminal), who appears to have had more compassion than Blueskin, who was a low ruffian; for when during a roadside quarrel outside an alehouse Blake knocked a man senseless into a muddy ditch, would have left him there to drown, had not Sheppard jumped in and rescued him.

Blake was also an associate of the notorious Jonathan Wild, and an account of the quarrel between them is found, *inter alia,* in that delightful book—chiefly noted for its pictures—Charles Knight's *Old England:* "Blueskin, one of Wild's associates," runs the account, "has obtained scarcely less notoriety than Wild himself. He, at last, fell under the mighty fiat, was taken, and sentenced to the gallows. Wild was to be a witness against him; and his conduct under these circumstances shows us how worthy he was to be the original of Fielding's history—how truly, in his way, he was great. A day or two before the trial Jonathan went to see Blueskin in the bail-dock. It is necessary to premise that £40 was then paid to those who were the means of bringing felons to the gallows— *blood-money,* as the payment has been popularly called.   To another prisoner Wild first addressed himself: ' I believe you will not bring £40 this time.   I wish Joe (meaning Blueskin) was in your case; but I'll do my endeavour to bring you off as a single felon,' that is to say, as one liable only to transportation. ' Then, turning to me,' continues Blueskin, for it is his narrative we are following, ' he said, " I believe you must die. I'll send you a good book or two, and provide you a coffin; and you shall not be anatomised." ' "   There is nothing in Fielding to surpass this.   Can anyone wonder that the maddened convict, drawing a clasped penknife, rushed upon his destroyer. That was not, however, a death in harmony with the peculiar greatness of Wild's life.

There is nothing romantic about Blake's life, nor yet any incidents noteworthy enough for record. His nickname—which he earned on account of his dark skin and often unshaven chin—has, perhaps, largely been the cause of much of his notoriety. He was hanged in his twenty-fourth year, on November 11th, 1724.

THE FLYING HIGHWAYMAN.

In the *Annual Register* for 1761 appears the following:

" The Flying Highwayman engrosses the conversation of most of the towns within twenty miles of London.   He rides three different horses, a grey, a sorrel and a black; he has done rare feats on

Hounslow Heath and has leapt over Colnbrook turnpike a dozen times within this fortnight."

I am sorry to have to take Harrison Ainsworth to task, for in addition to giving Dick Turpin a fame that really did not belong to him, he also tries to "steal more thunder" for his hero from Hawkes—who was *the* "Flying Highwayman" and not Dick Turpin. "Enamoured of his vocation," writes Ainsworth in *Rookwood*, "Turpin delighted to hear himself designated as the Flying Highwayman, and it was with rapturous triumph that he found his single-handed feats attributed to a band of marauders. But this state of things could not long endure: his secret was blown; the vigilance of the police was aroused; he was tracked to his haunts; and after a number of hair-breadth 'scapes, which he only affected by miracle, or by the aid of his wonder-working mare, he reluctantly quitted the healthy hills of Bagshot, the pampas plains of Hounslow (over which, like an archetype of the galloping Sir Francis Head, he had so often scoured), the gorsy commons of Highgate, Hampstead and Finchley, the marshy fields of Battersea, almost all of which he had been known to visit in a single night."

The Flying Highwayman's real name was Hawkes, and we find further mention of him in Grantley Berkeley's *Life and Recollections:* "Among the heroes of the road," he writes, "I must name Hawkes, commonly known as the 'Flying Highwayman' from the rapidity of his movements." Hawkes' eventual capture was due to some Runners disguising themselves as drunken rustic brawlers at an inn and thus putting the highwayman off his guard.

A good story is told by Grantley Berkeley that not long before the exeution the highwayman was visited in Newgate by a stranger who was anxious to buy his horse: "The highwayman understood the case, or so he thought, for his visitor was unquestionably a gentleman, and he well knew that such gentlemen sometimes found it expedient—by reverses of fortune— to play the High Toby. 'Sir,' said Hawkes to his visitor, 'I am obliged to you—but the mare won't suit you if you want her *for the road;* it is not every man that can get her up to a carriage!'

"This answer so amused the visitor that he advanced a sum of money to try to let the prisoner buy his freedom, but though the amount had often purchased the freedom of lesser rogues, the 'Flying Highwayman' was thought too dangerous to let go. The unknown visitor was no less a person than eccentric and wealthy Lord Coleraine."

The Flying Highwayman also figures in two incidents in Harrison Ainsworth's novel, *The Lord Mayor of London*.

Hawkes finally ended his career at Tyburn, and it is surprising that the *Newgate Calendar* has no mention of him.

"THE SKATING HIGHWAYMAN."

Can one who robs on the river be termed a highwayman—even if the Thames is sometimes called "The Silent Highway"? Yet Jonathan Simpson, though he chose the Thames for his depredations, used no boat; but, as an expert skater, his method was even simpler; he would overtake others on the ice, trip them up, and before they knew what had happened the expert thief was searching their pockets, and then, when the victim began to sit up and take notice, it was to see the Skating Highwayman skimming away. Of course, this original method had its disadvantages from the robber's point of view; it naturally meant ice; but in the great

frost of 1686 the Thames was frozen over for thirteen weeks, a circumstance
of which this ingenious thief took full advantage.

When the thaw came he was forced to take to horseback and the more
lasting road, where he was apprehended and sentenced to be hung. By
influence, and a little bribery, I expect, for we are told he possessed rich
relations, a reprieve was procured, which arrived in proper dramatic fashion
as he was actually waiting at Tyburn with the halter round his neck!

Simpson seemed to have been a witty rogue, and as he was riding back
to Newgate behind a sheriff's officer the latter asked him if he thought of
a reprieve when he came to the gallows. " No more," said Simpson, " than
I thought of my dying day."

" When he was brought to the prison door," the *Calendar* tells us, " the
turnkey refused to receive him, saying, as he was sent to be executed, they
were discharged of him unless there was a fresh warrant for his commitment; whereupon Simpson made this reflection: ' What an unhappy cast-off
dog am I, that both Tyburn and Newgate should in one day refuse to
entertain me!"

His robberies were numerous and he is said to have committed nineteen
in one day between London and Barnet, his victims including the Duke of
Berwick (natural son of James II.) and Lord Delamere.   Simpson was
finally caught, and the *Calendar* concludes with these words: " When he
was sent to Newgate he now found the keeper so much his friend as to
receive him; neither did Tyburn this time refuse to bear his burden."

SWIFT   NICKS.

It is curious that of the highwayman who actually *did* ride to York in a
single night we know practically nothing; there is no separate entry for him
in the *Calendar,* and he is mentioned only in connection with a confederate.
What sparse knowledge we have of him is collected from different sources,
and I have done my best from scanty material to bring together here what
is known of this famous (yet seemingly modest) night rider.

In the excellent preface to one edition of *The Calendar,* we read: " The
confusion attending the circumstances of Swift Nick's career is great.
A recent collector of Northern legends, the late Richard Blakeborough
(see *The Hand of Glory,* by J. Fairfax-Blakeborough), who was apparently
not conversant with Johnson or Smith's works, avers on the strength of
The Records of York Castle that Swift Nicks is the same as the highwayman William Nevison, but neither Smith nor Johnson, in a long account of
this worthy's life, makes any suggestion of his being Swift Nicks.   Nor,
earlier still, did Defoe in the account of the ride to York in his *Tour
Through Britain* (1724).   But why, on the other hand, did not Smith or
Johnson give the life of Swift Nicks, seeing he was so famous? The answer
is past all guessing. Turpin, whose life we know, did not ride to York;
Swift Nicks, of whose career we know hardly anything, apparently did."

We do not even know for certain what the Christian name of Nicks
was, but in a footnote to the foregoing account we read: " A possible clue
to Swift Nicks' Christian name may be found in a postscript to *Jackson's
Recantation, or, the Life and Death of the Notorious High-way-Man, now
hanging in chains at Hampstead. Delivered to a friend a little before
execution: wherein is truly discovered the whole mystery of that wicked
and fatal profession of Padding on the Road* (London: Printed for
T.B. 1674). (How they loved this lengthy half-titles in those days!) In
this pamphlet " Samuel Swiftnicks " tells the reader that " this is no fiction,

but a true relation of Mr. Jackson's life and conversation."

Apparently the most authentic account of the famous ride to York is that already mentioned of the author of *Robinson Crusoe:* "From Gravesend we see nothing remarkable," writes Defoe, "on the road but Gad's-Hill, a noted place for robbing of seamen after they have received their pay at Chatham. Here it was that the famous robbery was committed in the year 1676, or thereabouts; it was about four o'clock in the morning when a gentleman was robbed by one Nicks on a bay mare. Mr. Nicks, who robb'd him, came away to Gravesend, and immediately ferry'd over. He came to York the same afternoon, put off his boots and riding cloaths, and went dress'd as if he had been an inhabitant of the place, not a traveller, to the bowling-green, where, among other gentlemen, was the Lord Mayor; he singling out his Lordship, study'd to do something particular that the Mayor might remember him by, and accordingly lay some odd bett which should cause the Mayor to remember him; and then takes the occasion to ask his Lordship what o'clock it was. Upon a prosecution which happen'd afterwards for this robbery, the whole case turn'd on this single point. The person robb'd swore as to the man, place and time. Nicks, the prisoner, denied the fact, and alleg'd that he was as far off as York at that time, and that particularly the day of the robbery he was at bowls on the publick green, and to support this he produced the Lord Mayor of York to testify.

"This was so well attested that the jury acquitted him on the supposition that it was impossible the man could be at two places so remote on one and the same day. There are more particulars related of this story, such that King Charles II. prevailed upon him, on assurance of pardon, to confess the truth to him privately, and that he own'd to His Majesty that he committed the robbery, and how he rode the journey, and that upon this the King gave him the name or title of Swift Nicks."

Charles II., who, with all his faults, loved a merry rogue as much as he loved a pretty face, was apparently better than his word, for we can trace his hand in the first part of the following paragraph, which is all the *Calendar* has to say of this intrepid hero: "Nicks was afterwards made a captain in Lord Montcastle's regiment in Ireland, where he married a great fortune and afterwards lived very honest."

In *The Romance of the Forum* there will be found a full and clear account of how Nicks performed the famous ride, for which another now generally gets all the credit.

I think, however, though we know so little of him, that he was the real hero of the famous equestrian feat round which so much controversy has raged; for besides Nicks, Nevison and Turpin there are other claimants to this feat; notably a soldier in the seventeenth century, who performed this ride in a single night, starting from a camp on Hounslow Heath, though we are told he used four horses ere he saw York Minster.

Still another claimant is given in Kirby's *Scientific Museum:* "In 1606 John Leyton, groom to James I., rode between London and York in one day, *for six days together.*" It does not state how many horses he used each way for what might be called this "mass production" ride to York. Apparently in those times riding to York seems to have been as popular a diversion as swimming the Channel is now.

THE QUAKER HIGHWAYMAN.

Jacob Halsey was born of wealthy parents and brought up strictly in the Quaker faith, and so zealous was he that we read "he pretended to be wonderfully gifted and the spirit abounded so powerfully that he frequently held forth in the meetings of the Friends." The "spirit" seems to have moved him a little too far one night, however, for when he heard a mysterious voice, "Jacob, where art thou?" he jumped out of bed and, running to the window, cried out, "Here am I! Oh, what is thy will?" Then the voice answered, "Arise presently, Jacob, my beloved, and go to the church and break all the windows." Immediately he got a long pole and did so, for which he was carted off to prison, apparently still without suspicion that the voice was that of one the *Calendar* calls "an arch, unlucky weed"—in other words Jacob was having his leg pulled!

In prison, his parents being wealthy and the prison laws very elastic in those days for those who could pay, he was known as a "Wet Quaker" (a modern term for the seventeenth century), or one who would drink, and as he was fond of standing treat to the other prisoners he soon became popular (another modern trait!).

When at liberty he remembered the talk of his fellow-prisoners, and it seemed to this simple youth that the life of a robber was more interesting than that of a strict Quaker, so he ran away and took to the road. He forsook his former quiet grey garb and dressed his new part as well as any, but "nevertheless" we read, "he would always rob in the language of the lambs."

His methods were old but his language was new to the highway robbers profession, for meeting with "a wicked old usurer" he addressed him thus: "Look thee, friend; I am not like one of those profane ones, who spoil men in the terrifying words of "Stand and Deliver," but an Israelite that spoils an Egyptian with good humour and peace; so open thy purse-strings and lend what thou hast, without grumbling."

Another time Jacob accosted a clergyman on the road in this manner: "Friend, imagining thee to be some Philistine going to spoil an honest Israelite for tithes. I must make bold to spoil thee first; wherefore, thou wicked one, deliver thy mammon to the righteous, that he may convert it to a better use than to exhaust it in gluttony and pride. Otherwise I shall send thee to the bottomless pit before thy time is come."

The poor parson was forced to deliver his scanty purse, but this canting highwayman found his next intended victim of sterner stuff, for when he tried the same "sermon" on the Earl of Westmorland his lordship was unreasonable enough to run him through before he had finished the opening paragraph!

The first of April in the year 1691 saw this hypocritical rogue hanged.

THE SWEARING HIGHWAYMAN

Most highwaymen were probably not unacquainted with the ungentle art of using expletives, but it has remained for Edward Wicks, a knight of the road, to be the only one (as far as I know) who actually earned any money by it. Since it happened on Hounslow Heath the story is perhaps worth the telling here. Once again the *Calendar* is my informant (with reference to another source) for the account of these "few well-chosen words!": "Ned Wicks, meeting with Lord Mohun ("Dog Mohun," Swift calls him; it was he who helped kill Mumford and fought the Duke of Hamilton) on the Heath near Colnbrook, attended by a groom, he commanded his lordship to stand and deliver. His lordship now meeting with his match, it put him into such a passionate fit of swearing that Wicks, not willing to be outdone in any wickedness, quoth he, 'My lord, I perceive you swear perfectly well *extempore;* come, I'll give your honour a fair chance for your moneys; and that is, he that swears best of us two shall keep his own and his that loseth.'

" His lordship agreed to this bargain, and throwing down a purse of fifty guineas, which Wicks match'd with a like sum; after a quarter of an hour's swearing most prodigiously on both sides it was left to his lordship's groom to decide the matter, who said, ' Why, indeed, your honour swears as well as ever I heard a person of quality in my life; but, indeed, to give the strange gentleman his due, he has won the wager."

Owing to a similarity of name Wicks is often confused with Nicks, the genuine York night-rider, but a glance at their dates will refute any connection, the latter performing his feat in 1676, while Wicks was not hanged until 1713, aged twenty-nine.

THE CHURCHWARDEN HIGHWAYMAN.

Yes, there actually was one, strange as it seems, and it came about thus. In 1781 two highwaymen usually known as " The Weston Brothers " (for such they were) began their career of crime by stopping the Bath Mail on Hounslow Heath. They did so well in their " profession " that they were able to retire. So amazing was the effrontery of these two villains that they bought an old manor in Sussex and set up as country gentlemen. George was actually chosen churchwarden. A strange detail proved his undoing, for in a description of him posted up when he was " Wanted " it was stated that one of his thumb nails was, after an accident, the shape of a parrot's bill. Some sharp-eyed person noticed this—perhaps when the worthy churchwarden was making the collection—and it led to his arrest. Joseph was taken, and the Weston Brothers eventually swung at Tyburn— doubtless still wearing their Old School ties!

If those more modern Western Brothers, who entertain us over the wireless, ever read these lines, I hope, when they bring their libel action against me (despite the different spelling), they will remember I stated that their " ancestor " was *also* a churchwarden.

THE PIEMAN OF HOUNSLOW HEATH.

It seems that our old friend Simple Simon was not the only boy who met a pieman! In the *Newgate Calendar* the sub-title to the heading " Henry Goodiff " reads: " A Boy condemned to death for robbing a Pie Man, who had swindled him on Hounslow Heath, of a few half-pence, March, 1794 "—it might almost be called a moral story, so beloved at that period, of the boy who was not quite so simple as the legendary Simon.

It seems that upon Hounslow Heath he met one of those knavish pastry pedlars, who cheat boys and ignorant country clowns in pretending to toss up for his penny pies.

" Poor Goodriff staked his *all*—a few pence—with the pieman; but, alas! he lost his fortune without even touching one of the savoury bits. Stung with disappointment he attacked the pieman, and forcibly took from him the miserable pittance of which he had been cheated. This was, in the eye of the law, a highway robbery.

The boy was actually sentenced to die; on the representation of the case to the Privy Council His Majesty's pardon was granted on condition the boy served in the Navy. Anyhow, he found the value of pie!

A HIGHWAYWOMAN—MOLL CUTPURSE.

In these days it is no surprise to find women competing with men in even usual spheres of activity; but in the eighteenth century it was considered remarkable. Yet it was not unknown; there were even women prize fighters (a novel, *Bruising Peg*, tells the story of such a one), and there was the famous woman soldier, whose story is told in G. R. Gleig's *Chelsea Hospital*, where she is buried. Incidentally she shot a highwayman with his own pistol on Hounslow Heath, where he attacked a waggon in which she was riding.

Women thieves there have been in plenty, but their stories do not concern us here, but there were two, Joan Bracey and Moll Cutpurse, who actually bestrode horses and robbed on the highway as well as any mere man. The former we can ignore for the present, for her activities lay far away from our Heath, but the latter did much " business " there.

Even of this famous High Tobywoman there is not a great deal to tell, in spite of the originality of her calling. In the short biography found in that journal which delighted ladies of a former day, *La Belle Assemblee*—and there was nothing more French about it than the name—we find (in 1811) the following brief, but interesting, memoir of our " heroine ": " Mary Frith, alias Moll Cutpurse, was born in London in 1589. Her early propensities formed a striking index of her future habits, for female attire, and the needle, were as irksome to her as running, cudgel-playing and fighting were consonant to her desires. When she arrived at a state of womanhood she took to wearing man's apparel.

It was the custom then for ladies and gentlemen to wear their purses hung to a girdle, and Moll was famous for attending places of public resort to cut them off, for which she obtained the name of *Cutpurse*

She likewise practised on the highway with much repute, till having robbed General Fairfax on Hounslow Heath, for which she was condemned to die, but purchased her life by paying the General two hundred guineas; She was the first Englishwoman that ever smoked tobacco.

A monument was raised to her memory in St. Bridget's Churchyard, and the great Milton wrote the following epitaph, which was engraven thereon, but was destroyed by the great fire in 1666.

The epitaph is of twenty-two lines, and begins:
> " Here lies under the same marble,
> Dust for Time's last sieve to garble."

Moll Cutpurse is famous, of course, but it is less known, I think, that so noted a poet wrote an epitaph for a highway robber—even a female one. She died in 1663, aged 74.

It is quoted in full in the *Calendar*, which gives an account of the famous incident on the Heath: " A long time had Moll robbed on the road, but at last, robbing General Fairfax of two hundred and fifty jacobuses on Hounslow Heath, shooting him through the arm for opposing her, and killing two horses on which a couple of his servants rode, a close pursuit was made after her by some Parliamentarian officers quartering in the town of Hounslow, to whom Fairfax had told his misfortune.

Moll is the heroine of Thomas Middleton's play—which he wrote in collaboration with Thomas Dekker in 1611 — *The Roaring Girle,* or *Moll Cutpurse,* and there is also a theory that she is the counterpart of Defoe's heroine in *Moll Flanders,* but there is little likeness, beyond the name, between the two ladies. Moll Flanders is a far more feminine character than Moll Cutpurse, but it is possible, and even likely, that Defoe borrowed certain characteristics from the earlier heroine.

In Kirby's *Remarkable Characters* there is related a tale, *The Intrepid*

Female; it concerns the actual adventures of Mary Anne Taylor, whose story is based on that of Moll Franders and Moll Cutpurse. Most of Mary Anne's life she passed as a man, taking the name of John Taylor, and serving both in the Navy and Army. "I had formed an acquaintance with Haines, the well-known highwayman," she related, "who some time after was hung in chains on Hounslow Heath for shooting a Bow Street officer.

"GHOSTLY" HIGHWAYMEN.

I recently found, in a magazine of 1845, an article *Musings by an Old Toll-Gate on Hounslow Heath.* Which particular one was not specified, but it is a good word-picture that we read: "You see nothing around for miles but the lonely heath, and you think of the long winter nights, when the hours of darkness hang over the silent scene. You recall the winds which blow all night long and the awful roaring of the tall trees, mingled with the heavy showers that beat upon the windows, sounding like robbers breaking through. Near at hand stands a gibbet-post where a murder was committed, and the gibbet-irons swing and creak in the wind.

"Or maybe that someone who destroyed himself is buried at the cross-roads, as was the custom, and all the country-folk believe the spot is haunted, for at twelve o'clock nobody knows what he has seen. Drunken farmers on horseback have been chased, and timid ploughboys have had to run for it; and the old toll-man has had to come out to one fainting, another speechless and a third with his hair standing on end, and if you believe but half there never was such a spot where 'bogles' laid wait and caught you unawares. One woman's all in white, and another without a head. You could never see their faces, but you heard the rustle of their garments and felt the cold air as they glided by, and if you approached they vanished.'

Whether we believe in these heathen spectres or not (of which there is even more than quoted) there is no doubt about the next sentence: "There are many instances of highwaymen riding up to the gate at midnight and paying the toll with a bullet, and many a fight with the Runners has taken place by this old turnpike gate on the heath." The anonymous writer adds a note on this spectre-land: "What a countryside of dreamy old supernatural lies is this heathland; nothing you can prove or disprove—but it is common gossip round many a country hearth in this part of Middlesex."

*   *   *   *   *   *

I have told elsewhere of my attempt to see a heathen spectre and its failure. The nearest to beholding anything of this sort was the following incident. I was riding along a lonely road one night between Hatton and Cranford. I had dismounted to light my pipe, and on looking up this is what I saw—a wild, desolate midnight heath, with a spectral oak in the foreground. The wind blew fiercely and the jagged branches, scantily covered, waved to and fro. A formless wrack of clouds streamed across the sky, giving a mysterious tone to the moonless expanse above, with a fine mist sweeping parallel to the horizon. Beyond the heath-like fields stretched out into endless blackness, where fancy conjured up indefinable shapes merging into space.

At the base of the oak was a shrouded figure on horseback, and I could see the animal's head more plainly than the rider, who had his cloak wrapped around him. I could not see his features, for a black mask covered the upper part of his face and the lower was covered by his mantle, which he held up with one hand while the other seemed to grasp a large horse-pistol, the long barrel of which protruded from beneath his cloak.

It was all very real, and had the mysterious figure cried " Stand and deliver!" I do not think I should have been surprised, even if startled. The masked horseman never moved, however, and I cried aloud, " Ho there, Dick Turpin!" and clapped my hands. The horse moved off into the blackness behind, taking its silent rider with it.

*   *   *   *   *   *

I passed the same spot next morning and tried to solve the ghostly affair. The tree was still waving its gaunt branches, and even Black Bess (an old brown cart-horse) was looking over a gate. Far from being a spectral steed it was friendly enough to share an apple. All the rest of the phenomena had dispersed with daylight, and so the Great Heath Mystery remains unsolved.

A friend who believes in spooks scorned all prosaic explanations, and was much annoyed with me over the incident. He was convinced that I had been, though he is not Irish, on " the verge of seeing the Unseen." He says that if I had not been a fool and bellowed like a stupid bull I might have been held up by a spectral highwayman! When I pointed out that it was at least *something* to have scared a ghost he was quite shocked at what he termed my levity. I fear, however, that ardent spiritualists are not always over strong in the " saving grace."

*   *   *   *   *   *

A good " Howler " is always worth hearing, so that must be the excuse for ending this chapter with one from a schoolboy's essay on the eighteenth century, where he wrote: " In those days for gentlemen to take ladies pillion-riding on horseback when travelling over such places as Hounslow Heath was very romantic and dangerous, as most of what are now roads were then only bridal paths."

CHAPTER XVIII.

The " Robin Redbreasts."

IMPRESSIONS of the " Robin Redbreasts," as the Bow Street Runners were known from their scarlet waistcoats, from the Penny Dreadful type of highwayman story, will give a distorted view of that really competent body.

In this class of " literature " they are usually represented as totally inefficient fools, easily outwitted, who spent their time hanging round the alehouses. That they *did* frequent these places is true, because, as often as not, their quarry was to be found there.

The Bow Street Runners were established in 1749. Perhaps in the very early days there were cases of thief-taking conducted on the same lines as the famous Jonathan Wild; thief-taker and thief were often in collusion, and hence, as Dickens phrases it, the officer who knew how to turn his occupation to profit found that his principal compliments were got under the rose.

The Runners disappeared after the introduction of the new police system in 1829, although the old name seems to have lingered on for some years. In *Oliver Twist*, published in 1838, the London police-officers who go to Chertsey are termed " Runners," but in *Bleak House* (1853) the same type of men are called " detective officers."

(307)

Anno Quarto & Quinto

GULIELMI & MARIÆ.

An Act for Encouraging the Apprehending of Highway Men.

 Hereas the Highways and Roads within the Kingdom of England, and Dominion of Wales have been of late time more infested with Thieves and Robbers then formerly, for Want of due and sufficient Encouragement given, and Means used for the Discovery and Apprehension of such Offenders, whereby so many Murders and Robberies have been Committed, that it is become Dangerous in many Parts of the Nation for Travellers to pass on their Lawful Occasions, to the great Dishonour of the Laws of this Realm, and the Government thereof.

4   Gggg 2   For

FACSIMILE OF ACT AGAINST
HIGHWAYMEN, 1692.

MAY TURPIN,

THE

QUEEN OF THE ROAD.

A ROMANCE.

By the Author of " Dick Turpin, a Romance of the Road ;" Jack Sheppard and
Jonathan Wild,' &c., &c.

RICHLY ILLUSTRATED,

THE NEWSAGENTS' PUBLISHING COMPANY (LIMITED),
147, FLEET STREET, E.C.

1864.

A PENNY DREADFUL COVER.   *Lent by Mr. Barry Ono
and Mr. Joseph Parks*

More than one explanation of the name Runner has been offered. It was an old name for a messenger. Swift speaks of the " runner to the post-office," and another writer defines a " Runner to a Gaming-House " as " one who gets intelligence when the constables are out." " Set a runner to catch a runner " was evidently an early rendering of " set a thief to catch a thief."

The usual costume of Bow Street Runners, for they had no regular uniform, included a blue dress-coat with brass buttons, with the bright red waistcoat. Dickens, writing in 1862, said he remembered (presumably some years earlier) these red-breasted functionaries very well as standing about the door of the office in Bow Street. " They kept company," he wrote, " with thieves and the like, much more than the detective-police do."

One of the best books on the old time Runners is Percy Fitzgerald's *Chronicles of Bow Street Police Office* in which will be found the whole history and many of the genuine adventures of this force. Though Bow Street itself lies without our scope it was really closely connected with Hounslow Heath through the number of highwaymen tried there.

No more famous magistrates sat on the Bench than the three Field-ings. The first was Henry Fielding, " the father of the English novel," who first occupied that position in 1753; he was succeeded in 1761 by his brother Sir John, the famous Blind Justice, and perhaps the cleverest law-giver who ever served there. Then, after an interval, came William Fielding, the son of Henry, who was there in 1822, in which year we hear of him giving evidence before a committee of the House of Commons, and speak-ing of his father as " the author of Tom Jones."

Henry Fielding's experience as a magistrate—his official title was Jus-tice of the Peace for Middlesex—furnished him with the material for his book *Enquiry into the Increase of Robbers;* and also gave him much " copy " for his grave satire *Jonathan Wild the Great.* It is perhaps of interest to note in passing that part of his greatest novel *Tom Jones* was written while Fielding was living at a cottage in Back Lane, near Twickenham Green, in those days adjacent to Hounslow Heath. He was the originator of what is known as " Fielding's Plan "; a scheme to protect the suburbs within twenty miles of London, then almost at the mercy of highwaymen, by means of small subscriptions from residents. This was mainly operated by the blind brother, who became a terror to evil-doers.

" The alehouse keepers, stable-keepers who let horses to hire should constantly read the advertisements inserted by Mr. Fielding in the *Public Advertiser.* The first would not then harbour a rogue; the second would never furnish a highwayman with a horse without knowing it time enough to detect him and save the horse."

There is a good deal more in this strain; it seems that the malefactor was allowed plenty of time to escape, while the " Flying Squad " of those days was put into slow motion.

Sir John Fielding, like his brother, had a keen sense of humour, and, utilising his experience, published some advice to the public in reference to thieves, the form of which has a quaint turn. " It was," reads one account, " printed on a sheet and given in the *Description of London and West-minster* published in 1776; and to this he added " *Proper Cautions* to mer-chants, Tradesmen and shopkeepers, Journeymen, Apprentices, Porters, errand boys, book-keepers and Inn-keepers; *also very necessary* for every person going to London on business or pleasure."

Then there are what he calls "Sky Farmers," "one of whom dresses himself extremely genteel and takes the character of a private gentleman. He is attended by two men, in the character of country farmers, with clumsy boots and horsemen's coats. 'The objects pitched upon' are charitable old ladies, and after having stopped their post-chaises, the Sky Farmer tells a dreadful story of losses by fire and flood to the utter ruin of these poor farmers, whose wives are also down with small-pox. A book is produced by the Sky Farmer, who is undertaking this disagreeable duty out of pity, with the names of all the nobility and gentry who are supposed to have already contributed." The Sky Farmer seems to have been a cross between a highwayman and a confidence man.

In *The Chronicles of Bow Street* we read of the Patrols, who were really mounted Runners. "To Sir John Fielding," writes the author, "the public were indebted for the introduction of a useful check on highway robbery, so simple and obvious in character that it is astonishing it was not suggested before. Knowing the unprotected state of the roads in the environs of the city, the notorious Hounslow, Blackheath and other unguarded commons, his energetic mind conceived the idea of an organised force, which, however small, would still furnish protection. A few men, well armed, patrolling the lonely roads, and meeting each other at fixed points, was the idea. . . . so successful was the plan of a patrole that it was extended under other magistrates. It is a popular delusion that until the advent of the New Police in 1829 the safety of London was entrusted to the incapable "Charlies," or watchmen, who were supposed to perform their duties by constantly sleeping in their watch-boxes. But, in truth, there was an efficient body of patrols, mounted and on foot."

Another energetic magistrate, a little later than Sir John Fielding, was Sir Richard Ford, who in 1805 formed "The Bow Street Horse - Patrole." He himself undertook the direction of it. "In that year," we are told, "highway robberies in the various country roads leading to London became very frequent, and this practical mode of checking the abuse was adopted. Their uniform was an odd one, consisting of a leathern hat, blue coat with yellow metal buttons, blue trousers and boots, with the invariable scarlet waistcoats, while they were armed to the teeth with cutlass, pistol and truncheon. They were all splendidly mounted and were awkward customers to encounter on the high road.

"The officer in charge," we read, "was directed to make himself known to all persons they met in carriages or on horseback by calling out 'Bow Street Patrole.' The highwaymen were much disturbed by their operations, and we constantly hear of encounters and captures." The force was found so efficient that another was formed, with the rather Irish name of "The Police Dismounted Horse-Patrole," whose duty it was to protect the roads lying between the beat of the horse-patrole and the city.

This was communicated to the public by means of such newspapers as then existed, as this account testifies: *The Middlesex Journal* 1770. From a plan of the patrole lately settled, it is desired that persons who may be robbed will not only leave notice at the turnpikes, but give immediate information at the Public Office in Bow Street.

The deeds of the Runners often found their way into the popular ballads of the period, but they were also mentioned by Lord Byron in his *English Bards:*

> " When Little's *leadless* pistol met his eye,
> And Bow Street myrmidons stood laughing by."

This had reference to the farcical duel in 1806 between Tom Moore, the poet, and Francis Jeffrey, of the *Edinburgh Review,* which was stopped by the Runners before a shot was fired. Through a wag altering the word " bullet " to " pellet," as a jest upon literary belligerants, in a newspaper account it was actually believed (though untrue) that the pistols were loaded with wads of paper instead of lead.

In *Chronicles of Bow Street* we read much of the " Charlies," or old night-watchmen; and Fitzgerald's book contains many good stories which might form a true supplement to Pierce Egan's spirited fiction; such stories as " Gentleman Jehus making most of a Jarvey " has the real touch of the *Tom and Jerry* period.

Before we pass on here are one or two stories from this *Chronicle,* the most quotable of books. " William Cobbett and the toll-keepers: The agitator Cobbett, having taken up the subject of turnpike overchargings, contested the matter so sturdily that he became a terror to the pike-keepers from his frequent summonses, and was actually allowed to go through the gates *free.* In 1823 he laid information against several turnpike-keepers for having taken too high a toll from poor men who kept one-horse carts on the western roads leading out from Hyde Park Corner. The tolls of these roads were rented by rich Jews, against whose long purses poor men are unable to contend.

" Cobbett went to several turnpikes and told the toll-collectors that if they did not desist from their extortion he would call them to account. Finding the extortion still going on he obtained summonses against several toll-collectors."

The following story not only has elements of humour, but is remarkable for the extreme care the " insulted " lady takes to hide her identity, the only clear part seems that it happened " somewhere in Middlesex."

It is extracted from the *Morning Chronicle* of 1825:

> Middlesex to wit, Kitty —— of —— in the town of ——, spinster, maketh oath that William Clement, a person of evil mind, did maliciously contrive to vilify, disgrace and injure this deponent by desiring to commit an outrage upon and murder her, on the 4th day of October within the said town of ——, in the county of Middlesex.
>
> (Signed) Kitty ——.

The terrible deed contemplated by this desperate villain was that in a critique of a concert, at which Kitty Blank was singing, he was guilty of a *jeu d'esprit* by stating that Handel had been known to have a singer thrown out of a window, and that it was a pity sometimes that such a " Concert pitch " was not renewed. No names were mentioned, but Miss Blank actually took this case to court and declared that she thought the *publisher* of the paper intended to murder her ! It is said that the " laughter in court " nearly stopped the case, though the magistrate had solemnly to bind over the defendant to keep the peace.

*　　*　　*　　*　　*　　*

The personel of the Bow Street Runners does not call for special mention, with one notable exception. If they had a " Big Five " in those days I do not know; " We are Seven " is the nearest I can get, for the chief amongst them was John Townsend, supported by John Shayer, John Vickery, Daniel Bishop, Samuel Taunton, William Salmon and George Ruthven (I feel I ought to end with " Uncle Tom Cobleigh and all " !)

Of these stalwarts Townsend stands out, as Dick Turpin among highwaymen or Sherlock Holmes in detective fiction.

" Townsend was an active Runner from 1786 till the end of the system," says one account, " a bold and energetic officer, he was much feared by criminals with whom, unlike some of his fraternity, he was never in collusion.

" Townsend had charge of the arrangements for the execution of Jerry Abershawe, the highwayman. After many narrow escapes and bold adventures Abershawe was caught at last and executed at Kennington, whence his body was hung in chains at Putney Bottom on a gibbet erected near the scene of his crimes. Townsend said that if one went to see the body there were a hundred thousand. He received information that there was a plot to cut down the corpse; so, taking ten of his officers with him, he watched through the night at the foot of the gibbet, hoping to catch the bold interferers with the law's savagery in the act. But he had been misled; no attempt was made to touch the criminal's body, and Townsend and his associates had only the discomfort of the night-watch."

A " gate " of 100,000 to see a dead highwayman—a modern Cup Final could hardly equal this. Such, however, were the " pictures—The Thrillers— of 1795." I have tried to identify the actual spot where the gibbet stood; the only clue being a remark of Townsend's: " The only difficulty is its being so near Lord Spencer's house; but we went down and pointed out a particular place; and he was hung at the pitch of the hill." This would be the rise of the slope towards Kingston Hill on the Putney side, opposite The Robin Hood Inn. One account states that the present church is on the site of the gibbet.

Those who want to hear more on this topic should consult the *Evidence of the Police Committee* held at the House of Commons in 1816, from which these notes about Abershawe are extracted; but there is another quotation in which our Heath is mentioned. It is given in question and answer form:

Q. " The activity of the Bow Street officers has infinitely increased of late years?

A. (By Townsend) " No doubt about it, sir. We used to have ten or fifteen highway robberies a week, we have not had one lately. I mean persons on horseback, on Hounslow Heath, Wimbledon or Finchley Commons. Now people travel safely by means of the new horse-patrol.

Q. " Do you think any advantages arise from a man being gibbeted after execution?

A. " Yes, I was always of that opinion. Say two men are hanging by the roadside, folk say, ' Why, these are hung and gibbeted for robbing on the highway,' and so the thing is kept alive. If it was not for this robbers would die and nobody know anything of it. But now where we hanged five highwaymen, say in 1788, we only hang one now!"

It was said to be Townsend who also told the Committee, with reference to the technical details of a new type of " drop " for the scaffold, that " though this would take twelve criminals at a time, it would really only hang ten *comfortably!"* The famous Runner was, apparently, quite serious, and failed to see the grim humour of his words.

In the *Chronicles* there are many other stories of Townsend, who seems to have been a " character "; and his association with royalty, which also finds a place in G. W. Abbot's gossipy book on Regency days, *Life of an Octogenarian:* " Townsend, the head of the Bow Street Police Office, was, in his way, one of the greatest men of his age. He had a quaint blunt John Bull style about him which pleased the aristocracy and even royalty. No one dared speak so freely as he did, and once when he called on the Duke of York, the Prince said to him, ' Well, Townsend, what is the world talking about to-day, eh?' ' All about you and Mrs. Clarke, your Royal Highness,' replied Townsend, boldly mentioning the scandal that was occupying the public mind. ' Ah, well, I don't care about that, Townsend.' ' Of course you don't,' answered Townsend, ' your Royal Highness would be a damned fool if you did!' and the Prince laughed heartily at this candid reply."

Here is a last story of the famous thief-taker, from *As the Crow Flies,* which says: " Townsend, the celebrated Bow Street Runner, used often to ride as an armed escort before the coaches containing Government money. Townsend was a little fat man, who wore a flaxen wig, kerseymore breeches, a blue straight-cut coat, and a broad-brimmed hat. He was daring, dexterous and cunning, and his merits, manners and odd sayings were much relished by the Royal Family. On one occasion Townsend, having to escort a carriage to Reading, took with him a friend, Joe Manton.

" Soon after reaching Hounslow three footpads stopped the coach, and Joe was just going to draw trigger, when Townsend cried out, ' Stop, Joe, don't fire! Let me talk to the gentlemen.' A glimpse of the moon revealed Townsend's dreaded features to the thieves, who instantly took to their heels; but he had already recognised them. In a few days his rough and ready hand was on their collars."

*   *   *   *   *   *

There was an earlier Bow Street Runner, though that body was not founded officially at the time, in Captain John Allen, who in 1637 was a great thief-taker. Owing to his efforts five of the most notorious highwaymen of the time was captured and executed, while many others, whom he had denounced, fled through fear of him. The Lord Chief Justice reported that as a result of Allen's activities several counties had " been in quiet " ever since. Soon after the Captain was ordered on foreign service—and all the highwaymen came back.

*   *   *   *   *   *

Those who wish for further news of the Runners can also refer to Gilbert Armitage's *History of the Bow Street Runners;* while of course they have been brought into stories innumerable, such as *The King's Gift,* by W. H. Morris, and many others of a like nature.

Oblivion, however, has overtaken both thieves and thief-takers. Bow Street Runners have gone the way of the " Charlies," beadles and parish constables; while the name and fame of the once dreaded Johnny Townsend, and his fellows, are known only to those who care to trace the byways of our social history.

CHAPTER XIX.

The Heath in Bookland.

I. The Heath in Literature: Prose.

THIS chapter must of necessity be like the bookcase that is always complete but never finished; to quote extracts from six books would make it complete in a sense, but to quote from sixty would be no guarantee that sixty more had not been missed. However wide the field of research, another—or many more—examples can always be found.

Research of this sort entails a good many things—a moderate initial knowledge of the most likely sources, enthusiasm, energy, the quick picking up of clues, solid hard work—and a little luck; and even then you may miss something just "round the corner." I have found items by pure chance in places as far apart as Worthing and Dundee, miles away from Hounslow Heath (there is a Hounslow in Scotland and another in Essex, but few have ever heard of them); I have found them in London second-hand book shops, in local libraries, in my own study (in unsuspected places sometimes), and perhaps most of all in the Reading Room of the British Museum.

A word of explanation re this chapter's title may help: by the first Literature is meant that wide range generally included under that head, but in the second "Literature" is meant those lurid productions, more popular in past generations than now, some often designated "Penny Dreadfuls" and some even earlier productions.

The extracts quoted now are from novels and general books rather than those dealing with topography, which, however, will also have mention. No special order need be kept, for with the authors writing of bygone days a chronology of publication dates would be of little moment here, though they will be found in the Bibliography.

Hounslow is mentioned, though not actually visited, in *Oliver Twist;* when Bill Sikes and Oliver are on their way to Chertsey on burglarious intent—at least as regards the former—near Kensington "an empty cart came up. Seeing 'Hounslow' written on it, he (Sikes) asked the driver with as much civility as he could assume, if he would give them a lift as far as Isleworth." A little later we read: "At length they came to a public-house called the Coach and Horses, a little way beyond which another road appeared to turn off, and here the cart stopped." Oliver and his sinister companion disappeared along that road—the place is now known as Busch Corner. There is a pleasant glimpse of the Middlesex countryside in Dickens' description of the journey of these ill-assorted wayfarers, through Hampton, Sunbury, Halliford and Shepperton, till the county boundary is reached by Chertsey Bridge. I regret it is too long for quotation (and in this case a *precis* would destroy its "flavour"), as much of the country was in bygone days part of the Heath of Hounslow. Dickens must have known this country well, for *Oliver Twist* was partly written while he was living (in 1838) within a mile or so of Busch Corner, and the route of Sikes and Oliver must almost have passed near the novelist's home. This house is still standing, by St. Margarets Station at East Twickenham, and is known as No. 4, Ailsa Park Villas, a picturesque row of pleasant, old-fashioned

190

houses standing back from the road in long front gardens.

Dickens' "clues" are usually fairly clear, but the slipshod methods of some authors in the topography of their stories is amazing, especially if the period is set back over a hundred years; in fact I actually heard a "defence" of this by someone who said that what did it matter if it were a long time ago? Could anything be more fatuous? Places were in exactly the same position then as now. I could quote numerous cases, but two will suffice, both in books by well-known living authors. In one the coach from Brighton to London is made to pass through Uxbridge! And in another a rider sets out from London on the Western Road and then crosses the Thames to go to Putney in *Middlesex!* (an obvious muddle-headed confusion of the modern Putney Bridge Station, which *is* in that county). But worse follows, for the next morning the traveller again crosses the river to the north bank, described as in Surrey, on his way to Guildford! Where he ended up is a mystery! I know that in every boook written by a human being there must be *some* errors—otherwise it would be machine-made and unimaginative—but there is a limit in such things.

In Julian Hawthorne's novel, *Dust*—a better book than its drab title indicates—there are some little touches of Middlesex topography that are pleasing. In matter of strict accuracy a carping critic might find fault with the coachman's description as he drove along: "That's Twickenham Church, ma'am. Mr. Pope's villa is a bit further down (sic). Yonder Mr. 'Orace Walpole's place." At the period of the book (1816) Pope's house had been demolished four years.

There is one excellent thing about this book that might be imitated by some writers who leave readers to guess at haphazard the period of their tale. Julian Hawthorne devotes the first chapter to a short, but clear, account of his period, with a few historical notes — and, what is more valuable in a "period novel" which thus is more than a strictly historical one—some few remarks on costume, literature and social life of the time; all of which gives a clear idea of things before the tale proper begins.

Here is a delightful little picture of one of those old eighteenth century houses, once so numerous in Middlesex, but now fast disappearing. It is interesting to pick up the topographical clues; for instance: "Bowling along easily on the westward road some seven miles from London, the horses tramped through the narrow, winding street of a sleepy little town, wearied out, as it were, with the burden of its historic associations, and drew up at last before a wrought-iron gateway in a high brick wall, the bricks cemented with green moss and covered with ivy. The gate having been thrown open by the alert footman, the horses tramped through it, and up the gravelled curve of a drive, overshadowed with fragrant lime-trees, until the driver pulled up before the gabled portal of an elderly, but comfortable and solid-looking, edifice, faced with white plaster and dignified by projecting eaves. . . . A large cool, shadowy hall received the travellers; beyond a broad staircase, and opening inward to the right of it, a vista of a spacious drawing room, with windows opening upon a verandah and a rich lawn at the back of the house."

In those days this description would have applied to half a dozen houses on the high road between Brentford (the sleepy little town) and Hounslow, and even to-day I think I could almost pick out the house. I will not give away this clue, but leave the joy of the hunter to the reader, should he traverse this road.

Here is another picture of a rider lost on the fringes of Hounslow Heath, though in this case the clues are more definite; though the Heath is not actually mentioned by name, the context makes its position clear. It is as well to know that Kew Bridge is always referred to as Brentford Bridge in this book—the latter, strictly speaking, being the one over the Brent. "At Brentford Bridge the rider mistook his way," writes Hawthorne, and, crossing the Thames there, was soon plunging through the obscurity that overhung the Isleworth side of the river. Sometimes the leaves of low-lying branches brushed his face, and sometimes his horse's hoofs resounded over the hollowness of a little bridge. By and by the horse stumbled at some inequality of the ground and nearly lost its footing as the rider emerged into more open country on the fringe of some heathland. He put his horse to a walk as he fancied he heard a faint, intermittant noise on the road before him; and he peered through the darkness ahead for the first glimpse of the approaching horseman."

Now there is no doubt that the scene of this was the borders of Hounslow Heath, and it might be naturally assumed with a mysterious night rider coming suddenly upon the scene, that an encounter with a highwayman followed. The riders, however, knew one another and proceeded on their way together.

In another part of the book, though, we are not disappointed, for there is a short, but vivid, account of an encounter near Hounslow with a knight of the road. The attacked party is narrating his experience: "My highwayman was not so ceremonious as the best of the old-fashioned ones. I heard his horse overtaking me at a gallop, and I drew aside to let him pass. But he rode straight against me—and nearly threw me. As I turned towards him he held a pistol up and fired at me. The ball knocked off my hat, but missed me. I had a heavy riding-whip and I struck at him. I think I must have hit him across the wrist; at all events, he dropped the pistol. Neither of us had spoken a word. A flash of lightning showed me that he was a large man, dressed in dark clothes; he put his arm across his face, as if to prevent my seeing it. The thunder was very loud, and my horse plunged and burst his girths; and I slipped to the ground, and when I got on my feet again I was alone; my highwayman had disappeared."

I suppose I am so used to "expecting the unexpected" with regard to finding news of Hounslow Heath in unlikely books that it came as a mild shock when the position was reversed. When I found H. C. Bailey's book, *The Highwayman,* with the opening scene set in Middlesex in the year 1714, I naturally expected some news of our Heath; the more so when I read in the first chapter: "It was late in a wet autumn, and all the clay of Middlesex slippery as butter and, withal, affectionate as warm glue. Having kept to the highway, though its miles of mud and water were, on the surface, even worse than the gleaming brown furrows of plough land."

I read on, and Chapter I. certainly lives up to the title, with the "hero's" rescue of two ladies whose coach was beset by knights of the road near Whetstone. After this episode the book deals almost entirely with political plotting, and not another mention of highwaymen do we find—and no word about our Heath—until the last chapter, when there is a rather weak attempt to justify the title, which it seems is used symbolically, because a girl tells the "hero" that he has a "stand-and-deliver stare" and that he is "a highwayman because you pillage us all. Love, honour, you win it from all." The book is quite good, save the title, which should be *The Jacobite* to fit the story.

THE HIGHWAYMAN'S HOLE.
Green Man, Hatton.

Drawing by N. Mayger

"MURDER COTTAGE." WHITTON.

Photo lent by Mr. Dudley Barton

Despite lengthy digressions, which wander far from the road, both literally and metaphorically, De Quincey's essay, *The English Mail Coach,* remains probably the finest thing in its kind in English literature. It is an epic of all the highways in the land, yet it can truthfully be said that beautiful little idyll concerning "Fanny of the Bath Road" takes place on one of ours. You must remember Fanny, the granddaughter of that coachman who "showed rosy blossoms on his face deeper even than his granddaughter's—*his* being drawn from the ale cask, Fanny's from the fountains of Dawn." De Quincey, though giving a hint that may lead us away from the Heath, does not state definitely *where* Fanny used to wait for the coach whose passenger fell in love with her, so we are at liberty to choose our own location. Mine is at the end of the oak-lined lane that leads to Cranford village, and I chose this because recently I actually saw her there in the flesh. I was riding along the Bath Road one morning when at this spot I saw a pretty girl in a light chintz dress and broad-brimmed hat, which wanted but little imagination to change into a high-waisted gown and poke bonnet of Regency days. Into my mind flashed at once a picture of Fanny of the Bath Road waiting for the coach. While I rode slowly by a "coach" actually did come up and carried my dream-Fanny away—for it was a motor-'bus, but the driver did not look the least like her grandfather!

I picked up recently a copy of *The Farmer's Lawyer: Or Every Country Gentleman His Own Counseller* (1774), a quaint old work, especially the chapters on "Highways" and "Turnpikes." Some of the laws then in force might be revived with advantage to-day. Here is one: "Forasmuch as evil-disposed persons that do damage or deface by carving any toll-gate, mile-stone or bridge on the highway shall be committed to the House of Correction there to be whipped." Just the thing for initial-carving fiends.

Or again: Anyone in charge of a vehicle on the highway that shall drive it to the annoyance and inconvenience of any of His Majesty's lieges, whether on horseback or on foot, shall, if lawfully convicted, be judged guilty of felony, and shall be transported for seven years." An excellent thing for motor-cyclists, and certain car drivers, too!

The book is full of delightful bits, such as: "To prevent floods there shall be no dam digging on streams by the highway"; or this entry, under "Game"—of most mysterious import: "By the Black Act (whatever that is) any person appearing disguised in any warren where hares are kept shall be guilty of felony without the benefit of clergy."

The King, however, seems to come into his own quite a lot in these pages; for instance, he is to have one hogshead in every twelve of cyder made in this country and a like amount of a mysterious drink called mum—though it has no connection with Mumm apparently. In fact the King, as far as the highways were concerned, lived in a land flowing with milk and honey; for under "Beasts at Wild on Turnpike Road" is:

"If a milch cow be found straying upon the highway half shall belong to the King."

"A swarm of bees in the highway may be seized by the King."

What the King was to do with his half cow, or how he was to seize the bees, is not explained; perhaps it was the pondering on these problems that drove poor George III. mad!

That R. D. Blackmore knew and loved the Heath, and in fact *all* Middlesex, is evident from his book *Kit and Kitty: A Story of West*

Middlesex; probably the finest novel devoted entirely to this county ever written. In that book there is a chapter, " The Giant on the Heath," which describes an exciting rescue of a girl from two villains who had imprisoned her in a lonely cottage. Even to-day it is possible for a close observer to follow the " clues " given by Blackmore, for instance the sentence: " There is, or at least there used to be, along the back of Hounslow Heath, a lane which leaves the great western road on the right."

We are told how the rescuer " took the next turn towards Harlington. He is a very tall man and is admonished by a woman who helps him in his enterprise. ' If they do see you, why, they'll take you for the Giant of the Heath—the old highwayman as was hanged in chains not a hundred yards from here—my father seed him often; and when he fell down he took to walking through the fuzz.' " This " ghost " has, I fear, ceased to " walk " here long ago.

To continue the " story ": " Bill, with many glances around, and heartily wishing himself at home, set forth towards the cottage, which was known as Struck-tree Cottage, because the lightning came and scorched the old oak. As he passed beneath the shattered tree he looked up with a shudder at the jagged fork, naked stubs, and contorted limbs, expecting the dead highwayman to clank his ghostly chains. Presently he came to a dark elbow of the track across the turf, and a clump of Scotch firs, bowed by the west winds, overhung the way, and made it sombre as the grave. Before him was a square building on the verge of the Heath and surrounded by bushes and a wooden palisade."

There is no space here to follow further this rescue, which is successful, and when the villains pursue in hot haste the "Giant of the Heath" crams two sallies over their heads so forcibly that they are powerless " as a dog-fish in an eel-cruive." A sally, it may be mentioned, is an old Middlesex term for the large wicket baskets of fruit growers.

In this case the period of the book is important, for it represents that of about 1860, and not the usual eighteenth century. We read here of many interesting things, of red inns that still exist—such as the Crooked Billet by Shortwood Common—and landmarks, such as the clump of Scotch firs still noticeable on the old Drill Ground on the Staines Road, together with old county customs. Here is an illuminating passage: " As he approached the inn the wind brought him the burden of a drawling song, drawled as only a Middlesex man—who can beat all the North and even West at that— can troll his slow emotions forth." Even to-day, seventy years after, the old Middlesex drawl is not quite extinct, as I have discovered in talking with old rustics at village inns.

We soon get back to the eighteenth century, for the next book I pick up for reference is *Roderick Random*, in which Smollett lays a scene here: " Strap rode up to the coach door, and told us, in a great fright, that two men on horseback were crossing the Heath (for by this time we had passed Hounslow) and were making directly towards us." In *Esmond*, also, Thackeray mentions this ever-present fear: " Beatrix's departure took place within the hour, her maid going with her in the post-chaise, and a man armed on the coach-box to prevent any danger of the road, and another man was sent to follow the coach and not leave it till it had passed over Hounslow Heath." In *Humphrey Clinker* also we find mention of high-waymen—as might be expected.

Goldsmith knew Hounslow and its surrounding districts well — in his

Citizen of the World there is a chapter laid in Brentford, and The Three Pigeons in *She Stoops to Conquer* is said to be taken from The Three Pigeons in that town, an inn of some fame in its day, now demolished. It is claimed, too, that Crackskull Common was Hounslow Heath, about the same distance from the inn in the play and in reality; the name fits in quite nicely (or nastily!), but somehow I always think that when the playwright mentions "the gibbet on Heavytree Heath" it was these memorials of horror on Hounslow's adjacent waste he had in mind.

Some of the adventures of Joseph and Parson Adams in Fielding's *Joseph Andrews* take place on the western road to London. While nothing of particular note happens on Hounslow Heath, as a novel of eighteenth century road life it is full of most picturesque detail. Smollett and Richardson, as well as Fielding, also can be read for many wonderful pen-pictures of this period; in fact it was Fielding who wrote in *Tom Jones:* "Hounslow Heath naturally suggests the idea of highwaymen."

When I read Jeffrey Farnol's highwayman story, *The Shadow,* there came into my mind, through an association of dual personalities, the doings of the Golden Farmer, whose doings can be read fully in Johnson's *Lives of the Highwaymen.* The likeness in this case, however, is probably by chance, for the incidents of the stories are quite different. Another story very similar is Richard Karverne's *The Grey Man,* except that the "hero" is a sailor instead of a parson. The latter again appears in Gilbert Sheldon's novel, *Bubble Fortune,* and as a respected citizen in Mrs. Gaskell's *The Squire's Story.* In fact the *Dr. Jekyll and Mr. Hyde* idea with regard to highwaymen seems a common plot.

A mild mystery of the Heath, though of a totally different nature, is contained in Austin Dobson's delightful *Ballad of Beau Brocade,* which tells us how the "Plymouth Fly" was saved by the outwitting of the highwayman by Dolly the chambermaid. The place of this happening is, I am almost certain, intended to be Hounslow Heath; for although no actual spot is mentioned, it all happened on "the London side of Bagshot" and they first heard the news of the affair at Staines, through which town the Plymouth coach would have to pass before it crossed the Heath.

The poem is an eighteenth century vignette, which no one could write better than Austin Dobson; it is too long to quote (and "snippets" would spoil it in this case), but read it if possible in the edition with Hugh Thomson's illustrations; they make the verses live, for this artist's work, combined with Austin Dobson's writing, form a perfect collaboration when the theme is eighteenth century England. This ballad must not be confused with Baroness Orczy's novel, *Beau Brocade,* also a highwayman story, and one that goes with a swing too.

In Baring Gould's curiously titled book, *Bladys of the Stewponey,* there is much about highwaymen, with a dance on the Heath, but not of Hounslow; though our Heath does pop up in some very unlikely places, as in the life of a banker by A. B. Blackie, called *The Bank Parlour,* where there is a story, "The Highway Attack," in which the Heath figures.

In *Highway Dust,* by G. G. Sellick, we have a highwayman story proper (to use a heraldic term); this is a book which the knights of the road and their doings form the main theme, rather than an incident. It is a well-told, swiftly-moving story, in which Hounslow, its Heath and some of its old inns form part of the background.

All lovers of highwaymen yarns — and the most prosaic of us would probably confess to a secret liking for them—cannot but admire that spirited volume, *The Hand of Glory*, which is a mine of information, in which romance, imagination and fact are cleverly blended. Its sub-title, " Grandfather's Tales and Legends of Highwaymen," is enough to set our expectations going—and they will not be disappointed.

These stories were originally collected by R. Blakeborough and edited by his son, J. Fairfax Blakeborough, who reminds us that many of the tales were told to his father first hand by old folk who could remember the stage-coach era.

A Tale of the Road—in 1791, by M. A. Butterworth, is a good highwayman yarn, set in desolate heath-like country strongly reminiscent of Hounslow.

Perhaps the most unknown highwayman book, and I have never seen it mentioned in any list of such stories (though I know such a one could never hope to be complete), is *The Life and Death of Gamaliel Ratsey: A Famous Thiefe of England*. He was executed in 1605, and in the same year appeared the sequel, *Ratsey's Ghost: Or the Second Part of his Madde Franckes and Robberies*.

Highwaymen: A Book of Gallant Rogues, by Charles J. Finger, is a throughly entertaining book on English highwaymen by an American. He has drawn on his imagination very largely and swallows greedily every legend without the least doubt or sifting of what evidence there is. He has tried hard to be very English and on the whole has succeeded quite well, though a few Transatlantic touches are noticeable; I do not mean those so glaring as to make Dick Turpin exclaim " Oh, yeah," or urge on Black Bess by crying " Atta, baby!"—it is more in small details he shows that his knowledge of English life is gained more from books than experience. Nevertheless I enjoyed the book thoroughly; it moves swiftly, and I even like the Ride to York. What matters where if it never took place.

The author relates a good story of Turpin: " Once, according to tradition, Dick surprised Mr. Pope of Twickenham as he walked in the fields, but found nothing on the man except a bundle of papers the poet seemed to be trying to hide, so after looking through them the highwayman tossed the bundle into a hedge. Seeing the little man run up to his papers, Turpin, full of suspicion, took them again, suspecting some hidden treasure he had overlooked, but there was only scrawling writing. So the thief returned the papers and was handed a gold chain which had been overlooked, knowing nothing of the treasure that lay hidden in the Essay on Man. For all that the highwayman was twitted shortly afterwards by the witty and charming Mrs. Ballenden when he stopped her coach on Hounslow Heath. When he called on her to deliver her jewels she flung her rings in his face, calling him a dull boor who did not know real treasure from silly gold, she having in mind the Twickenham affair. But what she meant he did not understand."

It is obvious that the writer has never visited the district that was once Hounslow Heath, for he writes: " More than fifteen miles Claude Duval rode that evening, going past Longford, Drayton and Cowley, across low rolling hills, down a valley of tender green threaded by a silver stream, then riding between two rows of thatched cottages, each with its glory of climbing rose bush and bank of sunflowers, he came at last to Uxbridge." He gets the position of the places in the right order — which could be ascertained from a map—but I'm afraid there are mighty few "rolling hills and valleys" between Longford and Uxbridge.

An article in an old magazine of 1835 describes how a party of people propose to take a country walk and decide to "devote this splendid day to the ancient palace of the kings at Hampton." They choose a curious route. By omnibus (no vulgar abbreviation, you notice, for a 'bus was then a novelty, and respected) to Isleworth and then intend to walk to Hampton Court—a roundabout way, but certainly interesting. Here is the description of their arrival in Isleworth: "We passed through Brentford and left the omnibus a little beyond the turnpike, and tread the earth with a feeling of independence. The sweet scent of the wallflowers, so plentiful in the gardens for miles on the road, have well prepared us for the full enjoyment of the perfumed breeze. Let us go joyously along the road; we meet with some dust, but the hedges are green as we advance, and we feel a difference in the air, and our spirits begin to dance within us. See that country house; its hospitable hall, with door wide open; and see the vista through the glass door at the end—the true old-fashioned *comfortable* garden. We could well stop here, and pass away the day on the smooth-shaven lawn, listening to the hum of the bees, and breathing the fresh air redolent of sweet odours. Are we only eight miles from London? I feel though we were a hundred!"

Unluckily for their idea of getting to Hampton Court they pushed on a little too far, instead of turning to the left at Busch Corner—and eventually they found themselves on "Hounslow's dreaded Heath!" The story is told with an eye for picturesqueness—as in the account of the old Middlesex garden—and not without humour. I imagine them to have been young people (hikers of a hundred years ago), with the inevitable "wag" of the party, who told them ghastly tales of highwaymen, so that "several of the young ladies screamed in afright and clung to their escorts for protection against an imaginary Dick Turpin."

In 1835 the Heath was mainly enclosed though, and no mounted highwaymen were left, but it is possible a footpad or two may have lingered on; but though the Heath had changed, human nature was much the same—and I don't suppose the swains made any objections to "protecting" with their manly arms the "frightened" fair. It does not say if they reached Hampton Court—possibly they found the Heath attractive enough for one day.

Recently I bought for twopence Charlotte Yonge's novel, *Love and Life*, simply because its sub-title attracted me: "An Old Story in Eighteenth Century Costume" had possibilities. Frankly, I have read better stories, but as a "topographical detective," both on the road and on paper, which is one who finds keen interest in following up "clues" from thinly disguised descriptions of actual places round London, I found this book a real joy.

I think telepathy must have guided my purchase, for I did not examine a good deal of it was laid in the districts near Hounslow. So once again the Gods of Chance, which lead us up some strange gardens at times, on this occasion led us once more to our own Heath.

Highwaymen figure, rather lightly considering the period and place, in these pages, but we get glimpses of old Brentford, Twickenham, Longford, and other Middlesex villages on, or near, the road to Bath, and most of all of an estate called "Bowstead Park," which lies "in the country beyond Brentford." There are other "clues," but I am practically certain that

" Bowstead Park " is Cranford Park. Assuming this, the story at once
doubles in interest, for even now, in spite of vandalestic changes, the
eighteenth century flavour has not departed from this delightful village
just off the Bath Road. It is obvious that the authoress knew this district
well, by a dozen little remarks which might escape the general reader, but
which, to one who also knows this countryside, are illuminating.

We get a glimpse of how the mail coaches were used to distribute news
(noticed at more length in another chapter) in *Jackanapes*, Mrs. Ewing's
delightful, if rather sad, little story, which interested me as a child, but
now appeals to me far more, with its delicate air of Regency days, an
" atmosphere " helped by the characteristic drawings of Randolph Caldecott.

Here we read of how the news of the victory of Waterloo was brought
to the village of Goose Green, good news mingled with sad, for with it
came the news of the death in battle of Jackanape's father. " But soon a
crowd gathered round the George and Dragon," runs the account, " gaping
to see the Mail Coach dressed with flowers and oak leaves, and the guard
wearing a laurel-wreath over and above the royal livery."

There is a slight mention of highwaymen in this book, but in passing
only and a little disjointed; for the wonderful black mare of the captain,
who elopes with Jackanape's mother (as a girl) gives the villagers cause
to think that he " was   a certain well-known Gentleman of the Road."
This is obviously meant to be Dick Turpin, for who could the mare be but
Black Bess?   But I am afraid Mr. Richard Turpin had wooed the Hampen
widow seventy-six years before they rode off to Gretna Green.

Lord Lytton's *Paul Clifford* is a novel in which highwaymen play a
leading part and they dash across our Heath, and many another road on
the outskirts of London, in breathless fashion. It is essentially a novel of
movement and any " quiet " bits seem but a prelude to adventure. Here is
a typical paragraph, certainly a spirited word-picture of a Heathen adventure in the " good old days ": " It was a frosty, clear night. The dusk of the
twilight had melted beneath the moon, and the hoary rime glittered from
the bushes. On went the horses briskly, their hoofs sounding cheerily.

" The rapid motion of the carriage—the bracing coolness of the night—
and the excitement occasioned by the forethought of danger, all conspired
to stir the languid blood of Lord Mauleverer. He felt his pistols. ' In this
country,' he said to himself, " I have only been robbed once by highwaymen. Then it was my fault for having unloaded pistols.'

" It was a pisturesque spot by which the carriage was now wheeling, a
small tract of forest-like land lying on either side of the road. To the left
the green Heath bears away among the trees and bushes. At the time we
speak of the country was quite wild and few places could be more adapted
for robbery. Mauleverer looked anxiously from the window. To the left
three dark objects were just discernable in the shade; a moment more and
they grew into the forms of three mounted men." Then the fun began!

Stanley Weyman's novel *The Castle Inn* has a good deal about life on
the western road and a little concerning the highwaymen on Hounslow
Heath without any special passages that lend themselves to quotation. Many
short stories—such as Frankfort Moore's *Highwayman for an Hour*—speak
of the Knights of the Road as riding over " The Heath "; although no name
is mentioned we are safe in assuming, especially when the scene is laid
near London, that a large proportion of the writers *were* referring to
Hounslow Heath, for when the period is the eighteenth century the names

Highwayman and Hounslow were almost synonymous.

A short story of the road, with an unexpected ending, is Bernard Cape's *The Five Insides,* in which a wax figure is cleverly used in the robbing of a stage coach. The ghost of a highwayman on a white horse plays a leading part in that fine short story *Grogwas Ghost,* by Hafren; an almost perfect yarn marred by a vague ending. Curiously enough a white equine spectre also appears in my own highwayman tale of the Bath Road, *The Mysterious Steed,* published some years before the former, but which, I frankly own, is not as good as the other story.

In the *Diary of a Young Lady of Fashion,* by Cleone Knox, adventures on the road are merely hinted at: " our journey was uneventful enough, for though the talk was of nothing but Highwaymen, not a sign of one did we see."

There are some clever touches in this book and show a pretty wide study of eighteenth century life. The capture of the highwayman in bed in the inn at Finchley is well told and the description of a night at a country inn of the period is quite likely to be a touch of truth:—" Spent a vastly uneasy night reclining in a chair in a wrapper, my feet on another chair, the bed being too miserably dirty for my taste, was also loath to disturb the fleas and cockroaches who made it their habitation."

Cleverer " fake " historical stories, however, are those of Brinsley Moore, whose fine highwayman yarn of the Bath Road, *Mrs. Biddlecombe's Diamonds,* is so well constructed from imaginary memories and letters that it might deceive anyone. In it appears the Marchioness of Cranford—a Middlesex title Debrett's pages never knew. Another story by the same author is *The Purple Domino,* in which highwaymen on the Bath Road play their usual role.

In *Brentwood of Brentwood,* one of those interminable serials which our ancestors loved—or apparently so, for they had plenty of them—which appeared in *Lloyd's Penny Weekly Miscellany* for 1845, is a highwayman episode, about the feeblest I have ever read. In an old bookseller's catalogue (1868) there is an intriguing title, *The Royal Highwayman,* but no author is given.

A Gentleman of the Road, by Horace Bleackley, is a fine romance of the eighteenth century, with some good " road stuff " in it; a book to be read and enjoyed. There is actually a chapter entitled " Hounslow Heath," and here is an extract from it, which speaks of a typical Heath scene in the old days: " At eight o'clock they were still a mile from the village of Bedfont. The breeze had dropped and the sun was setting in a cloudless sky. Suddenly, from down the road a few hundred yards ahead, there came a terrified shriek, followed by shouts. With one impulse Dick galloped forward. In a little while he met an agitated post-boy, running towards them, and then as a chaise, standing beside a tall oak tree, came in sight the cause of the clamour was evident. The scene was a common one. A masked horseman was holding a pistol to the head of the remaining postillion, while another alongside the carriage was having an altercation with the passengers within through the open window.

" He allowed his horse to amble slowly towards Hounslow; only once on his journey did his mind turn from the matter in hand, a ghastly object recalling him to the work-a-day world. It was one of those innumerable gibbets with which the roadway over the Heath was lined, and in the clear moonlight he was able to perceive that the body of a young man was hanging in its chains. Prompted by morbid curiosity he paused a moment, when he saw at a glance that he was gazing upon the remains of a notorious knight of the road who had paid the penalty of his crimes at Tyburn."

There are many other highwaymen stories that I have enjoyed, among which I remember *The Finding of Huggins*, by Frank Davis, *The Two Highwaymen*, by H. D. Lowry, *Black Kerchief Dick*, by Margery Allingham, *His Grace o' Gunne, A Tale of the Road*, by J. Hooper. Then there is Defoe's engaging rascal, *Colonel Jacque*, and Francis Warmen's *Captain Moonlight*.

A whole host of books that deal with highwaymen and road life, in varying degrees of detail, could be quoted. A few more cases will be appropriate here, perhaps. In Mrs. de Crespigny's pleasing novel of early Georgian days, *The Rose Brocade*, we meet a Captain Rook o' the Road, whose profession is not hard to guess, more so when his headquarters are stated to be "a wooded dingle on the edge of a desolate common." This might well be our Heath, but as most of his other exploits seem to have been in Surrey I suspect his hiding place was there too; but so be-sprinkled was Middlesex with highwaymen that she can well spare the "honour" of one to her sister county.

Who can write better of the eighteenth century than Agnes and Egerton Castle? In *French Nan* is a well-told highwayman yarn—not on our Heath, it is true, but in another part of Middlesex, "the waste lands of Fulham"; though in another chapter we see the coach traversing Hounslow's Heath. The incident mentioned is the "camouflaged" highwayman—so beloved of novelists—but it has all the glamour of a real hold-up on the road. In *Horses and Hounds*, by "Scrutator," are several highwayman stories, but none of a less conventional kind as to warrant special quotation, and the same might apply to Georgette Heyer's *The Black Moth*, an eighteenth century story—with its share of highwaymen incidents usual for that period.

In Oswald Crawfurd's novel, *The White Feather*, a good part of which is laid in Middlesex in the days of Queen Anne, though I'm afraid the author's topography gets a bit adrift at times. For instance, in a pleasant pen-picture of the riverside at Hampton Court he says: "That evening the Queen had gone by water, and in no state, to sup with Mrs. Masham at Twickenham, down the river, and this it was, perhaps, that had tempted one or two couples of gentlemen to saunter along the broad towing-path that parts the river from the palace gardens towards Twickenham village. A mile down stream from Hampton Court is a sharp bend of the river, and here the pathway cuts the new road that leads to London town by way of Hounslow, Brentford and Hammersmith."

Anyone who went to London from here via Hounslow would be going back on his tracks; nor is there such a road as he mentions—nothing nearer than Hampton Wick, and that is three times as far down stream as the mythical road of which he speaks.

In *The Heiress of Bath*, an anonymous story of 1855, which deals with the western city in the late eighteenth century, there is a highwayman episode on the Bath Road, in which the chief knight of the road bears a name of which the slightly altered spelling does not disguise its place of origin: "Three horsemen, armed and masked, were grouped together at the entrance of a wood that opened on the road. Captain Honoslow was conspicuous by his half-furbished military costume and mein."

Christmas Eve at Lonethorpe Manor, by W. W. Fenn, is a typical

A PENNY DREADFUL COVER. *Lent by Mr. Barry Ono and Mr. Joseph Parks*

A PENNY DREADFUL COVER.

*Lent by Mr. Barry Ono
and Mr. Joseph Parks*

highwayman yarn, with a mild mystery, not very hard to guess, interwoven into it. The scene of the action is obviously disguised, but one or two clues would fit Hounslow Heath nicely.

In Hazlett's delightful essay *The Fight*, we get a passing glimpse of our road. He wanted to get to Hungerford, but found all the coaches gone and started to walk—" At any rate I would not turn back; I might get to Hounslow, and so be on my road next morning "; but eventually the author was picked up by the friendly driver of the Brentford Stage and finally transferred to the Bath Mail. He also relates various misadventures of others, especially of " the owner of a one-horse vehicle who scorned to ask his way, and drove right on to Bagshot, instead of turning off at Hounslow." All through this essay the touches of road-life in 1822—even highwaymen find a small place in it—are as interesting as his account of the fight itself.

In *The Visionary*, by Sarah Symons, a quaint story in the typical mid-Victorian manner, there is just a glimpse of highwaymen, while part of the scene of the tale is laid at Twickenham.

" All is not gold that glitters," and all stories that speak of highwaymen are not about the genuine variety. The word is often used as a simile. For instance, when we read the title *Highwayman and Highwaymaid*, by Albert Treherne, we might reasonably think it to be of our present subject, but it is a story of the American War of Independence; again in Marriott Watson's *The Adventurers* there is a chapter, " We Turn Highwaymen," but it is used figuratively—though a fine yarn nevertheless.

In Charles Johnstone's curious book, *Chrysal: Or The Adventures of a Guinea*, there is an incident of a Middlesex highwayman, who seems to have been, as regards mounts, the opposite of Dick Turpin, for he was noted for his *white* mare; rather a distinguishing mark for a night rider.

More entertaining still is the account, in the same book, of an adventure on the road. The description of the different types of passengers in a travelling-waggon is masterly, and the scene at the inn is full of a rather broad humour; it all reminded me of Rowlandson's pictures put into words.

A book, of an earlier period, that also reflects such road-life scenes is Joan Parke's *Travel in England in the Seventeenth Century*, one of the most fascinating works I have ever read, and one of the richest fields for the explorer of road-lore. Quotation from it is impossible, for obvious reasons. There is a chapter on highwaymen, and of course Hounslow Heath plays its usual part as a stage for their activities; one of which is rather out of the usual run, for here we read an account of a pitched battle near Bedfont between a band of highwaymen and a collection of exasperated travellers and country folk, who put the road-knights to flight.

In *Tom Heron of Sax*, by E. Everett-Green, there is a good highwayman episode of the conventional sort, which turns out to be a " put up job."

Another of what may be called the mock-cum-real highwayman stories is *The Lord of Burleigh*, by Bernard Capes, in which the amateur—playing the role of knight of the road to enable him to run off with a fair maiden—unexpectedly meets the real thing and saves the lady—and so on!

A type of " spoof " highwayman yarn is one in which the title, *The High Toby* (in the volume of short stories, *Behind the Monocle*), is not the only deceptive part; it is a modern story of the road.

Although Ainsworth's famous novel, *Jack Sheppard* (1839), is known to all, how many know Defoe's *Jack Sheppard*, which appeared over a hundred years earlier, and being, with his *Jonathon Wild,* one of his lesser known works, of which a surprising number exist.

There is a story entitled *The Last of the Highwaymen,* by W. W. Fenn, which has good topographical touches of the roads round London, and where we see the shadow of Jerry Abershawe—or rather the gibbet on which he hanged so long, while *Simple Simon,* by Caroline Marridge, is not without some humour on the road.

Both the Bath Road and the Exeter Road figure in many stories of the old days. There is Frankfort Moore's *At The King's Head, Charming Miss Hulbert,* by " C," and *The Mad Brat,* by Agnes and Egerton Castle, an adventure of *Pamela Pounce,* all of which deal with various adventures on these two highways, though there are many more tales that do likewise.

The " fake " highwayman story is a popular type, under which heading comes R. Murray Gilchrist's *The Homecoming of the Heir.* The latter has a supernatural touch, but for real " spooky " highwayman yarns I could recommend *The Bank of Shadows,* by Arthur Morrison, and *The Legend of Newbury Castle,* by N. G. Thwaites, the latter being partly laid in Middlesex.

I think, however, that *Hangman's Loan,* Edward Albert's brilliant short story, is one of the weirdest and best told I have read for years. It has as a " hero " a highwayman on a gibbet. To give away the idea would be to spoil it for the next reader—it can be seen in *Chambers Journal.*

I wish a ghost story could be produced actually of the Heath—and surely its legends are incomplete without one?—but the best I can do to supply the deficiency is to tell a story from the pages of *The Supernatural in Crime,* a section of an old book on Roguery. The story is not called " The Ghost of Hounslow Heath," as it might have been, though this would have been a romantic enough title; it aspires to something even more hair-raising, " The Ghastly Spectre of the Lonely Farm."

" In 1744," begins this story, " a gentleman of fortune took lodgings at a farm on the borders of Hounslow Heath, as he said his physician had ordered him country air after an illness, and because, as a boy, he had lived in a neighbouring village he felt a desire to visit once again the scenes of his childhood. After residing some weeks at the farm he announced that he had had the misfortune to lose his brother, who lived in London, and who had expressed a wish to be buried in the village churchyard where he had played as a boy.

" The body, in a white shroud, was accordingly brought in a very handsome coffin and placed in the best parlour. The funeral was to take place the next day, and the lodger went out to make the necessary preparations. He was out late, and the farmer and his family retired to bed. A maid-servant was left up to let the lodger in and make him some hot punch. The girl was alone in the kitchen, when a tall, spectral-looking figure in white, with a bloodless face, entered and clapped itself down in a chair. The maid was terrified beyond expression at this awful apparition. Uttering a loud scream, she fled through a side door to the parlour; there she received a fresh shock: the coffin lid was raised up and the coffin was empty. The corpse was walking!

" She ran and awakened her master and mistress and communicated to them some portion of her fright, when the horrid spectre made its appearance and sat down in a chair in the bedroom, without them having observed how it entered. This chair stood by the door, so that no one could escape without passing close to the apparition, which rolled its glaring eyes so frightfully, uttered hollow groans and distorted its features so horribly that they could not bear to look upon it.

"The farmer and his wife hid beneath the bedclothes in a cold sweat, while the maidservant sank down insensible. At the same time the whole house seemed to be in an uproar; for covered as they were they could still hear an incessant noise and clatter, which increased their terror. At length all became perfectly still in the house. The farmer ventured to raise his head and to steal a glance at the fatal chair, but the ghost was gone! In time they plucked up courage to examine the house. The whole place had been stripped by artful thieves, and the gentleman had decamped without paying for his lodging. It turned out that he was no other than the accomplice of a notorious highwayman (who was hanged soon after for another crime) and that the supposed corpse was this arch-rogue himself, who had whitened his hands and face with chalk, put on the shroud and merely counterfeited death. About midnight he quitted the coffin and appeared to the maid in the kitchen, and then, seated at the door of the bed chamber, acted as a sentinel.

I am sorry that our ghost story of the Heath had such an ending after all, but it was the only "supernatural" story I could find of these parts, for in spite of all the dark and bloody deeds committed on Hounslow Heath I have yet to come across, either on paper or verbally, any account of the ghost of a highwayman, or his victim, ever appearing on the scene of the crime. Surely this is very remiss of the Ghosts' Trade Union—or whatever body governs the bodiless. The ghost of the masked Dick Turpin astride the gallant Black Bess would certainly be a more romantic shade than the Wailing Lady or the Murdered Monk, and far less hackneyed.

Were the ghost of a highwayman to appear on the Great West Road nowanights I think the chances are that he would get far more shocks than his intended victims, who, if they were not "speeding" too much to notice him at all, would probably have a vague idea it was something to do with "the pictures"!

Another "fake" highwayman story, apart from any spooky business, is *My Grandfather's Wager*, by C. T. C. James. One of the best of its type, it is rendered more interesting for us because it is laid on Hounslow Heath. In fact the local colour is extremely good and the description of the road between Hounslow and Colnbrook is both true and romantic.

The "biter bit" is another popular type, and one of the best of these I have read is an anonymous one entitled *An Unlucky Raid*, while still another nameless writer has given us a good yarn, this time of Fielding's Horse Patrole, in *A Road Story*.

Susan Fielding, a novel by Mrs. Edwardes—written in the sixties of last century—is an old-fashioned story that suits its setting: a village on Hounslow Heath in those days, a period which might be called the "inter-regnum" of the roads, after the bustling coaching days and before the coming of motors, when the Heath villages were quiet and sleepy.

"It was a drowsy, silent afternoon early in summer," the book begins. "The outlines of the scarce-clad trees showed lifeless against a neutral-tinted sky. The dull white London road, brisk thoroughfare in the old coaching days to all Western England, looked duller than usual as it stretched away, without a spot of colour to break its monotony, across Hounslow Heath. Even the canal seemed to drone in a sleepier voice than was its wont as it stagnated by under the wilderness of poplar, alder and sycamore that grew around the Powder Mills."

The author speaks of the heroine on a bridge watching " the dreary Heath and drearier overshadowed stream "; though later she writes in happier vein of the Heath, which, however, must have been pretty well enclosed by the period of the book. The heroine is the orphaned daughter of a Brentford bookseller, but the tale is set in the village of Halfont—in which it is easy to detect Bedfont under a thin disguise. It is curious how she mentions most places by their right names, except the real setting of the story—but I suspect that some of the characters were drawn from life and a slight camouflage (a word then unknown) was necessary. As a story I have read better books than *Susan Fielding*, but its setting is delightful and made all those ghosts of a not very long ago yesterday much more real than if the place had been imaginary.

Mr. Herbert Gibbs, of Bedfont, whose knowledge of the district is so extensive, tells me that he always understood that the house mentioned in this book has its prototype in the old mansion of Spelthorne St. Marys.

We see the influence of the Heath's reputation rather than any direct reference in Farquhar's play, *The Beaux Stratagem*, where we find Hounslow as a personal name, one of a gang of thieves.

It is rather curious that three poets and writers of the same name, though no relation (as far as I know), all have some connection with this district. These were the three Whiteheads. From our point of view the least known is the most important. This was Charles Whitehead (1804-65), who was the author of *Lives of the Highwaymen* and *The Autobiography of Jack Ketch,* the hangman, both published in 1834, in which, especially the former, figure many " heroes " of the Heath.

The second was Paul Whitehead (1710-1774), who once lived at Colne Lodge, Twickenham Common (now the Green), a house still standing, but in his day on the fringe of the Heath, and he wrote of the view from the back of the house:

" High tow'ring pines, like Titans, scale the skies,
And Lebanon's rich groves on Hounslow's desert rise."

He was a member of the Hell Fire Club and one of the Monks of Medivenham Abbey, described in *Chrysall* and other books.

The last Whitehead was William (1715-1785), who succeeded Colly Cibber as Poet Laureate. He was a tutor to the Jersey family at Osterley Park for some time.

A good description of the Heath in the " good " old days is to be found in *The Mirror* for 1844 in a series of articles, *English Life in the Eighteenth Century*, in the chapter entitled " Highwaymen ": " If the Strand and Holborn were considered dangerous, such a spot as Hounslow-heath was almost impassable, for this was the notorious haunt of the most daring highwaymen. This was their stronghold, full, said tradition, of subterranean caves and ambushes. Every tree was an object of suspicion, every bush was supposed to be the lurking place of robbers, and the hardy traveller who dared to cross the Heath after dark was momentarily affrighted from his propriety by a mysterious shadow.

" There were gentlemen highwaymen, flying highwaymen, and generous highwaymen. Highwaymen who took to the road for pleasure and for " glory "—highwaymen who had appeared at half a dozen different places in as many minutes—and highwaymen who, like Rob Roy, levied contributions from the rich to bestow on the poor. In short, the fireside tales which were told of the mounted robbers of the eighteenth century were innumerable; each had some mysterious air of romance connected with his history, and each rode a bold-faced nag and carried a brace of pistols. The extracts that could be taken from the newspapers and journals of the time, concerning robberies on the Heath of Hounslow, indeed of any open space round London, would be endless in variety."

Humour does not often enter into highwayman yarns, but that of the hypochandriac coachman on the Bath Road certainly has a grain or two. It is told in Walter Thornbury's entertaining book, *Cross Country*. It was heard, like many good yarns, at a country inn: " My father was a coachman and drove the Bath Stage for many a year. Now my father, the friend of every landlord and a favourite with the buxom barmaids, had one failing— he had fancies about his health, which was really as good as could be. Yet he never travelled without a draught of physic in each pocket, which, occasionally breaking over a lady's parcel, made a pretty mess. And his waistcoat pockets were lined with tin, in which were lozenges and pills; and he had a habit of feeling his pulse at the smallest provocation.

" He was driving one night and was telling a military gentleman how they were prepared for highwaymen, though as a matter of fact the guards blunderbuss had never been discharged within the memory of man. Away they went, with a fresh cup to stimulate their courage. My father even harangued the passengers as to the manner they should cross Hounslow Heath, as he thought a show of firearms and a determined manner might have a good effect on those highwaymen who heard of it. This proposal was met with loud cheering, especially by the military gentleman, who kindly consented to look to the priming of all the passengers' pistols.

" The coach suddenly stopped, to the horror of the passengers; voices were heard in the darkness and the trample of horses. Our military friend leapt out, armed with all the defensive weapons, and pulled my father down. The supposed military gentleman was really a highwayman. ' Ladies and gentlemen,' he cried, ' oblige your humble servant by handing me your bullion.' There were murmurs of resistance, so he presented a pistol at the window. ' I have here,' he said blandly, ' a friend of the most persuasive eloquence, who never fails to convince those whom I cannot.' He held his hat; in a moment it was filled with watches and guineas.

" ' Now I've one more account to settle, Nimming Jack,' he cried to a flashily-dressed companion whom no disguise could turn into anything but a second-rate knight of the road ' bring the old gent forward.' They dragged my father along. ' I've no money, gen'lemen ' he cried, in terror, as his tormentors, shouting with laughter, emptied his pockets of pills, lozenges and physic enough to fill a beaver. ' Open your mouth ' they cried,' and they rammed and poured the whole lot down his throat.

" The highwaymen rode off, and when the passengers would have fired at the retreating figures it was found that the obliging military gentleman had primed all their pistols with pepper instead of gunpowder! So the coach, lightened of its valuables, entered Hounslow with a sick coachman and crestfallen passengers."

In an interesting book with a too-long title, *The Early Years of Stage Coaching on the Bath Road,* by William A. Webb, we have much information on this theme, though not so much concerning the Hounslow roads as might have been expected. Much of these western roads is also found in Stanley Weyman's novel, *Sophia.*

Several times in these pages I have been on the verge of boasting that I had found a ghostly highwayman, and in *Six Ghost Stories,* by Sir T. G. Jackson, I nearly did so, for in the tale *The Red House* Jerry Abershawe figures, but not at the ghost. This story, set near Wimbledon Common, has a strong topographical interest, for part of the scene is laid at an old house still standing, and the " disguise " is of the thinnest. A good story, well told.

Notorious Highwaymen (in Timb's *Romance of London)* will interest many, while May Wynne's *Terror of the Moor* is a stirring tale in which these gentry figure; though I think an even better story is *A Tale of the Road,* by M. A. Butterworth, a highwayman story of 1791 and extremely well told. We should not forget, too, the exploits of Tom Faggus in *Lorna Doone,* for which Blackmore, as a Middlesex resident, found plenty of material around him.

A recent novel, in which Dick Turpin is the " hero," is *They Ride Again,* by Collin Brooks. It is the old conventional re-hash, in which Beetles, Peters and O'Flynn, the old Penny Dreadful characters, are brought to light again. Judged as a tale alone it might pass muster with the ignorant, but to anyone with even an elementary knowledge of the subject it is merely irritating. Historically it is the veriest hotch-potch I have ever read. Turpin is made a " pupil " of Nevison, who died twenty-two years before Dick was born; and Sixteen-String-Jack is introduced as a companion of Turpin, but Rann was not born till after Turpin was swinging at the end of a rope. These are but two of the errors; we need not go into the others. What a pity such slipshod work is produced; a glance at the *Newgate Calendar* would have corrected all this.

To be fair to the author, he hints in his preface at the " Dreadful " nature of his story, though apparently (we hope, for his sake) quite ignorant of its gross inaccuracies in chronology.

An equal historical " hash " is found in *The Long Day Closes,* by Beatrice Tunstall, a novel in which Turpin is mixed up in the Jacobite '45 rebellion. It must have been his ghost, though, for he was hanged six years before that date.

In closing this account of the books dealing with the Heath and its former inhabitants—permanent and nightly—there are several books that should be mentioned. One of these is Samuel G. Short's interesting little account of the district, *Southall and its Environs,* with pictures by the author; this contains brief accounts of many places of the Heath country that we have noticed here. Then there is Rev. E. R. Milton's *Hounslow through the Ages,* a most interesting little work, especially those parts dealing with mediaeval days, which the author has, apparently, made a special study. The section *Hounslow* in Walter G. Bell's fascinating book, *Where London Sleeps,* is a chapter we could wish were longer.

There is a good account of a stout walker over Hounslow Heath—in the year of The Indian Mutiny—described in a pamphlet entitled *The Pedestrian's Wallet,* by Kit Trampington, a walker along the Highways and Byways of Merrie England.

The name is probably a *nom de rue,* and he begins with a quotation from Henry Morley: " There are some, nay many, miles that have left green memories to me, and that have built themselves obelisks surmounted by immortals in the cemetery of my soul." This thought was in his mind, he says, when he started over the Heath—and the same theme has often been in mine on this same historic ground—for he tells us that he slept at an inn at Hounslow, and goes on: " A glorious June morning; the balm of flowers stealing through the latticed windows of a pleasant old inn a few stone-casts from the famous Heath of Hounslow. After a look from the pretty oriel, where I heard ' the breezy call of incense-breathing morn,' I went forth into the beauty-haunted places of dreamland, and thought of snug old-fashioned hostelries ahead, with amenities of courteous landlords; sweet-smelling fires of wood and cool flagons of honest barley-wine.

" In a few minutes I was treading the main street of this little Middlesex town on my way to its more famous Heath. There was not a rift in the sky, nor scarcely a breeze afloat, as I, pedestrian-wise, took the road. I was in fine trim, a light heart, a droit or two in my bag and a regular thieves exorciser in the way of an orthodox English ash-stick (remembering the once evil reputation of the ground I was now on)."

One is tempted to follow honest Kit on his wanderings, but having seen him over the Heath, we must leave him to the luck of his rambler's road.

* * * * * *

Plays that deal with highwaymen are not so numerous as books, but the old-time melodrama loved Dick Turpin and Black Bess, and I have seen a toll-gate leaped on the stage in a more recent revival—by H. A. Roberts, I think—of this old theme; while not many years ago a London theatre presented a play by Jefferson Farjeon called *The Highwayman.* " The hero," wrote a critic, " was sufficiently original and unbusinesslike to refund all he had stolen and rest content with riding off with ι lady." Another play of interest here is *The Bath Road,* by Francis Neilson, in which the action is set in the early nineteenth century.

An entertaining book that should be read by all interested in this theme is *Crime and the Drama,* by H. Chance Newton; it deals with many of these old-time highwayman plays, including the stage version of *Paul Clifford* and H. H. Milner's once so popular *Dick Turpin's Ride to York.* There are several omissions, however, that certainly ought to be represented in such a book.

Those of us, however, who were lucky enough to see the Hounslow Fageant, written so brilliantly by G. E. Bate, saw a real presentation of a highwayman episode on the Heath, among many other episodes. I wish space allowed for more about this pageant, which impressed me very deeply as a wonderfully imaginative piece of work.

For those who like horrors I would recommend *The Hangman of England,* by Horace Bleackley—it is illustrated with curious old prints of this grim subject—and there is even an account of a hang*woman!* Then, if this is not enough and more intimate histories of these vagabonds are required, let the reader turn to the entertaining pages of an old book, *The English Rogue Revived,* where he will find a little truth wrapped up as fiction, but far more fiction disguised as truth! Again, there is a book with a similar title, but probably more authentic as regards facts—*The English Rogue,* by Richard Head and Francis Kirkman. Both these books deal with a " tribe " as strange as uncivilised Africa could produce.

Those who wish to read more on gruesome subjects — especially the hanging of highwaymen—should refer to *Bygone Punishments,* by William Andrews, a book of grim memories on the pendant theme.

I hinted at the beginning of this chapter the difficulty of finishing it. Almost every day I am finding fresh examples of books that should have inclusion here, both those dealing with highwaymen and others of the general topography of the district. Some of these are of real interest, and so I make no apology for introducing, at the end of the chapter, several fresh examples.

We will take the highwaymen first. In some, though not all, editions of *Rookwood* we find a most interesting note concerning Turpin's writing of the famous Ride.

" The Ride to York," wrote Ainsworth, " was completed in one day and one night. The feat—for feat it was, being the composition of a hundred ordinary novel pages in less than twenty-four hours—was achieved at " The Elms "—a house I then occupied at Kilburn. Well do I remember the fever into which I was thrown at the time of composition. My pen literally scoured over the pages. So thoroughly did I identify myself with the flying highwayman that, once started, I found it impossible to halt. Animated by kindred enthusiasm, I cleared every obstacle in my path with as much facility as Turpin disposed of the impediments that beset his flight. In his company, I mounted the hillside, dashed through the bustling village, swept over the desolate Heath, threaded the silent street, and kept an onward course, without pause, without hindrance, without fatigue, with him I shouted, sang, laughed, exulted and wept. Nor did I retire to rest till, in imagination, I heard the bell of York Minster toll forth the knell of poor Black Bess."

In Eden Phillpots' old-time romance, *The Lovers,* we find a chapter " A Gentleman of the Road " and we are not disappointed to meet the expected highwayman, though he plays no very great part in the main story.

The Gallant Lover, a novel by H. St. John Cooper, is another " amateur highwayman " story, in which the "hero" takes to the road to recover certain papers. It is not really a highwayman story in the true sense, but a well-told exciting yarn of the early eighteenth century and worth reading. It adds a point of interest to us here to see by the preface that the book was written at Sunbury.

A more strenuous gallant is met with in *Bare-knuckle Lover,* by Louis Golding, in which the hero beats three fully-armed highwaymen with his fists alone!

The Crimson Falcon, by Nita O. Thompson is a novel of a similar type, in which the " highwayman " is a disguised baronet; while a disguised highwayman also plays a part in *Stand and Deliver,* by Draycot Dell, a good boy's story. There is a little about Hounslow, but more of Hampstead, where part of the story is laid at the Spaniards Inn. The tale departs a little from fact, as Turpin is said to have been killed at a fight at this old hostelry. However, the story is treated in an original way, as to find the solution to it the reader has to do a jig-saw puzzle (given with the book) which discloses the final details of the plot.

In *Talbot Harland,* one of Harrison Ainsworth's lesser known novels, Claude Duval figures a good deal; I rather doubt the historical accuracy of this story; for instance, the famous dance with the lady from the coach is made to take place in Kent—though we have the evidence from many sources that this took place on Hounslow Heath.

Also Claude Duval—after various aliases—is made to commit suicide in a morass after a duel with the Duke of Buckingham, and it is said that

OLD FARMYARD, MOGDEN. *Photo by H. M. Adcock*

'THE WHITE MANTLE." *Photo lent by Messrs. W. T. Mann & Sons*
Oak Farm, Worton.

the Duval who was hanged was merely a "miserable pretender." Again an historical "hotch-potch" I am afraid.

In *Vanities and Vicissitudes* Ralph Nevill tells some good stories—one of Hawke, "The Flying Highwayman," in a Middlesex lane, but too long to quote. Camden Pelham's *Chronicles of Crime* (1841) is a "hashed-up" Newgate Calendar, though not without interest.

The Days of Hogarth, sometimes known by its sub-title, *The Mysteries of Old London,* by G. W. R. Reynolds, has, not unnaturally when we consider the period, a good deal in it of highwaymen, as also has the same author's other novel, *The Rye House Plot.* Reynolds also wrote *Robert Macaire: or The French Bandit in England,* though the "hero" was not a bandit in the modern sense of the word—but a highwayman. Another French road-knight (whom Claude Duval made popular) is found in Louis Gallert's *Captain Satan.*

The Scarlet Rider, by Bertha Runkle, lives up to its provocative title; while *Diamond Cut Diamond,* by F. W. Gumley, is a good yarn.

We have already had occasion to mention H. B. Marriott Watson's *High Toby,* and in connection with this should be mentioned its two companion volumes—*Galloping Dick* and *The King's Highway*—though it should be noted that the second volume does not deal with the Galloping Dick of real life (Richard Ferguson), but with a Dick Ryder, a purely fictitious character. *Willowdene Will,* by Halliwell Sutcliffe, is a good highwayman yarn, as also will be found *The Brown Mask,* by Percy Jarvis Brebner (Christian Lys), and *Tom Tufton's Travels* and *Tom Tufton's Toll,* by E. Everett-Green. In *The Brown Mask* is a highwayman with the unusual nickname of The Galloping Hermit, while in *Willowdene Will* one of the stories is laid on the Heath and has a scene in The White Hart at Cranford.

In Paul Creswick's *At the Sign of the Cross Keys* we find some stirring highwayman episodes in the Heath country, of which I like the author's description: "This countryside is not without some claim on Beauty's bounty just here. The gentle, verdant fields, with their dotted hedgerows, the few elms scattered here and there—venerable, yet bending away from the attack of the north wind, which ravages cruelly this part of Middlesex—all lend themselves to the poet's mind as material, humble, yet not to be despised."

Lieutenant Barnabas, by Frank Barrat, is a good eighteenth century story—partly in Middlesex—with its usual quota of highwaymen; while *The Mystery of St. Dunstan's,* by Thomas Wright, though sounding like a modern "thriller," is in reality an early eighteenth century story, partly concerning the doings of one Dick Potter, a highwayman. *The Adventures of Denis,* by M. Bramston, is another eighteenth century story in which highwaymen figure.

Highwaymen have even been brought into educational works—which as part of eighteenth century life is as it should be — for in *The Long Journey: The Tale of Our Past,* a most entertaining volume by Laurence Housman and C. H. K. Marten, we find a chapter on the Knights of the Road; while Arthur L. Hayward has written the *Boys' Book of Highwaymen,* an abridgment from his larger work on this subject. Recently a play with the title of *Black Eagle* was broadcast over the wireless; most people thought this name to be that of a Red Indian chief, which it certainly sounds more like than a night-rider on the Heath.

There are few more topographical touches we should not miss before this long chapter is closed. In Ainsworth's *James the Second* we find

mention of Hounslow, chiefly in connection with the camps, while in the
immortal *Three Men in a Boat* we read of Sunbury, Kempton Park, Halliford, Shepperton and Staines.

In *The Plain Green Chariot* we hear something of the Middlesex highways, though save a brief reference to " the western road out of London "
there is little of the Heath country; its association is more with " the little
town of Willesden," which was " roused from its rural repose " by the events
of the tale. I'm afraid it is wide awake enough now, yet the period of this
story is less than a hundred years ago—in 1838.

In *Scribes and Pharisees* William Le Queux paints rather a depressing
picture of Hounslow in the " 'nineties." The author was at one time editor
of the *Middlesex Chronicle,* but I'm afraid his mind was too full of mysterious beautiful spies and foreign noblemen who do all sorts of impossible
things for him to appreciate—or even to realise—the wonderful story that
lay then unfolded in the surrounding countryside.

In Albert Smith's novel, *The Adventures of Mr. Ledbury* (1844), there
is a good deal concerning places covered in this book, though too late in
date for anything on highwaymen. There is a certain amount, however,
about road-life, and the account of the drive from London to Ascot on
race-day is one of the best of such descriptions I have read.

It has a word-picture of Hounslow in the most pathetic period of its
existence—just after the death-knell of the coaching era had left it stranded
and forlorn. " They rattled through the long street of dirty Brentford,"
we read, " and cleared the canal; here the party felt they were getting
into the country, delivering themselves up to the *abandon* of rural life . . .
when they arrived at Hounslow. The tradesmen were beginning to open
their shops, and all the inn-yards bore token of preparation for the
approaching business of race-day, being filled with grooms, post-boys and
horses. There are legends extant going to prove that in the olden time,
when railways were not, coaches and chariots used to pass through
Hounslow many times in the day; and these derived some confirmation
from the apparitions of various aged and decrepit post-chaises drawn out
before the doors, to whose dusty and mouldy forms water and blacking had
united to give a temporary renovation."

If space allowed I should like to go with the travellers further, for
there is quite a good description of the Heath country, which begins:
" Beyond the town (Hounslow) all was quiet again. It was a fine clear
morning, and there was a light vapour floating about the distant hills that
betokened the approach of a hot noon, whilst the hedges and the turf at
the side of the footpath were sparkling in the bright June sunshine; for
the day's influx of travellers had not yet begun to powder them with dust,
until they were all reduced to one uniform brown." Passing through Bedfont, where they annoyed the toll-gate keeper by badinage, they came to
Staines, and here we must leave them.

The Conservancy of the Thames is an interesting old book of 1745
wherein all sorts of odd river lore are mixed up with a history of the fishing
and fish of the old-time Thames, with many notes of places on the banks,
though the writer is often at fault on the latter; his knowledge of fish far
exceeded that of topography. His descriptions, however, have a quaintness
that make them worth reading. He has not a great deal to say of the
Middlesex villages, dismissing Sunbury (which he calls Sundbury) as " a
place that has not much to boast of, unless several good Houses, and being

situated by the side of so delightful a River "; while Laleham, he tells us, is a " place of but little account chiefly inhabited by Fishermen; who would they but abstain as much from Fishing illegally amongst themselves, as they seem willing to prevent Foreigners from London coming up hereabouts to do so, there would certainly be a much greater Quantity of, and better Fish than what there is in these Parts at present." It speaks volumes for the isolation of these Middlesex villages two hundred years ago when Londoners are looked upon as foreigners! It is interesting to note that the Crane is referred to in this book under the name of " Hounslow River."

There have recently appeared in *The Builder* some articles, *Changing Middlesex*, written and illustrated by Martin S. Briggs, F.R.I.B.A. The writer has brought a keen and artistic mind to bear on this pathetic subject, and I read his articles with real enjoyment, albeit with a certain sadness. It would be easy to quote from these articles if space allowed, especially those bits that deal with the preservation of what is still left to us of the country's beauty spots. The writer is a little unfair to Hounslow, I think, but with this exception I endorse almost everything he says.

* * * * * *

These stories jostle each other so quickly through the mind that it is often hard to get one on paper before it is crowded out by its successor; and so we must at last finally leave this interesting, but elastic, theme, not from want of material, but simply from an overwhelming *embarras des riches*. It has indeed been a feast of literature of all sorts and conditions, but true to tradition it has its skeleton, for which I am responsible. I have compiled a book that will never see publication; it is made up chiefly of newspaper cuttings of advertisements of building estates that have spoiled some favourite corner of this district, which has meant the demolition of an old historical mansion—such as Fulwell Park to quote one case only— or an old farm—a belt of woodland or meadows. It is one of the most depressing books I know, and I never open it without a curse at those who advertise " Live in the country " and then do their best to destroy it.

I call this volume *The Black Book of Middlesex;* but I keep it among my collection of books on the county, both historical, topographical and " association books," to which I am adding to almost daily, as it deals with what is perhaps the saddest phase of all in the wonderful story of Middlesex —but it is a veritable Skeleton at the Feast.

II. The Heath in Verse.

There is a sort of " no-man's-land " between the two parts of this chapter, " The Heath in Literature " and " Literature of the Heath," and that is verse. This, too, might be sub-divided in much the same way— under Poetry and Verse—but as it is even harder here to draw the line we must include all under one heading. This theme has never made the subject of Great Poems of England, and many verses have been brought in in other places as more appropriate, but this very incomplete " Anthology " of Highwaymen Verse may not be without interest. Again strict chronology is of no great account here. Once more we can begin with Charles Dickens, who has written certainly the best-known verses in connection with the Heath in *Pickwick Papers:*

" Bold Turpin vunce, on Hounslow Heath,
His bold mare Bess bestrode-er;

> Ven there he see'd the Bishop's coach
> A-coming along the road-er.
> So he gallops close to the 'orses' legs,
> And claps his head vithin;
> And the Bishop says, 'Sure as eggs is eggs,
> This here's the bold Turpin!'"

Dickens did not write these verses himself, but adapted some old-time ones, for in *Driven from Home,* a story of Penny Dreadful type—but like most of those bearing this name its only criminal propensity is exaggeration and over-painting—there is a verse:

> " The guard from the step did drop,
> But the coachman would keep on,
> Till bold Jerry made his pistol pop,
> And prevailed on him to stop,
> With a bullet in his nob,"

which seems to have a common ancestor with the lines in *Pickwick.* In an old-time ballad, *Dick Turpin and the Bishop,* the same story is told in a very much longer and more rambling form.

Scott follows next, for in *Rob Roy,* though a Scottish book, it is of a Middlesex highwayman he writes:

> "Twixt Kensington and Brentford then
> Did boldly stop six honest men."

In Gay's *Journey to Exeter* we find a few lines on Hounslow Heath; not actually mentioned by name, but what other heath is there between Brentford and Staines?—

> " Three dusty miles reach Brentford's tedious town,
> For dirty streets and white-legg'd chickens known,
> Thence o'er wide shrubby heath and furrowed lanes,
> We come where Thames divides the meads of Staines."

A street ballad of 1739 commemorates an exploit of the Heath's most famous hero, in the year of his execution:

> " On Hounslow Heath, as I rode o'er,
> I spied a lawyer riding before.
> 'Kind sir,' said I, 'ain't you afraid
> Of Turpin, that mischievous blade?'
> O rare Turpin, hero! O rare Turpin, O!
> " Says Turpin, 'He'll ne'er find me out;
> I've hid my money in my boot.'
> 'Oh,' says the lawyer, 'there's none can find
> My gold, for it's stitched in my cape behind.'
> " As they rode down by the Powder Mill,
> Turpin commands him to stand still.
> For my mare she wants a saddle cloth.'
> Said he, 'Your cape I must cut off."

Another ballad of the time is *Dick Turpin and Will Davies.*

> " One night when mounted on my mare,
> To Hounslow Heath I did repair,
> And saw Will Davies hanging there,
> Upon the gibbet bleak and bare,
> With a rustified, fustified, mustified air!

" Says he, ' Dick Turpin, here I be,
Upon the gibbet, as you see;
I take the matter easily,
 You'll have your turn as well as me,
  With your whistle-me, pistol-me, cut-my-throat air.
" For never more shall Hounslow see
A highwayman of such degree,
Appearance and gentility,
As Will who hangs upon this tree,
  With his rustified, fustified, mustified air.' "

While here is another:

" And one fine morn to take the air he mounts his gallant mare
And galloped over Hounslow-heath, to find what happened there,
His barkers from their holster-beds put out their muzzles black,
And his borer sharp swung in its sheath, and glitter'd at his back."

This ballad has been varied according to locality described, but as the *Lives of the Highwaymen* points out, it might apply to any eighteenth century heath in the neighbourhood of London.

In Ainsworth's *Rookwood* will be found many highwaymen verses, such as " The Game of High Toby " and " The Pledge of the Highwayman," in which locality is equally interchangeable, and the same may be said of " The Robber's Song " in *Paul Clifford,* where is also " Old Bags' Song ":

" Are the days gone, when on Hounslow Heath
  We flashed our nags?
When the stoutest bosoms quail'd beneath
  The voice of Bags?"

In an old ballad of 1674, *Robbery Rewarded,* is a highwayman's farewell:

" Adieu, vain delights, bewitch us no more,
Our former ill-courses we now do deplore,
Our crimes upon earth hath bereaved us of hope,
The thread of our lives is spun out on a rope.
We rob'd night and day,
Upon the High Way,
And spent it on wine and on wenches and play.
But to this sweet meat sowre sauce must be had,
For the gallows is still the reward of the Padd."

Many people misquote *The Beggars' Opera;* in Lord William Lennox's book, *Coaching Anecdotes,* the same error occurs, and in many others, which all seem to copy from each other instead of going to the original source. It was *not* Captain Macheath who made the well-known remark, " Let us take to the road," nor was it a remark; it was the first line of a song. It is sung by Mat-o'-the-Mint, an associate of Macheath, while the latter " sits down melancholy at the table."

Mat: " Let us take to the road;
    Hark! I hear the sound of coaches,
    The hour of attack approaches—
    To your arms, brave boys, and load,
    See the ball I hold!"

Another speech by Mat-o'-the-Mint that is often attributed to Macheath is the following:

Mat: " We were just breaking up, to go upon duty. Am I to have the honour of taking the air with you, sir, this evening upon the *Heath?* I drink a dram, now and then, with the stage coachmen, in the way of friendship and intelligence; and I know that, about this time, there will be passengers upon the western road who are worth speaking with."

The highwayman's mention of the "western road" leaves little doubt that the heath he meant was that of Hounslow.

The Beggars' Opera caused a sensation, even in the "broader" days of the eighteenth century. "There came a cry," writes Dutton Cook in his monograph, *Captain Macheath,* "that the play was immoral, and of course after that the boxes filled more than ever, for how could anyone form an opinion until he had seen the performance several times!" Human nature alters little through the ages.

"Sir John Fielding," continues the account, "declared that fresh cargoes of highwaymen were brought before his magistrate's court as the result of this play. The Archbishop of Canterbury censured it as an encouragement to vice, by making a highwayman the hero. Dean Swift, on the other hand, commended its morality as it placed vice in an odious light,' and Gibbon thought it tended to the 'refinement of highwaymen.' Tom Walker (the actor who played Macheath) had a different audience from modern times. Then they lived in the days of Sixteen String Jack, and had very definite ideas about highwaymen." This is not quite accurate, as Rann was much later than the opera, but there is truth in the next sentence: " Who knows how many gentlemen in the boxes and pit had been stopped on Hounslow Heath? They required a *bona fide* highwayman, not an exquisite."

In the *Bon Gaultier Ballads* are some verses, "The Death of Duval," which, as the title indicates deals with his passing rather than his exploits, which are but faintly reminiscent in the verse:

> " With step majestic to the cart advances
>   The dauntless Claude, and springs into his seat.
> He feels that on him now are fixed the glances
>   Of many a Briton bold and maiden sweet."

There is swing and movement in this Coaching Song—of the period of about 1830—in a book, *Rambles with an American in Great Britain,* by Christian Teare:

> " Changing at Hounslow; and time for a snap!
>   Trim little damsel in pinner and cap;
>   Peter, the coach-guard, will vouch for the tap—
>   Calls for a measure and drains it.
>   Chestnut and roans and a flea-bitten grey,
>   All in a fidget to gallop away,
>   Tossing and stamping—' As good as a play!'
>   Peter asserts and maintains it."

Some of these ballads may not have been great poetry, but their main value lies in their reflection of the period; for instance these lines, which tell us how the pedestrian at Hounslow forced his way

> " Through coaches, drays, choked turnpikes, and a whirl
>   Of wheels, and roar of voices, and confusion;
> Here taverns wooing to a pint of 'purl,'
>   There mails fast flying off like a delusion,"

certainly give us a glimpse of the busy scene at this spot for over 150 years; while the following extract, though a little confused to modern ears, with its over-use of capitals, gives a hint of some quarrel, whose forgotten details might let in a good deal of light on our understanding of it. It is termed *On Mail Coaches:*

> " Thus the Conclave of Fools, Tommy Todd and his Tools,
>   Their Anathemas deal at Mail Coaches;
> And like Zealots of Yore, thrump up Lies by the Score,
>   Which Thin Proselytes swallow like Loaches.
> Then Palmer, whose Brain can alone Guide the Rein,
>   Like Apollo thy Course daily run;
> And never let Fear Slack thy whole Career,
>   Till the Dog Star eclipses the Sun."

In *Brennan on the Moor,* a song really concerning an Irish highwayman of this name, we find this verse:

> " A brace of loaded pistols he did carry night and day,
> He never robbed a poor man all on the King's highway;
> But what he'd taken from the rich, like Turpin and Black Bess,
> He always did divide between the widows in distress,"

which is interesting here to show that it was Turpin's exploits on Hounslow Heath, among other places, that obviously "set the standard for other highwaymen," but the truth is probably spoken by one commentator of Turpin's mentioned in the above verses when he says: "Nobody, we suppose, would have been more astonished than Turpin (except Black Bess) at having such benevolence imputed to him."

A friend who knows I am collecting these highwayman songs sends me a copy of the famous "In a box of a stone jug I was born," with its lilting chorus, "Nix my dolly, pals, fake away." This, however, though certainly a thieves' song, is associated with Jack Shephard, and he was certainly no highwayman; a burglar and prison breaker, a footpad possibly, but who ever heard of Jack Shephard on a horse? Besides he was essentially a "town bird." I doubt if he ever got as far into the country as Hounslow Heath; there is a tradition of him at Dollis Hill, but that is about his limit, I fancy, of travels into the wilds of Middlesex.

I have in my collection a large number of highwaymen stories of all shapes and dates, and sprinkled among these are many verses, most of them probably adapted from the prolific source of eighteenth century scrap-books and romances. The dates are not quoted in most cases, but it is not hard to place them, though they are general enough to cover a fairly elastic period; many of them, too, bear a strong likeness to one another, for, like all popular stories, they have gathered embellishments as they have been sung by itinerant ballad singers or round alehouse fires.

Of course, encounters with the Bow Street Runners were favourite themes for the ballad maker, and there is certainly movement in these lines from the romantically titled story, *The Hermit of the Glade:*

> " There was riding and gibing, and rabble and rout,
> And the forest re-echoed the Bow Runners' shout;
> There was hurling and whirling, o'er brake and o'er briar,
> But the course of Dick Turpin was swift as wildfire.
> Whipping and spurring would nothing avail;
> Dick laughed at their curses and scoffed at their wail.

'My foot's in the stirrup!' loud rang his bold cry,
'Bess answered my call; now her mettle I'll try!'"
While in *The Phantom Highwayman* we read:
" Hark how the horses charge! in, lads, in!
The fight is fast, the wounds begin;
O, how they cry!
Room for the bold highwaymen, armed with thunder!
See how they break the bluecoats' ranks asunder!
O, how they fly!"
And the following lines in *On a False Trail* seem to indicate a special incident, no doubt popular at the time:
" The Runners went a-huntin', a-huntin', a-huntin';
The Runners went a-huntin' to cop Dick Turpin, O.
They thought they'd got the rumpad, the rumpad, the rumpad,
But copp'd instead another cove rigg'd up in Dick's old clo'."
A poetical touch seems to have been desired by the writer of the following, found in *The Masked Man of Mystery:*
" Now the moon puts her black nightcap on,
And every star its light is hiding;
And forth to the Heath is the highwayman gone,
His matchless cherry-black prancer riding.
Merrily over the common he rides,
His crepe-covered vizard drawn over his eyes."
And again, in *That Rascal Blueskin*, the romantic and sternly practical seem combined:
" The white-faced moon—who cares—who cares
If down upon us she peers and stares?
Laugh to scorn her glare, and loudly as ever
Shout as I show myself, ' *Stand and deliver.*' "
In the same story are the verses that might be called " The Highwayman's Warning ":
" And when backward Bess's ears are inclined,
It shows she sniffs ill in the wind.
This caution you will bear in mind,
Beware of the bloodhounds behind!"
Claude Duval and his exploits have always been popular with the ballad writer, and this verse, in *A Hot Corner*, is typical:
" Pledge! Pledge in a bumper each kind-hearted maiden,
Whose bright eyes were dimmed at the highwayman's fall;
Who stood by the cart, with sorrow o'erladen,
Bemoaning the fate of the gallant Duval!"
The real " hero " of our Heath, however, in spite of the Gavotte incident that took place here with the Frenchman, was undoubtedly Dick Turpin—who might be termed nowadays " The All-British Highwayman," and in a story bearing the suggestive title *The Hero of Hounslow Heath* we find him —or his personification—seated securely on the throne of popular favour:
" There's not a king, should you search the world round,
So blithe as the King of the Road to be found;
His pistols his sceptre, his saddle his throne,
Whence he levies supplies or enforces a loan."
While the retrospective type of verse is not without its admirers, such as *The Highwayman's Parting Song,* which begins: " I was a wild and wicked

**INTERIOR OF THE GREAT TITHE
BARN, HARMONDSWORTH.**

From an old print

THE GREAT TITHE BARN.
HARMONDSWORTH.

Photo by the Author

DAWLEY FARM, HARLINGTON.

Photo by the Author

youth " and goes on to narrate a whole catalogue of misdeeds.

Recantations seemed popular among highwaymen; the best known are two seventeenth century ones; that of John Clavel—*A Recantation of an ill ledde life* and Jackson's *Recantation; or the life and death of the Notorious Highwaymen now hanging in chains.*

Both these are contained in Old Broadsides; and all those who love such things, as I do, should see the facsimile collections in *Broadside Elegies*, by J. W. Draper, and *The Pack of Autolycus*, by H. E. Rollins.

Of modern bards Alfred Noyes shares with Austin Dobson the claim of being the writer of the best highwayman verses. Three of his poems on this theme are notable—there is *The Great North Road*, in which he meets the ghostly pedlar who tells him tales of bygone days and finishes with the verse:

> " Rogues were they all; but the white dust assoils 'em!
> Paradise without a spice of devilry would cloy;
> Heavy is my pack till I meet Jerry Abershawe,
> The Gay Golden Farmer and the Hereford Boy."

Then there is *The Ballad of Dick Turpin*. Again what matters it if the famous ride was never performed by his hero? Can we resist the magic of the lines:

> " By Crackskull Common, and Highgate Heath, he heard the chase behind;
> But he rode to forget—forget—forget—the hounds of his own mind.
> " And cherry-black Bess on the Enfield Road flew light as a bird to her goal;
> But her Rider carried a heavier load in his own struggling soul.
> " And the little sleeping villages, and the breathless country-side,
> Woke to the drum of the racing hoofs; but missed that ghostly ride."

Possibly the best of all Noyes' poems on this subject is *The Highwayman,* which tells, in stirring words, of romance and tragedy, and finishes with the fine stanzas:

> " And still of a winter's night, they say, when the wind is in the trees,
> When the moon is a ghostly galleon tossed upon cloudy seas,
> When the road is a ribbon of moonlight over the purple moor,
> A highwayman comes riding—riding—riding—
> A highwayman comes riding, up to the old inn door.
> Over the cobbles he clatters and clangs in the dark inn-yard.
> He taps with his whip on the shutters, but all is locked and barred.
> He whistles a tune to the window, and who should be waiting there
> But the landlord's black-eyed daughter, Bess, the landlord's daughter,
> Plaiting a dark red love-knot into her long black hair."

And all those who are too old, or too dull-witted, to fail to feel the thrill of this stirring poem have my sympathy.

* * * * * *

Those who like music with their romance should turn up that charming —but forgotten—little operetta, *Knights of the Road*, written by Henry A. Lytton and music by A. C. Mackenzie.

There is quite a pathetic note in the lines *Hail Hounslow*, by an anonymous writer—a parody on the *Deserted Village*—which deplore the state of Hounslow after the passing of the Coaching Era:

> " Hail, Hounslow! primest town upon the road,
> Where coaching once in all its glory showed.

Once, Hounslow, there was many a gallant team,
The dragsman's pride, the helpers' fruitful theme,
How dashingly they swept up to the well-known door,
Where rest awaited when the task was o'er.

    .   .   .   .   .

Once it was thus—another age appears,
And Hounslow's smiles, alas! are turn'd to tears.

It is rather a depressing ditty, the swan song of a place once the busiest
spot for coaches in the world, and goes on to describe how all are gone—
coachmen, post-boys, guards, ostlers, grooms, boots—and even " Bessy's self;
the bar's fair toast ":

" Whose winning smile was so well known to fame
That for a ray each traveller duly came—
E'en she—so hopeless Hounslow is thy case—
Hath packed her traps and bolted from her place."

Another requiem, of 1838, is *The Lay of the Last Hangman*—a parody
of the last minstrel—verses in which Jack Ketch's regret might be the
people's joy, for his bewailings are occasioned by the fact that with the
end of the coaching days there are no more highwaymen to catch and
hang—

" The last of all the Jacks was he
Who thought of Tyburn's triple tree,
For, well-a-day! their date was fled,
His throttling brethren all were dead."

But last of all perhaps the most suitable verses to quote are those
grim lines of Charles Mackay's *The Phantoms of St. Sepulchre's*—that
church adjoining old Newgate Prison, where the highwaymen took their
last ride up the Tyburn Road (now Oxford Street) and were swung into
eternity—or, as one of these phantoms says to another, the poet—

" And I hung and swung in the sight of men,
And the law of blood was satisfied."

III.   The " Literature " of the Heath.

Although so prolific, the " Literature " of the Heath has produced little
that is quotable; the information in the tales of the " Penny Dreadful "
type is mostly apocryphal and with little historical value, though from a
study of popular reading matter of a bygone age these publications are
sometimes useful, as well as of intrinsic worth to the collector.

It is no exaggeration to say that one of the old Dick Turpin penny
books of about 1830 is now worth far more than its light weight in gold;
while the Broadsides usually sold at executions, and the Street Ballads of
Catnach and other publishers of this type of " Literature " are rarer and
more valuable still.   In many of these Hounslow figured in the dashing
" biographies " of Dick Turpin and his fellow knights of the road, with most
lurid woodcuts, though as regards the Broadsides the most popular picture
seems to have been a crude representation of the last scene of all—that of
the " hero " hanging on the gallows, with his " last dying words."   A remarkable family likeness existed between these criminals—as the same cut was
used for all.   The drawing is so bad that it made little difference.

One story among my collection—a page out of Lloyd's *Entertaining
Journal* for 1844—is entitled *The Midnight Murder: A Legend of Hounslow
Heath,* and it begins: " Towards the close of a November day a solitary
traveller stopped at a lonely inn on Hounslow Heath."   No clue is given as

to the inn, but after an opening like that anything might happen—and it does!

Many of these stories—now looked upon as boys' books, but in earlier days eagerly read by adults also—have mention of actual inns and landmarks in the district that can still be identified. There is one, *On a False Trail*, whose first chapter is entitled " At the ' George,' Hounslow," a hostelry still standing, though somewhat altered. The story commences with Dick Turpin and Tom King "making their way from London, intent on arriving at the snug little retreat on the borders of Hounslow Heath; barely, however, had they gained the broad expanse of waste land than the snow had swooped down on them like an enveloping blanket."

Another story, *The Treasure Trail*, which begins across the Heath at Staines, introduces Dick Turpin and Sixteen-String-Jack (Thomas Rann) *together*. This is quite impossible—the former was hanged in 1739 and the latter in 1774—many years apart! So either Turpin would be nearly seventy or Rann in long clothes! Both rather awkward ages for a highwayman. With unconscious humour the anonymous author states that all his characters are fictitious! The characters are genuine enough, my unknown fellow-scribe, both Turpin and Rann were real men; it's your dates that are fictitious! Even a boy's book should be moderately accurate; a glance at *The Newgate Calendar* would have put him right; had he chosen Jerry Abershawe or Robert Ferguson (Galloping Dick) as a companion to Rann he would have been on safe ground, chronologically.

In another story, *Good Highwaymen Rejoice*, the same error is made; but more surprising is that in *The Dark Woman*, where Sixteen-String-Jack is said to be transported in 1816!

It would be possible to give the titles of many more of these boys' highwaymen stories, such as *Black Masks and Pistols*, or *The Christmas Coach*, but it would serve no good purpose, for they are really very much alike. Their chief interest is trying to pick out local landmarks, but without lengthy quotation it is impossible to pass all my discoveries on; for those, however, who are interested in such things the easiest to obtain nowadays are the following: *Dick Turpin;* one of Dick's publications about 1880; *The Dick Turpin Library and The Claude Duval Library*, published by the Aldine Company about thirty years ago; and Newnes' *Dick Turpin Library*, which can be bought to-day — all these stories, however, bear a strong family likeness! The earlier you go the more lurid the illustrations are.

Nowadays boys do not read highwayman stories as much as an earlier generation—their interest is now more centred in horse-power than in the power of the horse, but there have been one or two quite good yarns of this nature published recently, notably *Young Jack* by Herbert Strang, with Brock's fine illustrations, and *Nut Brown Roger and I.*

It is always easier to find another example than it is to end a chapter of this description; so as a finale I will choose the story *Stand and Deliver* by Charlton Lea (not to be confused with the book by Elizabeth Villiers, which bears the same title, though published years later), which is certainly not without humour, a grace often lacking in the very early ones! This yarn concerns a certain Lord Mayor of London, one Joshua Ponderberry, a fictitious name, it is presumed. The tale opens with Ponderberry reading a letter:

"Written on Hounslow Heath. My Lord,—As I understand you have offered Five Hundred Guineas for my capture, I shall deem it a pleasure to wait on you personally at the earliest moment—you will then have the opportunity of making me a prisoner with your own hands, and thus save your money.—
(Signed) Richard Turpin."

The story, of course, concerns the carrying out of this suggestion, naturally to the great confusion of the Lord Mayor and the further grandisement of "our hero."

In 1842 there was produced, at the City of London Theatre, a play *Claude Duval: The Ladies' Highwayman*, by T. P. Taylor. It is in one act and the scene is laid at "The Marquis of Honeybunn's mansion at Hounslow. Temp. 1669." There is no scene actually on the Heath, though it is mentioned.

I have mentioned a fair number of highwaymen stories and more would only "clog" the text; but for the benefit of those interested I will give the names of a few more:—

By Charlton Lea: *Driven from Home; Masked Man of Mystery; Secret of the Old Mint; Night Riders of Bagshot Heath; The Fatal Word; Dark Deeds; Mark of Vengeance; The Road to Tyburn; League of the Death's Heads.*

By Stephen H. Agnew: *Knights of the Moonless Nights; The Jaws of Justice; The Hounds of the Hills; The Shadow of Death; The Spectre of Black Hand Court; the Black Vampire; A Mystery of the Great West Road.*

Although the details of these stories are on the lurid side they are certainly not inaccurate in detail and show a good deal of research into the life and times of the period; especially in those of Charlton Lea, who prefaces his series of stories with a very sensible foreword, part of which I will quote, as it really bears also on this present book: "The object of these stories, dealing with the life and extraordinary adventures of one of the most daring law-breakers, is not to extol vice or throw a glamour round a career of crime. Much has been written about Dick Turpin; his name even now is a household word, though his character has been painted in the blackest colours. But there are two sides to every picture; and one is always the brighter.

"A crime punishable by death a hundred and fifty years ago would now scarcely merit a day's imprisonment. In those days a man, through some thoughtless freak, might easily find his neck in danger. His only chance of escape lay in flying the country, and to gain means for this he was driven to rob. Once on the downhill path the life was only too alluring. Money came swiftly and went as easily. It was thus that highwaymen were made."

* * * * *

It was my good fortune recently to inspect the famous Barry Ono Collection of "Penny Dreadfuls," of which I had heard but not previously seen. A wonderful experience, for Mr. Ono's claim to have the largest and finest collection of such books in the world is certainly justified.

I wish space allowed for a fuller description of these books here, for standing in Mr. Ono's library I had only to mention this or that edition when the next moment it was in my hand. It was like magic!

For the sake of those interested I give below a selection of this really great collection, which includes items so rare that Mr. Ono told me that he had been accused, by other collectors, of inventing the titles for effect. Having, however, myself seen and handled these books I can bear testimony to their existence, of which I own quite frankly I had never heard until this wonderful visit.

Among these exceedingly rare items are included *May Turpin: Queen of the Road* and *Tom Turpin.* Both, of course, are entirely fictitious characters. Then there are several rare items that have a special interest for us here, such as *Hounslow Heath and its Moonlight Riders; The Black Rider of Hounslow Heath; Will Dudley: or the Scarlet Riders of Hounslow Heath*, by W. L. Emmett. While most of these "Bloods" are anonymous, certain ones bear the names of writers known among collectors of this class of "literature," such as *Red Crepe: A Tale of the Highway and the Heath*, by Malcolm J. Errym (in *The London Miscellany,* 1866); *The Blue Dwarf*, by Percy B. St. John—probably the most fantastic and far-fetched of all such stories; it even takes Dick Turpin and Black Bess among the Red Indians on the American prairies! The most accurate and authentic of such books from an historical point of view is probably *Dick Turpin,* by Henry Downes Miles.

Many of these stories contain mention of Hounslow Heath and its old inns, and if space allowed I should have liked to have quoted some choice bits. Selection would not be easy from such a mass of material; and anyhow, I am afraid that such extracts would not add a great deal to our genuine knowledge of the dist .ct—for historical accuracy was not one of the things over which these old writers worried unduly.

Many other titles could be mentioned, a few of which, though by no means even vaguely approaching a complete list, may not be without interest here. There is *The Lone Hut on the Heath; Moonlight Jack; Black Hawke, the Highwayman; Laughing Dick; The Royal Highwayman; Black Bess; Life on the Road; The Black Highwayman; Blueskin; Dashing Duval: The Ladies' Highwayman.* Another of Malcolm Errym's productions was *Nightshade: or Claude Duval the Dashing Highwayman*, while *The Black Mask: or the Mysterious Robber; Jack Rann: Sixteen String Jack: the Noble-hearted Highwayman; Jerry Abershawe; Turnpike Dick; Tom King, the Dashing Highwayman* (a favourite sub-title); *Tom King and Jonathon Wild; Spring-heeled Jack; Townsend the Runner; Dick Turpin's Ride to York* (a "hardy annual"); *Turpin and Bess*—all true to the same lurid type.

Some of these "Dreadfuls" are noted for certain distinguishing features, such as: *Tyburn Dick: The Prince of Highwaymen,* is *not* about Dick Turpin; *Colonel Jack: or the Life of a Highwayman* has no connection with Defoe's similar title; nor have *Paul Clifford: or Hurrah for the Road!* and *Gentleman Clifford and his White Mare* the least to do with Lytton's hero in the book with the same name. *Newgate or the Flying Highwayman* deals with the doings of Hawke, whom we have already met on Hounslow Heath elsewhere in these pages; while *Captain Macheath, the Daring Highwayman*, makes the hero an actual person, which he never was, despite a certain popular belief. *Tyburn Tree* deals with McLaine, who was real enough, and whose name, as well as that of Macaire, has helped to confuse the minds of readers with the purely fictitious Macheath.

One of the earliest of all "Dreadfuls" of this type is *Lives of the Most*

Notorious Highwaymen, published by Lloyd in 1837, which purports to be more of a history; while *Gentleman Jack the Highwayman, or Life on the Road,* also published by Lloyd in 1850, easily holds the record for longevity, for, so popular did it prove, that it took *several years* to run in serial form. *Jack Rann,* by James Lindridge, has the double distinction of being *very* rare, but also fairly accurate.

All these, and many more, are to be found in Mr. Barry Ono's library, the fringes of which I have merely touched upon; and I cannot do better than close this brief account of that unique collection by quoting a paragraph from an article by this famous collector himself.   It is entitled *Dick Turpin Literature,* and the portion that so interested me reads: " The oldest Turpin relic in my collection is a cheap book, published 1800-20, but as clean as if just issued.   The title is *The Life and Adventures of Richard Turpin, a most notorious Highwayman, comprising a Particular Account of all his robberies, HIS RIDE TO YORK, and his Trial and Execution for Horse Stealing, 1739.*   I print RIDE TO YORK in capitals as the antiquity of this little book destroys the theory that W. Harrison Ainsworth   invented   this   legend   in   *Rookwood.*   One   of   the   most original yarns was *The Schooldays of Dick Turpin*   We also find Turpin as the hero or sub-hero of a whole host of other highwaymen stories, such as *Red Ralph: A Romance of the Road in the Days of Dick Turpin; Nan Darrell: the Highwayman's Daughter; The Night Hawks of London, or the Noble Highwayman,* and so on."

This article is intensely interesting, as it shatters a well-believed theory that it was Harrison Ainsworth that first attributed to Turpin the Ride to York; which, I must confess, I shared until Mr. Ono put me right.

Thousands who know Mr. Barry Ono as the famous variety artist, and originator of " The Old Time Music Hall " Sketch—and he is as great an expert on the bygone " Halls " as he is on Penny Dreadfuls—know one side of his versatile character only; and added to this his cheery and sporting personality made my visit to him a delight.   It made me feel strangely ignorant, however, on the " Dreadful " side of Highwayman Literature; as fascinating in its way as the pure historical with which I have a nodding acquaintance; but I left Mr. Ono's house (with tremendous difficulty, a magnet was pulling me back to those fascinating shelves) a good deal wiser on this particular topic than when I entered it.

Another interesting writer on the literature of Dick Turpin is Joseph Parks, who shares with Mr. Barry Ono enthusiasm for, and deep knowledge of, his subject.   Mr. Parks is known to all lovers of the old " Dreadfuls " as the Editor and Publisher of that excellent little magazine *The Collector's Miscellany*—it is issued at Salturn in Yorkshire—a mine of information, both in the text and illustrations, of the old highwaymen stories.

A rather curious thing happened recently; a friend sent me a " Blood " (one of the *Jack, Sam and Pete* series, written moderately recently as such books go).   The author was Gordon Maxwell, and he was under the impression that I had written it.   I had never heard of it, however, nor even of my double-fellow-author-namesake.   Mr. Barry Ono tells me, however, that some years ago (about the 'nineties) there *was* a writer of semi-Dreadfuls of that name.   If he is still alive possibly someone will accuse him of writing *Highwayman's Heath*—by way of reprisal.

In the well-known *Slang Dictionary* (Hotten's Edition, 1859) we read:

"Ainsworth's *Rookwood* and *Jack Shepherd*, and similar books, are
abounding in cant words, placed in the mouths of highwaymen. The Dick
Turpins and Jack Shepherds of the early and middle part of the last
century made cant popular. . . . They are not inserted as jokes or
squibs, but as selections from the pocket dictionaries of the highwaymen
of the day. One piece of information is conveyed to us, i.e., that the
'knights' or 'gentlemen of the road' using these polite words in those
days of highwaymen were really well-educated men—which heretofore has
always been a hard point of belief, notwithstanding old novels and operas."
    In spite of this view, however, I think this question is still open to
doubt. In the section devoted to Rhyming Slang, once so popular, it is
not without interest for us here to find the entry "Teeth—Hounslow
Heath." The best contemporary books on thieves' slang are those of
Thomas Dekker: *Lanthorne and Candle-Light* and *The Bel-Men of London*,
both published in 1608.

*   *   *   *   *   *

    I hope this chapter—in all its three sections—is not too much like an
annotated bibliography; yet, looked at broadly, that is what it really is.
Nor does it claim to be complete; such a list would need a volume to itself—
but what a volume it would be!

BOOK FOUR.

CHAPTER XX.

A Place of Crowded Memories where its Great House is a Slice of English History.

ISLEWORTH, as regards this book, is in a paradoxical position. Strictly
it should not be included, yet looked at broadly it is part of the whole
scheme.
    This is simplified if we divide it into Isleworth Town and Isle-
worth Hundred, for whereas the former is east of Hounslow and outside
the confines of the Heath, yet both Hounslow, and what is left of the
Heath, are now in the Hundred of Isleworth (Gistelworde of the *Domesday
Book*) though formerly in the Hundred of its own name. The "mystery"
of *Domesday* referring to the Hundred of Hounslow, instead of Isleworth
has always been rather a puzzle. It seems that the change was made in
1390 and that the *Domesday* compilers were in error in calling the Hundred
Hounslow; which they adopted from the fact that the Court Leets were
held there—but the Hundred should have been Isleworth, as it is now.
That even the Domesday compilers were human enough to err is comfort-
ing to later topographers.
    I propose, therefore, to adopt a half-measure here to suit the case,
mentioning the chief points only in Isleworth's long and interesting history, perhaps pointing to a "signpost" or two on the way, for the highways and byways of Old Isleworth are crammed with fascinating stories.
    Isleworth's riverside by the church is one of the most picturesque spots
along the Thames. On a sunny day it has a lazy, to-morrow-will-do sort
of air, which is refreshing these bustling days.
    There has been a church here since Saxon times—and even before
this it was said to have been a Roman compitum or landmark, and to-day
foremost in the view is the old church, for the tower is said to be four-

teenth century work and perhaps built by William of Wykeham, though the main body is of quite respectable age, except one end. One account describes this building (before the alterations) as the " ugliest church in Middlesex "—somewhat of a libel, but thereby hangs a tale.

We learn a good deal of " Churchwarden Gothic," and Isleworth Church, though not Gothic, has certainly suffered from churchwardenism; for when it was decided, in 1701, to rebuild it, Sir Christopher Wren was asked to prepare plans. This he did, but they did not please the churchwardens, who thought they could do much better themselves! So they scrapped Wren's plans and drew their own, *which they used!* The result was a dull, heavy building, which earned this nickname. Some 60 years ago, however, alterations did something to nullify this slight and it certainly can be truthfully said few churches have a finer position—at the end of Syon Reach, facing Kew Gardens and the Observatory meadows.

Next in prominence is the " London Apprentice " Inn, with its quaint old window overlooking the river. Its name gives the clue to the festive nature of its gatherings in bygone days and in the eighteenth century it was well-known to the night riders of Hounslow Heath as a convenient bolt hole, whence the river could be crossed to escape the Runners.

Beyond is the long island of osiers, which adds to the picturesqueness of the view and only half hides the old houses and wharves—with probably a sailing barge or two unloading, which gives the place a suggestion of an old seaport though a little spoilt by the ugly mill—and beyond it all a glimpse of a green riverside round the mouth of the River Crane—and one or two old mansions towards St. Margaret's.

It is a peaceful scene and that it has not altered materially in close on sixty years is proved by Thorne's description: " Isleworth extends for three miles along the Thames, where the river first becomes sylvan, Kew Gardens and Richmond Lower Park lining the opposite bank. The first mile from Brentford is occupied by the ducal park and palace of Syon. Then comes the ivy-clad church and mill, the riverside village, with its good old-fashioned, red-brick, middle-class residences, shops, wharves and boat-houses, and in front the long willowy eyot. Farther on and wider apart are fair and stately seats, with velvet lawns sloping to the river, and girt with shadowy trees; and ever and anon, and more frequently as we approach Twickenham, varied with clusters of modern houses."

Isleworth has been " free wharf " since mediaeval days and even now barges can load and unload without paying dues.

A much earlier, and quainter, description is found in " The Isleworth Survey " of 1635, which strangely tells us that Middlesex is " part of the Kingdome of the East Saxons "—surely Middle Saxons is more correct— and it goes on to say that the " ayre of Istelworthe is wonderful, temperate and healthful," and of the county in general it adds that it is " of a generality level, the soile for the most part fertile; one of the leaste in quantity, but not in dignitie, famous for many auntient expeditions, but notable that within her continente is situate that ever flourishing London, the metropolitan of the islands; with her little Sister Westminster . . . and still spreading her foundations to the admiration of the Christian Worlde."

As we have already commented, the fact that Middlesex contains London has been as much her curse as her blessing; to say nothing of " Little Sister " Westminster (since 1635 grown into quite a big girl); and as for

London spreading her foundations to the admiration of the Christian Worlde—well, some of the building now going on upon the fringe of London seems designed rather to please the Powers of Hell.

* * * * * *

In the main the history of Isleworth is a peaceful one and, its village chronicles—apart from the "great folk" who chose it as a habitation—show that it was agricultural; even now, despite changing times, a good deal of fruit is cultivated here. It has been, however, the scene of two striking events, for the Battle of Brentford was mainly fought in Isleworth, while nearly four hundred years earlier it was the scene of what has been described as an "historical riot," the details of which we read in Holmsted's *Chronicles:* "About the beginning of Lent (1264) the Constable of the Town, Sir Hugh Spenser, and a great multitude of citizens went to Thistleworth and there spoled the manor place of the King of the Romans (Richard, Earl of Cornwall, and brother of Henry III.), and then set it on fire, and destroyed the water-mills." For this act the Lord Mayor of London and chief citizens were imprisoned and fined to pay for the damage.

In the *Black Book of the Exchequer* we find details of this damage and the cost of making good Isleworth Manor House, which is chiefly interesting now as the only description extant of this old house, the very site of which is not accurately known. Here is the description slightly abbreviated: "There was an inner court surrounded by a moat. In this court was a hall with a basement chamber and a kitchen. There was also a chapel with chambers called the King's Chamber and the Queen's Chamber. These buildings had tile roofs and three chimneys. A "larder house" nearby was covered with straw. Outside the moat was the outer court and a granary, all tile roofed; a grange for the horses and for oxen, and a "dayhouse" were straw thatched. Surrounding this court was a cloister, and a watermill and windmill on the estate."

Lysons has a note regarding this house: "The site of Isleworth Palace, or ancient Manor House, is not exactly known; but it seems probable that it was behind the Phœnix-yard, called in old writings the *Moted Place.*"

* * * * * *

A study of the old houses, in which Isleworth is particularly rich, both past and present, affords much interest, *en route* and in books, but save for the notice of a few chief ones space again forbids. Some that still exist are no longer private residences, but used for convents and schools. We will take a glance first at those which can still be seen.

The largest of all is Kilmorey House, which was built for (though never occupied by) the eccentric Earl of Kilmorey. It is now the Royal Naval Female School. The mansion, a typical eighteenth century porticoed structure, stands on the river bank, in a fine garden. Next to it is Gordon House, called after Lord Frederick Gordon, but formerly occupied by Lord Kilmorey. It also possesses fine gardens, which were originally said to have been laid out under the supervision of William IV. The house is now also used as a school. Kilmorey House itself is said to be visited by the ghost of the old Earl—though this story is rather nullified by the fact that he never lived there—he died before the house was ready. He was a most eccentric man and apparently his ghost is keeping up this reputation by haunting the wrong house! There is said to be another ghost hereabouts—that of a girl murdered in a barge some hundred years ago (the story of the murder is told in the Countess of Munster's book).

If the spectres of the Earl and the girl ever meet I do not know.

I was recently told a story (by a former pupil of the R.N. School) of the reason "the front of the house is at the back," or so it is said because of the pillared portico facing the river. It is related that when the mansion was completed Lord Kilmorey found he had not enough money to pay for it, so it was sold. This so annoyed the old Earl that he used to take a chair and sit in front of the house all day, which in turn annoyed the new owners, so they built a new front facing the grounds, where the Earl could not see it. How much truth there is in this story I cannot say.

In *My Memoirs* the Countess of Munster has an interesting chapter on Isleworth in the reign of William IV. The authoress lived at Rails Head (now Gordon House).

The Sailor King seemed fond of assisting in the arrangement of Isleworth gardens, for at the Convent next along the river bank, now known as Nazareth House, but formerly Isleworth House, he is said, after a visit to Lady Cooper (widow of Sir William Cooper, Chaplain to George III.), to have ordered the Syon Vista in Kew Gardens to be cut to open up a view of the Pagoda from this garden, the beauty of which he admired.

Another old-time mansion, now a convent school, is Gumley House, a large building opposite the Fire Station. It was built at the end of the seventeenth century and occupied in Queen Anne's reign by a Mr. Gumley, a wealthy glass-manufacturer, who had a beautiful daughter. The combination of the money bags and the lovely maid proved the fate of William Pulteney, afterwards the Earl of Bath, who married the girl and spent the money. The Earl—famous as a politician and minister during the reigns of the first two Georges, and rival of Sir Robert Walpole and friend of the latter's son Horace—lived at Gumley House after his father-in-law's death, when the mansion was a centre for the fashionable world of the day.

The Belle of Isleworth seems to have had all the whims and fancies of a spoiled beauty, and Pope, in *The Looking Glass*—a reference to the source of paternal wealth—thus writes of her:—

> " With scornful mein, and various toss of air,
> Fantastic, vain and insolently fair,
> Grandeur intoxicates her giddy brain,
> She looks ambition and she moves disdain,
> For other carriage grac'd her virgin life,
> But charming Gumley's lost in Pulteney's wife."

Later the poet adds pointedly:—

> " O could the sire, renown'd in glass produce
> One faithful mirror for his daughter's use!
> Wherein she might her haughty errors trace
> And by reflection learn to mend her face."

Nearly opposite Gumley House is the smaller Silver Hall, which was built in 1801 on the site of an earlier building. Lysons has an interesting note as to the origin of its name (referring, apparently, to the original house): "The house called Silver Hall (now a school) on the south side of the Twickenham Road was built by John Smith, who was created a Baronet in 1694. His arms are over the piers of the gate. After his death it was in the occupation of Lady Harcourt, widow of the Chancellor. It was afterwards the property of Mrs. Oliver (whose maiden name was

Silver), mother of Silver Oliver. This circumstance, it seems, gave the house its present name; had I not been informed of it, I might have ascribed it perhaps to a different cause; for on or near the same spot is described in Glover's old map a house where resides 'Mr. John Broad, the famous metallist.'"

It is a pleasing specimen of the smaller country house of the period and set in a delightful old-world walled garden, through which runs a small stream. But what a high wall—I nearly broke my neck and incurred the suspicion of several passers-by in trying to climb up to look over it—for the house is still a girls' school.

Isleworth is in places a veritable walled city and most of these walls are high and unclimbable—they knew how to build walls in the 18th century. I have managed to look over some, but the majority are too high, and, of course, if you are seen climbing a convent wall (which mostly abut on main roads), whoever is "fool" enough to believe—however true it may be—that all you wanted to see was the house and garden! On pointing this out to a dear old lady she innocently remarked, "But then, you will find that all decent-minded people would believe you"—to which I might have replied—quoting Ben Travers—"But where are you to find the decent-minded people!"

Some of these gardens can be seen from the river, however, for those with tender consciences or who are bad climbers.

Another house that can best be seen from the river is the delightful old Ferry House, near the church. Originally a dower house of the Northumberland family, it is, I think, one of the most picturesque eighteenth century residences in the county. Its interior is as pleasing as its exterior, though in this case I did not have to climb any wall to gain admittance. It was many years ago, in pre-war days, when I first entered its hospitable portals, but it seems like yesterday. My brother and I had come up in the night and anchored in *The Penguin* off that garden, and I remember how in the early morning I went on deck and saw Ferry House. It seems that the occupants of the house were as interested in us as we were in their house—the yacht was a sea-going vessel of a rig strange to Thames-side dwellers—and our "Mutual Admiration Society" ended in a sporting invitation to two hungry mariners to breakfast.

*　　*　　*　　*　　*　　*

Among the famous houses of Isleworth now gone may be mentioned St. Margarets (which once stood next to Kilmorey House), and over whose grounds is built the district bearing its name. It was the seat of the Marquis of Ailsa, whose name is curiously muddled in various sources: in Tombleson's *Thames* he is referred to as the Marquis of Aylesbury, while on an old print I possess (engraved in Germany) he figures as Lord Halesby.

Lacey House, another riverside mansion that is gone, was built by the owner of Drury Lane Theatre, of that name, though it is best known as having been the residence, for a short time after their runaway match, of Richard Brinsley Sheridan and his bride.

It may have been a memory of this district which caused Sheridan (many years later) when his son asked him for some money, to reply: "My dear Tom, you will find a case of loaded pistols upstairs and a horse saddled. The night is dark and Hounslow Heath is but a mile beyond Isleworth." To which the son made answer: "I understand, father, what you mean, but I tried it last night. I stopped Peake, your treasurer, who told me you had been beforehand and robbed him of every sixpence."

The best known of all Isleworth's departed mansions was Kendal House, so called from the favourite of George I., the Duchess of Kendal, who resided here. In *The Good Fellows' Calendar* it is quaintly related how: " This gracious sovereign once, while *doing the tender* with the Duchess of Kendal, promised her that if she survived him, and if departed souls were so permitted, he would pay her a visit. The superstitious Duchess on his death so expected this that a large raven, flying into a window of her villa at Isleworth, she was persuaded it was the soul of her departed monarch, and treated it with respect and tenderness." This story is also to be found in Horace Walpole's *Reminiscences of the Courts of George I. and II.* Thackeray also refers to it in satirical vein in *The Four Georges:* " After his demise a great raven flying in at the Duchess of Kendal's window at Twickenham (Thackeray is slightly adrift in topography, Kendal House was definitely in Isleworth) she imagined the King's spirit inhabited her sable visitor. Affecting metempsychosis—funereal Royal bird. How pathetic is the idea of the Duchess weeping over it!"

The German Duchess was not popular with the villagers of Isleworth, who, on account of her tall and angular appearance, nicknamed her " The Maypole."

The mansion was subsequently opened as a place of public entertainment, and we read in *The Daily Advertiser* of 1750: " Kendal House, Isleworth, near Brentford, Middlesex, eight miles from London, will open for breakfast on Monday. The room for dancing is 60 feet long, and all the other rooms elegantly fitted up. The orchestra is allowed to be in the genteelest taste, being housed in an octagon in the Corinthian order. Ladies and gentlemen may divert themselves with fishing; near are two wildernesses, with delightful rural walks, and through the garden runs a rapid river, shaded with a pleasant grove of trees. Great care will be taken to keep out disorderly people. There is a man cook and a good larder."

This account—so typical of the eighteenth century—seems to have drawn the town, and the place enjoyed a measure of success. In a song called " Modern Diversions " printed in the *Universal Magazine* in 1753 we read:

> " To opera, assemblies,
>   Or else to masquerade,
>   New Tunbridge, or to Kendal House;
>   And this shall be the trade.
>   We'll sally out to breakfast,
>   And hear the fiddles play;
>   And there we'll revel, feast and dance,
>   And make a merry day.''

It appears, however, that Kendal House was not the earliest place of such amusement here, for in the *General Evening Post* in 1734 there is an advertisement of " The Isleworth Assembly " held at Dunton House—a place whose site is now impossible to identify.

Lord Byron was a frequent visitor to Hope House, Isleworth, and in early copies of *Don Juan* are some stanzas alluding to his host here, which, for some reason or other, are deleted from later editions of the poem.

An interesting story is told of Thanet House, an eighteenth century building in the Twickenham Road. It will be noticed that two cottages are built on either side of it, attached to the larger house. The reason of this was supposed to be for protection against the highwaymen and other desperate characters which then infested this lonely district. This strange arrangement was known in those days as " The Hen and Chickens," though in this case the " chicks " were meant to protect the mother instead of the usual way of things.

* * * * * *

Many other famous folk resided in Isleworth. Perhaps the most interesting is Thomas Chandler Haliburton, better known as " Sam Slick." Although always described as an American humorous writer, he was a Canadian by birth, and lived in later life at Isleworth, and is buried here. For some time he was M.P. for Launceston.

Another author who made the village his home was George Manville Fenn, who lived at Syon Lodge, a house recently demolished, that stood outside the park gates. His book, *Brownsmith's Boy*, is laid mainly in an Isleworth market garden.

A more famous writer than either has a slight connection with this district, for at Syon Park House—easily distinguished by its gazebo—now the Queen of Clubs Club, also just outside the park gates (but I believe actually in Brentford End), Percy Bysshe Shelley was at school; while Rennie, the famous engineer, was another pupil. I wonder which was the inn, said to have been on Hounslow Heath, where, many years later, Shelley had his famous " bacon feast." He always despised this dish—till ne smelt it cooking at this inn, and then had three big helpings. A curious story by which to remember a poet, but I have heard it related several times by people who had probably never read a line of his poetry. Shelley in *Laon and Cynthia* writes of his schooldays here:

" When I walked upon the glittering grass
And wept, I knew not why; until there rose
From near the Schoolroom voices that alas!
Were but one echo from a world of woes—
The harsh and grating strife of tyrants and of foes."

Near Shelley's old school, just past Syon Park gates going west, is the Coach and Horses Inn, mentioned in *Oliver Twist;* and this is spoken of in Harper's *Old Inns of Old England:* " The case of the ' Coach and Horses ' at Isleworth is remarkably well observed when we consider that the reference is only in passing. Indeed the topographical accuracy of Dickens, where he is wishful to be accurate, is astonishing; for Dickens apparently visited the scenes and from one eagle glance described them with all the accuracy of a guide book. . . . The ' Coach and Horses ' is unquestionably the house of which Dickens speaks, and was built certainly not later than the dawn of the nineteenth century." The house has altered little since the days when Dickens knew it.

An old Isleworth inn, some centuries old, and whose demolition I regret, is the picturesque old " Chequers," which has associations with the old highwayman days.

That the river scenery at Isleworth and Brentford influenced the growing mind of Turner is a thought as pleasant as it is true. An article in an old magazine *(Young England*, 1885) bears this out. It is entitled " The Dunce who became a Great Painter." The boy had not been well, so the London barber, his father, " decided he wanted a change of air and scene and it was arranged that he should visit an aunt at Brentford. What a change from Maiden Lane. Brentford was then a rural village, with the additional attractions of a wider river bordered by picturesque wharves, windmills, and lively with barges and wherries. Who that remembers the growing delight and fascination with which his first acquaintance with riverside scenery was associated will doubt that his rambles round Brentford and Isleworth have much to do with his love of nature and art?

" At Brentford he was sent to a school kept by a Mr. White, but he was fonder of drawing boats and churches than of learning dry columns of spelling, or sums. Frequently when Mr. White thought him working on a problem he was sketching birds, trees or some object visible through the schoolroom window. And in order that he might practice his art for the gratification of his schoolfellows some other urchin would secretly work out his sums for him."

Then follows a delightful paragraph: " Nor was it only in school that he indulged his taste for art. On going to and fro from the academy he embillished the walls and palisades on the way with chalk drawings of poultry or other live stock. And for thus defacing others' property the boy was often soundly whipped by his schoolmaster.

Even after he left Brentford his art was sternly discouraged, for one who called himself an art master in London said to Turner's father in despair: " Your boy is impenetrably dull; he blots and smears his drawing paper and sketches trees in the margins when he ought to be drawing rhomboids. The boy will never do any good, better make him a tinker or a cobbler instead of a perspective artist.

The account ends with the pungent remark: " Turner was pronounced perfectly hopeless in the very line in which he afterwards distinguished himself; his example as an illustrious dunce is almost unique. What a satire on the cocksure judgment of schoolmasters and professors! In 1789 his master said he would never be able to learn perspective—twenty years later he was Professor of Perspective at the Royal Academy. And now his merest sketch is worth more sovereigns than would cover its surface."

I heard from an inhabitant of Brentford that there was an old man living there a tthe time of Turner's schooldays who had a little more sense than the schoolmasters and used to encourage the boy to draw and to give him half-a-crown for his coloured sketches. Where are they now? I often wonder if they will ever come to light in some old Brentford house—when they would probably be thrown away as rubbish.

We read in Thorne: " Lord Baltimore, Secretary of State to James I., one of Walpole's *Noble Authors,* and the founder of the Colony (now State) of Baltimore, had a summer residence at Isleworth, but where it stood we know not."

This riverside village seems to have been a favourite with Secretaries of State, for Sir Ralph Winwood, who also held that office under James I. and the Duke of Shrewsbury who occupied the same position under William and Mary, were also both residents here.

There have been other notable residents of Isleworth who have left little trace of their stay behind them, such as Sir Edward Walpole and the Earl of Warwick.

In some ways the most interesting resident of Isleworth was Sir Joseph Banks, the famous naturalist and President of the Royal Society, who for many years lived at Spring Grove, on Smallbury Green, towards Hounslow. This old house, which named a district, stood where the Spring Grove Polytechnic (formerly the residence of Mr. Pears, the soap magnate);

is now situate. Sir Joseph lived at Spring Grove for many years and died here in 1820, when he was buried at Heston.

Of his life in Isleworth and the surrounding country a good deal can be gathered from various sources; we have already noticed his experiments in sheep farming. A rich and generous man, he used his wealth to good purpose, and many men of science less fortunate than himself had cause to bless him, while H.M.S. " Bounty "—on which the famous mutiny occurred in 1787—was fitted at Banks' expense.

Sir Joseph's best known benefaction, however, was the fitting out (again at his own cost) with apparatus of H.M.S. " Endeavour " in 1768, and he himself sailed with Captain Cook on that memorable voyage of discovery. It is to Banks that we owe the name of Botany Bay for the spot where the British flag first flew over the Australian continent. The name was given on account of the wonderful variety of flowers and plants that met the eyes of the explorers—the beauty of the place was afterwards commemorated by the foundation of a convict settlement!

The obvious derivation is not always the correct one, but some people strain the imagination too far to find alternatives; this is brought home by a story I was told quite seriously, and that was that the *flowers* had nothing to do with the giving of this name, but it was really caused by Banks spreading his pink blotting paper, in which he kept his botanical specimens, out to dry on the shore, and that he had so much of this that it covered the whole harbour shore and gave the appearance of growing flowers when seen from the ship. Now Sydney Harbour is a big place and to cover the shores of it in this way would have meant several fleets of ships, laden with nothing but blotting paper, sailing continually for some years from England.

Although we can dismiss this absurd idea, there is another little story in connection with this name in which more credence can be placed, at least I like to think so, though is is merely my own idea. It is this. Banks used to roam about the Middlesex countryside in search of botanical specimens, and there is between Enfield and Potters Bar an isolated hamlet—it is but an inn and a few cottages—set in what is almost hilly country (for Middlesex), and in these grassy undulations there is in summer still a wonderful profusion of floral beauty to be seen, and the name of this place (and marked on maps as such) is—Botany Bay. My theory is that this was named by Banks as a botanical happy hunting ground. Now was the Middlesex hamlet named after the Australian bay or *vice versa?* Personally I incline to the former, for the " bay " is merely a figure of speech. I suggest that after his return from Australia Banks " discovered " the Middlesex beauty spot and named it after the Antipodean one. I can bring no actual proof of this—but it is a few miles only from the naturalist-explorer's home at Spring Grove. Anyhow, if the reader has a more feasible explanation of this name on the Middlesex map, bearing in mind the circumstances, I am willing to hear it. Had it been " Botany Hills " it is possible that this Middlesex hamlet gave its name to the Australian settlement—I should like to think this, but frankly I suspect it to be the other way round.

There is a good deal of interest lying round the mouth of the River Brent, but it really is outside our present scope. I have seen it stated that the word Brent is old English for frog and that the stream was so called from the number of these reptiles living on its banks. This may or may not be so; but there is another " mystery " of far deeper interest, for in a number of *The Home Counties Magazine* is a provocative paragraph relating to a "lost" village hereabouts; not lost in the generally accepted term of such places, but a complete disappearance from map and memory

Here is the reference: "In the grant of King Edgar to the Monastery of Thorney, which, though known to be a forgery, can hardly be later than 1100, a Middlesex name is mentioned in the list of lands given to the monastery—Bleccenham.   This name is said to have entirely vanished. In *Anecdota Oxoniensia,* by A. S. Napier and W. H. Stevenson, it is stated that Bleccenham (or Blechenham) lay somewhere near the River Brent. The name was in existence after the Norman Conquest, for a Thomas de Blechenham is mentioned in fires of 1226 and 1316, as we see in Hardy and Page's *Middlesex Fires.*

It would certainly be interesting to find out if there is any record existing of the exact places where these lost villages were situated.   The writer of the paragraph quoted adds: "I should be glad to learn if these names survive in local memory. Sometimes a word, which has escaped the notice of the Ordnance Surveyors, will be found in a clump of trees or an isolated farmhouse." I fear, however, these names are too deeply sunk in the quicksands of the years to give us much hope of discovering any clues now, though I should much like to identify the site of the lost village on the banks of the Brent.

*   *   *   *   *   *

There is a story told by one of Banks' biographers which may have some bearing on the Botany Bay idea, which relates how Banks at school was so immoderately fond of play that his attention could not be fixed to his studies. At the age of fourteen a change came over the boy, which was accounted for by the fact that one fine summer evening he was walking down a Middlesex lane (if in the place now known as Botany Bay is not stated) which was clothed with flowers, and he was so struck with their beauty that he resolved to study botany. During the holidays he found an old book in a lumber room, without a cover and minus several leaves, but it described the plants he had seen and gave engravings. This was Gerard's *Herbal.* He carried the book back to school in triumph and was soon able to turn the tables on his former instructors."

It may not be inappropriate here to quote part of the amusing verses written by Rev. James Walcott—under the name of "Peter Pinder"—which commemorate the famous occasion when Sir Joseph Banks was arrested on Hounslow Heath by the Bow Street Runners as a footpad. The unfortunate President of the Royal Society was merely gathering botanical and natural history specimens, but this the Runners would not believe, for Sir Joseph, though a generous-hearted and brilliant man, was rather plain.

" Sirs, what d'ye take me for?" the Knight exclaimed—
    " A thief," replied the Runners, with a curse;
  " And now, sir, let us search you and be damn'd "—
    And then they searched his pockets, fobs and purse.
  But 'stead of pistol dire, and death-like crepe,
    A pocket handkerchief they cast their eye on,
  Containing frogs and toads of various shape,
    Dock, daisy, nettletop and dandelion.
  Yet would not alter they their strong belief
    That this, the pris'ner was a thief.
" Sirs, I'm no highwayman," exclaimed the Knight—
  " No, there," rejoined the Runners, " you are right—

KNELLER HALL, WHITTON. *Block lent by Middlesex Chronicle*

WHITTON WOODS. *Photo by the Author*

THE RIVERSIDE, ISLEWORTH.

Drawing by Donald Maxwell

SYON HOUSE, ISLEWORTH.

From a print of 1783

A footpad only. Yes, we know your trade.
Yes, you're a pretty babe of grace;
We want no proofs, old lodger, but your face;
So come along with us, old blade."

And so poor Sir Joseph was actually taken before a local magistrate—when the mistake was discovered.

Near Spring Grove House was a lane known locally as Hangman's Lane (though I do not think a gibbet ever existed here) that is *said* to be the scene of this exploit. I very much doubt it, however; it was more likely to have been on the wilder parts of the Heath itself.

Most of the eminent scientific men visited Spring Grove during the residence of Sir Joseph, who became one of the foremost men of his day. An extract from a Road Book of 1818 tells us, in rather stilted language: " On the right, before we entered Hounslow, is the seat of Sir Joseph Banks; a neat mansion, with considerable gardens, where curious plants are reared with care and assiduity. The proprietor accompanied Captain Cook round the world and is now president of the Royal Society, and has long been distinguished for his researches."

A more intimate sidelight on the Isleworth household is given in *A Book for a Rainy Day*, by J. T. Smith, who tells us: " The house of Sir Joseph Banks was kept for many years by his sister, a learned lady, who had as great a passion for collecting coins as her brother had for botanical researches. Her dress was that of the old school; her quilted petticoat had a hole on either side, for the convenience of rummaging two immense pockets, stuffed with books of all sizes. This petticoat was covered with a deep stomacher gown. In this dress I have frequently seen her walk, followed by a six-foot servant with a cane almost as tall as himself. Miss Banks, when she wanted to purchase a broadside in the streets, was mote than once taken for a member of the ballad-singing confraternity. And yet this same lady, when she was in the prime of life, had been a fashionable whip, and driven a four-in-hand in the Park."

Sir Joseph left his magnificent library and unique botanical collection housed at Spring Grove to the British Museum.

* * * * * *

Parish registers, kindred documents and some monuments always have a real interest (when the corn is separated from the chaff), especially when the affairs of " The Great House " play their part and tell, even as a mournful echo, of many whose names are known in history, alongside the " short and simple annals of the poor." Isleworth is no exception, and here we find the influence of Syon House mingling with the humble lives of the villagers.

The first event worth noticing was, however, in pre-Syon days. It was an extraordinary strike in 1586 by the villagers against an unpopular tax; the strike consisted of leaving their hearths and homes to such an extent that the place became almost a deserted village. Here is Lysons' account of this strange event: " A remarkable depopulation of Isleworth happened in the fourteenth century, which is thus recorded: There was an ancient custom that the tenants of the manor should pay a certain sum of money called the ' Diseyne ' (amounting to eight marks), to the lord, besides the customary rents. The sum was levied, in an equal proportion, upon all males of fifteen years and upwards. In the year 1586 the tenants prayed for relief, stating that formerly the payment of this sum had been no great burden, the number of the inhabitants being such that it amounted only to one penny each person; but that the place was then so depopulated that it was six times as much, which occasioned many to leave the place; by which means the burden grew still heavier. In consequence of this petition the 'diseyne' was remitted for four years." As we hear nothing of this affair subsequently it looks as if this strangely-named tax was dropped.

An event which shocked the villagers even more occurred in 1535, when Rev. John Hall, their vicar for the last fourteen years, was hanged at Tyburn. Despite the proximity to Hounslow Heath, this was not for a sudden temptation to turn highwayman on the good vicar's part, but he died for his conscience, as he refused to acknowledge the supremacy of Henry VIII. It seems a little strange that the King's vengeance should at this stage of his reign (he had been twenty-six years on the throne) descend on this Middlesex vicar.

The clergy seem to have afforded one or two incidents worth recording here, among which we find the singular fact of Dr. Turner, the herbalist who laid out Syon House Gardens and who held a licence to preach in Isleworth Church, was, though only a layman, appointed to the Deanery of Wells. Further mention of him will be found, by those who wish, in Wood's *Athenae Oxonienses;* but we need not follow him there, for Dr. Turner's interest, as regards Isleworth, was more botanical than parochial.

Probably one of the fiercest battles that ever raged on the Heath was a parochial one between Isleworth and Heston concerning an alleged enclosure by the former.

The document (quoted at length by Aungier and Lysons) is pre-Reformation and is entitled—with a fine scorn of precis writing—"The Answer of the parishioners of Istylworth on controveries, debats and stryves to the wronge byll of complaynte made agaynste them by John Bygge, constable of the hundredth and lordship of Istylworth, and the parishioners of Heston, for goynge so in process you weke, as hereather folowith."

The archaic spelling throughout is rich; I wish space allowed me to quote it in full, but here is an " edited " account.

The parishioners of Isleworth depart from the Parish Church, as was their wont, " in Godd's pease and the King's, intending no malyce, no gruge agaynste any other parishe, but only to goo with their processyon." For a while all was well, till the procession reached " Babar bryge and sayde a Gospell there, as they ever have done of old tyme "; but on the return march, keeping strictly to their " dyche-syde tyll they kam nyghe unto the grete hawthorn stonding in the saide heth," their troubles begin. For the fierce parishioners of Heston, also processioning, march up.

That they are on the warpath is soon evident. A deputation step promptly forward and demand of Isleworth's " formoste banner-man, Jonn Browne," that he and his friends shall studiously avoid the ditch-side, to which the stout standard-bearer replies they " wold not, synce the dyche is within the bounds of Istylworth." This reply seems to have annoyed the Hestonians, for " with that kam John Bygg and swore an othe: ' Knave, wold thow not avoyde the waye? Then I shall throw thee into the dyche!' " Bygg, it seems, was a man of his word, and into the " dyche " went Bannerman Brown, flag and all!

That was the prelude to battle, and there stepped from the ranks of Heston two doughty warriors named Chylde and Dewell, " ryotously blustrynhge and blowinge like tyrants and madde-men and they did begyn shulderynge other of the banner-men into the dyche." The battle continued to wage furiously, until the disputed " dyche " was full of wet and struggling humanity. The warlike Hestonians were gaining a strong advantage and looked like gaining a famous victory, when overtures for peace began to be thrust forward by the Vicar of Isleworth and other " honeste men of Istylworth, with their cappis in their hands, who did entreat in Godd's name and the Kyng's to kepe pease, and to suffer them pleasably to goo and pass homward to Istylworth."

At first the Hestonians (including their " wyffes "), whose blood was up, would not listen to peaceful pleadings, and raised cries of " Pull Istylworth Crosse, and take away the Crosse of Istylworth from such bloudye caytiffs and a vengeance on all the parishe of Istylworth; for they have undon us, to dych in and take in our comyn." Peace, however, was gained at last and a truce was granted and the men of Isleworth returned homewards, philosophically consoling themselves with the thought " that they had byn lyke to have made manslaughter had they not byn wiser and more dyscrete than the said John Bygge!"

Nicholas Byfield, who was Vicar of Isleworth from 1615 to 1622, and author of several now quite forgotten theological works, was said to have been a friend of Shakespeare and to have been visited at this riverside rectory by the dramatist himself. I can find no actual proof of this, though if so Shakespeare must have made a special journey from Stratford, for it was long after he had left London for his native town and a year only before his death. (The Byfield stigmatised by Butler in *Hudibras* was the son of this vicar.) In 1723 there was a particularly gory assault and murder of a girl named Anne Bristow on Smallberry Green; the then incumbent, Rev. Richard Coleire, preached so powerful a sermon on the event that it was published, with embellished details of the horrid happening, as a pamphlet; no doubt a best-seller, for such things were the thrillers of the "good" old days!

There is an echo of real literature in two other entries, for here was baptised, in 1617, Dorothy, daughter of Sir Robert and Lady Sidney. This girl was afterwards rendered famous in Edmund Waller's poem, *Sacharissa,* under which name she appears. One annotator of the poem states that he had searched in vain to discover the time and place of her birth and had perused the registers at Penshurst in vain. Had he looked at those of Isleworth he would have found what he wanted, for Lady Dorothy was born at Syon House, whilst her grandfather (the Earl of Northumberland) was in the Tower. The other echo of literature was concerned with a death instead of a birth, for Margaret Howard, Countess of Orsery, whose marriage to the Earl was the subject of Sir John Suckling's beautiful ballad, *A Wedding,* lies buried at Isleworth.

Another interesting record is that of the wedding in 1679 of Lady Elizabeth Percy, of Syon House, to the Earl of Ogle. A few months later he died, and the young widow soon after married Thomas Thynne, who was murdered by Count Koningsmark in September, 1682; on May 30th following the twice-widowed lady married Charles Seymour, the " Proud " Duke of Somerset — and thus she had three husbands before she was seventeen!

An entry in 1632 is intriguing in the record of the burial of " John Queat: A Dwarf." Was he the nominal prototype of the dwarf Quilp in *The Old Curiosity Shop?* The names have a similar sound.

The next entry we shall notice has a smack of early " food reform " about it, for among the minutes of the vestry is entered a licence in 1661 given by the Vicar of Isleworth to Richard Downton and his wife allowing them to eat meat in Lent, " for the recovery of their health, they being enforced by age, notorious sickness and weakness to abstain from fish."

One account of Isleworth I read stated that no visitor to the church should miss " the Halfpenny Monument to Mrs. Tolson, a great benefactress to the parish." The name is that of the sculptor—and not the cost—of the monument. The lady died in 1750.

There is not much more to detain us among these registers; the mention of Richard Blyke, who was buried in 1775, always reminds me of a terrible cockney. It is pure association of ideas, though, for this gentleman was a learned collector of topographical data. Another worthy gentleman—said to be a rich merchant—in the eighteenth century left money for a sundial that would tell the time at Jamaica, Moscow and Jerusalem. It is certainly a source of mild mystery as to *why* he should imagine that the villagers of Isleworth in those days—most of whom had probably never even *heard* of these places—should be seized with a sudden desire to know the time there.

I was told by an enthusiastic amateur topographer that he had made a unique discovery at Isleworth—he had found the grave of John Gilpin! This was strange, for his real name was Beyer, Gilpin being but an invention of Cowper's; still I want to solve this " mystery " one day. My friend was right—up to a point; for Samuel John Gilpin was certainly buried there in 1882, whereas John Beyer died in 1791, though I do not know where he is buried.

* * * * * *

They have all passed on—Earls and Countesses almost as forgotten, I'm afraid, as Giles, and Mary his wife, villagers, to whom London was but a far-away echo—and among all the epitaphs of those of high or low degree there is one which, for its very simplicity, lingers in the memory far longer than the gruesome eighteenth century ones ever can. It is but a few words, written by some sorrow-stricken mother who, in a pestilence, had lost all her five children at once. They are buried in one grave and the stone bears the simple and touching words:

" My beloved ones have gone down into the garden to gather lilies."
Poor soul; but she has joined them now—in the garden.

* * * * * *

There are several minor literary men, and a few others, who lived at Isleworth, whom it may be worth while to notice in passing. Let us take a lady first—Mrs. Oliver. She was the widow of a painter, Peter Oliver. After the husband's death Charles II. bought his collection of miniatures and paid the widow by an annuity of £300. When, however, Mrs. Oliver heard that the King had given the pictures to his mistresses she expressed herself strongly concerning the King's " goings on " with these ladies. Some kind friend carried her remarks to the King, and he was so annoyed that he at once stopped her pension; but he did not return the miniatures.

There is Richard Whitford, a monk, known by his *nom de plume* " The Old Wretch of Syon," who in 1507 wrote his *The Martilage in Englyshhe as it is redde in Syon with addicyons.* This was printed by Wynkyn de Worde in 1526. He also printed *The Orcharde of Syon* (in *The Harleian MSS.*), by Sir Richard Sutton, Steward of Syon Monastery.

William Cave was Vicar of Isleworth in 1691, and here he wrote several books, once well known but now forgotten, including *Lives of the Fathers* and *Historia Literaria.* Another literary vicar was William Drake, in 1777, known in his day as an antiquary.

There died at Syon Park Cottage in 1854 one George Field, a writer on chromatics and a practical experimenter in colours. Sir Joseph Banks told him that madder could not be grown in England, but Field eventually managed to do so in his garden at Isleworth.

George Keate lies buried here—it was also his birthplace. A minor author and poet of the eighteenth century, his work is little read to-day; he was certainly versatile, for his work ranges from *A History of Geneva* to *A Journey to Margate*, and from *A Voyage to the Pellew Islands* to *The Distressed Poet.*

The full chronicles of Syon should be read in *Syon Monastery*, by G. F. Aungier, as a religious house, while its historical side appears in most county histories. Nevertheless, its story is too vivid to be ignored here, though space allows mention only of the salient points concerning one of the most interesting places, not merely in Middlesex, but in all England.

The greater part of riverside Isleworth is formed by the grounds of Syon House, now a seat of the Duke of Northumberland, but at one time perhaps the most famous religious house near London. The original building, of which all trace is gone, was founded in 1415 by Henry V.; at the same time he founded one at Sheen, just across the river, and in Shakespeare's play it is to these two places the King refers:

"And I have built
Two chantries, where the sad and solemn priests
Sing still for Richard's soul."

Henry took this step partly on the advice of Archbishop Chicheley, who afterwards founded All Souls College, Oxford. An interesting account of this appears in Professor Burrows' *Worthies of All Souls.* Chicheley himself officiated at the opening of the monastery.

The Isleworth foundation was for both sisters and brethren and the former were known as the Daughters of Sion. The rules of the order were strict, and silence was enforced. Quaint signs were invented for communication, of which old chronicles record over a hundred. The following, for use in the refectory, will give some idea of them:

Vyneaire: Drawe thy forefinger from thyne ere to thy throte.

Ale: Make the signe of drink, and drawe thy hand displaied afore thyne eer dunwarde.

Fysshe: Wagge thy hand displaied swellings in manere of a fisshe taile.

Mustard: Hold thy nose in the uppere parte of thy right fist and rubbe it.

Brede: Make with thy thombes and two forefingeres a round compasse.

Egges: Make a token with thy right forefingere upon thy right thombe to and fro, as though thou should pile egges.

Salte: Phillippe with thy right thombe, and the forefingere over the left thombe.

Meal times at the monastery must have been interesting; though to the uninitiated asking for wine might suggest suicide, while the requesting of fish would resemble lunatics playing at birds.

Additions to the rules of Syon Monastery are preserved in St. Paul's Cathedral Library. They were discovered among some ancient manuscripts by Rev. R. H. Barham—writer of *The Ingoldsby Legends.*

The original monastery was situated where St. Margarets now is, and was dedicated to " Our Saviour, the Blessed Virgin Mary and St. Bridget." The latter, by the way, was a Swedish and not an Irish saint.

In a little volume, *The Myroure of Oure Ladye,* specially written for use of these sisters, we get an insight into the life in this community; more especially from Rev. J. H. Blunt's comprehensive introduction.

The literature of Syon is extensive, and some we may notice here. There is *The Pardon of the Monastery of Syon,* while in Burnet's *History of the Reformation* more will be found. Two very interesting accounts exist in manuscript form only (they can be seen in Hounslow Library)—one is *Isleworth Syon's Peace* of 1656 (chiefly legal) and E. J. Lines' *Isleworth Chronicle.* An eighteenth century account—brief but interesting—of Syon is found in *The Diaries of a Duchess*—1716-1776—edited by James Greig.

In 1431 the monastery was moved to approximately the site of the present Syon House. The life of this monastery was quite short, for in 1539—or 125 years only since its foundation—it was suppressed by Henry VIII. The Report of the King's Commissioners charges the nuns and monks with gross misconduct, and tradition asserts the existence of a tunnel beneath the Thames from Syon to the monastery of Sheen, to further the intercourse of the inmates of both houses; but even if the former charges are true, for though the Commissioners may have exaggerated matters a little for their own ends, there was probably some truth in the charges—mediaeval monks and nuns were not as blameless, I'm afraid, as biassed history would have us believe, I doubt the tunnel idea.

Another cause for the suppression of Syon was the reputed complicity of the inmates with the proceedings of the Maid of Kent. There seems to have been some truth in this, for one of the Commissioners reported that he "had ordered the confessionals to be walled up, for that hearing of outward confession hath been the cause of much evil and treason." The Holy Maid of Kent was certainly imprisoned at Syon, where she was visited by Sir Thomas More.

The nuns founded a new convent at Lisbon, and carried with them the keys of the old monastery as an assertion of their rights. A later Duke of Northumberland, many years after, visited the Lisbon convent and presented the sisters with a silver model of Syon. "We still hold the keys," said the abbess. "We've altered the locks now," replied the Duke.

The subsequent story of Syon belongs to history, for though in 1557 Mary (of Bloody memory) restored the monastery, the revival was short-lived. "Thirty years had passed," writes Fuller in his *Church History of Britain,* "since the dispersion, most of the elder nuns were dead and many of the younger had forsaken their vows and married. However, with much ado, joining some new ones to the old they made up a competent number." Two years later Protestant Elizabeth reigned and it was again suppressed.

To those who would read more on this subject I would refer, in addition to Aungier's book, to Dugdale's *Monasticon* and Wright's *Suppression of Monasteries.* The historical story of Syon is perhaps more interesting even than its monastic one, and certainly fuller of incident.

The first use to which the King who made matrimony his hobby put Syon was as a prison for the unfortunate Katherine Howard, and from here she went by water to the Tower—and never returned. Not many years after another procession was seen on the Thames, this time up-stream, for when Henry died his body was taken from Westminster to Windsor by water. "The funeral procession," says one account, "was unusually magnificent, even for those days. The journey took two days, the first stage being to Syon House, where the procession rested for the night, and divine service was celebrated for the repose of the King."

It is said that the present right-of-way over Syon Park was because the body of Henry VIII. was taken there. This is quite possible, for the passage of a dead body is still said to create such a thing.

A rather gruesome piece of history (or legend!) is that during the Great Plague a "Dead Pit" was made in Syon Park and that bodies were brought down by the barge-load. I do not believe this for one moment, it was too far from London for one thing, and the loading and unloading of the bodies would not be a task that would be undertaken in the circumstances.

With all his faults Henry was a great Englishman and had enough pluck to throw off the Roman Catholic yoke and allow England to have her own Church without taking orders from foreigners.

Edward VI. gave Syon to the Duke of Somerset, the Lord Protector, who pulled down the monastic buildings and erected a mansion for himself. He also made a botanical garden under the superintendence of Dr. Turner, known as "The Father of English Botany," which was famous in its day (1563). Some account of it appears in Turner's *Herbal*.

On Somerset's execution in 1552 Syon was given to John Dudley, afterwards Duke of Northumberland, whose son, Lord Guildford Dudley, married the King's cousin, Lady Jane Grey. In Elizabeth Strickland's *Tudor Princesses* will be found an account of how Lady Jane was offered the Crown of England here:—"When the King died Lady Jane was brought from Chelsea to Syon House to meet the assembled Council, and to receive, as she wrote in her diary, 'That which was ordained for me by the King.' She was forced to accept the Crown, being 'suffused with blushes' at the homage paid to her. She spent the night at Syon and the next day, with great pomp, she was taken by river to the Tower." Poor, unhappy "Nine Days' Queen," the victim of Northumberland's over-reaching ambition, she never returned to Syon.

There is a simple and more quotable account of this episode in Mrs. Roe's *Uncrowned Queens*, in which she writes: "The innocent object of Northumberland's ambitious plans was spending a few weeks of the glorious summer weather at Sion House, near Brentford, in the company of her young husband, and in the enjoyment of her favourite books. On the morning of the 10th of July, while walking in the garden, she was summoned to the house to receive a deputation 'bearing the King's commands.' Jane was surprised to find a company assembled there. The Duke informed her that the King was dead, and had bequeathed his Crown to her. Northumberland knelt at her feet, and the rest were going to follow his example when Jane—at first struck dumb with surprise—began to comprehend her position and, overwhelmed with grief and terror, fainted. When restored to consciousness she declared that she could not accept the Crown; but, finally yielding to their wishes, she sank on her knees and said: 'O God, give me strength to rule as to my country's good.' That same afternoon she was conveyed by water to the Tower."

There is a mention only of Syon House in Ainsworth's *Tower of London;* a book in which it might be expected to find more, as it deals with Northumberland and his unhappy victim—the only part of their tragic story dealt with here is Cavalcade on the Thames that left peaceful Isleworth for the storms of London.

After Lady Jane's execution Syon House became Crown property again, and in 1563 a survey was made, as it was intended that the Court should meet here because of the plague then raging in London. Apparently for some reason it did not come after all, *and there is no traceable record of Queen Elizabeth ever having slept here*—a distinction which can be claimed of few houses of any size or age in England.

James I. gave Syon to the Earl of Northumberland, of whom it is related: " A suspicion arose that this Earl, who was a Privy Councillor, was connected with the Gunpowder Plot, and although the suspicion appears to have been groundless it involved him in severe penalties. The Court of Star Chamber stripped him of his offices, fined him £30,000 and sent him to the Tower for life. After fifteen years in prison and the payment of £11,000 he was eventually released, and returned to spend his last years at his Thames-side mansion."

There is, in connection with the Gunpowder Plot, another of those interesting sidelights in Syon's story that County Chronicles ignore, and which we find in *Epochs and Episodes of History*, where it states that the night before the proposed blowing-up of Parliament, Percy, one of the conspirators, " lived with his august relative at Syon," and it was probably this that set tongues wagging. The chief thing, however, is the account, as brief as the visit, of the arrival of Guy Fawkes himself at Syon on that evening, for we read: " Fawkes rode to Isleworth to tell Percy what of the preparations and how well their plans had succeeded. This so affected Percy that he came away from Sion House with Fawkes and accompanied him to London."

The next Earl of Northumberland made many alterations in Syon House, or rather Inigo Jones did for him. This Earl was a Parliamentarian and after the surrender of Charles I. the King's children were taken to Syon House. Here their royal father, who was a prisoner at Hampton Court, was allowed to visit them—perhaps the most pathetic of all the minor incidents in Syon's long and eventful story.

While the Great Plague of London was raging one of these children visited Syon in different circumstances, for it was here that Charles II. held a Council meeting during the pestilence in July, 1665. Evelyn writes of this in his Diary: " Went to Sion, where His Majesty set at Council during the Contagion; when business was over, I viewed the seate belonging to the Earl of Northumberland, built out of an old Nunnerie, of stone, and faire enough, but more celebrated for the garden than it deserves; yet there is excellent wall fruit and a pretty fountaine."

In the October of the same year his fellow diarist, Pepys, was also at Syon, when we read how he spent the night at Mr. Povey's house at " Branford," and the next morning he records: " Up about seven o'clock, Mr. Povey walked with me to Syon, and there I took water to London."

It was at Syon that Princess (afterwards Queen) Anne came to live after her quarrel with Queen Mary.

About the middle of the eighteenth century the estate came into possession, by marriage, of Sir Hugh Smithson, afterwards created Duke of Northumberland, and it is from him that the present family is descended. " It is to this Duke," writes Thorne, " that Syon House owes its present form, and the gardens much of their beauty. Calling to his aid Robert Adam, he entirely remodelled the exterior, and altered and fitted the interior with great magnificence. Adam was very proud of his work, and Horace Walpole claimed a share in the internal arrangements."

BEDFONT CHURCH.
Showing the Peacocks as they are
to-day.

This assumption is based on a letter Walpole wrote to the Earl of Hertford: " I have been this evening to Syon, which is becoming another Mount Palatine. Adam has displayed great taste and the Earl matches it with magnificence."

It was Adam who designed the well-known Lion Gate, which, however, did not please the fastidious Horace, for he writes: " Mr. Adam has planned a magnificent gateway and screen for Syon. It is all lace and embroidery, consequently most improper to be exposed on the high road to Brentford." Adam's gateway is there still for anyone to form a less biassed opinion.

It is, perhaps, of interest here to note that it was a natural son of this Duke who founded the famous Smithsonian Institution in America. This was James Macie Smithson (1765-1829). His mother was a cousin of George Keats of Isleworth and a great-grandniece of the " Proud " Duke of Somerset, once owner of Syon House.

The walk across Syon Park on the land side is full of interest and gives a sense of real country, with a fine view of the mansion, though not its best side, as the view from the river is far finer. Perhaps the best point of all to see the house and park is from the Surrey bank by Kew Gardens. It is one of the most beautiful views near London. True, there may be houses more beautiful than the square, castleated pile of Syon, but its wonderful situation redeems it. About 1770 Richard Wilson painted his famous view of Syon Reach; this I compared with a recent photograph taken from the same viewpoint. They are practically the same picture —the only difference is the lion. That came here in 1874 from the Old Northumberland House in the Strand. There is a story that a former Duke, who had been worsted by some City financiers in a deal, had the lion turned round so that its backside faced the City, to show what he thought of it! It is now facing east again, however, so perhaps the City has been forgiven. How much truth there is in this I cannot say—probably none, though eighteenth century " humour " was fairly broad.

Surely it is a wonderful thing to find no change in this view after 160 years and only seven miles from London. It is a very favourite " game " of mine to sit on the towpath facing Syon and reconstruct its wonderful history. Try it; you will see some marvellous ghosts—or nothing at all, according to your imagination.

And yet, incredible as it may sound, there was recently a proposal to turn Syon Park into a *Sewage-farm!* Ye Gods!

* * * * * *

A more famous artist even than Wilson has also pictured Isleworth, for one of Turner's *Liber Studiorum* plates represents the end of Syon Park, showing the " Temple " boathouse and the mill beyond—both there to-day. Turner's picture is certainly interesting, but for scenic beauty Wilson's is the better of the two.

When I was gathering " local colour " for my book, *Just Beyond London,* I was talking to an inhabitant of Isleworth, who told me that the old barge (using the word in its earlier sense) in this boathouse was the actual one in which Lady Jane Grey was rowed to the Tower. I mentioned this in good faith, but soon after the book was published I had a letter from a stranger who in turn had received one from the Duke of Northumberland, saying that I was wrong on this point; the old boat had fallen to pieces long ago and that the barge in question dated only from the end of the eighteenth century. So, thanks to the Duke's interest, I am able now to make the correction.

* * * * * *

Before we leave Syon Park to explore other parts of Isleworth there is one aspect of it to which I should like to draw the reader's attention—an aspect that, as far as I know, has never before been brought into any book on the district—and that is its primordial one; for the history of Syon—or what is now that estate—goes back into the dim past.

I was led into making a little research into this a few months ago by some very interesting notes in *The Morning Post* by a writer who uses the *nom de plume* of Peter Simple. "This morning," he writes, "I walked along the Thames from Kew Bridge to Richmond. I know of no stretch of river scenery which provides so much food for delight. The lion-crested front of Syon House, standing battlemented and unassailable amidst its parkland, like the last fortress of feudalism, and Old Isleworth, with its mill, its sailing barges and its venerable church tower, these are things which belong to the heart of England.

"Somewhere between Strand-on-the-Green and Syon Reach there is a spot to which a local tradition once assigned the name of 'Old England.' To-day I tried to identify it—but without success. One or two of the older inhabitants remembered the name, but none could say for certain to what part of the river bank this name was given. The shifting population, the severance of the old links and the changing face of England have dealt harshly with the household names our forefathers knew; and 'Old England' has passed from our ken as completely as the submerged Kingdom of Lyonnesse."

Much as I like that imaginative paragraph, I totally disagree with Peter Simple. He assumes that because no local inhabitant knew quite where it was that Old England is no more. I can assure him that his picturesque simile is only half-right.

Submerged though it may be at high tide, at others it is very clear to view. Local folk, I have found, often know very little about the place in which they live, and it often remains for the "foreigner" to dig out their history for them. "Old England" is that part of the river's bank that lies on the Middlesex shore between Brentford and Isleworth.

At one time it was all in one "piece," but it is now divided into three parts. The first is the wooded island just above Kew Bridge, behind which is the old bed of the river, the new cut on the Kew Gardens side being artificial. The second is that part now occupied by the G.W.R. dock and sidings by the mouth of the River Brent. The third, and by far the most important from our point of view, is a few acres forming that strangely wooded triangle of the Syon House grounds just beyond the railway property and before the open meadows.

By the courtesy of the G.W.R. I was allowed to investigate from their premises, but, of course, it is not open to the public, so I would advise the explorer to go to the Kew towpath and use his eyes (or better still a field-glass) from that vantage point open to all. On a map in Brentford Library this corner of Syon Park is definitely marked as "Old England" and it is certainly all that is now left of it in its pristine state. The best time to see this is in the winter, when the view will be unimpeded by the screen of foliage.

The gazer will see across the river a rather weird sight; a tangled wood with trees growing in strange and fantastic shapes, at high tide half out of the water and overhanging the small creek that runs up the centre of the wood. More strange, however, are these fantastic trees at low water, when they stand out from the green, slimy sedge in all their gauntness. You can look up the waterway into the heart of this strange wood, where even by day it always seems twilight as if a pall screened the sun's rays from that mysterious solitude.

To me it always seems like a magic wood; one that Arthur Rackham, S. H. Sime or (most of all) Gustave Doré might have conceived in their most grotesque manner. Yet it is no fairy wood; no self-respecting fairy would be happy in such a place. Rather it is a haunt of gnomes, goblins, or even something more sinister and evil! It is true I have never seen anything more harmful in its depths than an otter or a heron; but that is how it always strikes me.

Were Conan Doyle's *Lost World* suddenly to materialise in England I can imagine no better setting for the prehistoric creatures than this primordial wood.

Frederick Turner, the local historian, writes: "At Brentford many years before the coming of Julius Caesar, this part of the Thames Valley resembled a vast and expansive lake, on luxuriously wooded banks and islands of which ferocious creatures of extraordinary size and character fixed their habitation and over which, we may assume, the primitive homesteads of a prehistoric people were raised."

Among these animals the writer mentions Hippopotami, African and Asiatic elephants, Irish elks, wild oxen, reindeer and mammoths.

Nor were these all, for Professor Boyd Dawkins adds to the list. "Hippopotami haunted the banks of the Thames," he writes, "there were wolves also, and foxes, brown bears, wild cats and lions of enormous size. Grisly bears and boars lived in the thickets and at night hyenas assembled in packs."

Anyone can see in Brentford Museum the remains of some of these animals, as well as many articles of pottery and weapons, found in and near "Old England," and I was particularly interested in part of the skeleton of an Hippopotamus dug up only about five years ago when the Great West Road was made—a long link in our island's history, disturbing the resting place of an Hippopotamus to make room for motors!

The primitive homes mentioned by Mr. Turner were lake, or pile, dwellings; for this spot was in later years the site of such a place. "Near the mouth of the River Brent," writes Wood Martin in *Lake Dwellings*, "piles have been discovered marking, as it is supposed, the site of an ancient water town," and Crawford in *Prehistoric Invasions* adds: "The site known as Old England at Brentford is a most remarkable one and it appears very probable, if not certain, that a pile village existed there on the marshy ground between the River Brent and the Thames."

It appears that some fairly recent researches were carried out here, for in E. C. Vulliamy's *Archaeology of Middlesex and London* we read: "In 1928 the remains of a Romano-British pile dwelling were examined on the edge of the alluvial meadow-land known as Old England at Brentford, at no great distance from the line of the Romans' highway. It cannot be said that they were discovered at that time, for their existence had been long known to Mr. G. F. Lawrence, but it was due to his enterprise, backed by the *Daily Express*, that serious work was attempted on the site.

The results were hardly spectacular. It was found that the remains were those of a rectangular hut, lying below the present high-tide level. The work had to be done rapidly between the tides, in circumstances by no means favourable. The work was carried out under the expert guidance of Dr. R. E. Mortimer Wheeler, Keeper of the London Museum, who gives details of this hut and a Roman pot found in it, which are of great interest, though too long to quote, and he concludes with the remark: " This poor riverside dwelling was probably that of a humble Briton, and perhaps one that was never occupied for any length of time."   Another such hut was dug up later in Syon Reach.

It was here that Caesar crossed the Thames in B.C. 54 in chase of Cassivellaunus, of which Sir Montagu Sharpe gave a vivid account in his *Antiquities of Middlesex*, but this is really quite " modern " history concerning this spot; and here it was that Edmund Ironside drove Canute and his defeated Danes across the river in A.D. 1016, and the Battle of Brentford was fought between the Cavaliers and the Roundheads in 1642, but these last two events seem so recent, compared with the brontosaurus days, as almost to be " Stop Press!" The most fascinating story of " Old England " lies in prehistoric times, and we are lucky in these changing days to see this little bit of strange woodland left, whose history is so marvellous, almost unchanged since antediluvian times.

Not the least marvellous part is that it is but six and a half miles only from Hyde Park Corner—within easy " hiking " distance. It is perhaps, the most wonderful " picture " among the many strange things that the Fringe of London has to show. The " entrance " is free and the tax nominal—all that is asked for the latter is the application of a little imagination. Yet in spite of this free show I doubt if half a dozen folk a year ever see it, that is knowing what it is, and being aware that they are gazing at a spot that has altered very little since the days long before England was inhabited by human beings at all!

Since I wrote this account of " Old England " and the " Demons' Wood " I have had the pleasure of a talk with Dr. R. E. Mortimer Wheeler, who undertook the excavation of this spot. He referred me to the quarterly review *Antiquity* (1929). Here is a most interesting illustrated article telling the story of his work in search of the remains of the lake-dwellings. I " discovered " this prehistoric wood before I had heard of Dr. Wheeler's article, of which I quote a paragraph, in rather more official style than my own account. " The Old England meadow," he writes, " is seamed by small water-channels which are, in some cases, dry under normal conditions, though one of them regularly carried the overflow from the lake in the grounds of Syon House. It seems likely that, at junction with the Thames, the Brent at one time formed a delta over this low-lying ground and that these water-channels are a remnant of this feature. To-day the meadow ends in a vertical ledge of alluvium, four feet or more in height, which marks the normal extent of the high tide.

" Below this ledge, for a distance of forty feet or more, the foreshore slopes gently downwards, and is in most places covered with a deposit of alluvial slime. It then slopes more sharply towards mid-stream, and, at a varying distance below the low-tide level, drops at a still deeper angle where the river-bed has been dredged for navigation."

Some further notes on this strange bit of " water-country " is found in A. G. Linney's interesting book on the Port of London, which shows another side of this surprising region.

I would advise all interested to read Sir Montagu Sharpe's account of this part in his *Middlesex in British, Roman and Saxon Times*, which is the best I know. He reminds us, with regard to the lake-dwellings, that we should not forget that in the early days there was a fishery at the mouth of the Brent, owned by the Abbot of Westminster and the Bishop of London; wattle hurdles were used in this and some of the finds may be remains of these.
      *   *   *   *   *   *

A marvellous story this of Syon; a story to stir the imagination as one sits and gazes on those beautiful water-side meadows in the centre of which stands the mansion in its fringe of noble trees.

I have only touched briefly on this wondrous tale, it could be extended a hundred-fold, for Syon is truly a little patch of English history—and yet in a book that modestly describes itself as *A Comprehensive Road Gazetteer: in which is set forth every item of interest for the traveller by coach or chaise,* and published in 1817, all the author could find to say of it was: " On the left is Syon Park, a seat of the Duke of Northumberland, almost a martyr to the gout."

In an equally brief but slightly earlier note, however, there is a touch of romance, for we read in a Government Report under " Promotions for 1764. The Earl of Northumberland of Sion House in Middlesex, to Vice-Admiral of all America."

I wish in view of this appointment I could round it off by stating that the American Admiral had a steward who rejoiced in the name of " O. Gee," but I can truthfully say that his father had; and if you go into Isleworth Church you will see his bust—" Sir Orlando Gee, d. 1705, Steward to the Earls of Northumberland and Registrar of the Admiralty."

In Syon House is a wonderful map, a partial copy of which can be seen in the church labelled: " Syon map of Isleworth 1623." It is worth study and contains many interesting features and quaint bits not found on ordinary charts. It is mentioned at some length in G. A. Cooke's *Description of Middlesex,* an early nineteenth century volume, which may be conveniently quoted here: " In one of the rooms at Sion House is a survey on vellum of the Hundred of Isleworth, full of historical anecdotes, of which the late Bishop of Carlisle communicated this account:

" ' Having lately been to view the Earl of Northumberland's seat at Sion in Middlesex, I met with a curiosity there which tends to illustrate the local antiquities of the neighbourhood which, together with those of the county of Middlesex, have been less attended to and more imperfectly described, though so near the metropolis, than the remotest parts of the kingdom.

" ' It is a map or survey on vellum of the *Hundred of Isleworth* about three yards long and two broad, framed as a picture and hung up in one of the apartments. It was made temp James I. and points out every gentleman's house, with the name of the owner, in Isleworth, Twickenham, Whitton, Brentford, Hounslow, and other adjacent villages.

" ' In a corner of the survey is written, " At Isleworth a capital palace is said to have belonged to Richard, Earl of Cornwall, brother to King Henry III., destroyed by the Londoners." The site of this palace is not marked in the survey, but I suppose it was the same where, temp. Henry

IV., stood a royal mansion on the spot where the Earl's house stood; for in an ancient record entitled "Palatia regis" occurs Istleworde. Not the least tradition remains now of there having been such an house here; for I took some pains to discover the scite.'"

* * * * * *

There are one or two threads that may be gathered together before we leave Isleworth and its vicinity. One of these concerns the little-known chapel that once stood at Brentford End, just outside Syon Park Gates, of which we read: "At Brentford there are three bridges over the Brent, which tradition says were built by a clothier. At the foot of Braynford bridge was the chapel of All Angels, now quite perished.

"All memory of this chapel being lost, and Camden, Norden and other writers silent about it, I shall point out its original from a record in the augmentation-office: an indenture bearing date 1530, in the will of Hugh Dennis, between his executors and the abbess and convent of Sion, and the prior of Sheene, touching the endowment of certain alms-houses for seven poor men, and the founding a chantry for two priests in the chapel of *All Angels, by W. Braynford bridges,* lying within the manor or Istelworth, near the monastery of Sion, and held of the said abbess, which were to celebrate masses daily for the souls of King Henry VII., the said Hugh Dennis, Esq., and Mary his wife, and Master John Somerset. It further appears by this indenture, the said almshouses and chantry were endowed with rents issuing out of the manors of *Osterley, Wykes, and Portpole* (alias Grays-inn) all in the county of Middlesex, and were under the patronage of the abbess of Sion.

"The dedication of the chapel is unique in this kingdom. Many churches and chapels were dedicated to St. Michael; and one near Exeter to Gabriel, whence the place is now called *Clyst Gabriel,* though the chapel is demolished.

The account also contains some other notes on the district which are worth quoting: "The rivulet which empties itself in the Thames here and turns some very large corn mills is styled in the survey *Isleworth river,* and described there as enlarged by an artificial cut from the Colne. I suspect that the original name of this stream was *Ise,* one of the Celtic names for *water,* and from thence perhaps it was called Isleworth."

* * * * *

In 1642, in spite of the Battle of Brentford, an incident happened here that caused far more excitement, and that was a personal visit from his Satanic Majesty to the town; for we read in an old Broadside:

"Terrible Newes From Brainford.

"A perfect and true relation of one Thompson, a waterman, who on Thursday night began to drinke at an inne a Health to the Devil; at which falling dead against the table; with the Devil himselfe appearing in the Room visible. At the burial of the sinful wretch his corps seeming heavy at first, but the coffin afterwards as light as if there had been nothing in it."

Presumably the burial was of the impious waterman (though the text might read otherwise). No clue is given to identify the inn where this exciting happening took place.

There was quite a "Hitler touch" about the mediaeval bridge that spanned the Brent, not far from one end of Syon Park; Christians were allowed to cross free, but Jews were charged a half-penny each.

Brentford has its own story in history, but we have no space for it here and it is rather out of our scope; but it is a wonderful record all the same; and it is a surprise to discover in certain ancient Latin documents that Brentford is styled the capital of England.

Stories seem to cling round the bridges about here, for that at right the other end of the parish, over the stream that divides Isleworth from Twickenham, is called Ivy Bridge, yet in the Isleworth Survey of 1635 it is "Mother Ivey's Bridge." Who this village worthy was, however, who gave it her name cannot be ascertained now.

There is perhaps the most amusing account, however, of this bridge in an old record. Ivy Bridge was once known as Twickenham Bridge, and in this document appears this paragraph:

"Twickenham Bridge: It cost the parish in building the sum of   It was at last obliged to be taken down, and a new one erected (under the eye of Mr. Paine) and this cost   and was begun in 17   and finished in 17   "

There is a human touch about this account that is refreshing; and shows that topographers have not altered much the centuries over. It is easy to leave blanks in the MS. and then forget to fill them in. Even the eagle eye of Mr. Paine was caught napping on this occasion.

*   *   *   *   *   *

I know of no place so rich in almshouses as Isleworth, for besides those on the main roads one is often meeting them in those quaint brick-walled walks that are another quaint characteristic of this place; and long may both survive. The oldest almshouses are those built by Sir Thomas Ingram in 1664, though the best-known are Tolson's, that picturesque little group by the river. Built originally in 1750 (but I fancy partly rebuilt), there is a romantic little story attaching to their foundation. Mrs. Tolson, a widow in very poor circumstances, kept a small school in the village; on becoming blind she had to give this up and became destitute; when a wealthy relative died and the poor, blind widow found herself suddenly rich, when, as a mark of gratitude, she founded these.

Names of new roads sometimes show woeful lack of imagination in failing to fix the scene of some historical building or personage, but far worse is the deliberate altering from a name that tells a story to some meaningless or hopelessly conventional title. There are several instances in Isleworth, but one will suffice and that is St. John's Road, formerly Brazil Mill Lane, a corruption of Brass Mill Lane, which recalls a mediaeval craft that flourished here in early days. When these old Brass Mills were founded is uncertain, but in 1593, when Norden wrote his *History of Middlesex*, he spoke of them as old-established. "Thistleworth is a place scytuate upon the Thames," writes the old surveyor, "not far from whence, between it and Worton, is a copper and brass myll, wher it is wrought out of the oare, melted and forged; many artificial devices there are to be noted in the performance of the worker and the workmen make plates of both copper and brass of all syces little and great, thyck and thyn for all purposes; they also make kyttles. The hammers, some of wrought and beaten iron, some of cast iron, of 200, 300, some 400 lbs. weight, are lifted up by an artificiall engyne by the force of the water."

When these mills ceased to function is also not quite clear. Mr. G. E. Bate, in his valuable little book (and he probably knows more about it than I do) tells us that he found the site marked on an early seventeenth century map as that of a " Decayed brass mill "; though Rocque's map of many years later (1745) marks the mills quite clearly.

Another old local industry was pottery, but that has also been abandoned for over 100 years; I believe, however, that Isleworth ware is still valued by collectors.

St. Margaret's, now a purely residential district lying between Isleworth and Twickenham, is, as we have seen, where the original Syon Monastery was situated, and where, before its foundation, as Stow tells us in his *Survey of London:* " Simon de Montfort with the barons pitched their tents in Thistleworth Park."

It was one of de Montfort's adherents who celebrated in verse the sacking of the Palace at Isleworth (referred to earlier) and of the claim for £30,000 compensation, mentioned in the lines:

" Thirtti thousent pound asked he
For to make the pees in the countrie."

These verses were said to be the first in which the Norman vernacular was introduced, for hitherto all the minstrels' songs had been in Saxon, and Bishop Percy claims that this poem marks the beginnings of a new era in English poesy, which certainly gives Isleworth a place in an interesting byway of our literature.

A more recent mansion in St. Margaret's, of which there is also no trace, was Twickenham Park, usually quoted as having been the " house of Lord Bacon "—though there was no such person in English history. This is not a " point " in the Shakespeare—Bacon Controversy; a little thought will elucidate the " mystery."

Tradition has it that during Lord Verulam's residence here he was actually visited by Shakespeare, though I can find no direct evidence of this.   Possibly Shakespeare, annoyed that Bacon was writing his plays, went to see what was to be done about it! Anyhow, this argument is as sensible as many of the far-fetched Baconian theories.

Bacon lived at Twickenham Park in 1593.   In the British Museum there is a memorandum drawn up by him, which states: " Let Twitham Park, which I sold in my younger days, be purchased for a residence for deserving persons to study in, since I found the situation of that place convenient for the trial of any philosophical conclusions." While living here Bacon wrote his *Essays* and *Novum Organum.*

The house was subsequently occupied by the Countess of Bedford, and here she was visited by well-known poets of the day, including Samuel Daniel, Michael Drayton and John Donne—who refers to it as " Twickenham Garden."

In 1676 Evelyn writes in his *Diary:* " To Twickenham Park, Lord Berkeley's country seat, to examine how the bailiffs and servants ordered matters." It was from here in the early part of the seventeenth century that David Winckebooms painted his well-known landscapes of the Thames Valley.   One is of Twickenham Park, with Morris-dancers and hobbyhorses in the foreground.

The " few notes " about Isleworth seem to have become rather elastic, and yet I left out a good deal. It is a deceptive place, at a casual glance one might not suspect it had so full a story—but casual glances are unreliable things where the history of bygone Middlesex is concerned; there are always treasures beneath the surface.

CHAPTER XXI.

Where the Population varies from a dozen to fifty thousand in a day.

THE story of the little Middlesex hamlet—it is not large enough to be a village and is not a parish—of Mogden is curious. The average person has never heard of it at all and often thinks you are mispronouncing Morden in Surrey, if you mention it. Yet Mogden has a population (visiting) often numbering over seventy thousand, while its population (resident) can hardly number a dozen.

It lies amidst meadows; it has one picturesque farm, a few cottages in a lane that is all—unless we count an Isolation Hospital hidden amongst the trees and a gravel pit as part of the " amenities " of the place.

I have been in Mogden and pondered on the banks of the small river, a branch of the Crane that forms the " delta," that flows through its fields, and have been as lonely as if I were in the heart of Devonshire, and on another occasion I have been as jostled in those " quiet " lanes as if I were in Piccadilly Circus on Boat Race night.

This anomalous mystery is easily explained, for Mogden lies behind the Rugby Football Ground at Twickenham and its lane is used as a short cut to the tram route to Isleworth—and yet I am certain that among those seventy thousand visitors not a dozen know its name.

The small road leading to Mogden from the Whitton Road has recently been enlarged, it was but a bush-fringed lane a short time ago, and I am always afraid that the place will be " discovered " and laid bare for the Jerry-builder. It is one of the places, were I a millionaire, I would buy just to save—an unheard-of hamlet, still rural and peaceful but eight and a half miles from Marble Arch, is surely worth preservation. Yet I know full well—fools that we are—it will soon be swept away by the devastating hand of " progress."

Mogden is not marked on most maps of the county and Thorne in *Environs of London* and Walford in *Greater London* ignore it completely, so we may assume that it was as unknown fifty years ago as it is to-day.

Not far away is Worton, almost as unknown to the general public, but quite a " metropolis " compared with tiny Mogden, for Worton boasts of a village street with two inns, one which bears a sign that I cannot remember having seen anywhere else—The Labouring Boys. Oak Farm, a typical red-roofed eighteenth century farmhouse, is a pleasing feature in this village, which, however, is more notable for three fine country mansions still standing in its borders—but for how long?

There are mentions both by Thorne and Walford in accounts alike in wording though different in detail. Here they are. Thorne says: " Worton was a royal manor till Henry VI. gave it to Sion monastery. It is now the property of the Duke of Northumberland. Worton Manor House, a good modern mansion, in the Worton Road, midway between Isleworth and Hounslow, was at the close of the last century the residence of Colonel Fullerton." While Walford tells us: " Worton Hall, in Worton Road, midway between Isleworth and Hounslow, is a modern mansion and perpetuates the Manor, once a royal manor, which was granted by Henry VI. to the Monastery of Sion. In some records it is called the 'Manor of Eystons,' thus perpetuating the name of a family which for three generations in the fourteenth century resided here."

In the *Catalogue of Ancient Deeds* we read: " In the second year of the reign of Edward IV. there was a grant by Richard Sunbury of Houndeslowe, Co. Middlesex, husbandman, to Wm. Yorke, Gentleman, of land: 'part at le merehegge abutting westward on the road leading from Worton to Kyngiston, and part in Worton in Langfurlange abutting on le Short-furlange.' "

Both these houses mentioned are here still, though which is on the site of the original manor I am not certain, but my personal " vote " is for Worton Hall. There is another old house nearby, and all three of about the same period of the eighteenth century.

The Manor House—I was sorry to see a board up announcing it is for sale—stands at the corner of a road from which it and its fine range of stabling are effectively screened by a high hedge round the grounds. Next to it is Worton Court, distinguishable by its turret. The fronts of both houses are all that can be seen, but they are enough to suggest that the backs may be even more picturesque.

Worton Hall, a few minutes further along the road, can be seen clearly by any passer-by, and it is worth stopping to see. It is one of the finest types of period architecture—late eighteenth century. In every sense it is typical of its age, both in the building and in the lawn in front with its fine cedar-tree in the centre.

At the rear are film studios, and if they ever want a scene for a " costume film " here it is ready to hand without any setting needed, a chance which has already been utilised, probably. I remember once standing by that gate for nearly an hour peopling the old place with visions of my imagination—as real to me as if I had seen them on the screen—in fact, more so than a good many impossible ones I have seen at " the pictures." The mental ones conjured up by this fine old Middlesex country mansion were vivid; I have seen a post-chaise or a yellow barouche with its bewigged postillions drive up to this old pillared doorway and have observed " My Lady " descend with her high-powdered hair and hooped dress of fine brocade, handed down by her escort garbed in a flowered coat and silken breeches.

Then the scene would shift, a few years pass by, and I would see the old house as it was in the Regency days; a meeting-place of the dashing Corinthians and the Bucks of those stirring times; and even a solitary highwayman prowling round would sometimes come into the picture, for at one time this old mansion stood on the fringe of the Heath.

Yes, they were vivid pictures by that gate, and I am afraid that I have at times stood there, lost in " past-dreams," long enough to incur suspicions as to my motive, for it is no new thing for me to find that one who comes to steal so innocent a thing as an impression may be misunderstood by the unimaginative. I once saw that I was very curiously watched by three or four " hobbledehoys." I spoke to them, asking some question or other in connection with the house; of course they knew nothing of what I wanted to know, but they looked sheepish and drew away suspiciously. When I passed them later in the village street I say them eyeing me as they whispered together. I expect it was a matter of surprise to them not to hear that Worton Hall was not visited by a "cat burglar" that night. "For, after all, as I ses to 'Arry, I ses, wot was 'e o doin' of standin' there lookin' at the 'ouse for over an 'our if 'e weren't tryin' to find aht 'ow to break in? Why, I even seed 'im go a peepin' rahnd the back arterwards. I reckon we scared 'im orf"—and the cute fellows probably looked upon themselves as guardians of the village.

Worton has lately been "blessed" with two marks of progress, a sewage farm (why they are always called "farms" is one of the mysteries of nomenclature) and a building estate, which are, frankly, ruining this former old-world spot. I'm sorry to end on a note of tragedy—for each time one of these Middlesex villages is spoiled beyond any possible chance of recovery it *is* a very real tragedy—but I am compelled to speak the horrid truth.

CHAPTER XXII.

How a noble Duke made the desert smile where now Jerry the Builder is doing his horrid worst—and how I missed the Bloody Post.

WHITTON, though one end of it is now almost part of Hounslow, still contains enough of individuality to make it worth the exploring. Traces of its old village life luckily still linger, and have defied the builder, who has, however, nevertheless done his best to spoil the place. The lane down by the old Manor House, itself recently renovated and "improved," is even now threatened with a row of shops, which, by the time these words are in print, will be a horrid reality.

The chief interest in the past in Whitton lay in its famous seats; indeed, this is true to-day, though one has been altered beyond recognition and the other two swept away altogether.

As one approaches Whitton along the road from Twickenham, a large mansion is to be seen on the right, whose extensive outbuildings, as the corner is turned, give the clue, even to a stranger, that this is no longer an ordinary house, and at times discordant sounds greet the ear.

In fact, any nervous traveller, unacquainted with the district, passing here in the dark, might well suppose it to be the home of "witches and warlocks at a dance," judging by the weird noises that issue therefrom—suggestive of a competition between wailing nuns and other ghostly visitants and a cats' concert on the tiles. This is nothing more alarming, however, than a reminder that this place is a Home of Harmony, and the sounds are but different brass instruments being played in different keys in different rooms during practice time. For this building is Kneller Hall, now the Royal Military School of Music, where bandsmen are trained.

Once known as Whitton House, it is an imposing building rather after Wren's style. though not designed by him. It was built by Sir Godfrey Kneller, as a summer residence, in 1710. The famous artist, court painter to four monarchs, spent much time and money on it, even taking a hand himself in assisting Louis Laguerre to paint the hall and staircase, once the chief internal glory of the house. Little remains now, however, of the original building except the front.

Kneller lived here for many years, and here he died. He was a churchwarden and a J.P. for Middlesex, doing his duty as a country squire with as much enthusiasm as he painted pictures, among which were the famous Hampton Court beauties and the Kit-Kat Club portraits. He was born at Lubeck, in Germany, and first rose to fame by his portrait of Charles II.; created a baronet by George I., he died at Whitton House in 1723.

Many anecdotes are told of Kneller—who had all the eccentricities of genius—during his residence in the village. He was, too, a man of inordinate vanity, and it has been said that he " bragged more, spelt worse and painted better " than any artist of his day.

Kneller's neighbour was Dr. Ratcliffe, the well-known physician, and the two were friendly, till a quarrel arose in a curious way. A door was made between the two gardens to allow more ready access for visits to each other. Kneller found, however, that the Doctor's servants picked his flowers, so he sent word to Ratcliffe that he intended to nail up the door. " Tell him that he may do anything he likes to it but paint it," was the angry doctor's reply, to which the artist retorted, " Well, he may say what he will, for tell him, that I will take anything from him except his medicine."

Dr. Ratcliffe had a great objection to paying bills. A gardener who had done some work at Whitton, after many fruitless attempts to get his account settled, caught the doctor in a chaise at his own door and demanded the liquidation of his debt. " Why, you rascal," cried Ratcliffe, " do you pretend to be paid for such a piece of work? You have spoiled my flower-bed and then covered it over with earth to hide your bad work!" " Doctor," replied the gardener, " mine is not the only bad work the earth hides!" " You dog, you," returned Ratcliffe, " are you a wit? Then you must be poor; come in and you shall be paid."

As a magistrate, Kneller's ideas of Justice were original—but perhaps not altogether wrong. The most quoted instance of this is his discharging a starving wretch who had stolen a leg of mutton and giving an opulent butcher a stern lecture for dragging the fellow before him, when it was proved in evidence that the butcher had taunted the poor man upon his ragged condition in comparison with his own well-fed sleekness.

This incident was commented upon by Pope in his *Imitations of Horace:*
" Faith in such case if you should prosecute,
I think Sir Godfrey should decide the suit,
Who sent the thief who stole the cash away,
And punish'd him that put it in his way."

Pope, his neighbour at Twickenham, was a close friend of Kneller, and paid frequent visits to the artist; and when such characters met, it is not to be wondered at, that many of the tales told of happenings at Whitton House should centre round these two men of genius. On one of his visits here, it is related that Pope, in an ironical tone, was congratulating Kneller on the great improvement in his works over those of Nature, and regretted his absence from the Creation. Kneller was equal to the thrust and parried it quickly, with a glance at the misshapen little figure of the poet, remarking, " Well, yes, I think I should have made some little things better."

On one occasion, however, the vanity was taken out of both of them, by Kneller's nephew, a Guinea trader, as the three sat in the Whitton garden. " Nephew," remarked Sir Godfrey, modestly, " you have the honour of seeing the two greatest men in the world, before you now," with a wave of his hand, indicating Pope and himself. " I don't know how great you may be," replied the Guinea man, " but I don't like your looks.

Why, I have often bought a man better than both of you together, all muscles and bones, for ten guineas."

Art and Artists, James Elmes' old fashioned book of anecdotes gives a dream related by Kneller to Pope and other guests at Whitton House. "Last night," he told them, and the story reflects his vanity, "I had an odd sort of dream. I dreamt I was dead and found myself in a narrow path between two mountains. Before me I saw a door and a number of people about it. I went on towards it and when I got nearer I could distinguish St. Peter by his keys, with some others of the apostles; they were admiring the people as they came in. When I joined the company I saw several seats at a little distance. As the first approached for admittance St. Peter asked his name and religion. "I am a Roman Catholic " replied the spirit. "Then sit down on the right hand " said St. Peter.

"The next was a Presbyterian; he was admitted after the usual questions and told to sit opposite. My turn came next and St. Peter very civilly asked me my name. I said it was Kneller, whereupon St. Luke, who was standing by, turned and said, ' What! the famous Sir Godfrey Kneller from England ? ' ' The very same, sir ' said I, ' at your service.' On this St. Luke embraced me and made me a great many compliments on the art we had both practised in this world; he entered so far into .the subject that he forgot the business for which I came. At last, however, he recollected himself and said ' I beg your pardon, Sir Godfrey; I was so taken up with the pleasure of conversing with you; but, apropos, pray sir, what religion are you ? ' ' Why truly, sir,' says I, ' I am of no religion.' ' Oh, sir,' says he, ' will you be so good then as to sit where you please?' "

According to Pope Kneller's vanity clung to him to the last, for when the poet came to visit his friend two days before his death, he says he found him sitting up in bed contemplating a design he had made for an elaborate tombstone for himself. It was upon this occasion that the following conversation is said to have occurred : " Mr. Pope was sitting by Sir Godfrey's bedside, and seeing him so impatient at the thought of going, told him he had been a very good man and no doubt would go to a better place." " Ah my friend, Mr. Pope," said he " I wish God would let me stay at Whitton."

There was some doubt as to where Kneller actually was buried. The monument in Westminster Abbey (whether the one he was designing on his deathbed or not, I do not know) has led many to believe that he was interred there; but that is not so. It is said that he refused burial in the Abbey with the remark " They do bury such fools there," and that he asked to be buried in his Whitton garden and that this was accordingly done; but Cobbett, in his *Memorials of Twickenham,* says that no trace of the grave even was found there—and it is hardly likely to be unmarked. The monument now in the Abbey was originally at Twickenham Church, and it is now generally considered that he was buried there after all.

Kneller's epitath was composed by Pope, who described it as the worst thing he ever wrote, but the first two lines are good:

" Kneller, by Heaven, and not a master taught,
  Whose Art was Nature, and whose pictures thought."

Pope was not the only poet who mentioned Kneller, and the others include Dryden, Prior, Addison, Steele and Tickell.

Charles Knight tells us in his *Old England:* " The news of the landing of the Prince of Orange was brought to him (James II.) as he sat to Kneller for his portrait, which was to be given to Pepys, but, instead of hurrying away, he bade the artist finish the picture, that his friend might not be disappointed.   This is about the most graceful incident we can remember of James's history."   Another account states that this occurred at Whitton, which was so convenient to the Hounslow Camp, but this is obviously wrong, as Whitton House was not built at that time.

John Smith, the celebrated mezzotint engraver, who died at the age of ninety in 1742, was frequently employed by Kneller and lived for some time with him at Whitton.   Some interesting details of Kneller's life here will be found in F. C. Hodgson's *Thames Side in the Past*.

After Kneller's death, the mansion passed into the possession of Sir Samuel Prime, and in 1847 it became a Normal Training School, of which Dr. Temple, afterwards Archbishop of Canterbury, was Principal.   In 1857 it was purchased by the Government for its present purpose.

Although little of Kneller's original house is left, the place is still worth a visit, for the grounds are still beautiful, especially that part at the back of the estate, where the River Crane has been widened out with most telling effect to form some of the prettiest views—of which this river has many— in its course as it winds through Middlesex.

The history of the other big estate in the village is, perhaps, even more interesting.   This is (or was, unfortunately) Whitton Place, which was built, soon after Kneller Hall, by the Duke of Argyll.   The grounds were extensive and mostly taken from Hounslow Heath by a special grant from the Crown.   He spent large sums in improving his estate and planting it with Scotch firs and cedars of Lebanon, and other exotics, some of which survive to this day.   A description of these Whitton trees can be found in Gilpin's *Forest Scenery*.

The Duke was sneered at, as a " treemonger," by Horace Walpole, whose prejudiced mind could not bear to think of any garden in comparison with his own at Strawberry Hill—albeit a wonderful spot.   Walpole, however, had to own that we are indebted to this Whitton garden for the introduction of many foreign trees and shrubs into England.   Almost every tree here was raised from seeds planted in 1725, in a special nursery the Duke maintained on the Hounslow Road, where he raised a large Chinese summer-house.

There is still to be seen in the Park a delightful old walled garden, with a fish pond in the centre, which I am told was one of the places where the Duke reared some of the rarer plants that adorned his estate.

Argyll's arboriculture, however, did not escape the wits of the day, and the following verse—which Pinkerton curiously enough attributes to Walpole, who never wrote it, though he expressed himself especially diverted by it—was once the " laugh of the town ":

> " Old Islay, to show his fine delicate taste
> In improving his garden, purloin'd from the waste,
> Bade his gard'ner one day to open his views
> By cutting a couple of grand avenues:
> No particular prospect his lordship intended,
> But left it to chance how his walks should be ended.
> With transport and joy he beheld his first view end
> In a favourite prospect—a church, that was ruin'd:
> But alas, what a sight did the next cut exhibit,
> At the end of a walk, hung a rogue on a gibbet.
> He beheld it and wept, for it caused him to muse on

> Full many a Campbell who died with his shoes on.
> All amazed and aghast at this ominous scene,
> He ordered it quick to be closed up again,
> With a clump of Scotch firs that would serve as a screen."

The ruined church was that of Twickenham, lately damaged in a storm. The writer was the Rev. James Bramston—author of *The Man of Taste*—who called his effort *An Epigram on Lord Islay's Garden at Whitton.*

In spite of the wits—or because of them—the Duke's house became the centre of the fashionable life of the day. The grounds were finely laid out and adorned with the statuary so loved as garden decorations by eighteenth century folk; and, of course, with plenty of sham ruins. These last were almost a religion with the old-time landscape gardeners; and I have known cases where genuine antiquities have actually been removed to erect them. There was, too, a Gothic Tower, the remains of which existed until quite recently in romantic desolation.

" Among other monuments," runs one account, " was a celebrated group in marble by Gabriel Cibber; the figure of a Highland piper and his dog. It represents the piper described by Defoe in his *Journal of the Plague Year*, as taken up for dead and carried off to his burial in the dead-cart, but awakened from his trance just as he was about to be thrown into the pit, sitting up in a cart and playing on his pipes, to the great affright of all present, after which he recovered. The group was, in later years, removed to the Gardens of Stowe."

The only remains of the former lavish display of statuary are the medallions to the gateway to Argyll Lodge, which (though the ironwork is new) are the original ones that adorned this gate in the days of the Duke.

A good account of the Duke's house and grounds that is worth attention deserves parting mention; it is in *The Description of Middlesex* (1775) —and afterwards the writer adds that he " finds nothing remarkable or worthy of mention till he reached Staines." All I can say is he must have been mighty unobservant.

The later history of this estate is concisely told by Thorne, when he writes: " After the Duke's death, the house changed hands more than once and the trees and plants were mostly removed: the choicest were transplanted to Kew Gardens about 1762. The property was at length purchased by Mr. Gostling, who divided the grounds into two parts, reserving one in which was the Grand Conservatory, which he converted into a villa for himself; the other, with the Duke's house, he sold to Sir William Chambers (the architect of Somerset House).

" Whitton Place in the hands of Chambers underwent many alterations. He converted the house into an Italian villa, and laid out the gardens with fish ponds, orange groves and aviaries. After Chambers' death, the property was re-purchased by the Gostling family, and was for a while the residence of Sir Benjamin Hobhouse, M.P. After Hobhouse vacated it Whitton Place was taken down and the grounds united again with Whitton Park, as Gostling had named his part of the estate.

" Nothing is left of Chambers' (i.e., the Duke's) house; that which was built on the site and partly out of the Duke's conservatory, is the seat of Miss Gostling. The park is large and fairly wooded. In it are two good sheets of water and a tower. The firs and cedars, now 150 years old, are magnificent." In *Peeps into Gardens about Twickenham*, by Mrs. Hampden.

Pye, a quaint and rambling (in more senses than one) book written in 1775, there is a good description of this house and gardens.

Those who would read more of Chambers, for his story is an interesting one both in and out of Whitton, are advised to read the chapter on him in Beresford Chancellor's *Lives of British Architects* and Trystan Edwards' Monograph on the same subject.

Whether it was the Duke's Chinese Summer-house that attracted Chambers to the place I do not know, but it is certainly not an impossible conjecture; for Pinkerton tells us: " In early life, Sir William Chambers made a voyage to China and was ever afterwards impressed with the beauties of the Chinese style of gardening. With these views, he built the Pagoda in Kew Gardens and wrote a *Dissertation on Oriental Gardening.*" Here, again, the wits of the day had another ' smack ' at an owner of Whitton Place, for very soon after appeared a reply with a ' snappy ' title of *An Heroic Epistle to Sir William Chambers, Kt., Comptroller-General of His Majesty's Works, and Author of a late Dissertation on Oriental Gardening, enriched with explanatory Notes, chiefly extracted from that elaborate Performance.* This was written by William Mason:

" Now to our lawns of dalliance and delight,
Join we the groves of horror and affright;
This to achieve, no foreign aids we try,
Thy gibbets, Bagshot, shall our wants supply;
Hounslow, whose heath sublimer terror fills,
Shall with her gibbets lend her powder-mills."

The sentence in the *Dissertation,* to which these lines apply, with reference to China, are: " There scenes of terror are composed of gloomy woods, gibbets, crosses, wheels and the whole apparatus of torture are seen from the roads. Here, too, they conceal in cavities, on the summits of the highest mountains, foundaries, lime-kilns, and glass-works, which send forth volumes of flame and continued columns of thick smoke, that give to the mountains the appearance of volcanoes."

This was enough for the satirist, who suggested that Hounslow Heath could supply all that China could in this way, and adds: " Now, to produce both these effects, viz., the appearance of volcanoes and earthquakes, we have substituted the occasional explosion of a powder-mill, which (if there be not too much simplicity in the contrivance) it is apprehended will at once answer all the purposes if lime-kilns and electrical machines, and imitate thunder and the explosions of cannon into the bargain."

Hounslow Heath, in the old days, was certainly nothing if not versatile. To return to the estate. The account quoted was written in 1870. and further drastic changes have occurred in the intervening half-century. The house of Whitton Park is now itself demolished (some twenty-five years hence) and most of its grounds cut up. Part of the gardens of the " Argyll-cum-Chambers-cum-Gostling " estates are, however, still preserved. The owners of the property are very sensibly, and with a fine public-spirited thought, trying to save them from being built over. They are now a private park, to which the public are admitted by favour. Much of the place is left wild and beautiful woodland, and forms an ideal pleasaunce, for here are some of the original trees planted by the Duke, and camping in the meadows and woods is allowed. There are tennis-courts for those who want them and the lake has been cleaned for bathing.

Since this was written changes are in the air; Whitton Park is threat-

DICK TURPIN AND TOM KING:
Two Famous "Heroes" of the Heath.

Block lent by Middlesex Chronicle

ened by the builder, though some efforts are being made to save it. If it is lost it will be a loss that Whitton may well mourn.

It is, of course, rather more civilised now than it was a few years ago, when, by an act of delightful trespass, I first explored these grounds; it was then a piece of the wild, and I was not surprised to learn, subsequently, that it had been filmed for a scene in an African jungle—and this but nine miles from London. The impression is still very vivid in my mind of the sense of loneliness and solitude I felt as I stood in the dusk of a summer evening by that lake and watched the last hues of sunset fade away through the wodlands over the water—it might well have been an African forest in reality, instead of pretence.

There have been, I am told, some half-dozen films taken in Whitton Park; in addition to the African jungle, a Chinese lake-village, complete with junks, and an old-English village church, built only to be set on fire, have each had their passing existence in these old Middlesex woods.

Recently as a contrast to the make-believe romances of Whitton Park a real life one has been seen here, in the form of a Gipsy Wedding, in true Romany style, such as would have delighted the heart of George Borrow.

In *The Romances of Whitton Park* (which appeared in the Jubilee Number of the *Middlesex Chronicle*) we have a true story, with the delicate flavour of an old-time novel, of the one-time heiress to these fair lands. I wish space allowed for its reproduction—a precis of it would ruin it.

I hope the scheme to save this Park succeeds; it deserves to, as such ideas of preservation are all too rare in these days of vandalism. It is certainly a place for memories, and I have sat on the ruins of the Gothic Tower—like a rural edition of Macaulay's New Zealander—and dreamed of past days in this fine old place which I should be very sorry to see ever disturbed by the spoiling hand of Jerry, the Builder. Argyle House, with its fine gardens, is their latest victim.

Other notable residents of Whitton include Sir John Suckling, the seventeenth century poet, who was born here in 1609. This accomplished person succeeded to the residence of his father at Whitton, and passed much of his short life in the retirement of the village. Vincent Corbet, father of Bishop Corbet, once had a nursery here; he is buried at Twickenham and his epitaph is by Ben Johnson, who wrote of him in his poem *Underwoods:*

" He has a mind as pure and neatly kept,
As were his nurseries, and swept
So of uncleanness or offence
That never came ill odour hence."

Suckling has one minor niche in the Temple of Fame, as he is credited, according to the D.N.B., of being the inventor of Cribbage!

It was in a farmhouse at Whitton that Dr. Dodd, the eighteenth century divine and author of the *Beauties of Shakespeare*, was in hiding when he was caught and subsequently hanged for forgery, in spite of the unavailing efforts of Dr. Johnson, and other influential people, to save him. An old account of Dr. Dodd contains the illuminating statement among the category of his misdeeds that " he once sank so low as to become the editor of a newspaper."

Wilkes, in his poem *Hounslow Heath,* had perforce to mention Whitton, since it is dedicated to the chief resident in the village, the Duke of Argyll. We do not learn a great deal, however, from these verses, though the following lines are not without interest:

> " Four large patrician elms behind the town
> (True as a beacon to the trav'ller known)
> Their lofty boughs with ancient pride display,
> And to fair Whitton point the cheerful way
> Whitton demands her verse—the Nine conspire,
> To swell my numbers with poetic fire."

These old elms were once famous landmarks on the Western road, and Pinkerton, writing in 1870, in his notes on the poem, says: " I have often fondly thought that the two old elms, still standing opposite the Bell public-house at Hounslow, were the remnants of those trees. But Wilkes expressly states that they were ' behind the town,' and according to Rocque's map of 1754 they were about thirty yards down Bell Lane on the way to Whitton." Bricks and mortar have long since swept away all traces of these venerable trees, unless the suggestion that those in the garden of Alverstone House, just behind the Bell, are the ones. They seem hardly in the right position; though possibly they are contemporary.

Whitton, chiefly on account of its famous inhabitants, is usually given a passing paragraph in most old topographical books, sometimes rather carelessly compiled, I am afraid, as in the case of *A Picture of Places near London*, 1803, which misinforms us: " Whitton Park is another of the numerous houses of Middlesex which deserve to be visited by the stranger, having been inhabited by two eminent artists, Sir Godfrey Kneller and Sir William Chambers, each of whom exercised his professional skill in the embellishments of the house and garden." Neither of these artistes, however, happened to have lived at Whitton Park; the former lived at Whitton *House*, and the latter at Whitton *Place*. It is, I must confess, a little confusing at first to have three houses as near in name as they were in proximity, and the casual paragrapher may perhaps be excused.

Whitton Church, though modern, with little to interest the rambler, is not unpicturesquely situated in a tree-clad " island " at the junction of two roads, one leading to the Lord Nelson Inn, near which are one or two other houses that speak of the former village days, though these buildings are rather swamped by modern ones.

In *The Book of Oddities* is a reference to an estate, said to have been situated between Twickenham and Whitton (though I can find no trace of it now) named Pepper Park, which was held on an extraordinary tenure— a man left it to his son on condition that he did not grow a moustache— if he did so, he was to forfeit the estate. Nor was this in some dim forgotten age, but within living memory, in 1862.

Whitton Woods are now no more, their last outpost has succumbed to the builder and the only trees remaining are now in the back gardens; yet, if my memory serves me rightly, they were extensive and lonely enough, even since the Great War, to rise to the notoriety of a murder—so they, at least, ended their days with the some fame as was theirs when they were once part of Hounslow Heath and the scene of nightly terror.

I was told a story concerning one of the few trees still remaining at one end of the building estate: in the trunk was found embedded some lengths of old wire rope, and this was said to have been used to hang the last highwayman on the Heath. You may believe this if you please; but was *wire* rope ever used for this purpose? And, moreover, would Tyburn be robbed of a " spectacle " by the hanging of a knight of the road with no one to look on but a few villagers?

Murder and suicide would seem to have been centenary events in Whitton, for just about one hundred years later (in 1869) we find a note in the parish records: "The Vestry expressed their sympathy with the family of the late Mr. Kyezor, of Whitton, who for years had taken great interest in the village. This gentleman was cruelly murdered by one of his tenants, Thomas Haydon Green, aged eighty-two, who committed suicide immediately after his vindictive act. Green (whose real name was Edwards) was the man who revealed the intentions of Thistlewood and the Cato Street Conspirators to Lord Harrowby in 1820."

I am indebted to Mr. Dudley Barton, of Sussex Cottage, who formerly lived in the "Murder Cottage," for some interesting details of this building, which still stands in the village and to which still clings a faint odour of this crime of long ago. They tell me in the village of a lane at the back of Kneller Hall formerly known as "Cut Throat Lane," on account of the murder of a girl by a soldier. If this crime is fact or legend I do not know; but I have come across numerous "Cut Throat Lanes," which is usually a corruption of "Cut Through Lane," or a short cut. I hate to spoil a gory story, but it is probably the real explanation of the name—I rather fancy the soldier and the girl were invented to fit it.

In his book on Twickenham R. S. Cobbett has one or two interesting notes about Whitton, among which we find: "It is situate about a mile and a half from Twickenham and on the edge of Hounslow Heath. By the Isleworth Survey, anno 1635, there appear to have been several warrens planted by Sir Robert Brett, Sir Simond Harvey and Sir Humphrey Line, also another planted, and a capital house begun by a Mr. Gromesditch, and finished by Sir H. Line. It appears to be called the Warren House in the Survey; and this land is said to be very stony; the country is flat.

"A small stream runs through it, called Burketts Brook, over which is an ancient bridge called Whitne Bridge. This brook comes from the Uxbridge river, passes under Twickenham Bridge to the Thames at Isleworth. This brook is the River Crane. Whitton was a notorious resort for the highwaymen who in the old days infested Hounslow Heath. Horace Walpole mentions a gentleman who was robbed there at one in the afternoon. A footpad after his death, having attained unenviable celebrity, lay in state here."

In the old parish records there is mention of a certain curiously named field in the village: "In 1678 Edward Adams and two others were admitted to two acres called the Bull Land, lying in Whitton, near Shoemakers' Pray . . . upon trust to maintain a sufficient bull for the common use of the inhabitants. There is no trace of this land later than 1705, when it is supposed it was merged into some other estate, though I believe a certain payment is still made on its account. Even more curious is the name "Shoemakers' Pray," though its derivation seems to be lost.

* * * * * *

A final and personal story to end this chapter may not be without interest—or humour. I read in Lysons, and several other books, including *The Exeter Road*, a paragraph that roused my curiosity:

"THE BLOODY POST ON HOUNSLOW HEATH.

"On the Heath between Whitton and Hounslow is a post commonly known by the name of The Bloody Post. It is thus described on each of its four sides: 'Buried here, with a stake drove through his body, is the wicked murderer John Proctor, who cut the throats of his wife and child and then poisoned himself. July 6th, 1765.' Underneath is a bloody hand grasping a knife."

Well, they buried him at four cross-roads, with a stake through his inside, in the approved fashion of the day, and this post, with its gory "illustrated" account of the tragedy, became the "thriller" of the district. I have since found it marked, under its gory name, on several old maps, and though all traces of this grim memorial have long since gone, I thought I would try and ascertain if a memory of it still existed in the minds of any local worthies who might be qualifying for the honour of being the Oldest Inhabitant.

So one day when I met a greybeard in the village street who looked eligible for that qualification, I asked him, "Do you happen to know the whereabouts of the Bloody Post?"

He glanced at an envelope I held, upon which I had written a few notes, but evinced no surprise at my question and replied, 'Why, yes, sir, you can't mistake it; it's down the road next to the butchers."

Here was luck indeed, I thought, and hurried off wondering how I came to miss such a thing. I found it all right, just as my old friend had said, standing up by the roadside, painted a bright blood-red—the village pillar-box!

CHAPTER XXIII.

Passes from the peace of Queens' Gardens to a place that caused Hounslow to be known among the Big Noises.

LIKE many Middlesex villages, the chief attractions of Hanworth lie away from that part through which the high road passes; in this case but a cluster of cottages, one or two shops, and The Brown Bear and the Oxford Arms.

Perhaps the most pleasant way to approach Hanworth is from the Hounslow side and to turn down a lane by the old-world little inn, The Jolly Sailor—though what a sailor found to be jolly about when this inn was named, in an inland spot "sacred" to soldiers and highwaymen, is more than I can imagine. At the end of the lane in question the rambler will find himself on a green opposite the church and the picturesque old Tudor Court.

In the "old" days of a few years ago there was a footpath walk across the Park to Feltham, and a very pleasant way it was, too; this walk is still there, but sadly changed; it is a dusty lane bordered by a high fence.

Writing in 1893, H. S. Vaughan, in *The Way About Middlesex,* says of this spot: "The view on entering the gate is delightful, the ponds on the right, with the overhanging trees and patches of water-lilies, reflect the graceful forms of the lofty elms in front of the church, whose picturesque lych-gate and half-hidden spire are pleasing sights."

There are no ponds now, nothing but an uncultivated piece of waste land, though probably in a transition stage, and with a little care it could still be a very beautiful spot, in spite of the sad felling of some of the fine old trees in the vicinity—not those near the church, luckily.

It is here the main interest of Hanworth lies. The church, prettily situated, replaced an ancient structure in 1685, and will not detain the wanderer long. The old church-house is gone too, at least I could not find any signs of it, which is quaintly mentioned in the Chantry Roll for Middlesex of 1547 as being "used for the assembly of persons to dryncke thereat and to gather money for the reparacion of the Church."

An even older building now claims our attention near the lych-gate. This is now known as Tudor Court, but it is the old stables of that place mentioned by Camden when he speaks of the "delicious champaign about Hanworth which so pleased King Henry VIII. that he made a hunting-box there."

Until quite recently it was picturesquely derelict, with a rather neglected air, but all this is altered now. A few years ago it was restored and converted into residences, with good taste and an eye for the artistic that is commendable; while the old-world courtyard gardens are exceedingly beautiful. Where these end and "Queen Elizabeth's Gardens" begin I am not sure, nor does it matter, as they are equally delightful. The latter are attached to the mansion on the estate, Tudor House. About this it is kinder to say little; its name is a complete misnomer, it is a large and ugly mid-Victorian structure, built in 1873, and looks it. Set in so wonderful a garden, it seems like a Profiteer in Fairyland.

Writing in 1875, Thorne, in his *Environs of London,* says: "The grounds, now called Queen Elizabeth's Gardens, retain much of their old-world character, and contain old yews, pines and cedars, ponds and waterfalls, but the property is now announced for sale, and may become the prey of the builder." History repeats itself, for though it has survived this last risk for over fifty years, it is again in danger; much has already been built on and most of the remainder is "ripe for building." I should imagine that the Tudor Gardens are safe—though you can never be certain of anything nowadays. The speculative builder would willingly line the road to Heaven with semi-detached villas if he thought he could make a profit.

The building that succeeded Tudor House—and the original Hanworth Park—was not the oldest one on the estate. This was on the orchard island, still surrounded by a moat; a very delightful spot, but there is nothing left of this old building—known as Hanworth Castle—though it is possible to make out a few remains of the ancient drawbridge.

Legend has it that the castle was originally built by the Danes, who made the moat. The latter may be true enough; we know they made moats round their camps in other parts of Middlesex, but that they built a castle is unlikely; the Danes were not great builders, their methods were rather those of "pirate than pioneer." Hanworth Castle was probably Norman, or even Saxon, and out of its remains was built the hunting-box of Henry VIII. It was finally destroyed by fire in 1797, although even by that time it had been so altered that little of the original structure remained.

There is an excellent ground plan of the old buildings at Hanworth to be seen in the *Victoria County History of Middlesex,* Vol. 2. For some occult reason Vol. 1 is not yet published.

When I came upon this wonderful garden and saw it as a vista through an open doorway in an old wall—one of the happiest ways of discovering such a place—I felt rather like Alice in Wonderland when she saw the garden through the small door, with the difference that I could, and did, go through at once. Trespass? Possibly, but I would willingly have spent

a night in a police cell for my " crime " than have missed the thrill of this
discovery.   I sat on a seat and smoked a reflective pipe, peopling in my
imagination this old-world pleasaunce with those folk of bygone days who
walked here.

Two ladies passed and eyed me (as an interloper) rather curiously, but
they did not speak. Soon after a man came up and asked, quite courteously,
what I was doing—I said I had come in to steal.   Instead of appearing
shocked, he laughed and asked what I hoped to get; when I replied " Impressions " he was quick-witted enough to understand, and said he could
aid and abet me.

He proved to be the estate bailiff, and may I often be caught in the
sin of trespass with such happy results.   It was he who showed me the
remains of the old drawbridge over the moat, as we went to explore the
site of the ancient castle, among other interesting things, not the least of
which was the old stone coat of arms of the Duke of St. Albans—a former
owner—which one day will, I hope, be restored to its proper place over the
main gateway to the courtyard.

My friendly captor even took me on to the roof of the modern house
to show me the bird's-eye view of the old Tudor Court, and a panorama it
was, and gave one quite a different impression of the place than when seen
from the ground level.

At the end of our tour, instead of " seeing me off the premises," as a
privileged trespasser he showed a fine and rare tact. We had reached the
old gardens and had said " Good-bye," when he added, " I disturbed your
dreams before, and now, with a little more added to your knowledge of
this place, perhaps you would like to combine them; so I will leave you
alone. Don't hurry away." And he went off and left me once more with
my visions. Again, I say, a rare tact.

*   *   *   *   *   *

Before we go on to explore the newer Hanworth Park, which has very
little historical importance in comparison with the original estate, it will,
perhaps, be interesting to take our minds back into the past to the
beginnings of the manor.

In his *History of Middlesex*, written in 1816, Brewer says " Hanworth
is a small and rural village on the south-west of the dreary flat of
Hounslow," which might almost be its description to-day, save for the fact
that the Heath is now cultivated, but the writer has also the most concise
summing-up of the early days of the place when he says " Hanworth appears
in the Domesday Book to be derived from Haen and Worth, signifying a
small village in a wood," which is likely enough.   The actual description
in Domesday is this: " Robert holds the manor, which answers for five
hides, under Earl Roger.   The land is three carucates.   One villane holds
a hide; five others have each a virgate, and there are two cottars.   There
is pasture for the cattle of the village.   The total annual value is 40s.; in
the reign of King Edward the Confessor it was worth 60s.   It was then the
property of Ulf, a domestic servant of the King."

To show how a little knowledge can be a dangerous thing, even in
topography, I was told by a villager that he had heard that Hanworth Park
once " belonged to a housemaid."   It was not until I looked up the
Domesday Book that I understood how the description of Ulf, once a noble
lord atached to the Court, gave rise to the statement.

The owners of the manor up to the thirteenth century are very obscure, but in 1294 it passed from the Hamden family into the possession of Thomas Dayrell. With its various owners for the next two centuries we need not concern ourselves here, their names are long forgotten. In 1519 its real history may be said to begin, for in this year it became the property of the Crown.

George Cavendish, in his *Life of Wolsey,* tells us that the King "had a place and parke at Hanworth for hunting, in which he took great pleasure; and to it the French ambassador and his suite were sent, by the King's desire, there to hunt and spend the day until nighte, whilst a great banquete at Hampton Court was preparing."

Lawsuits are often dry enough things, though occasionally they yield us glimpses of bygone days. This is the case in one, in the reign of Charles II., concerning enclosures at Hanworth. It contains many interesting details of this estate and is known as " An answer filed in Equity respecting the Park and Common of Hanworth in Middlesex." (Reprinted in full in the Transactions of the London and Middlesex Archeological Society, Vol. 1, 1860.)

" The Manor of Hanworth," runs the account, " became the property of the Crown in the reign of Henry VIII., and was the occasional residence of either himself or of his children. In 1528 we find him inviting Cardinal Wolsey to make use of it, on account of the prevalence of the plague.

" Princess Mary was resident here in February, 1538, and again in August, 1543. After King Henry's death the manor was occupied by Queen Katherine (Parr), upon whom it had been settled, in dower; and it was here that she spent, in the summer of 1547, a few happy weeks with her new husband, the Lord Admiral Seymour, the Lady Elizabeth, then fifteen years of age, remaining a member of the family. Here it was that the Lord Admiral indulged in those familiarities with the princess which were afterwards made a grave charge against him: tickling her in her bed, in order to wake her in the morning; and in the garden, cutting her gown, which was of black cloth, into a hundred pieces. It is right, however, to mention that on both occasions the queen was present, and a partaker in the misdemeanour."

In the *Progresses of Queen Elisabeth* these early days at Hanworth are mentioned rather quaintly, when we are told how, " At Hanworth in the garden, Seymour wrated (sic) with her and did cut her gown into a hundred pieces, being black clothes." On another occasion we read how " they tycled (sic) my Lady Elisabeth in the bed."

Although the husband was afterwards held to blame for this horse-play —and it apparently was nothing else—his wife was the instigator of what the *Burleigh Papers* calls " a violent romping scene, before the princess had left her bed." Nowadays we should probably call it a pillow-fight and take no more notice of it, though it got the admiral into hot water subsequently.

" It is clear, then, that whatever Katherine Parr may have in merits, the morals of this widow did not render her a fit duenna to the future Queen of England," writes one historian on these episodes, " happily, however, her stay at Hanworth did not last long after this, for a violent scene took place between the royal step-mother and the princess."

This was not Elizabeth's last visit to Hanworth, however, for in 1578, the Duchess of Somerset entertained her here, when the Queen sat for her portrait to Cornelius Ketel; and again, in 1600, Elizabeth hunted in the park and dined in the mansion with Sir Robert Killigrew. This was nearly fifty years after the pillow-fight; I wonder if she remembered it.

It is the two sons of Sir Robert Killigrew, that give Hanworth its only connection with English literature, but the link is interesting.

In 1605, William, the elder son, was born here. He became gentleman-usher to Charles I. and had command of a troop of horse, which guarded the King's person during the Civil War. His literary fame rests upon three plays, *Selindra, Pandora* and *Ormasdes,* all written in the year 1665, or thereabouts, but now forgotten.

His younger brother, Thomas, was not only more famous, but also more notorious; he was far cleverer than his elder brother and far less respectable. He was born at Hanworth Park in 1612—that is according to most biographies, although Lysons records that he could not find his baptism recorded in the registers, and goes on to state that he had seen in a Bible in a certain library an entry (said to be in the dramatist's own handwriting) to the effect that "he was born at Lothbury, London, on February 7th, 1611."

Anyhow, this does not sever his connection with Hanworth, for even if not actually born at the mansion, he certainly spent his boyhood there. In 1633 he became a page to Charles I., and his best-known play, *The Parson's Wedding,* was popular before the Civil War. After, he resided with the English Court during the Commonwealth, where he wrote several other plays; in fact, his nine plays were all written in a different city.

At the Restoration he returned and was appointed Groom of the Bedchamber by Charles II. He built a theatre where Drury Lane now stands and produced many plays, including some of his own. Like most of the Restoration dramatists, Thomas Killigrew was witty and profligate, two qualities (especially the latter) that seem to have been required in obtaining royal favour from the Merry Monarch.

The story of Hanworth Park in the seventeenth century is so concisely told in the *Answer in Equity,* already quoted, that we may let this document take up the tale once more. "At the beginning of his reign, in the summer of 1603," continues the account, "King James I. paid a visit to Hanworth, and there conferred the honour of knighthood on ten gentlemen. Hanworth became the country seat of one of his Scottish favourites, James Hay, Earl of Carlisle, and in 1627 it was granted by Charles I. to Sir Roger Palmer and Alexander Stafford. These are supposed, by Lysons, to have been trustees for Sir Francis Cottington, another royal favourite, then Chancellor of the Exchequer, and afterwards Lord Treasurer.

"Sir Francis was apparently settled at Hanworth some months before, for in April, 1627, Sir Peter Wiche, Knt., was married at Hanworth to 'Mrs. Jane Meredith, a virgin, and a daughter of Sir William Meredith,' and who was a sister of Lady Cottington.

"In the following year Sir Francis was busy in his improvements at Hanworth, and in a letter to Lord Strafford he describes the growth of a long brick wall about the gardens, and provision for 'a multitude of pheasants, partridges and wild-fowl,' that were to be bred there; the erection of a large room with a fountain and other rare devices, and 'an open gallery painted by the hand of a second Titian'" (Reubens).

"He looked forward," the account continues, "'with glee to the amazement of the barbarous Northern folk' that inhabited that part of Middlesex, when they should see the well-cut hedges and dainty walks."

A foot-note breaks up the story, but it is worth quotation, for it was evidently written in defence of the Middlesex peasantry of Hanworth.

TUDOR COURT, HANWORTH.
Queen Elizabeth's Old Stables, now
modernised.

OLD BRIDGE, CRANFORD PARK. *Photo by Miss Bessell*

From a print of 1857

AFTER THE EXPLOSION.
Hanworth Powder Mills.

" Probably," it tells us, " Sir Francis included *all* his countrymen under the term of Northern barbarians, and was anxious to show them the horticulture he had learnt at Madrid."

" The old porter with a long beard was like to have a good revenue by admitting the strangers that would flock to see these rarities," goes on the story, to which Sir Francis adds a personal touch: " My wife is the principal contriver of all, who with her clothes tucked up, and a staff in her hands, marches from place to place like an Amazon commanding an army."

In 1631 Sir Francis Cottington was created Baron Cottington of Hanworth, a title which expired with him in the year 1653. In 1635 he here entertained Queen Henrietta Maria, as noted in *The Stafford Papers:* " My Lord Cottington, about a fortnight since, entertained the Queen and all her Court at dinner at Hanworth, where she was well pleased. In 1638 he received a grant of free warren and licence to inclose 100 acres within his park."

This was the beginning of a long and bitter controversy between the successors of Lord Cottington and the villagers of Hanworth. The litigation is given in full in the *Transactions* and is interesting reading, but briefly it refers to " a certeyne quantity of comon or waste ground lying open and uninclosed called Hanworth Comon, conteyning 300 acres, the soyle of which did belong to the said Lord Cottington."

The trouble was that Cottington enclosed more than he had licence to do and that the villagers broke down the fences and declared the land still common land, which the subsequent owners of the estate were claiming. Strangely enough, the result of this law-suit is not given in these pages, but as we find in 1750 the then owners of the property paying £6 per annum to the poor in lieu of some portions of the waste enclosed, we may assume a compromise between greedy heirs and angry villagers.

Speaking of the glories of Hanworth, and the alterations, Cottington said of the country folk: " They will wholly neglect the sight of Hocus's dog, and Hocus himself will confess that calves with five legs, and the puppets themselves, will be nothing in comparison with this sight." Walter Jerrold comments on this: " The reference to Hocus (apparently the name of a showman) is curious; it suggests that ' hocus-pocus,' which seems to puzzle the dictionary makers (it is said to be a corruption in the vulgar tongue of the words ' Hoc et corpus ' used in the Mass) may derive from some old-time showman of the time of Charles I. It may be worth noting that recently at an Easter Fair not many miles from Hanworth, a misfortunately abnormal calf, pent in a tiny tent, was drawing the coppers of the curious."

During the Civil War Lord Cottington went to serve the King and his estates were confiscated by the Parliament and subsequently given to the regicide Bradshaw. Cottington died before he recovered the lands, which were, at the Restoration, restored to his cousin and heir, who sold them, in 1670, to Sir Thomas Chamber. By an intermarriage with the Chamber family it became the property of Lord Vere Beauclerk, Baron Vere of Hanworth. From this nobleman it descended to his son, Aubrey, Duke of St. Albans, of whom Horace Walpole wrote plaintively from Strawberry Hill to Sir Thomas Mann, in 1791: " The Duke of St. Albans has cut down all the brave old trees at Hanworth, and consequently reduced his park to what it issued from—Hounslow Heath; nay, he has hired a meadow next to mine for the benefit of embarkation and there lie all the good old corpses of oaks, ashes and chestnuts directly before the windows, and blocking up views of the river."

In that delightful book *Royal Houses Near London*, written and illustrated by Major Benton Fletcher, we find something of Hanworth. He is not correct, however, in saying that there is no mention of it before the sixteenth century, as we have seen, but he gives us an interesting addition when he says it was first enclosed as a game preserve by Sir John Crosby—builder of Crosby Hall—and that the first keeper when it became a Royal preserve was Sir Richard Weston.

The author also relates, not without humour, his first visit to this place. "The old Manor House," he says, "which withstood the attacks of Cromwell's men, was finally destroyed by fire, but a couple of Tudor kitchen chimneys are left to mark the site. The enclosing moat, surrounded by a great walled-in space, tells of the extent to which the gardens stretched during the zenith of Hanworth prosperity. Ancient yews and a mulberry tree remain as sentries.

"A five-step mounting stone and a carved Royal coat of arms lie about the garden. (I was told by a resident that the latter was that of the Duke of St. Albans.) High up, and built into a brick pediment, the smiling face of a terra-cotta bust looks down on the general ruin. When pointing this out to the writer, a gardener exclaimed, 'They do say as that head is a portrait of Annie Bowling.' In the Rectory of Hanworth some pieces of heraldic glass, including a royal coat of arms, have been inserted in a window, but there is little above ground to enable us to visualise the former appearance of the great house long since departed. There is only left the said sweet smile of 'Annie Bowling' to give animation to the scene of desolation."

The old Manor House at Hanworth was burned down in 1797, and the present mansion of Hanworth Park was re-built on rather higher ground, and here the second owner resided. This was Henry Perkins, the brewer, who, however, seems to have had a soul above beer, for he possessed one of the finest private libraries in England. This is notable as being a very rare example of a man having both the desire to buy many expensive books and the means to gratify that wish; for it is usually that those who wish to buy literary treasures have not the means, while those that have the means often have not either the desire to buy books or the brains to understand them, if acquired.

The unusual combination of the bibliophile and the brewer seems to have been a man of rare taste in literature. "Under the tuition of the learned Dr. Parr," writes Walford of him, "Mr. Henry Perkins acquired his love of books, and the bulk of his library was obtained between the years 1820 and 1830 from the great English and Continental sales. Among his treasures (sold under the hammer in 1873) were several curious MSS. of the thirteenth and fourteenth centuries, two copies of the famous Mazarin Bible, and a large number of ancient Bibles, Evangelaries, Missals, Books of Horns and Pontificals. There were many very choice works of legends including Lydgate's *Seige of Troy* and *The Romance of the Rose*.

Parr was a famous scholar in his day and was born at Harrow, where his father was an apothecary, in 1747. He was a master at Harrow and Stanmore. He died in 1825, and once was the centre of a curious literary controversy. In 1809 an anonymous book appeared called *Guy's Porridge Pot*, which was an attack on Dr. Parr. Walter Savage Landor defended Parr with a poem entitled *The Dun Cow,* to which the writer of the former book retorted with *The Dun Cow Roasted Whole,* containing scandalous aspersions upon Landor. How the matter ended I have no idea, but perhaps the writer of the libels did well to hide his identity, for Parr is described as being " bold and arrogant," while Landor is said to have been a man of " violent prejudices and ungovernable temper."

* * * * * *

The present Hanworth Park, from which a good distant view can be obtained near the church, is an imposing rather than a beautiful building. Thorne, writing about fifty years ago, calls it " a well-built commonplace mansion, with colonnade, and tall clock-tower, from which a wide prospect is obtained," and this exactly describes the place to-day.

It is now a County Club attached to the London Flying Club, and when I " reported for trespass " to the Secretary I received a sporting permission to go where I liked.

The Park itself is now of little interest, save to those interested in flying, most of the trees have been cut down and the little river put in places through a pipe and turfed over.

The mansion itself, now equipped as a most comfortable club-house, stands in a wooded oasis and from the air looks very like a dark green island in a light green sea. In one corner of the Park is a strange mound, which I was told was a prehistoric tumulus, but I subsequently discovered that it was the remains of an old ice-house—I came across, in the village, the son of a man who helped to construct it some fifty years ago.

The gardens are beautiful, velvety lawns and shady shrubbery walks, though that part which pleased me most was the old-English walled garden, which though dating only from 1905, as a wall-plaque tells us, has about it an air of ancient peace that is delightful, with its tiled paths, box hedges cut in topiary art, and a riot of colour in the flower beds. I spent some time here, in my favourite pastime of dreaming of the past times—although the noise of aeroplane engines all around somewhat disturbed my thoughts.

The old walled kitchen gardens—now partly turned into hard tennis-courts, and the old stable-yard now quite innocent of horses and used for parking cars—did not take kindly to these modern innovations. Artistically, it would have been wiser to have left them in their pristine state, however useful they may be in their new guise.

Two incidents, not without humour, brightened my visit to Hanworth Park, although in the first case the laugh was distinctly against myself. Across the Park flows the Cardinal's River. This is crossed by several wooden bridges, and on one of these I came across a young man in flying kit gazing reflectively into the water. I gave him good-day, which he returned, and then I spoke of this river and its history.

The young man listened intently and seemed to be taking an intelligent interest in the history of the little river that ran beneath us, but when I had finished my " lecture " he turned to me, most politely saying, " *Pardon, m'sieu, mais je suis francais; je ne comprends pas ce que vous dit.*"

The second incident also concerned a young man, but this time English; in fact, he was so proud of having been to Eton that he mentioned it five times in the first ten minutes. We got into conversation in the lounge of the Club and he told me he was down there trying to get a flying job. He was a nice boy, of the typical " public school type," but not bursting with over-much intelligence; for when we were discussing the history of the

place he told me that he thought that the house we were in was the original
hunting-box of Henry VIII.—despite the fact that the house is blatantly
late Georgian, even to an untrained eye.   I don't think they included a
course in period architecture in the curriculum at Eton in his day.

He seemed surprised when I told him when it was built and said he
had seen it in a guide book.   I replied that it must have referred to the old
house, or if it said this one, the book was merely wrong, and warned him
against accepting all he saw in print as gospel truth.

" But you tell me you write books," he replied.

" That may be; but there are books *and* books."

" And what are yours?" he laughed.

" Oh, mine is, I hope, an ' and book.' "

When we parted he said, " Well, good luck to your guide book."

" But I'm not writing one, mine is a rambling history and never meant
to be taken as a literal guide."

" But," he answered, " I thought you said yours was a Handbook."

Floreat Etona.   Which reminds one of the " Life " of Pellessier in the
old Follies programme—by Arthur Wimperis, if I remember rightly—which
contains the information: " At the age of fourteen a family council was held
to decide whether the boy should be educated or sent to Eton."   In the case
of my young friend it seems rather a pity that he was not sent along the
alternative road.

*   *   *   *   *   *

When Mason wrote in his *Heroic Epistle* in 1773,

<blockquote>
" Hounslow, whose Heath sublimer terror fills,
Shall with her gibbets lend her powder mills,"
</blockquote>

he voiced a dread those living in the district feared as much as the knights
of their roads; for the chance of being blown sky-high was an even more
devastating possibility than being robbed.

When exactly powder mills were first established on Hounslow Heath
is uncertain, but it was at an early date, for Walford writes: " It is said
that the first gunpowder manufactured in England was probably here; for
we are told that one William of Staines was employed by Edward III. in
1346 to make the gunpowder which enabled him to gain the victory of Crecy,
the first battle in which powder was used."

It was during the latter half of the eighteenth century that these
powder mills were the most active, both in production and eruption, as the
many paragraphs, culled from the old journals, testify, of which a few
extracts may prove of interest: " March, 1758.   The powder mills at Hounslow blew up to-day, but happily no lives were lost."   The accident gave
rise no doubt to this paragraph in *The Reading Mercury:* " Reading,
March 12.   Last night about nine o'clock a slight shock of an earthquake
was felt at Colebrook and other places between London and this town, but
we do not know if any damage was done.   The shock was also felt here."
" August, 1758.   Two powder mills at Hounslow blew up with about
600 weight of powder."   " December, 1758.   At night about twelve o'clock a
store of gunpowder at Hounslow took fire and blew up.   Several windows
300 yards distant from the works were shattered.   What might be the cause
is unknown, but in many places it was supposed to be an earthquake."

" September, 1770.   Two powder mills on Hounslow Heath blew up, by
which accident one man was killed."   Here are two accounts of the same
incident in 1772, one from *The Annual Register* and the other from *The*

Ladies' Magazine: About half after nine in the morning three powder mills on Hounslow heath blew up. The explosion was felt throughout the cities of London and Westminster and the inhabitants were greatly alarmed, supposing it to be an earthquake. The shock was also felt as far away as Gloucestershire and Worcestershire." " Yesterday morning exactly at half-past nine o'clock eight powder mills blew up at Hounslow heath by the explosion being communicated from one to another; the shock was so great that there was scarce a pane of glass left whole in the parishes of Twicken-ham, Brentford, Teddington, etc., most parts of London and Westminster likewise felt the shock, and imagined it an earthquake; happily no lives were lost, but one man was most terribly scorched." A little later in the same magazine appeared the following paragraph: " The inhabitants of Brentford, Hounslow, Twickenham and Isleworth, etc., have advertised for a meeting to petition Parliament for the removal of the powder mills on Hounslow Heath, as not only the inhabitants, but travellers (they being so near the high road) are now in eminent (sic) danger thereof."

This explosion was probably the one Mason had in mind when writing his H*eroic Epistle* in the following year, and it is certainly the one Horace Walpole wrote about in his *Letters,* dated January, 1772, just after he had returned to Strawberry Hill and found eight of his stained glass windows broken, besides other damage. " My shattered castle," he wrote, " never did look so Gothic in all its born days. You would swear it had been besieged by the Presbyterians in the Civil Wars, and that finding it impregnable they had vented their holy malice on the painted glass."

Another sidelight, not without humour, on this particular explosion is found in a newspaper that appeared not long after, which might well have been labelled " A Shocking Ghost." " About the time of the explosion at Hounslow powder mills," runs the account, "some families at Stockwell were terrified with the rattling and breaking of china, which they attributed to a supernatural cause. One lady was so firmly persuaded that some invisible agent was concerned that she discharged her maid, whom she suspected of having intercourse with the wicked spirit, and when she was gone, as no more mischief ensued, consoled herself that she had got rid of so dangerous an inmate."

Gilbert White's village of Selbourne, in Hampshire, felt these shocks, for in his *Journal,* under the date 1772, we read: " An extraordinary con-cussion in the air which shook people's windows and doors round the neighbourhood." To which a footnote is added: " The concussion felt Jan. 6th was occasioned by the blowing-up of the powder-mills near Hounslow. Incredible damage was done."

" April 24th, 1774. Sunday, about noon, a powder mill on Hounslow heath blew up, by which accident two persons lost their lives. The above happening during the time of divine service the congregation in Isleworth Church were so terrified, imagining the church was falling, that they hurried out with the greatest precipitation.

" September 25th, 1774. After the explosion at Hounslow powder mill a man's head was found more than a quarter of a mile from his body." The worst explosion of all, however, seems to have been the one recorded in January, 1796: " Between eight and nine o'clock this day the powder mills at Hounslow, owing to the wheels not being properly supplied with oil, took fire and blew up with a dreadful explosion, which not only terrified the inhabitants of the place, but alarmed the City of London. Three men at the works were killed and the flames reached a boat in the mill river, in which were thirty barrels of gunpowder, set fire to the whole and blew up with a terrible explosion; the man in charge being shattered to bits and the boat blown clean out of the water. Not a vestige of the mills is left standing and Hounslow-heath is covered with bricks and tiles, and the mangled remains of the unfortunate sufferers. The houses in Hounslow, Isleworth and Brentford have suffered considerably; the Crown Inn at Hounslow and the King's Head at Brentford have not a whole pane of glass in the windows; and the inhabitants were so terrified near the spot that they not only forsook their dwellings, but a number of women and children, through fear, appeared half-naked in the streets, expecting every moment that the houses would fall and bury them. The scattered limbs of the victims were, by order of the magistrates, collected and deposited in the Churchyard. The loss of the valuable manufactory is estimated at near £20,000." Of course, then, as now, the commercial side had to be brought in in the midst of tragedy!

July 4th, 1812. This morning about twelve one of the powder mills at Hounslow blew up. Two men were knocked down, but not killed. Their bodies presented a most shocking spectacle, they were so charred and black that they could scarcely be known. A surgeon was sent for, who advised them being conveyed to St. George's Hospital, which was done, in a caravan used for conveying powder to London. The groans and screams when they were moved were distressing."

Under August, 1813, there is an entry: "This morning at twenty-five past six o'clock two of the powder mills at Hounslow blew up. The concussion of the air was so great that it set the bells ringing at Brompton Church, a village near London, some ten miles distant."

These accounts all have a tragic sameness about them, but as a last example might be quoted (slightly out of chronology) one that had, perhaps, the most extraordinary result of all; for there is an old print that shows a general exodus from London of the terror-stricken population, and we read: "When the tremors of what is termed 'The Last Earthquake of London' were felt in 1750 it is placed on record that the Gambling Set at Whites Club laid wagers whether it was an earthquake or the blowing up of Hounslow powder mills." There is certainly no doubt that Hounslow Heath provided the Big Noises of the period.

The last one, as far as I know, was somewhere about 1904, and this one I heard myself. I was a schoolboy and living at Teddington (about two and a half miles away). I can remember how on a summer's evening we all rushed out of the house (like the people in former days) when we heard the deep double "Boom! Boom!" What damage was done I do not know, but quite recently I heard a humorous sidelight from a man who was living at Stanwell (four miles away) at the time. In the village was an old man, long stone deaf, who was working in his garden at the time of the explosion, and when the double "Boom" rang out he stood up with a pleased smile and remarked to his grandson, "Bless my soul! Why, that's the first time I've heard the cuckoo for thirty years!"

Both the "sublimer errors" and the Heath are now things of memory only, for the last explosion, like the last "Stand and deliver!" is but an echo of the past. The powder mills, in use up to just after the Great War, are now standing idle and forlorn. There are really two of them, one at Babers Bridge on the Staines Road, and the other at Hanworth—as a matter of fact I believe the latter are actually in Twickenham parish, though really nearer Hanworth. I have no doubt that the recorded explosions took place at both, but probably more at Hanworth, for they are the original ones of Mason's poem and the site of the mills of mediaeval days.

They stand in a park of some hundred and fifty acres, and though the buildings and workshops are now half dismantled, the place is well timbered and picturesque, with a few cottages still occupied, and big earthern "dumps" where the gunpowder was once stored. At the end of the long drive can be seen the old Shot Tower. Quaint, but derelict, it stands like a Tower of Mystery on the wooded banks of the River Crane which flows through the estate.

*   *   *   *   *   *

Even as I write these lines changes are taking place, other noises than gunpowder explosions are now heard; for the builder's hammer is beating a requiem to the old Hounslow Powder Mills.

At the moment the estate resembles, at one end, a lumber camp in Canada; giants that were once part of the Great Forest of Middlesex, are falling before the woodman's axe—or being unromantically pulled over by a steel hawser and a traction engine. Soon the dumps will also be levelled, and then when all is flat and treeless "progress" will be satisfied.

The only thing they cannot conceal is the River Crane, which flows through a wooded dell. Here is a splendid chance to show how in estate development necessity can be turned into virtue, and a belt of woodland should be left on both river banks. The estate developer is not (seemingly) over-gifted with imagination, and it will be interesting to see here how he will adapt what nature has so well begun for him.

CHAPTER XXIV.

Where East meets West, and of a village known through the most famous of Middlesex legends.

EAST BEDFONT is the most typical roadside village in all the Heath country and certainly the most picturesque of those that lie directly upon the King's two highways across this region.

If a hill village is said to "cling" to the mountain side, or a lowland one to "nestle" in the valley, how is one dominated by the road in a flat country to be described?

Bedfont owes its existence mainly to the travellers that have passed through in bygone days. We could say it "hangs on to" the road, an ugly term, if expressive.

Fifty years ago Walford wrote of the place: "Bedfont, formerly called East Bedfont to distinguish it from West Bedfont, lies on the high road about equidistant from Hounslow and Staines. With its long village green and pond, both fringed with fine elms and other trees, and its string of houses and cottages retreating so gracefully behind their gardens on either side of the road, it has a quaint and primitive air, which would hardly lead one to believe that he is within thirteen miles of the great metropolis. The quaintness of its appearance is increased by its little Norman church, with its wooden towers and dwarf steeple and its pair of trim and formal yew trees cut into shapes of peacocks."

Some thirty years later, C. G. Harper in his *Rural Nooks round London* writes: "To return to East Bedfont, which travellers along the high road between Hounslow and Staines must needs know, because they are bound to pass through it. Traversing that road it comes as a pleasant surprise from the enclosed fields on either hand, opening out as an entirely unexpected common, with a real pond and real ducks in it, and an, if possible, even more real village church in the middle distance, with an odd compromise between a flint and stone tower and a wooden bell-cote. The side of the church looking on to the common is almost wholly obscured by two huge yew-trees cut and trimmed to resemble peacocks."

I am glad to say that there is really very little I can add to either of these descriptions, even after the lapse of a good many years.

It will be noticed that both writers mention the yew-trees, as is only natural, for the "lions" of Bedfont are peacocks (to be Irish).

Thomas Hood it was who really made these trees famous, in his poem *The Two Peacocks of Bedfont.* In these verses the actual story is too wrapped up in words to be very clear to the casual reader, though it has glimpses of the old-world village life that are pleasing.

> " Alas, that breathing vanity should go . . .
> To haunt the peaceful churchyard of Bedfont."

These lines are the motif of the poem, which tells of two haughty maidens who lived in this village "once upon a time" and relates how:

> " Each Sabbath morning, at the hour of prayer,
> Behold two maidens, up the quiet green
> Shining, far distant, in the summer air
> That flaunts their dewy robes and breathes between
> Their downy plumes—sailing as if they were
> Two far-off ships—until they brush between
> The churchyard's humble walls, and watch and wait
> On either side of the wide-opened gate."

So overbearing were they in their fine silks and brocades that for their pride they were turned (it is not quite clear by whom) into peacocks and destined to stand here for ever as a punishment; the birds being subsequently, and miraculously, transformed into trees cut in their shape.

> " And where two haughty maidens used to be,
> In pride of plume, where plumy Death had trod,
> Trailing their gorgeous velvets wantonly,
> Most unmeet pall, over the holy sod;
> There, gentle stranger, thou may'st only see
> Two sombre Peacocks.—

. . When this poem first appeared in the *London Magazine* in 1822 Hood added the note: "If any man, in his unbelief, should doubt the truth and manner of this occurence, he may in an easy way be assured thereof to his satisfaction, by going to Bedfont, a journey of some thirteen miles, where he may behold with his own eyes the two peacocks.

" They seem at first to be of yew tree, which they greatly resemble, but on drawing nearer he will perceive cut therein the date 1704.

The date is rather overgrown now but when the trees are properly trimmed can still be traced. Another version of the legend has it that the trees were cut into this shape at the cost of a dissappointed suitor of one (or both) of the haughty maidens, "who, having been rejected with a

.

BEDFONT CHURCH AND "THE PEACOCKS."

From a print of 1807

wholly unnecessary degree of contumely, described them as proud as peacocks and considered this the best way of typifying them."

So we can take our choice of these two stories of the origin of these trees, which I hope will long remain to remind us of this quaint legend of old Middlesex.

In spite of Pope's satire in *The Guardian* these trees have long been popular favourites. There are several old prints of them, but I have what is rarer still, and that is one showing them *as girls*.

In the article, *The Crow Flies*, the bird does not alight at Bedfont, but still he " poises his jetty wings over the red roofs of the old posting village." The Crow, of course, mentions the Peacocks but he puts forward a slightly different reason for the poem, and though the wise bird cannot be right simply because the legend is far older than Hood's day, it is not without interest. " This poem," runs this account, " arose from the poet, having one day seen two peacocks struting in flaunting pride and displaying their jewelled plumes among the humble grassy graves of Bedfont churchyard. This contrast he surrounded with Stothard-like pictures of a country Sunday; hand coupled urchins in restrained talk, anxious pedagogue, pompous churchwarden stalking soemnly along, gold-bedizened beadle passing flaming through the churchyard gate, conscious of the world's approval."

In the *Chronicles of English Counties* there is a variation of this legend, where it says: " Bedfont is noteworthy for its curious yew-trees in the churchyard, trimmed into the faint presentment of two fighting cocks, birds in which, according to tradition, the parson of the parish once took a fond delight. After Bedfont all is straight road, stumpy trees, stiff hedges and deep ditches till we reach Staines." In Lewis's *Topographical Dictionary* (for 1835) these trees are also described as cocks, but I do not think there is any doubt as to the truth of the peacock legend—as far as such things can have truth.

The church itself, overshadowed, I am afraid both literally and metaphorically by the trees, is worth exploring, especially for its fine Norman doorway and its thirteenth century wall-paintings, discovered during restoration in mid-Victorian days. Lovers of the curious will find in this churchyard a tombstone dated the 31st of February, and another stating the deceased to be " 361 years of age."

The village has altered little. It is still peaceful, with its cluster of cottages by the Bell Inn and its larger houses by the church, of which Bedfont Lodge and St. Mary's are pleasantly reminiscent of eighteenth century days. There are one or two larger houses on the south side of the village and on one of the gateways are two bronze medallions of peacocks, apparently modern work.

It was this house—Bedfont House, a fine eighteenth century mansion— that tradition states to have been the residence of the two original " Peacocks," though their names are lost in the mists of the past.

According to some accounts Bedfont was at one time a Roman station, for in a field between here and Feltham there were dug up some years ago a number of Roman coins, mixed with arms and bones and the vestiges of some barrows of uncertain date. The place is called Bedefunte in the *Domesday Book,* where it is described as being held by " Richard of Walter, son of Other." The name, in bygone days, was variously spelt Bedfound and Belfont. The well-known Bedfont Turnpike-Gate stood between the Longford River and the village, and part of the old Toll-house still remains.

Bedfont's history in the past was, in the main, unexciting, but in the early seventeenth century there were happenings that are not without interest. In 1636 there was an outbreak of plague in London, thought to be spread by paper made from old rags. " One of the offending paper-makers was William Bushee, who had set up a mill in Middlesex, midway between Hounslow and East Bedfont. He was summoned ' for grindynge ragges in his paper mill that came from London, whereby one of his servantes became infected with the plague.' "

Paper (which was then mostly imported from abroad), however, continued to be made and Middlesex has another "triumph," for in 1675 a patent was granted to Eustace Burneby for "making all sorts of white paper for the use of writing and printing, being a new manufacture, never practised in any of our kingdoms or dominions." Burneby must have had some success, for three years later a book was presented to the king, "being printed on English paper and made within five miles of Windsor by Eustace Burneby, esq., who was the first Englishman that brought it into England." His mill was at Stanwell, but its success was short-lived.

The old Boundary mark of Windsor Forest is at Bedfont, for in former days the forest included a large tract of country that became the heath of Hounslow. Pope knew both forest and heath well, and in his poem *Windsor Forest* he has these fine lines descriptive of this part:

" Ev'n the wild heath, displays her purple dyes,
And 'midst the desert, fruitful fields arise,
That crowned with tufted trees and springing corn,
Like verdant isles the sable waste adorn.

After the church the next interesting building in Bedfont is the inn, The Black Dog, on the roadside a mile outside the village; it is immortalised by George Colman (the Elder) in his *Random Recollections:*

" Harvey, whose inn commands a view
Of Bedfont's church and churchyard too,
Where yew-trees into peacocks shorn
In vegetable torture mourn."

I cannot understand how the church could ever have been seen from this inn, it is quite impossible now and the juxtaposition of the two buildings cannot have altered—it must be poetical licence.

The former keeper of this inn, Peter Harvey, was a notable man in his day, and his inn was famous not so much for its cellar, which no doubt was excellent, as for a special sauce made by the landlord, of which he was very proud, and hereby hangs a romance of trade.

Here is an account of it, quoted from a recent advertisement: " It seems a little thing on which to hang fame—a sauce. But this was a wonderful sauce. Epicures in London spoke of it with bated breath and shining eyes. It was the masterpiece among sauces. When Peter's sister Elisabeth married Mr. Lazenby, a London grocer, Peter opened his heart. For a wedding gift he gave her his most cherished possession—the recipe of his sauce. And Elisabeth made the best of it . . . and so out of a wedding present there grew the business whose name to-day is a household word, " Elisabeth Lazenby and Son." Elisabeth married in 1776, but the fame of the sauce still clung to the Black Dog, and even after the death of Harvey it became the most famous rendezvous round London for the Driving Clubs so popular with the Regency Bucks and Corinthians — as evinced by Thackeray's mention of them in *The Four Georges,* one of many sources.

The inn was both a distinction and a half-way house to Windsor, and Charles James Apperley, better known as "Nimrod," writing in 1836 in *The Road*, tells us that the B.D.C., or "Benson Driving Club," which still holds its rendezvous at the Black Dog, Bedfont, is the only survivor of those numerous driving associations whose processions used, some twenty years ago, to be among the most imposing, as well as peculiar, spectacles in and around the metropolis.

Nimrod has a good deal to say about these "gentlemen-coachmen," mentioning among others the famous whip, Sir John Lade, and the celebrated "Tommy Onslow" (afterwards Lord Cranley), who was the subject of the well-known doggerel epigram:

> " What can Tommy Onslow do?
> He can drive a phaeton and two.
> Can Tommy Onslow do no more?
> Yes—he can drive a phaeton and four."

Nimrod's book also has some interesting pages on the different vehicles of the early nineteenth century—the whiskies, stanhopes, tilburies, dennet, and other forgotten conveyances of those days, forerunners of the more familiar gigs and dog-carts—he even describes the buggy, which, like many other things thought to be American in origin, is really old English.

Speaking of Hood's lines on the village, *The Crow* says: " The musing poet little thought of what Bedfont used to be in the Regency times, when the Four-in-Hand Clubs' vehicles rattled up to the Black Dog. Those were the days when baronets drove coaches, boxed the watch, smote the Charlies, wore many-caped coats, and were sudden and prompt in quarrel. Lord Sefton's and Colonel Berkeley's turn-outs were specially superb, the horses perfect, the equipments in refined taste. The society lasted in full vigour for upwards of twenty years. Mr. Akers, one of the most spirited members, in his enthusiastic desire to resemble a regular real coachman, filed a chink between his front teeth to enable him to whistle to his nags in the orthodox manner. It was not a very high ambition, but it led Mr. Akers to a coach-box and left him there finally planted."

There is also mention of these driving-clubs' " runs " to Bedfont in the *Autobiography* of the famous sporting Squire Osbaldaston (edited by Sir Theodore Cook): " Sir Harry Peyton was leader of the Benson Club; its chief rival was the Four-in-Hand Club, of which Osbaldaston was a member." He relates an incident in connection with Bedfont: " We never took the same road as Sir H. Peyton," he tells us, " for fear of collision, which might have ended in racing. They generally drove to Bedfont, between Hounslow and Egham . . . the road gives plenty of scope to try the qualities of the nags. No galloping under penalty of dismissal from the Club.

" Our teams were nearly matched. Just before the end none remained but Buxton, Lord Hawke and myself. Hearing a team close behind me I turned back, and to my surprise they were galloping; the next moment the team passed me at full speed with nobody on the box; the horses were running away. It was within twenty yards of a Turnpike gate; luckily it was open, and to my amazement the runaway team never touched it, they galloped up a lane where they came to a standstill, being unable to get any further; wonderful to relate neither the carriage nor the horses were injured. Lord Hawke, however, who was thrown from the box, was so badly hurt that his life was despaired of for a time, though he eventually recovered."

Sir Harry Peyton, like most whips of those days, was also the subject
of versification.

> " The road, the road, hurrah for the road,
>   In tandem, gig or phaeton;
> We love to be with the gay and free,
>   When tooled by matchless Peyton."

While in another set of contemporary verses, *The Song of the B.D.C.*, which
goes into personal detail of the amateur drivers, we again find his name:

> " Those were the days when Peyton's greys
>   To Bedfont led the way, sir,
> And Villebois followed with his bays
>   In beautiful array, sir.
> Then Spicer, too, came next in view
>   To join the gay procession.
> Oh, the dust we made—the cavalcade
>   Was neat beyond expression
> " No turnpike saw a fancy team
>   More neat than Dolphin sported,
> When o'er the stones with Charley Jones
>   To Bedfont they resorted.
> Few graced the box as much as Cox;
>   But there were none I ween, sir,
> Who held the reins 'twixt here and Staines
>   More slap up than the Dean, sir."

In *Down the Road: The Reminiscences of a Gentleman Coachman* there
are some stories of Peyton. " A Dandy of those days," says a commentator, " valued driving over all other accomplishments; the Four-in-
Hand Club eclipsed its rivals, and not only was the power of managing
four spirited horses in a workmanlike way esteemed above all virtues and
attainments, but the professional knights of the whip were regarded as
oracles and heroes, as the pages of the contemporary *Sporting Magazine*
testify: " We remember with a smile how learned men in the
House of Commons stated that no wheeled carriage in the world
could safely voyage at the perilous speed of fifteen miles an hour!"

Frequent references are found in old books of the " dangerous speed "
of the coaches towards the end of their career; here is one of many: " When
the stage coaches reached the almost incredible speed of twelve miles an
hour it caused great alarm in the public mind. Lord Chancellor Campbell
relates that he was frequently warned against travelling in the mail-coaches
on account of the fearful rate at which they flew, and instances were given
him of passengers who had died suddenly of apoplexy from the rapidity of
the motion." Speed hogs at twelve miles an hour!

In Captain Mallet's *Annals of the Road* he writes: " The Black Dog at
Bedfont, which no longer exists (I cannot understand this, it certainly *does*
exist to this day, and as far as I can observe seems to be the same building
as in Regency days, save for some minor alterations), used to be the place
where the B.D.C. always dined and where they had their private cellar."
In the same book we find this interesting paragraph: " It happened that
His Majesty (George IV.) changed horses at Bedfont soon after the Club
had dined. On being informed that his carriage was at the door they
drank his health with three times three."

These scenes of the Black Dog are recalled to us in the old sporting prints of the period. Mallet has many stories of the various members and episodes connected with those old driving clubs, but one anecdote will have to suffice here. Speaking of a certain member—his name is immaterial—he says: "He is one of the Old School and very entertaining. In the evening he is a good bit of company. After five bottles of hock, which he could put under his coat without the slightest inconvenience, he has often been seen to fill a bumper and place the glass on his head, during which time he would sing a song, in which not only every coachman's, but every horse-keeper's name between London and Plymouth was introduced. At the same time also he would go through the manoeuvres of hitting, wheeling and leader without spilling a drop of the wine; and after he had drunk it off he would run the empty glass up and down the large silver buttons on his coat with very singular effect."

There was at another time a very different type of diner at the Black Dog, for Lord Castlereagh, the famous statesman of Regency days, was once the guest at one of these club meetings here. A strange figure, I always think, for so hilarious a gathering, this much misunderstood politician, who stalked so tragically across the pages of history, and whose *body was cheered* by the mob as it passed through the streets for burial in Westminster Abbey, so hated had been the man in life.

He had cut his throat with a penknife, and is perhaps best remembered by Byron's " gloating couplet ":

" So *he* has cut his throat at last. He! Who?
The man who cut his country's long ago,"

though I think that the lines of Shelley have a tragic horror that is more haunting:

" I met Murder on the way—
He had a mask like Castlereagh—
Very smooth he looked, yet grim;
Seven bloodhounds followed him."

As Philip Guedella wittily remarks in a review of a book on Castlereagh (*The Foreign Policy of Castlereagh*, 1812-1815, by C. K. Webster): "How rarely statesmen seem to realise the unwisdom of annoying poets." Yet Castlereagh was a great statesman who did good work for England, and who has never had full justice done to him till the publication of Professor Webster's masterly study.

Another story concerns the Black Dog (though I cannot give chapter and verse for the statement), for it is said to be here, at a driving club dinner, that Sheridan made a bitingly true remark. Before dinner he addressed the assembled guests: " Now, gentlemen, shall we drink like beasts or like men?" Someone (with a tolerance rare in those times) replied, " Oh, like men, of course, we don't want to be beasts." " Then," answered Sheridan, " we can get disgustingly drunk; had we drunk like beasts we should have had to stick to water."

Yes, stirring scenes and strange people has this old inn seen, both inside its walls and on the road outside. It looks peaceful and picturesque enough to-day as it stands—a little lonely—beside the road to Staines, dreaming, as a building dreams, of all those it knew in bygone days, who have now passed their way down a Longer Road on which there is no returning.

* * * * * *

Since writing the foregoing "The Secret of the Black Dog" has, I think, been solved. It is quite a mild mystery, of how the landlord managed to see the church from so far off and why one writer spoke of the inn as demolished. It was really Mr. Herbert Gibbs, who lives at that charming 300-year-old house, The Spinney, nearby, and who has such a wonderful knowledge of this part of Middlesex, who cleared it up. I mentioned to him how I could not understand these points, and he said that there was once *another* Black Dog on the site of a house called St. Stephens at the corner of the Green overlooking the Church. This, Mr. Gibbs says, was the inn mentioned in the verses and where the Driving Clubs of Regency days used to meet.

This elucidates everything, though it is to be regretted that this old inn has gone; the present house on the site, a plain stucco building of mid-Victorian days, is soon, I understand, to be partially demolished itself for road widening. It is said that the foundations, and perhaps the cellars, of the old building remain, while the picturesque red-roofed stable at the back is certainly the original one, which saw so much activity in the days of long ago.

The present inn on the Staines Road towards Hounslow calls itself the " Old " Black Dog; if it is really older than the more famous building, or if it took the name on the demolition of the green-side inn, I do not know. Perhaps, like the two Magpies on the Bath Road, there may have once been two Black Dogs on this stretch of highway.

On the Staines Road, opposite Bedfont Lane and not far from the existing Black Dog Inn, is a house known as Newhaven. This was the home for some years of the famous racing novelist, Nat Gould, towards the close of his life. In *Racecourse and Battlefield* we find something of Kempton Park and the district generally; I expect there are others that also deal with the local racecourses, but I confess I have not read all his numerous turf romances.

＊　　＊　　＊　　＊　　＊　　＊

The isolated hamlet of West Bedfont, although but a few cottages, a tin chapel and the Three Crowns, a small alehouse lying half hidden among the meadows and quite unknown to travellers of either the Staines or the Bath Roads, has a special mention in the *Domesday Book*. In fact of the two Bedfonts it is the " senior," mentioned as *the* Bedfont, while the other, though now a much larger and more important place, was distinguished by the prefix " East " as of only secondary importance.

Mentions in *Domesday* are much alike, that is why I have not quoted them in every case. I have kept to no special rule; the chance of some small point has often decided the matter, but everyone can look them up in Lysons, or in the special *Middlesex Domesday* in the British Museum. In the case of West Bedfont, however, I will quote a *precis* of the entry, as it is the only claim to fame possessed by this little hamlet:

" Walter de Mucedent holds the manor of Bedefount under Walter Fitzother. The land is four carucates. There are two villanes who hold four hides; two others have two virgates and one border has five acres. The priest has one virgate and there are two slaves. The meadowland is equal to two oxgangs and there is pasture for the cattle of the manor."

The mention of priest is curious; there is certainly no church there now, nor can I find any record of there ever having been one; yet in the entry under *East* Bedfont, where there is a church dating from Saxon times, there is no mention of a priest. The simple explanation probably is (I know how " professional " archaeologists hate these straightforward explanations) that the priest from East Bedfont church lived, or anyhow farmed, in the neighbouring parish.

Lysons, in his *Parishes of Middlesex*, takes up the story: " In the year 1235 James, son of William de Haverhill, granted to Andrew Bukerell his homage and service of the whole manor of West Bedfont."

Dugdale's *Monasticon Anglicanum* tells us that the son (also Andrew) of Bukerell gave the manor of West Bedfont to the Prior of New Place, who held it under Brian de Windsor in 1399. . . " In the year 1415 this manor was vested in the Abbey of Chertsey, who exchanged it with Richard de Windsor for the advowson of Stanwell." This de Windsor died in 1428 seised of the manor of West Bedfont, then valued at 40s. It was included in the exchange between Lord Windsor and the King. In 1570 it was described as the Manor of West Bedfont, alias Bedfont Court, parcel to the manor of Stanwell.

Thorne and Walford waste no words on this place—about half a dozen each, and those almost contemptuous in their brevity—yet I found it a very peaceful spot in which to wile away a summer's afternoon. It has no " lions," there is nothing striking about it; the most exciting thing one can do is to drink a glass of beer at the little inn. Perhaps it is these negative qualities in this rushing world that give it its charm.

There is, or was, one good house in West Bedfont, the picturesque River Court, which is said to be the site of the already mentioned Bedfont Court. The fine red-brick house, with its old gateway, which has been recently demolished, stood on the banks of the Cardinal's River.

The demolition of River Court—which is to be regretted—shows up the hideous corrugated-iron works in the fields behind. These gaunt derelict buildings ruin the view on that side of West Bedfont, which otherwise can have altered little since it figured in *Domesday;* it was meadows then and it is meadows now, and I hope it will remain such for years to come.

An entry in a copy of *The Gentleman's Magazine* (early nineteenth century) is the only piece of " news " I have found about this place: " West Bedfont was the birthplace of Thomas Swain, an eighteenth century bell-founder. His foundry was at Longford."

I am afraid I have never heard of this worthy before, nor can I locate any bell-foundry at Longford; but possibly his "wares" still call the faithful to worship from the belfries in some of the peaceful Middlesex villages in the surrounding countryside.

CHAPTER XXV.

Of an old town once a thankful journey's end, and where the still waters of History are found to run deep.

THE story of Staines is a quiet one, for while there is much of it, there is no special thing that gives it prominence—such as the Peacocks at Bedfont, or the Tithe Barn at Harmondsworth. Staines has pursued its way quietly through the ages without changing much, till recently, and even now it is lucky enough to retain some of its character of an old county town.

I think, however, the description in *The Way About Middlesex* a little too scrappy: "Staines is an old and respectable town, but beyond that calls for no remark." History can be "dug out" of even less likely sources than this.

When I said there is nothing of prominence here I had not forgotten The London Stone (not to be confused with London Stone some seventeen miles away), which, though notable, is certainly not prominent as far as its situation is concerned; you might be in Staines a hundred times and never see it. If, however, you care to cross a meadow it is plain enough and worth a visit.

It marks the boundary of the jurisdiction of London on the upper Thames, and bears (or bore) the inscription: "God preserve the City of London. A.D. 1285." Its pedestal is chiefly remarkable for the number of different dates, commemorating various ceremonies, forgotten Lord Mayors and Aldermanic worthies. The first date is 1781, when the stone was raised to its pedestal; in 1812 the Conservators claimed the river, and in 1816 somebody else did something, though it is not quite clear what it was. In 1826 the Conservators viewed the river and proudly recorded the fact. In 1839 there was another ceremony, but it is impossible to read what it was. The latest date is 1857, but what happened then is left entirely to the imagination!

Until recently the Lord Mayor was *ex-officio* head of the Thames Conservancy, and it is in this capacity that Tom Hood humorously writes:

" Conservators of Thames from mead to mead,
   Great guardian of small sprats that swim the flood,
   Warden of London Stone."

The derivation of the name Staines has caused much controversy. Vaughan tells us: "The name is derived either from this stone or from a Roman milestone upon the ancient road to Silchester, which crossed the river here; the former is more probable. It was the custom of the Romans to place stations at fixed intervals along their roads—usually at each tenth milestone—and there is no reason why Staines alone among hundreds of such posts should have been known as the 'Town' at the milestone."

The argument against the town having been called after the stone of 1285 is simple, but convincing, because it was known as *Stanes* in *Domesday*, and its mention in the *Anglo-Saxon Chronicle* as Stana (a stone). Another idea is that it got its name from the stone causeway leading to the bridge in Roman times.

THE OLD BRIDGE, STAINES.
From a print of 1804.

THE LONDON STONE, STAINES.
Lord Mayor's visit about 1840.

Drawing by Donald Maxwell
Lent by Mr. Geoffrey Bles

"BRUGES IN MIDDLESEX."
River Colne at Staines.

The "stone" theory seems most general and is supported by Lysons and Dugdale: "Its name is derived from the Saxon *stana*, in allusion to the London mark stone which was erected in 1280." (Dates seem to vary between 1280 and 1285.) Dr. Taylor, in *Words and Places*, also takes this view: "Staines is so called from the stones bounding the river jurisdiction of the Lord Mayor." It will be noticed that he is the only one who uses the plural.

Against these theories it may be argued that both dates being after Saxon times why should it be called by a Saxon name? This looks as if an earlier stone (or stones) may have existed, which may have been either the Roman milestone or the approaches to the bridge, or even the stone piers of the bridge itself. I think Walford is the wisest (and certainly on the safest ground) when he says "the stone may be either Roman, Saxon or Norman."

As a last quotation there is Hall's *Book of the Thames:* "Staines was the site of one of the earliest bridges in England. The Roman road, which Dr. Stukeley calls the 'Via Trinobantica,' to the west crossed the Thames here, and the Roman station at this place is called, in the *Itinerary of Antonius,* Pontes, so that even then there was a bridge across the river." It proves more than that, the literal words used, "Ad Pontes"—by the bridges "—so we can assume that there were more than one bridge here when the Romans came, for the several mouths of the Colne would, of necessity, be also bridged. The smaller bridges were probably of wood, but the Thames bridge might have had stone piers, as Hall adds, "And so given the place its name," may be at a later date, but there is no doubt the *Roman* name was Bridges and not Stone.

Staines was one of the many places claimed as the spot of Caesar's crossing of the Thames, and here, as in the case of the names, we enter into the realms of controversy, even more strenuous than formerly. A good deal of this is, I am afraid, rather futile, for in Professor Lethaby's *London Before the Conquest* we find on two facing pages no less than ten different theories, by varying authorities, of this crossing. The explanation is easy, I think. Has it ever occurred to these learned, but apparently simple-minded, gentlemen that a general of Caesar's brilliance might have deployed his forces for this manoeuvre; or again, what proof have we that he crossed the river once only? He may have done so a dozen times for all we know, which would validate all these claims at once.

I do not profess to be half so learned as the professors who quarrel so on these archaelogical disputes, but I think if they brought a little more simple common sense to bear on the solving of these riddles they might find them easier. But then, if they did, they would find perhaps they had no excuse for their wrangles after all—and that would be so disappointing!

There is a good deal about Staines in the *Domesday Book:* "The Abbot of St. Peter holds *Stanes* for nineteen hides. There is land for twenty-four ploughs and pasture for the cattle of the village. Pannage for thirty hogs and two arpents of vineyard . . . four berewerks (hamlets) belong to this manor and they belonged to it in King Edward's time."

A little closer study of this description reveals the watery nature of the place, for we find entries absent in "inland" parishes. There were six water mills—probably on the Colne mouths—two "wears," probably on the same river, for there would be no Thames lock weirs in those days, and the mention of two different sections of meadow land leads us to assume, probably correctly, that one portion was dry land and the other water meadows.

It may have been a water mill referred to in the old chronicle: "Edmund de Westell, vicar of Heston, anno 1366, gave a mill, 34 acres of land and 5s. rent in Stanes and Stanwell to the Priory of Hounslow."

This study of old village life is full of fascination, especially the *Domesday* part, but space forbids further mention, but those who wish to read one of the most concise, yet imaginative, accounts of this theme should consult the chapter " Norman Villages and the *Domesday Book* " in *English Villages*, by P. H. Ditchfield.

The old writers always refer to the River Colne as " The Coln Ditch," but this means no disrespect to this charming little river; it was but the term for a small waterway, and it is said that Staines was once surrounded by a moat, all of which has gone except a portion known as Penton Ditch.

Looking for vestiges of the past when we know definitely they have existed is sometimes hard work enough, but it is rather discouraging to amateur antiquarians to find evidence that that for which they are seeking has never existed at all! It was this way with a few researches I tried to make to discover the whereabouts of the Old Abbey in Staines—the only Abbey in Middlesex, if we count Westminster as in London County.

Both Speed's *Religious Houses* and Weever's *Funeral Monuments* state that a Benedictine Abbey existed in Staines in Saxon days, the monks of which served several adjoining parishes, and add that the abbey (one says it was a priory only) was founded by Ralph, Lord Stafford. I was not at all successful in my discoveries and gave them up when I read in Noewcourt's book that " the Priory of Staines in Middlesex alluded to by several writers is really situated at Stone, in Staffordshire."

B. C. Halahan puts forward an ingenious theory regarding the line " Let me bring thee to Staines " in *Henry V*. " I had always assumed," he writes, " that the above referred to Staines between Richmond and Windsor. But from ' a tavern in Eastcheap,' of which Mistress Quickly was hostess, to Staines must be by road nearly twenty miles. I suggest, as an alternative, ' to Staines ' means the Stane Street, running from London Bridge to Chichester. This would have been as good a way as any for Pistol, Nym and Bardolph to have " shogged " to Southampton. From the tavern in Eastcheap to the south side of London Bridge would have been a reasonable distance for her to have gone with the adventurers. To walk nearly twenty miles to Staines, and back alone by the wilds of Hounslow Heath seems neither reasonable nor likely." There is certainly sound reasoning in this idea.

Beyond the Inigo Jones tower the present church of Staines is too modern to have much history, but as the site of an ecclesiastical building it is very ancient; for we are told that it is certain that the Norman church—demolished in 1828—was not the earliest there. We learn, on the authority of Leland, that in Saxon times Emengoldis, daughter of King Wulfhere, before the year 700 A.D., built a small chapel in the forest here. This was probably a small and simple building of wood, and we also learn that as far back as the ninth century a structure of this description was standing here, and that the rude tenements of the Saxon town clustered around this early " God's Acre." This little oratory was, in due course, probably superseded by a church of stone.

The small woodland sanctuary has an imaginative touch, even though it is now hard to visualise, when we notice the bare and treeless country (compared with former days) outside the town. Yet Hughson, and many others writers, remind us: "Staines forest extended from this place to Hounslow. The manor was one of those given by Edward the Confessor to the Church of Westminster. The Vicar of Staines held it under the Great Abbey by a curious tenure, namely, that of supplying two large wax candles for the altar of St. Peter's Church, to be burnt on the eve of the Epiphany. After the Dissolution Staines became vested in the Crown and was given by James I. to Lord Knyvet."

Because the history of Staines is a quiet one it is often dismissed rather scantily in many gazetteers and guide-books. Here is a typical entry, from Cassel's *Thames and its Story*: "Staines, new and suburban as it now appears for the most part, is as old as any place in England. Staines is by no means bereft of all antiquity, modernised though it be. Near the church is Winicroft House, a Tudor building which some good folk, innocent of architecture and chronology, soberly assign to the reign of King John."

The anonymous author of the above paragraph might have withheld his covert sneer at the innocence of the good folk, and spent his time finding out the correct name of the house. There is no Winicroft House; I suppose he means Duncroft House. The beam and the moat!

Here is Walford's account: "Quite close to the vicarage is Duncroft House, at one time the property of Lord Cranstoun. It is said that King John slept here the night before signing the Magna Carta at Runnymeade, but the tradition may be doubted. The house is late Elizabethan, or early Jacobean. The room said to be King John's has a fine oak chimney-piece, curiously inlaid, and the timbers of the upper part are massive. An earlier structure may have occupied the spot, but no trace of it exists."

In the days of Hounslow Heath's "glory" Staines was a busy place; more from reason of posting than changing coach-horses, it was too near Hounslow for that; but it shared with that town a feeling of dread or relief, according to whether the crossing of the dreaded Heath was in front or behind the wayfarer. A thankful Journey's End either way.

Walford gives a brief, but probably typical, account of Staines as it then was: "Lying as it does, in the good old coaching days, on the high road to Salisbury, just one stage out of Hounslow, Staines was a large posting town and its inns were numerous. Many of these since the days of railways have been turned into private houses.

"If not literally the 'half-way house,' Staines was at all events one of the resting places, and a halt for changing horses on the 'royal road' to Windsor. Hence the town was a favourite with good old George III. and Queen Charlotte; and hence probably it came to pass that royalty took part in the ceremony of opening the new bridge over the Thames.'

❋   ❋   ❋   ❋   ❋   ❋

In the history of most towns unconsciously humorous incidents often crop up among others to brighten the sometimes rather dull annals of bricks and mortar. In the case of Staines I have found, in various places, more of these than in many towns whose history has greater interest.

For instance, an old Gazetteer states that two annual fairs are held in Staines, one for horses and cattle, and another for onions and toys. Another solemnly informs us that "Staines consists of a straggling and irregular street and two large breweries." If the latter were there first it might account for the former, though no definite news of this is given.

Two other items quaintly remark: "An army of the Danes crossed the river at Staines in 1009, but on hearing of the intelligence of the army from London turned back." It is easy to see the meaning of this, which might have been more clearly expressed, but the following item is clear to the obvious: "Staines is composed of houses on one side of the main road; on the other side are more houses forming a street."

Another book states: "Staines has a plain, but comfortable Church, one corner of which fell down during morning service in 1828." It is in connection with the rebuilding that Walford tells us that "the Architect was chosen by competition and secured his election to the job by sundry presents of oysters and cods' heads and shoulders to the sapient committee to whom the choice of an architect was entrusted." So can we be surprised that the result was described as "an imitation Gothic structure of the poorest type"?

The parochial accounts are not without humour. Here are a few from the seventeenth century, chiefly remarkable for their contrasting values:

1657. "To going to London by water, 6d.," which is reasonable enough seeing that the distance is some thirty-five miles, though the next item seems to smack of the profiteer: "To ferrying over the river to Church, 1s."

1659. "To excommunicating Pritt, 17s." Pritt's crime is not divulged, but it cost a good deal for those days. Perhaps it was this rash expenditure that put the value of husbands so low, for the next item reads: "To a poore gentlewoman to ransom her husband, 6d." Again no explanation is given to whom the ransom was to be paid; perhaps it was to the gipsies, for highwaymen did not hold to ransom. The country round here was densely wooded at that time, which would offer good cover to the Romanies.

To return to the Church records there are several further items with tragedy and humour intermixed. It is rather quaintly stated, again in the seventeenth century, that "the Bishop of London was appointed to present to Staines fit curates removable at pleasure," apparently after the manner of chessmen. Again we read: "The demesne lands granted to the Vicar of Staines are described in a terrier bearing the date 1610 to consist of 54 acres." One commentator on this paragraph is careful to point out that a terrier in this case is a book or roll containing particulars of land measurements, and that it has no connection with dogs! He is right about the land, but wrong about the dogs; for both words are derived from the most elementary source of all—mother earth.

In 1768 the parish records contain mention of a mishap probably common enough, which, in this case, ended in tragedy, for on December 5th of that year we find entry of the burial of several persons who "were drowned at New Year's Bridge at Staines, passengers in the Exeter Coach."

About a hundred years earlier we read: "1662. To putting ye Kynges armes round a belle, £2." The spelling and date give this entry a touch of unconscious humour.

Curiously enough a King's indiscretions have a real echo here, for with reference to the churchyard Walford states: "Lady Letitia Lade, who lies buried here, was a cast-off mistress of the Prince Regent, who married her to his coachman, one Mr. John Lade, whom he knighted as a reward for his pliancy in the matter, or for his skill in handling the ribbons. It is said Sir John Lade is also buried here, but his name is not recorded on the tombstone."

Readers of *Rodney Stone* will recall how Letty Lade pulled the leaders across in the race from Brighton to London between Sir Charles Tregellis's tandem and Sir John Lade's coach and four. Conan Doyle, however, says she was the widow of Rann, the highwayman—Sixteen String Jack, one of the "heroes" of Hounslow Heath—who was hanged in 1774. Of course, it is possible that she was both the mistress of a prince and the wife of a highwayman, though hardly likely, I think, even in the rather "free" life of the last decades of the eighteenth century. Besides the dates do not quite agree; the events in *Rodney Stone* occur in 1802, when Lady Lade would be much older than depicted in the novel.

Readers of another author of an earlier age—Dean Swift—will not forget how the prude Phillis, having run off with her father's groom John, the couple settled down to lead a cat-and-dog life as landlord and hostess of the Blue Boar Inn, which will now be looked for in vain,
"They keep at Staines the Old Blue Boar,"
while Taylor, "The Water Poet," describing a coach journey in the seventeenth century, writes on another old inn here:
"To Staines that night at five o'clock we coasted,
Where, at the Bush, we had bak'd, boil'd and roasted."
There is another anecdote connected with a Staines inn, though which one is not recorded. A lady of fashion in the eighteenth century is said to have cut with a diamond on a pane of glass the following inscription: "Dear Lord D—— has the softest lips of any man in England." Foote, the actor, coming into the room soon after, scored underneath the following couplet:
"Then as like as two chips
Are D——'s head and lips."

*   *   *   *   *   *

There is an unusual description of Staines in the "forties" of last century in *The Adventures of Mr. Ledbury,* by Albert Smith, where we read: "There are certainly places in Great Britain more frivolous and dissipated than Staines. The trivial occupations of slight minds—evening parties, dramatic representations, public entertainments, and the like—are not there in vogue, but orderly *reunions,* sedate meetings, and placid society, are in the ascendant. It always tempts lively visitors to reflect upon what a place it might be if it were not what it is. There are noble inns, but few travellers; there is a fine bridge, but few things go over it; a capacious institution, but few lectures; or rather a fair complement of lectures, but few auditors; a goodly river, but few boats; capabilities for all kinds of amusements, dispositions for none." In another part of the same book will be found the rather more exciting details of a "spooky" adventure on the river between Staines and Laleham.

On this part of the river is Jamnagar House, formerly the home of "Ranji" (as we all knew and loved him rather than by his official title). This house was formerly Thorncroft, the home for many years of Sir Edward Clarke, the eminent Victorian lawyer.

*   *   *   *   *   *

The story of Staines' bridges is a remarkable one, for in the course of six years we find records:
1797. A new stone bridge built which collapsed.
1801. A new iron bridge built which collapsed.
1803. A new iron bridge built which collapsed.

After the fall of the third the old wooden bridge, which had luckily been left standing, was again brought into use and carried on till 1832, when the present stone bridge was built.

A contemporary account of the state of affairs in 1806 is found in Lambert's *London Environs:* " Here is an elegant stone bridge over the Thames built from a design by Thos. Sandby, R.A., but owing to some of the piers having given way it has not yet been opened. An iron bridge having been thrown over the river, which is equally useless from the abutments being insecure; and the wooden bridge is the only one passable."

This grand old veteran showed it had life to the last, for it spanned the ages as it did the Thames. Its age is uncertain; it is generally attributed to the Romans, but it is older than that (as we saw in the *Itinerary of Antoninus*). When the Roman road to the west—now the Staines Road—was made and a military station formed at Staines it is probable that a stronger bridge was built for the marching of the Legions.

In 1262 three oaks from Windsor Forest were granted by the King for the repair of this bridge, which for many centuries was the only one above Kingston and London, hence the importance of it, especially as it helped to connect London with Portsmouth and Windsor. It is stated by several historians that the Barons probably chose Runnymeade to enforce John to seal the Magna Carta because of the convenience of this bridge in asesmbling their forces from different parts of England.

This old bridge has quite a niche in English Literature, especially about the seventeenth century, and something of its history can be read in the following four books of that period: *Thame Isis* (1632); John Taylor's *Last Voyage* (1641); *Cosmo's Travels* (1669); and Ogilby's *Travellers' Guide* (1669).

So as we stand on the modern bridge let us give a thought to the older structure, whose beginning is lost in the mists of the past, and whose end is almost within living memory, which besides carrying the travellers on the western road on their lawful occasions, has also played its part in the making of English History.

*   *   *   *   *   *

We can close this chapter with one or two further items of general interest. " In 1407 King Henry IV. wrote to the Privy Council from Windsor, stating that his physician forbade him to ride to London on account of an injury to his leg, and therefore he was journeying by water. He hoped to be at Staines that night, and to reach London three or four days later." A leisurely journey, but a delightful one in those days, when hardly a house would be seen on the banks of The Silent Highway, and the Great Forest of Middlesex would stretch down to the water's edge.

The trial of Sir Walter Raleigh, in 1603, took place in the Old Market House at Staines; he was confined in the Tower of London, so why Staines was chosen for his trial, as one old chronicle distinctly states, is a fact I cannot explain.

Our last item shall be a local puzzle. On an old map of the county are the mysterious words, on Staines Moor, " Bone Head "; not that Bone Heads are rare, but what does it mean on a map?

CHAPTER XXVI.
Where a Highwayman's Hiding-Hole can still be seen.

HATTON has suffered almost more than any other Heath village from the arterial road; its peacefulness has not been so much disturbed as cut in two. It is still rural and sleepy—though now threatened by the builder—but in two halves; one being where The Green Man Inn and the large mansion of Temple Hatton are situated, and the other, mostly fields in that part lying towards Harlington Corner, where we find that picturesque eighteenth century mansion known as Hatton Gore.

The name Temple in connection with this village is interesting; it probably indicates that in some remote period of its history the land was the property of the Knights Templar.

Not much of the house of Temple Hatton can be seen from the road, here and there a portion of the grey mass of the building shows through the trees, for the estate, now a convent school of St. Anthony, is well wooded.

Baron Pollock, the famous lawyer of Victorian days, once lived here, and he certainly needed a large house, for he had twenty-five children, forty grandchildren and four "greats." Many stories are told in the village of their former "squire," how even to the last he never wore spectacles, and other personal details, but the two that interested me most both contain a grain of humour. One concerns his boyhood and one his later life. The first happened when he was at St. Paul's School, from which he ran away because he said there was no one there capable of teaching him any more. The irate headmaster called on his father, but the latter had to confess that he had no hold over the boy, who never returned to school. The master was furious and declared that his late pupil "was born to be hanged." Years after, when the boy had risen to be Attorney-General, the father and the headmaster met again, when the latter said, "Well, my boy didn't turn out so badly after all, doctor!" "Ah, my dear sir," replied the master, "didn't I prophesy long ago that he would one day occupy an elevated position!"

The other story is of an occasion when Pollock was Lord Chief Baron of the Exchequer, and on one summer day when his carriage came to take him from one assize town to another he thought he would ride outside rather than in the closed vehicle. He said to his chief clerk, who had been with him for years, "Now, Coleman, you and your son ride inside and I will go on the box; but they mustn't know that I am the judge as we go along. You must ' do the judge,' and mind you do it well." The journey progressed, and at a wayside inn the driver stopped to water the horses; the landlord came out and inquired of the assumed servant on the box if "his lordship in the carriage would be pleased to take any refreshment." "My Lord," said his representative on the box, "will your lordship take anything here?" Coleman, carrying out his instructions, immediately answered, "Oh, certainly; a bottle of champagne, please."

The wine was brought and drank by Coleman and his son with great politeness, when the clerk remarked to the landlord, "Give my man on the box a glass of beer, my good fellow, I daresay he is thirsty, and he will settle with you." This was done, and the Chief Baron, who had a keen sense of humour, was fond of telling this story against himself, and always declared that he enjoyed the beer as much as he did the joke.

One of Baron Pollock's grandsons is Lord Hanworth, who took his title from the neighbouring village, and whose book on his grandfather, *Lord Chief Baron Pollock,* has a chapter, "Family Life," which contains mention of Hatton that is full of interest. "By the end of the fifties," we read, "my grandfather came to prefer living at Hatton rather than staying in town . . . the house is still to be seen in proximity to the new motor road where it leads to the old main road to Staines. As his family grew up the house at Hatton was enlarged and the garden developed, for he was devoted to it, and trees were planted with judgment and taste. When he had originally gone to Hatton the Heath of Hounslow reached nearly to the house itself. Gradually farming cultivated the Heath, and brought development to the estate, to which he had added from time to time.

"He was devoted to Hatton, which he spoke of as being 'the product of no Long Vacation plus willingness to work.' In 1834 he bought 'Little Hanworth Park,' as it was called in contrast with Hanworth Park . . . the estate comprised 300 acres of farm land, through which the sluggish river, the Crane, passes. There had been a good house on the property when it belonged to the Tollemaches, but this was destroyed by fire in 1806, leaving only the pump that had been in the scullery standing, as indeed it was in my day, for the use of the farmer whose farmhouse was a remnant of the stables of the Tollemaches.

"There was some shooting at Hanworth; good enough, at any rate, to afford General Peel some sport, for he used to come over from Marble Hill. . . . Time, and in particular the Great War, has changed the face of this oasis in the midst of houses creeping out from the outskirts of London; and although part of the estate is still farm land, the Southern Railway have taken a portion for shunting.

"Yet one feature happily remains. On the banks of the Crane, and on the little eyots that are washed by it—some of which, rather curiously, and from the enclosure of this area from Hounslow Heath, belong to Isleworth parish—there still flourishes the beautiful wild balsam, *noli-me-tangere,* which, with its translucent green foliage and rich orange flowers, mark Hanworth as a favoured spot, for it is one of the few places in the South where it is to be found. Its habitat is generally Northern England and North Wales, yet here within twelve miles of Hyde Park Corner it forms one of the beauties of the later summer and autumn."

There are some delightful stories of the Baron's guests, of which the two following are, perhaps, the best: "On one occasion Thackeray came down to stay for a Saturday to Monday at Hatton, and upon arrival greeted my aunt with the words: 'How do you do, Miss Pollock? Dickens has killed his mother, so mine must continue to live on.' This seemingly alarming sentence did not refer to a tragedy—but merely to respective characters in *David Copperfield* and *Pendennis.*"

Another story refers to Sir David Wilkie, the famous artist, who was a guest at dinner when a question arose as to whether a crack in a pane of glass had been caused from inside or outside; and when asked his opinion he excused from giving any on the ground that he was a painter and not a glazier.

THE BEDFONT "PEACOCKS" AS GIRLS.

From a rare 18th century print

Baron Pollock married, as his second wife, the daughter of Captain Richard Langslow, who lived at Hatton, "where my grandfather had a cottage to which his children were sent for a change of air." The Baron always praised the air of Hatton highly—there was no arterial road then to poison the atmosphere.

The Baron died in 1870, at the age of eighty, and is buried at Hanworth.

* * * * * *

Hatton to-day, despite the changes, is a picturesque and pleasant spot, with its farms and village pond (now rather diminished) and the old Green Man Inn, a little modernised, I'm afraid, since the Highwayman's Hole was first built, and where it is said Dick Turpin, and other knights of the road, used to hide from the Bow Street Runners. To those who do not mind getting in a sooty mess this hole at the back of the fireplace can still be explored.

Curiously enough the two books to which the modern rambler round London owes most for information both practically ignore Hatton. Thorne gives four lines to it and does not even trouble to index it, while Walford, though he gives it a place in the index, dismisses it in one line. Even worse, Brewer's *History of Middlesex* has no mention at all of it.

Probably the best account (if pre-war) of Hatton yet written is in C. G. Harper's delightful book *Rural Nooks Round London*, where we are told: "Taking a cross road over what was once Hounslow Heath we come to the singularly retired hamlet of Hatton. On the way nothing is seen but acre after acre of rich orchards, marvellously brought into being out of what was not so very long ago thought to be valueless land. The wealth of fruit from these once derelict acres is remarkable, and it is a pretty sight in early spring to see the yet bare branches of the fruit trees so far as eye can reach with pure white or bright yellow flowers beneath them.

"Hatton, amidst all these rural activities, is to the last degree simple and innocent. There is no guile at Hatton; not a church, and I do not think there is a shop " (a village stores is there now). " The place seems so idyllic—but there is an inn at Hatton, and although it and the hamlet are now sufficiently unspotted from the wicked world, it was not ever thus.

" Indeed it was once far otherwise, for when a solitude vastly different from the existing state of affairs brooded over the level heath, the highwaymen found Hatton the hub of the wild. A glance at the map will explain this, and why they found its solitary little inn so convenient to their sly trade. Even highwaymen and footpads sometimes wanted food and drink and a rest. They were sufficiently daring to practise their trade on the Heath by day as well as by night, but they could not, individually, carry on day *and* night. I suspect they worked in eight-hour shifts. Coming off at dark at the cross-roads, the gallant fellow who had sat so long waiting for the coaches wanted refreshment, and found it, and hiding, too, at the Green Man at Hatton, whose landlord was the confident of all his tribe, harbourer and comforter of the wicked, keeper of a kind of early safe-storage for stolen valuables.

" Now the situation of Hatton was peculiar. In those times its position in the rare-visited back-country of the Heath, between the two famous coaching highways, was, in a manner, highly strategical. Hatton commanded from an almost equidistant position between the Bath and Staines Roads, most desirable from the highwayman's point of view."

The present appearance of the Green Man, comments the author in conclusion, shows a place "looking as innocent as the foregoing description would lead us to expect, but there was an ingenious hiding-hole for highwaymen in the tiny, countrified parlour of the inn, in which occasionally the hard-pressed fellows were hidden, not without sad happenings to their fine clothes, as may be suspected, as the hole is at the back of the fireplace. Sometimes the Runners came to Hatton and enquired curiously about those affairs, when those who were 'wanted' had to crawl into the darksome, and at times uncomfortably warm, hole. It is here even now and is a famous relic.

"For the rest Hatton is empty of interest. Until recently there stood an old wooden pound hard by, but a tree, Coronation or other, has been planted in the place of it." Much as I like his account, I do not agree with Harper when he says Hatton is devoid of interest; I managed to find a good deal; in fact, he contradicts himself, for he writes in another of his books, *The Old Inns of Old England,* after describing this old inn, "it seems a bower of rustic simplicity, standing at Hatton—'Hatton-in-the-Hinterland'—as one feels tempted to style it; a rural cross, 'the world forgetting, by the world forgot,' tucked away in the beautiful orchard country between the angle formed by the two old coach roads west of Hounslow. It is to-day (1906) a beautiful spot, as I have said, where the pink and white of the apple blossom delights the eye in spring, and the daffodil grows. The old pounds and the pond where the ducks quack and dive, in front of the Green Man, make an idyllic picture, unspotted from the world."

The writer then goes on to give another description of the famous Hole, and altogether refutes his own words with reference to the interest to be found in this little village, an interest, despite changes, still there to-day. He also tells us that the fields round Hatton remind him of Millet's picture "The Angelus," and the simile is very apt. It bears out what a friend, whom I took there one day, remarked of the countryside between Hatton and Stanwell. "This," he said, "reminds me very strongly of Flanders Fields." Again a true simile.

The sign of "The Green Man" is significant, for as Larwood's *History of Signboards* tells us, wherever this appears over an inn it is an indication that the district was once well wooded, for though sometimes called Robin Hood, the representation is that of a forester.

I found interest both outside and inside the Green Man; for conversations in old country inns can be most entertaining, as I found in this little Middlesex hostelry. In company with "the lads of the village" of the older generation we had pretty well exhausted the highwayman topic, in which the district still takes a lively interest, and I had listened to the landlord's amusing tale of how, quite recently, a man for a bet had climbed into the sooty Hiding Hole, only to find on emerging, black but triumphant, that the layer of odds of ten shillings against this feat being performed, not having the necessary capital to pay up on losing, had "silently stole away" while the winner was proving otherwise, so the latter found it a dirty business in more senses than one.

After we had all enjoyed this yarn, more graphically told than my brief outline, one of the yokels made the remark: "I wonder if the gent 'as 'eard about So-and-So's cottage?" This was pointed out to me; it was one of the most picturesque in the village, but I knew no special story about it, so I sought information.

It seems that this story has never appeared in print before, but has been handed down, with variations, from father to son for generations. "Its where the Bishop 'id, sir," said one. Now in the stormy history of the mediaeval church no doubt prelates have had to do strange things, but I had never heard of one forced to hide on Hounslow Heath. "No, it wernt no Bishop wot 'id there," broke in another, "it were a King." Discussion at once arose and opinion seemed divided into Bishops v. Kings. "You don't mean Tom King?" I queried, for it seemed feasible that Turpin's fellow-highwayman should have taken refuge here. "No, sir," interposed an old man who had not spoken before, "it wern't no 'ighwayman—it were *seven* Bishops wot 'id 'ere."

This view, though it suggested a pathetic picture of these seven ecclesiastics crowding into this small cottage, at least gave me a clue as to the date of the story. Obviously 1688, when seven bishops had a great influence on the Heath camp if never here in person, but why they should he hiding here was more than I could fathom. "I tell you it wern't no bishops," broke in the chief adherent of the King theory, "it were a King right enough."

"Well, 'oo the gent wants to see is Dick Whittington," added another of the company. What on earth this thrice-mayor of London had to do with the Seven Bishops was beyond me, but before I could make inquiry a shadow passed the window. "Why, I do believe as 'e is 'ere now," said the speaker; but the shadow passed by, and it was not a man at all who entered when someone opened the door—but a *cat* solemnly walked into the bar! Certainly a striking coincidence, but it proved to be the inn cat and had no connection this time with Dick Whittington.

We talked a good deal more on the subject and some sort of enlightenment gradually came to me out of the various wild opinions. It seemed that "Dick" Whittington was a local farmer, his real name was not Dick, I believe, but it obviously clung to him. It seemed that he was credited with knowing the true facts, so I called on him but was unlucky to find him out. To cut several long stories short, I subsequently managed, from different sources, to piece together the tale of that cottage.

According to local tradition this building, and it is certainly old enough, was the headquarters of King James II. while he was with the army at the Heath camp, when the tidings of the Acquittal of the Seven Bishops was brought down, though it is usually stated that the actual news was received in Lord Faversham's tent, apparently somewhere near the cottage, which, now divided into two, was then a single farmhouse.

Well, there is the story, and somehow I believe it; these village legends, when the chaff of the gossip of ages is separated from the corn of possible fact, often have a strange knack of containing a basis of truth.

* * * * * *

I next encountered Mr. Dietrich—a great character in Hatton and a brave man. He always wears a top hat; not that this is so much heroic as inconvenient, but when you know that Mr. Dietrich wears a top hat *and* rides a "penny-farthing" at the same time you will realise that he is made of stern stuff, and a man of high ideals. He is a man of parts also, for besides mending the village bicycles he is also the only (as far as I know) travelling tonsorial artist in Middlesex—to call him the village barber seems lacking in respect—for Mr. Dietrich rides round to different farms on his lofty anti-whisker mission, and will, or so I am told, shave a customer by the roadside. I have never seen him perform the latter operation, but one day I hope to be the "victim"; to be shaved by a hedge-barber, complete with topper and high-bicycle, would be an experience both novel and picturesque.

    *   *   *   *   *   *

There is not much more to say about Hatton, except to deplore the motor accidents that seem a daily happening there. One can hardly drink a cup of tea at Hatton House, a most delightful old Middlesex farm suddenly exposed to view by the cutting of the new road, and now turned into a Road House, without hearing a crash or seeing some smash outside the windows.

When I call this place a Road House I mean one of the better sort; not the awful places that go under this name sometimes, which seem to attract all the brainless fools who have cars, but care nothing about an old farmhouse, unless it is ruined by a ghastly jazz-band and garish decoration. Your real lover of Old England avoids such places as the Devil shuns Holy Water.

For those who would read a little more of Hatton, especially of the Green Man and similar places in the olden days, I would advise a perusal of Rudolf de Cordova's most interesting article Highwayman Inn, in *Cassell's Magazine* (1905).

CHAPTER XXVII.

Where Caesar's Legions camped and of a meeting with The Last Wolf in England.

T URN down from the Bath Road by the Three Magpies (not the *old* Magpies) and you will come upon a road as rural as anywhere in England. It is not, perhaps, scenically wonderful, but for detachment from London, or any urban interests, it would be hard to find its equal; there is a calmness and serenity about it that is soothing in a mad rushing world.

At the beginning of the road, on the left, is a small brick building, once a chapel, or it has that appearance, but now some municipal office, I believe; though I look upon it as the Headquarters of the Middlesex Agricultural Society, for it is there I always stop to read their notices.

This little building is, in a sense, a landmark, for in the strip of woodland behind is—or was, for there is no trace of it now to the casual observer —the Roman Camp, about which Stukely, and others have written.

The newly-erected corrugated-iron buildings and tall iron chimneys—some sort of brick works—have not improved the landscape near the Roman Camp; but let us hope, as iron structures, they may be temporary.

Near here is a curious notice—it has been there for years: "No Gipsies or Totting allowed." There have certainly been gipsies here recently, to my knowledge, and if, as I have been told, Totting is a corruption of "Touting," this part of the notice has not always been strictly observed—as I have also discovered!

There is nothing else in King's Arbour to detain us, and soon the road gives way to Heath Row, though that place is little more than a few cottages and the village " pub," The Harrow. There are two fine old farms in this village, both on the right of the road; the first, notable for its large stackyard, is Heathrow Hall on the old maps, and the second farm, a little further on, reminds me strongly of one of those delightful old farmsteads met with in the Weald of Kent, minus the oasthouses.

It is said that King's Arbour got its name from the fact that here was a stable used by George III., who would not use inns for changing horses, but kept an establishment of his own. This may or may not be true, but if it is why are there not many more King's Arbours on various roads?

Edward Ironside wrote, in 1797: " *Hethrow*, or as formerly written *Heathrow*, has a very considerable fishery for lamperns, a small kind of lampreys, which are used as bait by the English and Dutch in the cod and turbot fishery barges. Large quantities are fetched by the Hollanders during the demand for the fisheries from November to June. The usual price is 6s. per hogshead; afterwards they are sold for as many pence." All traces of this old-time industry seem to have now disappeared.

In Heath Row are some old cottages—of which a picture appears here— which might be in the heart of Devonshire, for their antiquity, their picturesqueness, and lonely situation. Very few people ever see them, for so few go along this road, which leads only, and by a roundabout way, to Stanwell, which is far easier to reach by other routes; no motorist would " waste " his time (thank Heaven!) on this mere by-road with the arterial horrors so near.

Perry Oaks is even smaller; a few scattered cottages, a delightful old farm and some orchards and meadows—and there it is. It is hardly a hamlet, even, but it is nevertheless a beautiful spot. Few have ever heard of it, and if you ask the average person if they know it they look at you as if you were enquiring for a place in Cumberland, or some equally far-away place, instead of one hardly a dozen miles from London. In fact, Perry Oaks, though certainly on the map (and not all of them), is only just so; and therein lies its charm.

Lysons has a brief mention of this place, which he informs us. " The Manor of Perry Place (now called Perry Oaks), described as a parcel of the demesne of the Manor of Harmondsworth, was demised in 1587 to Sir Christopher Hatton for 21 years at a rental of £8 per annum. . . The estate was granted to Lord Paget in 1603." This is all it has of historical fame, yet it has a most romantic memory, which came to my notice quite by chance, as some of the rambler's best clues do.

In *All the Year Round* for 1868 is this arresting paragraph: " Hounslow Heath was once an oak forest that spread its green boughs from Staines to Brentford, and there is an old tradition that the last wolf in England, killed centuries ago, was hunted down at Perry Oaks in that neighbourhood." This was great news; but no references are given as to the sources of this information, nor could I trace in any books on the county any other mention of this incident. It was enough, however, to set me to try and find out more. That a great forest once covered this now open land we know, and even many years after any wolf roamed here Samuel Pepys got lost in it: " 1665. I went to the new post-house at Charing-Cross and there got horses to Hounslow. So to Staines, and there, by this time, it was dark, and got a guide, who lost his way in the forest, till by help of the moone I led my guide in the way again."

One autumn afternoon I happened to be at Perry Oaks for no particular reason (sometimes the best reason of all). Though certainly now denuded of forest, it is still lonely enough for any wolf to make its home. Twilight was fast closing into night as I sat on a field gate, smoking, and let my imagination run riot, trying to picture what the place must have been like in those far-off days when giant oaks covered the now cleared ground, and the traveller might meet the dreaded wolf in any forest glade. It was a stimulating mental picture and I dreamed on. In front of me, about fifty yards across a clearing, was a clump of trees, thick enough to fade into dark shadows in the interior.

I was gazing at those trees, whose roots were hidden by a slight ground mist, and their blackness rather allured me. All at once I was conscious of a rather uncanny feeling; for out of the darkness gleamed two green eyes. I watched, fascinated. Yes, it was no hallucination—it was a wolf's head!

Had my imagination been so strong as to conjure up visions? In another moment the body of the animal came into view, turning at a right-angle to the trees and making its way across the field in front. There was no mistaking that profile; the long "lolloping" gait of a wolf is peculiar to that animal, and the jaws were open showing the great fangs, with the tongue hanging out at one corner.

I did not move, but still gazed spellbound. There was not a sound, no footsteps were audible, but without a doubt there was the shadow of a huge grey wolf, magnified and slightly distorted by the mist. It was terribly real —and yet so unreal!

I confess sometimes to being a dreamer, but I do not "see things." Ghosts have always dodged me; even though I have sought them in their haunts. Was this, then, to be the beginning; this spirit from the past appearing on the very spot where tradition said that the last of its race in this country expired with the hunter's arrow through its quivering heart?

If the beast had just passed across the view, and so out of sight, I might still think that I had seen the ghost of England's last wolf, had not a diversion occurred that brought me to earth. A whistle sounded close by, and the animal turned quickly and made towards the gate. A man emerged from the copse, his footsteps, like those of the wolf, deadened by the grass.

The mystery was cleared up, for when the "wolf" got near I saw what it was—a large Alsatian dog. It was, nevertheless, a strange coincidence that the first cousin to a wolf should thus suddenly appear on this spot at the time my thoughts were on this subject.

I spoke to the owner of the "ghost wolf" and he joined me in a friendly pipe. He was much interested and amused when I told him my story; though he lived at Stanwell he had never heard the legend of the Last Wolf of Perry Oaks, which was no surprise to me; I am getting used to finding how little folk know—or apparently care—of their own districts.

The "wolf" was quite friendly, and when I patted his handsome head and called him Fenrir, his owner, a pleasant but entirely unimaginative young man in plus-fours, quite missed the allusion to the fabulous wolf of Scandinavian mythology, and solemnly stated the dog's name was Rex.

* * * * * *

When the man and "wolf" had gone on their way I sat for some time deep in thought, for which I had much food. Naturally it was of wolves and all the verses I had ever read regarding loupine matters—their themes, anyhow, if my memory was not exactly word-perfect.

There were Thomson's lines in *Winter*·
> " Cruel as death, and hungry as the grave!
> Burning for blood; bony and gaunt and grim!
> Assembling wolves in raging troops descend."

Then Shakespeare's lines from *Henry IV.* were certainly more appropriate for the district I was in:
> " O, thou wilt be a wilderness again,
> Peopled with wolves, they old inhabitants."

While Chaucer's words:
> " A wolf there lay before him at his feete,
> With eyen red, and of a man he eat,"

were sufficiently gruesome to please any sensation lover, as were the ones (I do not know who wrote them):
> " The wind leaps over the flat of the fen,
> And jangles the chains of the poor dead men.
> *(And oh! and oh! 'tis the death of the day!)*
> The wind falls down from the edge of the scar,
> And ruffles the pool where the dead men are,
> *(And hark to the howl of the wolf so grey!)*"

Appropriate enough for Hounslow Heath in the old days, though the lines that perhaps lingered most in my mind were some powerful ones *'Twixt Dog and Wolf*, which, curiously, I came across only a week or so previously. Again they were anonymous:
> " A dog is howling at the court-yard door;
> Within the horses drag their halter-chains;
> Behold! the world is full of misty rains;
> And from a near pinewood into sight
> Steals one grey wolf!"

These lines, especially the last two, were quite applicable to the present case; I *had* thought of quoting them to the owner of the "wolf," but I refrained after the little episode of the name; I was afraid he would tell me that the clump of trees was an orchard and not a pinewood.

* * * * * *

The next day I went wolf-hunting—in the forest of books. The quarry was two-fold; to find out more about the tradition of the Last Wolf of Perry Oaks, and, if unable to do that, to learn something of the Last Wolves in England. In the former I drew blank, in spite of one " warm " scent, as you will see, but in the latter I ran my quarry to paper.

It is fairly easy to find references to wolves in England during mediaeval days, it is their later history in our island that has been lost in the mist of years. In Anglo-Saxon days, as we read in Camden's *Britannia*, these animals abounded " in great numbers in England and in the tenth century, in the reign of Athelstane, places of retreat were often erected in order to protect travellers from being devoured by wolves." In 1281 Edward I. instituted a Royal Commission on the subject of wolves, and issued a mandate, which stated: " The King to all bailiffs: Know ye that we have enjoined our dear and faithful Peter Corbet, that in all forests, parks and other places in which wolves may be found, that he may destroy all these wolves with his men, dogs and engines."

In spite of the dear and faithful Peter and his engines, wolves continued to flourish, and in 1320 we find a man, bearing the significant name of John le Wolfhunt, holding lands from Edward III. on condition that he "did chase and destroy all wolves that might come into the King's forests being adjacent to the said lands."

Some forty years later—in 1366—one Thomas de Engaine held lands by the service of finding "at his own proper costs certain dogs for the destroying of wolves, martin cats, wild cats and other vermaine" within certain northern counties and also "Oxford, Essex, Buckingham and Middlesex."

This was my "warm scent," but though it proved the existence of wolves in the same county, it did not throw any light on the tradition of Perry Oaks. Still it was something.

Since writing this luck has favoured me and I *have* discovered a direct reference, for in a mediaeval account of Harmondsworth (quoted elsewhere) there is an actual mention of a special swineherd to watch over the pigs in the surrounding woods to guard against wolves. In those days (1100 A.D.) these woods extended to Perry Oaks.

We learn from Baker's *Chronicles* that when Edward IV., in 1474, invaded France there were presented to him at the time, by the French king, Louis XI., among other gifts, "a wolf and a wild boar, beasts at that time in England."

Here chance entered into the search, as it so often does, and I found a clue in an unusual way. I was looking, on a different quest, through Coke's *Institutes of the Laws of Enlgand*, a book one would not ordinarily associate with romantic memories, when I came across the following illuminating statement: "There be many beasts of the forest in England. The hart in summer, the hind in winter; the buck in summer; wolf; the fox; the martin and capreolus, the roe." This was written in 1628, though Pennant's *British Quadrupeds* gives 1680 as the date of the last wolf in Northern England.

I hate to destroy a Legend of Hounslow Heath, but I really think that the famous wolf must have been the last in *Southern* England, probably before the disaforestation of the Warren of Staines of which Perry Oaks was a part, which occurred as we have seen in 1227.

Coke was a former owner of Osterley Park, and we find a record that on "January 3rd, 1598, Brigitta, daughter of Edward Coke, Attorney General (afterwards Lord Chief Justice) was baptised in the Chapel of Austerlie in Heston Church.'

As a magazine paragraph about a wolf first drew my attention to Perry Oaks another may be quoted in conclusion, this time from *The Ladies' Magazine* for 1751: "We hear from Hounslow in Middlesex that the neighbouring villages have been very much alarmed this fortnight past by the appearance of a Wolf that broke loose from a Person that show'd a Collection of Wild Beasts at Hounslow Fair. It has destroyed several sheep and calves, and it is feared will do much more Damage, as it cannot at present be pursued without doing great Harm to the standing corn. It has been seen by several persons and the owner has offered a Reward of One Hundred Guineas to anyone that will take it unhurt, which has made Numbers attempt it, but to no Effect, it being very Swift."

Here our information ceases. Whether or not it got as far as Perry Oaks and gave birth to the Last Wolf Legend is a mystery. It is a coincidence that in my cutting-book I came across a recent newspaper paragraph, which reads: "Four sheep were killed and thirty injured by an Alsatian dog on a farm at Heath Row; watch was kept and the dog was shot." It is but

THE LAST WOLF IN ENGLAND.
A Legend of Perry Oaks.

From an old print

Photo lent by Sir Montagu Sharpe

"OLD ENGLAND."
A remnant of primæval woodland
between Isleworth and Brentford.

a mile or so from Perry Oaks; I hope it wasn't my friend " the wolf."

It is strange how so many things " tie up " with the highwaymen; now there is no connection (except metaphorically) between one of those gentry and a wolf, yet in John Ashton's *Social Life in the Reign of Queen Anne* we read (and the italics are the author's): " The highwayman who roamed Hounslow Heath and other roads near London certainly carried his life in his hand—he was a *Wolf's Head*, and, everyone's hand being against him, he was shot at whenever he could be. And now wolves, highwaymen, and the Heath itself where they both once roamed, have all passed into the limbo of half-forgotten things.

CHAPTER XXVIII.

Where Lived the captor of Guy Fawkes, and other annals of an old village.

IF Goldsmith were alive to-day and came exploring with us—a thing he loved to do—I wonder which would be his " Sweet Auborn "— " the lovelist village of the plain "—of Hounslow ?

Even if his wandering wraith asked me that question I should have to think hard before giving a definite answer—if I could do so at all. I think my final choice would rest between Stanwell, Cranford and Harmondsworth, and even then, their respective charms weighed in the mental balance, I'm not quite sure which would turn the scale.

We have now arrived on our wanderings at Stanwell, which it is good to find still a village and not a camouflaged suburb, in spite of the Council houses at one end, which, to be fair, have not obtruded themselves here so blatantly as in many places .

It is still a typical Heath village as Walford reminds us in *Greater London* (1883) : " Up to the beginning of the nineteenth century upwards of 500 acres of land in Stanwell parish were an open waste, of which some 350 acres formed a portion, or continuation of Hounslow Heath. This state of things, however, is now altered, and what was once barren and profitless has now been turned into green pastures and smiling cornfields."

Equally true to-day, and Stanwell, lying as it does between the old Staines Road and that horror called an arterial road, which has scored the face of rural Middlesex, is still peaceful and one is able to stroll about and admire it in comparative security. It is built more or less in the form of a cross and is certainly a very " complete " little place, for here we have almost everything that goes to make up an old English village—the fine old church, the green, the wayside inn, farms and cottages, with what are generally known, rather snobbishly I think, as " better-class " houses on the outskirts—and last but not least, a " great house " ; in this case, Stanwell Place.

" The country round Stanwell is flat, but green and pleasant, especially on the Bucks side," writes Thorne. " It is a secluded village, of a few humble cottages, some better houses standing apart in well-sheltered grounds or pretty gardens. The little green might tempt the sketcher. In the centre stands a huge old elm, beyond it is the wheel-wright's shop, with an occasional flare from the forge, and in front a wild array of broken carts, ploughs and trunks of trees. Close at hand are two rustic inns, ' The

Five Bells' and 'The Wheatsheaf.' Over the churchyard yews and elms rises the village spire. Old men and children give life and colour to the foreground."

This was written between fifty and sixty years ago, and just as applicable to-day; even the wheelwright's and the old forge are still there; and this in an age when to revisit most places round London after a lapse of even a year is often to find them altered for the worse. Even the old men and children in the Stanwell word-picture are still there, though it may be that the latter have now become the former, whose originals have joined "the rude forefathers of the hamlet" in the village churchyard.

Stanwell still dreams the days away amidst the fields—or so it seems to a tired Londoner who may find himself in this peaceful spot—for about it yet lingers an air of rural peace that is very delightful so near London. There are many houses and cottages of undoubted antiquity and to two of the latter I see the inscription "Old World Cottages" is attached; I have often heard such buildings so called, but I have never before seen it actually written up as a definite name. Yet, why not? In this case it is certainly true enough.

Another thing that will intrigue the lover of the curious is a whale's jaw archway in a cottage garden. The exact history of this is vague; I am told that it was brought here by an old sea captain who came to this pleasant anchorage towards the close of his life's voyage; a likely explanation and it may be so; anyhow, true or not, it has become a local legend.

Stanwell church is large for it's situation and forms the fourth side of the picturesque "square" of the green. The building has Norman work in it, but is, perhaps, more notable for the possession (rare in village churches) of a clerestory, which, however, is modern, dating from a mid-Victorian restoration.

This church was once the property of Chertsey Abbey, Richard de Windsor having exchanged the advowson for the manor of West Bedfont, but came into the possession of the Crown at the Dissolution. It was formerly famous for its Easter Sepulchre, formed out of one of the tombs (fully described in Bloxham's *Gothic Architecture;* while in Horace Walpole's *Anecdotes of Painting* will be found further details of the sculpture on Knyvet's tomb).

Dr. Bruno Ryves, author of *Mercurius Rusticus,* an account of the sufferings of the Royalists, was vicar of this parish; he was deprived of his living during the Civil War, but recovered it at the Restoration.

The church registers contain some curious entries, without anything that calls for special attention, though the following is not without interest, under the burials:—

"William Rowls, killed in a duel at Cranford Bridge,
by Jack England, July 1st, 1784.

Then there is a note that Andrews, Lord Windsor, gave " a public house, known by the name of The Horns, and 12 acres of land, for the purpose of beautifying the Church."

I was intrigued by finding a note that in 1632 " 19 and 4/5 infants were baptised at Stanwell." There being no account of the quaint old-world ceremony by which four-fifths of an infant was baptised, I presume this to be something in the nature of an average.

The registers, of course, contain many names, in addition to those that appear in other parts of this chapter, that we have not space to notice save in passing, though I am tempted to record one or two for the reason that it is rather remarkable that this little village, up to the end of the 18th century lying in the midst of the wild heath of Hounslow, and quite away from civilisation, should have attracted so many of the " quality " in times when that word meant a wider social gulf than exists to-day.

Sir John Bankes resided in Stanwell up to the Civil War, for we find entries of births and burials of several of his children between the years 1636-42. Here is Lysons' account of him: " Sir John Bankes, who is stiled by Clarendon in his *History of the Rebellion* as a man of great abilities and unblemished integrity, was made Attorney General in 1634 and Lord Chief Justice in 1640. He was a zealous loyalist, but so highly esteemed by all parties that among the propositions made by Parliament in 1642 was a request that Sir John Bankes might be continued Lord Chief Justice. His constant adherence to the King, however, and probably his Lady's gallant defence of Corfe Castle, rendered him afterwards so obnoxious to the Republicans that his estates were confiscated and it was voted that he should be exempted from pardon."

Bankes did not live to the end of the Civil War, dying at Oxford in 1644, where he is buried. The heroic Lady Bankes whose deeds are historical, lived to see " the King enjoy his own again." She came of a well-known Middlesex family, the Hawtreys of Ruislip.

Sir George Nares, the famous 18th century lawyer and Justice of the Court of Common Pleas, was born at Stanwell in 1716. While in 1738 and 1744 we find, respectively, the records of the burials of the Hon. Brig.-Gen. Murray and the Hon. Charles Murray, brothers of the Earl of Dunmore.

The Hon. James Bertie, son of the Earl of Abingdon, who died at Stanwell in 1735, became possessed of the manor through his wife, who was daughter and heiress of Lord Willoughby.

Stanwell seems also to be a favourite place for weddings in the 18th century and what more picturesque setting could be desired—for we find entries:—

> 1712.—Sir William Osbaldston, Bart., married to the Hon. Catherine Bertie.
>
> 1729.—Sir Peter Soames, Bart., married to Miss Aleathea Philipps.
>
> 1774.—Sir Hungerford Hopkins, Bart., married to Catherine Stanhope.

So it goes on, and Stanwell contains in its registers these marriages, births and deaths of its quality and peasantry alike, whose lives, grand or simple, all make up the story of this pleasant village on the Heath.

There are some interesting tombs in the church, notably the 15th century one of Thomas Windsor (father of Lord Windsor) of Stanwell Place, who left a curious will with intricate instructions. Among other bequests were twenty wax torches, four for Stanwell and one each to the sixteen nearest churches in the county of Middlesex.

Of greater interest, perhaps, is the more ornate marble tomb of Lord Knyvet and his lady in the chancel, the work of Nicholas Stone, the well-known 17th century sculptor. It seems, as far as we can now judge, an excellent likeness of Knyvet, showing him in his robes with the ruffle and pointed beard of the period.

The tomb bears the inscription " Under this stone are buryed the bodies of the Right Honourable Lord Knyvet who deceased this 27th of July, anno d'mi, 1622 and of his Lady Elizabeth, his wife, who also dyed the 5th of September following in the same yeare."

This Lord Knyvet was a gentleman of the Privy Chamber to Queen Elizabeth. He was knighted by James I. and created Warden of the Mint. The King presented him with the Manor of Stanwell in 1603, and later raised him to the peerage. Such confidence had the King in Knyvet that he trusted to him and his wife the upbringing of his daughter, the Princess Mary, who, always a delicate child, eventually died whilst living at Stanwell Place.

It is not these facts, however, that constitute the real interest we have in Lord Knyvet to-day; it is for a much more romantic reason, for it was he who caught Guy Fawkes in the cellars of the Houses of Parliament.

. Because he received the warning letter in connection with the Gunpowder Plot Lord Monteagle is generally looked upon as the discoverer of Fawkes, but the popular imagination has attachetd the label to the wrong hero of this adventure. It is true Monteagle started the investigation, but it was Knyvet who actually made the arrest. History books—especially school ons—are responsible for this misunderstanding, usually mentioning Monteagle but not Knyvet. Memoirs, however, leave no doubt of the part played by the latter and the incident is told fully in many histories.

How Knyvet came to be the discoverer of Guy Fawkes was due to chance and not choice, for when Monteagle's letter was shown to James I. he ordered a search to be made in the cellars of the House, and it was in his official capacity as a Justice of the Peace for Westminster that this duty fell upon Knyvet. A contemporary account tells us " Sir Thomas Knyvet was sent to make a search in the vaults underneath the House of Lords and coming about midnight, with some of his company, found a man standing without doors in boots, and turning over some billets and faggots there laid (under the colour of winter fuel for Thomas Percy, who had hired house hereunto), discovered thirty-six barrels of gunpowder; the person in boots being one Guido Faux (Mr. Percy's servant), who should have put fire to the train upon the first day of the Parliament."

It is curious to note that mention is made twice of the fact that Guy Fawkes was wearing boots; it surely would have been more in keeping with a hidden conspirator if he had discarded them.

The details of this Roman Catholic wholesale murder plot, which came so near to being successful, were eventually confessed to Knyvet by Fawkes, who naively told his captor that " had he been ready he would have blown him up, himself and House and all."

There is a grain or two of truth, perhaps, in the statement that the only man who ever went into Parliament with the firm idea of doing his duty was Guy Fawkes. I like, too, the anecdote of the boy who, after reading about The Gunpowder Plot, said to his father: " But *why* did Guy Fawkes want to blow up the Members of Parliament? ' " Ah, my boy," was the reply, " When you are my age you will understand ! "

In *Epochs and Episodes of History* there is a picture of the capture, which shows Knyvet in the very act of laying hands upon Fawkes. The likeness to the effigy on the tomb in Stanwell is striking; possibly the artist may have used it as a model, or perhaps the pointed beard gives it the resemblance.

The following night, so this account goes on, Sir Thomas Knyvet, suspicious that all was not well, made a further search, with the result we know.

I give this account for what it is worth; it is interesting, but there are weak points in it; if Monteagle and Suffolk had no suspicion why did Knyvet suddenly have doubts?

This account is notable, for besides this mention of Sion House at Isleworth, it makes mention of a meeting of the conspirators at White Webbs Park, near Enfield; so Middlesex, by reasons of two of its famous mansions being used by the plotters and a Knight of the Shire capturing the most notorious one, has reason to be proud of its links with that first 5th of November, the anniversary of which has banged its explosive remembrance through three centuries.

Yet who remembers Knyvet? Although the famous, or infamous, Guy is known the world over, and has added a new word to our language and a fresh figure to the pageantry of the streets at a certain period of the year, few people have ever heard of his discoverer, although in this Middlesex church, so near London, there exists such an excellent likeness in marble of the finder of one whose many "ragtime" effigies have not the slightest resemblance to the original.

The home of Lord Knyvet, Stanwell Place, is still to be seen, though much altered since his day. It stands at one end of the village, not far from the church, and described by Thorne as "a spacious modern mansion; formal and dull outside, commodious and richly fitted within." I do not agree with the "formal and dull" part, perhaps time has mellowed it somewhat, and a fire in 1904 probably accounts for further alterations. Anyhow, it is a stately building now, if not exactly a "show place" architecturally. Its setting would redeem many uglier structures, and here again the fifty years old description of Thorne might have been penned yesterday when he writes of this house "it stands in a park of moderate size, rich in timber, especially elms and chestnuts, with a branch of the Colne flowing through it and forming a lake, with swans and all desirable amenities, and approached through stately gates which indicate a former more magnificent mansion."

Those gates are there to-day, still stately and beautiful, and long may they stand. I have seldom seen more romantic-looking gates—one almost waits for the yellow barouche, complete with postilion in powder wig, yellow waistcoat and high boots, and the eloping couple en route for Gretna Green. Those gates might have stepped straight out of an old-world picture of Regency days by Marcus Stone or S. E. Waller; and I can never pass them without sitting on the humble and more rural five-barred gate leading into the field opposite and "wasting" half an hour in dreams—a wonderful tonic, though my practically-minded friends probably think me a fool for my pains.

This house—or the manor—has a long history; soon after the Conquest it belonged to Walter Fitz-other (who came into England with William I.), whose eldest son, William, being Warden of Windsor Castle, took the name of Windsor. Also because, so it is said, that from the Manor House of Stanwell he could see the towers of the Castle across the watered meadows of the Colne. It continued in the possession of his family, Lords Windsor, till 1543, when it came under the taking ways of Henry VIII. The story is told by Sir William Dugdale from contemporary sources, when he relates how the king sent a message that he would dine with Lord Windsor at

Stanwell and was magnificently entertained, "whereupon the king told Lord Windsor that he liked Stanwell so well that he was resolved to have it; yet not without a more beneficial exchange. And the Lord Windsor, answering he hoped his majesty was not in earnest, it having been the seat of his ancestors for many ages, humbly begged he would not take it from him. The king, with a stern countenance replied, ' It must be,' and bade him go to the Attorney-General . . . who showed him a draught ready made of an exchange of his lordship of Stanwell in lieu of Bordesley Abbey, in Worcestershire, whereof being constrained to quit Stanwell, though he had laid in his Christmas provisions for the keeping of his wonted hospitality. All which he left in the house, saying ' They should not find it bare Stanwell.' "

According to some statement this oft-quoted story of the Christmas provisions is a myth; but I give it for what it is worth, though it is certainly a fact that the deed of exchange (which we are told was prepared beforehand) is still preserved in the Record Office, dated March 14th, 1543, by which time the Christmas turkeys must have been a trifle high.

The estate must have been considerably larger in those days, for in this deed the Manor of Stanwell is described as extending into the counties of Bucks, Berks, Surrey and Hants. Apart from Stanwell Place there are several buildings said to have once been part of Knyvet's property. As Mr. Herbert Gibbs reminds me one of these is to be found at Stanhope Farm, Messrs. F. and P. Smith's house in the village.

In Lord Windsor's will, dated only a few days after his forced leaving of the home of his ancestors, it is notable that he describes himself still as " Andrew Windsor of Stanwell " in the county of Middlesex, Knight, Lord Windsor, and ordered his body to be buried in the church of the Holy Trinity of Hounslow, in the said county of Middlesex."

Royal tyranny could command him to leave for an ' alien ' county, but it could not shake his loyalty, or alter his desire, to sleep his last sleep in his native Middlesex.

The estate continued in Royal ownership through the reigns of Edward VI., Elizabeth and James I., later it passed through various hands, including Lord Falkland and the Earl of Dunmore, till 1752 when it came into the possession of Sir John Gibbons, Bart., whose descendants still hold it.

In *The Village Labourer: 1760—1832*, by J. L. and B. Hammond, we find some interesting records of The Enclosures Act of 1798, which so affected this district, with special reference to the Stanwell portion of the Heath.

At the other end of the village from Stanwell Place stands a smaller but older building in the seventeenth century schoolhouse, a picturesque red-brick structure, with a stone inscription over the door.

It was while I was " trespassing " in the front garden to read this, that I was ' caught ' by the schoolmaster himself and my friendly captor and I had a most interesting talk on the history of Stanwell and Middlesex topography in general. In the course of our conversation, my captor said to me " I should think your name was Maxwell." As we were total strangers to each other this surprised me, and while I was forced to confess to the truth of his remarks, I asked how ever he knew. He laughed and replied, " There's no magic power in my knowledge, but you talk just like you write, and I've got several of your books inside—I'm the village librarian as well as the school master. As a student of Middlesex history I have been much interested in your chapters on a county most writers rather ignore." He was referring to certain chapters on *Middlesex Rambles* in *Just Beyond London*, *The Fringe of London* and *The Authors' Thames*.

I found Mr. C. E. Taylor—for such was my "captor's" name—a most interesting companion and I admired him for his loyalty to his native county and for being far-sighted enough to teach local topography as a subject to his pupils—such a thing may, perhaps, be the custom in Devonshire or Yorkshire, but rare enough I should imagine in "suburban" Middlesex, that "uninteresting" county so rich in history and romance.

* * * * * *

The antiquity of Stanwell is proved by its mention in old records (long. before the *Domesday Book*), where we find that it was at this place that the ancient Folk Moot used to take place for the Hundred of Spelthorne (anciently Speechthorn), an Anglo-Saxon division of Middlesex.

It seems to have kept up its reputation as a meeting-place for many centuries; later we find in the *Diary of Lord Melcombe* (better known as Bubb Doddington) that in the reign of George II. Stanwell Heath was the great rendezvous of the electors of Middlesex, before they rushed off to the rowdy poll at Brentford Butts.

Lysons tells us that "the name of the place has undergone no alteration in the mode of spelling, except from redundancy of letters, for centuries. Stanwell in the Saxon language is literally "the stone well." In *Domesday* "Stanwelle" is stated to have "four mills, yielding seventy shillings and four hundred eels, save twenty-five, and three wears, which produce one thousand eels; meadow for twelve ploughs; pasture for the cattle of the village, and pannage for one hundred hogs. Its whole value was fourteen pounds.'

It will be seen from this account that Stanwell was in those days a "watery" place, and it is so still in spite of more modern drainage of the water meadows of the Colne by Stanwell Moor. This river is rather confusing for a stranger to trace, as it flows in parts in three courses; the Colne proper is that nearest the Bucks bank.

Stanwell Moor is a pleasing spot and I shall never forget a "discovery" I made there once—that of a riverside cottage (not far from the weir) whose garden was a mass of flowers. It is hidden from the road and can only be reached by a winding path to the bank—it is one of those little "finds" that stick in the memory of the rambler.

Long after *Domesday* times Stanwell has become a "watering place" in another sense, by the building of the huge reservoirs at one end of it, whose banks have sadly curtailed the southward views from Stanwell Place.

The reservoirs are divided by a footpath, and it was while standing one evening at the western end of this that I had what is perhaps one of the most striking views of Stanwell and the country around. It was early twilight and across the "inland sea," where waterfowl were numerous, I could see the tall spire of the church outlined in the still water and the reflection of one or two lights as darkness deepened; I turned round and let my gaze wander in the opposite direction over the low-lying lands of Staines Moor, above which lay a white ground mist. The view here was even more remarkable; the sense of distance was forcible and that misty moor seemed to stretch almost to infinity, at least, I could not see the end of it. There was a sense of desolation about it, too, for the only sounds that fell upon my ears were the cries of the water-fowl behind me.

There was a mysterious quality that made a strong appeal to the imagination. Could it really be true that this lonely, desolate moorland was in the "suburban" county of Middlesex and that a little over a dozen miles away lay the largest city in the world, with its toiling, crowded millions? Yes, it was true enough, if hard to believe at the moment, and I descended to the roadway beneath, full of wonder, and a strange, rather indefinable sense of having seen a vision which most people miss—or at least ignore.

* * * * * *

It is an amazing thing how many people are anxious to show you the Crystal Palace! Why, I do not know, for when the Alexandra Palace is burned down it will be the ugliest building near London.

So when a stranger once accosted me on the top of Stanwell Reservoir, and remarked on the fine view, I was prepared for the worst. "Just you come here, sir," he said, "and look over there—Windsor Castle!" This was a relief, and then he pointed the other way. "Holloway College!" he said, proudly. This was bad enough, the third most hideous building within range—but I thought my fate had come when he pointed to the other corner, but "Harrow Church" greeted my surprised ears. There was one compass point left—to the S.W.—and I thought it had come at last; but to my intense surprise he pointed to a "splonge" on the horizon, and said, "Epsom Grandstand." I could hardly believe my ears! Four viewpoints and no Crystal Palace. *So in the end I showed him the Crystal Palace!* He appeared quite interested, and exclaimed, "Well, I never, so it is."

I consider this one of my topographical triumphs; I felt I had "got my own back" for the thousand and one times I have had this Giant Greenhouse pointed out to me from almost every height round London.

* * * * * *

I read recently in a newspaper of someone who was very proud because he had discovered, in the middle of Exmoor and twelve miles from a station, an old woman who had never been in a train in her life. Stanwell can beat this, for only a month or so ago I found a boy of fifteen in that village who not only had never been in a train, but who had seen one only in the far distance. A delightful isolation for a place almost on London's doorstep!

CHAPTER XXIX.

The Secret of the Moor.

I ONCE spent a summer night, when all respectable people were a-bed, in visiting different places that had once been part of Hounslow Heath.

I went alone, for though at times I felt that a companion would be cheery, I wanted to experience the full sense of loneliness of my environment. This I certainly did as I rode through sleeping villages and along deserted roads.

There was one place where the feeling of desolation was, perhaps, stronger than anywhere, and that was Staines Moor, that stretches north of the town. A ground mist hid my tracks at first and I had to be careful not to fall into many of the streams that traverse this lonely marsh and meadow land.

I sat on a gate part of the time and watched the mist gradually clear and the moon rise. My mind was busy with many thoughts, of highwaymen who might have made this moor a means of escape, though no coach would ever cross here, for in those days the existing roadway would be a quagmire.

As I sat there with my pipe as my only companion in those dark small hours I pondered on the real Secret of the Moor. It sounds like the title of a mystery novel, but though no novel it is still a mystery, which is that such utter and complete loneliness and desolation, with no house, cottage, barn or any sign of human habitation visible, should be possible so near the largest city in the world; but a few miles away eight million people jostled each other in crowded existence; yet here was I, if not monarch of all I surveyed, for I could see very little, as completely alone as regards immediate environment as Alexander Selkirk found himself.

There is a good deal of drivel written about the Home Counties, usually accompanied by covert sneers if the one be Middlesex, by people who simply do not know their subject; people who in " exploring " Essex get about as far as Barking and think they have seen the whole county, or when they have found Brentford go home under the impression that Middlesex has nothing more to show.

This is sometimes done by those who ought to know better. Here is a case in point. The writer is Miss Rose Macaulay, the novelist, in a review of Miss Charlotte Simpson's *Rediscovering England*: " To those who regard with disfavour," says Miss Macaulay, " books dealing with our more thickly populated counties, and called ' Unknown Surrey,' ' Unexplored Middlesex,' ' Lonely Bucks,' and the like I hasten to say that this book is nothing in this kind." Paradoxically Miss Macaulay has some interesting remarks about the Great Forest of Middlesex, but she is careful to explain that she is speaking of the eleventh century, apparently unaware that several clumps of it, one of over a thousand acres, still exist to-day.

Her chief sneer is kept to the end, when speaking of the type of books with which she begins, she calls them " Come-and-Ramble-with-me gush books." For the moment leaving " Unknown Surrey " and " Lonely Bucks." to look after themselves, we will deal with " Unexplored Middlesex." If

Miss Macaulay ever reads these lines—though she probably won't lower herself to read any book on Middlesex in case she found out something about it—I would like to put her to the test. If I give her sufficient clues will she meet me (duly chaperoned) at a certain point I will name in the middle of Staines Moor at a winter midnight?

I doubt if she would find it, for the spot I have in mind is really unexplored in spite of her sneers, but the attempt to find it would really be a revelation to her, I think (the chaperon would have to be chosen from those having no knowledge of the district), of how difficult to find even parts of so " urban " a county as Middlesex can be, and of how isolated such places are even at mid-day—let alone at the witching hour.

* * * * * *

Beyond the River Colne, at the western edge of the moor, lies Buckinghamshire, the first village in which is under a mile away. This is Horton, the early home of John Milton, before his blindness, of course, and he used to delight in roaming this countryside, the influence of which is clearly seen in the lines from *L'Allegro,* which owe as much to the Middlesex moor as to the adjacent county:

> " Meadows trim with daisie pied,
> Shallow brooks and rivers wide,
> Towers and battlements it sees
> Bosomed high in tufted trees."

A perfect little cameo of Staines Moor, the " towers and battlements," of course, being Windsor Castle.

Perhaps the shade of Milton still roams this lonely spot o-nights; if so, possibly Miss Macaulay would not like to meet it after her recent book *Milton,* which, as James Douglas pointed out in a review that was also a brilliant defence of the poet, was full of " shrewish sneers."

* * * * * *

Most writers ignore Staines Moor and the adjoining one of Stanwell. They think, I suppose, that there is nothing of interest there, and compilers of Guide (?) books usually leave them unvisited. There is one notable exception, however, and that is C. G. Harper's interesting account in *Thames Valley Villages,* where he says: " The neighbourhood of Staines is one of many waters. They divide Middlesex and Bucks. in the many branches and confluent channels of the Colne, and they permeate those widespreading levels westward of what was once Hounslow Heath, broadly known as Staines Moor. This watery landscape, now so beautiful, was once doubtless a very dreary waste. All moors and heaths carry with them in their very name the stigma of dreariness, just as when Goldsmith wrote. The name of a heath could only be associated with footpads and highwaymen, and to style a scene in a play ' Crackskull Common ' seemed a natural and appropriate touch. This ill association of commons long ago became a thing of the past, but we still couple the title of a ' moor ' with undesirable places, generally of an extreme sterility and associated in the mind's eye with inclement weather of the worst type. . . . Whatever Staines Moor may have once been, it no longer resembles those inimical wilds. It is, in fact, a corner of Middlesex endued with much beauty of a quiet, pastoral kind. In the midst of it and its pleasant grasslands and fine trees, with brooks and glancing waters everywhere, and here and there a water-mill, is Stanwell.

"At Stanwell the many noble elms of those parts are more closely grouped together and grow to a greater nobility, and at the very outskirts of the village is a finely wooded park—that of Stanwell Place. The especially fine water-bearing quality of those surroundings is notable in the scenery of that park, and has led of late years to the building of an immense reservoir."

We shall hear more of Stanwell in another chapter and we can return to the moors. An earlier account is not without interest, if a little depressing, for in Middleton's *Agriculture of Middlesex* (1798) we read: "Staines Moor and Stanwell Moor are, for the most part, on a gravelly bottom, but so often flooded and chilled by water, and so much injured by poaching cattle, that they produce little herbage till the end of May. The greatest improvement that could be made of these pastures would be effected by inclosure, embankment and the use of fen-mills." The two former works have been carried out since that day, but I have not seen any fen-mills here, though it is now drier than when these suggestions were proposed.

An ingenious theory has been put forward by Mr. H. Hepworth Thompson (writing in *John o' London's Weekly*) that while it is generally considered that the Magna Carta was sealed at Runnymede, this may have meant the island, but it also *may* have meant Staines Moor. "The document itself states," says the writer, "that it 'was given by our hand in a meadow which is called Runningmeade between Windsor and Staines.' Runnymeade, however, is a territorial name. There is a Runnymeade station a mile north of the actual meadow, as well as a Runnymeade rifle butts some distance away." The last two places are definitely on this Middlesex moor, and though the point cannot now be proved, I am afraid, it remains an interesting historical possibility.

If Staines Moor earns the title of the loneliest place in the county the tiny hamlet of Yeoveney, that is to be found in the middle of it, may almost be described as the loneliest group of habitations in it. It consists of a farm and a few cottages right away from any others, and at night is as desolate as a Dartmoor village. By day, however, is really the best time to explore this place, for then its situation is certainly beautiful; the surrounding country is rather flat, it is true, but it all seems to fit in the picture somehow.

The farm is an old manor house, and though the present building is a typical eighteenth century one it is built on the site of an earlier structure. For a long time it was empty and on that account the more desolate, and recently I committed the sin of trespass and explored it thoroughly; that is the outside, I was unable to get into the house without actually breaking in. The huge barns and farm buildings, some of the largest I have seen, interested me as much as the house; they were locked up, but cracks in the old boarding gave me glimpses into vast caverns of emptiness—an erie effect. In the great farmyard one solitary waggon (or hay-wain, to be both more picturesque and truthful) still stood, a large vehicle and cumbersome; why it had not been taken away with the rest of the farming stock I have no idea; its solitary position in an empty farmyard added to the general deserted look of the whole place.

At one time there was a chapel attached to this manor, and I read that when it was demolished one of the doors was preserved and built into the house, and to try and find this door was one of the objects of my search. It was not successful, none of the outside doors of the house bore the least ecclesiastical trace, and the great doors of the barns were far too big for anything less than a cathedral, had they answered the description otherwise, which they did not. If this door is inside the house still I cannot say, probably not, for it dates from mediaeval days.

It was in connection with the search for this door that an incident, not without humour, occurred. When I left the farm an old man was leaning over a cottage gate watching me. I spoke to him, hoping to gain information; though I did not get much he made a valuable suggestion to help in the search for the lost door.

"No, sir," he replied in answer to my query, "I never 'eard tell of no chapel door in the farm, and I worked there for years afore it were left empty. 'Ad this 'ere door got coloured glass in it?" I replied that it was unlikely, and added that it was probably of oak, possibly studded with nails.

My old friend shook his head again; but all at once his face brightened. "No, sir, I don't think there's no such thing at Yeoveney Farm, but if you really wants to see a chapel door there's one in Staines—at the Wesleyan Chapel!"

He seemed surprised when I told him that the one I sought was some seven hundred years old; he didn't seem to think much of it and expressed the opinion that it "were probably wore out by now"; but he went on to say that while he didn't imagine the Wesleyan Chapel door was *quite* as old as that, it was still a very good one, nicely varnished, with brass handles! He seemed anxious not to let the district down to a prying stranger in search of chapel doors!

Apart from doors I had quite an interesting talk with this old rustic, who, though a native of Berkshire, had lived for over thirty years in his present cottage on the moor. He, too, spoke of the loneliness of the situation, especially on winter nights when the white mists lay thick upon the ground—"What they caals in Barkshoir the White Lady." I asked him if he had ever seen the White Lady personally; he smiled rather queerly —a little sheepishly, I thought—and answered slowly, "Well, sir, I 'ave and I 'avn't. Modern folk *do* say as 'ow there ain't no such thing; but all I knows is if you is walking across the moor on a misty night you feel as if there might be *anything* lurking behind the fog. But p'raps its all nonsense arter all, and p'raps it ain't."

I could not "draw" him any more, he shut up like an oyster and seemed anxious to change the subject; so I must disappoint you if you are expecting to hear the full story of the White Lady of Staines Moor.

As I rode home this subject filled my mind (more even than the Wesleyan Chapel door) and I looked up "Village Superstitions" by Rev. P. H. Ditchfield, a Berkshire man, and deeply versed in his county's folk-lore, and with whom I have had many a talk. I did not find much, but this sentence is significant: "When the mist lies thick upon the ground the Berkshire peasants say it is the White Lady, a belief closely akin to the Dame Blanche said in Normandy to haunt streams." Well, there are enough streams on Staines Moor to make any water sprite happy, and I only regret that his fairly recent death prevented me taking this interesting piece of news to discuss with Mr. Ditchfield.

So I must leave the reader to follow up this clue and wish him good
ghost hunting on the lonely Middlesex moors.

* * * * * *

The historical facts concerning Yeoveney are not extensive, but
interesting. Lysons says: "Sir Nicholas Brembre, who was attained and
executed in the reign of Richard II., held for life certain lands, rents, etc.,
in Yeoveney, the reversion of which was vested in Thomas Bere, who had
assigned his reversionary interest to Thomas Walyngton, by whom it had
been again assigned to the Abbot and Convent of Westminster. These
lands were confirmed to the Convent by the King in 1397. It seems probable that this was the same estate which was called afterwards the Manor
of Yeveney, Yeoveny or Iveney, and was granted to the Dean and Chapter,
who for many years appear to have kept it in their hands. The family of
Dolben were lessees under the Dean and Chapter as early as 1667. The
lease was purchased of Sir William Dolben, Bt., in 1775, by the late William
Gill, Esquire, Alderman of London, and is now vested in his widow.

"In the endowment of the vicarage of Staines Yeveney is mentioned
among the chapelries to which the vicar was to present. The chapel at this
hamlet has long ago been dilapidated." For the last word we must read
demolished, as all trace of it had disappeared long before Lysons' time.

Hughson tells us very much the same as Lysons, while Walford has a
short note on it, and it was from the latter that I learned of the possible
existence of the mysterious door. "Staines Moor," he writes, "extending
upwards to Stanwell, consists of common-lands, over which the poor of
Staines have the rights of turbary (the right to cut turf).

"Yeoveney, a hamlet consisting of a farm-house and a few cottages,
about a mile to the north of the town, was an ancient chapelry attached to
the mother-church of Staines. Its chapel is long since disappeared, and
even its site is not known for certain, though an oaken door, said to have
formed part of it, is still preserved in the neighbouring farm-house."

One authority states that the site of the chapel was on the other side of
the road from the farm, a little towards Stanwell. There is not the slightest
trace of it now, even the foundation; for I have searched from this very
vague clue, with no better success than I had over the door.

Since I made my search I am glad to say that this fine old farmhouse
has been occupied and once more reflects delightfully the agricultural
pursuits of the county, as it has done for so many centuries. I see a change
was once foreshadowed, for in the *Reports for County Council of Middlesex*
(February, 1932) is a note: "The Yeoveney Manor Estate of 172 acres is
proposed to be turned into an Air-Port." Is this necessary? Hanworth
Park (The London Flying Club) and Heston Air Station are each only about
five miles away. Yet even this is better than houses; for an aerodrome
must, of necessity, keep *some* open "country." I am not a practical farmer
and I hear many stories of depression even in agricultural "London"; but
I should have thought that with the great hungry mouth of the metropolis
so near for transport that these often disused Middlesex acres could have
been made successfully to grow some foodstuffs we now import from abroad.
Perhaps this comes under the heading of politics, however, and of the inner
workings of politics I know even less!

CHAPTER XXX.

Concerns an "Earthly Paradise" — a Ghost — Buried Treasure — and 300,000 Glasses of beer.

POYLE is not so much a "lost" village as an undiscovered one. The difference is rather subtle; but to be "lost" a village must have once been discovered and then forgotten, or overlooked, as the tide of events swept past it. Poyle has never had any tide of events; it is now pretty much as it was a hundred years ago, and will be, it is to be hoped, a hundred years hence. It is a real piece of Unknown Middlesex. There is no church at Poyle—it is little more than a hamlet—but in the village chapel-yard, near the Punch Bowl, are some old tombstones, rare to find in such a building.

The Punch Bowl Inn on the old main road to Colnbrook is the "entrance" to Poyle, but it is the other end of the village street, by the small Golden Cross Inn, that the really picturesque part is to be found. Here are some old farms and delightful half-timbered houses, really ancient, and not those faked beamed atrocities that are being erected now and advertised as "Tudor residences' or "Elizabethean" (sic). Jerry's spelling is as weak as his building at times!

These houses at Poyle are a picture of Old England that has survived the terrible "progress" that is sweeping over Middlesex, and they are refreshing to the eye. There is one of them, I was sorry to see, half in ruins; one end seems to be occupied while the other is falling down, apparently by some die-hard owner loath to leave his old home before it leaves him. A villager once told me that Poyle formerly boasted an inhabitant who turned the scale at 25 stone. Perhaps he once leaned against this half-ruined house——.

Seriously, here is a chance where some rich American might step in with advantage and save the place; even if it were for erection overseas; for the old house cannot last long in its present state and to repair it would be to rebuild and thus spoil it. Instead of trying to buy historical old houses—such as "Jordans" in Bucks—let the American go to Poyle, where he could probably get hold of this house at a reasonable figure; and it is genuine.

Poyle Manor, a house pleasantly hidden among the trees, seems to have been discovered, for there is a gravel pit in the grounds by the main road, which does not add to its rural charm; the rich undersoil of these parts (witness the Staines Road) is often its undoing pictorially, whatever benefit it may be financially to its owners.

Poyle, if not just ignored in books on the county, is generally dismissed in a few lines. Thorne's *Environs of London* and Walford's *Greater London*, the two usual books of reference which cover this part, are typical. The former says "Poyle is a hamlet, with a few scattered cottages, an inn and a paper mill"; while the latter is not quite so graphic, for it tells us "Poyle is a small village near Stanwell." Neither account is very enlightening, it is to be feared, and quoted in this way reminds us of the witty remark of Sir James Barrie, at a cricket lunch to Mr. P. F. Warner, the former captain of this county—"When I first saw Mr. Warner bat he made one run; the second time he was not so successful."

In *The Antiquarian Repertory* we find: "A Liste of Arms of Knyghts of the County of Myddlesex in the reign of King Henry II.—1216-1272." In here appear the arms of Sir John de la Poyle of Poyle. This seems the earliest mention of this family, for he was evidently the father of William de la Poyle, mentioned in the *Harlean MSS.* as holding lands in Stanwell parish in 1267. This account continues: "William de Langdale conveyed this manor to John de la Poyle, Isabel his wife, and their heirs. He died in 1318, having demised the manor to Richard de Waledon." The reversionary interest, after the death of the said Richard, who was then living, was vested in Elizabeth, only daughter and heiress of John de la Poyle. It continued in this family for several generations; Sir Thomas de la Poyle died seised of it in 1424. In 1452 the manor was the property of John Geynesford, and in 1481 it was conveyed to John Catesby. In 1543 it became the property of the Windsor family, and was included in the exchange with Henry VIII.

Later it came into the possession of Lord Knyvet and later of the Gibbons family, who still hold it. Poyle Manor, sometimes called Poyle Park, on the site of the old house of the de la Poyles, has had various tenants, the only one of any particular note, as regards this chronicle, being Nicholas Hilliard, Portrait Painter to Queen Elizabeth. He took a lease of it in 1587 for twenty-one years at a rent of £11 3s. 4d. At the inquisition taken after the death of Sir Thomas de la Poyle in 1424 this manor was described as consisting of 100 acres of arable land, 40 acres of pasture, 40 acres of meadowland, three acres of heath land, and a water mill.

Fifteenth century rents at Poyle certainly had the virtue of variety, for within the space of sixty years we find the following:

Date	Description	Rent
1424	Pasture land	1d. an acre
1424	Wyld hethelande	4d. for 3 acres
1424	100 acres of arable land	£4 12s. 8½d.
1424	The Manor of Poyle (Quit Rent)	One Rose on the festival of John the Baptist.
1431	The Manor of Poyle (Quit Rent)	Four Capons on Hoc Day.
1452	The Manor of Poyle	The service of half a knight's fee.
1481	The Manor of Poyle	4s. 9½d. every 24 weeks.

The only thing I cannot understand is why Wyld hethelande, in those days quite unprofitable, should have been so expensive!

The most famous resident of Poyle Manor is now quite forgotten, except to a few collectors. Nicholas Hilliard (1537-1619) was a man of some pristine importance, occupying three columns in the D.N.B., and the only one of his name in that many-volumed work, which incidentally errs in describing Poyle as "near Stanmore, Middlesex." The right county, but the place is some sixteen miles away, as near the northern border as Stanwell is to the western.

Hilliard was a miniature painter and worker in precious metals and jewels. He was appointed "Goldsmith, Carver and Limner to Queen

Elizabeth," whom he painted both as a princess and a queen. In *Notes and Queries* there is an interesting paragraph concerning Hilliard (quoted from Augmentation Office Records): "From the memorandum annexed to a lease of the Manor of Poyle, in the parish of Stanwell, Co. Middlesex, dated 1587, it appears that Nicholas Hilliard was the engraver of the Great Seal employed at that period:

> "Memorandum—the said Lease to be for 21 yeares to the said Hilliard in consideration of his paines in engraving Ye Great Seale of England.
>
> "Fr. Walsingham.   W. Burleigh."

James I. continued to favour Hilliard and in Horace Walpole's *Anecdotes of Painting* is quoted the patent granted to the artist by that king:

> "Whereas our well beloved servant Nicholas Hilliard, Gentleman, our principal drawer of small portraits, and embosser of our medals in gold, in respect of his extraordinary skill in drawing, graving and imprinting, etc.; we have granted unto him our special licence for twelve years to invent, make, grave and imprint any pictures of our image or our royal family, etc.; and that no one do presume to do so without his licence obtained."

Further particulars of this will be found in Ryder's *Foedera*.

This was a source of much profit to Hilliard, as it empowered him not only to grant licences for the production and sale of the King's portrait, but also to seize such as were unauthorised.

It is, however, as the first English miniature painter that Hilliard is notable, and his works were highly esteemed in his day. Dr. Donne, in *The Storm,* written in 1587, testified that

> "A hand or eye
> By Hilliard drawn is worth a history
> By a coarse painter made."

According to some accounts Hilliard is said to be the author of an important treatise on miniature painting now in the Bodlean Library, though other accounts state that it was written by one of his pupils from his instructions, or, as we should now put it, more simply—he dictated it.

An American friend who was much amused when I pointed out to him the tomb of "O. Gee" (at Isleworth) may be interested to learn that I found a record of an old woman who died at Poyle at the ripe age of 103—and her name was Ann How!

* * * * * *

If I describe Poyle Manor and its grounds as an Earthly Paradise I shall but voice the impression it made on me one Sunday afternoon in summer. It was a hot day and I had been riding over the Middlesex roads since early morning, and in the late afternoon found myself in the charming little main (and only) "street" of Poyle village, and I sat by the roadside to rest. The smoke of many pipes was lost in the still air, and I would not swear that I did not lapse into dreamland for a few minutes; anyhow, no dream could have been more vivid than the wonderful waking vision that was to be mine a few minutes later.

This is how it came about. As I sat on that grassy bank a great "wall" of beautiful trees confronted me, through which I could see a glimpse of an old red roof and a glint of water. My conscience has never been very tender on point of trespass, so leaving my bicycle by the lodge I commenced

STANWELL PLACE.
The former house of Lord Knyvet.

Photo by the Author

THE OLD GATEWAY, STANWELL PLACE.
"One almost waits for the eloping couple of Regency days off to Gretna Green.

Photo by F. Ash

HIGHWAYMAN'S CAGE, CRANFORD

Photo by F. Ash

SEVEN MILES FROM LONDON.   *Photo by the Author*
Old Farm at Scrattedge.

to walk up the drive—for the grounds were that of Poyle Manor. More for the reason that it was Sunday afternoon than from any feeling of guilt at trespassing I intended merely to go but a little way up the drive and see what I could see. Yard, however, succeeded yard, some influence I could not resist led me on, till turning a corner suddenly I found myself confronted with the most delightful seventeenth century house I think I have ever seen; its setting in that old-world garden was perfect.

Retreat was impossible now; the only thing was to turn my trespass into permission—or get kicked out. I knocked at the door and sent my card in with a request to be allowed to explore. Nothing like "nerve" but in this case it was rewarded with rare courtesy. The maid returned with the message, "Mrs. Bain says will you do what you please." It was like suddenly getting a ticket to wander in fairyland. I have seldom spent a more delightful two hours than those that followed.

The garden and meadows extended to some fourteen acres, laid out with consummate skill. First there was the rose garden, a blaze of glory, from which lawns of living velvet ran down to the banks of the small river —a tributary of the Colne—that runs through this paradise. A great cedar, said to be four hundred years old, spread its branches overhead, while a strangely distorted catalpa lay beneath. To one side, separate from the river, was the moat with its floating carpet of water-lilies, access to which lay through one of the most curiously constructed gateways ever seen—a circular space in the middle of an old red brick wall—the effect was curious but pleasing.

The walled kitchen gardens were basking in the sun, with espalier apple-trees against the walls—as they should be in all well-regulated wall gardens. Passing through these I came to the river bank again, where stood a fine summer-house, which I was told dated from Queen Anne's reign. The sweet smell of new-mown hay led me to the meadows and a shady orchard beyond, from which a fine view of the house is obtained. A much older building had once stood here, but not much of it remained, it was a farmhouse at one time, I learned subsequently. I wondered what sort of a house existed here in 1267, the first date I had of the manor, not much more than a wattle-and-daub structure probably.

Up to the present I have heard no story of Queen Elizabeth sleeping here—a rare negative! Not even has Cromwell's name been suggested instead, but I *was* told that Ann Boleyn once lived here, though I cannot find the least historical evidence on which to base this legend.

* * * * * *

On going up to the house at the end of the explorations to convey my thanks to the Lady of the Manor (used figuratively; for those who like strict accuracy it may be said that Poyle is now a sub-manor to Stanwell, and the lord of both manors was formerly Sir Alexander Gibbons, and now, I believe, is Mr. H. Scott-Freeman, of Staines). I was very graciously received, and I am glad to say that in return for the kindness shown to a wandering scribe and a stranger I was able to clear up a little "mystery" by a small effort in topographical deduction.

"Before you go," said the Lady of the Manor, "I want you to see our staircase." I duly admired it, a really wonderful thing in dark carved oak and running round the first floor as a gallery. "How old is it?" I asked. "We don't quite know," was the reply; "it was not originally in this house at all. It's said to have been here about a hundred years and once to have belonged to Lord Uxbridge."

I did a bit of quick thinking and in a flash the truth came to me. "I think I can give you its history," I said. "But how can you if you have never seen it before?" "It was the name of Lord Uxbridge that told me," I answered. "I think you will find, too, that this staircase has been here nearer two than one hundred years—since 1739, in fact; for in that year Lord Uxbridge pulled down two wings of Dawley Farm, Harlington, Lord Bolingbroke's marvellous mansion. What is more likely than that the then owner of Poyle Manor House bought the staircase to save it from destruction and sent a farm-cart to bring it here; for Dawley Farm is only about four miles away. It seems feasible enough, though, of course, unless documentary evidence exists of the sale—which is not likely—it cannot be proved, but the theory is probably not far from the truth.

So it was with mutual thanks that the Lady of the Manor and I parted, though hers was the greater gift—I merely told her of the story of an old staircase, but she gave me a memory of that wonderful Old English garden that can never fade and where I still often walk in spirit.

*   *   *   *   *   *

I was talking to someone in the village after this visit and was asked if I had seen the Grey Lady. I replied that I had seen several ladies, but so far as I could remember none was dressed in that colour. My questioner laughed. "Oh, I mean the ghost, known as the Grey Lady." "Ghosts don't like me," I answered, "they always dodge me; but I like ghost stories, can't you tell me this one?" "I don't know that there is very much to tell and, of course, my ghost news is only what I have heard," answered my informant, "but I will tell you what I know." And this, "boiled down" from a rather rambling account, is what I heard of The Ghost of Poyle Manor.

The story begins in the seventeenth century, when the house was occupied by a cavalier and his lady, whom it appears were not on very good terms; anyhow, one afternoon the husband disappeared after a tiff, and some hours later the deserted wife—who was dressed in grey—happened to glance out of the window and was surprised to see a boat on the little river that runs through the grounds. In this boat was her husband; not that this was so very surprising. What astonished the annoyed wife was that in the boat sat a girl—a proper hussy, too. Slowly the husband rowed past the house and disappeared into the bushes.

"This husband must have been either a hero or a fool," I broke in, "to take his 'bird' on the river through his own garden, with the shady Thames backwaters not many miles away. He deserved all he got, and his homecoming must have been a tragic one; stern wife—rolling pin—in the true comic paper style."

"It was tragic enough," replied the narrator, "but not in the way you mean. When he returned there was no sign of his wife; at first he thought she had gone away in pique, but before long they found her—in the river—drowned. Since then her ghost is said to haunt the place, always looking out from the upper window on to the river for the faithless husband and his paramour. Some say, too, that her appearance presages death."

"Does the boat and its phantom occupants also appear?"

"That I don't know; I am thankful to say I have never seen them and I hope I never shall." I asked permission from the teller of this story if I might include it in my book; at the mention of a book the flow of eloquence ceased abruptly; a thing I have noticed several times. People who will talk volubly enough will close up like oysters if they find that what they say may possibly be recorded.

" Well," replied my informant in this case, " *I* can't stop you putting it in. I have only told you what is pretty well known in the village; but I would rather you did not mention my name in connection with it."

My friend seemed relieved at the desired promise being given, quite forgetting that I had no knowledge of his name, anyhow; for it was merely a casual conversation.

So there is the story of the Grey Lady for what it is worth—of its truth, or otherwise, no opinion is offered.

*   *   *   *   *   *

On my first visit to Poyle I chanced to ride down the road that leads over the Buckinghamshire border to Horton, with its memories of Milton. On the left of this road is a concrete wall, some twenty or so feet high and extending for about half a mile. It is overgrown with ivy in parts and obviously not modern. Wondering what it was I sought enligtenment from an old man leaning over a cottage gate.

" That there wall?" he said, looking up at it as though he had never noticed it before. " Oh, that's to keep the fish in." " Keep the fish in?" I repeated, rather mystified. " What have they got inside it—the Loch Ness Monster?" Apparently this old rustic had never heard of this fabulous beast, for he shook his head and replied solemnly, " No, sir, that ain't the name; I think they're trout." He did not appear to be very interested in the matter. He had lived in that cottage, he told me, over fifty years, but what mysteries lay behind that wall did not worry him seemingly, such was his bucolic mind; though rather refreshing to find such a thing in Middlesex, and so near London.

It is true we cannot rival the Scotch monster on the Heath to-day, but even since the days of the Brontosaurus Middlesex has had some little fame in this matter, for in a quaint old book, *Strange News for England: 1659,* is found the following: " Great and unheard-of wonders in the Thames off the Middlesex coast: where has been seen a huge and mighty fysshe much like unto a Black Bull, and a Mermaid, being a Fysshe so-called." What part of the Middlesex " coast " is not mentioned.

I stayed talking to this old man for a while, and when we left the subject of monsters and got on to that of highwaymen he brightened up a little; though even then our talk took a slightly nautical flavour. He asked me if I had ever " 'Eard tell " of Dick Turpin's Ride to New York, and when I asked if he rode on a Sea Horse the old man was quite sorry for my ignorance and told me all about Black Bess. My old friend was quite interested, however, in the price of a pint, and I expect down at the " local " that evening edified the company with a rambling story of " a strange gent wot was a-talking all about riding sea-monsters, but wot 'e meant I ain't got no idea!"

A passing policeman gave me the information I wanted about the wall. It proved to be part of the old Runnymede Rifle Range, built at the time of the Volunteer " boom " in the sixties of last century. The fish, I discovered, were hardly behind it at all, but some way beyond it, where there was some preserved water for anglers.

As I rode on my mind ran on those sixteenth century words of Sir Edward Dyer, " My mind to me a kingdom is." They are certainly true, though to give a person " a piece of your mind " might be construed differently from giving him " part of your kingdom!" But if a mind *is* a kingdom, *what* a lot of vacant thrones there are about to-day! Many people,

I am afraid, and it was probably the same in bygone days, suffer from that distressing complaint which might be called " Cowmindedness." To explain. A man and a cow walk down a village street together, and (presumably) both see exactly the same things; which are (sometimes) impressed on the mind of the man and not (again presumably) upon that of the cow. Though many seem to go through life with a bovine mental attitude.

A dozen cases could be quoted in proof of this, but one will suffice. During the war a bomb fell near a certain country church, with a curiously shaped spire—it had a canopy top that looked as if a snuffer had been put on it. It had been like this for some hundreds of years, yet an old man, born and bred in the village, seriously told me after the explosion that *this* had caused the church spire to collapse! Though he had *seen* it every day of his life, it needed a bomb to make him *notice* its strange shape, though the bomb had not affected it at all. Now this man was Cowminded!

People have asked me how it is I see things others do not. I claim to do no such thing, though occasionally I may remember what they forget. It might even be put—sometimes I may see things others look at, a subtle, but important, difference.

·　·　·　·　·　·

To revert for a moment, before we leave Poyle, to Nicholas Hilliard, those who wish to see his portrait will find it in certain editions of *Anecdotes of Painting.* A number of this artist's miniatures were in Horace Walpole's collection at Strawberry Hill, as well as one famous curiosity connected with him, and described as " A Lyttel Booke of Prayers written on vellum by Queen Elisabeth in six languages with a minature at the beginning of the Queen painted by Nicholas Hilliard."

His son Lawrence was also a miniature painter, though his work now is even less known than that of his father. Lawrence died in 1640, but no reference is given as to the date of his birth, though this was probably at Poyle.

Several of the miniatures of Nicholas were in the collection of Charles I., who purchased from the son a remarkable jewel, the work of the elder Hilliard. This contained the portraits of Henry VII., Henry VIII., Edward VI. and Queen Jane Seymour, and having on the top an enamelled representation of the Battle of Bosworth, with red and white roses.

" The portraits," says one old book on art, " are now at Windsor Castle, but the jewel has long since disappeared." The same chronicle has a story accounting for this disappearance. It says that it was stolen by a dishonest servant, who buried it " beneathe ye bushes in ye grounde at his master's former manor at Poyle," and then apparently forgot which bush, or else had no chance for recovery. This unlikely story is probably pure fiction— these old books on art are full of such anecdotes. Another old book that has some mention of Hilliard (and also of Peter Oliver, whom we met at Isleworth) is *Art and Artists in England,* by G. F. Waagen.

The story in the first book, anyhow, caused me some subsequent amusement. I was talking to the old night watchman at the pravel pit, and told him something of the former owners of Poyle Park, including the history of the lost jewel of Charles I. This last bit of very doubtful information caused far more interest than any amount of true facts concerning the place, and was, incidentally, the cause of my entering into a conspiracy against the King's Realm—that of the (intended) hiding of Treasure Trove!

"You say as 'ow there's jooels buried 'ere, sir?" asked the night watchman.

"Well, perhaps *a* jewel that once belonged to a king."

"Bless me soul, supposin' *I* found it. 'Ave you said anything to the foreman about it, sir?" he asked rather anxiously. I said I had not.

"Ah!" with relief, "then let's keep it dark, sir. I might find it poking about with me stick." The sin of avarice was eating into his heart. "'Ow much would this 'ere jooel be worth now, sir, five quid?"

"More like five thousand!"

The old man fanned himself with his hat. High Finance unnerved him. "Five thousand quid," he muttered, "bless my soul."

I did a rough calculation on the back of an envelope. Taking beer at 8d. a pint, this sum would represent three hundred thousand half-pint glasses. I mentioned this to the Watchman; he nearly fainted. "Five thousand pounds was so far beyond even his mental reach that he could never imagine possessing it; but he could grasp three hundred thousand glasses of beer, mentally at least!

"Then if I finds this jooel, sir, I could get all them glasses of beer for it?"

"Yes, if you could find a market for it." He misunderstood me, to him a market meant stalls. "I don't think I would try to sell it in a market, sir," he confided, growing cunning 'by suggestion,' "they might arst too many questions. Couldn't *you* sell it, sir, private like, and go 'alves?" This with lowered voice.

"I might," I replied, also *sotto voce*—as a good conspirator should speak, "so if you find it let me have it at once—fifty-fifty, you know!"

"That's it, sir, I'll begin to look this very evening. Three 'undred thousand beers," he muttered, as if the very idea had mesmerised him; it was practically owning a brewery. Then an uneasy thought assailed him, "You don't think, sir, as 'ow this 'ere diggin' for gravel is all a blind, and they is reely lookin' for the jooel all the time?"

I said I thought this extremely unlikely and, to give him courage to dispel horrid doubt and to urge him to energy in his Treasure Hunt, suggested an adjournment to the Punch Bowl. He accepted with simple directness—half a pint in hand was worth three hundred thousand in the bushes.

So after deducting in true business fashion the cost of the combined drinks we had to seal the bargain. I am now owner of a half share in a mythical 299,998 glasses of beer. Well, when the King's jewel is found, provided things work out as my fellow-conspirator imagines, I hope all my readers will join me at the Punch Bowl—Here's luck!

As we talked, for some unexplainable reason (unless old Omar's Bachanalian spirit was attracted by the fabulous pints) there came into my mind a verse after the Rubaiyat metre, which I jotted down and handed to my old friend.

He read it slowly:

"Here lies King Charles's jewel beneath the ground,
    Which, lost three hundred years, may yet be found;
And still be worth three hundred thousand beers—
    It's things like this that make the world go—hic—round!"

The Watchman was visibly disappointed. " Bless me soul, then there's someone wot knows of this; the man wot wrote this pome."

" No, I'm afraid I am guilty of writing it."

" What, is you a poet, sir? Why, I thought you was just a ordinary gentleman." I was not sure from his tone if I had risen or dropped in his estimation.

" Well, anyhow, I am a very ordinary poet," I replied, as we shook hand at the inn door, and I went on my way leaving my companion rather mystified over this distinction with a difference.

CHAPTER XXXI.
Of Queen Elizabeth's bread; and where she proved herself a sound sleeper.

HESTON has no separate mention in *Domesday*, as it was then included under Hounslow, though time has now turned the tables by including Hounslow with Heston and Isleworth; for Hounslow, strictly speaking, is no parish at all, one side of the High Street being in Heston and the other in Isleworth. Yet in spite of this the old name for the Hundred was Hounslow, though it is now Isleworth. This is not a puzzle, though it sounds like one, and why these changes all came about is not easy to explain.

The place was written Hestune in the reign of Henry II., and before then Hegeston—the enclosed town—though only a hamlet; another authority gives the derivation from Hese or Hyse, a ground overgrown with bushes.

Heston was of old famous for its fertility, and Norden describes it as: " A most fertile place of wheate, yet not so much to be commended for the quantitie as for qualitie; for the wheate is most pure, accompted the purist in many shires; and therefore Queen Elizabeth hath the most part of her provision from that place for manchet for her Highness's own diet as is reported." Camden in his *Britannia* also mentions this: " In the little village of Heston the wheat-flour whereof has been particularly made choice of by our kings for their own bread."

Another writer on the agriculture of the county, Cooke, in the beginning of the nineteenth century, proves that up to those days this village still held its own for wheat growing: " The lands about Heston are chiefly of a strong loam, and celebrated for producing the finest wheat in the country; the skin is thin, the corn free and bold, and the flour white; or, as the millers term it, fair. The rotation of crops are wheat, barley, with clover mowed twice, pease or beans to be gathered, and turnips."

It seems, however, that the district was famed for its wheat very much earlier than even Elizabeth's reign, for we find in the records of a place so far removed as Lambeth some old accounts (quoted in *The History of Lambeth*, by J. Tanswell. The original accounts are in the Public Record Office) for the Manor of Faukeshall (Vauxhall) in 1327: " In expenses of two men, with three horses and a cart, fetching wheat from Houneslowe, 2½d.," and again, " In the expenses of two labourers fetching corn from Hou:1eslowe, on the feast of St. Edmund the Archbishop, with the toll, 2d., also at Kingston Bridge, 6d., and in Great Nails bought for the repair of the Cart, 1d."

This wheat was probably Heston-grown, for the term Houneslowe would include it at that date. The last entry is doubly interesting, as it gives some idea of the route taken and a glimpse of what the roads must have been like to need " Great Nails " for repairs on the way. The journey, too, from Vauxhall to Hounslow in the early fourteenth century must have been through as wild and lonely country as could be found anywhere in England.

It is a natural transition from the grist to the mill and it is not surprising that this village was once noted for its fine old windmill, which, as a matter of fact, was really in Hounslow on the Staines Road, opposite the Review Ground, though always known as Heston Mill. A landmark all over the Heath, it was unfortunately burned down in 1892. This was probably on the same site as the mill of which we read in Lyson: " Edmund de Wastell, vicar of Heston, anno 1366, gave a mill, 34 acres of land and 3s. rent in Staines and Stanwell to the Priory of Hounslow."

We are reminded of the former mill in Thornbury's *Life of Turner*, where he speaks of the artist as a frequent visitor to Heston, as the guest of the Rev. Mr. Trimmer, the vicar, whose son relates some anecdotes of Turner's rambles through Middlesex in search of the picturesque. One in which he would cross Hounslow Heath is worth quoting. The period would be about 1830. " Turner had a gig and an old bay horse called Crop-ear," he tells us, " and in this he used to drive out sketching and take my father and myself with him. His sketching apparatus was under the seat. I remember once going on an expedition of this kind to Staines, where he made some sketches, from these he painted a picture which strongly resembles the place to this day. We went at a very steady pace, as Turner painted much faster than he drove." I wonder if the ghosts of " Admiral Booth " and Crop-ear ever amble along the Great West Road to-day?

The writer also describes how Turner used to stop frequently and the chances are probable that he made many drawings on Hounslow Heath, which he so often traversed; its wildness would have appealed to him.

" The Windmill, one of the *Liber Studiorum* plates, has been said to have been Heston Mill, but a glance at the picture disproves this. There is no lock-gate at Heston; but this mill is only a couple of miles away, just across Osterley Park, at Hanwell, where the River Brent and the Grand Junction (now Union) Canal part company at that spot where the six locks lift the stream up hill, and where, more curious still, there is a spot where three ways cross—road on top, waterway in the middle and rail underneath. The great asylum now stands where the old mill appears in the picture.

It is probable, however, that Heston Mill appears un-named in Turner's sketch-book, for he must have seen it every day during his stay in the village and is hardly likely to have neglected so picturesque and handy a model; and I should not be surprised if the plate " The Straw-yard "—a pleasing farm scene, with a glimpse of a flat countryside through the gateway—also owes its origin to this village. The plate " The Young Anglers " is, of course, known definitely to be on the River Crane, near where it flows into the Thames at Isleworth, not very far away. There are also several other subjects that I strongly suspect have a Middlesex origin.

In the *Life of Turner* there is another mention of the artist in this district, when it says: " Turner once went with my father and another to see the pictures at Osterley House, collected by Mr. Child. There was a splendid Gainsborough my father had once rescued from a garret. Of this picture Turner made a *memoniter,* a small drawing, in the evening." Richard Wilson also painted a good deal hereabouts, and there is a picture of his entitled " On Hounslow Heath," a delightful subject, with water in the foreground and a mill—probably that of Heston—in the distance.

*   *   *   *   *   *

The literary fame of Heston is rather meagre; and rests almost on Anthony Collins, the seventeenth century contraversial writer and friend of John Locke. Collins, once well - known, is now forgotten except to students of the literature of that period. He is said to have been born at Heston in 1676; his father was a resident of the village and is buried in the church, where two of his daughters were baptised, though Anthony himself was christened in Isleworth church.

Heston at the present time is alike a joy and a despair; the former for the things of beauty still to be seen within its borders, and the latter for the modern signs of "progress" that are fast spoiling the old-world atmosphere of this fine old Middlesex village.

The church may be included among the former, for though the nave was built in mid-Victorian days the tower is Early English, and the fifteenth-century lychgate is one of the oldest and most original in England, on account of its old machinery, though it probably would not work now. Thorne mentions it as it was some fifty years ago: " Heston village consists of three or four irregular streets converging upon a little triangular green, in the centre of which is a brick pound. About the village are several good old brick residences—the vicarage by the church is a comfortable looking example—one or two stately mansions and many cottages both good and bad. The village and the lanes are rich in large elms and walnut trees and the level meadows look green and flourishing.

" The church of St. Leonard is off the green, the entrance is by a large, picturesque old oak lich-gate, with one wide door turning on a central pivot and self-closing by means of a rude pulley-wheel in the roof, and a stone weight enclosed in an iron frame, a primitive but effective piece of machinery. The old church was one of the most interesting in Middlesex and when it was levelled to the ground it was in spite of earnest protests by architects and archaeologists. From the back of the churchyard there is a pleasant walk of about a mile by tall elms, and across a wheat-field, to Osterley House."

Though the old stone-weighted machinery of the lychgate can still be seen, there are inevitable changes since this was written, but luckily not so many that it is not easily recognisable even now. The pound is gone and crops of bricks and mortar have taken the place of wheat, while many of the old houses have given place to roads of modern villas. Heston Hall is one of them, but the fine old eighteenth century mansion of Heston House, on the turn of the road to Cranford, is still standing, with its picturesque gateways and old-world garden, though every time I pass it I fear to find it gone.

It was in connection with the former house that I was nearly led on a false trail. I was talking to an old labourer, who was telling me details of the house, and he surprised me by saying that Hogarth once lived there. My surprise was two - fold, firstly that he should know anything of that artist, and secondly that I had never heard of his residence here, for most

WOOD LAKE: OSTERLEY PARK.   *Photo by the Author*

"THE MONKS' FARMYARD":   *Photo by F. Ash*
Grange Farm, Heston, held by Hounslow Monastery 800 years ago.

of the details of his life in Middlesex are familiar to me. I questioned my informant closely, but he would not be shaken, and even "proved" his words by saying that he could actually remember *seeing him walking about the village!* This was startling news, for Hogarth had been dead 170 years! Enlightenment from another source solved this mystery and proved that the old labourer had spoken the literal truth when he said he had seen Hogarth in Heston. (The reader has probably guessed the solution. *A* Mr. Hogarth lived at Heston Hall, but if related to the artist I do not know).

We next discussed changes in the village; he was quite sad about them, and remarked, with unconscious humour, that now, after his evening pint at The Queen's Head, he sometimes had a job to find his way home! " But there's one thing, sir, as 'asn't changed. That there cottage," and he pointed with his stick to a ramshackle building across the road, one that seemed likely to fall to pieces any moment. " Bin empty for years," he added, " and what's more they can't find the owner. The Council boarded it up once, I don't know if they meant to repair it or pull it down, but the villagers soon 'ad 'em down. Wouldn't 'ave no interference with their rights. If there aint no owner, they sez, it belongs to us as much as to the Council."

We walked across to inspect the building. The half-broken door hung on one hinge, and in the semi-darkness I could see some old ceiling-beams. " Good beams those," I remarked to my guide. " Why, that was just what I was a-goin' to show you," he answered, in a rather disappointed tone. I was sorry to have damped the ardour of this rustic antiquarian and hastened to add: " Please go on, have they any special history?" " That they 'ave," he continued, brightening up at the chance of getting his story out after all.

I expected some long-rambling yarn about Queen Elizabeth, but I was agreeably disappointed. " Yes, sir," my narrator continued, pointing to the centre beam that spanned the whole ceiling, " that's it!" " That's what?" I asked. " The beam, sir," he replied, rather surprised at my ignorance. " Yes, I can see that; but what about it?" " That's where they found 'im!" " Found who?" " Why, Joe White?" He looked more surprised still. " Why, 'im what 'anged 'isself on that very beam!" He seemed astonished that I had not heard of this tragedy, which according to his account was one of the chief events of English History. Well, it probably was in this old labourer's life, even if the sordid story had no wider fame.

" There used to be a staple where the rope went," he went on, " but it's broke off. But that's the very beam, sir, for I 'elped to cut 'im down. Now *there's* something for your 'istory book, sir!" I must have mentioned that I was seeking local legends, and he did his best, so I am taking the hint. So if you go rambling in Heston you may still see that beam (if the cottage has not fallen down first) and I have no doubt that any villager will enlighten you on the history of the unfortunate Joe, if you have a taste for horrors.

I was sorry to see that the old Heston Post Office—part of a grocer's shop—has been demolished. It was said to have been 900 years old, and I am told that it has been held by the postmaster, Mr. Paines, and his family for 100 years.

There are happily, however, many things left hereabouts to occupy our attention, apart from suicides and old shops, especially in the Parish records. Here we read that Heston Church was once held by foreign monks, those of St. Waleric in Picardy, who surrendered it to Winchester College, who in turn gave it to the Crown. Curious old customs once held sway here, for not only were the lands in Heston inherited by the youngest son, in accordance with the law of Borough English, but an estate was once held here by an even stranger tenure, for in 1398 Edmund Fauconer (or Falconer) died seised of a house and lands under Queen Isabel, by a grant of Edward the Third, on the terms that he was bound to ride his demesnes among the reapers upon Bedrepe (Reaping) Day in Autumn; with a sparrowhawk in his hand, presumably a practical pun on his name. This field, once known as The Falconer's Field, is now part of Osterley Park.

Many humbler names have also disappeared in the march of time. Where, for instance, is Smoky Lane now, a former title of a Heston thoroughfare? We can guess how it got this name; probably from the gypsy fires where their caravans had rested, for the Heath was formerly a favourite spot for these wandering folk. Not, however, that they were very welcome visitors, rather the reverse, for in a chronicle of 1594 we read how: " At Heston five men, all late of London, yomen, were taken, tried at the sessions and had a true bill against them, merely because they were ' seen and found in the consort or society commonly called Egipcians, and that the same men did call themselves Egipcians and that they feloniously continued and remained there and elsewhere in the same county for the space of one month.'" For this " offence " three of the unfortunate men were actually hanged. Had a certain romantic episode which once took place between a young gypsy queen and myself (see *The Fringe of London* and the chapter " Of how *Lavengro* gained me the kisses of a Queen.") happened in 1594 anywhere near Heston, I am afraid I should have soon joined the grisly company on the Heath gibbets!

*   *   *   *   *   *

Eight hundred years ago the monks of Hounslow Priory, like the good husbandmen they were, took a pride in their monastic farm or grange (which is the original meaning of the word, though now used more generally) and the name still survives in Grange Farm, Heston, though its fields are no longer held by the brethren.

It is good, however, in these days of change, to find this fine Middlesex farm, one of the oldest in the county, still fulfilling its original destiny of feeding the multitude, albeit the hungry maw of London instead of the monks, and the pilgrims who gathered at their hospitable board to refresh themselves, probably to sleep also rather than face the unknown terrors of the wild and desolate heath that lay beyond its doors.

Grange Farm lies a little behind the main part of the village, by North Hyde and overlooking the meadows towards Cranford, where the Heston Airport is hidden by an orchard. I do not know if the pilgrims of old ever visited the farm, but I know of a twentieth century one who " discovered " it on a Sunday afternoon, and who, becoming so interested in the old farmyard and the curious semi-monastic window of the stable that he committed the sin of trespass, and was caught red-handed and kept a " prisoner " for the rest of the afternoon! In other words, Mr. J. J. Barker, the farmer, when he found me wandering about his farmyard, took a most sporting " revenge " by taking me on a tour of the house and farm-buildings. Seldom have I spent a more entertaining afternoon, as we compared notes of what we both knew about the place, till between us we managed to build up its long history through the ages.

The house shows its age best from the back, for the front is pure eighteenth century and most picturesquely set in a fine old garden, which combined make a delightful " cameo " in an old English setting which I trust will survive for many years.

The farm buildings are equally quaint and in keeping with the scene, in which cart-horses, haystacks and other rural " supers " make up this charming stage. I have been many times since to Grange Farm, which I own fascinates me, but much as I love the old place its most wonderful memory is that first afternoon when I was lucky enough to be caught trespassing. Mr. Barker told me, incidentally, that it was lucky for me his foreman did not catch me, for he is a terror to such " criminals." I am afraid, however, that so hardened have I become when a place really interests me that I have soothed breasts even more savage than that of a furious foreman!

I set out to write the history of Grange Farm, but do not seem to have made much progress. I have not written of the Shropshire women, who still come annually to work here, and live in a barn—there is quite a " Tess " touch about this. It is interesting to note, too, that Lysons, in 1795, mentions these Shropshire women as working on Heston farms in those days. Nor have I mentioned old Henry Little, the fine old Middlesex yeoman, who has worked on this farm for some sixty - five years (" Coom Michaelmas " probably). Good luck to him, for he is still able to do a job o' work, though not far off ninety.

These things, however, are more incidental than historical, and the real history I know of this farm is that it has carried on as such, without cessation, for some eight centuries, which, however, is about as wonderful a history—seeing it is only about ten miles from London—as that of any farm in England.

* * * * * *

Not long ago I lost my way completely between Heston and Lampton, despite the fact that I have traversed it dozens of times, which proves—if a thing so obvious needs it—that to leave anywhere on the fringe of London unvisited for a few months is to return to a *terra incognita*. (The schoolboy howler of translating *terra incognita* as " an unknown fear " has, in such cases, a horrible touch of truth about it!).

When I knew this walk it was by pleasant field-paths, shaded by noble elms, as rural a ramble as the heart could desire, but now it is all bricks and mortar and new roads all exactly alike. I had taken a friend over to Heston and had promised him this country stroll to finish up, and my horror can be imagined at what I found. Nevertheless we set out down Ichabod Road (as it *should* be called) for our destination. In the old days a rough bearing from the Church tower put one on the right track, and all was plain sailing, but now no tower was visible above the wretched houses. Still we pushed on in what we thought was the right direction; up this road and down that. Of course, as an old sailor, I should have got my direction from the sun, but I suppose my disgust upset me and I was careless.

On we walked, but it seemed a mighty long way. There happened to be few people about, but eventually we met two old ladies, of whom we enquired if we were yet anywhere near Lampton. They looked slightly alarmed and clutched their handbags as they told us we were nearly at Southall — in the opposite direction. Sadly we retraced our steps, and finally landed at Lampton. Again in the spirit of howlers we might write " sick transit "—for we were certainly tired of travelling that weary road.

I was prepared for the change in Lampton from a country village to a suburb, and The Black Horse from an old country inn to a modernised 'bus terminus; it is one of the many tragedies of Middlesex. Lampton Hall still stands, however. Once a fine old country house, not over picturesque in square yellow brick, but pleasantly situated. It is now rather like a lion surrounded by jackals. I admire the die-hard spirit of its owner, who refuses to sell it to Jerry the Builder, but continues to occupy it as of yore, when it lay lonely amidst the fields, when the Great West Road was non-existent and even the rumble of the stage-coaches came as a faint echo across the meadows from the main road a mile away. Now the grounds of the house have been cut into by the new arterial road, and cars scream by at all hours of the day and night where once was ancient peace. In its happier and more peaceful days Lampton Hall was often visited by Charles Dickens, who found in its lonely situation a quiet tonic after the bustle of London life——and now? *Sic transit*, indeed.

Another story has it that The Highlands, a fine old eighteenth century house in the Lampton Road, was once the residence of Dickens. I can find no evidence of this, but it is quite possible the novelist may have been a visitor here also.

There is not a great deal to see in Lampton to-day, beyond the houses mentioned, though the wanderer should not fail to notice the very fine signboard of the Black Horse Inn, painted by Mr. Lynwood Palmer.

* * * * *

Near Heston and Osterley are several little places still worth exploring, for though you will get some shocks, you may also have one or two pleasant surprises.

Scrattedge has never been a village even, hardly more than a hamlet in its happier days, but now it is almost swamped. Once it was a pleasant cluster of a farm or so and a few cottages in amidst the fields outside Osterley Park. The last remnants of its picturesque past, however, still exist in the delightful little Rose House Farm, with its quaint old semi-circular windows and old-world garden. Opposite, too, is an old cottage that must have been also there in eighteenth century days; practically all the rest is modern. The Great West Road has swallowed it up, as it has a good many other things, including Syon Hill Farm, where not long ago the Old Berkeley Coach used to change horses.

The farmhouse is still there, but empty and desolate, and its disappearance cannot be far off. Near here was once a beautiful old orchard, in the midst of which was a most picturesque little cottage—easily two hundred years old—and a delightful " rus in urbe." I shall never forget my disgust one day on visiting this and finding all the trees cut down and in their place a forest of iron posts and girders.

The Great West Road is responsible, I am told, for a death a day, and one might add a factory a week—a road of Blood and Ugliness. The only time it is bearable is at night, when darkness shields its hideousness, and when (to try and be fair to an enemy) some of the lighting effects are rather striking.

At the other end of the park is Wyke Green; picturesque but threatened.

It is still rural, with a farm or two, an inn, and an imposing eighteenth century structure in Wyke House, which bears no outward trace of its fall from its former station as one of the lesser mansions of the county—it is now a private lunatic asylum.

The little wayside inn—The Hare and Hounds—at Wyke Green has one pleasing and fairly uncommon feature. When it was " re-built " it was not re-built at all. This paradoxical statement is explained in this way: at the side of the present inn is a small building, which at a casual glance might be a stable. A second glance reveals the truth; it is the old inn intact and a picturesque little wayside hostelry. It is an idea that might be copied more often. I first visited this inn with Mr. W. Townsend, of Sunbury, who, having known the district some sixty years ago, much entertained me with stories of the old days. One of these concerned the last of the old bare-fist prize fights on Wyke Green, which had a rare flavour of bygone times about it.

At the other side of Wyke Green stand the main gates of Osterley Park, of which more anon, and on still another side of this estate is Norwood Green, recently one of the most beautiful places in this district, and even now, in spite of the filling in of the last of the " Dutch Canal " ponds and the disappearance of some of its old houses—witness Norwood Hall, the haunted house where once I searched in vain for the ghost.

North Hyde has nothing special to detain the rambler; the Grand Union Canal gives a glimpse of " nautical " life of Middlesex, when the gaily-painted monkey barges pass up and down on their lawful occasions. There is a large Roman Catholic Orphanage here, but what intrigued me most was a large empty house behind a high brick wall; one of the most extraordinary houses to find in a village; it looks like a typically London house of the larger type, such as might be found in Kensington, that had wandered out into the country and lost its way. Much as I deplore the passing of old houses, this particular one would not be much missed if it found its way back again.

If, as William Morris says, a park that is being cut up looks in anguish, but a garden cries, what does a village do when suddenly cut in two? Swears, I should imagine. This is the fate of Sutton, once a quiet little place, but now divided against itself by the Great West Road.

Were I a resident of Sutton I should curse this arterial horror more than I do as a wanderer; for it literally divides the place against itself to its complete damnation. Yet there are some good houses left here, notably Sutton Hall, a fine eighteenth century structure with an old-world garden; both house and grounds are a glimpse of bygone days that are pleasing. There are several other most picturesque smaller houses; there is The Thatched Cottage, Tenby Cottage, Sutton Cottage and The White House, the residence of Mr. Lynwood Palmer, the artist. And we must not forget The Gardens, an old farmhouse which, if a little swamped by newer houses, is still a delight to the eye.

Then comes the Road, but in the lane south of it are some more pleasing old houses, among which can be noticed Willow Lodge, Raglan Cottage, Sutton House and Sutton Lodge; while Orchard House, though more modern, is not unpleasing. This sounds a mere list of houses, but without detailed descriptions it is all we can do now; but a lover of old houses, or a student of eighteenth century architecture, could spend a less profitable hour than wandering in these two lanes—he could shut his metaphorical eyes as he crossed the arterial road, though he is advised to keep his literal ones wide open!

It was in Sutton Lane that the conspirators assembled to waylay William III. in 1696, but they were frustrated. The *Journal of the House of Commons* for that year states that a camp was formed at Hounslow Heath—this seems to have been a habit of Kings about that period!—" to circumvent a horrid and detestable conspiracy formed, and carried on by Papists and other wicked and Traiterous Persons, for assassinating his Majesty's Royal Person."

* * * * * *

Partly in the parish of Heston is the delightful demesne of Osterley Park, one of the most beautiful rambling grounds anywhere near London. There is a right-of-way across the park by the main road, and many paths often unknown to the public, which makes it better for those who do. The mansion, with its Ionic portico and four turrets, is seen in a striking vista across the larger lake, though even more beautiful is the tree-encompassed sheet of water on the right.

As we leave the house and lakes behind we see as fine a stretch of park-like meadowland as exists anywhere in England, although this spot is under ten miles from London. These broad acres extend as far as the eye can reach—a conventional phrase, but true in this case, as the park fencing in the distance is hidden by a belt of trees.

Linger in this fine old English park. It was never meant to be hurried through; it speaks too delightfully of an age when there was more time to contemplate and enjoy such things.

Its history, too, is long. The manor belonged to John of Osterlee in the reign of Edward I., and in 1443 it was held by John Somerseth, Chancellor of the Exchequer to Henry VI., who had founded a hospital and chantry for the fraternity of All Holy Angels at Brentford End, of which this manor formed part of the endowment. In 1508 Hugh Denys of Grays Inn bequeathed Osterley to the Convent of Sheen, and twenty years later the Manor was conveyed to the Abbess of Syon. At the Dissolution it was granted by Henry VIII. to the Marquis of Exeter, on whose attainder it reverted to the Crown. Edward VI. gave it to the Protector Somerset, but four years later, on the latter's execution, it went back to the Crown. In 1557 it was granted to Augustine Thair, and a few years later became the property of Sir Thomas Gresham, builder of the Royal Exchange.

Gresham enclosed a large part of Hounslow Heath to form his park, one of the first enclosures recorded, and built a magnificent mansion in 1577, and the next year it was visited by Queen Elizabeth——of course. In this case there is ample evidence of her visit (which is not always the case), for an account of it appears in Nichols' *Progresses of Queen Elizabeth.*

In Ward's *Life of Gresham*—though the story is first told in Fuller's *Worthies*—is the well-known tale of the wall. " Her Majesty found fault with the court of this house as too great; affirming that it would appear more handsome if divided with a wall in the middle. What doeth Sir Thomas Gresham but in the night-time sends for workmen to London (money commands all things) who so speedily and silently applied their business that the next morning that court was double which the night before had been single."

This circumstance gave the courtiers the chance to make several feeble puns; one saying that it was no wonder that he could change a building who could build a 'change; while another, referring with extremely bad taste, to differences in the knight's family, affirmed that any house is easier divided than united.

This story is also told reversed; how the Queen suggested that an existing wall would be better away and that the workmen demolished it in the night. So we can believe which we like, or both if we want to, for there probably is not much truth in either, and if the "wall" were more substantial than a wooden fence I should be surprised. Anyhow Elizabeth proved herself a sound sleeper—if any evidence is needed for this—by slumbering peacefully through all the noise of building—or demolition.

Gresham entertained the Queen sumptuously, and we read of a *Play at Awsterley* (written by Churchyard, though the MS. is said to be lost) having been performed in her honour, though Elizabeth had annoyance to bear here also, for in the *Minutes of the Privy Council* it appears that some of Gresham's park-paling was burned while the Queen was there, and that she was much offended, and had four men put into the Marshalsea Prison for the offence. The same record states that Gresham's great enclosure at Osterley was very unpopular, and that complaints against him by sundry villagers, for having enclosed common lands, were heard, but, of course, money overcame right then as now!

There is a good story told of the Virgin Queen and Gresham, the scene of which is given as this mansion, though I do not vouch for the truth of the yarn. An old farmer and his wife were at a London Art Gallery, and a picture of Adam and Eve, in the usual Garden of Eden garments, much shocked the old lady. " Shameless hussy!" she snorted, " What is the title of this picture, George?" Her husband, who was following with the catalogue, reading the titles out loud, unfortunately got the numbers mixed, and answered, " Oh, that's Sir Thomas Gresham receiving Queen Elizabeth at Osterley!"

One always has to write of Queen Elizabeth's sleepings with a certain amount of reserve; not that you are not on safe ground, it is *too* safe. There is hardly a house in the Home Counties more than a hundred years old (with 3 bed., 2 rec., us. off., bth., h & c) that tradition does not associate with this energetically sleepy monarch's visits. She must have adopted a form of " Two Houses Nightly " to have got through a quarter of her alleged visits in one lifetime.

The die-hard local legends should, I think, be placed in this order:— 1, Queen Elizabeth. 2, Oliver Cromwell. 3, The Secret Underground Passage. Some houses claim all three! In fact, it is only dates that prevent scandals, for I was once solemnly told in the grounds of Boston Manor, Brentford (not far from Osterley), by an old labourer that Queen Elizabeth once slept there with William the Conqueror! It happened to be William IV., with his lawful spouse Queen Adelaide; so my old friend did his best; he, at least, got the William right; more accurate than some " authentic " stories that I have been told sometimes.

Elizabeth made use of Gresham as a gaoler; for as money was saved by such an arrangement it became a practice with the Queen to quarter her State prisoners, or those she wished to keep under control, upon the richer gentry. Thus it was that Lady Mary Grey, sister of Lady Jane, was for some time an inmate of Osterley House, and although the knight petitioned the Queen to relieve him of this charge, she was obdurate and would not allow any change, and the unhappy girl was kept in durance (though

certainly not vile) here for several years.   She enjoyed a splendid residence,
at once a palace and a prison, and yet her only " crime " was that, alarmed
at her sister's sufferings in having married a powerful noble, the younger
sister wed a plebian youth of her own choice, and for this she was detained
in custody by the jealous Elizabeth, who disapproved of any who got married
without her consent.

Gresham had a paper mill at Osterley Park, which was the subject of
an Exchequer enquiry in 1584 to decide whether it encroached on the
Queen's highway, or injured the Queen's mills.   This was on the Brent
" near Cruxewell's forde." It was originally a corn mill and we read how
Gresham " joyned a paper myll therunto and yet used the same myll a corne
myll still and all under one roufe and dryven by one stream."

Though Sir Thomas Gresham is famous to most as the founder of the
Royal Exchange, another act of his had far more far-reaching effect upon
millions who have never seen, or perhaps hardly ever heard of, this building
—he introduced oranges into England.

The splendour of Osterley suffered eclipse on his death.   " No sooner
was he gone," writes his biographer, " than this fine seat began to fall into
decay," and Norden, the seventeenth century historian of Middlesex, writing
whilst Lady Gresham still occupied it, says, " Osterley, or Oysterley, the
house now of Ladie Gresham ,a faire and stately building of bricke, standeth
in a parke, well-wooded and garnished with manie faire ponds, which afford
fish and water-fowle.   It is also of great use for milles, as pepper-milles,
oyle-milles and corne-milles.   In the same parke is a very faire heronry and
sundry certain wilde beasts, for the increase and preservation whereof were
devised sundrie allurements, likewise fallen all to ruine."

The manor passed to Sir William Read, and after to Sir Edward Coke,
Attorney-General and afterwards Lord Chief Justice.   Of the Earl of
Desmond, the next owner, an amusing story is told in The Strafford Letters,
which relates how, in 1635, the earl ran away with his own wife.   Desmond,
who had married one of the co-heirs of Sir Montague Stanhope, came one
morning to York House, where his wife lived with the duchess during his
absence abroad, and hurried her away, half undressed and against her will,
to a coach and so carried her away.   In the night she put herself into
milkmaid's clothes, and had like to make her escape, but was discovered."
All ended happily, however, and forgiveness was mutual, and later he
brought her to Osterley, where she lived for years and brought up a large
family.

Sir William Waller, the Parliamentary general, was the next owner, and
after passing through one or two hands was bought by Sir Francis Child,
the banker.   Various alterations and rebuildings took place, but in 1770
Robert Adam completed the mansion as we see it now, incorporating
Gresham's turrets with his Corinthian portico; a little unusual, perhaps,
but not ineffective .

Soon after this Horace Walpole visited it and left a description of the
place in his usual flambuoyant and rather inaccurate style: " Oh, the palace
of palaces ;and yet a palace sans crown, sans coronet, but such expense!
such taste, such profusion. . . . Osterley is so improved and enriched that
all Percies and Seymours of Sion must die of envy.   There is a double
portico and is as noble as the Propyleum of Athens . . . there is a kitchen
garden that costs £1,400 a year, a menagerie full of birds, that come from a
thousand islands which Mr. Bankes has not yet discovered; and then in the

drawing-room are doorcases and a crimson and gold frieze, that I believe was borrowed from the Palace of the Sun; and then the park is the ugliest spot in the universe, and so I returned comforted to Strawberry."

The last sentence gives us the clue to Horace's venom—he was jealous of Osterley; a far finer and more interesting place than the gimcrack Strawberry Hill. The remark about the park at Osterley is just stupid. I have an old print of the place about this time which gives the lie to this statement; Osterley Park was then, and is still, one of the beauty spots of the county.

A description of Osterley, written in 1803, says: "This delightful spot, situated but nine miles from London, is in the parish of Heston. The park, finely wooded, is six miles in circumference. The house, rebuilt in 1760, is a magnificent structure, exceeding 140 feet from east to west, antd 117 feet from north to south. The apartments are spacious, and are fitted up with the richest hangings of silk, velvet, goblin (sic) tapestry and elegantly sculptured marbles; the decorations display the talents of Mr. Adam, the architect, and Zucci, the painter. From the lodges a spacious road is entered, between two fine sheets of water, which gives great beauty and variety to this part of the park. On the north shore of one of these is a menagerie."

With the exception of the menageries this description would apply to-day, so little has the place altered in a hundred and thirty odd years— may the next century and a third see as few alterations. By the way, I should much like to see a " goblin " tapestry! Just the thing for the haunted chamber in an old mansion/

The present owner of this estate is the Earl of Jersey, who I am glad is living there and not giving it up to the builder. It came into his family through a romantic elopement. The only daughter of Robert Child ran away with the Earl of Westmoreland; they were forgiven and subsequently lived at Osterley, and their daughter married the then Earl of Jersey. Family elopements, however, were still in the blood, for *their* daughter, Lady Adele Villiers, also eloped and fled to Gretna Green. It forms an interesting link with the past to know that the gallant captain, with whom the fair maiden ran away, died only about fourteen years before the outbreak of the Great War in 1914.

* * * * * *

In *Glimpses of Old English Homes,* by Elizabeth Balch, appears an illustrated account of Osterley, with a good deal of the interior of the mansion, not usually mentioned in most books that touch on this place.

Osterley Park, and the district generally, also appears in a book of a very different nature, for the boys' story, *Dick of Temple Bar,* shows a good knowledge of local topography, with the exception of the coloured frontispiece (obviously imported), supposed to represent a cottage between Isleworth and Brentford. It shows the building nestling at the foot of a high mountain! I am still trying to locate that mysterious peak of Middlesex.

CHAPTER XXXII.

The Other Cranford

NEAR where the Great West Road disgorges its traffic into the old Bath Road is Cranford Bridge. There is a picturesque oak-lined side road on the right, just before the River Crane.

No sign post tells the traveller where this shady avenue leads, and so the average motorist ignores it, which is a good thing, for were it more frequented it would spoil the peaceful charm that still clings to the delightful village of Cranford, lying half a mile off the main road.

Cranford, despite its wonderful history, has been strangely neglected by historians, and writers on various parts of England have given prominence to many places whose stories are far less worthy of record.

The *Domesday* account tells us: "William, son of Ansculf, holds the Manor of Cranford of the King, and it is held under him by Hugh. It is taxed at 5 hides. There are three carucates of arable land, one of which is in demesne, and the villans occupy the others. The priest has one virgate. Two cottars have two acres; and there are three slaves. The total value of the manor is 60s. per annum. When it came into the present owner's possession it was only 40s.; but in the reign of King Edward the Confessor, 100s. Tristan, the King's Thane, then held it."

In 1877 there was published *The Middlesex Domesday Book,* but it contains little of interest save a list of the landowners for that date.

Then we have Lysons' words on the parish boundaries: "Cranford lies in the hundred of Elthorne; the church is situated about a mile north of the Bath Road, thirteen miles from London. The parish is bounded by Hayes and Norwood on the north, by Heston on the east, on the west by Harlington, and on the south by Bedfont. It contains about 500 acres of land, of which about two-thirds are arable. There are about 80 acres of Hounslow-heath. The soil is for the most part a strong loam."

A writer on the county in 1816 says: "Cranford village contains several ornamental and spacious dwellings, and it is approached from the Bath Road through a long avenue of oak trees"; and despite the fact that more than a century has passed since this was written the words are as true to-day.

Cranford is really quite off the map of knowledge of most Londoners, several having confessed to me they had never heard of it.

It is remarkable that such a collection of old-world houses of good size should form this village in the middle of a desolate heath; for in the eighteenth century, when most of these houses were built, it stood in the centre of the bleak Hounslow Heath of evil fame.

Cranford is one of the few villages where the better class (a term I use for want of another) and moderately larger houses predominate, especially at the main road end.

Estates on the main road are now being developed, and are fast spoiling the outskirts of the village. I wish the National Trust, or some such body, could stop such vandalism. It makes one tremble for the ultimate fate of Cranford.

The first interesting thing that catches the eye of the wanderer as he enters the village proper is the round brick "Cage," or Lock-up; for it was in this that the highwaymen (when caught) were locked up and put in charge of the village constable by the Runners, till the delinquents could be taken into more secure custody. The cage itself is much as it was of yore, with the original iron door, though the barred window is gone. This addition, through which a captured highwayman may have glared at the crowd of curious villagers, bold enough now that he was under lock and key to approach, came to an undignified ending—it was stolen by a rag-and-bone man and sold for old iron. This interesting little building dates from 1810, and probably superseded an earlier one.

Springfield, a house not far away, is a delightful old place, with its red gabled roof and whitewashed walls; and its fine stone-pillared gateway of wrought iron work, while Stansfield House, with its dovecote in front and its range of quaint old stabling at the side, is also worthy of notice.

The former house was once the home of Grantley Berkeley, where he had a special cockpit made for the entertainment of his friends; the one for the villagers' general use was by the ford on the Bath Road. There is an account in his book of a "secret" cockfight at Cranford (after the "sport" had become illegal in 1849) which was disturbed by the arrival of the police.

There is, however, something at Springfield more worthy of notice; in the garden close to the road will be seen another round house, larger than the cage opposite. The taller structure was once the observatory of an astronomer (the villager who told me this was more romantic; he called him an astrologer). This was Mr. Warren de la Rue, who, we read, "made Cranford a place of interest to the world of science on account of the observations carried on here. The great reflecting telescope, and other valuable apparatus, were eventually presented to Oxford University, where they are now housed."

Nor do the pleasant old houses comprise all the things of beauty that are a joy for the present (I wish I could write for ever) in this quaint old village street. There were two ponds (now filled in), one a typical village pond, surrounded by white posts, and covered with duck-weed; and the other more in the nature of a "Dutch Canal," long in shape with a small wooded island.

Then also in the main street are two old farms, with hayricks and picturesque farmyards abutting on the roadway in the real old country style, and backed by meadows where the cattle gaze as peacefully as if the great motor road were a hundred miles away instead of one.

In the centre of the village once stood the old inn bearing the sign of The Queen's Head; a fine old building with its whitewashed walls and low-pitched red-tiled roof overhanging the quaint old porch, with an inviting-looking bench for weary wayfarers beneath the great tree outside, where one could rest, refresh and be thankful. The inside of this ancient house was also worth a visit, for if you knocked your head on one of the old beams in the low-ceilinged bar you at least had the satisfaction of knowing that the same beam probably knocked the heads of fourteenth century customers just as impartially; for the house dated from about 1350. Its Spirit Licence (one of the earliest in existence) dated from 1604.

I regret to have to write of this fine old place in the past tense, for though you will find a Queen's Head there now, it is not the original one. Despite strong local opposition from the saner residents it was demolished a few years back. The new inn, to be quite fair, is better than most new inns are apt to be; its architecture is quite pleasing, but it is not the wonderful old hostelry of picturesque memory. When *will* brewers see the folly of destroying these fine old English inns? In this case a just retribution has overtaken them, for the present landlord tells me that since the new building was erected the receipts have dropped to less than half. Well, it serves them right; perhaps the loss of solid cash will appeal to dull senses untouched by the artistic.

It is Queen Elizabeth's head that now adorns the front of this rebuilt inn. I wonder why; for the original building was probably called after a much earlier queen. The personality of Elizabeth was so strong that her memory overshadows that of other queens; whoever remembers being shown a bedroom in which Margaret of Anjou or Phillipa of Hainault slept?—whereas Queen Elizabeth's bedrooms——!

Another example of modern Cranford architecture is to be seen opposite this inn, where the new almshouses are situated. They are good in design and will mellow well. Originally they were to be let at the delightful rent of one shilling a year, but I am told that owing to the high cost of building this Tenants' Utopia was not realised.

As is only to be expected of an old inn that once stood in the middle of Hounslow Heath, numerous stories clustered round the Queen's Head in connection with highwaymen; stories some of which are probably true, the central figures in most cases being Dick Turpin, Black Bess and Tom King. That these famous folk often visited here is more than likely. The building figured in several films with highwaymen episodes, and I was told that one of them was "Dick Turpin's Ride to York"; so if in this film you see "An inn near York" you may be seeing all the time this old Middlesex hostelry.

The village was also filmed as the scene of an old-time wedding, in costumes of Regency days, and certainly round London I cannot think of a more fitting setting for such a picture than certain parts of Cranford. The only thing missing to complete such a picture is an old village church, and though Cranford Church is a beautiful old structure, it does not stand in the village street, but in the Park, to which delightful demesne we shall soon come.

*   *   *   *   *   *

Before we glance into Cranford's manorial history, which stretches back to pre-*Domesday* times, it may interest the reader to hear my pet theory that Cranford-on-the-Heath has a distinct connection with that more or less imaginary place described in Mrs. Gaskell's immortal novel. In the delightful pages of *Cranford* we are given to understand that we are reading the description of its prototype—Knutsford in Cheshire; yet all the same I should not like to state dogmatically that the Middlesex village had nothing whatever to do with the re-naming of the northern one in the book.

Mrs. Gaskell was born in Middlesex in 1810, and though she went north at an early age she revisited friends around London later, and what is more likely than she discovered for herself this charming village in her native county during some afternoon drive, and being struck, as well she might have been, with its quaintness, which must have been even more picturesque in her day (*Cranford* was published in 1851), she gave the same name to the semi-imaginary town of which she was writing.

Even to-day the Middlesex Cranford has clinging to it much of the old-world charm that the authoress depicted. No higher compliment can be paid to the Middlesex Cranford than to say that were a group of ladies to walk down its street to-day dressed in the costumes of the period, they would not look incongruous (were folk in modern dress out of sight) and would fit into the picture with the old houses that have not changed in the last century.

So I certainly do not think that it was chance alone that made Mrs. Gaskell take the name of Cranford for the book town. It is easy to imagine the stately Miss Jenkins, Miss Matty and Miss Jessie Brown—complete with dimples and poke-bonnet—in this picturesque old village street, that lies so near, and yet so far, from the modern bustle of an arterial motor road. Are there many places left, as near the world's largest city, of which this can still be said?

* * * * * *

It was my good fortune recently to listen to a wonderful lecture, "A Thousand Years of Cranford History," given by Mr. A. C. Marshall, a resident of many years. It is usually the fate of any wanderer who may write upon a place, that however much research he may make, to discover, sooner or later, someone who knows more than he does about the subject. In this case I was lucky enough to find this someone sooner, Mr. Marshall, and in a talk with him after his lecture I asked if he were going to publish it. He said he thought not, though as a matter of fact I should welcome such a rival. I want to be as honest a thief as possible and own up at once what "thunder" I have stolen from Mr. Marshall's talk. It is some of the intimate little stories of village life that find so welcome a place in county histories—for anyone can dig out facts from the latter. It was these touches, though, that gave spice and charm to his talk, and he blended them skilfully into his narrative as he unfolded to us the quietly interesting story of Cranford since the earliest times.

Mr. Marshall is well known as an author, and to his interesting guide to the district I am indebted. In his novel, *Black Bess,* he has shown an understanding of highwaymen and their ways which his long residence in the vicinity of Hounslow Heath has probably influenced.

* * * * * *

In the Bronze Age Cranford consisted of a few rude huts in the forest, and there was probably a Roman camp here. In Sir Montagu Sharpe's *Middlesex: In British, Roman and Saxon Times* there is a drawing of one of the Bonotini, or Roman Survey Mounds, still existing in Cranford Park. For hundreds of years Cranford altered little; for in those days, when the only "road" was a rough trackway through the forest, there was no inducement for the building of anything larger than a charcoal-burner's hovel. Few travellers came this way and the spot which is now Cranford lay too far from the Staines Road to be noticed, and the Bath Road did not then exist.

In mediaeval days there must have been a few cottages clustering round the Manor of the Knights Templar, for there is still a meadow known as The Quintain Field, where the village lads, as well as the knights, used to practise the art of tilting. One of these Quintains, or Tilting Posts, can still be seen at Offham in Kent.

So through the quiet centuries Cranford slept its peaceful way, till the eighteenth, when it woke up and took its place in the tide of the affairs of men and horses, for a busy place was Cranford in the old coaching days, at least that part on the main road, though the traffic would have affected the village less, which then, as now, was purely agricultural.

Although the first actual Mail Coach did not pass through the village till 1784—for the Mail Coaches were a much later innovation than the ordinary stage coaches—all through this century Cranford stabled hundreds of horses, for coaches and post-chaises. Among the coaches re-horsed at Cranford was the Night Bath Mail.

In those days it was impossible for two coaches to pass on the high humped-back bridge over the Crane. This bridge, built in the mid-eighteenth century to replace the wooden structure that spanned the ford of ancient days, was only superseded by the present structure a few years ago.

Mr. Marshall told me one curious little fact; he said that a letter to London reached its destination *quicker* by Mail Coach a hundred years ago than it does to-day by modern postal methods. I told him to be thankful that Cranford is still so delightfully off the map.

The close of the coaching era was the end of Cranford as a busy spot, for after the last Mail Coach had passed through the village in 1846 the place sank once again into a country sleep, which, luckily, parts of it still retain. It is true that a " counterblast " to the newly-formed Great Western Railway was tried, in the form of a Steam Road Carriage that ran through Cranford as far as Reading, but it did not survive long—it probably blew up; they usually did.

I recently witnessed a sight on the Bath Road at Cranford with a certain sadness of its own—an old stage-coach on a motor-lorry. Where it was going I do not know; I hope to some pageant and not to a coach-breaker's yard. I wondered if it ever passed through here in its palmy days, drawn by a spanking team of bays to the tune of the old coachguard's horn. It was a pathetic ghost, and as I saw it whizzing by at 30 m.p.h. it looked really unhappy.

There are several interesting things still to be seen in the vicinity of the Crane bridge, the chief of which is the old blacksmith's, which has been in the Greenbank family for about a hundred years. I have an old newspaper cutting, dated 1750, of a highwayman who had his horse shod at this very forge. The wanderer should notice, too, the old pumps, on both the Bath and the Staines Roads. They were once more numerous, but a few remain; they were used in the coaching days to keep down the clouds of dust that the horses' hoofs raised—though the other side of the picture was almost worse; the thick mud of winter being so deep as almost to stop the progress of any vehicle.

The man who caused the " downfall " of Cranford, as regards its coaching interest, by a curious chance lived there; for " The Cedars " was the home of I. K. Brunel (son of the builder of the Thames Tunnel) when he was Chief Engineer of the G.W.R. As he was also the designer of the " Great Eastern " it is possible that the plans for the giant steamship were drawn, or at least conceived, at Cranford. Some interesting facts of Brunel's life (who was responsible for the famous " Broad Gauge " construction) will be found in *Lives of the Engineers*, by Samuel Smiles.

There is another triumph for Cranford, humbler but more far reaching. Here was grown the first apple that has since achieved world-wide fame as " Cox's Orange Pippin." Mr. Cox lived for many years at " The Firs," and it was in his Cranford garden that he first experimented with this apple.

He was a retired brewer who turned fruit grower and also had nurseries at Colnbrook. He died in 1844 and is buried at Harmondsworth.

"The Firs," which stood on the main road, and was unluckily burned down a few years back, was an old mansion with an interesting history; for it was here that George III. lodged his dentist, so that, the place being almost equi-distant from London and Windsor, he should be handy for a sudden call for both.

I am not sure of the name of this dentist, but it may have been Dumergue, who certainly held this post at one time. He was a friend of Sir Walter Scott, who often stayed with him—as we learn in J. G. Lockhart's *Life of Scott*—so it is possible that the great novelist may have been among the distinguished visitors to Cranford.

There is another story connected with t his house with a touch of humour, and concerns the origin of the long avenue of fir trees still to be seen in what the builders of an estate have left of the grounds (I hope they will have sense enough to retain this row of trees). It is said that some time in the eighteenth century "The Firs" and the still standing Avenue House were respectively occupied by two elderly bachelors, who after being close friends became rivals for the hand of the same fair widow. The feud became so bitter that neither could bear the sight of the other; so one planted a row of fir trees to hide his neighbour's house, when, not to be outdone, his rival did the same. The finger of tradition points to the present double row of firs as the identical trees.

It is also from this village that the beautiful specimens of chrysanthemums known as "Cranfordia," "Cranford Pink" and "Hollicots" take their name. The latter is the name of a house in the main street, which has in autumn a veritable flower show in its front garden—a far better setting than all the cut-flower shows. In this picturesque old house is some specially fine old oak.

In connection with trees in this village there exists in the park an oak which, according to village legend, was grown from an acorn planted by R. B. Sheridan, after he had taken it from a shot pheasant's crop. The tree pride of Cranford, though, is undoubtedly the oak avenue at the Bath Road entrance to the village. I once met here with an American millionaire. He was both impressed and enthusiastic. "I would give ten thousand dollars each if I could take them to my own country home in the States," he said. "I've only got one oak there, but its not so good as any of these." I felt proud of being English, for these trees "belonged" to me at that moment, and I was richer (in trees) than a Yankee millionaire.

To force home the lesson I took a long short cut through Richmond Park, where oaks can be seen in a wider setting. My American friend was generous in his praise. "This is one of the times you score over us," he admitted. "I could buy a hundred of your wonderful old oaks, but all the dollars in America wouldn't buy a successful journey over the water for them—that is *to live* afterwards. I guess its one of the few things I've found in England that money can't buy—and frankly, I'm glad to find it. Yes, sir, you've sure something to be proud of in your oaks."

And yet the suburban builder would delight in destroying a forest of centuries old oaks if he could erect a few more miserable S.D. villas in their place. We are a strange people; but perhaps it is merely human nature not to prize a thing until you have lost it.

When the American asked me to write something in his album, to
remind him of our rambles in England, I wrote:

" In Memory of the Oak Avenue at Cranford in Middlesex.

" Old trees in their living are the only things that money cannot
command. Rivers leave their beds, run into cities, and traverse
mountains for it; obelisks, arches, palaces and temples, amphi-
theatres and pyramids rise up like exhaltations at its bidding; even
the free spirit of man, the only thing great on earth, crouchers and
cowers in its presence. It passes away and vanishes before venerable trees.

" Walter Savage Landor."

The American read these words slowly twice, and then remarked,
relapsing into his native language but speaking quite sincerely: " Gee, but
that's dandy." And now every time I pass this oak avenue the purport of
Landor's words comes into my mind. Already a building estate has appeared
on one side of this tree-lined road, and a vague dread is always in my
mind that one day——? I was told that it was once proposed (by what
set of criminal lunatics I do not know) to cut down these trees, but the
Berkeleys, who still own the land though they no longer live here, stopped
their demolition. It is to be hoped they will retain this power of veto.
It is bad enough to see one end of this wonderful avenue partially destroyed by the new inn, where some vandal has nailed to one of the trees
the notice " To the Public Bar," and on another fixed a flood - lighting
lamp; while the echoes of a dance band are vomited through an open window. Often I have stood in that avenue at night and, as I watched the
effect of the moonlight through the branches, thought of the line " The
moon has raised her lamp above." The old - fashioned lunar rays now,
however, are quite paled by some nice modern flood-lighting!

*   *   *   *   *

An account, written by Thorne some fifty years ago, would almost
apply to it to-day: " The parish of Cranford is large and level, the land
for the most part arable; there are broad wheat-fields, large orchards,
abundant timber-trees—altogether a fruitful, well-cultivated and pleasant
land, rather than one remarkable for scenery." About 1820 the enclosure
of Cranford fields began, for much of it was once wild heath-land; but it
still possesses the distinction of having the county's largest field, which
is just over 100 acres in extent and stands between the aerodrome and
the Bath Road. Up to about 1850 I am told that oxen were still used to
plough the Cranford meadows, and that many of the farm-workers—as
at Heston—were sturdy Shropshire women, who made the long journey
entirely by canal; a thing still possible to do, when most of our inland
waterways are neglected.

In former days grazing rights were an asset to the villagers, and there
is a case on record—about the time of the Enclosure Act—of an old woman,
named Mary Lewen, being granted three-quarters of an acre of ground
as compensation for the loss of her rights of grazing five geese. On this
land she built a cottage which is still standing opposite the Stag and
Hounds Inn, with a tablet " Lewen's Cot, 1819." The five geese of
Dame Lewen seem to have been as valuable as " the gintleman that pays
the rint " is to the Irish peasant.

Talking to a villager a little while ago I heard an interesting thing
in connection with this cottage. There is (or was) a " claimant " to it.

OSTERLEY PARK.

From a print of 1785

My informant was, years ago, on a job in London and happened to mention the name Cranford, when a fellow - workman, an old man named Lewen, asked him if he knew a cottage called "Lewen's Cot," and said that he was the rightful owner of it, but that someone had stolen his rights. In the absence of legal documents he was unable to prove his claim. How much truth there is in this I have no idea, though I have left out a good deal of picturesque detail; as the graphic touch about the claimant wandering up and down the length and breadth of England trying to find Cranford, and then discovering it a dozen miles from London; in which there may certainly be a germ of truth—more learned folk than this old labourer have made the same error.

    ✲   ✲   ✲   ✲   ✲   ✲

There are many houses in Cranford, apart from Cranford Park itself, worth mention. Some we have already noticed, but before we pass on a little concerning a few of the others may be of interest, though the list is nothing like complete.

There is the Red House, to which clings a faint memory of the once famous Berkeley scandal; for it was at this square house in the Harlington Road where lived the Hon. Morton Berkeley, who, though rightfully the sixth Earl, would not use the title as it would reflect on his mother's good name. Here he lived as a simple country gentleman, facing the great mansion which he refused to occupy. For this double renunciation we cannot but respect him. He now sleeps in the little church, to which his coffin was carried across the meadows on the shoulders of the villagers who loved him.

The Red House, with its fine vista over the park lands, even to-day is still delightfully rural, and Mr. Marshall's words, in his little book on the district, are still true of this lane: "There are probably few villages so near London with such rural surroundings as Cranford. The nightingale may still be heard and kingfishers and herons are not uncommon. At two points there are fords, or water-splashes, over the River Crane, and the views in Back Lane (on the way to Harlington) can scarcely be surpassed within a dozen miles of Hyde Park Corner."

Of the two fords mentioned by the writer one is that now bridged over the Bath Road, but the other is at the Hayes end of the village, and is crossed by a wooden footbridge. This ford is deep, as a warning notice says. There is some talk of a road, which I hope will never be built. Instead I would have the ford made wider and deeper; for it is this little strip of water alone that keeps the lorries from industrial Hayes tearing through Cranford, which would be the death-knell of the present peace of the village.

The hump-backed bridge over the Crane in the Harlington Road might well have been a packhorse bridge, and in all probability it was such in the old days. But we are wandering from the houses, a thing easy to do when there is so much of interest.

Just outside the Park gates is Hartlands, a long, white eighteenth century house, set in pleasant meadow-fringed gardens. This house, formerly known as "Bifrons," was once the dower-house of the Berkeleys. Close here and just inside the Park gates is the Rectory. I was told it was Tudor in origin, but if so it has been much modernised. As a matter of fact, I think my informant was mixing it up with Fuller's old Rectory (of which more anon). Anyhow, the present Rectory is a very delightful place—is there another rectory in the London Diocese so beautifully situated? I doubt it. A house of entirely different character is Cranford Hall, the square, rather ugly, early nineteenth century building on the Bath Road, with its bi-eagled gateway and seven blocked-up windows, a reminder of about the most stupid tax ever imposed on the community. This house has a fine walled garden with a beautiful cedar, a landmark for miles over the flat countryside. Cranford Hall, once a well-known boys' school, is now let in flats, the fate of many such old houses, though better than demolition.

We have already noticed the Queen's Head, and of the other Cranford inns much could be written. Once again I deplore the passing of the picturesque old Berkeley Arms, inseparably associated with the coaching days. Of the present Berkeley Arms I have already written and would rather say little more. It cost a lot of money—and looks it. It may attract the profiteer, for the waiters have real boiled shirts, but to have the best of old English wanderers' fare—bread and cheese and beer— would never do in such a "palace"—the lordly contempt of the boiled shirt gentlemen would be too crushing.

The White Hart opposite is better; for though re-built it is more in keeping with an English road. The stables are old and a reminder of busier days. I fancy the original White Hart was older than the Berkeley Arms, but neither of them was as ancient as the original Queen's Head.

There is mention of the White Hart, and a glimpse of the surrounding country, in *Coaching Days and Coaching Ways.* In C. G. Harper's *The Bath Road,* written in 1899, we are given a further glimpse of Cranford and its inns: "The houses grouped round Cranford Bridge were, some 70 years ago, built on the very borders of Hounslow Heath, whose dreary and dangerous wastes only formed a boundary here, beside the still waters of the Crane. At Cranford Bridge stands that fine old coaching inn, 'The Berkeley Arms,' and opposite 'The White Hart,' which must have been in those times a very haven of refuge in that wild spot; and way up the lane to the right hand lies the village and park, as pretty a spot as you shall find in a long day's march. Cranford village is rich in beautiful old mansions set in midst of walled gardens whose formal precincts are entered through massive wrought-iron gates.

"Cranford being situated in the midst of alarums and excursions caused by the highwaymen who infested the vicinity and kept the inhabitants in a state of terror every night, had a peculiarly urgent need for the 'Cage,' and it is, perhaps, because these gentry were expert prison breakers that this one is more than usually strong."

I once read that Mr. Pickwick stopped at the White Hart, Cranford, on his way to Bath. He may have done, but there is no evidence of it in the *Papers.* There is practically no topographical description of this journey. Mr. Pickwick certainly did stop at *a* White Hart on this trip, but it was at *Bath.* I wish Dickens *had* left a description of this Middlesex roadside village.

It is curious that the few writers who *do* mention Cranford make some strange errors; for another mentions "The Toll House in front of the inn at Cranford." Which inn? Nor can I find in the old Road Books (notably *Paterson's Roads)* that there ever was a turnpike gate here

A more stupid error still occurs in Pigot's *Topography of Middlesex* (1839), where the writer states: "Cranford is situated on the bank of the

River *Colne*, which is crossed by a bridge, *hence the name of the village.*" To hark back to the White Hart for a moment before we pass on. Here is another cage—and one that still has a living occupant! Not a highwayman this time, but a "lady," for Polly is really a remarkable parrot. Recently she stopped seven motorists in one week with a wonderful imitation of a burst tyre, followed by a most realistic hiss.

There is still another of the old-time Cranford inns that is now a memory only, with one small, and generally unnoticed, reminder of its former existence. On Mr. Nicholls' grocer's shop at the opposite corner from the Queen's Head can be seen an old iron bracket. This once held the sign-board when this building was an inn, with the curious name of "Who'd a-thought it?" Something of these old inns, and other charms of the district, will be found in *Picturesque Middlesex*, by Ernest Hill and Duncan Moule. It is one of the few ramble books that mention Cranford.

* * * * * *

The story of Cranford Manor is unusual; it began as one, became two, and is now one again. After the Domesday Survey (the exact date is uncertain) it was divided into two—and known as Cranford St. John and Cranford-le-Mote. The former was given by John de Cranford to the Knights Templar, and in the *Calendar of Patent Rolls* in 1301 is an entry: "Confirmation in mortmain of a charter to the Brethren of the Knights Templars in England and their tenants of Craunford, common of all his pastures and hethe within the bounds of the hundred of Istelworth to wit, from the town of Craunford to the town of Twykenham in length, and from the bridge of Babbeworthe Babbeuuorthepond to the town called Hundesleslawe in breadth, and to hold in frank almoin." This bridge is Baber's Bridge on the Staines Road.

Upon the abolition of the Order the manor became vested in the Crown until 1310; four years later Ralp de Monthermer was lord of the manor, and in 1328 it passed to Robert de Swalclyve. In 1333 Roger, Bishop of Litchfield, presented the living to Cranford Church to himself, by reason of the manor being in his possession. About 1363 the manor became vested in the Knights Hospitallers of St. John of Jerusalem, who two years later became possessed also of the twin-manor of Cranford-le-Mote, which up to that time had been the property of the Abbot of Thame.

In *The Pell Records* under " Issues of the Exchequer 1233 " we read: "Richard de Craneford in Middlesex paid 27s. 6d. for the Scutage of Porter " and later "Richard de Crankford (sic) fined half a mark for Licence to Agree." What these terms mean is not stated.

The monks continued to reside here until the Dissolution, and in 1543 the manors were granted to Lord Windsor, whose family disposed of them in 1594 to Thomas Crompton. Although the manors were still one there continued to be two distinct houses, that of St. John being where the present mansion now is, and the other to the north-east of the Church, where the remains of the moat can still be traced in the woods.

According to Lysons the joint history of the manors becomes a little vague about here; but apparently they became vested in the Crown again, for we find Elizabeth granting leases to Sir Gideon Amondisham (or Amsham) and George Needler. In 1603 the le-Mote house was occupied by Sir William Fleetwood, Receiver of the Court of Wards, but soon after this both houses were held by Sir Roger Aston, Gentleman of the Bedchamber to James the First, and Master of the Great Wardrobe.

Subsequently the moat house seems to have been used as the Rectory, for we find several of the writings of Thomas Fuller dated from here. The house was demolished in 1780.

The present mansion is best seen from across the river, but is worth inside inspection; a great rambling place in which it would be easy to lose oneself. It is said (though exactly *who* says these things is always a mystery) that the walls are four feet thick, as when the present house was built in the eighteenth century the older house was *not* pulled down but left *in situ* and the new one built completely round it. In the drawing room is a wonderful carved oak mantel dating from 1644, and the great kitchens and enormous cellars tell stories of busier days.

The stable-yard is spacious and built in a quadrangle, flanked by the great range of stabling where the old Berkeley Hounds were formerly kept. The old clock, that is said to have come from Hampton Court Palace some two hundred years ago, is still going. The belfry is most picturesque, and the old bell (now taken to Berkeley Castle) was cast and brought here some sixty years before Hampton Court was built. I was glad to see that the ancient weathercock, which formerly adorned these stables but in some mysterious way had managed to find itself on the Old Berkeley Arms, is now back again.

An interesting link with bygone times is to learn that the Berkeleys were the last of the old English families to maintain a private Jester, and I like to think that this " light-hearted loon," complete with cap and bells and merry quips so quaint and so terse, once added to the gaiety of Cranford House.

The gardens, rather overgrown just now, are wonderful, and the long green aisle in the woods behind them is one of the finest avenues of trees I have ever seen. In the grounds are two statues, which according to my village informants have strange histories, which the reader can believe or not. The first is that of a woman and child, originally at the end of the long water until some vandals overthrew it. This, I was told, commemorates an eighteenth century tragedy, when the mother went mad and drowned the child in the lake. Who she was, or why a statue was erected to mark this melancholy deed, I am unable to say.

The other statue, which is still there, has an even more remarkable story. It is of lead and represents a figure, scantily clad and not unlike the Dying Gladiator, with a rope round his neck. This, I was told, represents " Mark Antony, a famous pirate who was captured at sea *in the eighteenth century* by the Admiral Earl of Berkeley, who hanged him in Cranford woods." Even allowing for the name to have been mixed up why ever should the Admiral bring his captive to Cranford for execution? Was there no yard-arm on his ship? It is, perhaps, hardly necessary to mention the stories of the secret underground passage to Harlington Church. Every old house has tales of such passages, which in most cases never existed at all.

In connection with Cranford House, " history " once repeated itself. In Norris Brewer's *Beauties of England and Wales,* written in 1816, it will be noticed that while there is a plate of almost every mansion in the county, Cranford House is not represented, and in a footnote we find the reason: " The Countess of Berkeley refused us permission to view the interior of Cranford House. It may not be obtrusive to observe that the residence of Lady Berkeley is the only mansion appertaining to the nobility in the

County of Middlesex to which we have been denied admission."

Over a hundred years later another topographer tried to gain admission to Cranford House for the same reason. At that time the caretaker was a stolid ex-policeman who *was* going to admit me till I foolishly mentioned I was writing a book. This knowledge seemed to dry up the not very genial current of his soul, and his whole manner changed. He refused to let me in without sanction from his superiors, and at once became most guarded in what he said, and although he did not actually use the words his manner implied that anything I said would be taken down in evidence and used against me! The fact of a rambler wanting to see the mansion was nothing—but one who might write in a book what the ex-policeman said was obviously one of whom it was wise to be wary. I did not get in that day at all.

You will not find the ex-policeman there now, and I am glad that soon the Park will be open to the public. There was a scare that it was to be cut up for building, but now the Middlesex County Council and the Hayes District Council have shown fine public spirit in saving the wonderful old place. All honour to them.

I should here like to record my thanks to Mr. F. Sadler, Bailiff under the Berkeleys, for his courtesy and help on several occasions. Mr. Sadler has lived in Cranford all his life, and has a fund of stories, which I found most entertaining.

* * * * * *

The estate of Cranford Manor, if a little flat, forms a most pleasant stretch of English parkland, beautifully wooded in parts, especially where the River Crane is widened out as it flows in front of the mansion. The old stone bridge that spans these waters has been to me as a Kalendar of Country Delights. Within half-an-hour by car from the Marble Arch, its situation is as rural and peaceful as anywhere in the shires of England. Here have I watched the seasons and their change. Firstly when the snow has covered the fields like a white sheet and turned the woods adjoining into a veritable fairyland.

Though I have never seen a plunging pike, hungered into madness, in the river below it is not so long since they swam here, as well as wild fowl, for which the estate was noted. Curlew and snipe have made their nests in these lonely meads, while even the " dappled darlings " once raced across the same meadows, from the hunt kennels by the mansion. In fact, Cranford Park reminds me strongly of Kingsley's *Ode to the North East Wind*—the manliest poem in English Literature. Spring in Cranford Park is very beautiful, and nowhere can the awakening of Nature from her winter sleep be better observed than in this happy pleasurance. Midsummer has its own mature beauty, when the heat of the day can be tempered by woodland shade. And then the autumn—and I am writing these lines sitting on that bridge on a bright October morning—when Nature's magic brush has tinted so beautiful a scene for me, I am apt to think that this is the most entrancing picture of all; but then I think that of every season's panorama as it passes before me on this spot with its simple, but impressive, pageantry.

Is it to be wondered at, then, that I was utterly sick at heart when I saw a blatant board announcing that it was for sale as " Ripe for Development." I hardly know which I wanted to do first, weep as the angels weep, or swear as bargees are supposed to do. My first wish was for an axe, and then, seeing certain practical difficulties in the way, for a brush and some red paint to erase the offending expression and substitute "Mellowed for Preservation."

The term "Ripe for Development" in such a place maddens me. Estate Agents' jargon, it means nothing, and is almost as stupid as the term "A period house" used without qualification. What period? Queen Anne or Mary Ann? Ionic or Ironic? A modern semi-detached villa is a "period house." Saner thoughts have now prevailed, and most of this beautiful demesne is saved.

* * * * * *

In many a place in the Home Counties we find a book, apart from a local history, that tells us a good deal about it in former days, usually some biography or book of memoirs, and the glimpses thus given us are often of extraordinary interest. In Cranford, though there is no history of it yet written, we are lucky in finding two of the other type, which, though dealing with different matters largely, tell us a good deal about life in this little Middlesex heath village.

The first is the Hon. Grantley Berkeley's *Life and Recollections.* The author was a "roaring blade," very typical of the "twenties" of last century—the "Tom and Jerry" period—about which time most of the Cranford incident occurs. He was Master of the Old Berkeley Hounds, which introduce us to the writer's other book, *Reminiscences of a Huntsman.* It is the former book, however, that gives us the more vivid glimpses of Cranford.

Grantley Berkeley spent much of his time here, both at the mansion and at Springfield, and it is in his pages that we read the (alleged) authentic account of the famous ghost story of the old Cranford House. He relates how he and his brother Morton were about to go out at night after poachers: "It was my mother's rule that servants should be in bed at ten o'clock, and on the night of the ghost we were to go forth at midnight. My brother and myself were together, and well armed, and little inclined to be afraid of anything. We passed by the Still Room, intending by crossing the kitchen to reach the courtyard.

"The large old house was as quiet as death when we entered the kitchen. By the bottom of the table, near the great fireplace, a tall screen stood, and as I looked at it the glowing embers in the grate threw a glare of red light over the room, making the smallest thing distinctly visible, and falling full on the tall figure of a woman, divided from me only by the breadth of the table. She was dressed as a maidservant, with a poke bonnet and a dark shawl. On my entrance she slowly turned her head, and as she did so every feature ought to have stood forth in the firelight, but beneath her bonnet was an indistinctness of outline not to be accounted for.

"I said to my brother, who was behind me, 'Look.' As I spoke the figure seemed to glide rather than walk slowly on, up the kitchen towards the fireplace, while I locked the door and put the key in my pocket. Morton said, 'I see her; there she goes.' I had not said what I had seen and therefore could not have suggested the idea. On turning round there was no woman to be seen, so I asked my brother where she had gone. He replied, 'Up the kitchen, towards the screen.' 'Come on then,' I cried, 'let's catch her to see who she is.' Our impression was that it was one of the maidservants, and we proceeded, each taking a separate corner of the screen and meeting on the side next to the fireplace — but there was nothing there!

"Astounded, we commenced a search, looked up the chimney and into every nook and corner. But there was no living thing in the kitchen but ourselves. The windows were fast, and so high in the walls that no one could have reached them; the door was locked, and the only other door, into the scullery, we found locked and the key on our side. We hear of tables knocked by knuckles of ghosts, of pictures drawn by spiritual agency, of handkerchiefs floating in the air, of words written by unseen hands, not one word of which do I believe; but here I offer to my readers a fact impossible to be accounted for; an apparition visible to two persons who, when they saw it, thought to be a living body; each supposed it to be a woman, and fearless of spiritual agency pursued it, but in vain.

"The form resembled no one we knew, it came to indicate no treasure, nor to point out any spot of perpetuated crime; it came we know not why, and went we know not whither. The only rumour of a ghost we had ever heard arose from an occurrence that happened many years ago to my father. He had come down from London to Cranford, and as he went through the courtyard, one side of which is formed by the kitchen, he saw on the cellar steps at the end of this court, where was no other outlet, the figure of a man. It was nearly dark, but beneath the bright sky of the summer night the figure stood out from the sable hue of the descending arch as distinctly as in noonday.

"My father had brought down no male domestic, and he at once saw that the form was strange, so he advanced upon it with the words, 'Halloa, sir, who are you?' The figure answered him not, but receded down the cellar steps, and was lost in the darkness. My father ordered the spirit up from the vasty deep—the cellars under the old house are immense. As usual, however, with the spirits, the call was not obeyed, so my father remained on watch, and called the maid-servants. Leaving them clustered together at the entrance, candle in hand, he searched the place for the delinquent, but his search was fruitless. Of course, in this instance, there was the possibility of the figure being a 'follower'; and on that account might have been passed off by the maids."

Frankly these ghost stories are weak; in the second a possible explanation is given, and for the first, which the writer tries to cloak in mystery, the explanation seems even simpler. We must remember that those were "three bottle days," and as the two men were sitting up ready to go out into the cold, what is more likely than that they should have had a "wee drappie" to keep out the inclement night? The "ghost" probably *was* a maid-servant up after hours, and cute enough to evade two fuddled ghost-hunters. I was much interested to find, on my inspection of this kitchen, that the actual long table mentioned is still in its original position—but I saw no ghost.

There is mention of these ghosts in Charles G. Harper's *Haunted Houses,* but it adds little to our knowledge of the spooks in this old mansion; though the following description of this place is good: "The mansion is, for the most part, a heavy, scowling pile, rambling darkly, a mass of deep-toned red-brick, over much ground in the picturesque park; and a more or less 'modern' portion with a double-bayed front, furnished with verandah-roofs on the first floor, looking weirdly like heavy, half-closed eyelids, has not a much more cheerful appearance. To the distant view, the house and church, framed as it were by the sullen waters of the River Crane and dark masses of trees, look sufficiently eerie." Test this description after nightfall; you will find it true.

Here is another story of mysterious midnight happenings in this old house: "In those days," writes Grantley Berkeley, "Cranford House was as isolated and as lonely a place as is possible to conceive; and it was my father's custom to drive down from London with four long-tailed black horses, that took two hours to cover the twelve miles, on a Saturday night and to remain at Cranford till Monday. On one of these occasions he was accompanied by his sister, Lady Grannard. My father's favourite pointer, Doll, went with them in the carriage. After enjoying the extreme quietude of the place and rambling about the gardens, redolent of the perfume of flowers and musical with the voices of birds, they retired for the night.

"In the midst of this tranquility Lord Berkeley had sunk to sleep, Doll lying on his bed. Slumber had continued undisturbed for some time, when, on partially opening his eyes, he thought he heard a slight bustle outside the door. On listening the fact became more certain, for he distinctly heard the slow sliding of a hand on the panels, as if feeling for the handle, and then struck the lock and paused there in suspense. His pistols were lying loaded by his bed; he seized one and waited. He had no light and all was as dark as pitch. He could hear the handle of the door cautiously turned, and heard the door rub over the carpet as it opened to admit the intruder. Light as the step was he nevertheless was next aware of its stealing towards his bed.

"Doll was conscious, too, of the suspicious visitor, for her attention was rivetted. This puzzled him, for the dog would have flown at a stranger. Suddenly thump-thump went her tail. There was no one in the house, besides my father and his sister, that Doll knew (for they had brought no servants from London, and the dog had never been to the house before and did not know the servants residing there). So Lord Berkeley replaced his pistol on the chair, but with his strong right hand, and it was a powerful one, ready for any required action, he sat up in bed.

"The almost noiseless step came on, till the slight rustle that accompanied it proclaimed the object to be within reach. My father stretched out his hand, and he seized his sister's arm. With a shock she awoke—Lady Grannard had been sleep-walking, and but for Doll, and my father's knowledge of the dog's fidelity and his cool presence of mind, he might have killed his sister. The sagacious pointer had saved him from this frightful act."

The famous incident of the Earl of Berkeley and the highwayman has several versions. Here is the one usually related, quoted from my former book, The Authors' Thames: "The Earl, who had been robbed once by a highwayman and always carried loaded pistols, and vowed he would never yield again to one robber only. One night as he was driving over the Heath towards Cranford he was awakened by the sudden stoppage of the coach and a head peered in at the window. 'Now, my lord, I have you at last! You said you would never yield to a single robber—deliver!' 'Then who is that looking over your shoulder?' replied the Earl. Thrown off his guard the highwayman turned, when the Earl, drawing his pistol, shot him dead."

The Gentleman's Magazine for 1774 has a different version: "As Lord Berkeley was passing over Hounslow Heath one evening in his post-chaise the driver was called to stop by a young fellow, genteelly dressed and

OLD QUEEN'S HEAD, CRANFORD. *Photo by F. Ash*

CRANFORD HOUSE AND CHURCH. *Photo by F. Ash*
River Crane in foreground.

HESTON CHURCH.
From a Print of 1807.

mounted, but the driver, not readily obeying, the fellow discharged his pistol at the chaise, which Lord Berkeley returned, and in an instant a servant came up and shot the fellow dead."

Still another account of the affair is given by Grantley Berkeley: "As my father was proceeding across the Heath, rather nearer to the old precincts of the village of Hounslow than to Cranford, a voice called out to the postboy to halt, and a man rode up to the carriage window. The robber thrust in a pistol; my father caught the weapon, and thrust his gun against the body of the highwayman and discharged it. It set the highwayman's clothes on fire; nevertheless he rode away for some yards, and then fell dead. When the robber fell he was immediately joined by his accomplices. Lord Berkeley now got out of his carriage and, with his pistols, advanced upon them. The fellows fled, leaving the dead man."

It is surprising the interest this affair roused and the different mentions of it to be found. It appears in G. W. E. Russell's *Collections and Recollections;* and Horace Walpole, who never missed any gossip, mentions it twice in his *Letters;* while another account is found in an even more unlikely place, Lord Stanhope's *History of England.* Even the accounts of members of the Earl's family differ; that of his Countess being quite dissimilar from that of his sister, the Margravine of Anspach (the mother of Hon. Berkeley Craven, who figures in *Rodney Stone*).

Here is another adventure, from *The Ladies' Magazine*, 1808, when his lordship was in danger from a different cause: "The Earl of Berkeley, walking in his park at Cranford with his small son, was attacked by a deer, whose horns he immediately seized, and kept hold when thrown down and trampled upon by the furious animal. In this situation he desired the child not to be afraid, but to take from his (the father's) pocket a large knife, and to stab the deer. This the boy did and by frequent stabs caused the animal to run away. Lord Berkeley has recovered from the injury."

To return to Grantley Berkeley—who was probably the child referred to—his book is so quotable that it is hard to know where to stop. It is true he blunders at times on topographical details, such as describing Hounslow Heath *intersected* by the Thames and the Mole. Yet even though the book has its faults, they are those of a *live* book—so many are moribund! Take his chapter "Cranford House"; how crammed with romance it is. He speaks of the Coach and Horses Inn at Harlington Corner as "on the fringe of Harlington Common"; the name has now disappeared; and tells of boyish pranks on the Heath. A delightful chapter, and among the many other things the writer mentions are the shooting parties at Cranford, when the Duke of York, the Duke of St. Albans, "Punch" Greville, Sir George and Sir Horace Symons, and many others came to Cranford. Half the fashionable world seems to have congregated here in those days.

Then there is another chapter, "Highwaymen and Ghosts" (also mentioned elsewhere), which is even fuller of incident. We have already quoted from this chapter on the "spooks," and here are some on the other side of the picture.

The author mentions the famous "Highwayman Bishop": "The vicinity of Hounslow Heath also rendered it a convenient place for the nightly occupation of villains. Nor was the profession of highwayman confined to the lower classes; for even a dignitary of the Established Church was found on the Heath collecting tithes in a promiscuous way. This, the archives of the British Museum tell us, was the Lord Bishop Twysden of Raphoe, a member of the old Kentish family of that name, who was found suspiciously out at night on Hounslow Heath in 1752, and was most unquestionably shot through the body. A correspondent of *The Gentleman's Magazine* asks the question: "Was this the bishop who was taken *ill* on Hounslow Heath, and carried back to his friend's house, where he died of an inflammation?" This mysterious affair was never satisfactorily cleared up.

Again Grantley Berkeley writes: "Cranford adjoined Hounslow Heath and the incidents for which it long retained a terrible celebrity were often canvassed in my hearing. In these unadventurous times it is not easy to realise the spirit which influenced people, sometimes holding respectable positions, to imitate the heroes who lived on plunder. The wide unenclosed heathland was the resort of those who desired to better their fortunes at the expense of travellers; they became the haunt of mounted gentlemen who cried "Stand and deliver!" with a loaded pistol and a black mask, at the window of every chase or stage-coach."

To this he adds: "In those days Hounslow Heath was as celebrated for highwaymen as it was for plovers' eggs. Its thick furze bushes, thorns and wide extent, running as it did to Hatton, Harlington and Hampton Commons, made the pursuit of a malefactor on a fast horse very difficult."

A story is told of Berkeley Craven and Alvanley on the roads hereabouts: "Lord Alvanley was always ready with a joke. Once as he was with Craven in a post-chaise they were upset crossing Hounslow Heath. Indignant at the catastrophe Craven determined to give the first post-boy a 'taste of his quality,' but finding him an old man, simple remarked, 'Your age protects you.' Lord Alvanley 'went for' post-boy the second, but finding him a young, determined-looking fellow, wisely retired with 'And as for you, sir, your youth protects you!' "

W. A. Hirst has written an excellent little book in his *Rambles in the Home Counties*. It is a book I would recommend to all wanderers, but I hope the author will not mind if I take him to task for giving Hertfordshire history that belongs solely to Middlesex. The Battle of Barnet was fought entirely in Middlesex, and every foot of the unfortunate Admiral Byng's estate of Wrotham Park is in this county and not in Hertfordshire. In Hirst's book we find a not very flattering word portrait of this Cranford author. "Having passed through the village," we read, "by the noble grounds of Cranford House, and cross the little Crane by the footbridge. At this house Grantley Berkeley, an eccentric and turbulent character, spent his youth." George Meredith, in *Beauchamp's Career*, has drawn too flattering a picture of him as Everard Romfrey. The man was an insolent bully who brutally assaulted Fraser, the proprietor of the noted magazine, and afterwards fought a duel with Maginn, the Captain Shandon of Thackeray."

Hirst's opinion seems unfair; we have to remember the times in which Grantley was most active were not our times. They were the rough and ready, hell-for-leather days—hard drinking, hard swearing, hard riding and hard fighting times, not to be judged at all by our more kid-glove standards.

Opinions, however, seem to differ about Grantley. In that interesting book, *Within an Hour of London Town*, by "A Son of the Marshes," the author asks an old rustic if he knew Grantley Berkeley. "Knew him?" was the answer, "yes, I should think I did; knew him well and his bloodhound Druid. What he said he meant did Grantley. Folks round here couldn't make him out, nor his ways neither; but he had lots o' good qualities.'

Later the writer adds: "Referring again to the Hon. Grantley Berkeley, he said rustics wondered at his ways; his influence over birds and animals appeared like magic They said 'outlandish things followed him about; they se'd wild creatures feed out of his hand.' His power with them was truly marvellous. A most kind and considerate man Grantley Berkeley was; and as a sportsman and naturalist second to none; he claimed the respect and admiration of all."

Here in peaceful Cranford can still be found some who, when they were young, have seen an old man walking down the village street, visiting again the scenes of his boisterous young manhood. That old man was the Honourable Grantley Berkeley.

We ought to forgive much and see a deal of good in one who could write, as Grantley did, when he left (about 1829) the village I have learned to love as he did, though a century and more divides our impressions; and I can still find traces of what then surrounded him. "To those dear woods and fields at Cranford," he wrote, "then a long farewell. To the woods, where beneath the shading and faithfully silent trees the first vows of a boyish love reached the listening ear, and where the heart felt and expressed a spring that the summer of manhood has never surpassed. These woods, where in summer song-birds flocked from the more open and trodden fields to pour out their loving melody in security. Where the last quiet notes of the murmuring turtle-dove were taken up by the nightingale, and from eve continued through the night. To the river through the willows and the the park, where Miss Kemble, afterwards Mrs. Sartoris, once entranced my soul by singing to us — as the boat floated down the stream with us, memories of heroism and love. Adieu to all."

Grantley Berkeley, who died as recently as 1881, retained his interest in Cranford long after he had left it; and I can appreciate his feelings when he wrote, after a visit in 1865: "The site of former nocturnal poachings has now undergone a change. Enclosures have taken place; cornfields have sprung up in lieu of furze bushes, villas have filled the swampy gravel pits, where, as a boy, I shot snipe; and the gardens, full of roses and other flowers, have banished the bull-rushes. There are no heaths now, and where the peewit fitfully hovered and enticingly sheered away from her nest cultivation reigns supreme." I wonder what old Grantley would say to-day could he revisit his beloved Cranford.

* * * * * *

As we have heard of the ghosts of Cranford House this may be a suitable place to tell a little adventure of my own in search of another wraith in these parts, not, I am afraid, crowned with success.

It concerns a Grey Lady, who seems to play a prominent part in the ghostly history of West Middlesex, for it was at Poyle that I did not see another one. On the present occasion when I was asked, about 10.30 p.m., if I would care to explore a Haunted Wood I jumped at the chance quicker than I did subsequently from fright. This is a different spectre from the feeble shades that are supposed to haunt Cranford House, and is entirely a woodland spirit. What legend is connected with her is uncertain, but she is said to " walk " in the woods on the site of the old Moat House, and along the Beech Avenue, behind the present mansion. The former place is her usual *habitat,* I was told. So to the Moat Woods we went.

Speaking as an amateur I should say it was a suitable time for ghost hunting. Early spring had not quite forgotten that it was really late

winter, and a keen wind was blowing, and the moonlight rendered fitful
by scurrying clouds that moved the shadows here and there, as some player
in a fantastic game of midnight chess might shift his pieces on a giant
board. Every tree might hold a shade other than its own, every bush a
Lurking Something; and the strange voices of a woodland night demanded
our business in that home of mysterious possibility.

Anyone who has walked through woods by night knows that the stillness is liable to be broken by unexpected sounds, which, if not inexplicable,
are startling. The chirping of grasshoppers, the rustling of the dead leaves
as some small animal is disturbed, the whispering of the breeze in the
foliage overhead, the snapping of a dry twig underfoot, the rising to the
wing of a frightened bird and the piercing cry of the screech-owl, and, if
water be near, the croaking of frogs. All these strike upon the ear and
thrill the nerves.

How many of these night sounds we heard on this occasion I am not
prepared to say, but it was ghostly enough, for the only light we had was
a pocket torch, and the tall tree trunks stood in our path like grim sentinels
where the beams fell on them. First we had to cross the old moat on a
log; this moat is still half-full of water and nearly circular in shape, and
marks clearly the site of the old house where Fuller lived.

As soon as we entered the wood a ghastly shriek rang out. " The Grey
Lady is in good voice to-night," I said, " she welcomes us." I was assured,
however, this was an owl only; the ghost never uttered any sound. The
moon gave only a dim light, its uncertain beams being also obstructed by
the gaunt branches overhead. The undergrowth was thick and straggling
brambles formed " ropes " across our path that threatened to trip us up,
but we were soon in the centre of this woodland island. Here we stopped
to look about us, as well as the darkness would allow. It was certainly an
eerie spot and one in which any reasonable ghost should have been happily
miserable enough. As we paused we left for a moment the subject of
ghosts for one which, I must confess, was more interesting. One of my
conductors flashed his torch on the upturned roots of a large fallen tree.
To my surprise the roots were covered with bricks, embedded in the mud.
I examined one; from its shape I should say it was Tudor. My companions
then told me of the excavations they had made and the numerous short
passages they had found beneath the earth. I examined one of these
" secret passages," and though I hate to destroy romance I am pretty
certain they are the remains of an old drainage system.

I was then told the story of how tradition spoke of a secret underground
chamber beneath the foundations of the Moat House, and how the noble
family who held this estate for so long would never allow any excavating
to be made for it. Why, I have no idea, for the legend relates no hair-
raising story connected with it. So we can let our imaginations conjure up
what pictures they will of what lies unearthed in these haunted woods. If
there *is* anything in the story I should much like to be there when this
chamber of unknown mysteries is laid open.

As we sat here on the fallen trunk we turned our talk from archaeology
back to ghosts, and I was told what little there was to know about the one
supposed to roam these woods. I may say, in parenthesis, that both my
companions were young men and not at all the usual neurotic type who
believe in ghostly phenomena; nor did either claim to be " psychic "; yet
they both said that several times in these woods at night they were badly

scared by what they could not clearly describe. Some power of evil seemed abroad that affected them strongly.

They swore on their words of honour—and I believe them—that they were not " pulling my leg " or trying to make " my flesh creep," but sincerely believed all they said. As we talked I noticed the later it got—it must have been close on midnight by this time—that they became uneasy and fidgety. They owned though they were frightened, that these woods still fascinated them, and that they came here often—*together*. One said that he had actually *seen* the Grey Lady. It was just at dusk on an autumn evening when he saw what he took to be an old woman in a long grey cloak, walking up and down and peering about as if she had lost something; on his going down the woodland path towards it the figure vanished. The other young man confessed that he had never *seen* anything, only felt the evil influence.

I will not attempt to explain all this, but set down the facts exactly as I heard them; but I can honestly say that I felt nothing whatever, and, apart from the discomfort, would have no objection to spending the night by myself in this " haunted " wood. As a matter of fact I *did* return another night quite alone (and nearly fell into the moat getting over the slippery log) and spent about half-an-hour walking up and down. Perhaps the smoke from my pipe frightened the Grey Lady, for I saw or heard nothing beyond the usual woodland night sounds. No powers of evil forced themselves upon my mind, and I left that wood with a clean soul—if with dirty heels.

Again I hate to destroy a good story, but as regards the Grey Lady of Cranford Woods I think what my young friend saw *was* an old woman gathering sticks for her fire; she *may* have worn a grey cloak. What is more natural than this errand took her to the wood—and that, at the approach of a stranger, who might be someone in authority, this harmless trespasser disappeared.

Another explanation is even simpler still. Both these young men wore glasses, and having recently taken to them myself for reading; I have noticed that things behind one are often reflected in a shadowy form in front. I donned them on the night I returned to the woods alone, but I saw no reflected fellow-trespasser; apparently because no one else was there. But your hardened ghost-seer has a knack of rejecting the simple explanation.

Anyhow I owe a debt of gratitude to my two conductors—both good sportsmen—who did their best to give me a thrill. It was an evening of real entertainment, for though the " star " failed to appear, I saw some far more interesting "pictures" that night. These two young men going to explore the ruined house (or what was left of it) and finding the ghost reminded me of a scene in *Rodney Stone,* where he and Boy Jim go to explore the mysterious old house at Friars Oak.

* * * * * *

The second book that deals with Cranford, more modern if less known than Grantley Berkeley's, but running it closely for interest, is *By the Clock of St. James's,* by Percy Armytage, former Court Official. This gentleman was, I believe, a great-nephew of the former, and spent his boyhood at Cranford Park. He lived, until his recent death, at " Meadowbank," on the Bath Road.

I read his book with delight, especially the parts about Cranford. He tells us many stories of the village in earlier days; of its Great House and its Church. We must content ourselves with three extracts only; each a little cameo in itself, recalling " our village " some seventy years ago.

Here is the first: " Cranford is most vividly recalled to me by summer perfumes; hawthorn, meadowsweet, pungent and lush, fringing the banks of the River Crane; and every country scent and sound—these, to me, are Cranford. Situated in a healthy, rural stretch of country it is still one of the few bits of pastoral and woodland country within the span of a dozen miles from Hyde Park Corner. Industrialism is flinging its tentacles distressingly close, and there are now tall factory chimneys outlining the Grand Junction Canal, and the railroad to the west. Yet the present Rector of Cranford, Rev. Dr. E. P. Lewis, in 1926 watched an otter in the River Crane; and my memory, bridging a period of nearly seventy years, records almost every conceivable form of wild life in the immediate neighbourhood.

" To this day, in an ash tree hard by the watersplash, I will wager that in season you may hear the nightingale; and at sundown, gliding into the twilight, wild ducks come to sleep beside the ornamental water. Herons are frequent visitors and kingfishers are still by no means rare."

The author describes a journey from Cranford in those far-off days that has an interest of its own, when he tells us: " To a child travel is a great adventure, and I have indelibly engraved on my memory my first journey from Cranford to Berkeley. Clothed most unsuitably in a Little Lord Fauntleroy velvet suit, I climbed into a high-bodied chariot painted bright yellow; it was drawn by four horses and the postillions wore crimson liveries. There was only one seat inside, and this being reserved for my grandparents, I was accommodated by a brocaded footstool. The dicky behind was occupied by my grandparents' maid. The front of the chariot was enclosed by a sheet of plate glass, curtained at each end. From my lowly perch I first became acquainted with the eight miles of road between Cranford and Slough. From Slough to Stroud the coach, including the occupants, was taken by rail on a truck, horses again drawing it on the last stage of the journey. This was an ' inter regnum ' between road and rail travel."

The final extract is, perhaps, the best of all. I have been to that little church recently on a Sunday morning, and allowing for certain differences that the passing years have rendered inevitable, I can, from this visit, picture vividly the old-time scene of which he writes: " Here is just one lingering memory of Sunday mornings at Cranford whilst I was still a boy. The place, as I have remarked, was essentially somnolent and restful, so near London and yet so far removed from its hurly-burly; an unspoiled English landscape, where the lowing of the cattle and the melody of wild birds, mingled with other rural sounds, alone broke the stillness. The very atmosphere of the quaint old house set one in tune for the Sabbath, and, as the old church bell was tinkling, we assembled in the vestibule, each with a large Book of Common Prayer. We would await the coming of the Reverend H. W. Hickes, a genuine sporting parson, who farmed, hunted, engaged in all the prevailing amusements, revelled in a good dinner with vintage wine, yet never forget he was a parish priest.

" At about five minutes to eleven Mr. Hickes would arrive, always with the remark, ' We are ready now, Sir Maurice.' Thereupon, with Mr. Hickes leading the way as if it had been a funeral procession, and we following grandfather and grandmother, who were immediately behind him; the household marched solemnly into the church. The Rector himself handed us to the family pew and then disappeared behind an old three-decker pulpit, from which he presently emerged in a white surplice, which he afterwards changed into a black gown for the sermon.

"Years after I heard a clergyman announce, 'The choir will now render an anthem "God Preserve Us."' The story has become a chestnut, but that anthem might well have been associated with the barrel-organ then in use in Cranford Church; fortunately it could only plead guilty to the violation of three separate tunes. This alarming instrument was operated by the village schoolmistress, who vigorously turned the handle; her signal to commence being a lusty blast upon a whistle blown by Mr. Hickes. Thus, when the parson piped, the organ and choir, more or less concurrently, began, and the three tunes had to serve alike for Psalms or for the few hymns then in customary use, without the slightest regard for metre or length of line. After a brief address, usually of the harrowing hell-fire type, we all went home."

* * * * * *

There is no need to drag into the limelight the details of the Berkeley Scandal of 1828, which provided so much fashionable gossip. It concerned the marriage of the then Earl (many years before) to Mary Cole, the daughter of a Gloucester butcher. This marriage was declared irregular, so he married her again, and it was to settle which children should be considered legitimate that led to litigation. Finally it was decided that only those born after the second marriage should be allowed to succeed to the title; and even this was not considered satisfactory by the family, who claimed the first marriage legal. As we have already noticed, the Hon. Morton Berkeley, though declared by the House of Lords to be the earl after his father's death, refused to take the title.

After the Earl's death Cranford Park was left to his widow as a Dower House, and here the Countess who had been twice married to the same man continued to reside. Butcher's daughter though she might have been, she was a lady of character, and when, some time before her husband's death, she found his affairs in a deplorable condition and that the Earl never had a penny of ready money and was being swindled on all sides, she undertook to clear him of embarrassment if she were allowed the sole control for a year. So well did she succeed that at the end of that time the Earl was completely free of debt and his estates paying as they had never done before. So good was her stewardship that she continued to manage his affairs until his death.

Frances Ann Kemble, the actress, has left an interesting account of a visit to Cranford, and said of the Berkeleys "they had a vein of singularity unlike other people." Of the octogenarian Countess—"the beautiful daughter of a butcher" as she describes her—she tells a typical story: "On one occasion the old lady had her glass filled with claret so full till the liquid appeared to form a rim above it, and then raising it steadily to her lips, looked round the table, drank the contents without spilling a drop, and said, 'Not one of my sons could do that!'"

* * * * *

The mention of a priest in *Domesday* proves the existence of a Saxon church at Cranford. Almost certainly but a wooden structure, it probably stood about where the present building of St. Dunstan's now is. The first mention of a vicar here is in 1310, and though most of the present building is early eighteenth century, the tower is about 1400, though parts of the structure are said to be Norman.

Its situation as it looks across the park is, perhaps, the most beautiful in the whole county, and the actual picture of the old church itself is enhanced by the old lych-gate, built by a former Countess of Berkeley, and the fine old yew tree, said to be eight hundred years old.

This church is worth a visit; both inside and out it breathes a spirit of ancient peace. Apart from its history many stories are told of it, one of which relates how Jenner, the discoverer of vaccination, used to worship here while staying with a relative. It is probably too much to claim that it was at Cranford that Jenner actually made his famous studies on vaccination, yet it is not altogether impossible. In one account we read: " It was through his knowledge of country life that he made his immortal discovery in conversation with a milkmaid. The girl happened to remark that she had in the past contracted cow-pox, and was therefore immune from small-pox. By some curious chance the words stuck in his mind, and later formed the basis of a discovery that changed the whole conduct of human life."

Was this a Cranford milkmaid? Jenner probably took his walks abroad here to commune with Nature, as was his wont, and it might have been in one of these that he encountered the girl.

The visitor should notice the " music window " in Cranford Church, one of the first in England, I believe, to have the notes so shown. It is said to have been designed by Mendelssohn himself, in memory of a friend in this village with whom he used to stay. Luckily this window has survived the numerous explosions of Hounslow Powder Mills, which have shattered windows here.

There is a fine altar tomb of Sir Roger Aston, who, in addition to the posts before mentioned, was the King's Barber; though this latter title meant more than it sounds to-day; and also the King's Dentist, which in those days was inseparable from the work of a barber.

The actual wording on the tomb reads: " A diligent and trustie servant to James, King of Great Britain, France and Ireland, and for ye painfull and faithfull service he had donne." Was it thoughtlessness, or a subtle sense of humour, that describes a dentist as having rendered " painfull service "?

Another forgotten office has a passing remembrance, for here is buried " The High Constable of Hounslow Heath," an appointment held under the Crown, and no sinecure in the olden days. This functionary lived at Cranford in the midst of his activities.

There are several monuments of the Berkeley family, and one to Sir Charles Scarborough, physician to Charles II. and James II. He was the author of several medical works, and his *Syllabus Musculorum* was once a standard book. He was a friend of a great many well-known men of his time, including Cowley and Waller, the poets, and William Harvey, the discoverer of blood circulation, who bequeathed " my velvet gowne to my lovinge friend Mr. Dr. Scarburgh, as well as all my little silver instruments of surgerie." He was a close friend of Pepys, and on one occasion went with him with a Naval flotilla to Scotland. The ship on which Scarburgh was sailing was wrecked, and he was struggling in the water in grave peril, when he was rescued by Pepys himself in another ship.

The most interesting monument of all, however, is a modest placque,

"A BIT OF OLD ENGLAND."
Cottages at Heath Row.

Photo by F. Ash

THE OLD MAGPIES INN.
A famous Bath Road hostelry.

Photo by F. Ash

with a Latin inscription, to Thomas Fuller, rector from 1658 until his death in 1661. His witty suggestion for his epitaph, "Here lies Fuller's earth," was not adopted.

The famous author of *The Worthies of England* and many other works is too well known to need much description here. Most of his writing work was over when he came to Cranford, though *The Worthies* was not published until after his death, and it is possible that the last part was written here; and his last works, *Appeal of Injured Innocence*, against the attack of Peter Heylyn on the former's *Church History*, and his *Mixt Contemplations*, are actually dated from "Cranford Moat House." Though there is no mention of Cranford to be found in these books, in the latter there is a paragraph that may well have been engendered by the proximity of Hounslow Heath: "A traveller who had been robbed on the road enquired of a gentleman he met, who was also in a melancholy humour (a cause having gone against him), where he might find a Justice of the Peace, to whom the other replied: 'You ask for two things together, which singly and severally are not to be had. I neither know where justice is, nor yet where peace is to be found.'"

Fuller died at his lodging in Covent Garden, and his funeral was attended by "two hundred fully robed clergymen," which must have been an imposing sight in Cranford's quiet churchyard.

A story, both interesting and amusing, which concerns Fuller and Cranford (though it begins far away) is found in Rev. S. W. Christopher's *Homes of Old English Writers* (1875). The author was in Northamptonshire, and had been reading Fuller's *Appeal*, and where it was written. "Where was Cranford," he asks himself, "I must see the birthplace of his last book and his last living. I consulted Bradshaw, if perchance Cranford might be found there. There was one verily, on a Northants line. 'Do you know Cranford?' I said to a fellow-passenger. 'Oh, yes, it's not far off.' 'Then I shall get out there, I want to see the place where Fuller wrote his last pages and where his dust is resting.' 'I did not know he was buried here—near his birthplace.' 'Well, in his *Life and Works* it is stated he was buried in his parish church of Cranford; the writer speaks of it in a way which shows he knew of only one Cranford, and this must be the place.'

"I alighted, and was soon threatened with bewilderment. 'Is this the way to the church?' I asked an old man. 'Which church, sir?' 'Cranford Church.' 'Do you mean Cranford St. Andrews or Cranford St. Johns? This is the road to St. Andrews, and that to St. Johns.' I turned first to St. Andrews, a neat little sanctuary, but there was no memorial to Fuller and the sexton had never heard of him. I then went to St. Johns, a venerable pile, and which answered to my idea of Fuller's resting-place; but there was no remembrance of him. These two were both Cranfords, but not Fuller's.

"An inquiry at the village post-office discovered another Cranford, not in Northants, but in *Middlesex!* I started for Middlesex, laughing at my mode of acquiring geography! The place was within an hour of my home, while I had been looking in Northamptonshire.

"What was once wild open Hounslow Heath had become a cultivated enclosure when I passed over it on my way to the genuine Cranford. The old haunt of highwaymen and footpads was now overlooked by the military barracks; and the lone inn which once offered doubtful 'Entertainment for Man and Horse' had been supplanted by "The Traveller's Friend.' A sudden turn from the London Road brought me into a noble avenue of old oaks, leading to the village, which was the perfection of rural repose and beauty. On one side the picturesque houses smiled peacefully behind their bright screens of clipped beech; and the old willows were throwing their shadow over the clear waters.

A green lane, richly embowered with elms, led me to the gate of the Manor grounds, within which stood the village sanctuary. I enquired at the old rectory, with its quaint gables. The venerable parson himself guided me to the consecrated spot. Our road lay across the beautiful bright lawn, shut in amidst luxuriant foliage, with many an ancient oak and elm keeping watch and ward over this 'happy valley.' Nestling in the shade was the little church of venerable charm, which had once echoed to Fuller's reverent step. ' The house from which he dated his *Appeal* is no longer standing, is it?' I asked. ' No, it was taken down in 1780. It stood within a moat not far from here. Perhaps it was from there he also wrote his *Pulpit Sparks*. Dear good man, his Prayers have passed into Praise for ever.' "

Since I discovered the foregoing in Mr. Christopher's book I came across an old album of my mother's, and in it I found an entry written and signed by him in the year 1874—the year before the publication of his book and probably that in which he went to Cranford. I had never heard his name mentioned, but apparently he must have known my mother sixty years ago. A strange coincidence.

Fuller, as well as being a great scholar, was a charming personality, and who usually had a good word for everyone—if they deserved it. Was it not he who described a negro as " God's image carved in ebony "? Yet Fuller could be severe enough on fools and rogues, and it is related how Charles II. once remarked that he respected Fuller, because he was the only man honest enough to tell him what a scoundrel he (the King) was! It is a pity that Fuller did not write a companion volume to his immortal work, and call it " The Unworthies of England "; it might have been even more entertaining.

* * * * * *

Fuller's successor was John Wilkins, afterwards Bishop of Chester. The few details of his life at Cranford are not without a curious interest. It is a coincidence that a man who lived less than half a mile from what is now Heston Airport should have written a book *in the seventeenth century* on how to fly to the moon. Yet Wilkins did, and it is entitled *The Discovery of a World in the Moone*. It is a strange work and described as " partly scientific and partly imaginative "; rather more the latter, I fancy. Perhaps his ghost still hovers near the aerodrome to encourage less ambitious modern airmen who take short flights to the ends of the earth, but leave the moon for the spectral planes of the Flying Bishop.

Although Hounslow Heath witnessed nothing of the Bishop's attempts to fly (which did not get beyond his imagination) it saw something almost as entertaining; for in Wilkin's ingenious book *Mathematical Magic*, there is an account of " Land Sailing Carriage." They were once used on the Arabian desert, but they so intrigued the Bishop that during his vicarship of Cranford he constructed one for himself. We read in a quaint old book *Wonders of Art : or Remarkable Curiosities* how the inhabitants of the villages around Hounslow were amazed to see a clergyman careering over the Heath in his strange craft, which, in those superstitious times, must have savoured of Black Magic. The account does not record if the Bishop, thus engaged, ever encountered a highwayman. If so it is probable the

Knight on Winged Wheels was less scared than the Knight of the Road.
One old writer suggests that *Peter Wilkins*, Robert Paltock's book on
the Flying Indians, was so named after the Bishop. This may be, but
about a hundred years elapsed between the publication of the two books.
The writer who makes this suggestion rather quaintly adds: " But the difficulties on the way to the moon since Bishop Wilkins wrote are as great.
It was he who imagined that birds took their flight there, and that swarms
of gnats and flies descended from the same place."

Wilkins married Oliver Cromwell's sister, and it is stated by several
writers that for this reason Cranford Church never suffered at the hands
of the Puritan soldiers (who, tradition states, stabled their horses in three-
quarters of the churches in England) or fared badly from iconoclastic zeal.
The only snag about this otherwise plausible theory is that Wilkins did not
become vicar here until after the Restoration. It is one of those statements
that are repeated without even any mild analytical thought. That Wilkins
did reap benefit from his brother-in-law is known, but the saving of Cranford Church was not among them.

Wilkins also enjoyed the favour of Charles II., and was one of the band
of learned men whom that King incorporated as the Royal Society. By
temperament Wilkins might be called a "Middlesex Vicar of Bray," for we
read: "Being of an easy temper and accommodating principles he passed
through troublous times with a minimum of hardship." The solution
comes from Burnet's *Own Times:* "The pliability of Bishop Wilkins'
politics may, perhaps, be ascribed in a great measure to his mind being
occupied on matters more congenial to his disposition, as on all occasions
he exhibited a degree of forbearance which rendered him unpopular with
the bigoted of both parties." In other words Wilkins was wise enough to
place the humbug of politics at its true worth.

It is curious to note, as in the case of Fuller, that Noble's *Memoirs of
the Cromwells,* concerning the marriage of Wilkins, also places Cranford
in Northamptonshire. Lucky Cranford—to be but twelve miles from the
metropolis and yet so unknown.

*   *   *   *   *   *

Some quaint names are to be found in Cranford's Parish Registers.
There are Guthlanus Cordall and Mardocheus Brownell, rectors in 1564
and 1581; Sir Eusebius Pelsant, 1727; and in 1721 we find Lady Theophila
Ingoldsby—no wonder Cranford is a great place for legends. Strangest of
all (have you met a more curious name anywhere?) was a gentleman who
lived in Cranford in 1593, and rejoiced in a most extraordinary surname—
Richard Clinker-a-Dagger. If he were not a swashbuckler of the true
sword-and-cloak school, then Shakespeare was right, there *is* nothing in a
name. Yet it is probable, when we think of the tiny hamlet, so remote
from London, that was the Cranford of Elizabethan days, that the bearer
of this ominous name merely inherited it from some more energetic
mediaeval ancestor, while he himself was but a peaceful Middlesex yeoman,
concerned only with his crops and cattle.

It was at a cottage in the village that I was shown another reminder of
the past of a different nature. This was a china image of Dick Turpin
and Black Bess. It was eighteenth century Staffordshire ware, and might
have been valuable; but had it been solid gold it could not have been prized
more by the owner, who told me sadly that he once had a companion piece
of Tom King, but one day "Dick 'e fell agin Tom, knocked 'im down and

smashed 'im." A coincidence of fate in the china-image world, for in real life Dick was the accidental cause of Tom's death.

Cranford is a great place for legends, if village stories can be so dignified, and many an entertaining hour have I spent in talking to the villagers, and hearing their tales of bygone days. One of these is connected with the church and has a quiet pathos of its own. In the churchyard is a simple grave, marked with initials only, where lies a certain lady of title, who died soon after the late war. She chose Cranford as her last resting place as "the sweetest churchyard in all England." She did much for the welfare of the troops and shortly before her death she received a letter from a soldier thanking her and saying that when he came back he was going to leave a bunch of poppies from Flanders Fields on her doorstep. He gave no name, but the letter touched her, and at her own request it was buried with her. In some way the soldier heard of her death, and instead of leaving the poppies on her doorstep he went to Cranford churchyard and placed them on her grave.

The sublime and the ridiculous are never far apart, and the next story I heard was very different. An old man was telling me of a certain visit of King Edward (when Prince of Wales) to Cranford House, where it seems he was a frequent visitor. "Yes, sir," my informant told me, "and do you know one day when the Prince was down 'ere they got up a special Prize Fight; just as it were done in the old days. All the swells dressed up in white top 'ats and silk breeches. They 'ired two professional ' pugs ' to 'ave a real bare-fist fight, and do you know, sir, they brought 'em down from London *stripped to the waist in a closed van!*" When I suggested that probably the pugilists changed in some outhouse my old friend was quite shocked. That closed van, with the half-naked prize fighters in it, had been a cherished dream of his for years, and he wouldn't budge an inch. So I was forced to agree that it was a most picturesque touch—for, after all, who was I, a mere rambler, to upset the belief of years?

Several old people have told me they remember the Berkeley family in residence. They left some twenty years or so ago, I believe, and what impressed the natives was the number of vans of furniture that wended their way through the village street when they left. The number varied, some modestly putting it as low as five, and others as high as thirty. Anyhow, whatever the number, all agreed it was a thrilling spectacle, the like of which Cranford will never see again.

I have heard dozens of village legends, here and elsewhere, but this is the only place I have actually been an eye witness of the birth of one. To mention airily, "When I was walking through Cranford with the Prince" may sound boastful, but in this case it is true. I had taken an Indian Prince, who was studying agriculture in this country, just to show him what the "completely urban" County of Middlesex could do in this way. My Indian friend was much interested to hear that oxen used to plough the Cranford meadows, but got rather mixed in his dates, and, that method being still in use in his own country, mystified several worthy Middlesex farmers by asking them the comparative work per acre of a horse and an ox.

We finished up with a visit to Cranford church, by which time it was dusk, and it was here that the village legend was born. It came about in this way; as we turned a corner of the church we came upon a group of children, the eldest of which was about five. Now the Indian's dark skin and black beard, surmounted by his white turban, showed up in deep contrast in the failing light, and scared the children, who apparently had never seen an Indian before. They stood open-mouthed and speechless for a moment, and then let out a concerted shriek of terror—and fled for their lives! We paused in the shadow of the woods to watch events. What story the children told I have no idea; though I verily believe they imagined they had seen the Devil in person! In a few minutes several people rushed out from the house; two men were armed with sticks and another carried a lantern, as they frantically searched the churchyard. They found nothing, of course, though I expect by this time the story, which would lose nothing in the re-telling, has passed into another legend as The Ghost of the Churchyard. I daresay many ghost stories have even less foundation.

Yes, Cranford churchyard is a wonderful place for ghosts born of the imagination. Can anyone walk in an old country churchyard without conjuring up the life of the " rude forefathers " that sleep below? Anyway, I cannot. There is one wooden tomb " stone " here to " Edward Bishop. Yeoman, d. 1810." I often picture this old Middlesex yeoman of Regency days as he went about his lawful occasions in the surrounding fields and lanes. Then there is another tombstone to " Arthur Morris, d. 1929: son of Sir Lewis Morris, the poet." What association the family had with Cranford I do not know, but if the father knew this old church where his son lies sleeping it could not but have pleased him. He might well have written To the Setting Sun or Of Love and Sleep here, to mention two only of his poems. Read them in Cranford Churchyard (or with it visioned in your mind) and you will realise it.

It is a spot that might well attract poets. Perhaps Milton knew it as a young man, for his home at Horton was but a few miles away, and the scenery described in L'Allegro is very like that round Cranford; while Gray may have wandered the eight miles from Stoke Poges on a ramble and found further elegiac inspiration.

We have wondered elsewhere what Wilkes meant in his poem Hounslow Heath when he speaks of " Gay Crantford's Castle by the Muses named," and why the Muses, or Wilkes, should have called Cranford House a castle. Yet Cranford has a " Castle "—of sorts—guarded in true fairy-tale style by a Savage Beast (canine), or so I found by a mild trespass, which was turned into a courteous permission by the owner of the orchard in which it stands.

The " Castle " is up a lane alongside " Meadowbank " in the Bath Road. The building is a little disappointing for those who expect a real castle; it is a small double-turretted affair of irregular brickwork, one of those " mock antiques " which our great-grandfathers loved to erect to improve a " prospect." Wilkes could not have known it, for his poem is dated 1747, whereas that of the " Castle," shown thereon, is 1817.

Even if your tender conscience on the question of trespass, or the fear of the savage beast (who would have had my legs if I had not used my bicycle as a shield) should stop you seeing this " Castle," pause by the gate of " Meadowbank." Just inside on the right you will see the lodge, a quaint little thatched cottage, and if you are not looking at Thomas Hood's " minikin abode " I shall be extremely surprised. I feel as certain as one can be on what can never be proved that this was the place, for it answers all tests of " evidence " that the poet had it in mind when he began that curious poem A Fairy Tale with the lines:

" On Hounslow Heath—and close beside the road,
As western travellers may oft have seen,
A little house some years ago there stood, a minikin abode ";
while further on, such is the influence of highwaymen on this district, we
read:
" The little house became a coach once more,
And, like Macheath, took to the road again."
Cranford is a place that might well have inspired a great poem—of the
elegiac type; though Wilkes has a little more to say of the river here,
beyond the lines quoted in the chapter on the Crane, and those about the
Gay Castle that never existed, outside his imagination. He goes on to
speak of the fish that once abounded here, and may still for all I know,
though I do not suppose they would relish the chemicals that are so sur-
prisingly allowed to be pumped into this little river from some factory at
Hayes:
" The broad-shaped breams, and red-finned roaches here,
With bright-eyed perch, and spangled trout appear;
Dace, gudgeon, golden carp, and silver eel,
The deep recesses of the flood conceal."
The same writer speaks of the road that lies between Hounslow and
Cranford:
" Here should I wander o'er the southern plain,
Two lonely miles—t'indulge my pensive vein."
In 1747 it might have suited the thoughtful mind of a country parson,
but I fear now that his pensive vein would get a shock if he could revisit it.
I often try and visualise Hounslow's poet-vicar as he took his walks over
the Heath; and somehow there always comes into my mind an image of
Dr. Syntax in Search of the Picturesque, though there is no evidence to
suppose that Wilkes was like that eccentric cleric.

* * * * * *

There are many comparisons that could be made with regard to Cranford did space allow, but we must content ourselves with three as a conclusion. The first one is in a book I bought recently, in one of those penny
boxes that hold such fascinating surprises. It is called *Winter Sunshine,*
and is a series of essays by John Burroughs, an American who had as clear
an insight into, and as great an appreciation of, Old England as ever did
his fellow-countryman Washington Irving. What a refreshing counterblast to Hollywood and its inanities are such Americans.
In this book there is a sentence that might have been written of Cranford Church. Perhaps it was; who knows? The author has a good deal
to say of the London countryside. "When you see an English country
church," he writes, "withdrawn, secluded, out of reach of wheels, standing
amid grassy graves and surrounded by noble trees, approached by paths
and shaded lanes, you appreciate more than ever this beautiful habit of the
people."
In the *Domesday Tables*, edited by F. H. Baring, in the Middlesex
portion Cranford is called Cranfield throughout—a strange slip in a book
so accurate.
In *The Villages of England*, by A. K. Wickham, we find much fascinating matter on this topic, with a short but imaginative Foreword by Dr.
M. R. James. A useful appendix of the different counties is given, and yet,
though there is a sub-foreword from the writings of Thomas Fuller, no

word appears of the charming village where he spent his last years. In fact, while thirty-two different counties are touched upon, there is not even a passing reference to a single one of the many delightful villages of rural Middlesex.

* * * * * *

If this chapter on Cranford appears a little disjointed I would remind the reader that it is intended less as a history than as a series of impressions. Every time I go down to " Our Village " I seem to discover something fresh about it, and of all the places round London I think it easily holds the " Dual Crown," for many places have interesting stories, but have been spoiled artistically, and others, while retaining their picturesqueness, have little to say of their past.

Cranford scores in both ways; its story is one of the most vivid of any such places, and its present beauty can still hold its own. Nothing can ever dim the former, but so shortsighted and stupid are we in destroying what should be jealously guarded that I have misgivings as to its future.

Very true are the words of G. K. Chesterton: " The English village is a relic: it is even a miraculous relic, like that of a great saint."

I wonder what Fate has in store for Cranford—for a place can suffer martyrdom as well as a person.

CHAPTER XXXIII.

How bad grammar named an Earl, and an "Obscurity" that attracted all.

HARLINGTON has been described as the "metropolis of fruitdom"; apt enough, as it is the centre of fruit farms.

It is a straggling village which begins at the Coach and Horses Inn on the Bath Road at Harlington Corner, once known as "West End," and ends somewhere about Dawley Farm, which, though it appears to be in Hayes, is in Harlington.

Thorne, in 1876, says: "Harlington, a quiet rural village, with no marked feature, has a cheerful well-to-do look. The cottages have plenty of bright flowers in the front gardens, and apples and plums at the back. The country is level, lying at the north-west of Hounslow Heath, some 250 acres of which belong to Harlington parish. Much of the country is devoted to market-gardens and orchards, the cherry prevailing. The lanes are shady, and the country green and pleasant."

Again it is good to be able to record that no great change has come about—as yet! Many of the cottages in the village street date from the sixteenth century, while the chief inn, The White Hart, may be described as Ancient and Modern, for one end only has been rebuilt, which gives it a rather lob-sided appearance, which is not, however, noticeable in the other old hostelry, The Red Lion, at the corner of Cranford Road.

In the *Domesday Book* the place is written Herdintone, and known as Hardington or Herdyngton up to the end of the sixteenth century. The manor has passed through many hands, among whom are some well-known names, including Sir Henry Bennet, the famous Cabal minister, the Earls of Tankerville, Lord Bolingbroke and Lord Uxbridge. Of the two latter we shall hear more soon, and by far the most interesting of the remainder is Henry Bennet, for he became Earl of Arlington in 1664. He did not want to take that title, for he chose that of Harlington, but some bright official of the 'Erald's College was careless over his " H's," so when the patent arrived the new peer found that he *was* the Earl of Arlington! He protested, but was told that it was too late to alter it as " the proof had been worked off "; so the best they could do was to amend the patent to read: " The Earl of Arlington of Harlington in Middlesex." Arlington Street in Piccadilly also owes its name to this unfortunate slip. The irony of the situation is that there are over fifty places in Middlesex beginning with H—yet when they want to name an Earl after one of them they drop it!

Pepys mentions this incident, in September, 1665, when he tells us he was visiting his friend Mr. Povy, who had a country house near Brentford, and the latter pointed out the house: " He showed me my Lord Arlington's house that he was born in, in a towne called Harlington," and there is a footnote which adds: " Dawley House, near Hounslow, long the seat of the Benet family. Harlington, in which parish it is situated, gave the title of Baron and Earl to Sir Henry Benet: the aspirate being dropped (it may be said ' according to the custom of London '). The mansion was alienated by the Earl of Tankerville, to Viscount Bolingbroke, since when it has often changed owners."

Harlington Church—SS. Peter and Paul—is worth the rambler's notice. A priest is mentioned in *Domesday*, so a church existed there in Saxon days; the present building dates from Norman times, though much restored.

There is a fine Norman doorway, one of the finest in England, and thus described by one antiquarian writer: " The south doorway under the porch at Harlington Church is Norman and unusually good. It has zig-zag mouldings and one singular feature in the ornamentation of this doorway is that the outer member of the arch comprises a series of cats' heads, the tongues being fancifully carved. The pillars are of modern brick, but the capitals are Norman. The mouldings have been formerly cut away to admit the addition of a wooden porch of more recent date, finely carved." Another writer repudiates the cat's head theory (which was started by Lysons) and declares the tongues to be beaks!

" There are many other interesting things inside the church " continues the first writer, " notably the Norman font, an oak hour-glass, probably thirteenth century, an Easter Sepulchre, and a handsome carving thought to be the remains of an altar."

The monuments and brasses are worth inspection; one of the latter is a fifteenth century effigy of John Monmouthe, a former rector; it is part of a priest in a chasuble, but the inscription " Pray for the soul " has been deliberately defaced, probably by some Puritan incumbent. There are monuments to Sir John Bennet, Lord Ossulton and the Earl of Tankerville, and several to the de Salis family.

The most notable, however, is the tablet to Joseph Trapp, vicar 1733-47, with a poetical inscription. Trapp had a minor fame in his day for his literary work, though now quite forgotten. The following account, culled from Lysons, is worth passing notice: " Trapp was educated at Oxford and became an M.A. in 1702. In 1704 he published a tragedy called *Abra Muli; or Love and Empire.* In 1707 he was made Professor of Poetry at Oxford and his lectures, which were published under the title of *Prelectiones Poeticae,* gained him the character of a scholar and critic; his translations of Virgil and Milton were fatal to his reputation as a poet.

He was made a D.D. in 1727. Several volumes of his sermons have been issued."

Trapp, who earned no fame by his own literary labours, is now chiefly remembered as having been satirised by Swift in his *Journal to Stella:* "Your parson, Slap, Scrap, Flap (what d'ye call him?), Trap."

A clever epigram in verse, however, is attributed to Trapp, though judging by his other rather dull writings (in spite of the strange titles) it is doubtful if he really wrote it. It was composed when George I. gave a library to Cambridge:

" The King to Oxford sent a troop of horse,
For Tories own no argument but force.
With equal ease to Cambridge books he sent,
For Whigs allow no force but argument."

Among the earlier rectors of Harlington was John de Tewkesbury, the author of several learned books, of whom there is an account in Pitt's *Treatise of Illustrious Men*, and John Kyte, who resigned this living in 1510 and became Bishop of Carlisle.

Outside the church is a grand yew tree, still sound and green, one of the largest in England, and said to be as old as the Conquest. It is fully described in Louden's *Arboretum Britannicum;* the trunk measures over seventeen feet in circumference and its branches at one time covered a space of 150 feet. The clipping of this giant tree was formerly a village holiday, a ceremony abolished in 1825, since when the yew, formerly cut in topiary work, has grown as nature dictates.

In the vestry there is a quaint eighteenth century oil painting, showing the tree as it was. The antiquity of the yew is proved by its mention in Walter Johnson's *Byways in British Archaeology.*

It seems that Trapp was not the only poet that Harlington has produced, for in 1729 an engraving was published of this tree with verses by "Poet John Saxy," the parish clerk. Among the lines of this rural bard the best known are:

" So thick, so fine, so full, so wide,
A troop of Guards might under't ride . . .
It yields to Harlington a fame
Much louder than its Earldom's name."

The tower of the church contains six bells and the leads afford some good views, including Windsor Castle, and (as Thorne reminds us) *of course* the Crystal Palace!

The Parish Registers, as usual, are full of interest. They date from 1540 only, but a few of the items are worth mention. They are curious as containing the names of " travellers "—a result of the parish being about a day's tramp from London. There are several charities (some not without a touch of humour), though most are now obsolete. One rector left a sum for the repairing of his tomb, and though his body was subsequently moved to another part of the churchyard, the repairing of the empty tomb was continued for years—so as not to lose the money. Another parishioner left some land to provide a leg of pork for the bellringers on Guy Fawkes Day, and the land was known as Pork Half-Acre; and when the right of cutting the turf was taken from the villagers their protest resulted in the granting of fourteen acres set apart for this purpose.

In the will of " William Woodeson, Gent.," who was buried in 1786, is a curious item: " I order that my body be dressed in my last new shirt and

muslin neck-cloth and night-cap, and my plain night-gown and my little
pillow-case under my head. In my right hand my rusty old sword, which
always lay by my bedside, and in my left hand my Latin Testament." It
would seem that this gentleman, a little doubtful of his reception in the
next world, wanted to be prepared either for war or peace.

The adjoining village of Hayes, although it is really out of our scope
in spite of the very elastic borders of Hounslow Heath, has some even more
amusing parochial chronicles, at which we can glance as we pass. The
vicar's troubles in the middle of the eighteenth century, though annoying
enough to the good man at the time, are humorous. It seems for some
reason he had trouble with a rebellious choir, and at last, by reason of their
ill-behaviour, the vicar forbade them to sing in church at all. Nevertheless
the next Sunday they were all in their places, looking so meek that the
parson thought they had seen the error of their ways and repented; but he
was soon undeceived, for when the clerk gave out the hundredth Psalm the
choir started singing the fifteenth lustily. Things became even worse and
the choir got completely out of hand. One man sat in a front pew with a
pot of beer and a pipe, another rang the bells during the sermon, while two
more indulged in the refined amusement of spitting on the congregation
from the gallery.

*   *   *   *   *   *

Sub-Manors of Harlington are Pinkwell and Sipson, the former but a
few cottages till a row of bungalows was recently built, and the latter,
anciently known as Shepiston and Sibbeston, a purely agricultural village,
in which a large Baptist Chapel is the predominating feature, and a
thatched inn the most picturesque one. The name originally meant " The
Town of the Sheep."

The most vivid story of Harlington is told in C. G. Harper's *The Bath
Road:* " The times of the highwayman are, fortunately for the wayfarer, if
unhappily for romance, long past, and many of the once notorious haunts
of the knights of the road have disappeared before the ravages of time, and
the more destructive builder. A hundred years ago it would have been
difficult to name a lonely suburban inn that was not favoured by the highwaymen. Nowadays the remaining ones are, for those interested in the old
story of the roads, all too few.

" Perhaps this queer little roadside inn, the Old Magpies, is the most
romantic-looking among those left. It possesses a thick and beetle-browed
thatch that hangs over the upper windows like bushy eyebrows, and gives
those windows, the " eyes " of the house, just that lowering look which
bristling eyebrows confer upon a man.

" It is not only its romantic appearance that gives the Old Magpies
interest, for outside this house, so near to the terrible Hounslow Heath, the
brother of Mr. Mellish, M.P. for Grimsby, was murdered by highwaymen in
1798, when returning one night from hunting. The carriage was passing
near this inn when it was attacked by three highwaymen. One held the
horses' heads while the other two guarded the windows, firing a shot
through to terrify the occupants. They then demanded money, purses
and bank-notes being handed over. The travellers were allowed to go, a
parting shot being fired into the carriage. It struck Mr. Mellish in the
forehead. Coming to another inn nearby, called The Three Magpies, the
wounded man was taken upstairs while a surgeon was sent for. He came

from Hounslow and was robbed on the way by the same gang. Mr. Mellish, however, died, and the assassins were never caught."

The same writer retells this story in another book, *Old Inns of England,* in which he refers to Harlington Corner as Sipson Green, a name seldom used to-day save by old folk. There is a vignette of this part that is worth quoting: "No district was more affected by highwaymen in the old days than Hounslow Heath, and the fork of the road where the two great highways to Bath and Exeter set out upon their several courses at the west end of what was once Hounslow village used in those days to be decorated with a permanent gibbet, rarely without its scarecrow occupant in the shape of some tattered robber, strung up as a warning to his fellows."

The story of this murder is also told by Grantley Berkeley in his *Life and Recollections,* and is mentioned in several other books. Both inns are little altered since those days. It is rather curious that two inns, almost next door, should bear practically the same name, though quite different in appearance.

*   *   *   *   *   *

At one end of Harlington, standing up a long drive and behind a long wall, is an old house surrounded by an old-world garden and walled orchards. It is a delightful place altogether and breathes an atmosphere of other days, as well it might, for it was formerly one of the finest houses near London, where its owner entertained those whose names have now passed into the pages of History.

The house is Dawley Farm, or what is left of it, for the present building is but a fragment of Lord Bolingbroke's wonderful mansion; for though he loved to call it a farm, it was really an ornate and stately edifice.

Few houses have been more described in contemporary literature than Dawley, and we can let these tell its story, beginning with a letter from Bolingbroke himself to Swift in 1727: "I may get a day or two for Dawley, where I hope you will find me established. There I propose to finish my days in ease, without sloth, and I believe I shall seldom visit London, unless it be to divert myself now and then with annoying fools and knaves for a month or two." The next year he writes again to the Dean: "I am in my farm again and here I shoot strong and tenacious roots; I have caught hold of the earth (to use a gardener's phrase) and neither my enemies nor my friends will find it an easy matter to transplant me."

Pope's letters abound in references to Dawley, for the poet was a frequent visitor, where, as he writes to Mallet, he came to "try a course of asses milk," and it was on his return to Twickenham on one occasion in Lord Bolingbroke's carriage and six that he was upset in crossing the Crane and nearly drowned.

This account of the mishap appears in the *Chronicles of English Counties:* "Once in returning from Dawley in Lord Bolingbroke's coach Pope had an accident which is, in a literary way, historic. At Whitton, near Twickenham, a little river crosses the road, but this night the bridge was broken down, and the alternative ford was choked by a balk of timber, and my lord's fine coach was upset in the middle of the stream, and the poor poet soused in the water. The great Voltaire was visiting Lord Bolingbroke at the time, and wrote a graceful letter of congratulation to the poet on his escape."

Pope again writes while on a visit here: "I now hold the pen for my Lord Bolingbroke, who is reading your letter between two haycocks; but his attention is somewhat diverted by casting his eyes on the clouds—not in admiration of what you say, but for fear of a shower . . . he has fitted up his farm and you will agree with me that his scheme of retreat is not founded upon weak appearances. As to his temperature I can answer that (for one whole day) we have had nothing for dinner but mutton broth, beans and bacon, and a barn-door fowl. Now his Lordship is run after his cart and I overheard him yesterday agree with a painter for £200 to paint his country hall with trophies of rakes, spades, prongs, etc., and other ornaments, merely to countenance his calling it Farm."

Goldsmith, quoting this letter in his *Life of Bolingbroke,* observes: "What Pope here says of his engagements with a painter was after executed: the hall was painted in black crayons only, so that at first view it brought to mind the figures often seen scratched with charcoal, or the smoke of a candle, upon the kitchen wall of a farm-house. The whole, however, produced a most striking effect."

This strange scheme of decoration was known as Chiaroscuro, and was much in vogue at that time for semi-public buildings, and the reason that Bolingbroke's choice caused so much comment was, apparently, that he selected this style for a private house. It is said that on this, and other improvements to Dawley, he spent £23,000.

His sister, Lady Luxborough, writes in her *Letters:* "When my brother Bolingbroke built Dawley, which he chose to call a farm, he had his hall painted in stone colours with all the implements of husbandry, as one might see arms and trophies in some general's hall, and it had an effect that pleased everybody."

There is some description of Pope's visits to Dawley Farm in Edith Sitwell's *Alexander Pope,* an interesting book, in spite of its frequent touches of "Sitwellism," and its rather over-praise of the poet, who is almost cannonized, and the bitter vituperation against those with whom he quarrelled—not a few—and its super-vitriolic touches against Lady Mary Wortley Montagu.

In the volume of short stories, *Old Patch's Medley,* Marjorie Bowen's collection of historical vignettes, there is a tale, *Lord Bolingbroke and Two Ladies;* it has little concern with Dawley, except to mislead, for it mentions Lord Bolingbroke's famous country house *in Kent.* It is the old story— Hayes, Middlesex mixed up with Hayes, Kent.

In an oft-quoted poem entitled *Dawley Farm,* which appeared in the *Gentleman's Magazine* for 1731, these wall-drawings are mentioned, among other things, in connection with the owner:

> " See, emblems of himself, his villa stand,
> Politely finish'd elegantly grand!
> No gaudy colours deck the rural hall,
> Black light and shade discriminate the wall:
> Himself neglects what must all others charm,
> And what he built a palace calls a farm . . .
> Here splendidly obscure, delighted lives,
> And only for his wretched country grieves."

Bolingbroke, soon tired of this splendid obscurity and in 1735 went to France—partly because he could not help himself—and the following letters show the subsequent fate of Dawley. " Let we depend on you and Bathhurst," he wrote to Sir W. Wyndham, " for enabling me to live a cosmopolite the rest of my days. For this purpose you must dispose of

Dawley for me. To what purpose should I keep an expensive retreat where in all probability I shall never return." Again Alderman Barber wrote to Swift: "Lord Bolingbroke has been here a few days to sell Dawley to pay his debts; and he will return to France." Then Pope, writing to Ralph Allen, says: "Lord Bolingbroke executed his deeds for the sale of Dawley on Friday." In a subsequent letter (1739) the poet says that Dawley sold for £26,000.

The purchaser was the Earl of Uxbridge, who pulled down the house except the one wing we see still standing, and after passing through several hands it was brought by the family of de Salis, who held it until quite recently, when it was purchased by The Gramophone Company of Hayes, who courteously gave me permission to "trespass" as much as I liked.

Memories of the great days still linger round Dawley. One field near is still known as "The Lanterns," so named it is said because on grand occasions Bolingbroke had the road from Dawley to West Drayton, crossing the meadow, hung with lamps to guide his visitors. A more obvious link is: the long wall which, I was seriously told by a villager, was built by Lord Bolingbroke to keep out the germs of the Great Plague of London, and that the diamond-shaped purple brick markings were put in the wall as a. warning—apparently to the germs ! Despite the mixing of dates this description is not quite true. The wall was not built by Bolingbroke but by Lord Uxbridge, with the idea of keeping out vagrants who might have the small-pox, then raging in London. The long wall, broken in places, is still there, and the purple diamonds visible at intervals, though I do not fancy they have any significance beyond decoration.

The names of Bolingbroke's visitors would fill a book; for besides Pope the guests included Dryden, Swift, Gay and Voltaire—and many other folk who lived in the early years of the eighteenth century, when a visit to Dawley was "the thing."

Something of the famous Frenchman's visits here can be found in C. E. Vulliamy's *Voltaire*, where there is a chapter on his residence in England, though not so much as might have been hoped about Dawley. For those who wish to study this subject more closely are recommended *Voltaire*, by Richard Aldington; *The Young Voltaire*, by C. B. Chase; J. Churton Collins' *Voltaire in England;* and *Letters Concerning the English Nation*, by Charles Whibley. Lack of space, however, will not allow of more than this passing mention of these books here.

Nor is this the place to enter very deeply into the curious character of Bolingbroke, described by Augustine Birrell as "the most accomplished of all our political rascals" in *Men, Women and Books*. The views of so notable a scholar as Birrell must be respected; but somehow I find myself more in agreement with Professor Churton Collins in his opinion of Bolingbroke.

Now the canal and the railway pass through these beautiful grounds, and what are left round the old house are but a fragment of those of former days. At one one time the fate of this remnant of Dawley trembled in the balance, and it was in danger of demolition to enlarge the gramophone factory. Such an act of vandalism has, however, been averted and I trust finally stopped. To pull down this fine old house, with its wonderful silent memories, merely to add to the din of an already noise-racked world, would have been an unpardonable crime.

I wonder if science will ever be able to bring back through the ether the voices of the past? A hundred years ago the thought of being able to listen to people talking in America by turning a knob in England would have seemed as miraculous. If they ever do recall the voices of yesterday what a wonderful medley of words will issue from Dawley Farm. There is one voice I would wait hours to hear—that of Swift reading aloud to Bolingbroke, Pope, Gay and one or two others the manuscript of *Gulliver's Travels,* for this book was published anonymously and before it appeared the author read it to his friends, who were " in the know," at Pope's house at Twickenham, but unable to finish it in one evening the company assembled the next night at Dawley to hear the conclusion. Pope's house is gone, so Dawley alone remains where the echoes of the Dean's voice reading this book may still linger silently invisible.

The episode of the Dean's reading aloud, here briefly touched upon, I found an obscure book of eighteenth century memoirs, though I can find no mention of it in the usual records of Dawley. It is an illuminating thought—will it ever be reality, I wonder, to hear that magic voice?

* * * * * *

By a strange chance some time after I had written the above I heard a wireless play, *Alibi from the Air,* in which almost this identical idea was used. I am also told since that there is a book by " Gunpat " in which this theme is dealt with; and I seem to remember vaguely that Emerson once wrote something about " Sound being reproduced again." I have not time before this goes to press to look up these last two items (and the second might be a long job), but it seems that my idea has also occurred to others; two before I thought of it and one after. " Human wireless " perhaps; but it proves still more that there is nothing new under the sun—even in the air.

Walford calls this house Dawley Court, but this is misleading; for Dawley *Court* was at Hillingdon. It has recently been pulled down, it was a pleasant old house finely set in a small park. Not so old as Dawley Farm it was the subsequent home of the same family (de Salis) who were the last owners of the original Dawley.

Apart from Bolingbroke Dawley Farm has a history that goes far back into the past. It is mentioned in *Domesday,* and Lysons' account, incorporates this: " There is a Manor in this parish of small extent, but of very ancient date, called Dalley or Dawley. In the survey of Domesday it is thus described, under the name of Dallega: ' Alnodus holds the manor of Earl Roger (Earl of Arundel) as three hides....the total value is 30s. per annum. In the reign of King Edward (the Confessor) it was 60s. This manor lies within the manor of Colham, which it did not in the reign of King Edward. It was the property of Godwin Alfit, a servant of Wigot.' "

In 1316 this manor was the property of Gilbert de Barentone. It afterwards came to the Lovells and was by them conveyed to Robert Awbrey in 1540. They continued at Dawley till 1560. Sir Ambrose Coppinger died seised of this manor in 1605." Then came " the Earl without an aitch, " who sold it to Lord Tankerville, in whose time it was said that a small herd of the famous wild oxen from Northumberland were kept in the park at Dawley.

The next owner was Bolingbroke who sold it to Lord Uxbridge, who in turn disposed of it to the Earl of Berkeley, by whom it was sold in 1772 to Count de Salis, who held it until it passed to its present owners a few years ago.

It is of interest to note in conclusion that the name Dawley is derived from "Dole Lea"; the latter an old word for meadow, and the former an ancient term for anything that is given out—from which comes "dole" in its modern sense.

CHAPTER XXXIV.

Tells, among other things, of England's largest Tithe Barn, and of precious stones still to be found in Middlesex.

T O approach even a well-known place from an unexpected angle is a mental tonic. I felt this one bright autumn afternoon when, after a visit to Dawley Farm, I went to take another look, for old exploration's sake, at West Drayton, with its interesting church and fine old gatehouse, whose setting has not been improved by a building estate put up near, though I was glad to see that old Middlesex mansion of Drayton Hall, with its wooded grounds, is fighting the invader. Anyhow, a new fence round the estate has been erected, which does not look like surrender.

Although West Drayton is really out of our ken, as regards this book, an unusual fact concerning any place is of passing interest, and the following paragraph, culled from a mid-Victorian magazine, is sufficiently strange to warrant notice: "By West Drayton ,where the Coln makes its way in many devious channels towards the Thames, stood not long ago an old brick mansion called Burroughs—a moated grange with pensive shaded walks. Tradition has it that here the Lord Protector had a private dwelling —a retreat unknown to any but his closest friends, and not perhaps to more than one of those—and it is said that on Cromwell's death his body was secretly brought to Burroughs; and thus, while pompous obsequies were celebrated over some nameless corpse in Westminster Abbey, in this retired spot beneath the pavement of the hall the veritable relics of the Great Protector were interred.' There are many curious stories told about the re-burial of Cromwell, and we are at liberty to believe or not this one of the original burial.

On the occasion of this visit to West Drayton I strolled, for no particular reason, along the old elm avenue. At the end of the avenue, I paused, for, with my thoughts full of another subject, I did not realise at once what lay ahead; but this is what I saw. A large flat field with a pathway across it; at the end was a clump of trees from which emerged a cluster of red roofs and the bell-tower of a church. As I walked towards it I saw a long roof by the side of the church. Slowly it began to dawn on my rather absent mind what lay ahead; set so picturesquely against the sunset—it was Harmondsworth Church and the Old Tithe Barn.

I stopped and gazed at the view. I almost "drank' it in—if you can understand the term; it was like meeting an old friend unexpectedly, for, strangely enough, well as I know Harmondsworth, I cannot remember ever having seen it from quite this angle before. It is an impression that has never faded; it is so essentially an old Middlesex subject.

The part of the country that leads from the elm avenue to the village is marked on old maps as Harmondsworth Field; not because it is a field literally, but because this is a name hereabout in the county for any open

space; when it is not termed Moor. It happens, however, quite by chance,
that there is a Harmondsworth Moor—a separate place.

*   *   *   *   *

The usual approach to Harmondsworth is from the Bath Road, and I
know of few places more worth a visit. It contains two very rare things—
one that the most unobservant can hardly miss, and one that is practically
missed by everyone till pointed out. I mean the Great Tithe Barn and the
Ancient Mass Clock in the church wall.

With the exception of the Barn there is not a very great deal to see in
Harmondsworth. It is an old-fashioned, rather sleepy old place, which I
always find restful. There are some delightful half-timbered cottages in
the main street, which, if viewed without too great a juxtaposition of an
ugly building next to them, are worth examination; I believe they are sixteenth century.

Again it is good to be able to say, in quoting an old description of a
place, that it has not altered much in fifty years. Happily, despite drastic
changes in some cases, this can be said of more than one place in South-
West Middlesex, and one of these is this present village.

Here, then, is Thorne's account of 1876: " The village of Harmondsworth
is small, but there are some good houses on the east side; in the main street
are one or two half-timber cottages, with projecting upper storeys and overhanging thatched eaves, and a fine elm on what should be a green by the
church "—which is all very much as it is to-day.

The account continues: " The country is flat, the soil fertile, and the
occupations almost entirely agricultural. Large corn and green crops are
raised, with vegetables for the London market, and fruit is much grown.
Much of this parish once belonged to Hounslow Heath, but now all is
enclosed and cultivated, not an acre having been spared as open ground.
The scenery is tame, but trees are abundant, and often of large size; the
old Powder Mill River winds through the parish and the Colne runs along
its western border." Again much like it to-day, except that little corn is
grown now.

In *The Way About Middlesex* we read: " The scenery round Harmondsworth is of pleasant type, a trifle Flemish in character. Quaint red-tiled
houses and ancient black barns standing amid flat rich meadows, the latter
parted everywhere by narrow water channels, winding sluggishly beneath
pollard willows and alders." There certainly *is* something Flemish, or
Dutch, in the water-meadows by the many-branched Colne, where cattle
may often be seen knee-deep in marshy grassland, reminiscent of an oil
painting by Cuyp or other old Dutch master.

If you want to find these pleasant pictures go down the lane by the
Manor Farm, past the rather sordid but not unpicturesque cottages, whose
inhabitants are rough and ready in appearance and will probably scowl at
a stranger in a silent, resentful way. I have been told that these rude forefathers of the hamlet are really honest farm workers, who, though they
may certainly be a little rowdy on Saturday nights, confine their attention
to fighting each other and rarely molest outsiders. Anyhow, it is rather
refreshing, in these modern days, to be scowled at as an interloping
" foreigner "—only fourteen miles from London!

The watery nature of a portion of this parish had also caught the eye
of old Lysons, as it also had the compilers of the *Domesday Book*, as will be
seen later, and in those days there was evidently far more water-land (to

THE OLD PEGGY BEDFORD INN.

Photo lent by Mrs. Neal

OLD THATCHED SHOP, LONGFORD.
Once part of the Peggy Bedford Stables.

Photo by the Author

be slightly Irish) than there is now. This is what Lysons says: "The western branch of the river Colne separates the parishes of Harmondsworth and Iver; Cardinal Wolsey's river, the Old River, or Powder Mill River, and another branch of the Colne, run through this parish, between Longford and Colnbrook."

In *Where Traditions Linger* there is a pleasing description of Harmondsworth: "Pursuing our way westward from Harlington we will journey towards the village green of Harmondsworth, which has facing it a fine bit of half-timber worthy of Worcestershire. It is one of the prettiest bits of Middlesex we have, and it is to be hoped that the delightful old block of buildings, with overhanging upper storeys, will escape the 'restorer,' who has been on the warpath during the last decade. . . . The magnificent 'Gothic Barn,' the sole remains of the old Manor House of Harmondsworth, pulled down in the eighteenth century, is, we think, safe, otherwise a like fate might await it upon becoming better known. But for the lack of lofty windows one is reminded of the Great Hall of Eltham Palace." Probably this barn was constructed of oaks grown locally, for when it was built the Great Forest of Staines was in existence.

Thorne's description of the church is very like it is now: "St Mary's Church is large and interesting. In its present form it is mainly perpendicular, but it was rebuilt from an earlier church, parts of which were retained. It consists of nave with aisles, chancel, and a good (modern) wooden south porch, and a battlemented tower at the south-west. The body of the church is built of black flints, but the squared stones of the earlier building are worked up in the walls, and upon some of them carvings may be traced.

"Especially curious is the doorway under the porch. It is of very fair Norman work, and has been taken down from the original church and re-erected on a somewhat narrower scale. The arch is semi-circular, the innermost facia being flat, and ornamented with square panels, on which circles with crosses and leaves are carved. The lower part of the tower is of early date, the upper part is more modern. In it is a peal of five bells— of seventeenth century—and there is a clock bell in the open turret.

"Though the church was restored in 1863, the open roof is old; note the hammer-beam roof of the chancel aisle. On the south of the chancel are three sedelia and a piscina with a credence. The brasses which were on the floor, being detached, were placed in a chest, but stolen by the workmen at the restoration. There is an excellent late Norman font, large enough for complete immersion. From the top of the tower a view over the level country rivals that of Harlington, but is more open to the horizon."

Walford, some seventeen years later, has also something to say of the famous church door: "The south doorway is of Norman work, the chief feature of it is a range of birds' heads, the beaks being thrown over a moulding. . . . The village consists chiefly of scattered dwellings, many of which are in that ancient half-timber and plaster and thatched roofs, so favourable to the picturesque. There are also one or two old mansions, with cedars in the grounds."

It is a bold thing to disagree with Lysons, but in Harmondsworth his "sin" is of omission. He says: "I have not found any traces of a priory here in ancient records." In this he contradicts himself, for he mentions one account, but ignores others which I have managed to find.

It is true that they are not very numerous or in much detail, but they *do* exist. Beyond the *Domesday* account, Bishop Tanner tells us that "there was at Harmondsworth a cell to the Priory of Holy Trinity at Rouen, but no traces of it have been discovered recently." Cobbett mentions it in his list of religious houses at the Dissolution that there was an alien priory here, eventually granted by Edward VI. to Sir William Paget. He gives us few details, but Brewer is rather more explicit and tells us how it shared the fate of the alien priories when England was at war with France and was seized by Edward III. in 1340. There are also other accounts, most of which it would be but repetition to mention. One of these, however, certainly must have some reference here, as I do not think it has ever been published before. It is the most imaginative I have ever read of this place.

I am lucky to be able to quote from it, and am indebted to Mr. F. J. Philp, of Heathrow Hall, near Harmondsworth, for bringing it to my notice. The writer modestly hides his identity, nor does he give the source of the mediaeval document from which it is taken, but it is most vivid. He speaks of the discontent of the Saxon peasants at the harsh treatment of the foreign Abbot and Prior, which terminated in a Middlesex Peasants' Revolt, and the writer proceeds: " In 1100 A.D. twelve good men and true were required to declare on oath why they were so turbulent in the Manor of Harmondsworth: why they do beat the Prior and cudgel his priests. Nay, the Abbot himself during his visit was unmercifully whipt by them, and they answer:

" ' At the time of sowing every bondman in Harmondsworth had to plough and harrow two acres. The Lord Abbot supplies seed and we sow it: we have to fetch it from the Grange and our horse may not have a feed of it, but if any is over we must return it to the Grange. Those not wanted for ploughing must thresh in the Great Barn till sunset. At the hay harvest we must mow the Lord Abbot's hay. And all of this without pay. Those who are ill must do double work the next day or pay a fine as the Lord Abbot decrees. At the end of the day we may have as much hay as we can lift with a scythe, but this must be done in the presence of the Prior. If we put so much on our scythe that it break we are fined. At the end of the hay harvest the Prior may give us either a ram or thirteen pence. Everyone must help stack the hay, for which we are paid nothing. Every Saxon who has a horse and cart must carry hay to the Great Barn. . . . We have other work to do without pay, for when the Crier comes round at corn harvest we have to work from sunrise to sunset. At mid-day we get three loaves of bread for thirteen reapers. After the day's work we get soup of beans, bread, cheese and beer, and every two men a plate of meat which costs the Lord Abbot three-halfpence. Every year we have to clean the river from all weeds and we get no pay for this, but are given bread, cheese and beer and fish for every two men, and we must repair all the Abbot's fencing.

" ' We have free pannage for our pigs but if the pig is over one year we must pay one penny. We have to take our pigs to the Grange at Martinmass and if we cannot convince the Prior of the age of the pig we must pay three halfpence. No one is allowed to marry without the consent of the Lord Abbot and then a heriot beast must be paid.' "

There is more in this strain, and on it the writer comments: "Can it be wondered at that the Saxons in our Parish were always in rebellion. When

King Harold was Lord of the Manor he treated his people like friends. It was not till 1387 that the Manor was handed to William of Wykeham for his new school at Winchester, and thus for 300 years Harmondsworth had to submit to a foreign yoke." Conditions under William of Wykeham were very different for the people of Harmondsworth, for we read that then anyone working for the Manor had daily pay and food as follows—bread, cheese, butter, eggs, beef, beer, pork, mutton, ducks, salt fish and herrings. Certainly the fat of the land compared with the lean times under the Abbot. This insight into mediaeval labour conditions is interesting; I wonder what the present Labour Party would say to them!

At the end of this account are some verses, again anonymous, but headed: "The Spring in the Garden of the Manor Farm at Harmondsworth was known to the Benedictines as 'Our Lady's Tears.'" The verses are obviously "modern-mediaeval" and rather rambling. A reference to "far London" shows the isolation of Harmondsworth in those times.

It is curious to find an estate in Middlesex being seized by the King of England from a French King, yet this happened here, and of this we read: "King Edward the Third being at war with Philip de Valois seized his Manor of Harmondsworth into his own hands." Apparently it came originally into the possession of the French King through foreign monastic rights. It would seem that the French King got possession of it again by some means or other, for there is a note in the Middlesex Records: "It appears from Tanner's *Notita Monastica* that there was a Priory at Harmondsworth of the Benedictine Order, which was a cell of the Abbey of Rouen. In the extent of Manors belonging to the Alien Priories seized by the Crown in the time of Richard II. (1386) it is also mentioned."

So much for the history of Harmondsworth Priory. What little now remains of it I have carefully inspected, but all to be seen was a bush-covered mound; if any relics lay underneath I have no idea—it is certainly possible—though if excavation would reveal anything but a few crumbling walls is doubtful. Sometimes, however, our imaginations can build better pictures than realities.

* * * * * *

Apart from the monastic "lapse" Lysons has a fair amount to say of this place, and builds up in his own peculiar way a vivid picture of old-time Harmondsworth. His methods are rather different from those of Thorne, Walford, and, in a way, Hughson. Lysons does not give much of what might be termed narrative description, no pen pictures of old village life that can be so charming if handled well; he rather lets the reader build up his own impression "from information received." Both methods have much to commend them, so let us follow Lysons' for a while. Among the items of odd news he supplies are the following:

"In the survey or 1770 Harmondsworth consisted of 3,480 acres, of which 1,176 formed part of Hounslow Heath, more than any other parish."

"The name of this place in *Domesday* is Hermodesworth. *Worth* is Saxon for manor or farm, sometimes village. Hermode is probably a proper name."

Lysons quotes the *Domesday* extract in full, but as it differs little from many others it is hardly worth while to reproduce it all. It is interesting to note, however, that there were "Fisheries for a thousand eels" and that the inhabitants once had the right of fishery in all rivers and common waters within the manor on Wednesdays, Fridays and Saturdays. On the other days the rights, apparently, belonged to the monks.

" There is a Roman camp in Harmondsworth Parish not far from Sibiston." (This is at Heath Row, and noted elsewhere.)

" Traces of the moat round the Manor Farm can still be seen, supplied from the Duke's River." (A few traces can now be made out, but not so clearly as in Lysons' time.)

" You may meet the Cicutavirosa on the heath near Harmondsworth." (There is no need to take a gun! It was only a scarce plant, said to have been the species of hemlock with which Socrates was poisoned.)

So much for Lysons' notes, which the curious can expand at will by reference to his *Middlesex Parishes,* that monument of research and erudition.

Coming to more modern times, *The Records,* already quoted, contain an account of the discovery, some fifty years ago, of silver coins in the churchyard. They were found with the skeleton of a man. " Some of the coins," runs the account, " were inclosed in what might have been a purse; this leather receptacle was much decayed and unable to be preserved. About half the skeleton was removed, but no coffin was visible. The coins were of the reigns of Elizabeth and James I. The body was buried in its clothes.

" Had the body been found in the open fields, instead of in a churchyard, we could have supposed this person had been murdered by the highwaymen who infested the adjacent open country near Hounslow, and the victim only partially deprived of his valuables. This theory is destroyed by the deposit of the body in the churchyard, which would have led to the discovery of the murder.

" At the Battle of Brentford the fighting was within a few miles of here. At this encounter a wounded soldier might have fled in this direction and died here, or one of the slain have been brought here for burial, and the money buried with him in his clothes."

Those who wish to learn more on this subject should consult *Middlesex Notes and Queries* for 1896, where is an article by G. W. Redway, " The Battlefields of Middlesex."

With reference to the " military history " of the barn itself, I was told two stories in the village. One was that Cromwell's soldiers slept there, which is probable, so convenient a place would hardly be overlooked; and the other was that William the Conqueror drilled his troops *prior* to the Battle of Hastings. Apart from the extremely unlikely event of an invading force getting so far inland without being attacked, the story is frankly impossible, as the Conqueror landed long before the barn was built.

* * * * * *

Now we come to the details of the two most famous things in Harmondsworth, previously mentioned—the Great Tithe Barn and the Mass Clock.

We have heard a good deal already, however, of the former, which has been noticed by almost every writer on the village; but there are a few more remarks. Lysons is not very prolific, and says: " In the farm yard is a barn remarkable for its large dimensions, being 191 feet in length and 38 feet in breadth," while Hughson uses exactly the same words. Thorne and Walford though both having more to say, are again almost identical. Here is a composite account: "Immediately north-west of the church is a remarkable old Barn, the most interesting object of antiquity in this neighbourhood. It is monastic in origin. It is of extraordinary size and is divided into three floors. The walls are of conglomerate (Pudding Stone), found locally. The open roof is of massive oak, an excellent example of old timber work. The body of the barn is divided into a nave and aisles by two rows of oak pillars of immense thickness, which rest on square blocks of sandstone. But unusual as are the dimensions it was a century back much larger. It had then a projecting wing at the north end, so as to form an L. This wing was taken down when the Manor House was demolished, and rebuilt at Heath Row; it was then known as Tithe Barn to distinguish it from the original Manor Barn. The Manor House, which stood by the Church, was a rich and ancient pile; its many gables and ornamented barge-boards and other decorative work had got out of repair, and it was pulled down in 1774."

Perhaps the most imaginative account of the Barn is in the *Middlesex Transactions*: "The size of this barn is so vast, and its features so striking a character architecturally, that there are few buildings of its kind equal to it in the kingdom. As to its date, I am disposed to put it not later than 1375. In giving this somewhat vague date, the entire absence throughout the building of any marked decorative features must be borne in mind. The construction is that in use at the latter end of the fourteenth century. The general appearance is striking in the extreme, and has the solidity and grandeur inseparable from the works of those masters of building, the Benedictines.

"The excellent condition of Harmondsworth Barn, with its massive forest of sound oak timber, is also remarkable; and in spite of an exposed position with a great extent of roof in a flat country, subject to the full force of violent winds, no part of the timbering appears to have been dislodged. As an example of mediaeval carpentry of the best period it is, perhaps, unequalled; and one is almost afraid to think of it in connection with fire, to which, however, it will doubtless some day succumb. The barn is divided into twelve bays, with threshing floors at the third, seventh and tenth bays. Whether all these formed part of the original design may possibly be a question; at any rate they are old enough to be considered ancient."

I think the interior has been simplified since this was written, and the length given in various accounts seems to vary. I fancy 192 feet is the most accurate measurement. It is claimed as the largest Tithe Barn in England, though there has always been controversy over the odd inches! Of course every large barn may not be a *Tithe* barn. A general utility barn might be used on an estate, but a Tithe Barn was, naturally, intended for the tenth part that belonged to the clergy, and is always found near a church. Many barns are wrongly called Tithe barns.

The writer last quoted wrote prophetic words, for the wing removed to Heath Row may now be sought for in vain—it was burned down some years ago. Great precautions are taken to prevent such a tragedy at Harmondsworth, and notices prohibiting smoking inside are wisely displayed. It would hardly be thought necessary, but the crass stupidity of some people is amazing, for I was told of a recent visitor here *who strongly objected to putting out his cigarette before entering*. "Some cockney tripper, I suppose?" was my comment, "who knew no better." "No," was the reply, "that is the extraordinary part. He was an elderly man with a white moustache. He was at least dressed like a gentleman—in plus-fours. He looked rather like a retired colonel. He was most indignant when entrance was refused till he put out his cigarette."

The largest Tithe Barn in England—and that but a few miles from London—at the mercy of such vandals! Had he entered alone anything might have happened, for it is full of hay and straw.

* * * * * *

I recall with pleasure my first visit to this wonderful barn. I was caught trespassing in the farmyard (as usual) by the farmer, who again took a noble revenge by not only showing me the inside of the barn, but over the rest of the farm as well. The farmhouse, he told me, occupies the site of the old Manor House, part of the gardens being the original ones of the vanished mansion. What interested me most, next to the barn, was the orchard-field at the back. I think it is the most beautiful field in the county; the great wall of the barn on one side of it, the bush-covered mound in the centre, beneath which lies what is left of the mediaeval Priory. Part of the old moat can still be traced; gnarled trunks of fruit trees give a most picturesque look, to which the sheep beneath are unconscious "supers." The field is bordered by one of the branches of the Colne, and the flat, marshy fields stretch for some miles into Buckinghamshire. It is a peaceful scene and brings home the rather quaint description of Hughson —written in 1809—"The banks of the Colne by Harmondsworth, and the surrounding country, afford an extensive range of moorish meadows; which water-lands also accompany the course of other streams hereabouts."

From this field the pudding-stones at the base of the Barn are best seen. These are said to have been quarried locally, but exactly where no one seems to know.

Fine as the exterior of the Barn is it is the interior that really catches and holds the imagination. Here, as you stand gazing down the three Gothic arches that form the aisles it can easily be understood why it has been called "A Cathedral in Wood." It would be easy to force imaginative similie and describe how one almost saw this building as a great church with the monks at prayer—and so on.

To me it made no such appeal; despite its ecclesiastical look it has never seemed more than a place for husbandry—a word more suitable here than farming. There is an old flail kept here, a relic of the old threshing floor days, and though it is probably more modern than the monks, it was, at least, the type of instrument they used. It was the sight of this that fired my imagination, and I can truly say that as I have stood at one end of this barn and gazed down those dim, mysterious aisles—with one door shut this description is not forced—and seen in my mind's eye the old monks, with their robes tucked about their knees, beating the corn with their flails, as lustily as they would like to have applied the lash to the backs of unenlightened heretics.

I often wonder where those old monks are sleeping. Somewhere near, doubtless, for there was probably a burial ground attached to the monastery. I should like to have seen this old place in the days of its glory; so lost is it that not even a picture of it remains, though we have the barn to help in our mental reconstruction.

God rest your souls, good brethren of Harmondsworth Priory—if you will allow a heretic to say so. Near seven hundred years ago you built this Great Barn—and to-day it still stands a memorial to your piety and skill. May no cigarette (a word strange to your ghostly ears, who never heard of tobacco) of modern vandal destroy in a few seconds what even Time has not yet defeated through all those centuries.

* * * * * *

Now we come, as a finale, to what might be called the Precious Stones of Harmondsworth, for they are more valuable than diamonds or rubies, if not counted so by a world that cares for material values only.

These are the little flints to be seen in the outside wall of the Church, to the left facing the porch. Not very conspicuous at first, as against the more prominent artistry of the Norman doorway, these stones may easily be unnoticed unless the visitor knows of their existence. I must confess that I had admired the doorway many times before I became aware of the Mass Clock—for that is what those little stones are. It was a fellow-rambler I happened to meet in the Church who first pointed out this interesting little group to me. The Gods of Good Luck were kind to me that day, for my informant proved to be an expert on matters ecclesiastical—Mr. Herbert Mansford, the architect and lecturer.

Although there are other Mass Clocks—sometimes called by the uglier name of Scratch Dials, or Incised Dials—in England, this one is, as far as I know, the only one in the Home Counties, and the nearest to London.

Recently there were some interesting letters in *The Church Times* on this matter, in which learned authorities on the subject took part. To begin with, as everyone is not familiar with these dials, we can hear the excellent and concise description of T. W. Cole: "These Mass Dials are one of the most interesting survivals of mediaeval churches, especially as they are connected with so integral a function as the Mass. These dials are inconspicuous, being often incisions on the stone itself and often partly obliterated by lichen. But they are readily found if looked for, though many clergymen are sometimes unaware of them existing on their own churches.

"These Mass Dials are usually to be found on the south wall, or buttresses, and consist of a hole for the gnomen (which has long since disappeared), from which radiate certain incised lines, often enclosed in a circle, so that the whole forms a kind of clock-face known locally as ' scratch dials.' These are of very primitive form, dating usually from Norman times to the fourteenth century, and are distinctive from the ordinary sundial. Primarily intended to mark the hour for Mass, they often developed into general time-tellers for the village."

Letters were also printed from the authors of the two best-known books on the subject: Don Ethelbert Horne, of Downside Abbey, writer of *Primitive Sundials or Scratch Dials,* and Arthur R. Green, author of *Sundials, Incised Dials or Mass Clocks.* My own modest share in this correspondence was to point out to Londoners where, at Harmondsworth, they can see a Mass Clock for themselves; for this famous church relic (if a thing can be famous if practically unknown) I consider a real Middlesex " find," as I have never seen it mentioned yet in any book on the county.

It is always good to find in an old church an account of its history for the benefit of the wanderer; it is a kindly thought that should draw from all a few coppers for the poor-box. The account here is good, and tells us: " Lying on one of the Lines of the Roman Survey there would be at the cross-roads a Pagan Compitum, or village shrine, for Heathen worship. Many of these were converted to Christian use. . . . The Mass Clock on the South Wall is probably a thousand years old."

It was at Harmondsworth that I recently met with one of the most interesting characters it has ever been my good luck to encounter. It was on the occasion of one of those Ploughing Matches (organised by the Middlesex Agricultural Society), whose " Thomas Hardy touch " has always so pleased me; but as I have described one of these elsewhere in some detail it need not be reiterated, except an unusual one.

* * * * * *

I had been talking to a group of women farm workers, especially to one dear old dame, whom the others called Grannie, who told me she had worked on the same Harmondsworth farm for over forty years, and hoped soon to celebrate her jubilee of labour. Would that another " Labour Party " was as picturesque and as innocent of political guile.

As I chatted to these women I was aware of the figure of a man who was sidling up to me, who spoke in a hoarse whisper, though what he said I could not make out at first. When I turned to look at him a quaint figure met my gaze. He was short and dressed in clothes far too large. He must have been about seventy, with a wizened face, all wrinkles, clean shaven, and bright little eyes like a ferret, with a quizical humorous twinkle in them, a face that would hold attention anywhere, as it did mine then.

Yet it was not his face, nor yet his person, that I first noticed; it was two things he was carrying, one slung round his neck with cord and one in his hands. At first glance they looked like blow-bladders from some animal, but on a second look they proved to be solid and evidently whitish roots of some sort. I asked him what they were. " Mandrake Root," he answered, " the best medicine in the world—better'n all your doctors' muck. Now, what about a pennorth, sir?" " What's it good for?" I asked. He looked at me quizically again. " What 'ave you got, now, sir?" " Well, let's say diabetes." He chuckled. " Why, it's *the* very thing you want, sir," he replied, getting his knife ready. I am certain the answer would have been the same if I had said mumps or housemaid's knee!

He then scraped some of the root and held it out. " 'Ere you are, sir, just taste it." I did so and found it intensely bitter. All the while the old man was enlarging on its virtues; if he could be believed it was a veritable panacea. I mentioned several obscure diseases of which he had probably never heard—such as sebora—but that did not daunt him; apparently there was no complaint in the Medical Dictionary that this marvellous root would not cure.

I bought a chunk, which I keep as a curiosity, and give a scraping now and then to friends who wish to know the bitterness of life. What interested me most, however, was the subsequent talk I had with this quaint old Mandrake Root gatherer. He got it, he said, in a field near Poyle or thereabouts, and he always searched for it at night to dodge the police. Why it should be necessary to do this he did not explain; I think it was really put in for dramatic effect, for though I know little about the laws governing the finding of Mandrakes, I cannot imagine it to be a crime against the King's Realm. The old man knew all about the Biblical legend of the root,

AN OLD HOUSE AT POYLE. *Photo by S. J. Holloway*

OLD TOLL-HOUSE: COLNBROOK. *Photo by the Author*

LALEHAM CHURCH. *Photo by the Author*

FARM AT PERRY OAKS. *Photo by the Author*

and how it was supposed to shriek when pulled out of the earth, which, he explained, was only suction. Where he learned all this I do not know, for he hardly had the appearance of a student of folk-lore! He even knew the mediaeval legend of fastening a dog to the root to pull it out of the ground. for fear of evil spirits, and how the dog always died of fright when it heard. the mandrake scream!

The old man was delightfully candid about himself, for when I asked where he could be found—I wanted to see him again—he told me he lived near Poyle when he was not in prison, and that I could always ascertain. his whereabouts from the police! Not from the crime of Mandrake-pulling,. however, would he be in durance vile, he was too cute for that, but, as he remarked outspokenly, "Yes, sir, drink's me downfall." So I expect the saxpance I banged on Mandrake Root went down a liquid road.

But what a find. Not many distant counties could produce a Mandrake Root seller to-day. Yet in Middlesex—which, according to fools, "is all London, you know!"—here was one still plying his trade with roots pulled in the shire. I hope to see my old friend again, for surely such a character is worth further acquaintance—worth even the risk of joining him in the village lock-up after standing him a welcome pint at the village inn.

CHAPTER XXXV.

Of a bi-county town that fell asleep on the coming of the railway and luckily has not yet awakened.

IT has been the fate of Colnbrook twice to be left stranded by the tide of traffic; firstly when the stage coaches ceased to run, and secondly when the motors also deserted the narrow street for the broader way.

Colnbrook has the honour (or inconvenience) of being not only in two counties, but also in four parishes. Even the river from which it takes its name is here divided into four channels, crossed by as many bridges.

It is a sleepy old town and there is not much to see, but it is restful. There is no old church, however, which we somehow look for in such a place, for the present church is modern (1849) and hidden away from the main street.

It has replaced an older one, for Colnbrook forms, we are told, a "Consolidated chapelry" and the ancient chantry chapel formerly stood in the narrow main street, and was removed years ago by the commissioners of the turnpike roads, and a neat chapel erected in a more convenient part. The market-house was taken down at the same time."

This was written about 1850, so even at that date makers of roads were no more respecters of old houses than they are to-day.

Colnbrook, when incorporated in 1544, had a bailiff and twelve burgesses, a Market and Fair, to which was attached a Court of Pie Powder; all of which have long since disappeared.

The Court of "Pie Powder" sat when any mediaeval fair of importance was held; it was a court of summary jurisdiction to settle disputes between traders and to punish transgressors. "Pie Powder" is a corruption of Pieds Poudres—Dusty Feet—hence Court for Travellers.

One account of these Courts tells us that "they sat during the great fairs which sometimes lasted three weeks, and were attended by many foreign merchants, buying Gascon wine, Milan armour, Venetian glass, Genoese silk and velvet, Flemish clothes, Spanish iron, besides all sorts of English produce." It seems that the fairs of Colnbrook in the olden days were matters of some moment.

As befits a place in two counties and four parishes, its history is also "cut up "; in fact, Colnbrook seems divided against itself as much on paper as in reality.

Camden and Gale, the antiquaries, declare it to be the Ad Pontes of the *Itinerary of Antoninus,* but this statement is disputed by others, Leland placing it at Reading, Salmon at Dorking and Horsley at Old Windsor. Modern antiquarians are now agreed that *Pontes* was Staines.

Again Camden, in his *Britannia,* tells us that some of the small islands in this neighbourhood, formed by the different branches of the Colne, are supposed to have been the places where the Danes secured themselves against the attacks of King Alfred in 894; but this theory is contested by Bishop Gibson, who says that Camden has got the right name but the wrong river, and declares that it is the Essex Colne that was the scene of these happenings.

Drayton, writing a few years ago in his *Polyolbion,* makes it clear as to which Colne he refers, for he mentions it winding its way about Colnbrook " through the goodly grain of Middlesex."

The very buildings seem to enter into these controversies. In the Middlesex part of the town are some old cottages, with a quaint archway and some really beautiful gardens, that are known locally as King John's Palace. When I explored them I could find no real evidence as to how they got this name; the inhabitants all firmly believing that King John once had a palace of which these are the remains. Whether King John ever had a palace here or not, the present buildings are hardly old enough to be the remains of it. Another account is that John slept here the night before he sealed the Magna Carta at Runnymede; it is, however, always stated that he spent the night at Duncroft Hall, still standing, very much re-built, near Staines. Another version has it that the King stopped at the Ostrich Inn for refreshment on the way to Runnymeade, and that some of his retainers, unable to get in, went to this other house, then also a hostelry.

The issue is further confused by another King of the same name, for Edward the Black Prince, with his famous prisoner King John of France, was met at Colnbrook by Edward III., probably at this house.

It seems redundant to state that Queen Elizabeth slept at Colnbrook. Rumour has it that she did so at The Ostrich, The George and The White Hart. Three reasons are given for her so doing, the first being when she was carried a prisoner from Woodstock to Hampton Court, the second when her horse went lame on her way to Windsor, and the third when she was out hawking on Hounslow Heath, though which inn was used on each occasion we are not told.

Even the meaning of the name Colnbrook is in dispute, if the absurd derivation from Cole-in-the-Brook (which will be commented on later) is noticed. The derivation from its situation on the River Colne is the correct one. I feel all this is rather muddled history, but the topographical part, at least, is indisputable.

The chief places of interest in Colnbrook to-day are its inns, and they are picturesque enough still. The George, a comfortable-looking typical eighteenth century hostelry, faces the bend of the road as you approach the town from the Middlesex side. Older and more interesting, though, is the Ostrich Inn, just round the corner. It is this old place that gives Colnbrook its present interest.

It is a rambling, half-timbered, gabled building, standing on most days picturesquely aloof by the roadside as if dreaming of bygone times, when all was a-bustle and its quaint little yard echoing with the busy life of the road. Why on earth they wanted to spoil this living memory of a more artistic yesterday by erecting a gasometer just behind this quaint old inn-yard is one of the many mysteries of town "planning." I have a little booklet, issued by the proprietor of this old inn, outlining its history, an excellent example that might be followed by other inns. This booklet is interesting, though it concerns itself chiefly with crime — but the writer knew human nature. "There is something universal in the appeal of the story of any great crime," he says, "and if the years have mellowed its crudity, if time has quietly wrought happy changes in the theatre where it was worked out—above all, if the scenes to which it leads are now peaceful and beautiful—there is no little enjoyment to be found in recalling it."

After a brief resume of the quiet history of Colnbrook, which he calls " the best illustration nearest to London of a coaching town ruined by railways that it is possible to discover," the writer gets down quickly to his main theme, i.e., the inns, and notably The Ostrich.

"A very pleasing feature in connection with the ' Ostrich ' is its little cobble-stoned courtyard. Entering this, through a low archway, and then turning left on the cobblestones, one obtains a very pleasant and sunny view of steep roofs, dormer windows, dovecote and whitewashed walls with grape vines. The interior of the house is just as charming, a wide, old-fashioned staircase, giving access to the first floor, where there is some splendid oak panelling in the dining-room. Here, also, is the bedroom used by Dick Turpin, practically intact.

"This inn was a favourite resort of that famous highwayman. From here (the house being then known as the ' Crane ') he once had a narrow escape in the dead of night from the Bow Street Runners. He managed to get away only by jumping from his bedroom window into the courtyard, mounting his horse, leaping the hedge at the end of the inn's garden, and so over the Colne and away across the Heath. Amongst other curios at the ' Ostrich ' is one of the veritable pistols used by Dick Turpin."

We are also told of a curious little historical story of Colnbrook, not generally known. This concerns the early days of the Civil War. " On the day after the removal of Charles the First," runs the account, " from Windsor to London, for his trial in Westminster Hall, he was followed by his personal servant, John Dowcett, and a Knight, Capt. Fanshaw. It had been arranged that a messenger should be sent from the King in London to meet these two with instructions as to how his cause could best be served. They were not aware of the identity of the expected messenger and were somewhat perturbed. Dowcett, however, had met many messengers from the King and thought he would be able to recognise whoever was sent.

" As they rode into Colnbrook they were approached by a rider dressed in leather-jerkin and homespun breeches, who greeted them and said he had ridden from London that morning, and if they were going that way advised them to be very careful of some rogues further on. Being informed by the Knight that they were riding to London, the stranger invited them to an inn close by, as he wished to give them 'helpful information.'

"Dowcett was filled with misgiving, as he felt that the proper messenger should have asked further questions. He, however, trusted to Capt. Fanshaw and followed the pair as they turned through the gateway of the 'Ostrich' yard. Soon after entering the inn their suspicions were aroused by the behaviour of a number of men already there. They were quickly separated and overpowered, and each locked in different parts of the building, with threats of having their throats slit if they called for help.

"Within a few minutes a number of armed men rode into the yard, and their leader (Lord Richmond, the true messenger from the King) demanded news of the two travellers from the landlord. The latter denied all knowledge of them. Lord Richmond disbelieved him and threatened to raze the inn to the ground if they were not produced. The men from the inn then rushed out into the yard and set upon the new arrivals. There was a short and fierce fracas in which five of the ruffians were severely wounded and one killed.

Capt. Farnshaw had heard the sounds of the conflict and, guessing that help was at hand, shouted out. He was heard and very soon both he and Dowcett were released, and eventually continued their journey to London in the company of Lord Richmond and his armed men."

"Amongst the Colnbrook innkeepers of long ago," he continues, "was one named Buckingham, who made so much money at the 'George' that he got into Parliament, eventually in the golden pages of Debrett and died in sanctity—a pattern to all men.

"However, we are concerned here with what was, and still is, the most famour of Colnbrook's many old buildings, viz., 'Ye Olde Ostrich Inne.' It is a plastered, timber and brick, picturesque inn with a long projecting front and charming old-world air, and is one of the oldest, if not *the* oldest, in the county. The present Ostrich is the successor of a much more ancient building. There have been, in fact, several inns on this site. The first appears to have been a guest-house or Hospice, founded by one Milo Crispen, and given, in 1106, in trust to the Abbey of Abingdon 'for the good of travellers in this world and the salvation of their souls in the next.'

"It would seem to be from this circumstance that the inn derived its name, for it was early known as the 'Ospridge,' a kind of orthographic half-way house between the former 'hospice' and the present 'Ostrich.' The inn became in after years the resort of guests going to Windsor Castle; and here ambassadors robed themselves before being conducted into the Royal presence." In Froissart's *Chronicles* there is an account of four ambassadors to King Edward III., who "dyned in the Kynge's chamber, and after they departed, laye the same night atte Colnbrook."

Now comes the story of the "great crime that made Colnbrook famous," for, we are told, "besides being one of the oldest inns in the county, it has the blackest history of any, and if only half of its legends have the slightest substratum of fact, then this hostelry was the scene of some of the most gruesome crimes imaginable. How the inn managed to keep its customers after the dreadful murders committed in it during the reign of Henry I. (certainly not fifty years after the hospice was given to Abingdon Abbey) is inexplicable.

"At the time of the last murder at the Ostrich, a short record of which follows, the innkeeper's name was Jarman. He and his wife had long been engaged in the 'systematic removal' of wealthy guests, and had devised an ingenious murder-trap in the chief bedroom. On each occasion when they plotted a murder their conversation was always in these terms: 'Wife, there is now a fat pig to be had if you want one.' Whereupon she would answer, 'I pray you, put him in the hogstie till to-morrow.'

"The bedstead in this room was placed on a hinged trap-door above the brewhouse's boiling vat. A window at the back of a cupboard enabled the inkeepers to see if their victims slept. According to one record sixty murders were committed before the innkeeper and his wife were brought to book.

"Thomas Cole, a clothier of Reading, used this house freely. He carried large sums of money, and consequently he became a marked man. For some time he escaped. Once he fell sick, and luckily he lay elsewhere; another time London was aflame to the skies and he pressed on there. 'The third time pays for all,' said the innkeeper, but a friend came and lodged with him on his third visit to the Blue Room and so his doom was again postponed.

"The landlord was struck with the coincidences. His wife, the more desperate of the two, accused him of cowardice, when, on the clothier's next visit, he proposed that they let him sleep elsewhere than in the Blue Room. They argued violently, huddled over the brewhouse fire, and in the end she prevailed. Before retiring the clothier asked the landlord to sign a paper. *It was his will.* More than ever perturbed by this, and by Cole's outspoken presentiments of coming evil, the landlord again urged his wife to stay the business in hand. She was a little moved, but thoughts of the clothier's gold, and that this was really to be the last victim. . . ."

Now comes a dramatic pause, when the writer adds "Mr. Cole's horse went home riderless." He does not explain why the simple-minded Mr. Cole did not go to another inn if he felt so suspicious. "The body was found," he finishes, "in a neighbouring brook—thus the name of Colnbrook is derived from 'Cole-in-the-brook.'" To do the writer of this booklet justice, he does not swallow this absurd theory.

"The neatly-elaborated horrific pages of Edgar Allan Poe contain nothing so thrilling," adds the editor of this booklet, "nothing that so bears the stamp of having just so happened as this account of murder in the Blue Room of the Ostrich, written by a scribbling pamphleteer."

This inn finds a place in several other books, perhaps most pleasantly in *At the Sign of the Ostrich*, by Charles James, a novel of eighteenth century Colnbrook, as well as having some pleasing touches of the surrounding countryside. An enjoyable yarn of an old-fashioned flavour. Some mention of the inn is also found in Thomas Burke's *The English Inn*, a comprehensive book, but one in which it is rather hard to find the reference to any special inn, as it has no index.

There is mention, and several good pictures, of the Ostrich in a more elaborate book of the same title, *The English Inn*, by A. E. Richardson and H. D. Eberlein. A better account than these, however, is to be found in C. G. Harper's *The Old Inns of Old England*, where he writes: "The decayed coaching town of Colnbrook is little changed from those times. Still do the old red-brick houses on either side of the narrow causeway-like street wear their old-time look, and the solid red-faced 'George' Inn yet seems to be awaiting the arrival of the mail, or of some post-chaise nearing

London or setting out on the second stage to Bath.

"Once a market town, it is now a village, but it is still a place of inns ... the present 'Ostrich' is the successor of a much more ancient one. There have been several on this site. The first appears to have been a guest-house or hospice: *Quodam hospitum in via Londoniae apud Colebroc.*"

Even in the name of this inn of picturesque but sanguinary memory we are again drawn into mild controversy. Apparently from having been called the Crane it became the Ostrich. I do not think we need look for any deep archaeological reason for this change; I suspect that the old-time signboard painter was responsible, his bird probably would do for either; it was, doubtless, meant for a crane in the early days, a bird well known in England, but later, when the Middlesex and Buckinghamshire peasants heard of the big African bird they began to see a likeness of what they imagined it to be, and perhaps a new sign-painter tried to be "in the fashion," with variable success.

There is another smaller building hereabouts that is worth passing notice for its association with the coaching days, and that is the old Toll-gate House still standing on the Bath Road opposite the Punch Bowl Inn.

In *The Land We Live In*, by Charles Knight, written in 1848, there is a mid-period word-picture of deserted Colnbrook between the decline of coach traffic and before the rising of the age of petrol. " Along by lanes and field-paths," he says, " from which we have occasional glimpses of the Colne and always pretty peeps over the neighbouring country, we reach Colnbrook; but there we need not stay. That respectable-looking but apparently not very flourishing town, with its four bridges, is too well known to travellers on the western road—how few they are now!—to need description."

Here we must leave Colnbrook, resisting the temptation (at least on paper, though the reader can please himself) to explore beyond it, for I do not think that Hounslow Heath, even in its broadest days, ever extended beyond the Colne.

The beautiful and peaceful country towards Horton—with its memories of Milton—is here, where the Colne, a rushy stream with willowy banks, flows "through meadows trim with daisies pied"—to quote but one line from *L'Allegro* of the scenery said to have inspired the poem.

Explorers of this corner of Middlesex would do well to consult *Rambles Round Uxbridge*, Stephen Springall's useful book, which, if rather scrappy in parts is a good companion on the road, especially for those who like visiting churches, for its scope in this way is wider than its title indicates.

I like the story, from another source, of the Profiteer (query—do Profiteers explore churches?) who was once visiting a church in a Middlesex village. He was rather hazy in his topography, but when he saw over the door of a certain church MDCLX he proudly turned to his wife and exclaimed, " There, me dear, I told you as 'ow this village *were* in Middlesex and not Surrey as you would 'ave it!"

A little way back on the Bath Road from Colnbrook is the old Peggy Bedford Inn, which we have already noticed, but I came across some verses since that might have been inspired by this old hostelry in its sad and forlorn days. They are entitled *The Old Inn,* and are in *The Middlesex Book of Verse.* The writer is E. E. Barrett, and they certainly have a swing as well as an atmosphere. Here is one verse:

" Deserted on its lonely height,
With shuttered windows bare of light,
Its stout old walls moss green and grey,
Its rafters crumbling day by day;
With tileless roof beneath the sky,
And smokeless chimneys raised on high,
The grey old inn stands watching still,
Where four roads meet upon the hill."

Substitute " flat " for "height " and "two " for " four " roads—and you have the derelict Peggy Bedford.

Near here is a notice board by a field gate: " The World Explorers' Rustic Club." They have chosen a good spot; when they have finished exploring the world they may find a little of interest in this corner of " Unknown Middlesex."

EPILOGUE.

IN "ringing down the curtain" on the story of "Highwayman's Heath" many thoughts naturally crowd the mind. Of these we need deal with only one here. What will be the ultimate fate of this tract of country that lies, almost unknown to many, just beyond London's doorstep?

I am sorry to end on a note of tragedy, but 1 fear I know the answer only too well. Already the hand of the despoiler is apparent; it will become a suburb—horrible thought. Its fields and orchards will, in a few short years, become streets of unlovely villas; its centuries old barns will be demolished to build cinemas, as people will *pay* to see the supposed life of U.S.A. on the screen, when they will not trouble to glance at that of rural England for nothing. Village greens will be destroyed, old houses pulled down, old trees felled, and ancient forges, where anvil-music still rings out, become garages, with rows of hideous petrol pumps.

It *could* be saved—but it will not be. I know it would need a long purse, but it could be made self-supporting; its farms still carrying on with real agriculture and not becoming show places. Little need be altered, except, perhaps, to demolish a few blatantly modern buildings out of keeping with the old ones. Richmond Park was made in this way, though instead of creating a park we should be saving a countryside.

Surely it would be worth while to rescue this little piece of Old England before it is too late, where the city-weary could wander in the country and have the mental tonic of dreaming of past days amidst scenes steeped in romantic memories and history of our homeland. Luckily it is still possible to do this here—but again the haunting thought—for how long?

During the War I suppose I shared with millions of others thoughts of the land for which we were fighting; and in the long night watches of a North Sea patrol my mind often created visions of this old Middlesex countryside, which I was glad to find when I returned was still the same.

Every lover of his country should read Clough Williams-Ellis' wonderful book, *England and the Octopus,* in which the same thought is expressed, when he says: "We were invited to fight to preserve England; we believed, we fought. . . . We saved our country that we might ourselves destroy it." He says a good deal more, including some trenchant remarks touching these parts, of the spoilation of the old Bath Road and the baseness of the Great West Road. I wish space allowed for more quotation.

A writer in *The Daily Telegraph,* who signs himself "Middle Saxon," recently wrote an article of fine understanding: *Unspoilt Middlesex: A Cinderella of Counties.* He, too, foresees the end, though realising, as few do, how much of interest and beauty is still left. I agree with all he says, except, perhaps, the statement that Hounslow Heath in the old days possessed more gibbets than trees! His simile is, I fear, rather over enthusiastic for the "picturesque" sights of yesterday.

Another who sees the danger ahead is P. Crawfurth Smith in his spirited article *Save Our Countryside*: "Let us make war on the Jerry builder, and protect our countryside. He is allowed too much rein; he should be made to contribute extensively towards preserving as open land a large proportion of the property he develops." The writer continues to speak of the

384

Green Belt round London, a subject on which I have touched in this book. Even if it had been begun as recently as after the Great War it would have been almost an accomplished fact by now, instead of a dream of what never will be.

There is one more book I should like to mention before we finish, that will be welcomed by those who like to take their history in small doses, and that is T. Michael Pope's anthology, *Middlesex: In Prose and Verse,* a charming little book and an ideal pocket companion for the rambler. It was my good luck to be able to assist the compiler a little in this work, and by his recent death all of us who knew him—and the County of Middlesex as well—have lost a true friend.

It is, perhaps, inevitable in a book dealing with many places all so full of interest that notes, since accumulated, are bound to crop up. In fact almost every chapter, especially the topographical ones, could have had its appendix. I have resisted the temptation hitherto, but I feel that the following notes on so wonderful a spot as Osterley Park (see Chapter XXXI.) will be of interest, so I make no further excuse for inserting these particular ones here—though many more are omitted, so rich in story is this demesne.

* * * * *

For those who would read more of Queen Elizabeth at Osterley I would recommend Nichol's *Progresses* (which appeared about 100 years ago in that interesting old *Penny Magazine*). It is said that the stables here are part of Gresham's Elizabethan mansion, but though certainly contemporary, I do not think they were actually part of the house itself, for Mr. Arthur T. Bolton, author of that magnificent work on the architecture of the Brothers Adam, told me how, when they altered Gresham's house, they " lifted " it a story in a most ingenious way by building underneath the old mansion, so that the old ground floor is now the first floor.

* * * * *

The elopement of the Earl with the banker's daughter, already mentioned, has a curious sidelight. The young Earl was one day talking to Robert Child, and asking him what *he* would do if he wanted to marry a girl and the parents would not consent. " Why, run off with her, my boy!" replied the banker, not realising that it was his own daughter that was in question. And so the Earl did, as we have seen. Another story is also told of the second elopement, how when Lady Jersey (the mother) finally forgave the runaway lovers and consented to receive Captain Ibbotson, she remarked, after the first interview, that she had no idea that the middle-classes were so clean!

I am indebted for these stories to *Fifty-one Years of Victorian Life,* by Margaret Elizabeth Villiers (Countess of Jersey), a book full of entertainment and interest. The authoress mentions the sensation the elopement of Lady Adele caused at the time. The papers were full of it, and one broke forth into a long " poem," which is about as bad verse as I ever hope to read. Here is one verse—and it's enough:

> " Lady Ad. with love was mad,
> Just seventeen and no one bolder,
> And lately off to Gretna Green
> My Lady went and married a soldier.
> A captain of the 11th Hussars,
> In Cupid's net he had nicely caught her;
> Her father was a nobleman,
> And Addie was his Lordship's daughter."

In the book mentioned, and also in her other volume, *The Family of Villiers,* Lady Jersey mentions several other books that have to do with Osterley. She quotes some more verses by Lionel Ashley, whom they called "The Bard." He was the son of the famous Lord Shaftesbury. Written in 1887, the local interest is stronger than the poetry, I fear, but for the former I quote three verses:

> " In a cot may be found, I have heard the remark,
> More delight than in castles with pillars,
> But we find in the Palace of Osterley Park
> All the charms of suburban Villiers.

> " A Sunday in Osterley gardens and halls,
> That's a day to look onto and after,
> Its pleasures my memory fondly recalls,
> And the talk with its wisdom and laughter.

> " In a nice little church a grave sermon we heard,
> Which reproved Christianity flabby,
> And urged that in Heaven a place be preferred
> To a Jubilee seat in the Abbey."

The church, it is explained, was that on Norwood Green.

Osterley Park was a place of considerable fame in Regency days, when the beautiful and notorious Countess of Jersey was at the height of her influence. A great many stories are told of her for which there is no space here, except one clever epigram, for it was she who remarked, after hearing that the Prince Regent had personated both the King and Queen at a certain Drawing Room, that he was on that occasion *a sequence*—King, Queen and Knave!

The "notorious" Countess of Jersey, we read from the book already quoted, was the posthumous daughter of the Bishop of Raphoe, son of Sir William Twysden, Bart. "The Bishop," she writes, "was a celebrated character, as he appears to have combined the qualities of a highwayman with those proper to his profession. Visitors who dined with him at Osterley were often attacked on their homeward way, and if they shot in self-defence found their weapons missed fire. At last a guest was warned that the charges had been drawn. He reloaded, and on being accosted by a masked man fired, and his assailant made off. The Bishop was unable for some weeks to perform his episcopal functions. His enterprise earned him the name of "Slip-Gibbet." He used to hunt, and his prowess was the admiration of the huntsmen. At Hounslow he kept a pack of hounds, and there is a mysterious story to the effect that his death resulted from some encounter with his dogs. Others assert that it was due to the wound received on Hounslow Heath." We have met the Highwayman-Bishop before, however, in these pages.

* * * * * *

Lady Jersey mentions several other interesting books in literary personalities. Writing of a visit of James Russell Lowell, the famous American author, she says: "It is pleasant to recall him sitting in the garden at Osterley on peaceful summer evenings, enjoying especially that blue haze peculiar to the Valley of the Thames, which softens without obscuring the gentle English landscape."

She also tells us that Sir Herbert Maxwell was a frequent visitor there, and how in his novel *Sir Lucian Elphin* he adopted Osterley, under a different name, as the background for his scenes. She also quotes from Augustus Hare's *Story of My Life* much that is interesting. He wrote in

1890: "I went to Osterley, which looked bewitching, with its swans floating in sunshine beyond the shade of the old cedars. I told the Jersey children —splendid audience—a long story in a glade of the garden, where the scene might have recalled the *Decameron*." In another part he has a fine description of the interior of the mansion, and I like the touch (when the Duchess of Cleveland was a tenant) a few years earlier, when he wrote: "June, 1877. Lady Manners drove me to Osterley. The great wide park looked dark and dull under a leaden sky, the house as gloomy and ghostly as Bleak House. The old Duchess (Cleveland), stumping about with her ebony stick, seemed part of the place."

The old bridge in Osterley Park is one of the most interesting things on the estate, though hardly known to the general public. It lies in the fields on the Hanwell side. Some of the older folk in the village remember this bridge before it fell into its present sadly dilapidated state. One old man told me it was built by the Romans, as he had once seen Caesar's head carved on it! The same man also told me of a tunnel under the road through which the Roman army escaped after a battle! Anything so modern as the Romans, however, was scornfully denied by another village worthy, who quite seriously stated that he had always " 'eard tell as 'ow it were built by Adam!" By a strange chance, though this statement is naturally wrong, the bridge certainly *was* built by Adam. This paradox, however, is explained, not by the father of us all leaving the Garden of Eden to do this job in Middlesex, but by the fact that it was Robert Adam who was responsible for the work about 1770.

I made a special inspection of this old bridge (for once in my life I did not trespass, but got permission—a rare virtue of which I feel proud). The bridge spans what was once a stream, but now little more than a marshy dip in the ground, and the bridge itself is badly fallen into decay, and so overgrown with greenery that it is almost invisible from the road. I saw how the Roman idea grew up; the remains of what is generally known as " classical work " is apparent. Not far away is the Roman tunnel—a culvert under the road to a wood beyond to take off the surface water. I have seen pictures of this bridge in its pristine state, and I cannot help regretting that so fine a specimen of Adam work should have come to so sorry an end. There are other specimens of his architecture, however, beside the mansion—the Orangery, the Aviary and other buildings, which are most interesting, and can be seen by the public on those days when the private gardens are open in aid of the hospital.

Wood Lake—the lower of the two—is able to be viewed in bluebell-time by the same reason. This is a magnificent stretch of tree-fringed water. A friend recently returned from the New World said it reminded him of a Canadian lake in its picturesque wildness and sense of isolation. I told him it was something far more wonderful than that. Such a place might be expected in Canada, but to find it seven miles only from the world's largest city is almost a miracle.

I would advise everyone, when the next chance occurs, to go and see the gardens, and above all this wonderful lake—the general park can be viewed at any time—but these two things are without parallel, especially the latter, in the county. To the observant they tell a " story " of the marvels of Osterley Park far more vividly than these few notes of mine. If there are sermons in stones, there are volumes to be read in Wood Lake.

Even now, close as my researches have been, I know I have not discovered anything like all that has been written on the surprising district dealt with. I am not saying this from false modesty, expecting people to reply, " Oh, but look what a lot you *have* got." I know I have got a lot. I should be a fool if I did not, seeing the trouble I have gone through to find it out. I am convinced, however, that the " lines left out " of the present volume would make a sequel almost as long, for I have had to discard a great deal I should like to have included, to say nothing of what yet remains undiscovered.

Everything, in the topographical sections, is written from personal exploration, but places change so rapidly nowadays that if readers find a row of shops where I have described an old house, let them put the blame in the right quarter, and realise that I shall share their regrets.

* * * * * *

A friend who likes to " pull my leg " asked me why I had not found a quotation from *The Bible* with regard to Hounslow Heath? I replied that *The Bible* is so modern a book compared with the date of my beginning the story of the Heath, for the Brontosaurus was extinct long before it was written. Noah's great-grandson was the best I could do in this way, however, but I *did* find a quotation from *The Book of Jeremiah* that might well apply to the Heath country:

" Ask for the old paths, where is the good way, and walk
therein, and ye shall find rest for your souls."

What better advice for these worrying and strenuous days? So let us be thankful that hereabouts are still left a few such pathways, where we can take the prophet's advice.

* * * * * *

These are invisible threads holding men's hearts to Old England, stretching from hemisphere to hemisphere without breaking; and who can doubt, after reading these pages, that one of these threads passes over the old-time Heath of Hounslow?

THE END.

BIBLIOGRAPHY AND INDEXES.

THE dates in the Bibliography refer to publication and not to the period of the book's subject; these are added in the hope that it may be of some real use to future students of Middlesex lore. Some books bear no date, but the context will generally give the "clue."

My sincere thanks are due to Miss Florence Dawson for her help in these compilations; not only has her careful and accurate work aided me in a long and arduous task, but her wide knowledge of English Literature and History has also been of the greatest possible value.

BIBLIOGRAPHY.

ADDENDA.

THE following books, sometimes under their titles and sometimes not, have also been referred to or quoted from in the text, and should have acknowledgment.

After his Kind, J. W. Palmer
Anglo-Saxon Chronicle (1799)
Argosy, The (1882)
Ashmole M.S.S. (1677)
Autobiography (1828), Leigh Hunt
Autobiography (1887), W. P. Frith
Augmentation Records

Beacon Fires, A. Hill
Beauties of Middlesex (1850), W. Keane
Blue Book Royal Commission Book of Days (1869), R. and W. Chambers
Burleigh Papers, The

AUTHORS.

TOPOGRAPHICAL AND GENERAL INDEX.